Nomad

Borzu Qermezi sitting by a spring in front of his tent in summer pastures at
Hanalishah. August 1977.

Nomad

A Year in the Life of
a Qashqa'i Tribesman in Iran

LOIS BECK

University of California Press

BERKELEY   LOS ANGELES

University of California Press
Berkeley and Los Angeles, California

© 1991 by
Lois Beck

Library of Congress Cataloging-in-Publication Data

Beck, Lois
    Nomad : a year in the life of a Qashqa'i tribesman in Iran / Lois
Beck.
        p.   cm.
    Includes bibliographical references and index.
    ISBN 0–520–07003–8 (alk. paper). —ISBN 0–520–07495–5
(pbk.: alk. paper)
    1. Qashqā'ī (Turkic people) 2. Qermezi, Borzu. 3. Qashqā'ī
(Turkic people)—Biography.   I. Title.
    DS269.K3B42   1991
    955.05'092—dc20   91–14470
                                                                      CIP

Printed in the United States of America
9 8 7 6 5 4 3 2 1

The paper used in this publication meets the minimum requirements of
American National Standard for Information Sciences—Permanence of
Paper for Printed Library Materials, ANSI Z39.48-1984. ∞

Contents

List of Illustrations

Maps

Figures

Tables

Acknowledgments

This book was made possible by the warm and generous hospitality of Borzu Qermezi, Jehangir Khan Darrehshuri, and their extended families.

Manucher Dareshuri, son of Jehangir Khan Darrehshuri, has known Borzu Qermezi and other Qermezi people all his life. He read two drafts of the manuscript, helped to clarify the historical and political context, and answered many questions. He drew sketches of Darrehshuri territory that enabled me to see more clearly the spatial components of political organization. The final version reflects his knowledge and insight. Naheed Dareshuri, daughter of Amiramanollah Khan Darrehshuri and grand-daughter of Ziad Khan Darrehshuri, offered many perceptive explanations about Qashqa'i culture and society. An expert weaver, she drew the textile design that appears on the book jacket. Manucher and Naheed have been dear friends for over twenty years, and I am deeply indebted to them.

The final version of this book remains true to my conception of it from the time I first reread the journals I kept in 1970 and 1971. Still, many people who read the manuscript have helped me to elaborate and clarify. I appreciate the comments of David Edwards, John Bowen, Steven Caton, Julie Katz, Patty Jo Watson, and Richard Watson, all of whom read an early draft. Richard Tapper, Gene Garthwaite, William Beeman, and Edmund Burke III offered useful suggestions on a later draft. Leonard Helfgott, Jane Bestor, Mary Martin, and Erika Friedl provided pertinent remarks on the next-to-final draft. Mohammad Shahbazi, an Igdir Qashqa'i man who was born and raised a nomadic pastoralist, also read and commented on the manuscript. He helped me to understand more clearly which features of Qashqa'i culture and society were general and which were more specific to the Darrehshuri tribe and the Qermezi subtribe.

A Fulbright-Hays fellowship aided the initial research on which this book is based. The Department of Anthropology at Washington University in St. Louis provided some financial support for the production of the manuscript. Ernest Thomas Greene generously allowed me to include four photographs he took of Borzu Qermezi and his family in 1966. Maps 1–3 are based in part on an excellent map of Qashqa'i territory published by Gerhard Kortum in 1980, and I thank him for permitting me once again to use it. James Opie graciously offered me the designs used at the chapter openings. Mary Kennedy typed the tables and drew the maps. Mahmoud Amin helped me with Persian and Turkish terms. Rebecca Torstrick ably assisted me in St. Louis during my research in Iran in 1991.

Lynne Withey, assistant director of the University of California Press, offered encouragement from the beginning of this project, and her enthusiastic support contributed to my peace of mind during subsequent drafts.

Finally, I cannot imagine this book without also thinking about my daughter Julia. This book was the first major project I began after Julia's birth, and I saw that it was indeed possible to care for a child, do creative and fruitful scholarship, and teach full-time, all simultaneously. Julia sat in my lap and played in my study while I wrote the first draft and has been fascinated with each stage of the process since then. As this book goes to press, she and I will be living with Borzu Qermezi and his family, and I eagerly anticipate her reactions to them and their reactions to her.

Hanalishah, Qashqa'i territory, Iran—Spring 1991:

Borzu and I sit together in his tent in summer pastures and watch Julia chase after (and successfully retrieve) a lamb trying to follow its mother when she rejoined the herd. Although seriously ill, Borzu is as spirited and full of plans for the future as he was twenty years ago. He knows I have written a book about him.

I dedicate this book to Borzu Qermezi, to the memory of Khalifeh Qermezi, and to the memory of the seventeen young Qermezi men who were killed in the 1980s in the Iraq-Iran war.

Preface

I use actual names of people, tribal groups, and places in this account. If Mohammad Reza Shah and his regime had still been in power when I wrote this book, I would have used pseudonyms for the Qermezi subtribe and its members. Because this regime and its key officials were no longer in place in the late 1980s, I could describe their impact on this Qashqa'i group. A very different regime and a new set of officials emerged in 1979 along with some different policies and attitudes toward the Qashqa'i. Whatever the regime in power, Borzu Qermezi, for one, would have been disappointed had he become some imaginary figure in this account.

The language spoken by Qermezi and other Qashqa'i people has been influenced by the different linguistic backgrounds of their ancestors and neighbors and by the dialects of Persian and Luri spoken in the regions they frequented. The Qashqa'i used Turkish, Persian, and Arabic terms for people, tribal groups, and places. They sometimes Persianized Turkish terms, and they Turkicized many Persian terms. In this book I render these terms as they were spoken by most Qermezi Qashqa'i people. Literate Qermezi men wrote words for me in Persian/Arabic script, for Qashqa'i Turkish is not a written language, and I base my transliteration on the style suggested by the *International Journal of Middle Eastern Studies* and followed by many Middle Eastern scholars. I use "e" and "o" for short vowels and omit diacritical marks. It is difficult to represent Persianized Turkish and Turkicized Persian words first in Persian/Arabic script and then in Latin.

Other than personal, tribal, and some place names, I use few Turkish, Persian, and Arabic terms and phrases in this text in order to render it accessible to a wide audience. Such terms and phrases, when they do appear, are italicized on first use. Whenever possible, I rely on English equivalents. I apologize to Qermezi and other Qashqa'i people for converting their hundreds of terms and defining traits into such nondescriptive terms as "sheep" and "grazing land." I translate some place names into English. Other names of locations important in Iranian history, such as Arzhan Plain (Plain of Wild Almond Trees), remain partly or fully in the original. Figures B-5 and B-6 contain the Turkish/Persian and English equivalents of many places mentioned in the text.

The chapters Autumn, Winter, Spring, and Summer contain background and explanatory material and are self-contained. Almost all people mentioned in the text are listed alphabetically and identified in appendix A. Figures (including genealogies) and tables appear in appendixes B and C. A bibliographical essay contains a brief discussion of the book's most pertinent topics.

The central people in this account are Borzu Qermezi, his wife Falak, and their six children (Zolaikha, Mohammad Karim, Zohreh, Farideh, Dariush, Bizhan) still at home. His daughter Samarrokh was married to her cousin Asadollah. Borzu's two full brothers (Gholam Hosain, Abdol Hosain) and three half-brothers (Khalifeh, Ali, Jehangir) and their families are also prominent. Borzu's three hired shepherds (Aqaboa, Khodabakhsh, Mohammad Hosain) and his camel herder (Yadollah) and their families lived with or alongside him. Borzu's rivals Sohrab and Hajji Boa are mentioned frequently. Morad, Borzu's cousin and brother-in-law, was his closest supporter. Ali's son Akbar and Aqaboa's wife Katayun were particularly helpful to me and play important roles in the text.

I recognize that most readers will have difficulty remembering all the names and identities of this book's large cast. At times it may not be essential to know exactly who a particular person is. I suggest that readers remember the names mentioned above, rely on contextual clues for the identities of others, and, as desired, consult appendix A.

Introduction

Borzu Qermezi was the headman and political leader of a group of tribally organized nomadic pastoralists who were part of the Qashqa'i confederacy of southwest Iran. Members of this group accepted him as their representative, and outside authorities including Qashqa'i khans and Iranian government officials verified his position and supported him in it. This book contains an account of a year in the life of Borzu, his extended family, and his political group. I describe the day-to-day activities of this tribal leader interacting with his family and group on different occasions and in varying situations, from the most mundane to the sublime, from the most private and local to the national.

Nomadic pastoralism, it will be seen, is a complex and demanding enterprise full of decisions that must be made quickly, and a wrong choice can have serious long-term consequences. I provide a historical account of a way of life at a particular time and describe how it was affected by broad political and economic forces, as mediated through the specific constellation of local social relationships, themselves shaped by a variety of social and cultural factors. The lives I describe have an implicit narrative form embodied in the frame of time and the social structure.

Borzu and the people of the Qermezi group faced many difficulties in 1970 and 1971. This account, evoking the rhythms of the seasons in a way of life threatened by a host of pressures, details these vicissitudes and the strategies devised by Borzu and the others to cope with them. Expected winter rains did not fall, and the pastures and crops on which the people depended did not grow. The drought caused their debts to urban merchants and moneylenders to mount. Iran's government was increasing its control over the Qashqa'i, and the Qermezi group could not escape the expanding jurisdiction of central authorities. The government's applica-

1

tion of new policies concerning pastures, migratory schedules, animals, prices of pastoral products, and tribal leadership was jeopardizing the people's ability to conduct viable nomadic pastoralism. Non-Qashqa'i agriculturalists and livestock investors were encroaching on land upon which the group depended.

The major theme of this book is the continued viability of both Borzu's leadership and the seasonal migration. During the twelve months detailed here, Borzu's role as tribal headman shifted in response to political and economic changes in Iran as a whole. He gradually lost some of the political support upon which he had relied. The loss of this support from his group can be explained in part by people's resistance to him and their disapproval of his actions. At the same time, these people had been forced to adopt new economic and social strategies to meet circumstances Borzu could not change. They withdrew from him because of outside pressures that not only affected economic conditions but also made part of his role as headman obsolete. They did not need him as they once had, and he could not adequately assist them under the new circumstances.

Borzu's actions and attitudes sometimes seemed better suited to the past than to the circumstances present in 1970 and 1971. His occasional aggressive, belligerent attitude—which was often a pose—was appropriate to the period when leaders of the Qashqa'i confederacy had enjoyed a high degree of political autonomy and tribal members had controlled through force their seasonal territories and their right of migratory passage. Qashqa'i tribespeople had often been able to resist state incursions and rule, had dominated over a settled non-Qashqa'i peasantry, and had fought over boundaries with neighboring tribal groups. Despite Borzu's often astute perceptions of and reactions to changing circumstances, he was still frustrated by them, for they placed him at a disadvantage. He often noted to me as he confronted some adversary, "I would hit him if the government weren't leaning over my shoulder ready to arrest and imprison me."

This account is structured around topics relevant to Iran in the 1960s and early 1970s: the impact of the state in its many dimensions on tribally organized nomadic pastoralists; the economic and social strategies of nomadic pastoralists experiencing pressure on land and resources and in the market; the causes of the decline of nomadic pastoralism; the process of the settlement of nomads; the history of a small tribal group and the ways changing circumstances affected it; the role of a local-level tribal leader as a mediator and broker between two different kinds of political, economic, and sociocultural systems during a period of transition; the changes in a tribal confederacy's political hierarchy; and the ecological, economic, political, social, and cultural significance of the seasonal migration.

The attention I give in this book to political history is intended in part to explain Borzu's style of leadership. His actions, including those that may seem threatening, insensitive, or unwarranted, need to be understood in the context of the rapidly expanding power of the state and the diminishing power of tribal leaders and institutions. I attempt to blend a discussion of Borzu's personal style of leadership with the at-times catastrophic circumstances that befell him and his group, and I discuss the relationship between intragroup political dynamics and political and economic decision-making in the context of rapidly changing times.

I document, moreover, a way of life—the migratory cycle of nomadic pastoralism. The subtext of my account describes the conditions of possibility of that way of life and whether or not it could continue. Just as social relationships were affected by the migratory cycle, so too were they inevitably altered by the conditions of crisis in which that cycle occurred. The mediating thread in the account is Borzu Qermezi and his efforts to wield leadership by controlling the process of migration and its persistence. He effectively equated his leadership with continuation of the pastoral cycle, with the future of nomadic pastoralism. Hence the cessation of nomadism and the settlement of people in his group were politicized processes that implicitly and explicitly challenged his power and authority.

The framework of this book is the yearly round, presented through the four seasons. Seasons rather than weeks or years or some other measure marked the course of time for the Qashqa'i. Seasons marked, as well, the places where the people lived and traveled. Time and space were intermingled for them in ways often confusing to people not accustomed to such perceptions. The many, diverse activities of the nomads corresponded to times and places, so that cheese-making, for example, was associated with the summer season and the location where the producers spent that season. They might not have been able to tell an outsider what year or how many years ago the young child Farideh had been lost and been thought to have been abducted, but they were certain to identify precisely the season, the exact location, and the associated activity. Finally, each of the four seasons was also identified with a particular social group. People formed groups of varying sizes and components to meet the changing requirements of time, space, and activity in the different seasons. The framework of the four seasons thus enables me to describe and explain how people experienced and perceived the circumstances of their lives.

The period covered in each chapter does not exactly correspond with the ninety-some days of the official season. The Qashqa'i considered autumn and spring as the times to migrate, while during winter and summer they inhabited their seasonal pastures. They noted with ceremony the two solstices and two equinoxes. Most people knew exactly how many days had passed since the beginning of the current season and how many remained until the next one. They commented upon, and sometimes marked ritually, the seasonal midpoints. Each season people prepared for the next. They always carried with them a heightened sense of seasonal time.

By focusing on the activities of a man and a small group over one year's time, I avoid some problems found in many anthropological ethnographies. Anthropologists often generalize about a people without much explicit reference to time. Especially when they use the "ethnographic present" tense to describe conditions in the past, they deny the importance of history and the ongoing processes of change that are a vital part of all cultures and societies. I avoid impersonal generalizations by portraying one small group and the precise time in which its members lived. The events and circumstances of the particular year were both typical and atypical, and I explain what was unique as well as what was customary about the patterns and processes of life for Borzu and his group as they traveled through one seasonal round.

In this account I also stress broader issues and the wider context. Qermezi and other Qashqa'i people dealt daily and directly with the pressures of the state, the government, the national economy, and the wider and encompassing Iranian society. Their varied responses to changing political and economic conditions included their attempts to make nomadic pastoralism viable, combine agriculture with pastoralism, abandon nomadism and settle, assume new livelihoods, and form new socioeconomic and political alliances.

After hearing a seminar by a junior anthropologist on the history of an Indian family, an esteemed senior anthropologist commented, "Now, if only we had four hundred million of such reports, we would know something about India." In this book I focus on the particular in order to stress processes affecting Qashqa'i nomadic pastoralists in Iran in the late 1960s and early 1970s. In writing this account I have not, however, altered what I saw and experienced in a small group for the sake of presenting a more general, more widely applicable account. I hope that my descriptions and explanations of the small group inform general as well as specific issues.

Blending ethnographic and historical material, this book contains data unavailable for other tribal and nomadic pastoral people in the Middle East and central Asia. Through this example I explain why nomadic pastoralism was once an important part of this vast region and why tribal society has had such enduring and adaptable qualities. Even if it was possible to conduct long-term ethnographic research in Iran again, the material presented in this book would not be duplicated due to the rapid transformations brought about by the final seven years of Mohammad Reza Shah's rule, the revolution in 1978 and 1979, the establishment of the Islamic Republic, the Qashqa'i insurgency against the Khomeini regime in 1980–1982, and the passage of time. As a colleague of mine notes, this book is "a message in a bottle from the Iran that was."

The Qashqa'i Confederacy

The Qashqa'i people lived and migrated within and near the borders of the southwest Iranian province of Fars, which has long held strategic, political, and economic importance for the rest of Iran. (I use the past tense to correspond with the account that follows; many points I make here also represented Qashqa'i society through 1990.) Fars linked the Persian Gulf with the major centers of population on the central Iranian plateau. The presence of the gulf heightened the significance of Fars for the government capital in Tehran, established there at the end of the eighteenth century, and for foreign powers competing for influence in Iran and the wider region. The discovery of oil before World War I in Khuzistan province to the north, along with continued British domination in the Indian Ocean, the Persian Gulf, and Iraq after World War I, increased the strategic importance of Fars.

The provincial capital of Fars, Shiraz, served as a major urban, market, government, and religious center. The environs of the Zagros Mountains, which run from northwest to southeast in the province, were home to agriculturalists in the broad valleys of the lowlands and nomadic pastoralists organized in tribes and tribal confederacies in the foothills and the highlands.

The Qashqa'i people were part of a tribal confederacy of considerable size and power that played an important regional and, on occasion, national role in Iran in the nineteenth and twentieth centuries. Their leaders were prominent in Shiraz and the province and sometimes exerted influ-

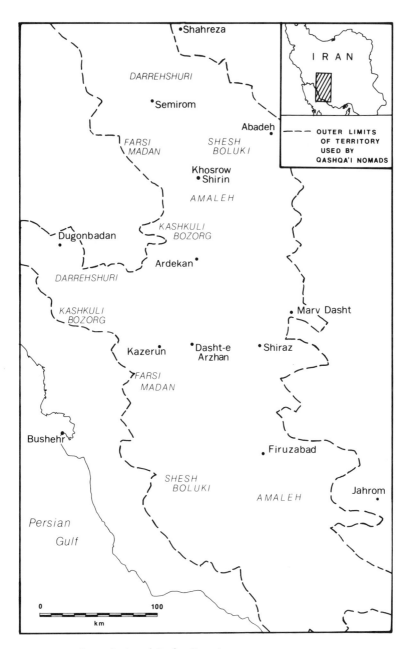

Map 1. Outer limits of Qashqa'i territory

ence on the national level. The confederacy itself was formed, probably beginning in the late eighteenth century, by a complex set of processes. Nomadic pastoralists in the area organized themselves as members of tribes and the confederacy for the defense of natural, economic, and social resources; the expansion of territory and power; and the right of migratory passage. In this organization, they followed existing patterns and improvised as circumstances changed. Urban and rural elites, both tribal and nontribal, relied on the military support available from a tribally organized society and also used its members as a means of securing wealth and labor. Unable to rule much of the countryside directly and in need of military support, revenue, and local law and order, provincial and state elites relied on tribal leaders and their followers for many of these tasks. Agents of foreign powers periodically exerted their own influence in southwest Iran, sometimes claiming to assist state rulers but always serving their own interests, and they too used tribal leaders and their supporters to effect the changes they desired. Hierarchically organized Qashqa'i leaders mediated these powers and the relationships they engendered, and, in so doing, they too played a major role in forming and sustaining the confederacy.

The formation and dissolution of tribes and tribal confederacies in Iran involved complex processes relating to local-level and wider factors. Tribes in Iran were formed out of the conjunction of people using and depending upon resources (land for pastoralism and agriculture, water, migratory routes, trade routes, and markets), external powers and pressures, and mediating agents (tribal leaders, government officials, regional elites, foreign agents, and outside analysts including social scientists). Tribes were useful ways of organizing people, from the point of view of the people themselves, their leaders, and external powers, all of whom could benefit by the organization. The local-level ties of tribally organized people were created on a voluntary basis according to principles and processes of kinship, marriage, coresidence, economics, politics, and friendship. These local-level ties did not create tribes. Rather, tribes were formed through the political affiliation of individuals and groups to local-level and in some cases higher-level groups and leaders. As representatives of their groups for the wider society, the state in particular, tribal leaders played a major role in tribal formation. The extent of supralocal, wider tribal ties is in large part explained by the geopolitical and strategic setting, the value placed internally and especially externally on local resources (natural, economic, social—including labor), the extent of external pressures (especially state and government intervention and influence), the ability of groups to organize and act in terms of their own interests, and the level of military expertise and power. As each of these circumstances altered, so too did the characteristics of tribal groups, leadership systems, and sociopolitical identities.

In *The Qashqa'i of Iran* (1986)—a sociohistorical study based on my anthropological research among the Qashqa'i, interviews with Qashqa'i leaders and others, and archival research—I trace the parallel and vitally interconnected processes of the formation of the Qashqa'i tribal confederacy and the formation of the state in Iran during the late eighteenth, nineteenth, and twentieth centuries. As the Iranian state developed and changed, it played a role in tribal and confederacy formation, while the paramount leaders of the Qashqa'i confederacy mediated among nomadic pastoralists at the local level, lower-level Qashqa'i leaders, regional and national elites, government officials, and agents of foreign powers. These paramount tribal leaders drew their power and authority from diverse sources: their tribal bases; their state, urban, religious, and even international connections; and the rural nontribal agricultural people they governed or controlled. By intention, the tribal leaders became indispensable mediators and brokers for these different sociopolitical and cultural systems. As they integrated these constituencies, they played key roles in consolidating people at the local level and linking them with wider systems.

In this new book I focus on the role of a local-level tribal headman as he attempted to represent and protect his small Qashqa'i group within a wider tribal context and faced with a dominant, encroaching state and society. I examine the ways that Qashqa'i people at the local level related to the hierarchy of Qashqa'i political groups and leaders, wider encompassing society, and state. From Borzu Qermezi's perspective, his role as a tribal leader was vitally connected with what he perceived as benefits to be gained from both local-level and wider contacts.

In these two books I offer views of the same general topic from three different perspectives. In *The Qashqa'i of Iran* I focus on the role of the state in tribal formation and dissolution and on the role of tribal elites as mediators under these circumstances. Here I focus on the third perspective, a local-level group and its leader and their relationship to the wider context in which they lived. Using these three perspectives (the state and the wider context, tribal leaders as mediators, people at the local level), I demonstrate how tribes were built and dismantled from processes occurring at different levels (from the top down, the middle, and the bottom up). This approach allows a comprehensive picture of tribal formation and dissolution as they relate to state and local processes.

Tribal groups in Iran at any given historical period took many different forms. They can be analytically placed along a continuum, with small, decentralized, relatively egalitarian kinship-based groups on one end and large, centralized, socioeconomically stratified nonkinship-based groups on the other. The former lacked leaders beyond local-level elders, while the latter held powerful and wealthy leaders who formed part of the Iranian elite and participated in politics on provincial and national levels. Small tribal groups joined larger ones when, for example, state rulers attempted to restrict access to resources or when foreign troops invaded. Large tribal groups divided into small groups in order to be less visible to the state and escape its reach. Intertribal mobility, particularly in the Zagros Mountains of western Iran, was a common pattern in the eighteenth, nineteenth, and early twentieth centuries and was part of the process of tribal formation and dissolution. Historically, tribal society in Iran contained both nomadic and settled components, and nomadic and settled tribal people relied in various ways on both pastoralism and agriculture.

Tribal groups in Iran, even small ones but especially large tribal confederacies such as the Qashqa'i, traced diverse ethnolinguistic origins for their members. Leadership and the construction (by the people themselves and by outsiders) of tribal and ethnic identities served to unite tribal groups and give their members a sense of solidarity. Tribal systems in Iran demonstrated continuing viability and resiliency in the face of changing circumstances. The ties of tribal people with their groups provided the context in which they lived much of their lives. Tribal ties and identities were more permanent and enduring for them than the affiliations and loyalties sought and sometimes demanded by rulers of Iranian states. States came and went for these people; tribes remained a constant.

The Qashqa'i people claimed origins in the ethnolinguistically diverse peoples of central Asia, the Caucasus, Iran, and Turkey. Their ancestors, they say, were Turks, Lurs, Kurds, Laks, Arabs, Persians, Baluch, and gypsies, among others. None of these labels implies a single group, origin, language, cultural system, or identity. Linguistic and other evidence verifies the diversity of the Qashqa'i. In the twentieth century almost all Qashqa'i asserted a Turkish identity in an environment dominated politically, economically, and numerically by ethnic Persians. By the mid-twentieth century almost all Qashqa'i spoke Turkish as a first language. Speaking Turkish and learning to speak it were part of the process of tribal and confederacy formation; along with other traits, language served to differentiate the Qashqa'i from most other people in southwest Iran.

The Khamseh tribal confederacy neighboring the Qashqa'i to the east was identified by its members and outsiders as "Arab," while its members too traced diverse origins. No single language marked people of this confederacy, despite the label. In southwest Iran in the second half of the nineteenth century and in the twentieth century, the label "Turk" meant Qashqa'i and the label "Arab" meant Khamseh. The label "Lur" identified the Luri-speaking neighbors of the Qashqa'i to the north and west, themselves often organized as tribal groups (Bakhtiyari and such Kuhgiluyeh groups as Boir Ahmad and Mamassani). The Qashqa'i considered themselves "Turks" and all others (whether Persians, Lurs, or others) "tajik."

To be Qashqa'i was closely connected with the practices, technology, lifestyle, customs, and values of nomadic pastoralism, but it also connoted a tribal organization, a hierarchy of tribal leaders, a shared history, a language, and a cultural heritage. Hence, for the Qashqa'i who temporarily or permanently settled in villages and towns, no necessary diminution of tribal identity occurred. A person's identity as a Qashqa'i held cultural and sociopolitical attributes and was often highly significant for settled as well as migrating Qashqa'i. The Qashqa'i were and are Shi'i Muslims, as were almost all other people in southwest Iran. Their religious beliefs and practices expressed their own perceptions of Shi'i Islam as well as regional and specifically Qashqa'i attitudes and customs.

In the middle of the twentieth century the Qashqa'i confederacy contained approximately 400,000 people who identified themselves as Qashqa'i and who affiliated to the hierarchy of political groups and leaders. Every Qashqa'i person was a member of a lineage, subtribe, and tribe and derived part of his or her identity from each of these groups. Everyone was a Qashqa'i as well as, for example, a Darrehshuri (tribal member), a Qermezi (subtribal member), and an Aqa Mohammadli (lineage member). Which of these particular labels was used at any given time depended on the context and circumstance.

The Qashqa'i confederacy consisted of five large tribes (Amaleh, Darrehshuri, Kashkuli Bozorg, Farsimadan, Shesh Boluki), some smaller ones (including Kashkuli Kuchek and Qarachai), and other groups. Each tribe was headed by a family of khans to whom members of that tribe's subtribes affiliated. The confederacy as a whole was headed by the small Janikhani (var. Shahilu) family, whose ancestors had formed the confederacy and who were and are the symbolic head of all Qashqa'i. Khans of the

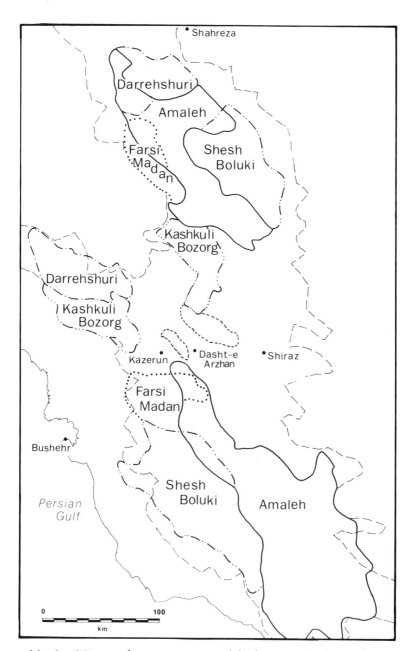

Map 2.   Winter and summer pastures of the five major Qashqa'i tribes

component Qashqa'i tribes allied with and supported the Janikhani family in different ways during their history.

In the nineteenth and twentieth centuries the vast majority of Qashqa'i practiced nomadic pastoralism in the Zagros Mountains in an area between Isfahan and the Persian Gulf to the south and southwest. Qashqa'i nomads inhabited winter pastures at altitudes from 600 to 1,500 meters in the Zagros foothills to the south, west, and northwest of the city of Shiraz. They migrated in the spring to summer pastures at altitudes from 1,900 to 3,300 meters in the alpine valleys of the Zagros north of Shiraz. The highest mountain peak in summer pastures is approximately 4,400 meters. Many Qashqa'i cultivated grain in their two seasonal pastures and depended on the harvest for their own bread and for animal feed. They produced meat, other pastoral products, and sometimes woven goods for sale in markets.

The Qashqa'i were socioeconomically stratified. Leaders of the confederacy and its component tribes constituted a wealthy elite whose income until the early 1960s derived primarily from a non-Qashqa'i peasantry whose land they controlled. They also extracted wealth and labor from their tribal followers but not to the extent of jeopardizing political support. Their economic position needs to be viewed in the context of the regional and national class structure rather than isolated at the Qashqa'i or tribal level. Qashqa'i khans exercised class rule in a larger Iranian context and hierarchical rule in a tribal context. They formed part of Iran's upper class. A second socioeconomic group contained non-elite Qashqa'i who served the khans as advisors, secretaries, overseers, and subtribal headmen. Members of the third group, the majority of Qashqa'i, used pastoral and agricultural land that was controlled by or under the influence of the tribal elite. They occasionally owed a tax to tribal leaders but were otherwise economically independent of them. Servants and workers of the elite, hired shepherds and camel herders, and specialized laborers made up the fourth segment of Qashqa'i society.

Qashqa'i people formed kinship, political, and local groups. They were members of patrilineages and sociopolitically defined subtribes. Their socioterritorial groups were based in part on membership in lineages and subtribes, but other factors such as economic contract and intergroup marriage also brought people into groups at the local level. Nomadic pastoralists set up tent encampments in pastures under the control of lineage and subtribal elders, subtribal headmen, tribal khans, and, since 1962, government agents. During the long autumn and spring migrations, the nomads traveled in groups that reflected the various ties that bound them.

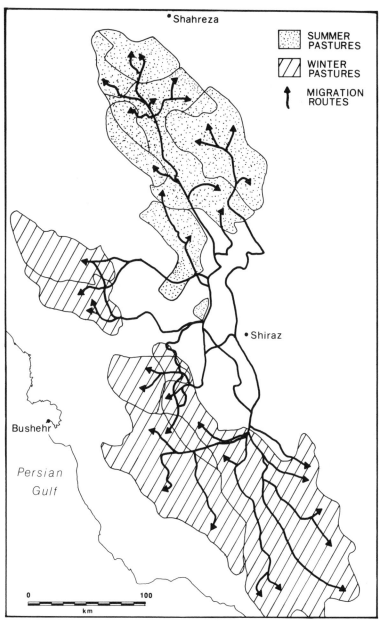

Map 3.   Migratory routes of the Qashqa'i tribes

Qermezi ("The Red Ones") was one of the approximately forty-four subtribes of the Darrehshuri tribe, which was one of the five major Qashqa'i tribes. Because of ongoing processes of subtribal formation and dissolution, in which groups joined together, split apart, and acquired and lost members (all processes to be seen, even in only a year's time, in the Qermezi group), the number of Darrehshuri subtribes fluctuated, and people could not usually determine definitively when one subtribe formally became two subtribes or when a subtribe no longer existed. The existence of certain subtribes such as Qermezi was not in question, but no one agreed completely with others about the rest. Subtribes within the Darrehshuri tribe were not connected genealogically. Members of each asserted their own unique history of how the subtribe formed and came to be part of the Darrehshuri tribe and the Qashqa'i confederacy.

Darrehshuri summer pastures were the most northern of the Qashqa'i pastures and bordered Bakhtiyari tribal territory to the north. Darrehshuri winter pastures, bordering the territory of Kuhgiluyeh Lur tribes, were in the western Zagros foothills near the town of Dugonbadan and far from the winter pastures of other major Qashqa'i tribes except for Kashkuli Bozorg. These two locations, combined with the historical independence of the Darrehshuri khans from the leaders of the Qashqa'i confederacy, gave the tribe a degree of autonomy that other Qashqa'i tribes lacked.

The Qermezi subtribe consisted of approximately one thousand people and included the members of five patrilineages and other associated individuals. Members of three of the lineages claimed a common—although unnamed and possibly mythical—ancestor, while the other two maintained traditions of separate origin. Lineage membership was almost always traced patrilineally; men and women were members of the lineage of their fathers. Men camped and migrated primarily with lineage mates. Women camped and migrated with the families of their husbands. People usually married within the subtribe, to a fellow lineage member or a member of one of the other four lineages. Everyone in a lineage was interlinked by kinship and marriage. A man's father-in-law, for example, may also have been his father's brother. Marriage between close relatives, particularly patrilateral and matrilateral cousins (especially first cousins), was the preferred pattern. Some people married members of other Darrehshuri subtribes and a few married members of other Qashqa'i tribes, and so most people also had more extensive ties. Everyone was connected by multiple strands of relationships within the lineage, subtribe, tribe, and confederacy. A few ties with other tribes and other groups extended people's links beyond these sociopolitically defined borders. The subtribe as a social entity was bounded in these ways and connected to similar and to larger entities.

At the local level the basic socioeconomic unit was the household, which was contained within a single tent. Headed by an adult man and usually containing a nuclear family consisting of a married man and woman and their children, households owned and tended their own herd and pack animals, used pasture independently, and made economic and political decisions. Upon marriage a woman joined the household of her husband's parents, and the young couple lived there until they decided to form their own independent household. The last son remained with his parents in the parental tent and cared for them in their old age. Most households holding more than a nuclear family contained a son's bride and possibly their young children or an elderly father or mother.

According to the earliest collective memories of Qermezi people, their men had always loyally supported and been closely affiliated with the Darrehshuri khans. Borzu's father Shir Mohammad, then Qermezi's headman, was killed in 1943 fighting in a war the Iranian army waged against Qashqa'i and Boir Ahmad Lur forces led by khans. Borzu's elder brother Khalifeh had also been a loyal headman.

In 1964 Borzu took over the headmanship from his ailing and dispirited brother. Combined with his aggressive attitude and imposing physical presence, the factors that led to his headmanship were the personal and effective ties he had developed with the Darrehshuri khans, his locally prominent role in a tribal movement against Mohammad Reza Shah (r. 1941–1979) in the 1950s, and his lucrative appointment as a khan's overseer of shepherds. As headman, his primary responsibility was to mediate on the subtribe's behalf with khans and, increasingly, government agents.

Borzu and the position of subtribal headman grew in importance when Mohammad Reza Shah divested the power of the top two levels (*ilkhani*, khans) of the Qashqa'i political hierarchy in the 1950s and 1960s. But in other ways Borzu and his position also lost some importance because their vital place in the chain of power and authority within this hierarchy was all but gone. Both changes resulted in his playing a new role, and he improvised as circumstances continued to change rapidly.

After the early 1960s the Qashqa'i fell under the control of many different, often competing government agencies. They perceived the Iranian military as an oppressive, vindictive force and the government bureaucracy as a virtually meaningless maze. Officials attempted to centralize control over the Qashqa'i, but in 1970 and 1971 their mandates were unclear and their agencies uncoordinated. They experienced administrative and other problems, in part because Qashqa'i nomads were dispersed over and mobile within a wide area of southwest Iran during the course of a year. Even in towns near winter and summer pastures, control over the nomads was decentralized in different offices whose personnel often knew little about the others' policies and actions. Qashqa'i people were forced to relate to each and to all agencies. One main reason a headman such as Borzu was so essential was that he was in a position to handle these contacts and other members of the subtribe ordinarily were not.

In most contexts Borzu was the undisputed headman of Qermezi subtribe, but two Qermezi men occasionally posed a challenge to him. Leading man in his own lineage and Borzu's father's sister's son, Sohrab was a thorn in Borzu's side and irritated him. Sohrab desired power and authority in the subtribe and received support from two Darrehshuri khans. Khans often noted that it was useful for them to support two men rather than one in a subtribe, for it gave them more control and a balance of power. Khans competed with one another for tribal support, and rival khans supported rival leaders at the subtribal level. Borzu sought expressions of loyalty from group members. Any man who could challenge this loyalty was a threat to him and caused him concern. Hajji Boa, Borzu's patrilateral kinsman who was settled in a village and offered to help the Qermezi people who wanted to settle, was such a man. He represented to Borzu the real and the potential loss of his political support.

Borzu, the Qermezi people, and all other Qashqa'i were experiencing the impact of wide-scale political, economic, and social changes in 1970 and 1971. In this book I depict the local-level circumstances resulting from changes occurring in Iran as a whole.

In the mid-1950s Mohammad Reza Shah had exiled the leaders of the Qashqa'i confederacy from Iran because of their support of Prime Minister Mohammad Mosaddeq before and after the 1953 coup d'état. The shah perceived them as posing a continuing threat to his regime. In the early 1960s he nationalized pastures and enacted a national land reform, which changed the relationship between the Qashqa'i and the land on which they depended. The state expropriated pastoral and agricultural land used exclusively by them, and non-Qashqa'i livestock investors and agriculturalists gained access to it. Simultaneous to the implementation of new land policies, the shah took steps to seize military and political control over the Qashqa'i people from the tribal khans and to place that control in the hands of government agents. Rural police (gendarmes) disarmed the Qashqa'i and subjected their seasonal migrations to military control. The shah's repressive secret police (SAVAK) engaged in ever-expanding surveillance and intimidation. Changes in the national economy (inflation, government-subsidized imports of meat and dairy products, the government's neglect of agriculture and pastoralism) were debilitating for the Qashqa'i. Officials promoting the rapid expansion of national education wanted to Persianize the Qashqa'i and other non-Persians, integrate them into a modernizing Iranian society, and substitute loyalties to the nation-state for loyalties to tribes and ethnic groups.

The impact of these changes on the lives of Qashqa'i nomads would become even more apparent in subsequent years. The process of their settlement and further incorporation in Iranian society was accelerated until 1978 and 1979 when Iran was swept up in a revolution that ousted the shah and brought forth the Islamic Republic of Iran. The paramount Qashqa'i leaders seized the opportunity afforded by the revolution to return to Iran after twenty-five years of forced exile. They sought to reestablish their position in the confederacy, region, and nation, but their efforts failed. After an insurgency they and other Qashqa'i waged against military forces of the Islamic Republic from 1980 through 1982, they were again forced out of potential leadership positions when the new regime won the military struggle and subjected the insurgents to imprisonment, execution, foreign and internal exile, and house arrest.

The Book's Genesis

I base this account of the passage of Borzu Qermezi and his group through the four seasons in 1970 and 1971 on the daily journal I wrote at the time. While living with Borzu's family and group, I kept three sets of notes. The main set related specifically to the topic of my doctoral dissertation research, which was a study of local organization among nomadic pastoralists. The second set contained material that I thought at the time was peripheral to the topic of local organization. I wrote down information as I learned it, regardless of its immediate relevance to my research topic. The third set was the daily journal. Every day without fail I wrote in detail about the previous day's activities and described events and interactions. Much of this description focused on Borzu's camp where I lived, but I also met daily with people in other camps and with outsiders of many kinds. Every day many people visited Borzu's camp, and I noted why they had come and what happened during their stay. Almost every day I visited other camps, either alone or accompanied, and observed the range of activities that occurred within the larger group. I often talked with people away from camps as they went about their daily tasks. During the two long seasonal migrations when the social environment vastly expanded, I kept a detailed record of daily activities, the physical and social terrain through which the group traveled, and the diverse interactions of Borzu's group with other Qashqa'i and with members of the wider Iranian society.

Most of what I wrote in the journal came from my observations and casual interactions and not directly from formal or informal discussions and interviews. When I talked with people and was able to take notes, I recorded information in the other two sets of notes. Later I augmented these notes with material I had not been able to write down at the time of the discussions. When I had some time to myself, I wrote in the journal about what had happened and what I had seen the previous day.

At the time, I never intended to use the journal for purposes other than to check details and the sequence of events. My other two sets of notes contained the information on which I planned to base the doctoral dissertation and other scholarly writings. While writing in the journal I never looked at the entries of previous days. After I completed the journal, the day after my final day spent with Qermezi people, I did not look at it again.

In 1987 I began to type on a word processor some handwritten notes I had taken during a second period of research among the Qashqa'i in 1977. Inspired by what I saw in those notes, I also typed other handwritten notes from the earlier period of research in 1970 and 1971. Having by 1987 forgotten some details of that period, I found the volumes of the journal I had written at the time and began to read. I was astonished to see the wealth of information it contained. My memory of the journal was that it held only ordinary descriptions and daily, by now probably unimportant and uninteresting, details. I was intrigued by the account of Borzu and his group during the time I lived with them. I saw unfolding before my eyes the ecological and economic crisis facing the group, the people's agonizing decisions to settle or remain as nomadic pastoralists, and the political and personal crisis coming to a head for Borzu. I often cried as I read the account, moved by the problems the people had faced and by my memory, now enriched, of them. I was saddened to read about individuals who had since then died. While of course nothing "new" was in this account, for I had witnessed and experienced all that I had written about, I was struck by the immediacy of events and the difficult circumstances of life for the people I had grown to know. Reading the journal in its entirety for the first time, I was surprised to see patterns emerge that

I am not sure I saw at the time of the original research. Although I had been preparing in 1987 to write another kind of book, the present work is the one I needed and wanted to write first.

Even though this account covers events in 1970 and 1971, I could not have written it in 1972 after my return to the United States. My first responsibility then was writing the doctoral dissertation. Professional and especially institutional pressures since 1972 required that I devote my energies to other tasks and projects. In 1972 I also did not yet have the necessary distance from the experience of living with this group. My reading of the journal then would not have had the impact it did many years later.

In 1977 and 1979 I returned to Qashqa'i territory to resume research on the Qermezi group and the wider Qashqa'i confederacy. In 1979 I studied British government, university, and museum archives in London to understand the interrelationship of Iran, Great Britain, and the Qashqa'i confederacy. The revolution in Iran in 1978–1979 had made possible a more explicitly political research on the confederacy. Since 1976 I have conducted research among members of the Qashqa'i political elite, some of whom had been in exile in Europe and the United States and were soon to be exiled again. The impact of the revolution, when the paramount Qashqa'i leaders seized the opportunity to return to Iran from exile to resume positions of leadership, and then the insurgency that this elite waged against military forces of the Islamic Republic from 1980 through 1982 have drawn my attention since 1978.

To prepare to write this book, I read through the journal once again and then reviewed all other notes I had taken during the period the journal covered. I begin the account with the autumn migration of 1970, continue it through the period of residence in winter pastures and the return spring migration to summer pastures, and end with the beginning of the next autumn migration of 1971. In this account I do not add my own presence beyond the few pages that follow. In the description of events occurring during the year, I always write from personal observation and experience. When I recount the group's notions of its own history, I rely on what Qermezi people told me.

Conditions of Research

Since 1963 and 1964 when I was an undergraduate university student in Iran and visited Qashqa'i territory, I planned to conduct anthropological research among the Qashqa'i. My original research proposal, written when I was a graduate student in anthropology at the University of Chicago, outlined my intentions to work among Qashqa'i nomadic pastoralists. My application for a Fulbright-Hays fellowship was approved by the Office of Education in Washington, D.C., pending permission of officials at the United States Embassy in Tehran. Vetoing the proposal, embassy officials noted that a woman could not conduct research in the mountains of Iran and certainly could not live among the Qashqa'i, whom they said were lawless and dangerous people. When, on my own initiative, I resubmitted the proposal to the Office of Education after having changed the group of study from nomadic pastoralists to villagers in the same area, embassy officials approved the application, and my fellowship was granted.

I went to Iran in November 1969, accompanied by Sam Beck, in order to conduct research among recently settled, formerly nomadic, Qashqa'i villagers. After a tedious bureaucratic delay in procuring official Iranian approval of the research (a delay all other foreign researchers were also experiencing, regardless of topic or group of study), Sam and I went to Shiraz to survey the surrounding area for an appropriate village. On a trip to the Kazerun area west of Shiraz in early spring, we saw thousands of Qashqa'i nomads beginning the spring migration to summer pastures. When we stopped along the road to wait for people and animals to pass by unimpeded, a boisterous, middle-aged Qashqa'i man came from a camp toward the road and invited us to have tea with him. At first I politely refused and then, on his insistence, accompanied him to his tent. I thought he might help us to find a group of settled Qashqa'i. As tea was being prepared, I saw a man slaughter and begin to butcher a young goat, and it dawned on me that we were expected to stay for a meal. I welcomed the chance to talk with a Qashqa'i family. Other men and boys from surrounding tents came to sit by the fire and talk, and women and children gathered nearby. The afternoon and evening passed pleasantly and quickly. The meal was not ready until well after dark, and our host expected us to stay the night. Before dawn people in the family were up and about, and they had packed up the tent and camp and were on the move before sunrise. After politely, reluctantly declining our host's offer to accompany him on the day's migration, we said our farewells and returned to Shiraz. I never expected to see him again.

Dr. Sirus Azarnia, director of the government's Office of Tribal Development (in actuality, office for the settlement of nomads) in Shiraz, helped us to locate villages near Qashqa'i summer and winter pastures. He also took us to an area where the government was settling nomads of the

dissolved Khamseh tribal confederacy. After seeing me talking with nomads in tents nearby, he asked me why I wanted to study villagers instead
of nomads. I told him that the United States government was apparently
worried about my safety, and he laughed. He then offered to introduce
me to several headmen of nomadic groups and promised to process the
necessary government clearances if one of them invited us to stay. He
advised me to write to officials at the United States Embassy, to inform
them of my possible change in plans, and see what their reaction would
be. When no response came, I took the silence as consent. I knew for a
fact that my letter had been received and discussed. Several weeks later
an embassy official told me informally and off the record that I could
follow my new plans without concern. He did caution me not to get killed
because, he said, my death would cause political problems for relationships, then rapidly intensifying, between Iran and the United States.

Azarnia introduced us to Jehangir Khan, a prominent Darrehshuri
Qashqa'i khan and a man who Azarnia said could be of help. Jehangir
Khan invited us to stay with him in his camp at Round Sun (Mehr-e
Gerd) in Darrehshuri summer pastures while we sought a group of nomads with whom to live. His sons and daughters were anxious to learn
or practice English, and we were glad to help. From midspring into the
summer of 1970 we remained as his guests while I began research in
Round Sun and the surrounding Darrehshuri territory on the tribe and
confederacy. During the wait for further Iranian government clearance,
Jehangir Khan and members of his extended family offered suggestions
about Darrehshuri groups. Initially they were reluctant about sending us
into the rugged Darrehshuri territory and on the long seasonal migrations, where they said living conditions would be difficult. With the exception of Jehangir Khan's brother Ayaz Khan, they had not been on these
migrations themselves for eight years, and they noted that even they
would find the two- to three-month treks arduous, accustomed as they
now were to new comforts. They finally settled upon the names of the
headmen of three Darrehshuri subtribes, and Jehangir Khan said we
would have a chance to meet the men when they each came on their own
business to see him.

The first two headmen invited us to visit, and as we were preparing to
go with one of them, the third one appeared. He was Borzu Qermezi, the
man who had entertained us, quite by chance, during the spring migration. We were astonished at the coincidence. I had not known he was a
member of the Darrehshuri tribe; I had not asked him about his political
affiliations. Borzu immediately invited us to live with him as long as we

wished, and we did not hesitate to say we would be delighted. We visited him in his summer pastures and talked with members of his group, and I continued research in Darrehshuri territory on the tribe and its organization. In late summer when I received, after another bureaucratic hassle, a government document permitting us to travel without restriction in Fars and adjoining provinces where Qashqa'i were located, we joined Borzu on the autumn migration. We remained with him and his family into the following autumn, after the Iranian military halted all Qashqa'i migrations until Mohammad Reza Shah concluded his celebration of twenty-five hundred years of the Iranian monarchy. When the ostentatious celebration ended, we stayed at Atakola, a new village near Darrehshuri summer pastures where some of Borzu's relatives had just settled. We returned to the United States in December 1971.

I had learned spoken and written Persian when I had been a student at Pahlavi (Shiraz) University in Iran in 1963 and 1964. In the years that followed I studied Persian, Arabic, and Turkish in colleges and universities in the United States. Sam knew none of these languages when we first entered Iran, but by the time of our departure he spoke Qashqa'i Turkish and especially Persian well. We began to learn Qashqa'i Turkish when we lived in Round Sun and traveled in Qashqa'i territory in the spring and summer of 1970. After we joined Borzu and the Qermezi group in the late summer, our knowledge of Turkish rapidly increased, and I needed to rely on Persian much less frequently than before. Because Qashqa'i people associated the Persian language with the government agents and urban merchants and moneylenders who harassed and exploited them, we tried to use Qashqa'i Turkish exclusively. Many Qashqa'i men were fluent in Persian because of their frequent contact with the Persian-dominated society surrounding them, but very few Qashqa'i women at the subtribal level knew much Persian because of their own limited contacts with Persian speakers. Qashqa'i men and women preferred speaking Turkish with us and were proud of our growing linguistic abilities. No one in the Qermezi group knew any English.

It was difficult to conduct research in Iran in the late 1960s and early 1970s because of the climate of fear that affected everyone. Agents and informers of SAVAK, the shah's repressive secret police, were said to be everywhere, and citizens and others never knew for certain what acts and forms of expression the regime would tolerate. Although I wanted to conduct research on Qashqa'i political organization, I understood that Iranian and American officials disapproved and might prevent it. My topic of research concerned local organization, which seemed to be less problematic although not as apolitical as pastoralism and its technology, for example. I wanted to avoid causing harm to the people with whom I lived and visited; I did not want to draw the attention of government officials to them. I avoided government offices in Kazerun and Semirom, towns near Qermezi winter and summer pastures respectively, even though I knew their personnel might help to provide information about the government's relationship with the Qashqa'i. I did not want to be in a position of answering their questions about my activities. My research permit was a long-term one that appeared to have no restrictions, but I never knew if government agents were applying pressure to have the permit canceled or raising questions with key officials about my activities. All government agents, in fact almost all non-Qashqa'i Iranians, were appalled and amazed that anyone would want to live with Qashqa'i nomads, whom they perceived as uncivilized, backward, and prone to violence and theft. Often officials' questions about what I was doing and why were probably harmless in the sense that they would not act on information they received, but I still gave short nonspecific answers. With outsiders I always avoided topics that appeared to be political.

Borzu was a superlative host for our entire stay. Even though he was under stress he seemed to enjoy our presence. When other Qashqa'i people invited us to visit or live with them, Borzu was concerned that we might leave him. He also worried that the climate and weather would be difficult for us and that we would not get enough food. I was concerned that we would be an economic drain on his household and would draw undue attention to him. After his many protests that we were his guests for as long as we wished, he ultimately did not interfere with our desire to contribute food. When we went to town we bought rice, flour, fruits, vegetables, dates, nuts, tea, sugar, live chickens, and eggs—all foods these Qashqa'i ate if they could afford it. We gave these supplies to Borzu's wife Falak when she was alone, so that he and others would not see us give food. We ate with Borzu's family during our entire stay and shared their own often sparse fare. Because of his responsibilities as group spokesman, he often hosted guests and visitors, and we shared in those meals as well. We usually accompanied him when members of his group invited him as a guest. When he traveled outside Qermezi territory to villages, towns, and cities and to the Darrehshuri khans' camps and urban residences, we rarely accompanied him.

We tried to reciprocate the hospitality of Borzu and members of his group in other ways. I mention these contributions because anthropologists sometimes appear not to understand the full economic (let alone political) implications of their residence among the people they have chosen to study, and they can be an economic burden. It must also be noted that these people often have little or no choice in deciding whether or not anthropologists are going to live with them and examine their lives. From the start, the relationship is unequal. And anthropologists rarely become hosts to the people they have studied and do not reciprocate in kind.

We gave Borzu, members of his group, and other people we visited such gifts as clothes, fabric, jewelry, knives, flashlights, and lanterns. We almost always gave items these people used themselves, and they especially appreciated the qualities of foreign-made goods and the gifts we had brought or had sent from the United States and Europe. When Falak fell seriously ill and finally received what passed in Iran as "modern" professional care, we provided financial help and also convinced government officials to reduce the large hospital bill. We frequently rendered first aid and rudimentary medical assistance and on occasion took people to Shiraz, Isfahan, and nearby towns for emergency care. We paid for treatment and medicine. We brought a medical team from Shiraz to inoculate people against smallpox and other diseases, and we invited veterinarians from the university there to treat and inoculate animals. We helped Borzu and his group obtain grain, fodder, and transportation from the government during the drought. After Borzu bought a pickup truck and then could no longer find or pay for a driver (for he never attempted to learn to drive himself), his son Mohammad Karim drove. When the son went to Kazerun for school examinations, Sam drove the truck, and Borzu was grateful. (I never rode in the vehicle during the migrations. Borzu provided me with his best horse.)

Through our acquaintance with Mohammad Bahmanbaigi, director of the Office of Tribal Education in Shiraz, we helped Qermezi children and young adults gain access to the tribal education program and further their education in town schools, particularly the tribal high school and the tribal teachers training program in Shiraz. When we could, we assisted Borzu and other Qermezi people in their encounters with hostile outsiders, including state agents and local notables. Outsiders constantly harassed Qermezi people and issued threats and demands, and we were sometimes able to deflect their attention. Borzu needed to bribe fewer individuals and give less money because of our presence. When I returned to Iran, twice in 1977 and once in 1979 after the revolution, I brought gifts for Borzu and his family and group members, and I did so again during my research trip to Iran in 1991.

Our main contribution to Borzu, at least in terms of how he evaluated our presence, was not directly economic. He used us to verify and enhance his social status in his relationship with members of his group, other Qashqa'i (especially the elite), Iranian officials, and members of the surrounding non-Qashqa'i society. Government officials and regional elites often challenged his status and emphasized what they perceived to be their own higher status. As long-term host to Americans, however, Borzu indicated that his status rose equal to or above them. He often proclaimed to people that we had been guests of Jehangir Khan Darrehshuri (a prominent, powerful man) and were now his guests. He was proud whenever Ayaz Khan Darrehshuri publicly and repeatedly invited us to live with him; we always said we were already guests of Borzu and were comfortable staying with him. He wanted us to impress others, and we were willing to comply. This dimension of our presence was the one he appreciated the most.

Borzu said we enhanced his entertainment of guests and visitors. A major part of his role as headman was serving as liaison between his group and outsiders of many kinds, whom he often hosted. He developed a repertoire of questions he would ask us, depending on the status and sophistication of these outsiders. His questions included: How many tribes are there in America? How many camels does your father own? Are there fat-tailed sheep like mine in America? How many days did you travel from America to my tent and by how many conveyances? How many years have you spent in school, and what is taking you so long to finish? He would lean back, smiling, as visitors expressed amazement at our answers. When Persian and Lur peasants claiming to be pious Muslims (and sometimes to trace descent from the prophet Mohammad) came to harass him about his sheep in their cultivated fields, Borzu would demand a list of the full names of the twelve Shi'i imams and then smugly listen while the peasants could not respond fully and I could.

Borzu appeared to take great pleasure in being our host. We attempted to respond in ways he would appreciate. As time progressed, we came increasingly to enjoy his company, and I believe that he enjoyed ours.

We shared with Borzu an appreciation of certain kinds of humor, and we savored the way he explained customs, events, and interactions. In a casual conversation about an entirely different subject, he would often nonchalantly mention something that he knew we wanted to know, and he would watch carefully for the first sign that we understood. He delighted in teaching us things we could not comprehend until he explained them. Early in our stay with him, he tore a large oak leaf into pieces to show me how the Qashqa'i confederacy was segmented (and then he stomped on a piece that represented a Qashqa'i tribe whose men had once stolen sheep from him). And late one night as we sat around the fire in the winter tent, Borzu hushed everyone, told us to listen carefully, and then questioned us about a strange bellowing, bubbling noise off in the distance. "What could that possibly be?" he kept asking, pretending to look puzzled himself. "Are there noises like that in America?" he wondered aloud. After sending out Sam and Yadollah with a flashlight to investigate, we learned that the noise came from a hobbled, agonized male camel in rut with a swollen flapping tongue and frothing mouth.

Borzu tested us about our growing knowledge of his group and its history and activities. When a man or woman we had not seen before arrived at his camp, he would quiz us about the person's identity by saying, for example, "This man's father's brother's wife's brother was shot in the battle of Semirom." We would have to piece together the connections ourselves, as he slowly, with relish, provided additional, often obscure, hints. Later he would boast to others about how we had finally managed to figure out who a particular "stranger" was. He would pretend to be miffed when it was clear we had learned something from someone else. I learned to tease Borzu in the same way he teased us, by, for example, using all-female links in describing who I had seen that day, when his style (and that of all men) was to stress ties among men, even though ties among women might have been much closer and hence simpler to explain.

It was with sadness that we finally had to leave Borzu's company.

There was no way to repay Borzu's hospitality completely, and I still worry about our having been an economic and emotional drain on him. For the opportunity he provided us, for us to have had the chance to live with him for over a year, under the difficult circumstances this book describes, there is no comparable measure by which we could have or could still reciprocate. I remain deeply indebted to his generosity and his open-mindedness to our presence.

Autumn

Borzu circled the large camp on his horse one last time. After shouting further unnecessary instructions to the others, he headed south out of the alpine valley of Hanalishah where he and his group had spent the summer.

Today they were beginning the three-month-long autumn migration to winter pastures four hundred kilometers away, a trek that would take them from summer pastures high in the Zagros Mountains to the Zagros foothills rising above the coastal plains of the Persian Gulf. Camels loaded with folded tents and other heavy baggage were anxious to leave too. They seemed to know the route and schedule already, for they rose to their feet and headed south, followed by men and boys. Women and children hastened to finish packing possessions and load them on donkeys and mules, and then they circled the campsite to check for forgotten and mislaid items.

Shepherds with their sheep and goats had left before dawn. These animals traveled more slowly than the pack animals so they could graze along the way. For the past month they had eaten fresh stubble in recently harvested fields. Now that this vegetation was depleted, herders were anxious to see what resources would still be available on the route ahead.

Borzu's group was part of the Darrehshuri, the tribe the Iranian government scheduled last to begin the autumn migration. Military officers falsely claimed that this tribe needed less time than the other Qashqa'i tribes to migrate because its winter quarters were closer. Officers also hoped to prevent crowding by allowing nomads in southern and central Qashqa'i summer pastures to be well on their way to winter pastures before the most northern group, the Darrehshuri, began its migration. To the dismay of Darrehshuri nomads, this government policy meant that they were unlikely to find much if any good grazing along the route because of the millions of animals that had already preceded them.

The autumn migration was different from the spring migration when herds grazed fresh wild vegetation. Then herders kept their animals on the high slopes of mountains and hills away from the cultivated fields of the valleys below. But in autumn no fresh vegetation grew and little was left of earlier growth, so herds relied on stubble in harvested fields and kept to the valley floors. Agriculturalists often tried to limit access to their fields to their own animals. They could not, however, forbid nomads to travel through the vicinity, for the migrators held not only government-decreed rights of passage but also rights to camp for "one day and one night" in any uninhabited location. Agriculturalists opposed this policy because it threatened resources they claimed for themselves. Nomads had used the migratory route's resources without much restriction for generations, and they resisted attempts to curtail their activities. Much of the natural pasturage on which they formerly relied was now obliterated, having been plowed under by agriculturalists. Grain harvested from land where pasture used to thrive was now consumed in villages and exported to cities and did not benefit the nomads, who vehemently proclaimed that they held inherent rights, at the very least, to the stubble remaining behind.

Water was another problem in autumn. During the spring migration, nomads usually found natural springs and streams in the mountains, and they benefited from melting snow and the last of the winter rains. During the autumn migration, they were forced to draw water in the valleys from wells, springs, and channels that were already claimed and protected by settled people. The two groups often met with antagonism.

Borzu rode ahead of the caravan of people and pack animals to confront with his authority and power any possible threats to the group. His companions had discussed the schedule and route to be taken, even precise campsites, during the past days and weeks in the relative idleness that preceded the migration. Still, Borzu wanted to alter plans quickly if other nomads were crowding the route or preempting his chosen campsites or if water was scarce. For weeks he had sought out news of conditions along the migratory route and the schedules of other groups, but he still expected to make decisions on a daily, even moment to moment, basis.

Borzu also rode ahead because he wanted to choose the most suitable campsite for his group and particularly his own tent. If he were not the first to arrive, he might lose this chance. A favorable spot, away from the track where other nomads would travel, was one with good grazing, water, and fuel nearby and some protection from the elements. Harsh winds and blowing dust, especially, were problems in autumn. He sought for himself a central location from which he could observe his traveling companions and others in the vicinity. The reputations of tribal headmen such as Borzu were known far and wide, but Qashqa'i and other people were often able to assess these men personally only during the migration. A large traveling party attested to the status of the central figure, and a large camp with tents arranged around his spoke to his leadership abilities. The headman needed and wanted a visible body of supporters. A central location for his tent was practical too, for he could call for assistance and send people on errands. People in his entourage provided support for his many and frequent guests and visitors.

While resident in winter and summer pastures over which they held customary and now some legal rights, these nomads could protect their families, wealth, and resources, but during the migration they traveled through alien territory and had only the defense the group itself could muster. Many, therefore, chose to travel in groups ranging from a few to thirty families to benefit from the support of allied people. A large traveling party provided protection through sheer numbers and enough men to track thieves and stolen animals. Theft of animals, always on men's minds, was the major threat during the migration. Nomads who lived as solitary families or in small groups in secluded locations in winter and summer pastures took the opportunity of the migration to join others. People who were drawn away by marriage or other reasons from their group of origin especially appreciated the migration. Men sometimes invited their sons-in-law to travel with them, and women and families who were separated by marriage enjoyed a chance to be together. People demonstrated their loyalty to the headman by accompanying him and received benefits in return.

The first day of the autumn and spring migrations, called "changing the stones," held special meaning for the Qashqa'i. Whenever they occupied a campsite where they planned to stay more than a day, they piled their possessions on a row or platform of stones at the back of the tent to protect them from ground moisture, dirt, and insects. The stone structure as well as the baggage on top symbolized home and family. People at Hanalishah planned the first day's move as a short one lasting less than an hour. Although they had changed their campsites at least several times while resident in summer pastures during the past three months, they still needed several days to adjust to the routine of daily packing and traveling. They perceived the first move as a practice one to test loads on

1.   Morad driving loaded camels on the migration

animals and rearrange baggage. A short first move also allowed people to return to Hanalishah to retrieve forgotten items.

In autumn, but not spring, these nomads were forced by the lack of natural vegetation to carry fodder for their animals, which meant extra burdens for pack animals. During the preceding weeks some men had borrowed or bought additional animals for transport and entrusted to settled kin or "village friends" the animals that were unfit for the months of hard travel ahead. Some settled people were glad to lend surplus animals, for they were then spared the expense and effort of feeding and caring for them during the harsh winter months when the area was heavily blanketed with snow and the weather bitterly cold.

First to arrive at the chosen site in the next valley, Borzu stood where he wanted his own tent set up and gestured to the others as they came into view to fan out around him. Other men, riding horses or mules, were usually the first of their families to arrive at the site so that they too

2. Abdol Rasul on horseback

could select their own spots. Sometimes the camp and even the tent sites were the precise ones used in previous seasons and years. They saw the fire pits they had dug and sometimes the row of stones for baggage from their last passage, which marked the exact spots where they had camped before.

Borzu's hired shepherd and camel herder chose sites close to him, and his herds would sleep between his tent and theirs for protection from thieves and predators and to prevent straying. Men most closely allied with Borzu camped nearby, and other men such as compatible brothers or men and their sons-in-law camped side by side a distance away.

By midmorning twenty households had arrived. Not all people pitched their woven goat-hair tents; the weather was good, the effort seemed unnecessary, and they anticipated an early departure the next morning. Some made shelters from the reed screens they ordinarily used as a base for the tent or from a wooden tripod covered with a blanket or tent panel. Piles of baggage also served as shelter. Borzu always wanted his tent put up because he needed a physical display of his leadership and, not incidentally, had the extra labor to erect it. Besides, he was apt to have guests or at least visitors, and therefore his place of residence was a more public space than that of others in camp. In an hour or so, his dwelling and possessions looked exactly as they had appeared early in the morning before the day's disassembling and transporting. Before the pack animals were completely unloaded, Borzu tapped a spot and instructed his camel herder Yadollah and his sixteen-year-old daughter Zolaikha to dig a fire pit and make tea. He located a carpet that had been draped over a camel's load, spread it on the ground, and placed himself conspicuously on it to oversee activities.

Once the tent was up, the baggage organized, and his thirteen-year-old daughter Zohreh on the way to a distant spring to collect water, Borzu prepared his lunch. The day before he had ordered the slaughter of a thin sickly goat that would not have survived the three-month trek, and he called to Falak, his wife of twenty-two years, to find him a sharp knife and a metal skewer so he could cut chunks of meat from a hind quarter and roast them over the fire. Smelling broiling meat, his sons four-year-old Dariush and three-year-old Bizhan rushed to sit close by him in hopes of tidbits. Although some families celebrated together the "changing the stones," Borzu observed the event privately over his kebab and flat bread. When he finished his meal he told Yadollah to saddle his horse, and then he abruptly left camp for Semirom, the region's economic and administrative center.

3.   Borzu inspecting the horns and pelt of a wild goat in front of his tent at Han-alishah. August 1977.

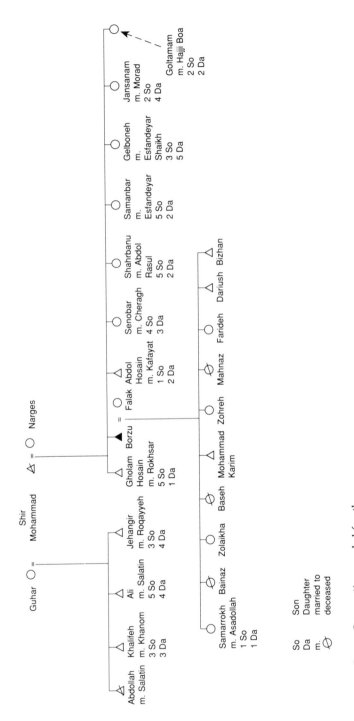

4. Borzu Qermezi's extended family

The government's Tribal Security Force in Semirom, a branch of the gendarmerie responsible for the military control of the Qashqa'i tribes, had not yet granted permission for the Darrehshuri to begin the autumn migration. Many nomads, however, had congregated in the plains of Semirom to await the decree. Borzu did not want to be crowded with other nomads while they waited together, but he also did not want to be the last to arrive at the staging area. At this time of year, headmen of many Darrehshuri groups frequently went to Semirom to await word of the departure date, or they sent someone in their place. Borzu often went himself because he also needed to settle affairs in Semirom offices from the summer and even years past before he left the area. For example, in early summer he had engaged in an escalating, then violent, conflict with a Persian man whom the government had permitted to cultivate at Hanalishah on the basis of its national land reforms of the 1960s. The two men had fought over water rights and the border separating pastoral and agricultural land. The cultivator had severed the ears of one of Borzu's donkeys; he claimed the animal habitually ate his ripening lentil crop. He had not filed a complaint with the gendarmerie or the Tribal Security Force because of his (correct) suspicion that Borzu had already bribed their compliance and gained some support. He brought his complaint instead to the secret police, which had caused irksome problems with government officials for both of them for weeks.

Political control over the Qashqa'i was decentralized, and no clear delineation of official responsibility was apparent. Although concentrated in Fars, Qashqa'i nomads used pastures and migrated in six other adjoining Iranian provinces. Different authorities and offices in many towns and the cities of Shiraz and Isfahan handled legal and political problems. A case brought to one government office in one town often had to be cleared up there, regardless of where the parties happened to be at the time. These patterns of decentralization combined with local rigidity were inconvenient and expensive for the nomads, who spent the year in four different, widely separated locations. The group with Borzu spent winter in Fars and summer in Isfahan province. Other members of his subtribe were found in two other provinces during the year.

To Borzu's dismay, the Tribal Security Force in Semirom had not yet received orders from its headquarters in Shiraz. He talked briefly with other men waiting there and then walked to the shop of Hajj Kalhaidar where he traded in summer. He bought most of his yearly supplies on credit from this shop and another one in Kazerun, the town nearest his winter pastures. Although he could purchase supplies with cash during the migration, he was not usually able to buy on credit then, and so he stocked up on goods in Semirom despite difficulties in transport. Some commodities were cheaper in Semirom than elsewhere and cheaper in late summer than at other times of the year, and he tried to calculate his potential savings if he was to purchase additional goods on credit here. But with the cost of interest payments, little if any savings seemed likely, so he abandoned the idea. Even relatively prosperous men such as Borzu were heavily in debt and unable to extricate themselves.

Most nomads acquired cash only once a year, in late spring or early summer, when they sold surplus sheep and goats. With this cash they immediately paid some debts to urban merchants and moneylenders from whom they had bought goods on credit and borrowed money during the previous year since the last sale of animals. Few were able to pay all the previous year's debts, and they again had to buy on credit and borrow money as soon as they had sold their animals. Interest rates were calculated by month, season, and year and could run as high as 100 percent per annum. Wealthy Qashqa'i men such as the Darrehshuri khans could borrow cash from moneylenders at a rate of 35 percent per annum, which was not an option available to other Qashqa'i who were forced to take commodities on credit at higher and compounding rates of interest. The lower interest rates charged by state banks were also unavailable to them. The nomads' only other major source of income came from pastoral products, clarified butter primarily, but also wool, goat hair, dried curds, and sometimes woven goods. Because of their dependence on merchant·moneylenders for goods, credit, and loans, they were obliged to trade their pastoral products with these men, always at prices much lower than if they sold them independently when and where prices were high, such as in the bazaar in Shiraz. Creditors who bought these products at below-market prices then sold them for their own profit.

Hajj Kalhaidar welcomed Borzu, and they sat and drank tea. He was a Persian man who lived in Semirom in late spring and through summer and in the town of Shahreza the rest of the year. The title of *hajji* was honorific only, for he had not made the pilgrimage to Mecca. He had traveled to a Shi'i Muslim shrine in Kerbala in Iraq; the preface to his name Haidar signified this pilgrimage—Kal being a shortened form of Kerbala'i. Men who traded with him gathered at his shop, and above it was a room where they could sleep, talk, and say prayers (which few Qashqa'i nomads did). The room was furnished with bedding rolls, tea-making equipment, and a water pipe. Kalhaidar read documents and wrote letters for Borzu, who was only minimally literate. Officials needing to contact Borzu notified Kalhaidar who relayed messages. One of Borzu's two mailing addresses was that of this shop. After he had sold animals several weeks previously, he gave cash to Kalhaidar who wrote a personal check to pay one of Borzu's creditors in Kazerun. Adjoining the shop was a room where Borzu and others stored goods they did not need on the migration or during winter or that were too heavy to transport. Partway through the migration, as the land became barren, Borzu would send a man with several mules back to Semirom to collect stored fodder for his animals.

In the late afternoon, after futile visits to see several government officials who had failed to return to their offices after lunch, Borzu returned to camp. His herds had arrived after his departure, and shepherds had driven them to nearby fields to graze on stubble and then up the mountain slopes to browse on shrubs. Milked every other day now, female goats would soon be dry. Ewes had stopped producing milk in midsummer. In a few days women would no longer milk or process the liquid, tasks not to resume until late winter, and they and their children already missed having the food.

Morad and Hasel, Borzu's campmates and kinsmen, saw him return and walked over to his tent to discuss strategy for the days to come. They had heard that permission to migrate had not yet been granted. They had all deliberated this problem for weeks and had undergone similar delays in years past. One year the military had not permitted them to migrate until the tenth day of autumn, despite the fact that the deteriorating condition of pastoral resources required that they leave Hanalishah twenty to thirty days before autumn began. By controlling the schedule and randomly selecting a date for the nomads' departure, government officials intended to discourage nomadism and otherwise exercise power over the Qashqa'i, whom they feared as a military threat.

Several men in Borzu's group who were anxious to reach winter pastures to protect vegetation there from trespassing herders had considered moving on ahead by themselves but were eventually dissuaded by the advantage of traveling in a large group. A few families could move along with the Amaleh, a Qashqa'i tribe that had already received permission to migrate, but twenty families could not move undetected, especially given the army's and gendarmes' checkpoints at mountain passes and other bottlenecks. Borzu was accountable for his group and would be held responsible if the authorities learned that any of the nomads had ignored government regulations.

The people migrating and camping with Borzu consisted primarily of his closest male relatives and their families. Given the high rate of in-group marriage, especially between first cousins, all these individuals were closely interrelated and linked in many directions through blood and marriage. The group also contained more distant male relatives who had married women from the core group. In addition, some hired shepherds and one hired camel herder lived with this group on the basis of contractual ties with animal owners. The men hired were almost always members of other subtribes, usually from within the Darrehshuri tribe, and sometimes distant kinship ties connected them with their employers. Hired herders were among the poorest Qashqa'i. They usually lacked pasture rights of their own, and they owned few herd or pack animals. Hired on a yearly basis, they were paid from eighty to 130 dollars, some food and clothing, and one goat or sheep at the end of their service.

Borzu owned three herds of sheep and goats, each holding close to three hundred animals. Two herds accompanied him on the autumn migration under the care of hired shepherds. One shepherd headed an independent household and camped with Borzu; the other, a young unmarried man, lived as part of Borzu's household. The third herd, also tended by a hired shepherd, used a different route and schedule in autumn and did not join Borzu in his winter pastures near the town of Kazerun. Because grazing was scarce there, Borzu hoped to lessen winter's risks by separating his herds. The third herd would rejoin him during the spring migration and stay with him in summer pastures.

Borzu was the headman (*kadkhoda*) of the Qermezi subtribe (*tireh*), one of the approximately forty-four subtribes of the Darrehshuri tribe. Defined by political and social ties, a subtribe consisted of people who gave allegiance to a common headman and who considered themselves to be a political unit. It was also an administrative unit for Darrehshuri khans and government officials.

The Qermezi subtribe contained approximately one thousand people organized in some 140 households. It consisted of members of five patri-lineages (Aqa Mohammadli, Imamverdili, Qairkhbaili, Qasemli, Kachili) and twenty or so other associated families. The five lineages shared a history going back five generations; political affiliation, intermarriage, and other social and economic ties connected them. Members of three of the lineages were said by some to descend from a common ancestor. The associated families also intermarried and cooperated socially and economically with the larger group. Borzu's lineage, Aqa Mohammadli, was dominant in numbers and power. His main rival, Sohrab, was the leading figure in Imamverdili lineage. Most of Sohrab's supporters were Imamverdili men although they occasionally relied on Borzu for liaison with government authorities. Qairkhbaili and Qasemli men also periodically used Borzu's services. Men of each lineage usually kept counsel with their own closest kin. Most men of these four lineages migrated with lineage mates in groups of from five to thirty families, often spread out over one or several days' travel.

Men of Kachili lineage had remained in villages after most other Qermezi people (and most Qashqa'i) had resumed nomadism when Reza Shah (r. 1925–1941), who had forced all Qashqa'i to settle in 1933, abdicated. Only a few Kachili people remained active members of the subtribe, which meant that Borzu, whose wife Falak was Kachili, was deprived of the support of her kinsmen. Unlike most men he lacked, via a wife, many affinal kin on whom to rely.

Borzu's traveling companions were primarily from his own Aqa Mohammadli lineage. Two Kachili men who were his wife's brothers accompanied him, as did Esfandeyar, a Qairkhbaili man who was married to his sister. Esfandeyar had fought against Borzu in the past and now hoped to establish a better relationship with him by offering support during the migration. Other Qermezi families not currently with this group, including some who shared Borzu's winter but not his summer pastures, would join him during later stages of the migration.

The subtribe was fragmented during the migration because of its size. Ninety or so Qermezi households regularly migrated between winter and summer pastures, too large a number to travel together. The subtribe was fragmented in winter and summer pastures because of scarcity of land; no single location in either seasonal quarters was large enough for all its households. Over the years, particularly since 1941 when migrations resumed, different groups defined primarily by patrilineal ties found different territories. Most Qermezi nomads spent winter in close proximity in pastures near Kazerun, while in summer they were more dispersed because pastureland in the high mountains was limited.

The men gathered in Borzu's tent agreed to continue to move slowly toward and then through the plains south of Semirom to the semiofficial staging area at Kumeh. They hoped to receive the government's permission before their arrival there. Officials forbade any Darrehshuri nomads to travel past Kumeh until they so ordered. Some families were already having trouble with too heavy loads, and the short distances to be traveled each day would benefit the pack animals. A few men decided to take advantage of the delay to transport sacks of straw and barley by mule to a village farther along the migratory route where a Qashqa'i merchant

5. Mother and two children on the migration

lived. They would store the fodder with him until the group arrived there. By then other fodder they carried would be gone.

Before dawn the next day, shepherds again set out early with the flocks, and as the sky became light the nomads began to pack up and break camp. They were traveling well before the sun appeared over the mountains. A new campsite was found in an hour, and people arranged themselves in much the same way as they had done the previous day. They would move a short distance the next day, and hence many chose again not to pitch tents, although a cool wind blew steadily, and it was chilly at night. Morad planned to go to Semirom for supplies, including kerosene for his lantern, and Borzu told him to stop by the Tribal Security Force.

During the group's slow, increasingly crowded passage south, Borzu often rode back to Semirom to handle transactions with merchants and government officials, but he still became bored and impatient sitting in camp all day with little to do. Several times he visited Round Sun, north of Semirom, where khans of the Darrehshuri tribe lived in elaborate tents until cold weather sent them to their village houses. Their economic interests were primarily in summer quarters, and they had cut back their herds and invested heavily in orchards and mechanized cultivation. Because they had not migrated with the tribe since 1962 and because most stayed in cities during winter, summer was now when they met with the tribespeople. Hoping to retain the khans' patronage, Borzu still regularly visited them bearing the customary gifts of lambs and kids.

Most men of Qasemli lineage had spent the summer in the mountains south of Semirom, and some came to see Borzu while he was in the vicinity. Some Qasemli men, mingling with Amaleh Qashqa'i nomads who had migrated earlier, were already gone, while a few others planned to travel with Borzu. Most Qasemli men spent winter in pastures southeast of Borzu's pastures, and he discussed the probable state of resources there with them. Lacking any direct contact since spring, women and children of the two groups enjoyed a chance to catch up on news, especially the summer's weddings (which men were more apt to attend than women), births, deaths, illnesses, weavings completed or sold, and men's disputes.

The migrations offered women, especially those married outside their own lineage, opportunities to visit. During the autumn migration they had less work and larger, more compact groups than during the spring migration when they milked, processed milk products, tended lambs and kids, manufactured goatskin bags, and scoured the countryside for wild plants. Their camps were smaller then and their tents more dispersed. During the more sedentary periods of winter and summer, women rarely left camp except to attend weddings, assist at childbirths, visit ill relatives, and mourn deaths.

Camps during the migration were governed by the same general rules and customs as camps in winter and summer pastures. People traveling with Borzu considered themselves a single social unit, and their many households also gathered into smaller units whose members were bound more tightly by rules and customs than were members of the larger group. When, for example, someone discovered at dawn that a camel was missing, people in the closest tents were more apt to postpone that day's move to help search than were people farther away. Families who camped together assisted one another, especially in emergencies. Each independent household was self-sufficient in equipment and labor for its daily functions, including herding and tending animals, but if a shepherd fell ill suddenly or a camel saddle broke, nearby people provided temporary labor, lent equipment, or assisted in repairs.

Some camps were more hierarchically structured than others. Men such as Borzu and his elder brother Khalifeh, Qermezi's previous headman, clearly presided over the people with them, and their camps were informally named after these men. Other camps, particularly small ones, were more egalitarian in structure and activity. Each was bound by an informal contract. When a man needed to leave the group, he was obliged to inform the others, especially the camp's leader if one existed, in time for them to make alternative arrangements if necessary. This custom helped to protect all households because each depended on the presence of others for assistance and defense. The nomads considered a household alone, especially on the migration, to be untenable and vulnerable.

People who camped together were supposed to respect one another's privacy. Men approached a tent only from the front, possibly by taking a circuitous route, so as not to surprise or catch unawares the people inside. They made a noise or shouted a greeting as extra warning, and the guard dogs were certain to run at the visitor and bark ferociously. Women were more apt to approach a campsite quietly and seek out the women and girls there, and the dogs rarely threatened them. Men sitting in a tent sometimes did not know that a woman visitor had come and gone. No one entered a tent without an invitation. Tents were usually pitched so that people in one could not look directly into another, but it was still considered impolite to stare even if circumstances permitted it. Hardly any private, unseen place existed within or by the tent, but people created space through mechanisms of social distance. They did not interrupt others' family quarrels unless physical violence seemed likely. Women dumped ashes from fire pits downwind and well away from other tents. Dust clouds raised by camels and donkeys, who luxuriated in rolling in ash heaps, thus blew away from the tents. People tethered animals so as not to interfere with others, and they kept herds well separated.

In a custom called the "neighbors' share," camp members shared meat and other scarce items. Even when women made a rice stew, they were sure to send some to the other tents. During the migration when many families traveled together, people shared with the nearest tents. Women considered it ill form if not improper to return a bowl empty. Some other item, even if only a few dates, was given in exchange. When women returned flour or raw rice, they first took a pinch and put it back into their own supplies as a way of ritually securing the bounty of their own households.

One ritual binding camp members was not observed during the months of the migration. When a household left camp—to begin the migration early, for example—women and children of the remaining households went to the vacated tent site at sunset, made a fire in the abandoned fire pit there, and sat for a few moments to remember the departed ones. The home fire was periodically lit in this way until the people who had departed were thought to have arrived safely at their destination. The ritual was believed to protect them during their travels until they were able to establish their new campsite.

People usually pitched their tents in a northeasterly direction to benefit from the early morning sun's warmth and to avoid the hotter sun of the afternoon. This alignment also made it difficult for people in one tent to see directly into the tents of others in camp. Women kept food, water, and most of the equipment they needed for their work along the right (facing out) interior and exterior wall of the tent. Three parts of the tent—the row of stones where baggage was piled, the piled baggage itself, and the fire pit (hearth)—held special significance and were symbolic of home and family. The pile of baggage was covered with a special long *gelim* (a flat-woven textile) or another woven item. People said they should not sit upon the piled baggage, step over or into an unlit fire pit, or throw anything (especially bread crumbs) into the fire. If they ignored these prohibitions, they said that some disaster would strike the home and family. They treated bread, the staple food, with care, for they believed it contained God's blessing. After a meal, women did not leave bread crumbs to be trod upon but carefully swept them up and scattered them outside for the chickens.

At night women and older girls pulled bedding from the top of the piled baggage where they had folded it in narrow sections early that morning. Families slept in a row on pile carpets and felt rugs with their heads against the piled baggage. A few men, including Borzu, slept on a thin mattress stuffed with cotton batting. Overlapping woven blankets covered the sleepers. Husband and wife sometimes slept side by side in the middle of the row, with infants and young children beside the mother. Girls in ascending order of age slept beside the mother, and boys in ascending order beside the father. The eldest children, most apt to stay up late and get up during the night and again early in the morning for chores, were at either end. When a son brought his new bride to the parental tent, they often slept to the far left of the row, sometimes behind a cloth curtain, or behind the piled baggage.

People viewed their tents as their focal points. When they told stories about the past, they gestured in different directions to recreate an event. The event, however, may have occurred somewhere other than their current location. When Borzu recounted the story of the time they feared his daughter Farideh had been abducted, he pointed in the directions people had searched. She had disappeared not from the place where Borzu was telling the story, but rather from a site along the migratory route

6. Gholam Hosain playing a flute in his tent

7. Itinerant peddlers showing fabric to Ali's family. Akbar's wife Dayeh Soltan is in the center.

several hundred kilometers away. When an itinerant peddler asked Falak if she had woven a particular gelim before or after she married, she replied that she had been "here" and motioned around the tent where they sat.

Almost every day during the early stages of the autumn migration, non-Qashqa'i peddlers made their rounds among the nomads. Some were urban-based and quite professional in their conduct and in the quality and array of goods carried (fabric, metal goods, teapots), while others came from nearby villages with chickens, eggs, and seasonal produce. Men in Borzu's camp expressed little interest in peddlers and often ignored them because they could buy the same items more cheaply in town shops. Women, however, were fascinated with the commodities. They did not have the same sense as men of prices in town, for they rarely if ever went there, and they traded household supplies (their own products as well as commodities men had purchased in markets) at disadvantageous terms for the items they desired. Peddlers often bypassed a tent if a man was present but would soon collect a circle of women and children if they were alone. Urban-based peddlers, who were always men, accepted dried curds, wool, and animal skins in trade, while village-based peddlers, who were sometimes women, accepted a wider range of goods including yarn and old goatskin bags. Cash was rarely used in the transactions.

Non-Qashqa'i beggars and dervishes also visited during the migration. Most beggars claimed to be *sayyids*, reputed descendants of the prophet Mohammad, or asserted other special connections with Islam. Qermezi men often chased them off or at least ignored them, while women, if alone, offered them tea to drink, bread to eat, and something to take such as a handful of raw wool or a piece of a sugar cone. Beggars and dervishes "wrote" and recited prayers, which women saw as possibly efficacious against illness and misfortune. These men were usually illiterate and uninformed about formal Islam, and they scribbled lines that looked like Arabic script to the women. Some women were skeptical about these men's powers to heal or otherwise change the course of events, but they feared the consequences if they shunned them or refused to offer them anything. Women often spoke of cases of illness, death, and catastrophe that had been caused by the curses of sayyids who felt slighted.

Thirteen days after Borzu and his group left their summer pastures at Hanalishah, the military permitted the Darrehshuri tribe, including Borzu's section, to migrate to winter pastures. The gendarme captain in charge of the Tribal Security Force offered no reason for the delay, and none was asked of him. Borzu and the others viewed "the hand of the government" as arbitrary. By now the weather was uncomfortably cold and windy at night at these high altitudes, and animals suffered from exposure and lack of sufficient food. Borzu's group set off early the next morning. As each day of the migration progressed, the group moved steadily south and lower in altitude, and so the weather did not worsen.

The migration of Borzu's group, along with all other Darrehshuri, took them southeast of Kumeh and then west as they veered away from Shiraz and the route that many other Qashqa'i nomads took. Many Qashqa'i headed straight south past Shiraz to winter pastures in the south of Fars province. Members of the Darrehshuri and Kashkuli Bozorg tribes, whose winter pastures were northwest of Shiraz, took a southwesterly route as they approached Shiraz. They avoided the congestion created by nomads seeking places to cross the swift and sometimes treacherous Kor River, and they escaped the military's heavy surveillance of this area. They also avoided the construction site of the massive Dariush Kabir Dam. When the dam was complete and the area behind it flooded to form a huge reservoir, most Qashqa'i nomads would have to find new routes. The physical and increasingly the social terrain restricted the nomads' migrations and in places caused crowding. Rapidly expanding cultivation aided

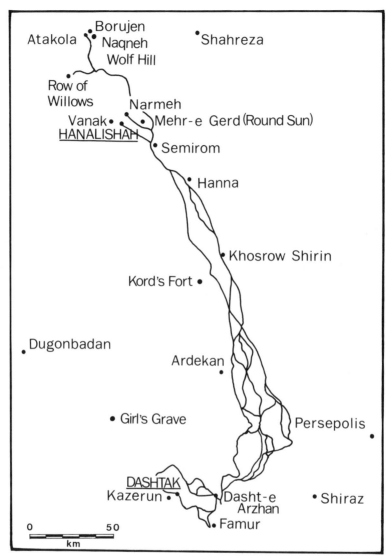

Map 4. Migratory routes of Qermezi subtribe

by new wells, motorized pumps, tractors, combines, and other new technology cut into customary routes. Most Qashqa'i nomads used different migratory routes on each seasonal passage; rarely did they repeat the exact routes they had taken previously. The different environmental circumstances in autumn and spring also created the need to alter routes and campsites.

8. Nomads and their animals assembled on the banks of the Kor River

Winter and summer pastures differed, as did the tone of the two migrations. In spring the nomads were excited and anxious as they anticipated fresh new grass in summer quarters and worried about getting there
before other pastoralists exploited it. In autumn they were more low-
keyed. No new grass awaited them in winter pastures, and they worried
most about the harshness of winter and the probability of winter rains
upon which their animals and crops depended. No one rushed to meet
these uncertainties, which would be resolved in their own due time without much human intervention. The natural vegetation men had tried to
conserve in winter pastures during the previous winter, for their return
the following autumn, was guarded by men who stayed at these sites all
year. No one stayed all year in summer pastures to provide similar protection, a situation producing anxiety during the spring migration.

Although people did not delay entering summer pastures, they did
devise strategies to delay entering winter ones. The winter territory of
Borzu's group, Dashtak, was a fixed and limited piece of land, and pasture
and water were sparse and inadequate. Men sought alternative pastures
toward the end of the migratory route for one or several prolonged stays.
They planned to move short distances every two days during the last
stages of the migration, and they would try to rent grazing land, a transaction that had been officially illegal since the national land reforms of

9. Woman preparing to cross the Kor River

the early 1960s. In his role as headman, Borzu would try to bribe government agents who would make it their business to be informed about his group's activities. At this early stage in the migration, Borzu and the others lacked sufficient details about resources at any of these locations, and so they postponed specific decisions until later.

The images of "grass" and "pastures" in the minds of many Western readers conjure up scenes these nomads rarely saw. Much of the land was dry and barren. Only in a few places along the migratory route in spring did they encounter grass with jointed stems and slender leaves. Otherwise, the vegetation upon which they relied took the form of scattered hardy ground plants and small shrubs. Reminiscing, men described lambs frolicking in new spring grass that was so tall and dense that one spotted only their ears occasionally poking from the lushness. Such memories were apparently not exaggerated: conditions for pastoralism had generally been much better before the 1950s. Since then, overgrazing and the destruction of trees and shrubs for fuel (which caused the loss of nearby ground vegetation) had created serious environmental degradation.

The migration from Kumeh to Arzhan Plain, west of Shiraz, took Borzu's group thirty-one days. Scarcity of water was a constant concern. The nomads sometimes traveled twice a day and on a few occasions at night to find adequate grazing and water as well as suitable campsites. Shepherds sometimes moved the herds at night so they would need less water to drink, and twice people traveled at night so that the pack animals would be less thirsty than if they traveled during the heat of the day. Every day after setting up camp, Borzu rode ahead on horseback alone or with a kinsman to scout the next day's route and reconnoiter possible campsites for the group. He noted proudly that he traveled three times the distance of other men on any given day and that his powers of endurance vastly exceeded theirs. He asked people he encountered questions about conditions ahead and the presence of other migrators.

Wild game was more plentiful during the autumn migration than during spring because of the new crop of young, the seasonal loss of vegetative cover, and the animals' patterns of movement. As men of Borzu's group traveled south, they often pointed out areas where they had shot game in the past. Mountain sheep and goats, especially the males with long curved horns kept as trophies, and gazelle were their favored prey. Hunting as a source of food and as sport was now denied practically all Qashqa'i, for the government had confiscated their arms in 1966 as part of a policy to render them militarily impotent. A Qashqa'i man's identity derived in part from his skills as a hunter, and all men were nostalgic

10.   Borzu mounted on his horse and armed with a rifle. On the autumn migration, September 1966. Courtesy of Ernest Thomas Greene.

about the past when they could demonstrate their skills and share and savor the meat.

Although no longer permitted to possess guns and rifles, Qermezi men always kept other weapons handy. They usually carried a shepherd's crook or club, especially while tending herds and always during the migration, in order to defend property and protect people. Some men carried a wooden club with an iron head containing spikes, ridges, or studs; others wrapped the club head with leather. A few said they had used a cow tail as a menacing whip. As a means of threat they also brandished short-handled wooden clubs used for pounding in tent stakes. Knives served utilitarian purposes but were also potential weapons. In fights men employed slings with leather or woven wool pouches, a weapon also used to down game birds and predators. In their gait and the prominent and proud way men held their weapons, they displayed themselves to outsid-

11. Borzu, his son Mohammad Karim, and his cousin Morad. On the autumn migration, September 1966. Courtesy of Ernest Thomas Greene.

ers as fearless, powerful men ready to strike. When they had been armed with guns and rifles, they were feared by settled people, and they attempted to maintain the posture.

Most men in Borzu's group stopped for a day near Jamalbaigi village. An Amaleh Qashqa'i man settled there was one of only two trading partners along the migratory route who offered them commodities on credit, and they took advantage of his services to replenish their supplies of flour, rice, and salt. He was also their only Qashqa'i merchant. They had taken goods on credit during their last passage through the area, and some repaid him now with the clarified butter they had produced in summer. A few men collected fodder they had stored with him during the early stages of this migration.

As Khalifeh and other men left the village, they recalled "a terrible hungry year" some forty years previously and its difficult autumn migration. Because of a drought they had harvested little wheat in summer pastures, and sparse grazing meant they had processed few milk products. By the time they reached the vicinity of Shiraz, their wheat flour was gone. They collected acorns from which they made flour and bread. They

12. Bride riding a camel on the migration. She temporarily covered her mouth and nose against the dust; Qashqa'i women otherwise did not cover their faces.

also ate wild plants and nuts. Some men stole food from villagers and pastoralists.

Borzu hoped to find suitable pastures near Arzhan Plain (Dasht-e Arzhan, Plain of Wild Almond Trees), a town and a region west of Shiraz on the road to Bushehr on the Persian Gulf. He needed to delay his group's arrival at its final destination at Dashtak, located at a lower altitude across a range of mountains to the west. Arzhan Plain was close enough to Dashtak for men to leave the migration temporarily in order to thresh their grain. It was also close enough to the town of Kazerun for them to reestablish contact with the merchants and moneylenders with whom they conducted business in autumn and winter.

As his group approached Arzhan Plain, Borzu traveled ahead by horse to survey the situation. Land in the vicinity was owned or controlled by Lur men in the town of Arzhan Plain and several nearby villages with whom he needed to negotiate. He did not trust these Lurs, but he preferred them to Persians. Although gendarmes enforced the government edict forbidding nomads to camp in any location longer than twenty-four hours during the migration, Borzu knew of strategies to placate them temporarily. He said also that if he obtained the compliance of local land-owners, he could avoid some difficulties with gendarmes. He eventually chose Wide Mountain (Kuh Pahn), an area of ample grazing and other useful resources, for an extended stay of ten to twenty days. He expected that he would be forced to pay the men who viewed this area as their exclusive domain.

The major difficulty with Wide Mountain was the lack of water, and Borzu's group had only occasionally been able to use the area for more than several days. As Borzu contemplated how to exploit the abundant grazing there, he refined a plan he had been considering for months. If only he could rent a truck and driver, he could transport water to Wide Mountain for animals and people and delay his arrival at Dashtak which was reported to have little grazing and no water. Famur, an area south of Arzhan Plain where his group usually went before going to Dashtak when the winter rains began or after vegetation began to grow there, was re-ported to lack grazing. This year he planned to bypass Famur.

The Ministry of Justice summoned Borzu to the courthouse in Shiraz concerning a case of highway robbery allegedly committed by Qermezi men years before. While walking through the Shiraz bazaar he unexpect-edly met Hajj Kalhaidar, his principal merchant-moneylender in Semi-rom. They discussed the shortage of water that was troubling nomadic pastoralists in the province, and Borzu explained his tentative plans to transport water to his group now prepared to enter the mountains above Arzhan Plain. Kalhaidar told him he was ready to sell his old pickup truck, for he had just bought another one in better condition. When Borzu asked him what he wanted for the truck, Kalhaidar suggested that he hire a driver if he wanted to buy a vehicle. He commented that he had earlier been talking with a Qashqa'i man who was looking for wage work.

Although Borzu had haggled for hours, even days, over the price of commodities with Kalhaidar in years past, they quickly agreed on a suit-able price for the pickup truck and the terms of payment. Borzu would take out a small cash loan once he reached Kazerun and would pay the remainder plus interest the next summer after he sold animals. He cal-culated the cost of the truck at one hundred sheep and one hundred goats, according to that summer's animal prices. Both men seemed pleased, and a bargain was struck. After inspecting the truck, they returned to the bazaar and with luck located the prospective driver idling in a carpet shop. Borzu agreed to hire him for two months until he himself and his fifteen-year-old son, currently in school in Kazerun, learned to drive. He wanted to use the truck immediately, but the driver said he needed a mechanic to check it and then would collect his family. He agreed to meet Borzu in Arzhan Plain in two days.

An exhilarated Borzu returned to camp. Since he had become headman seven years previously, his status had been somewhat ambiguous. He was wealthier than any of his kinsmen and supporters, and his lifestyle, especially the hospitality he offered and his network of contacts outside Qermezi, was much more elaborate than theirs. But he owned no land, unlike a few Darrehshuri headmen who were now prospering from their apple orchards and grain cultivation. And his status was nowhere near that of the Darrehshuri khans whom he admired and attempted in small ways to emulate. Although the decision to buy this particular vehicle was sudden and unpremeditated, he had wanted for years to own motorized transport. Ownership of land and vehicles separated khans and wealthy headmen from him and symbolized their difference. Now a proud truck owner, Borzu had assumed a new position more comparable to that of men he respected.

On a practical level, Borzu expected to profit economically from the purchase, especially now that Wide Mountain could be exploited more intensively. He would transport water there, and everyone's herds could graze to satiation without taxing their energies by having to walk long distances to water. On a local political level, he considered the benefits his new acquisition would provide. His supporters would become more dependent on him because of favors he could offer through use of the vehicle. This dilapidated green Toyota was about to change his life.

On Borzu's first night back at camp, he instructed his wife Falak to cook a large pot of rice and invited men in his immediate group to discuss plans with him. Over tea before the meal, he announced that he had bought a truck and would use it to transport water to Wide Mountain where he hoped to arrange for a stay of ten to twenty days. He asked the men if they wanted to cooperate in this venture, and he said he would charge each household a share, determined by herd size, of his costs. When several men inquired about the amount, he said he had no idea. None of them had much if any ready cash, and all were unwilling to undertake new expenditures, for they were heavily in debt and would have no income until the next summer. But they needed pasture and water for their animals for the next month and a half before the winter rains began, when they would enter their winter pastures at Dashtak, and they did not see any viable alternatives. Their animals were already suffering. Borzu emphasized that they would get a return on money spent now for trucking in water when they sold heavier animals next summer, and he reminded them of the lower mortality rates of well-tended animals. Many were currently pregnant, and everyone recognized that healthy ewes and does delivered heavier, healthier young. Also, the nomads were nearing Kazerun where men could secure loans now that most of them had recently paid some debts incurred there.

No explicit, verbalized consensus emerged from the meeting, as was customary, and men left to discuss the proposition in small groups as they often did under similar circumstances. On parting, Borzu said he still planned to move the next day to the mountains above Arzhan Plain, and from there they could make a judgment more accurately.

Early the next morning the group broke camp and traveled into the mountains behind the town of Arzhan Plain to Molla Nari valley where plentiful grazing was available. The nearest water was at several distant wells controlled by landowners in town. Shepherds watered their herds before entering the valley and would return to these same wells late in the day. For the next three days shepherds drove the animals to and from the wells, and many people spent most of each day transporting water by mule and donkey to camp for animal and human use. Goatskin bags soon proved inadequate for the job at hand, and some men bought large plastic containers in town.

The vicinity of the wells was crowded with the pack and herd animals of Qashqa'i and other nomads who were migrating in the same direction and trying to delay entering their assigned winter pastures. Some groups, including some people with Borzu, drew water from a government well by the asphalt highway, a longer distance away and dangerous because of fast-moving vehicles on the road but requiring less waiting time. The government had dug this well in 1968 for use during the construction of the road, not for the benefit of nomads.

Families with teenage sons in school in Kazerun sent word that they should come and help. Borzu's nephew Fathollah, the first to arrive, stripped off his city pants, which he wore over the loose-fitting pants that Qashqa'i men customarily wore. As he rode off on a mule with his sister to get water, his mother remarked how quickly he had become a nomad again.

Each time people brought water to camp, they filled shallow metal pans, called to shepherds in the hills to bring small groups of animals to drink, and shouted "ho" to the animals who ran downhill in response to the call. The hands of women and girls who did most of the actual handling of water, under chilly and windy conditions, were soon cracked, bleeding, and painful. By nightfall everyone was exhausted. Borzu and the others had watched with envy as a truck carrying barrels of water passed by their campsite on a dirt road leading farther into the mountains. On questioning the driver at the government well, Fathollah learned that Kashkuli Qashqa'i nomads had rented the truck.

On the evening of the third day at Molla Nari, men gathered again at Borzu's tent. They were now convinced that they could not continue for many more days to bring by pack animal the water they needed, and they accepted Borzu's plan and agreed to share expenses. Borzu still faced the problem of grazing land, however, and he described the day's inconclusive encounters.

Earlier that day four government forest rangers had come by Landrover to demand that Borzu leave Molla Nari immediately. They claimed that the government entitled men in Arzhan Plain to use the land exclusively for their own herds. Part of the Ministry of Agriculture, forest rangers were charged with the responsibility of controlling use of nationalized land. They were supposed to regulate hunting and grazing and prevent cutting of wood and making of charcoal. Borzu told the four men that he was migrating to winter pastures but needed to go slowly because of the lack of water there. Unsympathetic, the forest rangers retorted that they would return the next day with gendarmes to make sure he had left the area. With the forest rangers' unexpected arrival, Borzu had told Falak to prepare lunch for them, but they left before it was ready and did not even show the courtesy of drinking the tea that was prepared for them. A peasant showed up on donkey-back soon afterward with the same message. Although ragged in dress, he announced authoritatively that Borzu was trespassing and must report to the headman of the village farther up the road. Borzu ignored him and did not offer food.

Before Borzu could check on the watering of his animals, a Lur landowner from Arzhan Plain and his wife, children, and several subordinates unexpectedly drove into camp. Borzu ordered his shepherd to kill a goat for them, as his own and the landowner's status required. He broiled meat on skewers for the guests, and then they all ate a meat stew with the rice that had been intended for the forest rangers. On a trip to Arzhan Plain a few days earlier, Borzu had offered the landowner formulaic and customary greetings that included invitations to be his guest, but he had not expected him to respond. Now that the man was ensconced in his tent,

Borzu thought he might help to resolve the land problem, but the man offered no suggestions and seemed disinterested. He had come simply to enjoy himself and offer his family an outing.

Late that afternoon Hafez, Borzu's new driver, had arrived in camp with his family and their possessions loaded in the pickup truck. Driving through Arzhan Plain he had met by chance Borzu's son Mohammad Karim who had been able to show him the way to the campsite. Hafez, a Talehbazli Darrehshuri man, and his family had been settled near his wife's father for several years. He drove a tractor during planting seasons and looked for other paid work between plantings. He was not at all enthused about this job, especially having to live as a nomad again, but had lacked other options. Borzu pointed out a nearby site for Hafez's tent, and then they briefly discussed his work. Borzu sent several men from camp with him to Arzhan Plain to buy barrels for transporting water.

Early the next morning many people in Borzu's group traveled to Wide Mountain. Aware of the forest rangers' threats, they were also ready to use better grazing farther into the mountains. Their route took them up a long steep curving path through forests to Bear Canyon, surrounded by hills with oak trees and other vegetation. The day was clear and bright, with a nip of autumn in the air. Hafez made an early morning trip to the government well to fill the barrels and arrived at Wide Mountain as people were setting up camp. They transferred some water to basins that had been carved out of stone possibly hundreds of years ago and used since then by people from Arzhan Plain for making liquor. They stored the rest of the water in goatskin bags and their new plastic containers. Along with the camp's men and boys who provided the physical labor, Hafez made three more trips to collect water and another trip to buy barrels for storing water.

Riding in his truck for the first time and relishing his new status, Borzu visited the Lur headman and landowner of the nearest village as the peasant had demanded the previous day. Wide Mountain was government land, having been nationalized in the land reforms of the 1960s, but the headmen of this village and Arzhan Plain claimed that the Ministry of Agriculture granted them exclusive rights to the territory. Paying cash and promising more money in the future, Borzu convinced the village headman to allow him and his group of thirty households to stay for ten days on half the land.

Borzu was barely back in camp when the Lur headman of Arzhan Plain, along with an entourage of family and subordinates, suddenly drove up close to his tent. The headman announced he wanted to use

13. Narges (with a broken arm) and Katayun giving water to camels at Wide Mountain

Borzu's camp as a base for a hunting expedition. Borzu had invited him to visit as well, some days past, before he had known exactly who held legal rights to or at least claims over this land. A gendarme and three nonlocal Lurs, whose purpose on the visit was not immediately divulged, accompanied the headman. Borzu instructed his shepherd to kill a goat and ordered an elaborate meal for the many visitors. The village headman had informed him earlier in the day that the Arzhan Plain headman claimed rights over the other half of Wide Mountain. Understanding the importance of the occasion, Borzu treated the man and his party with respect and tended to many of their personal needs himself rather than leaving this task to his own subordinates as was customary. He served the headman tea and later poured water from a long-spouted pitcher for him to wash his right hand before eating. After lunch and a short nap, Borzu and the headman went for a walk to conduct business out of the gendarme's earshot. The headman had brought the gendarme to bolster his own authority at Wide Mountain, but he also hoped to negotiate privately without the gendarme's knowledge.

The three nonlocal Lurs, the headman explained, were hired herders of large commercial flocks who were contracting for grazing land before bringing the animals to this area. Owned by urban investors, such herds had recently become the bane of Qashqa'i pastoralism, for they consumed vegetation that the Qashqa'i had customarily and by tribal right controlled. With the political pacification of the Qashqa'i in the early and middle 1960s, Persian and Lur urban capitalists invested heavily in livestock and sent them into Qashqa'i territory under the care of non-Qashqa'i hired herders. They paid cash for grazing and were increasingly preempting customary Qashqa'i pastures. A few investors in Isfahan, Shahreza, and Borujen each owned as many as sixty herds, each containing four hundred or more animals. Darrehshuri pastoralists suffered more from these incursions than most other Qashqa'i pastoralists because their summer pastures were directly south of the towns where these herds originated.

The three Lur hired herders were responsible for twelve hundred sheep and goats now near Semirom and coming to Arzhan Plain in twenty days. The headman of Arzhan Plain had already agreed to rent them Wide Mountain, and they worried that other pastoralists such as Borzu would consume the grazing for which they had already consented to pay. The headman mentioned a sum he said would cover use of the area for the next twenty days, and Borzu assented. The Lur hired herders were displeased with the apparent agreement, although they were not privy to the details. They tried to draw the gendarme into the discussion, but he held a prior commitment to the headman and was willing to be a silent witness to the proceedings. The two Lur headmen with claims over Wide Mountain were apparently able to negotiate the area's use without much if any interference from government officials. The legal basis of anyone's actual rights was never demonstrated to Borzu. He did know it was illegal to rent nationalized land.

Not all thirty families who had been traveling with Borzu had come to Wide Mountain, and some others who had planned to join him for the final leg of the migration now did not. Some people were skeptical about the truck's ability to solve the water problem, and some were unwilling or unable to pay whatever expenses would be incurred. And most people, including those who had accompanied Borzu to Wide Mountain, were hesitant about the new monetary arrangement with him. He had not yet indicated the amount he would ask; he said only that people could pay according to their ability. They regarded that statement as vague and noted that if they could not pay a sufficient amount, he would extract other goods or services from them. They complained that Borzu was not always fair in his relationship with group members, and many feared becoming too close to or too reliant on him. They gave the example of the goat that he had killed for the previous day's meal; he had taken it from the herd of his younger brother Abdol Hosain while he was away from camp getting water.

Members of Qermezi subtribe, especially those who were most dependent on Borzu in his role as headman, were customarily obliged to provide him with goods and services to offset expenses he incurred and to compensate him for efforts he made on their behalf. They expected him to create a stable situation for them with government agents, tribal khans, local notables, and any other people who harassed them. If he fulfilled this role, they were willing to support him in his efforts and put up with what they sometimes regarded as arbitrary or self-serving acts. While Borzu saw the offerings of group members as just payment, others sometimes viewed them as enhancements to his own wealth and status, and they pointed out as evidence his already large herds and his vast, in their view often unnecessary, personal expenditures. They said they helped to support him in his already privileged position, while they themselves were without wealth and fell into deeper debt. Some men of the subtribe and most men who shared pastures with Borzu were willing to give him a sheep or goat every year or so to contribute to the hospitality he was required to offer. They reasoned that through such hospitality he settled

their disputes, negotiated for land, pacified potential aggressors, and upheld group honor. But they wanted to select this animal and to choose the
occasion to volunteer it. From birth, each animal had a specific intended
fate, and Borzu's selection from someone's herd in that person's absence
violated this plan.

When headmen such as Borzu had been formally part of the political
hierarchy of the Qashqa'i confederacy and responsible for linking their
subtribes to the tribal khans, they had received a portion of an extracted
tax as payment for their own services. Until 1962 when the government
divested them of this power, khans had collected annually 1 to 3 percent
of the herds of most tribal members. Headmen who served as the conduit
paid no tax themselves and retained a tenth of the collected animals.
Tribal members also paid their headmen directly in the clarified butter
they produced during two nights in spring at the height of milk production. By 1970 both these payments had stopped, but some tribal members
continued to support their headmen economically, and headmen expected
such payments for services they continued to provide their groups.

People's concerns about Borzu's fairness kept many men from getting
too close to him. They expected to be taken advantage of and sometimes
were, but they also did not completely appreciate how much he did for
their benefit. Qashqa'i nomads who lacked comparably effective headmen
were often in a worse economic situation than were the majority of Qermezi nomads. Also, families most closely associated with Borzu tended
to be wealthier and were afforded better and wider opportunities than
more distant families and families who held other affiliations. Qermezi
men using winter and summer pastures other than Dashtak and Hanalishah were forced to rent pastoral and agricultural land. Men with Borzu
at Dashtak and Hanalishah paid no rent because of his power and political
standing and his diligent, astute efforts on their behalf. Many Darrehshuri subtribes had broken up since the mid-1960s, and their members
had dispersed and often become impoverished, partly because no one was
able or willing to secure pastoral or agricultural land for them. Qermezi
people did acknowledge that they were advantaged economically over
many other Qashqa'i, and in charitable moments they credited Borzu for
their relative good fortune. They also appreciated such services as government liaison and his role in providing their children with formal education.

During the first few days at Wide Mountain, Hafez spent most of the
day driving to and from the government well on the highway. Different
groups of men and boys went with him to hoist water from the well to

metal containers which they then emptied into barrels standing in the bed of the pickup truck. When the truck returned to camp, people on board, along with additional help from tents in the area, transferred the water to barrels and other containers and to the stone basins. Every family brought shallow pans and watered their herds in sequence in an organized way. Keeping distant and aloof, Hafez considered himself a hired driver, not a wage laborer, and performed little physical work himself. On occasion Borzu rode in the truck so Hafez could drop him off in Arzhan Plain farther up the highway and later pick him up, but he did not do any physical labor connected with the water hauling either.

Other Qermezi families, some of whom had been reluctant earlier, saw the advantages of exploiting this grazing (and the disadvantages of their current locations) and moved to Wide Mountain after first securing permission from Borzu. Soon forty households were dispersed throughout the valley, their three thousand sheep and two thousand goats grazing in the vicinity. The largest camp at Wide Mountain was Borzu's, containing his shepherd, camel herder, truck driver, brothers, and cousins. His wife's two brothers were just over a hill within shouting distance. Other families were tucked into small ravines in camps of a few tents.

Hafez's efforts notwithstanding, Borzu's small pickup truck proved inadequate to supply the needs of everyone's herd and pack animals. On the ninth day at Wide Mountain, Borzu contracted in Arzhan Plain for more water to be trucked in. The cost per barrel covered use of a large truck, a driver, and gasoline; the nomads were required to provide all the labor. On the tenth day the rented truck arrived in camp to pick up workers, and for the next few days it made one or two trips daily. Hafez continued to take at least four trips a day, and on occasion a trip at night was necessary when the truck required repair in Arzhan Plain. Every family, even Borzu's, still sent several youngsters once or twice a day by mule and donkey to the wells to collect water for household use. People held high standards for drinking water and water used to make tea, and no one wanted to consume water that came from the open barrels.

Everyone at Wide Mountain, including hired shepherds and the camel herder, relied on the trucked-in water for their animals except for Borzu's younger brother Abdol Hosain (and, by extension, his hired shepherd). The two brothers disagreed about the extent of assistance that Abdol Hosain should be rendering Borzu, and Abdol Hosain was attempting to maintain his independence. He was not willing to camp alone or seek a new group, and so he accompanied his kinsmen to Wide Mountain, but he refused to speak to Borzu and ignored the trucked-in water. The two men were in a state of ritual, mutual avoidance, which would remain in effect until one or several prominent, neutral people successfully staged a semiformal ceremony of reconciliation. People saw Abdol Hosain leaving with donkeys and a mule early in the morning, alone (for his children were young), and returning six hours later fully laden and exhausted. Women of the two households were not constrained by the men's hostility, except when the two were present, and they freely interacted. Abdol Hosain's wife occasionally took water from Borzu's supply when Borzu was absent. Borzu's elderly, feisty mother lived with her youngest son Abdol Hosain and mediated between the two households.

Practically every location along the migratory route offered its own unique resources, and the physical environment of Wide Mountain was particularly rich. These nomads had not been in forests since the previous spring when they had hurried through the region, unable to exploit it as thoroughly as they wished. Stands of trees, oak and wild pistachio in particular, provided wood for tent fastenings and stakes, looms, clubs, shepherd's crooks, devices used in animal husbandry and for pack animals, household items, and talismans for camels and rams. Men manufactured some items on the spot or while herding, and others they would fashion from wood they took with them.

While men at Wide Mountain devised new techniques for watering animals, women and children exploited the terrain whenever they were not occupied with watering. Women gathered wild fruits, nuts, other plants, and minerals for food, medicine, dyes, and curing and tanning agents. After cleaning them, they bundled them in cloth tied with yarn, each bundle identified by odor and by the particular cloth, yarn, and manner of wrapping. They stored dyes, medicines, herbs, and spices in saddlebags fastened shut with a metal lock. Throughout the year women continually replenished their own supplies and assembled items to give as cherished gifts, especially to women who no longer migrated or who lacked access to such resources. Small groups of children at Wide Mountain rushed excitedly after nuts, berries, and greens to eat and tree sap to chew. Children, especially girls until they were eight or nine when their mothers first allowed them to cook, often did not get enough food, and so they foraged for themselves. Young men and boys set partridge and quail traps and also went after these and other game birds with slings and stones. Once people settled into a routine, they cut or collected and dried tall grass and leaves as fodder to transport to winter pastures.

Women and children especially appreciated the sedentary period at Wide Mountain. Tents and camps were in closer proximity than during the migration or in seasonal pastures. While resident in seasonal pastures women usually stated a specific purpose when visiting other camps. During the migration this custom did not always apply, but the hazards of alien territory, the dispersal of the nomads, and the women's heavy work loads usually prevented much intercamp visiting. At Wide Mountain women said they were protected by this relatively isolated spot and could frequent other tents and camps without risk. They gave small gifts to one another, and the terrain provided natural resources for these exchanges. They also gave figs, which they traded with Lur village peddlers for wool, yarn, meat, and skins.

Planning their major weaving projects for winter, women took advantage of this sojourn to prepare and dye yarn, braid ropes, and weave the small or less complicated straps, tent panels, grain sacks, and rough blankets. All year women spun the raw wool of their sheep and the raw hair of their goats into yarn. Any time a woman's hands were momentarily free, she pulled from her jacket a spindle made of wood and horn and spun the raw wool or hair she kept tucked up her sleeve. Women packed away the completed balls of yarn until periods such as this one, when they twisted and tightened the yarn by stringing it between two fixed objects such as a tent pole and a tree limb and spinning the stick on which the yarn was slowly wrapped. If the wool yarn was not to be used in its natural color, women dyed it with raw and processed substances and mordants, dried it, and rolled it into balls. By the time women arrived at winter pastures they expected to have ready all the yarn in the chosen colors for the one or two major items they planned to weave that season. Women plotted out their weavings years in advance and could describe each item in detail and sketch the design motifs in the dirt.

Shortly after their arrival at Wide Mountain, some of the nomads traveled ahead to winter pastures at Dashtak to thresh the wheat and barley they had planted there the previous year. Others went with them to collect grain already threshed by others. Many men planted one crop in late autumn after their arrival in winter pastures and depended on early winter rains. They sometimes planted a second crop in the middle of winter and relied on the rains to follow. For the harvest in early and middle spring, after the spring migration had begun, they either returned to winter pastures or entrusted the task to men who remained there all year. Men threshed, winnowed, and stored some grain right after harvest, and they left other harvested grain in piles protected by thorny bushes weighted with stones and would thresh and winnow it toward the end of the autumn migration. They stored grain in the town of Kazerun with merchants or in the tents and storage huts of men who threshed it. Men took some wheat to be milled in Kazerun and brought flour to their families at Wide Mountain. They stored straw, much needed as fodder for pack animals, at the threshing ground in well-protected piles or in huts at winter campsites. During autumn some men fed barley to pregnant ewes and year-old lambs to build up their strength for winter.

Men often cooperated in the tasks of cultivation in order to minimize the disruptions to nomadic pastoralism. One or several men agreed to plant, harvest, and thresh while their brothers or cousins cared for the herds and families of the cultivators during their absence. Men doing the work received a larger portion of the harvest. Men and their adolescent or older sons could divide the tasks of herding and cultivating without needing to cooperate with other households.

After the group's camels had transported baggage to Wide Mountain, Borzu's camel herder Yadollah drove most of them back to Molla Nari where water was close. When Yadollah returned the camels to Wide Mountain some days later, he told their owners that many were lethargic. When sores erupted in and around their mouths, he saw that they had contracted smallpox. They were sick for many days. Animals with the worst lesions were unable to eat or drink, and owners feared they would eventually lose them all. The cries of stricken young camels resembled those of human infants. According to a veterinarian in Shiraz, smallpox was making one of its periodic appearances in south Iran, and it soon reached epidemic levels. Although camels represented a significant portion of a household's wealth and were expensive to replace, no one in the group other than Yadollah, who was personally attached to each one, did much about their care, even after some died. A few men mixed barley flour, salt, and water and forcibly shoved balls of the mixture down the throats of camels that had been unable to eat. Eventually most recovered, but their temporary incapacity was a source of anxiety and an impediment to traveling on. People wondered how well the recovering camels would be able to cope with the sparse vegetation and scarcity of water of the impending winter.

On the sixteenth day after the arrival of Borzu's group at Wide Mountain, a Landrover sped up the dirt track, and four Lur men leapt out of the vehicle. They ran into camp to order Borzu to "pack up and get out." Their spokesman, quick to feign anger, shouted that he had been opposed to Borzu being at Wide Mountain at all and that the nomads had ruined the land and turned it to dust. They had not visited Borzu before, but he had known of them from Arzhan Plain and from previous migrations in

14. Yadollah feeding camels barley flour

the area. First they claimed to be government forest rangers, then on
questioning from Borzu stated that the Ministry of Agriculture autho-
rized them to protect the land and levy fines on trespassers. They claimed
to be headmen of Arzhan Plain and three villages to the west. Headman
was the title of a government-appointed overseer of a village or town, but
it was also used opportunistically, as in this case, by the extended families
of the actual appointees. The man ordering Borzu to leave was an uncle
of the headman of Arzhan Plain whom Borzu had already paid for twenty
days of pasturing at Wide Mountain. According to these men's calculations, this was day nineteen, and Borzu must leave by the next day. They
had added the three days the group had spent at Molla Nari to the sixteen
days at Wide Mountain. Borzu had not intended to depart and in fact was
just settling into the routine of water hauling. He had expected that his
financial investment in the water-transporting venture would run a
longer term.

While Borzu and the spokesman went off to talk alone, the other three men took a stroll along the dirt road. They spotted some gunnysacks hidden under bushes at the bottom of a ravine and discovered nine large bags of charcoal. Charcoal production on government land was illegal, and part of the claimed authorization of these men was to surveil and report on this activity. They sent for Borzu and the fourth man. Borzu proclaimed, too loudly, that a shepherd had told him about the sacks just that morning and that he had planned to notify the forest rangers in Arzhan Plain on his next trip there. The four men confiscated the charcoal and ordered several passing shepherds to carry the sacks to the road. A man driving to a nearby village stopped to satisfy his curiosity about the proceedings, and he soon agreed to buy the charcoal at going rates from the four men. The sacks would not have fitted into their Landrover, and the men had worried that the charcoal would disappear if they left it for transport later. They kept demanding to know who had produced it; it had obviously just been processed and packed. Charcoal was made in pits in the ground, and the smoke generated could be seen and smelled for long distances. Borzu reported that none of the nomads had known about the charcoal, a statement the men greeted with skepticism. Charcoal was often produced with the aid of kerosene, and Borzu pointed out that nomads carried none or only small amounts.

By relinquishing the charcoal to the four men, Borzu believed he had gained an advantage in the negotiations to come. They might be less greedy for bribes now that each had profited from the (illegal) sale of the charcoal. He knew that further payment was unavoidable but hoped to keep it low, considering the expense that he and his group had incurred to remain at Wide Mountain this long. Borzu stated his case to them. His group was slowly moving toward winter pastures that lacked grazing and water, and he had already paid two headmen in the vicinity for a twenty-day stay. Camels were incapacitated by smallpox and unable to transport their possessions. He said they needed another fifteen days. After a heated discussion the four men agreed to a ten-day stay and a payment that they split in complicated ways among themselves. Borzu watched with irritation the men's bickerings over the disbursement of the cash.

Borzu was angry after their departure. He said he was frustrated by a situation over which he exercised little control. If he had not bribed these men, they would have pressured gendarmes and forest rangers to force him off the land. As in his dealings with the other two headmen, he knew no facts about the legal status of these men's control over the land. They had never shown him any documents. But it was clear that these men and others like them enjoyed special relationships with government agents in the region. Simply passing through, Borzu could not adequately challenge them.

As he had handled the payment for the initial twenty days, Borzu counted the number of households present and assessed their ability to pay. Of the forty-four households now under his authority at Wide Mountain, twenty-four he considered too small and too poor to pay any amount. He divided the bribe among the remaining twenty according to herd size. Men paid him what they could, which he accepted without comment, even if the sum was lower than the suggested amount. What share if any Borzu paid (and he was more able to pay than anyone else) was not made explicit in these calculations, and no one confronted him directly about it. On other occasions and in other locations when he was forced to pay for use of land, he collected the same sum from every household if the overall payment was small. If the payment was large, as it was at Wide Mountain, he collected according to wealth.

This matter apparently settled, at least for the moment, Borzu and the men of his group turned their attention to the remaining stages of the migration. When the final ten days at Wide Mountain were over, they would move slowly and meanderingly toward their winter pastures at Dashtak by remaining at each campsite for several days and by staying within government regulations by still being "on the migration." They needed one more prolonged stay before reaching winter pastures because of scarce water and grazing there.

That evening Borzu's brother Jehangir invited some men at Wide Mountain to dinner, and they used the occasion to plan strategy. After the discussion, Khalifeh, another brother and the former Qermezi headman, drafted a letter in Persian to the government's forest rangers in Kazerun to request permission to remain an extra few days at Mahmud Begi Mountain, their last stop before Dashtak. He wrote that hired herders were illegally grazing large commercial herds at Mahmud Begi Mountain (as reported by men who had just returned from threshing). Several men coached Khalifeh's son Bahram in what to say in Persian when he delivered the letter. They told him to mention the smallpox epidemic and to plead that old men in his group, unable to climb mountains, needed special consideration. Four days later he returned from Kazerun to report that the request was denied.

With three days still remaining in their residence at Wide Mountain, yet another Lur landowner from Arzhan Plain, accompanied by a gendarme, rode into camp with Hafez. Hafez had driven to town for gasoline, encountered the landowner there, and was obliged to deliver him to Borzu as he had demanded. After a few stylized pleasantries the landowner began to shout at Borzu for the destruction his group had caused, and he ordered him to "pack up and get lost." Quickly becoming agitated, Borzu reminded him that he had paid for ten extra days and three still remained. The gendarme guided the landowner arm in arm away from the tent to calm him down, and later the gendarme and Borzu also took a walk together. According to the gendarme, the four men Borzu had paid in order to stay an additional ten days were not entitled to grant this permission, and other landowners in the area were now anxious for money as well. He suggested that if Borzu came to Arzhan Plain to sign a statement about the transaction with the four men, officials there would try to retrieve the money. Borzu wanted the money back but was not certain that formally notifying the authorities of his bribe was advantageous. It was illegal for private individuals to rent nationalized land.

The next day, after a restless night of deliberation, Borzu told his story to a gendarme officer in Arzhan Plain and signed a statement. The officer demanded a grazing fee from Borzu because he had been exploiting government land. (A year later the gendarmes finally extracted money from the four men but claimed they kept it in government coffers because the sum was just payment for the use of nationalized land.)

That same day yet another Lur headman, this one from a village west of Arzhan Plain, rushed into camp to harass Borzu about being at Wide Mountain. He had encountered Borzu's truck transporting water to Wide Mountain and hitched a ride. Word had spread that the nomads were vulnerable and susceptible to demands for money. Increasingly irritated at the situation, Borzu chased the man off and shouted that he was leaving the area for good in two days. Later in the day a gendarme came to Wide Mountain, also by hitching a ride with Hafez, to check up on any new charcoal production. Other than noting to Borzu that his ten days were almost finished, he was not much concerned about grazing and instead searched the surrounding hills for charcoal pits. He located several that were only a few days old, as ascertained by the smell, and destroyed them. Borzu claimed ignorance.

People with Borzu were beginning to see that the truck was a mixed blessing, that it enabled them to be approached in ways rarely possible before. The village headman would not have walked all the way to Wide Mountain, for it was a long steep climb up the mountain slopes. By exploiting the truck's convenience, he enhanced the style of his arrival and solidified his resolve to threaten the nomads. One night early in their stay at Wide Mountain, people had been awakened well past midnight by the sound of several jeeps coming along the road. Men in the jeeps kept the headlights off, surveyed the area with flashlights, and then left quietly. People getting up to investigate saw they were gendarmes. The next day they heard that gendarmes had been searching for smugglers coming from the Persian Gulf via back roads. Angry about this incursion, Borzu's coresidents at Wide Mountain blamed him and their forced encampment along a road, a setting they had always avoided in the past.

Borzu, in turn, complained about being harassed by outsiders who were irritable from hunger and thirst. The month of Ramadan, during which many Muslims fast from dawn to dusk, had begun some days earlier. Because travelers were exempt from fasting, he joked that the distance to Wide Mountain was perhaps great enough to allow the men annoying him to break the fast. And then they expected him to provide a tasty feast. Like other Qermezi people, Borzu did not fast and said he had never done so. The nomads often noted that they were good Muslims who did not need to prove their belief through what they regarded as an inconvenient ritual. They commented that the merchants and money-lenders who demonstrated their piety by ostentatious fasting and daily prayer also routinely violated Islamic law by charging them interest, lying, and cheating and, by so doing, nullified their fasts and prayers.

With the loss of camels from smallpox, some families hard-pressed for pack animals and needing to travel slowly in the days to come left Wide Mountain early. A few families at Wide Mountain did not share winter pastures with Borzu and came to take their leave. No explicit farewell was said. Although this was a formal, ritualized occasion—a time when people recognized the authority of the headman—Borzu and the ones departing simply commented on the route ahead, and he issued instructions to be relayed to others.

Midmorning several days later, Borzu's group struck camp and moved down the mountain slopes toward Molla Nari where it had been before coming to Wide Mountain. The distance to winter pastures could be covered in six days, but people traveled only short distances each day and took twelve to sixteen days depending on the health of their pack animals, the resources along the route, and their desire to reach the ultimate destination.

As the nomads left the mountains above Arzhan Plain, they and their herds were jostled by twelve hundred sheep and goats tended by the hired herders who had rented Wide Mountain for the following period. A wealthy urban investor paid a wage to these herders, Lurs from the moun-

tains southwest of Isfahan, to tend his animals. His sheep and goats were
a smaller breed than those owned by most Qashqa'i and were more resilient in adverse conditions. By using pastures at times of the year when
most Qashqa'i nomads were elsewhere, the hired herders often exploited
resources the Qashqa'i were conserving for their own use later. They traveled between pastures with great speed. When they overtook Qashqa'i
nomads moving in the same direction, the Qashqa'i herders became anxious and disturbed. Hired herders were armed, a means of protection and
power the Qashqa'i were forbidden by Iranian law. These herders were
easily identified, for they traveled without women and children, carried
only minimal gear packed on donkeys, slept in canvas pup tents, tended
large herds of small-breed animals, and wore distinctive dress (wide-
legged black pants and round black skull caps made of felt).

Borzu's group entered the plain in front of the town of Arzhan Plain
and followed along the edges of the asphalt road leading in the direction
of Kazerun. They spent a few nights just past the end of the asphalt road
and then traveled near the less busy of the two vehicular roads to Kazerun. In several locations gendarmes forced them to break camp and
move.

On the trip through the hills and valleys south of Arzhan Plain, Borzu
encountered several of the alleged headmen who had harassed him during
the past month. One of them, now herding donkeys loaded with water
bags, had arrived at Wide Mountain in style in a Landrover and had authoritatively ordered him to leave. Struck by the contrast in the man's
two appearances, Borzu told Hafez to floor the accelerator and swerve
close to the man, which showered him with gravel and dust, and then to
back up. In order to enhance this small act of revenge and demonstrate
the reversal of their statuses, Borzu shouted sarcastic greetings to the man
from the luxury of the cab of the pickup and told him not to work too
hard.

Once over the difficult and rugged Pass of the Girl and then the Pass
of the Old Woman, the nomads descended into the foothills above the
plains of Kazerun. Most Qermezi men who were not members of Aqa
Mohammadli lineage wintered near the passes or at Famur to the south a
short distance away, and they parted company from Borzu. Many men
formally visited him just beforehand. Men of the two groups would often
meet in the town of Kazerun in the months to come, but women and
children, not to see one another again until spring at the earliest, parted
sadly.

The families heading to Molla Balut and ultimately Dashtak set off together. The release of tension in the group was noticeable. Although no one was looking forward with pleasure to the harsh season to come, they were glad to have finished the migration, with all its uncertainties, and to be away from alien territory. Once in their customary and designated winter pastures at Dashtak, they exercised some control over resources and were much less vulnerable to incursions.

Molla Balut, the "autumn pasture" of Borzu's group, was located below Dashtak in the foothills of the mountains. People found the land dry and barren ("only rocks," they said with dissatisfaction as they kicked at a few), and they set up encampments to wait impatiently for winter rains to begin.

Winter

Borzu and Khalifeh walked down a slope to Zulfaqar's tent and solemnly entered, each in turn saying a short prayer in Arabic. Men sitting in the tent quietly rose to their feet and moved to make a place for the newcomers. First Khalifeh and then Borzu were urged to take places of honor in the rear of the tent against the piled baggage. The occasion for the gathering was to commemorate the death of Zulfaqar six months earlier. Ritual observances for the family occurred on the day of a death, on the third, seventh, and fortieth days thereafter, and on the first anniversary. Some families observed every anniversary that followed, many commemorated all their dead on several special days of the year, and some said a prayer for the deceased every Thursday. Zulfaqar's family had marked his death on the customary days, but because it did not migrate to summer pastures, people now ending the migration had not earlier had a chance to mark ceremonially his passing.

Although originally part of Ipaigli, a once powerful and now disintegrated subtribe, Zulfaqar had considered himself and was considered by others to be Qermezi. He and other members of his extended family had lived and intermarried with Qermezi people for years, and Khalifeh and Borzu had represented them to outsiders. Zulfaqar had earned people's respect as a literate man and an expert in ritual and religion. He had been poor, and one of his teenage sons was Borzu's hired shepherd.

As soon as the nomads had reached Molla Balut, Zulfaqar's wife Kokab prepared to host them. Her eldest son Alibakhsh sacrificed one of the family's forty goats and invited men for a meal. She borrowed a carpet, large serving trays, and tea glasses from Borzu's wife Falak. Helped by neighboring women and girls, Kokab and her daughters cooked rice and a meat stew behind and to the side of the tent, out of sight of the guests.

The men uttered an Arabic prayer in unison before eating, and the women wailed in sorrow. As the mourners thought about Zulfaqar, they said they also remembered their own deceased loved ones for whom he had officiated at funerals.

In addition to its ritual significance, this gathering was the first occasion for men to discuss plans for moving to their Dashtak winter pastures in the mountains above. Several families had already pitched winter tents there, and others had begun to prepare their campsites. The main problem was the lack of water. Families already camped at Dashtak drove their herds down the mountain and past Molla Balut several times a day to a well in the plain below, and they transported water from the well by mule and donkey for household use. Another problem, which Borzu mentioned in passing, was his truck. Vehicles could not travel to Dashtak, and no road between Molla Balut and Dashtak could be built because of the rough and rocky steep terrain. Using the truck to haul water as at Wide Mountain was impossible here. Every family would have to transport its own water until winter rains began and the basins that men had constructed at Dashtak would fill. A third problem concerned Borzu's rival Sohrab, sitting next to Khalifeh. The respect that Borzu held for the occasion prevented him from lashing out at Sohrab, who was making what Borzu said was a ridiculous claim to pasture rights at Dashtak.

Borzu's youngest brother Abdol Hosain was also on people's minds. After he had formed his own independent household, he had shared pastures at Dashtak with Borzu and then with Gholam Hosain, his other full brother. Gholam Hosain's and Borzu's pastures were limited, however, and Abdol Hosain no longer wanted to reside with Borzu. Borzu had allocated him a campsite and grazing at Molla Balut, an area lacking vegetation and natural protection from rain, wind, and cold weather. Although Abdol Hosain and Sohrab were friendly, a sentiment enhanced because Abdol Hosain's wife was Sohrab's niece, Abdol Hosain was disturbed that Sohrab camped at Molla Balut and jeopardized its sparse grazing. He said he wanted to share Borzu's own pastures at Dashtak. The two brothers were not yet on speaking terms.

Subtle pressure within the community placed Borzu in a difficult position. He was, after all, the headman responsible for all group members as well as Abdol Hosain's elder brother. People temporarily camped at Molla Balut could see for themselves how impossible it would be for Abdol Hosain to graze his animals there for the next three to four months. If Borzu allocated grazing at Dashtak to Abdol Hosain, a man who currently lacked rights there, he provided an advantage to Sohrab who was making his own claim to Dashtak pastures. In Sohrab's case, some legal precedent existed, for he had been part of the original Qermezi group when it first came to Dashtak, and he had spent winters there before finding other winter pastures. The main evidence government officials sought in order to establish land claims was proof of prior residence, and hence Sohrab might win his case. At the conclusion of the meal, these issues still unresolved, men stood up and murmured another prayer as they left the tent. Women once again began to wail.

While waiting for winter rains before entering Dashtak, Borzu and his group usually spent a month or so at Famur to the southeast or high in the mountains above Dashtak, but both places lacked water and vegetation this year. The problem with Molla Balut was the lack of grazing. The stubble from wheat and barley they and others had harvested in the spring was long gone, and the region in general at this and lower altitudes was too hot and dry to sustain much if any vegetation except during a brief growing season in winter and early spring. Also, no fuel was available at Molla Balut, and already people had transported many loads of wood and brush from Dashtak. A government well was located several kilometers down the slope in the plain. Borzu's cousin Morad noted wryly that it was a Qashqa'i's fate always to lack some necessity: if water was available, grass was not; if grass was available, fuel was not; if . . . The problem for Borzu and the others was where to camp, where to graze, and where to get water, and these three tasks were at the moment conducted in three separate places, a problem especially troublesome for households with limited labor. Due to deliver their lambs any day, ewes would need special attention and be an additional drain on labor.

The next day men climbed up the steep path to Dashtak to evaluate the territory. Most decided to continue for the next few days to send herds there for grazing and then set up camp in the mountains before many lambs were born.

In the meantime Borzu cajoled some men into creating a path for his truck between Molla Balut and the gravel road farther down the slope past the well, so that he could transport water to camp and more easily travel to the nearby town of Kazerun. For the moment the truck remained by the well, and Borzu and his driver Hafez walked to and from camp. Other families relied on their own labor and pack animals for water.

A few days later Borzu decided to move his household to Dashtak. The process took four exhausting trips that lasted from before dawn to well after dark. Although the distance to the new campsite was short, the terrain was steep and rugged. The route led up a dry stream gorge filled with rocks and gravel, slippery for pack animals. Borzu made his initial trip with water and empty barrels, for he needed to establish a water supply at the new site. On the second trip he transported the winter tent and its accompanying equipment, and on the third trip he moved his family and household goods. On the final trip, in the dark, he brought sacks of grain and more water.

Borzu had complicated these efforts when he had attacked his hired shepherd Aqaboa as he led the herd from camp before dawn. Problems had been brewing between them, but the tension of the day apparently got the best of Borzu. He was barely restrained by men who rushed to stop him from doing Aqaboa serious injury. The shepherd had been hard-pressed in his job, especially since arriving at Wide Mountain, because of the extra hauling of water, the night grazing (animals not being satiated during the day), and driving animals great distances to water. He was tired from the long trek between the well in the plain below Molla Balut and the grazing high on the mountain slopes at Dashtak. He had not left early enough to suit Borzu this morning, thereby provoking the attack. Unable to hit back because of his status and that of Borzu, Aqaboa chose one of the only options possible. He ran to his own tent not far from Borzu's, angrily jerked out the stakes, which collapsed the tent in a heap (an act symbolic of the rupture of social relations and the bonds uniting campmates), and stomped off alone toward Kazerun. This act of protest left Borzu without a shepherd at a crucial time. Although people were increasingly reluctant to work for him, they did understand his need for help. Morad released his own shepherd to substitute for Aqaboa, while Khalifeh sent Hasan after Aqaboa to convince him to return to work. Aqaboa worked under a yearly contract, had not been paid his full salary, and could not afford to forfeit the previous months' labor.

Two days previously the first lamb had been born. For the trip up the mountain Borzu's thirteen-year-old daughter Zohreh nestled it and four newly delivered lambs in a bag strapped on a donkey, ordinarily used for carrying goatskin water bags. With wooden pins she made a small pocket in the bag for each lamb.

As Borzu's family and others struggled up the rough incline of the dry stream gorge to Dashtak, they could see at the top of a hill a lone tree surrounded by piles of small rocks. On reaching the summit, some people paused to place a rock or pebble by the tree and turn around to look across the wide valley at the distant mountains beyond. Several youngsters scrambled up the piles of rocks to place their own in the tree's branches, and some girls tied strips of cloth to its twigs. Remarkably standing when no others remained, the tree was called an "old stork" and was believed to be capable of sending across the valley to a saint's tomb (too distant to see) the prayers and vows that people uttered as they placed their small offerings. Not even the avid charcoal makers from Kazerun and villages in the valley had touched the tree when over time they had destroyed all others. Borzu's brother Ali noted with a chuckle that if Qermezi people had been smart many years ago when they first came to Dashtak, they would have filled every tree with rocks and rags, thereby preventing the region's Persians and Lurs from deforesting the area. The nomads were skeptical of the beliefs of the people settled in the region and viewed these ritual acts as superstition, but they did not mind adding a rock "just in case."

Between trips to and from Dashtak Borzu oversaw the process of pitching the large winter tent at his campsite. The nomads used three different campsites during their residence in winter pastures. Each was located on the plot of land Borzu allocated to them at Dashtak. Entered first, the autumn campsite was usually in a depression or shallow ravine for protection from wind and rain but not where sudden torrents of water could threaten people and livestock and destroy property. People cleared away rocks and debris and then leveled the place where they pitched the tent. They constructed a stone barrier around the edge of the tent, and a shallow trench served to direct water away from the tent's interior. The winter tent, different from the one used in summer and on the migrations, was stored in Kazerun during other seasons. Both tents were rectangular in shape and woven from goat hair, but the fabric of the winter one was coarser and thicker for protection from rain, snow, and cold. The winter tent was enclosed on three sides with an entrance at one of the two narrow ends. Wooden boards supported by poles raised the roof to a peak to help the runoff of rain. This tent was often longer than the summer one to accommodate a reed pen for lambs and kids in the back. Near the tent a rudimentary uncovered pen freshly made of brambles helped to protect the herd at night.

A week to three weeks later, depending on the onset of heavy rains and colder weather, people would move to their winter campsite, close to the autumn campsite but located in a more protected area such as a deeper ravine. There they had built and improved over the years several animal and storage huts as well as a pen for the herd. The few families who camped near the steep gorge leading to Molla Balut at the south of Dashtak relied on natural caves to protect animals and store straw and equip-

15. Fortified winter campsite of Morad, Abdol Rasul, and Naser.

ment. Near the winter campsite men had dug basins for the collection of rain and surface runoff, and these became their sources of water.

Between the forty-fifth day of winter and the beginning of spring, as the weather became warm and people and animals did not need as much protection, they would move to the spring campsite in more open terrain. Like the autumn campsite, this one lacked semipermanent structures such as huts and animal pens.

Sixty-five independent households, most of which were Qermezi by origin, shared winter pastures at Dashtak. These families were organized in eighteen camps of one to ten tents. Each family occupied a specific winter campsite and enjoyed exclusive use of demarcated land as pastures. Almost all camps were located about halfway between the cliffs and gorges to the southwest and the steep incline of the mountain slopes to the northeast. Half a kilometer or more separated each camp from its neighbors to the northwest and southeast.

The physical nature of the terrain at Dashtak helped to define and bound these pastures, and government allocations of land and use of adjoining territory by other people gave further definition to the area. High mountains stand above Dashtak, while in the other three directions sedentary agriculturalists and nomadic pastoralists (Qashqa'i and others) exploited resources.

People at Dashtak perceived themselves to be physically and socially isolated as well as restricted and contained. The mountains to the northeast and the cliffs and gorges to the southwest left only one easily traversed route running northwest and southeast through the territory, which enabled Dashtak's residents to keep track of people entering and passing through their land. At the northwest and southeast entrances Borzu placed as guards marginal families who wanted to better their relationship with him but who were not crucial to the group in case of incursions and encroachments. These families were new to Dashtak, held no customary or legal land rights, and were either not Qermezi by origin or members of Qermezi lineages other than Aqa Mohammadli. Bulverdi Qashqa'i nomads occupied pastures to the southeast, while Qarachai Qashqa'i, Bulverdi Qashqa'i, and Kuruni Kurds inhabited pastures to the northwest. Also to the northwest and southeast, Lur, Persian, and Arab villagers from the Kazerun valley and vicinity cultivated grain, often illegally, and for years had encroached on land the government allocated to Qermezi as pasture. They also cultivated at lower altitudes to the west below the cliffs and gorges and to the north and south of Molla Balut.

The actual name of these mountainous winter pastures was Sar-e Dashtak (Above the Plain), but the nomads simply called it Dashtak (The Plain).

As Borzu and a few other Qermezi men sat around the fire at the autumn campsite after their arduous day of moving and setting up camp, they talked about Qermezi history. These discussions and similar ones to follow were part of normal conversation, not only on cold nights by the fire but on many different occasions. They offered entertainment and were ways of passing time; they also transmitted knowledge and history via oral tradition to Qermezi children who learned who they were and from where they came by listening to these lively conversations.

Political History

Qermezi people stated that their ancestors became part of the Darrehshuri tribe (and hence the Qashqa'i confederacy) in the second half of the nineteenth century during the rule of a powerful, prominent Darrehshuri khan, Hajji Boa Khan (d. 1873). (Hajji was part of his personal name; he had not made a pilgrimage to Mecca.) They said that Hajji Boa Khan spotted Ali, Vali, and Yuli in a battle near a graveyard at Baiza. These three brothers were said to be ancestors of the members of three Qermezi lineages. One brother, strong and red-faced, hoisted a gravestone and threw it at the enemy. Awed, Hajji Boa Khan asked, "Who are these strong red [-faced] people?" (Hence, the derivation of the name Qermezi, "The Red Ones.") Darrehshuri khans took these "red" men to Qashqa'i and other tribal sporting contests to use them in competitions, and they also relied on them in raids and for war. They noted, "Qermezi is the sword of the khans." Reputedly, Qermezi men could steal an object when no one else could and escape without being caught.

The Qermezi group contained members of five patrilineages and other associated people. Many of them stated that the ancestors of Kachili and possibly also Qasemli lineages were founders of the group and that the three ancestors (Ali, Vali, Yuli) of Imamverdili, Qairkhbaili, and Aqa Mohammadli lineages joined the group as shepherds and servants. Other people stated that Kachili was not part of the original group at all and instead married into the three lineages slowly until it too became considered Qermezi. A few people asserted that the red-faced man who had thrown the gravestone was the ancestor of Qasemli lineage and that Qasemli ancestors were the original Qermezi.

The Qermezi group held "Black Qermezi" and "Red Qermezi" components. Men in the lineages stemming from the three brothers, the so-called Black Qermezi with dark-skinned faces, maintained their military and physical skills which they periodically offered to Darrehshuri khans. Members of Qasemli and particularly Kachili lineages, said to have light facial complexions, were the so-called Red Qermezi. Because Kachili men had been horsekeepers for Darrehshuri khans and part of their personal entourage, Red Qermezi became synonymous with being the khans' servants. The servants of Qashqa'i khans enjoyed prestige within the wider tribal system, but Qermezi people often derided Kachili men for what they said were their subservient roles.

Darrehshuri khans reported that ancestors of the Qermezi group were horsekeepers for Gudarz Kikha, son of Hajji Boa Khan and for a short time at the end of the nineteenth century the *kalantar*, chief khan of the Darrehshuri tribe. When Gudarz Kikha's brother Ayaz Kikha became kalantar, Black Qermezi men sought autonomy from the khans. Ayaz Kikha reduced the power of other Darrehshuri khans and *kikhas* (equivalent or lower in status to khans), including Gudarz Kikha. Many Red Qermezi men remained as servants of the Gudarzkikha branch of the khan family. Later some of these men, members of Kachili lineage, joined the entourage of the Ayazkikha khans, where they were still found in 1970.

Some Qermezi men stated that members of three of the five lineages were related patrilineally because of their ties to the three brothers, while others declared that the three apical ancestors were not brothers or even related but had simply allied at a time when Hajji Boa Khan was building his support. Qermezi men and women regarded members of the five lineages as interrelated and pointed to the intersecting kinship and marriage ties. Men of the three Black Qermezi lineages interacted frequently while men of Qasemli and Kachili lineages maintained some territorial and social distance. Women were less apt than men to stress differences among them according to lineage affiliation because they were more likely to reside with and depend upon people of other lineages.

Each of the five Qermezi lineages held its own reputation within the larger group. Men, bound more closely than women to their own lineage, were more apt than women to characterize the other lineages negatively. Most Qermezi men who were not part of Qasemli lineage routinely referred to the lineage as Nafamlar, "Those Who Are Stupid," and considered Qasemli men as lacking in power. An Aqa Mohammadli man noted, "Ahmad Khan and Musa Khan [two Qasemli men] own large flocks, but they can't answer a simple question, and so they are of no account." Men regarded the ability to speak intelligently and convincingly as being of prime importance. Most Qermezi men who were not members of Kachili lineage considered Kachili men as little more than servants, which in fact many of them had been. Qairkhbaili, "Forty Extended Families," was sometimes also said to be "forty voices, all saying something different" (that is, they could not agree on anything). They were known for their physical power.

People often characterized Aqa Mohammadli and Imamverdili men by what they perceived were the negative and positive traits of their respective dominant figures, Borzu and Sohrab. Both were aggressive, large, stocky men full of ambition. They exhibited commanding, authoritative personalities and held charismatic qualities. In any gathering, people's attention was riveted on the two men. People envied Aqa Mohammadli men for the benefits that close association with Borzu and the headmanship often brought, but they also joked about these men becoming hapless victims of Borzu's dreams and schemes. Imamverdili men were said to make contradictory statements to different people. Sohrab in particular held a reputation for causing antagonisms between Khalifeh's and Borzu's supporters by passing rumors about one side to the other. (Borzu did not gossip and said he had no need to do so. He generally kept to himself much of what others told him, and people trusted his confidence.)

The names of Aqa Mohammadli, Imamverdili, and Qasemli lineages each derived from ancestors, Aqa Mohammad, Imam Verdi, and Qasem.

16. Sohrab armed with a wooden club. On the autumn migration, September 1966. Courtesy of Ernest Thomas Greene.

The suffix -li, often used interchangeably with -lu, indicated "people of." Qairkhbaili, "Forty Extended Families," was a descriptive name. Kachili derived its name from *kachi,* a mixture of flour and milk. People recounted the story of the mother's brother of Abbas, reputed ancestor of the lineage, who was short of wheat due to a drought. Camped by the migratory route, he milked his sheep, mixed milk and flour to conserve flour, and offered some to people who traveled by. Kachili people sang the rhyme, "I made kachi, I poured it [into bowls], people coming and people leaving ate it, and thus we got our name."

Five men representing four of the five lineages had served as headman of Qermezi subtribe, as far as they could remember. The group many people regarded as the originator of the subtribe was Kachili, and Yunes Ali was their headman. Molla Qoli of Imamverdili, the next headman, was known for his expertise in religion and ritual. He was Sohrab's father's father's brother's son.

Borzu's father Shir Mohammad of Aqa Mohammadli lineage took over the headmanship and held it until his death in 1943 at the battle of Semirom between the Iranian army and allied Qashqa'i and Boir Ahmad Lur forces. Fighting alongside Darrehshuri khans against the army, he was shot and killed while attempting to capture an army machine-gun nest. Ten bullets pierced his body. In 1970 this war was the most significant in Qashqa'i memory, and stories about the war and Shir Mohammad's bravery were intertwined for Qermezi people.

Rostam Khan of Qasemli lineage had been installed as Qermezi's headman by Nasrollah Khan Darrehshuri for three months during Shir Mohammad's tenure. Darrehshuri khans were divided into two rival groups (Ayazkikhali and Aqakikhali) that competed over receiving tributes paid by the Darrehshuri subtribes. Nasrollah Khan, head of Aqakikhali, wanted Qermezi's tribute and needed to install a headman loyal to him, and so he captured Shir Mohammad, held him in chains in the camp of the ilkhani (paramount leader of the Qashqa'i confederacy), and appointed Rostam Khan. Hosain Khan Darrehshuri, head of Ayazkikhali and recipient of Qermezi's tribute, freed Shir Mohammad who promptly resumed the headmanship and kept it until his death. Khalifeh, Shir Mohammad's eldest living son who had assisted his father, took over the position when his father was killed.

After the battle of Semirom, Ziad Khan Darrehshuri appealed to the ilkhani Naser Khan, to offer a tribute to Shir Mohammad's sons on account of the loss of their father. Naser Khan expressed his gratitude for loyalty by allocating Khalifeh and his brothers a fifth of the rent from property he controlled near Semirom. Khalifeh in turn gave part of the income to Ziad Khan in recognition of his intercession.

In 1954, following the 1953 coup d'état during which the paramount Qashqa'i khans opposed Mohammad Reza Shah, the Iranian government held a referendum in order for headmen and elders of Darrehshuri subtribes to vote for the Darrehshuri khan of their choice. The shah wanted to divide up the interests of the Darrehshuri khans and split up powerful subtribes such as Qermezi. The Darrehshuri khans were themselves divided in the extent to which they were loyal to the shah. When Zeki Khan and Ja'far Qoli Khan (now head of Aqakikhali) sided with the shah after the coup and claimed new land in Darrehshuri territory, Jehangir Khan told the government that only a formal vote would indicate which khans the Darrehshuri people actually supported. Khalifeh and Borzu voted for Mohammad Hasan Khan, while the two men's rival, Sohrab, voted for Ziad Khan. Few Darrehshuri men voted for Zeki Khan or Ja'far Qoli Khan, which indicated, among other things, the tribesmen's prevalent anti-shah sentiments.

Sohrab had been close to Shir Mohammad, his mother's brother (a relationship often characterized by affection) and the man who had raised him when his own father was unable to care for his family. Wounded in 1943 at the beginning of the battle of Semirom during an act of bravery, Sohrab won the support of several Darrehshuri khans. Khalifeh, the new headman, was not as strong a personality as his father Shir Mohammad, and by 1945 Sohrab was challenging his authority and vying for the position. He migrated early from winter and summer pastures in order to force a division between his and Khalifeh's supporters. Darrehshuri khans collected an annual tribute from the subtribes, channeled through headmen, and Sohrab wanted the benefits of its collection and payment. The government referendum of 1954 crystallized the informal separation of Qermezi into two groups. Since that time, Qashqa'i people and others often spoke of Qermezi in terms of "Khalifeh's [later Borzu's] group" and "Sohrab's group." To reward Sohrab's loyalty, Ziad Khan allocated summer pastures to him and his supporters at Wolf Hill. Mohammad Hasan Khan and Jehangir Khan allocated summer pastures to Khalifeh and his supporters near Wolf Hill. These three Ayazkikha khans wanted to challenge the power of Ja'far Qoli Khan, head of Aqakikhali whose base of strength was there.

Almost all Aqa Mohammadli men supported Khalifeh and Borzu, and almost all Imamverdili men supported Sohrab. Most Qairkhbaili men backed Khalifeh and Borzu until a dispute over Dashtak pastures in 1966 when many of them temporarily joined Sohrab along with key Qasemli and Kachili men. Qasemli men were usually independent but sometimes sought assistance from Khalifeh, Borzu, and Sohrab concerning land, khans, and the Iranian government. Most Kachili men settled in villages in the 1930s and ceased to rely on Qermezi's headman. Some were part of the Darrehshuri khans' entourage and received their patronage and mediation.

Khalifeh served as headman for twenty-one years and then said he could no longer be effective. After two of his adolescent sons died through accident and illness, he became despondent and ill. In 1964 he gave his briefcase holding documents relating to the headmanship to his younger brother Borzu and said, "The task is yours if the people agree." No one openly opposed the change, and no man other than Sohrab sought the headmanship for himself. Khalifeh's eldest son Bahram was still too young and inexperienced for the job. Borzu had assisted Khalifeh in sub-tribal affairs with the government and khans for years. During Khalifeh's last few years as headman, Borzu had increasingly assumed responsibility for Qermezi's external relationships, a task he performed with growing effectiveness.

Jehangir Khan Darrehshuri had played a crucial role in Borzu's rise to power. He had paid special attention to Borzu as a young man accompanying his father and then his brother as they carried out their political duties. He saw the need for a strong leader in the subtribe, one who was able to challenge Sohrab who had already received support from the preeminent Darrehshuri khan, Ziad Khan. Khalifeh was not proving to be the powerful leader that his father Shir Mohammad had been.

The beginning of Borzu's rise to power coincided with the 1953 coup d'état in support of Mohammad Reza Shah against Prime Minister Mohammad Mosaddeq. The event provided Borzu with the opportunity to become involved in a small way in national politics. When the coup succeeded, Mohammad Bahmanbaigi, Zeki Khan Darrehshuri, and Ja'far Qoli Khan Darrehshuri formed a pro-shah coalition to secure government favors, influence Qashqa'i and Darrehshuri politics, and gain control of tribal territory. A member of the Amaleh tribe and son of a loyal supporter of the Qashqa'i ilkhani, Bahmanbaigi saw the opportunity to seize Qashqa'i leadership for himself when the paramount Qashqa'i khans allied with Mosaddeq and then continued to oppose the shah following Mosaddeq's fall from power and arrest. Bahmanbaigi, Zeki Khan, and Ja'far Qoli Khan brought Kuhgiluyeh Lurs to fight for their interests in Amaleh and Darrehshuri territory. Jehangir Khan Darrehshuri organized a coun-

17. Jehangir Khan Darrehshuri and his granddaughter Maral. Maral was a premedical student at Temple University in Philadelphia in 1991.

terforce of Mosaddeq supporters, young aggressive men of loyal Darreh-shuri subtribes. Borzu Qermezi was among them and quickly proved his power and ability. Jehangir Khan and his pro-Mosaddeq, anti-shah supporters prevailed in the local struggle, and Borzu became known as Jehangir Khan's hero. Darrehshuri khans informally bestowed the title of *beg* (var. *baig, bai*), "honorable man," on him, a title usually reserved for older men and headmen of subtribes.

Jehangir Khan appointed Borzu as supervisor of his shepherds to reward his loyalty, strengthen him further, and "give him a face" (honor, reputation) so that he would be in a position to compete successfully against Sohrab and eventually take over the headmanship. By molding young men with potential in selected subtribes, Jehangir Khan enhanced his own power and broke up power blocs within the tribe. He wanted to create supporters who were not already affiliated to his uncles Ziad Khan and Zeki Khan. By selecting Borzu, Jehangir Khan also continued his support of the sons of Shir Mohammad who had gallantly died fighting in the government's war against the khans. It was this last explanation and not the others that Qermezi people gave for Jehangir Khan appointing Borzu as supervisor.

A supervisor of shepherds (*mukhtabad*) achieved honor from holding the position and being in the khan's favor. He also received material rewards in the form of free grazing, exemption from the khan's animal tax, one lamb for every one hundred animals supervised, and clarified butter. The supervisor hired and oversaw the khan's shepherds dispersed throughout Darrehshuri territory, and he organized branding and shearing, reported the year's gains and losses to the khan, and coordinated the delivery of wool to him and the transport of animals to market for sale. Borzu served as Jehangir Khan's supervisor until 1968 when the khan no longer needed someone in that position because he had steadily decreased his herds and animals. In 1970 the khan owned two herds—previously he had owned ten or more—and dealt directly with his two hired shepherds.

The origin of Borzu's wealth also stemmed from his connection with Jehangir Khan. In 1962 Mohhi ed-Din Kashefi, a wealthy Persian industrialist in Isfahan, advanced Jehangir Khan $6,700, with which he bought eight hundred year-old lambs and kids. Borzu hired shepherds and oversaw the care of these animals. Several years later Borzu and Jehangir Khan sold the animals, returned the $6,700 to Kashefi along with half the profit, and divided the other half of the profit, $3,200, between themselves. With his $1,600 Borzu bought year-old lambs, which became the core of his wealth and the source of his expanding herds.

In 1966 the government ordered that the Qashqa'i be disarmed and held Borzu, as Qermezi headman, responsible for collecting the group's guns. In performing this task he became better acquainted with army officers in Kazerun. That same year an intra-Qermezi fight over Dashtak pastures broke out, and Borzu frequented government offices in Kazerun as he tried to handle the dispute. These two events—confiscating weapons and negotiating a conflict—fortified him in his position both with the government and with his group.

In 1967 Borzu received official recognition as Qermezi headman from the Tribal Security Force, which was charged with the responsibility of controlling the Qashqa'i tribes. That year the government had transferred the Tribal Security Force from the army to the gendarmerie and vastly expanded its authority and power, in response to the outbreak of protest in Fars province against the government's attempts to implement land reform and other changes. The Tribal Security Force had been created after the battle of Semirom in 1943, according to an agreement between paramount Qashqa'i leaders and government officials that the government's contact with the Qashqa'i would be through this army agency and that it would not otherwise interfere in tribal affairs.

The Tribal Security Force designated and affirmed the position of subtribal headmen as a primary means of centralizing control over the Qashqa'i. The force required Borzu as headman to submit a list of men in the subtribe whom he represented. After Sohrab submitted his own list, the force recognized both men and created a file for each, with their photographs attached. Because their main task was now serving as liaison with the government, and because Borzu was more skilled and qualified in this regard than Sohrab, Borzu was the generally acknowledged headman of the entire subtribe. He was proving to be more adept in helping the nomads to adjust to the many political and economic changes then occurring in Iran. Sohrab lacked literacy and an effective manner with government officials, skills becoming mandatory in a modernizing Iran with a rapidly expanding bureaucracy and government apparatus. Despite the nationalization of pastures and the national land reforms then taking place, which were debilitating changes for most nomadic pastoralists in Iran, Borzu was able to secure pastures for many families in the subtribe, while Sohrab managed to perform this service only for himself and a few close supporters. If Sohrab had been able to acquire long-term pasture rights for his supporters, most of whom were Imamverdili men, he could have formally created a separate subtribe. But he had not done so, and his supporters continued to rely on Borzu for liaison with the government.

Borzu and Sohrab were large, physically powerful, aggressive, and often bellicose, traits that had been essential in the past when physical force was often used to achieve desired ends. In a rapidly transforming Iran, however, other traits had become more important. Qermezi people often noted that a headman was now needed for "office work" (governmental and bureaucratic tasks), and Borzu was more qualified and effective than Sohrab. Sohrab remained unsuccessful in his challenge to Borzu. He sought and received the continuing patronage of Ziad Khan Darrehshuri and his son Amiramanollah Khan, while Borzu's patrons remained Jehangir Khan and his brother Mohammad Hasan Khan.

In 1970 Jehangir Khan and other Darrehshuri khans still addressed Borzu as "Borzu Beg," sometimes, it seemed, slightly in jest. Beg was a title bestowed by Qashqa'i khans on men at the subtribal level who performed loyally and bravely. No specific function or role accompanied the title; it was primarily honorific and recognized past deeds. Thirty or so Darrehshuri men, mostly headmen and former headmen, held the title,

and khans relied on them for political and military support. By the time
Borzu was established in his headmanship, the government had already
undercut the power and authority of Darrehshuri and other Qashqa'i
khans. By calling Borzu "beg," the khans recognized his elevated status
and recalled past times. The slight humor that accompanied the reference
was not intended to demean him. Rather, the khans were amused by their
use of a nearly obsolete title, one that had often been conferred after acts
of bravery in battle. They noted that Borzu would still have been a "real"
beg if circumstances permitted the khans to govern as they had in the
past.

Qermezi and other Darrehshuri people used the term "kikha" when
talking generally about the Darrehshuri khans. "Khan," they said, was a
government-bestowed title and conveyed a formal and distant relationship. The men they supported were "kikha," a term conveying a closer
and more friendly relationship. Darrehshuri khans in 1970 used "khan"
to refer to active tribal leaders of the two main branches (Ayazkikhali and
Aqakikhali) of the khan family, while "kikha" referred to men of the
seven minor branches. Khans were more prominent and powerful than
kikhas. Khans in fact talked and joked about the "insignificant" *kikhali*
(the kikha families) in a slightly deriding tone. Darrehshuri people, especially those who lacked any direct contact with khans, often used
"kikha" (and occasionally "khan") in a generic sense with no personal
reference. "Kikha summoned us to war, and we went," they said, without
indicating which particular khan it was.

Until 1945 members of Qermezi subtribe had spent winters in Darrehshuri territory at a place named Girl's Grave (Qez Mazareh) between
White Grave (Gur Espid) and Nurabad on the border of Qashqa'i (Darrehshuri and Kashkuli) and Boir Ahmad Lur land. In a famous battle at
the beginning of the twentieth century, Ayaz Kikha Darrehshuri and his
son Hosain Khan captured Girl's Grave and other parts of the Mahur
region from Kashkuli khans. Needing a strong force along the new border,
Ayaz Kikha assigned Girl's Grave to Qermezi subtribe because its men
were known to be powerful, courageous, and reliable. Girl's Grave now
marked the Darrehshuri–Kashkuli–Boir Ahmad Lur border, and it remained a place of contention for these three tribes. Hosain Khan controlled the territory until 1933 when Reza Shah ordered all Qashqa'i nomads to settle. The Qermezi group remained year around at Girl's Grave
until 1941 without much contact with the Darrehshuri khans who had
settled in or near summer pastures. In the interval Reza Shah had arrested
Hosain Khan and then executed him in 1937. When the British and So-

viets forced Reza Shah to abdicate in 1941, almost all Qermezi people immediately resumed their seasonal migrations.

A violent confrontation in 1945 with Boir Ahmad Lurs forced the Qermezi group to leave Girl's Grave permanently. Even in 1970 Qermezi people told the story of the conflict and subsequent flight in detail and with passion and excitement. This event more than any other left a lasting imprint on them, and they dated many historical events not by years but as occurring either before or after the flight. The story explained why they occupied winter pastures at Dashtak, far from the territory of most other Darrehshuri. It also expressed internal political tensions that were still disruptive in 1970. In 1945 an imminent split within the Qermezi group was postponed when two rival men and their supporters came together in self-defense against external aggression.

The story begins with the aftermath of Shir Mohammad's death in the battle of Semirom in 1943, when Sohrab began to challenge the authority of Khalifeh, the new headman, and vie for the position. At the end of winter in 1945 Sohrab held a meeting to announce that he and his supporters were ready to migrate to Naibur, the first stage of the spring migration. Na'amatollah, Sohrab's mother's brother's son and a young but respected Aqa Mohammadli man, stated that he and others were not ready to migrate because they still needed to harvest that season's opium and grain crops. The day after Sohrab left with his group, Na'amatollah decided he ought to discuss the matter further with him, and he set out on his horse to find him.

A short distance away a kinsman shouted to Na'amatollah that he had seen twelve thieves coming on a raid to steal Qermezi sheep. Na'amatollah galloped back to his tent to get another gun. His cousin Khalifeh who was nearby rode with him to repel the thieves, Boir Ahmad Lurs from the neighboring territory to the northeast. When the thieves saw the two men approach, they split up, five slipping into a ravine near charcoal pits and seven escaping a distance away. Having no difficulty following their tracks in the tall spring grass, Na'amatollah and Khalifeh found the seven thieves hiding behind oak trees near a cave. The thieves shot at them. A bullet cut through Khalifeh's leg and entered his horse's stomach. The horse fell to the ground, and Khalifeh, thrown free in the fall, rolled behind a few rocks. Partially hidden behind a small wild almond tree, Na'amatollah was shot in the stomach. As he fell he shouted to Khalifeh, "I am dead." Khalifeh yelled back, "Don't be afraid," and returned the fire. The seven thieves fled to a ditch in a dry riverbed.

Khalifeh called to a kinsman who had followed them, and he retrieved

Na'amatollah's gun and horse for Khalifeh. Hearing gunfire, other Qermezi men hastened to the scene. Seeing Na'amatollah's body they shouted, "They killed our brother. Let's kill them." They found the seven thieves hiding and killed five of them outright. Another was severely wounded and left to die. They captured the seventh and interrogated him about his companions and their occupations and place of residence. Then they debated his fate. Some said they should promptly kill him because Qermezi women would certainly kill him if they brought him back to camp as prisoner (for he had killed their "brother" too). A few men suggested that they release him, but they all agreed that if they did so, he would send others to take revenge. The decision was made. Sardar shot and killed him.

Na'amatollah's father brought his son's body back to camp, and kinsmen buried him that night. Early the next morning Jehangir rode to Sohrab's camp to seek armed support in case an attack came, and another man traveled to Zeki Khan Darrehshuri's camp to report on the fight. Sohrab and his brother Darab came the next day. On their way they searched for the five missing thieves in order to kill them so that they would be unable to report the story to the families of the men already dead. They located the five thieves, one of whom shouted to ask about the fate of their companions. Darab shot one man who fell and then escaped into the forest (and later went insane), and the other four fled.

Zeki Khan Darrehshuri came promptly with an armed contingent to escort the two Qermezi groups (Na'amatollah's and Sohrab's, now temporarily united) away from the area and to help in case a revenge party of Boir Ahmad Lurs chased after them. They migrated together for three or four days until well away from Boir Ahmad territory and the scene of the fight. A dervish sent by the families of the seven dead men traveled after the group to ask where the bodies were so he could bring them home for a proper burial.

Out of fear of the Lurs' revenge, Qermezi people never returned to Girl's Grave. They had abandoned unharvested opium and grain crops as well as Shir Mohammad's house, fruit garden, and other permanent structures. Members of two other Darrehshuri subtribes seized their pastures. The Lurs never sought a settlement of the unresolved conflict. The possibility of exchanging women in marriage, often the solution to such disputes, was out of the question from the point of view of the Qermezi people involved. They would never, they said, give their precious daughters to thieves. While they might consider giving a girl in marriage to another Darrehshuri group with which they were feuding, they would never under these circumstances give a girl to another tribe, especially one that was not Qashqa'i.

The Qermezi group migrated to summer pastures, and Khalifeh and Sohrab consulted with Darrehshuri khans about finding new winter pastures. The resumption of Qashqa'i nomadism in the aftermath of Reza Shah's abdication had caused a shake-up in land allocations, and Darrehshuri and other Qashqa'i tribal khans were attempting to expand their territorial interests. Several Darrehshuri khans anxious to spread their influence in the direction of Kazerun said they would help Qermezi people find pastures there. Ziad Khan suggested a place named Dashtak in the mountains above Kazerun. Khalifeh and Sohrab said later that they were glad to have gone there because it was far from the influence and interference of khans. They also appreciated the proximity of Kazerun, a better, more convenient market for them than their former market at Dugonbadan, and they thought that government authorities there might protect them against the Boir Ahmad Lurs if they sought revenge.

History of Dashtak

When the Qermezi group first arrived at Dashtak in the autumn of 1945 after having migrated from summer pastures, the territory was already rented by Bulverdi Qashqa'i and Kashkuli Qashqa'i nomadic pastoralists from two Lur landowners in Davan village in the mountains east of Kazerun. During the first winter the landowners allowed the Qermezi group to share Dashtak with the other two groups and collected rent from all of them. At the beginning of the second winter Bulverdi pastoralists tried to expel the Qermezi group, but it was larger and drove out both the Bulverdi and Kashkuli by force of arms during the second and third winters. Because it paid more rent than the other two groups, the Davan landowners did not object to the expulsion. Qermezi people used the pastureland exclusively from that time. In 1945 some Kashkuli were still living in houses they had built at Molla Balut, below Dashtak, when Reza Shah had forced all Qashqa'i nomads to settle. When they left the area they abandoned the houses, and the ruins were still standing in 1970. Kuruni Kurds, also at Dashtak and on its northern border in 1945, remained as competitors for the land.

Qermezi men paid the Lur landowners rent in cash at the beginning of winter when they arrived from summer pastures. They also owed them a New Year's gift in March of one goat and six kilograms of clarified butter. In 1964, as part of a nationwide program of nationalization, officials from the Land Reform Organization of the Ministry of Agriculture confiscated Dashtak from the Lur landowners and declared it government land. In 1965 the government entitled Borzu, as headman of Qermezi, and members of his group to use Dashtak as pastures without charge. The group was obligated to occupy Dashtak every winter regardless of the condition of pastoral resources. If one winter the group went elsewhere, it would lose its rights to Dashtak, and the government would reassign the land to other pastoralists. In 1964 and 1965 the Qermezi group continued to pay rent, pressured by the former landowners who were no longer legally entitled to collect it, because the pastoralists wanted to cultivate land on the perimeter of Dashtak that the landowners still controlled. After 1965 they no longer paid any rent.

Borzu tried to relocate some families at Dashtak in 1965, and a fight between Aqa Mohammadli and other Qermezi men erupted. Although Dashtak was territory the government assigned to Qermezi subtribe, Aqa Mohammadli men controlled the best and largest plots. Borzu favored his own lineage over the others. Ultimately he wanted to force the brothers Sardar and Sepahdar (and their many soon-to-be-independent sons) of Qairkhbaili lineage from Dashtak and allocate their section to Aqa Mohammadli men such as Abdol Hosain. Saying that no other space was available and as harassment, Borzu sent an Imamverdili man to share Sepahdar's camp. Sepahdar refused to take him in. Borzu then told Sepahdar to release some pastureland to Khalifeh who needed more grazing. Sepahdar again refused. When Khalifeh and his son Bahram grazed their animals on Sepahdar's land, Sepahdar and Bahram fought. Most men of the other three lineages opposed these moves and sided with Qairkhbaili men.

Nearing the end of the spring migration, Qermezi men and women fought over the Dashtak issue. In the fray, many were injured and twenty-three sheep of Aqa Mohammadli men were stolen by a Qairkhbaili man. Borzu accused Sepahdar and his sons of complicity. Khalifeh filed a complaint at the gendarmerie stating that two of Sardar's sons possessed guns illegally and had stolen his sheep. The two sons were arrested and imprisoned until a merchant in Kazerun, patron of Qairkhbaili men, posted bail and paid for their release. The next winter, leopards attacked and killed or injured twenty of Sepahdar's goats. Sepahdar's son Esfandeyar cut the dead goats with a knife to make it seem as if they had been killed by a man. Sepahdar blamed five Aqa Mohammadli men for the slaughter and filed a complaint at the gendarmerie. Borzu handled the case and paid legal costs.

During the next two years the dispute raged. "Every day" each winter, people said later, "war" broke out at Dashtak as men from the two sides encountered one another during their daily routines. Qairkhbaili men, formerly fully supportive of Borzu, offered aid to Sohrab in his quest for the headmanship of Qermezi. Later, when Sepahdar saw that Sohrab had failed to secure pasture rights for members of his expanding group, he withdrew his support. In 1968 two Imamverdili men mediated the dispute between Borzu and Sepahdar. They said to Borzu, "The fight is finished. Sepahdar is your mother's brother" (which he was). They took Borzu to Sepahdar's tent, and in the presence of Khalifeh and Sepahdar's sons the two men agreed to cease fighting.

In 1966, still piqued by the government's confiscation of Dashtak and the loss of the rent, the former landowners sent 150 of their peasants on a raid to reclaim the land for cultivation. They chose a day for their incursion when they knew many Qermezi men would be in Kazerun. One hundred of the men prepared to plow Dashtak land with as many teams of horses, mules, and plows and the other 50 were to serve as guards. Aiding them were 12 Boir Ahmad Lur men from Boir Ahmad territory to the north and Qarachai Qashqa'i men who pastured just north of Dashtak and wanted to expand their own land. The origin of the Davan landowners, settled in the mountains east of Kazerun for several generations, was Boir Ahmad Lur, and they continued to identify themselves as such and to rely on Boir Ahmad support.

Qermezi people described the invasion by saying, "A lion came from the forest, and no man or woman was there." Only 2 Qermezi men and 1 non-Qermezi hired shepherd were close by that day, and they urgently sent children to alert other men in the territory and the mountains above where they were tending herds. Qermezi women in the vicinity joined in the defense, and other women hearing about the fight "jumped on mules and rushed to battle." At the height of the conflict, 13 Qermezi men and 30 women faced the 150 peasants and their supporters. Both sides, including women, sustained injuries. The peasants, beaten back, surrendered the fight and abandoned horses, mules, plows, clothing, and food in their haste to escape. They were never to return in such a group again. (The former landowners' incursions every year thereafter were always more subtle.)

When the violence ended, Hasel rode to Kazerun to report to Borzu, who filed a complaint at the gendarmerie and brought armed gendarmes to Dashtak to investigate. Later that winter the Davan landowner who had instigated the raid agreed to pay legal costs and make peace. Gendarmes brought him to Borzu to make the final settlement, and the abandoned property was then returned.

One government document for Dashtak listed Borzu and four close kinsmen (Khalifeh, Jehangir, Morad, Mansur). It gave some discretionary power to these five, especially Borzu in his role as headman, to add and remove families as they saw fit. Another document listed the forty-four men who had occupied the territory when the government transferred rights to Qermezi. Since 1965 some of them had settled in villages, and Borzu assigned new men to their places. Several others of the forty-four had died, and their sons filled their places. As political alliances changed, some men left Dashtak for other winter pastures, and Borzu allowed entry to others who had been elsewhere. He exercised control and wielded power, and his decisions carried weight with the government authorities who held jurisdiction over the area. These officials, however, could and did make independent rulings that undercut Borzu's authority, and a few men residing at Dashtak or wanting to move there had caused him problems. Borzu's rival Sohrab was a case in point.

All five Qermezi lineages were represented among the 65 men heading independent households at Dashtak (22 from Aqa Mohammadli, 17 Qairkhbaili, 7 Imamverdili, 4 Kachili, 1 Qasemli). Twelve of the other 14 men originated from other Darrehshuri subtribes, and 2 were from the Amaleh Qashqa'i tribe. Six of the 14 were shepherds or camel herders hired on a yearly basis. With one exception they lacked independent pasture rights at Dashtak, but they could herd their own few animals along with those of their employers. One of the 14 was the teacher assigned by the government to Qermezi subtribe, and another was Borzu's hired driver. The other 6 men had wintered at Dashtak for many years and had established long-term relationships, sometimes fortified by intermarriage, with Qermezi people. Twelve of the 14 men (the teacher and driver being the other two) were poor, and most performed services for their Qermezi neighbors. These 12 often considered themselves and were considered by others to be Qermezi. The names of the subtribes and tribes from which they originated were, however, often affixed to their personal names as a way of distinguishing them from Qermezi people in the five lineages. The 12 were Qermezi in the sense of being part of an active sociopolitical community. Attacks on Dashtak or its inhabitants put all 65 men on the defense. Borzu represented the 12 men to outsiders and served as their patron.

Ten to 13 of the 65 men stayed with their families at Dashtak year around unless the heat was intolerable, and these too were among the poor. Each owned a small herd of ten to forty goats (for sheep did not flourish in this climate), a few of which they sometimes sent on the migration to summer pastures with their kin and neighbors. For added income, they planted and harvested the grain of people who migrated, and they sold in Kazerun firewood, charcoal, wild almonds, and sap from wild almond trees. During the scorchingly hot weather of late spring, summer, and early autumn, they lived in huts made of branches, reeds, and grass and packed away their woven goat-hair tents which they said the sun would destroy.

Most Qermezi nomads who were not at Dashtak wintered in pastures to the southeast in close proximity to one another. Twenty-three Qasemli and Imamverdili men were at Famur, 9 Imamverdili and Qairkhbaili at Sweet Well, 11 Imamverdili and Qairkhbaili at Seven Girls, and 6 Imamverdili, Qasemli, and Qairkhbaili in Sorkhi Lur tribal territory. Five Qasemli men were at Basht near the town of Dugonbadan to the northwest. All these nomads occupied nationalized land, but Persian and Lur men who still held power over the areas illegally forced them to pay rent for pastures and cultivable land.

In 1953 Jehangir Khan Darrehshuri had rented a large expanse of cultivable land and pasture at Famur to the southeast of Dashtak and turned it over to Qermezi subtribe. The land was part of a religious endowment (*vaqf*). He collected a fifth of the harvest brought in by Qermezi men, then paid five thousand kilograms of grain as rent to an agent of the religious foundation and kept the rest. Khalifeh served as overseer of the crop, calculated the amount each man owed Jehangir Khan, and received 3 percent for his efforts. Some Qermezi families cooperated in order to exploit simultaneously the cultivable land at Famur and the grazing at Dashtak. One or two men of each association grew grain and vegetables at Famur while other men herded their combined animals at Dashtak. When land reform confiscated Famur from the religious foundation in 1962, and Jehangir Khan no longer wanted to rent it, Qermezi men concentrated their agricultural efforts at Dashtak and Molla Balut and ceased their cultivation of vegetables.

In 1965 Borzu and Ahmad Khan, principal figure in Qasemli lineage, sought and received a document from the Ministry of Agriculture enabling their groups to continue to use Famur as winter pastures. Their petition was made on the basis of their prior residence there. Nomads heading to Dashtak usually stopped first at Famur for a month at the end of the autumn migration and then went to Dashtak when rain had filled the basins there and new vegetation was soon to appear. Members of

Ahmad Khan's group went to Famur at the end of the autumn migration and stayed through the winter. Every year the Persian headman of the nearby village of Qal'eh Moshiri forced the group to pay rent even though the land was nationalized. He threatened them with expulsion if they did not pay. He bought the compliance of government agents, who claimed ignorance of his illegal practices, except on one occasion in 1966. That year the headman had illegally sold the pasture rights of Famur to Qermezi nomads and to an investor in Isfahan, whose five thousand animals consumed all the vegetation. Borzu reported the violation to the gendarmes, who jailed the headman on the basis of Borzu's and Ahmad Khan's legal rights. Borzu expelled the commercial herds. Although he and the Qal'eh Moshiri headman eventually reconciled, the headman continued to demand, and received, illegal rent from Qermezi nomads at Famur.

External Political Relationships

In 1945 when the Qermezi group abandoned its customary winter pastures in Darrehshuri territory (where many Darrehshuri khans resided seasonally) and sought pastures to the southeast near Kazerun, it lost its frequent association during the winter with these khans. In 1943 Jehangir Khan had moved his winter campsite to Famur and was close to the Qermezi group when it arrived. When land reform confiscated Famur pastures in 1962, he rented a house in Shiraz for the winter. Ziad Khan, preeminent Darrehshuri khan, spent winters at Polo Field Canyon near Kazerun, but by 1970 he was not directly involved in most tribal affairs because of government restrictions and advancing age. Borzu, Khalifeh, and Sohrab occasionally visited several khans in Shiraz during winter, and Borzu sometimes stayed at Mohammad Hasan Khan's house while he conducted government business relating to subtribal affairs. Because of their move near Kazerun, Qermezi people did not often see other Darrehshuri in winter. Most Qashqa'i nomads associated with members of their own tribes in winter and summer pastures.

As Darrehshuri nomads migrated south in autumn, the Tribal Security Force in charge of Darrehshuri affairs moved from Semirom to Dugonbadan in the Zagros foothills in time to take charge of problems arising there when the tribe arrived. Almost all Qermezi people in winter pastures, however, lived near Kazerun 130 kilometers southeast of Dugonbadan and fell under the general authority of the regular gendarmes, forest rangers, land reform officials, army, police, secret police, and officials of the Ministry of Justice. Because Qermezi was part of the Darrehshuri tribe, certain official matters continued to rest with the Tribal Security Force in Dugonbadan, a division of responsibility and jurisdiction that often caused confusion and uncertainty. For example, during the previous winter Borzu had frequently traveled to offices in Kazerun, Dugonbadan, and Shiraz to find out how he could regain the gun the government had confiscated from him in 1966 and what documents would be required. He was unsuccessful in his quest. At other times the distance of the Tribal Security Force meant that it did not interfere in Qermezi affairs, and Qermezi men, especially Borzu in his role as headman, were more autonomous. Peasants, landowners, and others holding grievances against Qermezi men were not likely to take their complaints all the way to Dugonbadan. They would have brought them to the force had it been in Kazerun, just as peasants and other aggrieved parties sought the force's assistance in Semirom when they fought with Qermezi men residing at nearby Hanalishah. Gerdarme posts at Mirror Bridge and Famur to the southeast shared some control over the Qermezi group with gendarme headquarters in Kazerun. Borzu often traveled from one to the other to handle business.

The Iranian military presence in the Kazerun area was greater than in the Semirom area, largely because of the strategic location. The road between Bushehr on the Persian Gulf and Shiraz passed by Kazerun and was one of the few major routes between the gulf and centers of population on the Iranian plateau. Commerce on the road was heavy and increasing, especially the transport of goods to and from the port of Bushehr. Smugglers regularly used roads in the vicinity to carry contraband from the gulf, and bandits and highway robbers lay in wait for them.

The military presence also related to land reform and intertribal borders. The as-yet-incomplete nature of land reform and the nationalization of pastures created disputes over land. As with many other areas of Iran, a relatively small number of people controlled a large portion of the cultivated and cultivable land and exercised power over a vast, often landless peasantry. Peasants now expected their own land, while landowners were devising ways to retain control. In addition, the Kazerun area was situated between the territories of three major Qashqa'i tribes and bordered on Mamassani and Boir Ahmad Lur tribal territory. Control over the intervening regions, particularly the increasingly important agricultural areas, was in dispute. Pastureland was rapidly shrinking, and tribally organized pastoralists as well as expanding numbers of herders hired by urban investors vied for the remaining land and resources.

Qermezi people were affected by many national policies and programs such as military surveillance, land reform, controlled meat prices, and formal education, but, like many other rural and provincial Iranians, they were not well situated to comprehend fully the rationale behind them. Also, the ways in which policies were implemented at the local level did not necessarily coincide with the intentions of policymakers. Implementation varied within the broad territory these nomads occupied. Local government agents and agencies competed and conflicted with one another, and rampant corruption and abuse of privilege were always evident.

If Mohammad Reza Shah saw or learned about the abuses and self-aggrandizing practices of lower-echelon government agents, Qermezi people said, he would immediately stop them. Although the nomads occasionally talked about writing letters and petitions to him directly, they perceived him as unreachable and never did write. They did not support the shah in either word or deed, but in 1970 they did not have any specific reason to oppose him. Their opposition was directed against the government agents they actually encountered. They said these men did not serve the interests of the Qashqa'i, the shah, the government as a whole, or Iran.

Borzu received a more sophisticated interpretation of national policy from Jehangir Khan Darrehshuri and the khan's advisors, Habib Aqa Zahedi and Faraj Aqa Zahedi, while the other nomads derived their information from Borzu, merchants, moneylenders, and rumors encountered in towns.

Qermezi people had a vague concept of "Iran." Through their many and frequent encounters with government agents, they were aware of a broad political and military authority over which they had no control and which periodically oppressed them. The association was negative; they perceived no positive benefits from this authority. The nomads did not consider themselves Iranians, but they recognized, of course, that they lived within a larger political entity named Iran. They expressed no sense of loyalty to Iran or its ruler the shah and gave no indication that they shared a citizenry with the non-Qashqa'i people who harassed them. Students in the tribal school and in Kazerun received instruction in Iranian geography, history, and patriotism and were told to respect Iranian symbols including the flag and the shah's portrait, both of which were prominently displayed in every school tent and classroom.

External Economic Relationships

Winter was a time of economic hardship for Qermezi and other nomads. What cash if any remained after the sale of animals in summer and the repayment of debts was long gone, and they again depended on urban Persian and Lur merchant-moneylenders to sell them goods on credit and advance them loans. Merchant-moneylenders charged higher rates of interest for credit and loans in winter than in summer because of the greater risks and the distant time of repayment and because the nomads did not have their own products to exchange. Unlike summer when the nomads traded pastoral products (fresh and clarified butter, wool, goat hair, dried curds) and sometimes gave them as "gifts" (yogurt, cheese), none were forthcoming during winter.

The nomads conducted business with at least one merchant-moneylender in Kazerun, and men such as Borzu, who needed wide urban networks as well as multiple sources of cash and credit, often relied on three or four. Each man sought his own unique set of merchant-moneylenders in Kazerun and Semirom, an intentional practice serving to keep many of them from falling under the economic domination of any single creditor.

Merchant-moneylenders in Kazerun, the nomads' economic center and the center of the wider region as well, offered the same services (storage, a mail address, message delivery, letter writing, assistance with the government) as their counterparts in Semirom, and their shops provided a gathering place and a safe haven for women on their rare visits to town. Merchant-moneylenders were generically called hajjis, although only a few had actually made a pilgrimage to Mecca. Others had traveled to pilgrimage sites at Kerbala in Iraq (adding Kerbala'i to their names) or Mashhad in northeast Iran (adding Mashhadi). Only one Qashqa'i shopkeeper, a Farsimadan man who sold secondhand coats, did business in Kazerun.

The nomads complained that merchants constantly tried to trick them by referring to intentionally illegible records, by making incomprehensible calculations, by changing the terms of agreement after transactions, and by confusing them with different weights.

When the metric system was officially introduced in Iran in 1935, the many differing weights and measures found in the country were made to correspond. One *sang* ("stone") was to equal 1 kilogram, and 1 *man* was to equal 3 kilograms. Despite these official changes, other weights of man continued to be used. The Qashqa'i encountered many different ones, the most common equivalents being 3, 3.5, 4.75, 5, and 6 kilograms. In winter pastures and Kazerun, a man usually weighed 3 or 5 kilograms, while in summer pastures it usually weighed 6 kilograms. Some goods were associated with specific weights. Wool and goat hair were usually weighed with a 6-kilogram man because this weight was used in summer pastures where nomads sold these products. Rice was often weighed with a 4.75-kilogram man, for this weight was used in the rice-producing areas of Kamfiruz in Qashqa'i summer pastures. Wheat, wheat flour, and barley, produce these nomads cultivated themselves in winter and summer pastures and also bought and sold in both areas and along the migratory route, were weighed differently in different places and at different seasons. Wheat in Semirom in summer was usually weighed with a 6-kilogram man, while flour ground from this wheat at the same place and time was often weighed with a 5-kilogram man. The price of grain rose and fell and rose again during the year, which complicated conversions.

Merchants told nomads trying to pay for goods they had taken on credit many months before that they had used a 6-kilogram man and not a 5-kilogram one, and hence they charged for more goods than they had actually given. The profit for merchants was increased by the added interest on 6 and not 5 kilograms of goods. When nomads and merchants traded goods, as they usually did instead of using currency, merchants often used different weights of man for the two commodities being exchanged, in order to confuse the nomads. As Iranian currency increasingly replaced commodities as the stated value of goods, even though commodities were still exchanged, calculations were further complicated in ways beneficial to merchants. To confuse the issue even more, interest rates were always computed in Iranian currency although often paid in commodities. Merchants usually required the nomads to pay the going price of goods at the time they paid their debts, but only if the price was higher than when they had taken possession of them. Thus nomads often did not know the ultimate cost of goods they took on credit.

Many Qashqa'i men preferred using a man weighing 4.75 kilograms, equivalent to thirty gun cartridges, the only item of standard weight that all Qashqa'i had possessed. Even after the army confiscated guns in 1966 and men no longer carried cartridges, this weight remained important. As they dealt with different weights in different places, some men mentally converted all their purchases and sales into the 4.75-kilogram man. Most merchants wanted nothing to do with this weight.

In the 1960s when the government introduced new land policies and stepped up its control over Qashqa'i nomadic pastoralists, many urban merchant-moneylenders began to invest in herd animals. They took advantage of the economic decline suffered by nomads during this period and exploited an animal contract called *nimsud* ("half profit") that nomads had previously used for their own profit. Under these new conditions, nomads who were heavily in debt were forced to turn over half ownership of a portion of their herds to their creditors. The creditors then subtracted from the debt the amount of money this half represented, and the former full owner of the animals was obliged to tend them without compensation until the contract year or years ended. At that time the contract, if not renewed, was terminated, the animals sold and the income divided between the two men. During the run of the contract, the two men shared the clarified butter and the wool or hair these animals produced. Through this contract nomads were released from part of their debt, but they lost the labor and investment of capital (shepherd's wage, pasture rental, fodder, purchased water) necessary to tend the animals their creditors now partly owned. Under this arrangement, nomads became the indentured herders of what had been their own animals, with no guarantee that they would profit at the end of the contract period. They were obligated to trade their pastoral products, at below market price, with the men who owned part of their herds, which brought additional profit to their partners.

Nomads hated this form of nimsud contracting and all that it implied. It often increased rather than alleviated their level of debt and, for some, brought about or furthered their impoverishment. A man's status was partly determined by the portion of his herd under contract to others— that is, by the extent of his economic dependency. Nomads distinguished between being in debt to a merchant-moneylender and having him interfere in decisions concerning the jointly owned herd (as was his apparent right) and, by extension, in other aspects of nomadic pastoralism. They viewed this intrusion of a non-Qashqa'i outsider, a person they looked down upon, even despised, and who lacked any understanding of the complexities of pastoralism, as a violation of their identity and the integrity of their way of life. The main reasons the nomads gave for wanting to abandon nomadic pastoralism were their inability to get out of debt and their loss of full ownership and control of their herds. The previous summer most men in Borzu's group had sustained losses when they sold their nimsud animals. They had tended these animals for a year or more without profit.

In a less exploitative use of nimsud contracts, an urban investor advanced money (or, less commonly, animals) to a nomad. The nomad bought animals, usually year-old rams and bucks, tended them for a year or more, and sold them. Depending on the terms of the contract, the nomad either returned the initial investment plus half the profit to the partner or gave him half the money from the sale, in which case the nomad and partner shared equally in any profit incurred or loss sustained. Under this form of nimsud contracting, the partner rarely interfered in the nomad's pursuit of a livelihood, and usually no debtor relationship, beyond the obligation to pay when the animals were sold, existed between them. Most of the capital (money, animals) for these contracts came from towns and a city to the north and northeast of Qashqa'i territory. Borujen was the main source for Darrehshuri nomads. One urban investor there owned 170,000 sheep and goats that he sent to graze in Darrehshuri and neighboring territory. Some of these animals fell under this form of nimsud contract, while the rest were tended by hired herders. Another investor owned ninety herds, sixty of which were nimsud and the rest under hired herders.

Urban investors could profit from owning herds in 1970 while most Qashqa'i nomadic pastoralists could not because investors had ready capital and could also acquire government loans at 8 percent interest a year. Most nomadic pastoralists operated at a deficit and paid up to 100 percent interest a year. Investors had few or no expenses beyond the initial purchase of animals or their acquisition by default on loans. They exploited a cheap source of labor and often used pastureland free of charge.

Shortly after Borzu and his family settled down to sleep on their first night in the winter tent at the autumn campsite at Dashtak, they heard a few drops of rain hitting the roof and were amused at their luck. Early the next morning Borzu awoke to find Hasan waiting patiently by the fire outside where Zolaikha had just baked bread. Khalifeh had sent him to settle the conflict between Borzu and his shepherd Aqaboa who, refusing to accompany Borzu to Dashtak, had remained at Molla Balut. Irritated by the trouble he had caused for himself the day before by his attack on the shepherd, Borzu issued only a few general complaints, and then Hasan went to find Aqaboa. Later in the morning Borzu saw his shepherd at a distance heading toward the herd to relieve the temporary herder from the day before. Borzu and Aqaboa said nothing to one another about their dispute (until the occasion, some months ahead, of the next attack when each would speak his mind).

Six lambs were born during the day, and Aqaboa's job was made more

18. Aqaboa and a newborn lamb

difficult with each succeeding birth. Once a day he drove the sheep down the mountain slope to the well in the plain below Molla Balut, and once a day these animals drank water Borzu's daughters and son transported by mule and donkey to the campsite. Twice a day he pulled new mothers out of the large herd, left the rest of the herd under the care of his young son, brought the ewes to camp, and matched them with their lambs so they could nurse. For a few nights he slept in the open with the herd, protected only by his felt cloak. Later, when he could find someone to watch the herd, he would bring his family and tent from Molla Balut to Borzu's camp. In the meantime Borzu relied on Aqaboa's wife Katayun to haul water to Molla Balut.

Most ewes, especially first-time mothers, needed help during delivery and the first few days of nursing. Ewes who delivered out of anyone's view sometimes wandered back to the herd, and someone would search for the newborn lambs before predators could eat them. In cleaning off their lambs' faces, ewes began to become familiar with their smell, but for a few days most experienced difficulty finding their lambs and then allowing them to nurse. If bonding was slow, shepherds vigorously rubbed the lambs on their mothers' fat tails to transfer odor to the lambs, and on occasion a shepherd put his fingers into the birth canal and then rubbed them on the lamb's back and tail to help the mother identify her offspring.

Aqaboa discovered one of Borzu's sheep wandering alone, part of her intestines hanging entangled with the afterbirth, and she soon died. He did not have a knife or sharp stone to slit her throat while she was still alive. He found her healthy lamb hidden under a bush and, by wiping scent on the orphan, paired her with a ewe whose lamb had died after birth. The surrogate mother soon regarded this lamb as her own. Aqaboa transferred lambs whose mothers produced insufficient milk to other ewes by the same technique. Some young nursed from two ewes. Later, when kids began to be born, does and lambs, or ewes and kids, would be paired in the same way when death or disability struck one member of a natural pair. Aqaboa loaded Borzu's dead ewe on a donkey to bring her to camp. He told his children to chase animals well away from his path, for if they saw her, he believed they would sicken and the pregnant ones would miscarry. The ewe's meat was considered ritually impure and hence inedible because she had died before her throat could be cut and blood could flow out. Several days later Falak traded the skin and wool to an itinerant peddler for turnips, onions, and potatoes.

By the third day of residence at the autumn campsite, sixteen lambs had been born. They could not yet find their own mothers when the pen

19.   Zolaikha opening the lamb pen at the back of the winter tent

at the back of the tent was opened, and practically everyone in camp spent an hour matching pairs and assisting each in nursing. People sang and made rhythmic sounds to encourage lambs to suckle and ewes to be patient. In time, lambs would hear their mothers as they approached the campsite, well before any person saw or heard them, and would bleat anxiously and jam together where the pen opened. When released, they ran out, each quite remarkably making a beeline for its own mother. Anxious as well, mothers learned to wait in the same place every time for their eager offspring. Aqaboa often sang, "Salbeh [woman's name] with colorful eyes offers comfort. The ewe bleats and locates her lamb."

For ten days Borzu's daughters and son, with others occasionally assisting, spent most of the day transporting water from Molla Balut to camp. His driver Hafez carried water by truck from the well to Molla Balut, and Borzu's family drew its supplies from the filled barrels. His daughters Zolaikha and Zohreh loved these six-hour trips, despite the fatigue, for on their passage through Dashtak they talked with people along the way. Women and girls remained in camp unless tasks demanded otherwise, and the lack of water at Dashtak was an acceptable excuse to get away.

The Qashqa'i divided the season of winter into segments, to help them cope with the most difficult days. The "first forty" days took them from the last days of autumn into winter. During this segment they prepared their campsites and animals for the rigors of the more arduous days to come. The main part of winter, when conditions were the worst, was termed the "big forty" and the "little forty." During the forty days of the "big forty," most of the animal deaths occurred, and during the twenty days of the "little forty" that followed, conditions were still severe but less harsh. Then came the "time of spring" just before the vernal equinox when they hoped for favorable circumstances. A shorter version of this scheme for dividing the season consisted of the "big forty" and the "little forty": the first forty-five days of winter, which were the worst, and the second forty-five days of winter when "grass, milk, and cheese" were plentiful.

On the first day of the "first forty," a member of each household gathered wood and tucked it away in a storage hut to save for the vernal equinox when that year's crop of lambs and kids would be branded. By saving the wood and then burning it in the branding fires, the nomads marked ceremonially the beginning and ending of winter and the birth and survival of animals.

No season was as harsh as winter. Its severity began with lack of rain and increasing cold, followed by torrential rainstorms during which animals would not eat or drink. Bitterly cold windy weather followed the rain. Snow soon covered the mountain peaks above and often fell on the camps below, causing further problems in herding and grazing. Although the snow cover on grazing lands did not last, the cold weather accompanying it did, and animals suffered. Sufficient rain and snow were, however, necessary to fill the basins on which the nomads relied for water and to moisten the ground adequately for vegetation to grow. The nomads' grain crops also depended on this moisture.

The many predators living on the rocky mountain slopes compounded these problems. Often traveling in pairs and working together to foil the vigilance of shepherds and guard dogs, wolves were the greatest threat, especially when sheep and goats were hungry, weak, and under duress from the weather. Foxes regularly attacked the nomads' chickens, even when they were protected at night in coops and in overturned baskets partially buried underground. Wolves took advantage of the clamor to attack sheep and goats. People said that if they saw a fox, a wolf was sure to be lurking somewhere close. Occasionally leopards (their gray spots of summer turning to gray stripes in winter) also made deadly assaults on herds. Striped hyenas were able to lunge at the throat of a sheep and then drag the dying or traumatized prey across its own shoulder in order to escape with it. Because most predators attacked at night, herds were usually penned and protected then. On moonlit nights shepherds took flocks to graze, always alert to the danger of losing strays to stalking wolves, leopards, and hyenas. When sheep and goats were weak from lack of food and water and suffering from extreme cold and wind, predators attacked in daylight. Sheep, more docile and meaty and less dangerous than the horned goats, were their main targets. Other than hyenas, these large predators did not often succeed in carrying off an entire animal because of the noisy defense raised by guard dogs, shepherds, and others, but they caused injuries that often proved fatal. Vultures sought injured and defenseless animals, including newborn lambs and kids not yet retrieved by shepherds. Circling vultures usually indicated the location of a trapped, injured, or dead animal, and someone always went immediately to investigate. At least two varieties of scorpions were present, one whose sting could be deadly to both people and animals. Some snakes were poisonous.

People often used a single term, "predator," to cover all predators, large and small, dangerous or not, even the harmless hedgehog. They sometimes shouted, "Predator!" to scare small children who were misbehaving. Children would then look around frantically to determine the actual nature of the threat.

As Borzu settled into his autumn campsite, his kinsman Mohammad asked permission to join the camp of his father Arghvan and his brother Qahraman, just to the north. Because Qahraman's animals encroached on Borzu's land, Borzu told Mohammad no room was available there and offered him space by Mansur at the edge of Dashtak. Mohammad, who had pitched his tent near Borzu's as he awaited the decision, announced he would join his father regardless of what Borzu said. Reacting to the insolence, Borzu retaliated by hitting him. Men witnessing the attack restrained Borzu and sent Mohammad away while they solved the conflict. They disagreed about Mohammad's status. Although he said, "Dashtak is the place of my mother," a few men stated that he did not have a right to grazing. Others noted that his father Arghvan had been with the Qermezi group when it first came to Dashtak and that Mohammad, like his two brothers currently resident at Dashtak, should be entitled to pastures in the way that any son would be. Khalifeh, who had already given space in his own camp to another of Arghvan's sons, asked his son-in-law Amir Hosain who camped alone if he would accept Mohammad. Amir Hosain consented. Acquiescing to the mediation, Mohammad moved his tent, and everyone agreed that Amir Hosain was better off not isolated. Some weeks later Mohammad quietly joined his father Arghvan's camp. Borzu heard about the move but issued no public objection. For the rest of the winter, people jokingly referred to the camp as "Mohammad's" when formerly they had always called it "Arghvan's."

Borzu had given Falak's kinsman Hasan a campsite on the far northern edge of Dashtak, actually on the other side of the border, on territory considered by Lur men in Davan village to be their agricultural land. Before coming to Dashtak, Hasan had received grazing land from Ja'far Qoli Khan Darrehshuri, but when he expressed a desire to return to Qermezi territory, Borzu rewarded him with space, albeit marginal, and he was grateful. Every year two men from Davan tried to extract a tax from Borzu for use of this land, and every year he threatened them with physical injury. When Hasan arrived at Dashtak in late autumn, he plowed a plot of land for grain cultivation, but Davan peasants replowed it for themselves, and he lost the seed he had sown.

The problem with Abdol Hosain, still camped at Molla Balut and lacking a place to graze his flocks, had not yet been resolved. Borzu let the issue of his younger brother rest in his mind for a few days and then reluctantly made a decision. He sent word via Aqaboa that Abdol Hosain could send his shepherd and herd to Borzu's site and use the grazing there. Partly because of the added burden to the site's vegetation of another household's pack animals, especially camels, Borzu instructed Abdol Hosain to leave his family, tent, and pack animals at Molla Balut and perhaps move them later to the southern edge of Dashtak. Soon people would need the extra protection of the winter campsite, and Borzu indicated that no space was available at his or any other camp. Some natural protection was found by the dry steam gorge, and he decided that Abdol Hosain should stay there. But perhaps more pertinently, because the two men were still not speaking to one another, neither wanted to share the same campsite. Abdol Hosain especially did not want to be trapped into doing chores for Borzu, as his younger-brother status might stipulate and as his dependency on him would certainly require. Also, campmates were obliged by custom to assist one another, but Abdol Hosain could not see himself falling into that pattern. He refused to help Borzu as much as Borzu wished, a continuing source of conflict between them.

Although people joked about a man being separated from his means of livelihood, they were sorry about the rift between the two men (their relatives, after all) and the punishment Borzu administered. The task of every herd owner was to practice sheep and goat husbandry. Of course Abdol Hosain could visit his herd, they said, but how was he supposed to spend the rest of his time? He needed to decide daily about supplemental feeding, treatment of injuries and illness, and other crucial matters upon which his subsistence depended.

The next day Borj Ali, Abdol Hosain's hired shepherd, brought the herd to Borzu's camp and erected a small shelter at a site pointed out by Borzu where the animals would not mingle with Borzu's animals at night. Narges, mother of Borzu and Abdol Hosain, transported newborn lambs on donkeys and placed them in a small pen in the shelter she would tend. Twice a day Borj Ali drove the herd to the well below Molla Balut, so for the moment Abdol Hosain was able to oversee his animals as they traveled by his camp. He occasionally brought water to Borj Ali for animals unable to travel far. On these trips he ignored Borzu and hardly looked in the direction of his tent. Later, Borj Ali moved his family and tent, now containing the lamb pen, to Borzu's camp, and he offered the site further protection from wolves. Narges returned to Abdol Hosain's tent.

Borj Ali's residence at Dashtak demonstrates the web of relationships that connected practically everyone in and associated with the Qermezi group. Even hired shepherds, almost always non-Qermezi men who worked for a salary for a year or two before finding work elsewhere, were often linked to this group in noneconomic ways. A Bulverdi Darreshuri man, Borj Ali was Abdol Hosain's mother's sister's son's son; Narges's sister had married a Bulverdi man whose grandson sought employment as a shepherd. Few Qermezi men who were able to hire a shepherd wanted to hire a close kinsman, for they said the two sets of ties were incompatible, and control over the shepherd was compromised. If, however, distant ties of kinship and marriage existed, then obligations were better respected, resulting in more dependable herding. In this case, Narges mediated the relationship between her son Abdol Hosain and her sister's grandson.

Borzu's cousins Morad, Abdol Rasul, and Naser were having their own problems with pasture space at Dashtak, but for the moment they were trying to find a solution themselves. The section of land these three brothers shared had originally been intended for one household and 100 to 200 sheep and goats. When they first came to Dashtak they were part of one household. Now the three brothers were independent, each with his own herd and pack animals (totaling 600 sheep and goats, 20 camels, and 15 donkeys), and the grazing and water available were inadequate. They agreed that the best solution was to take turns using the section. Every winter one brother would stay at Dashtak while the other two would find alternative pastures. Each brother, however, wished to be the first to stay at Dashtak and told the others to be the ones to leave first.

Borzu wanted the teacher to live in his camp so that he could exercise control over him, use his skills for reading and writing documents, and rely on his sophistication and erudition when interacting with government agents and other outsiders. Adequate space for the two tents was lacking, however, and the teacher had said he preferred to be located elsewhere. He pitched his own and the school tent in the large camp of Khalifeh and his brothers. Borzu's and Khalifeh's lands at Dashtak were adjoining and stood at the center of the wider territory, a convenient place for children coming from other camps.

Teachers from the Ministry of Education had taught at Dashtak for six years, beginning in 1956. In 1962 the Office of Tribal Education in Shiraz began to assign teachers to the dominant section of Qermezi subtribe, at Dashtak in winter and Hanalishah in summer. The tribal school had operated for eight years, and five years of education were now available. Twenty-three children attended school, including several Qermezi children from Famur pastures who lived with relatives at Dashtak when school was in session. Although one goal of the program was equal opportunity for boys and girls, no family was currently sending girls to school because, people said, their labor was needed at home. During the eight years, eight girls had attended school but only four of them had finished the first year. Three of these, daughters of Khalifeh and Borzu, had completed four years of school. Borzu and especially Khalifeh valued formal education for their daughters. The status of these girls, already higher than that of other Qermezi girls because they were daughters of headmen, was slightly increased by their education.

The Office of Tribal Education was run by Mohammad Bahmanbaigi, an Amaleh Qashqa'i man who believed in the importance of education for the Qashqa'i if they were to adapt to the transformations of a modernizing nation-state. He selected teacher trainees from Qashqa'i subtribes and sent most graduates back to their own groups. No Qermezi child had yet attended teacher training school and become a teacher. Bahmanbaigi assigned as Qermezi's teacher Mohammad Qoli Naderi, a Naderli Darrehshuri man whose subtribe prided itself on its high level of education. Mohammad and his new bride lived in a round white canvas tent next to the round white canvas tent of the school.

Six Qermezi boys, all members of Aqa Mohammadli lineage, attended school in Kazerun. They had completed five years of school in the tribal program and qualified for admission to government-run public schools. Because the academic-year schedule interfered with the seasonal migrations and the changing residences in winter and summer pastures, their parents lost their labor during much of the year. In late autumn and winter the proximity of Kazerun to Dashtak meant that these boys could return home on Friday and other school holidays. Parents regarded the room, board, and general expenses as a heavy but necessary burden. They valued formal education and the literacy their sons achieved and, perhaps equally important, their growing ability to deal with Persians and Persian-dominated society. The boys lived together in Kazerun and interacted primarily with one another and with other Qashqa'i boys there. One of the six, Borzu's son Mohammad Karim, was difficult to get along with, but the other five remarked that he sometimes needed their help in a fight.

Borzu often traveled to Kazerun during these initial days at Dashtak. Because of the effort of descending the mountain slopes by foot to Molla Balut, driving with Hafez to and from Kazerun, and then climbing from Molla Balut to Dashtak, he often stayed overnight in town at the home or shop of a merchant-moneylender. To his dismay he found that running the pickup truck brought unexpected expenses, including frequent repairs, and his debts were already substantially higher than they had been the previous year. But he enjoyed being seen in Kazerun in his truck with his hired driver, both visible signs of his prosperity and status, and some of the time he spent there lacked any practical purpose.

Whenever Borzu was gone for a day or more, he immediately inspected the herd and pack animals on his return. He quickly surveyed the tent and camp and ordered people to rectify problems he spotted, such as an overcrowded lamb pen, a worn halter, chickens pecking at a gaping sack of barley, or a dead animal lying too close to the tent. He complained that his family and campmates did not act on their own initiative. They did know what raised his ire and usually tried to make corrections just before they expected him to appear. A flurry of nervous activity always erupted whenever they heard news of his imminent arrival. His wife Falak often sent a child or shepherd to watch from a nearby hill and signal when Borzu approached so they could be ready. He wanted fresh hot tea on arrival and expected a good fire, clean water ready to boil, and a carpet newly laid out by the hearth for him to sit upon.

Borzu reported that the problem with his rival Sohrab had escalated, for he was still pushing his claim to pasture at Dashtak, including Borzu's own campsites. When the Qermezi group first came to Dashtak in 1945, Sohrab and the headman Khalifeh were temporarily allied. After several years at Dashtak, Sohrab and his immediate supporters found other pastures to rent over the mountains east of Kazerun, and there they stayed during winter until 1969. That year Sohrab asked the government's forest rangers in Kazerun to give him a place at Dashtak, but they replied that the land was in Borzu's name and that none of their documents listed Sohrab as a resident. They told him he needed Borzu's written authorization. Borzu did not want Sohrab at Dashtak and would not comply. Sohrab pressed his case with gendarme officers and government officials and tried to get a ruling on his position from Darrehshuri khans, who professed ignorance about the current legal status of the territory. Dashtak was not, nor had it ever been, territory under their control. Still, Sohrab hoped that the khans could influence the officials who held jurisdiction over the area.

For several years Sohrab had reportedly bribed the former landowners of Dashtak to encourage them to cultivate their old lands. One of them saw that Borzu now owned a truck and offered to help him construct a road to Dashtak, but Borzu flatly turned him down, for he said he knew it was a ploy to enable the landowner to transport his own tractors and plows to the territory. Every year the landowners sent peasants to plant illegally at Dashtak, and Borzu wanted to prevent further encroachments.

As soon as Sohrab arrived this year at Molla Balut (an unauthorized residence, according to Borzu), he signed statements at gendarme headquarters in Kazerun and at the gendarme post at Famur that he had indeed resided at Dashtak in previous years. He bribed officials at each place so that they would process the papers through bureaucratic channels. Borzu called a meeting of men who held rights to Dashtak, to assess the level of support they would offer him in his fight against Sohrab. Two of Sohrab's brothers, although not invited to the meeting, were among the current residents of Dashtak, Borzu having given them a place someone had abandoned a few years back. The brothers offered passive support to Sohrab and did not try to influence Borzu, for fear their own place would be jeopardized. No one at the meeting expressed willingness to help Sohrab.

The main evidence Borzu hoped the government would assemble was available in school records, but he doubted that any officials would make the effort. For the past fourteen years, five teachers on government salary had taught Qermezi children at Dashtak and had kept records (although no one knew where they currently were). On Borzu's next trip to Kazerun he suggested to the gendarmes, who had summoned him to sign a statement, that they locate the five teachers to ask them if Sohrab's children had ever attended school at Dashtak. Because they had not, Borzu hoped this evidence would be adequate to prove that Sohrab had not been a Dashtak resident. Meanwhile, the gendarmes were applying not-so-subtle pressure on Borzu for a bribe by frequently mentioning the sum that Sohrab had already paid. Borzu continued to rely on government documents allocating him and others, but not Sohrab, pastures at Dashtak. He eventually prevailed in this conflict, but only after months of agitation and not until the end of winter when people turned their attention to the spring migration. In the meantime Sohrab remained at Molla Balut, and Borzu did not attempt to force him to leave.

Men at Dashtak took advantage of the period between the end of the autumn migration and the beginning of the winter rains to plow and plant wheat and barley. Families with pasture rights at Dashtak could cultivate any portion of their allocated land. Cultivation on these nationalized pastures was forbidden by Iranian law, which government agents appeared to ignore totally. Men chose small plots near their campsites so they could watch for trespassers, and they enclosed them with high stone barriers to protect crops from herd and pack animals. They used wooden plows they made or bought in Kazerun and mules and horses as draft animals. Many families also planted at Molla Balut, but its disadvantage was that it was far from their camps and vulnerable to destruction of crops by herders from other groups. Molla Balut, an alluvial fan, profited from the runoff of water and soil deposits from the mountains above. The area often received more rain than Dashtak, and agricultural yields were often higher. Many families tried to plant small plots of wheat and barley at each location. Labor was the limiting factor because of simultaneous and essential pastoral chores and because the harvest came only after the beginning of the spring migration. Men returned to winter pastures to harvest or contracted with someone who lived there all year to harvest for them. They hoped to provide most of their yearly needs for grain and straw through these efforts, but rarely in recent years were they successful. In a dry year they were under stress, for they had to buy large quantities of grain and straw on credit in town.

The totality of crops harvested at Dashtak belonged to the cultivators, while a fifth of the crops harvested at Molla Balut was owed the landowner, a Persian sayyid in Kazerun. The cultivable land at Molla Balut had not been and would not be subject to land reform. The Persian owner had subdivided his large landholdings in the Kazerun valley among his many family members shortly before land reform was implemented in Fars, and each of them became legally entitled according to new laws to hold on to a certain amount of land.

Because of his literacy and the respect people held for him, Borzu's elder brother Khalifeh had always served as overseer of the harvest. By observing ripening fields or piles of harvested grain, he estimated in writing the amount of grain to be threshed, and cultivators later paid a fifth of the estimated amount to the landowner. For his services, Khalifeh received 3 percent of each person's harvest at Molla Balut.

Qermezi men had formerly grown opium poppies at Dashtak and Molla Balut, but their close proximity to Kazerun meant that they had to discontinue this lucrative production when the government banned the use and unauthorized cultivation of opium in Iran in 1955. They had produced opium for sale only; no one in the Qermezi group smoked opium.

Lacking independent land rights, hired shepherds and camel herders at Dashtak were not entitled to cultivate. They could not earn extra income by helping others to cultivate because their jobs consumed their time; their labor had already been purchased by the owners of the herds they tended. Some men who remained at Dashtak all year also lacked independent land rights and earned use of pastures there by helping others to cultivate. The inability to cultivate independently contributed to the continuing poverty of these two categories of men. Qashqa'i nomads were finding that they could not profitably engage in pastoralism without cultivating. Agriculture was often the activity separating pastoralists of moderate means from poor pastoralists.

Rain fell intermittently during the ninth night at the autumn campsite. The next morning shepherds reported that it had fallen quite heavily at Molla Balut. Everyone sensed that a storm was brewing because of the wind and dark clouds, and Borzu instructed his campmates to prepare for its arrival. Aqaboa pounded in tent stakes more securely, tightened tent ropes, and then laid branches weighted with stones over the ropes and stakes to secure the tent further. Women and children cleared and deepened the trench around the tent, and boys banked several small gullies on nearby slopes to deflect the flow of water. Aqaboa affixed a tent strip as a rain shelter over the tent's entrance, dug a new fire pit inside, and lined the pit with stones. Borzu sent Zohreh to the winter campsite to collect straw stored in huts there, in case it rained heavily for several days and pack animals were unable to graze on natural vegetation. With the help of his small children, Aqaboa fortified the rudimentary uncovered pen for sheep and goats, and Falak sent Zolaikha to bring green branches from nearby wild almond trees to line the lamb pen for warmth. Borzu noted that the sheep were tossing their heads from side to side and vigorously flapping their ears, a sure sign of rain. He did little actual work himself and would do little in the future unless a crisis was imminent.

Having given instructions, Borzu went to check the gorge of a nearby dry stream. The gorge was filled with boulders and rocks, and in places, he said, water from torrential rain occasionally pooled but did not last for more than a few days. For years he had contemplated improving these natural formations. Now that he owned a truck, he imagined building a road from Kazerun to his winter campsite, hauling cement to fortify these pools, and diverting the flow of water so that mud and rocks did not fill them up. These alterations would give him a clean, dependable source of water for part of the season. He talked about hiring a mason and ten laborers from Kazerun to do the actual construction, with help from ten Dashtak men and the Qermezi boys on vacation from school in Kazerun. First he needed a road to Dashtak, and he set off to the winter campsite farther up the mountain slope to determine where it should run. Because of the rough terrain he could not build a road to the autumn campsite, but men and pack animals could carry construction materials from the winter campsite to the gorge.

That night it rained heavily, and in the morning the soaked roof of the tent steamed from the heat of the fire inside. Borzu hurried to check the gorge, but not enough rain had fallen or run off fast enough to cause pooling there. He then checked the basins in several locations in his territory. They too were still empty; the ground needed a good soaking before rain would pool there. His daughters went off as usual to Molla Balut for water.

Two days later another storm appeared to be forming, the sky darkening and a steady wind blowing from the north. Again people hastily prepared for it. They deepened and widened the trench around the tent and banked the tent's base with more dirt and rocks. Zohreh reported that the first kid of the goat herd had just been born. Borzu instructed her to tell Khodabakhsh to move this herd to the autumn campsite from Molla Balut, where he had kept it since the end of the migration in order to conserve grazing at Dashtak. The young shepherd would need assistance once kids began to drop. With the oncoming rains Borzu expected that he would now be able to water both his herds at Dashtak, which would save effort for people and animals.

Borzu owned three herds of close to three hundred animals apiece, and two of the herds had accompanied him on the autumn migration. The herd of large "Torki" sheep with dark and multicolored fleece (along with a few adult male goats that led the herd) was tended by Aqaboa, who was Amaleh Qashqa'i and Borzu's stepmother's brother's son. Aqaboa's Qermezi wife Katayun was a member of Borzu's lineage; they had four young children and an independent household. The herd of goats, also of the large "Torki" breed, was tended by Khodabakhsh, teenage son of Zulfaqar whose family resided all year at Dashtak. Khodabakhsh was by origin Ipaigli Darrehshuri, but for all practical purposes he was Qermezi, and he lived as part of Borzu's household. Borzu's third herd, white-fleeced sheep of the small "Araqi" breed, was tended by Mohammad Hosain of Qasemli lineage. They spent the winter in pastures near Dugonbadan a long distance away, joined Borzu on the spring migration, and stayed with him in summer. By separating his two herds of sheep during autumn and winter, when the environmental conditions for pastoralism were the worst, Borzu hoped to prevent disaster striking them simultaneously. By keeping Mohammad Hosain and the third herd close by in spring and summer, Borzu exercised control over the production of milk and wool and the selection of animals for sale.

Like all Qashqa'i pastoralists, Borzu could identify and describe in detail each of his animals by its physical and behavioral characteristics. He knew the maternal pedigree of each one and could point out inherited traits. Aqaboa, Khodabakhsh, and all other herders periodically counted the animals under their care, and if the number came up short, their quick survey of the herd told them which specific animal or animals were missing. Even without counting, their glance at a herd was often sufficient to warn them that a single animal was missing.

No other Qermezi man owned two, let alone three, herds. The twenty-one Aqa Mohammadli men (excluding Borzu) at Dashtak each owned, on average, 135 sheep and goats (including nimsud animals). Of these twenty-one men, Khalifeh owned the largest herd (245) and Nader the smallest (20). The number of sheep and goats necessary to support a household depended on such factors as family size, its ability to cultivate, success of the harvest, other income-producing activities, hired shepherds, nimsud animals, and existing debt. Men owning 30 animals and having other income, such as from charcoal production, were not in debt and in fact could not buy on credit or secure loans because of their poverty. Men owning the largest herds also had the greatest expenses and were the ones most deeply in debt. Borzu's debts totaled $8,000, Khalifeh's $2,000, and Ali's $3,000. The shepherd Aqaboa stated that 20 to 40 animals were the minimal number for his family of six to survive, while Borzu's nephew Akbar and his bride, newly established in their own household, said 150 were necessary if no other major source of income was present. Borzu noted that a nuclear family could not subsist on fewer than 60 animals and that "a good life" (which he defined as having rice, guests, and a change of clothes) required 200 animals.

Fifteen of the twenty-one Aqa Mohammadli men (excluding Borzu again) at Dashtak owned camels, for an average of 6 camels each. Of these, Khalifeh owned the most (12) and several men owned 2. Borzu owned 15. Aqa Mohammadli men were wealthier on average than men of the other four Qermezi lineages.

The moment Borzu's wife Falak had arrived at the autumn campsite, she had constructed a loom outside the tent and began weaving a *jajim* (a flat-woven textile). She said that as soon as the rains began all weaving would cease. Seeing the frantic preparations for the storm, she reluctantly completed a pattern and dismantled the loom, carefully rolling up and then wrapping the incomplete textile to store in the relative dryness of the tent. She complained that she would never be able to tighten the warp and weft strands properly when she set up the loom again and that the edges of the finished blanket would be skewed. She regretted that, without weaving, she would be "without work" for a while.

It rained heavily for a day, and people were immobilized by the wind, wet, and cold. Rain drizzled through the roof of the tent, and everything inside became damp. The lanolin-rich fibers of the goat-hair tent swelled and tightened to form a waterproof barrier for all but the heaviest, most persistent rains. Aqaboa and Khodabakhsh periodically took their herds to graze, but when the animals huddled for protection and would not eat, the shepherds returned them to camp. Borzu released small groups of lambs and kids in the tent for needed exercise and a relief from the crowded pen. He sang in Luri, "My cows are thin and my tent is wet" (a Boir Ahmad rhyme) as he watched them cavort. The shallow basins constructed for each camp slowly filled with rain and runoff, and pools formed in the gorges. For the moment at least, water would not be a problem. People dreaded the cold weather following rainstorms more than they did the rain itself, and the next few days were bitterly cold and windy. Again animals ate poorly or not at all.

On two nights wolves breached the rudimentary pen for sheep and goats and seriously wounded several animals. Aqaboa hung patches of an old tent strip over the barricade of brambles where the wolves had entered, to frighten away other wolves coming to make a similar attack. Borj Ali erected a flag made of tent fabric over the pen containing Abdol Hosain's animals, for the same purpose. Wounded sheep, vulnerable to cold weather and further attack, stayed in Borzu's tent behind the pen for

20.   Zolaikha filling a goatskin bag from a basin at Dashtak

lambs and kids. Aqaboa hoped to kill a wolf with a stone shot from his sling, so he could hang one of its paws, as a warning to other wolves, over the pen of these vulnerable young animals.

During the next ten days it rained again several times, but not hard. Fearing worse weather to come, Borzu decided to move to the more protected winter campsite farther up the mountain slope. Although all other families at Dashtak had already settled into their winter campsites, Borzu preferred to move on a symbolically significant date, and so he had waited, at no little discomfort to his family, campmates, and animals, until the winter solstice. He appreciated the symmetry that this conformity to ideals provided him. Camels that ordinarily transported heavy goods were still at Famur with Yadollah, to conserve vegetation at Dashtak, and the move took much of the day with loaded donkeys and mules making many trips to the new site.

Borzu's winter campsite filled the bottom of a sheltering ravine and was partly hidden from the view of passersby. The winter tent was pitched again but over a cleared and leveled platform covered with gravel and rimmed by a small barrier of mud and rocks. Channels to deflect the flow of water surrounded the tent. A small hut with a stone base and a roof of branches and reeds stood near the tent's narrow front entrance. The men who cultivated for Borzu stored straw there after the spring's grain harvest. At the autumn campsite women and girls had cooked and performed other tasks in the tent when the weather was poor, but at the winter campsite they used the hut. They would often disappear from public view during the next few months, to enjoy the warmth, relaxation, and privacy of the hut. Women ate as they prepared meals, often by spooning food from the pot as it cooked, instead of having to hand all the food to men as they did in the tent. A less substantially built hut stood a short distance away. It protected horses, mules, donkeys, and injured sheep and goats during inclement weather and at night.

A fortified uncovered pen for sheep and goats constructed of a rough stone wall about a meter high with a barricade of brambles jumbled on top was on the northwest slope of the ravine. Tree branches served as a gate. Aqaboa pitched his tent close to one end of the roughly rectangular pen, and Borzu instructed Borj Ali to set up his own tent at the other end. Both families listened at night for predators. In two weeks when Yadollah would bring the camels from Famur, he would pitch his own tent down the ravine near Aqaboa's. Unlike most others at Dashtak, Borzu did not share his campsite with close relatives, all of whom feared being imposed upon to do chores. People sharing his space were hired workers and

21. Borzu's winter campsite at Dashtak after a light snowfall

their families. A large basin, now filled with water, stood to the east of the camp. Borzu's grain plots were at Molla Balut and Dashtak near the campsites of men who cultivated for him.

Land surrounding the campsite was Borzu's exclusive grazing area, and specific but unmarked boundaries separated his territory from that of his neighbors to the northwest and southeast. Land farther up the mountain slopes was community property and was also exploited illegally by Lurs and Persians for firewood, charcoal, sap from wild almond trees, nuts, fruit, and game. Borzu and other residents of Dashtak carefully watched their allocated territories to prevent trespassing and tried to keep their own animals away from the land of others. Sheep and goats were always under supervision, but camels, free-ranging and troublesome to tend, often had to be retrieved. Borzu and Sohrab hired camel herders, but other men relied on family members who held many other taxing responsibilities. While resident at the autumn campsite, Borzu had often been irritated by Qahraman whose camels kept crossing the boundary these men shared and eating vegetation Borzu had been conserving for his own animals for use in winter. Members of his camp were constantly on alert and quickly drove off others' camels. He reserved one small basin on his land for camels, and shepherds kept sheep and goats away on the belief that they could contract illness by sharing water sources.

Once settled into the winter campsite where they would remain for two to three months, Borzu's daughter Zolaikha and the shepherd's wife Katayun set up a loom for a pile carpet Zolaikha wanted to weave for her dowry. The job took all morning. After they had wrapped the warp threads and then attached a tripod to the rest of the loom, they each said, "In the name of God, the most merciful, the most compassionate." The blessing came only when weaving could actually commence. Seeing from her own loom that they had affixed the tripod, Borj Ali's wife Afsar yelled over a greeting to wish them good luck.

Women and older girls at Dashtak knew the details of each other's weaving projects and always asked about the progress made. They inspected one another's work when afforded the opportunity. They asked men and boys visiting from other camps to describe the weaving of their family members and female kin. Men often examined looms when they visited, out of curiosity, but also to be able to answer other women's questions. They were sometimes the conduit for information about dyes, designs, and techniques. Stopping by Borzu's camp one day, Askar asked his cousin Zolaikha about a particular gelim motif for his sister-in-law. Unmarried and newly married women, especially, competed with one another over the speed and skill with which they wove.

Samarrokh came to see her sister Zolaikha's new carpet and offer suggestions about the pattern. She complained that her husband Asadollah had just killed one of her goats to prepare a meal in honor of his grandmother. Still part of his father's household, he possessed no animals of his own. When the two had married, many people had given Samarrokh sheep and goats, which formed the nucleus of the herd they would possess when they created their own independent household. In the meantime, the animals were regarded as hers, but Asadollah tended them and was responsible for most decisions. Men did not talk about animals their wives owned, but women always knew their exact numbers and condition. A woman married for twenty years could still point out in the herd all the animals that stemmed from her wedding gifts. Women complained that men sold, traded, ate, and gave away women's animals rather than their own. One man quietly remarked that he was trying to rid his herd of all animals belonging to his wife so that he would not have to be drawn into arguments about them anymore.

When lambs were a little more than a month old, children began to herd them during the day between nursings. One child (for Borzu's animals it was his six-year-old daughter Farideh) was placed in charge, and other children in the camp went along to help and play. True to their image, lambs did indeed leap and frolic, and keeping up with them to see that they were out of danger was a serious responsibility. A week later kids were also released from the pen, and children were kept busy with these rambunctious animals. No grass grew, but green shoots on bushes and small trees were available, and children broke them off or bent down tall branches to ground level. Once they located a food supply, while they watched the young animals, they constructed their own tiny camps: sticks and fragments of fabric for tents, stones and thorny branches for sheep pens, twigs and bits of yarn for looms, and rocks and pebbles for pack and herd animals, all carefully scavenged and hoarded for these occasions. They built small fires by the tents and pretended to bake pieces of bread they had smuggled from home. Children often sang to the young animals as they browsed. Their favorite song was, "We are coming [to the rescue]. The kids flee because a wolf is coming. The lambs flee because a khan is coming." Later, as the lambs and kids matured, became more venturesome, and needed other kinds of vegetation, older children assumed the shepherding and took them to the higher mountain slopes.

Farideh kept a small doll she had made out of wood and cloth scraps

22. Farideh and her miniature tent

rolled in the waistband of her skirt, her only safe place for a treasure. Her mother, sisters, and even Borzu often yelled at her to straighten her strangely hanging skirt, and she looked sad as she reluctantly tugged at the hem. They never knew the reason it hung so crookedly.

Tired of the long walk between Dashtak and Molla Balut and of having to depend on others to transport supplies from Kazerun, Borzu began his road-building project. A passable route for his truck already existed from the outskirts of Kazerun up a dry riverbed and into the immediate foothills. This track, which would need to be improved, had been used regularly by Lurs and Persians transporting firewood and charcoal by mule and donkey from the mountain slopes. The problem for Borzu was the fifteen kilometers between these foothills and his own campsite at Dashtak on the mountain slopes to the east. Many dry riverbeds and streambeds, falling sharply in altitude, cut through the area from northeast to southwest. The route Borzu envisaged traveled along the summits of ridges and descended into and rose out of many rocky ravines.

Borzu sent word to a few specific men that he needed a road crew right away, a message, he said with a smile, that would simultaneously reach everyone at Dashtak. At dawn the next morning twelve men, most coming "voluntarily," converged at Borzu's tent, and they set out on foot for the most distant section of the track near Kazerun. Borzu had decided that if he could not build a road all the way to his campsite, he could try to prepare one to the edges of Qermezi territory, in which case he would leave his truck there and relocate the family of a subordinate to stand guard.

Performing this kind of task for the group headman was new for the men at Dashtak. In the past, men most dependent upon him had periodically offered a day's labor for shearing, branding, or transporting animals to town for sale, but a long-term project such as road construction had never been implemented before. Many men were willing enough to assist Borzu for a day, but when they saw the amount of effort a road would require, they became irritated and anxious, especially because this period was a crucial one in the care of their own animals. The first forty-five days of winter placed heavy and troublesome demands for labor on them. This pattern of obligatory assistance was one with which they were familiar, however, for until the mid-1960s Darrehshuri khans had occasionally requested support from their subtribes when they formed military contingents, brought tribal delegations to the Qashqa'i ilkhani's camp, sheared their many sheep and goats, began orchards, and built walls around their gardens. Group loyalty was measured in part by the number of men who responded and by their ability to complete the task at hand. Borzu was not a khan, however, and the days of the khans' requisitioning labor were ending.

The twelve men setting out with Borzu included his young son-in-law, two young men who hoped to (and probably would) be his sons-in-law, a man who planted his grain, three boys on vacation from school in Kazerun, his wife Falak's two brothers, a man he recently gave pasture at Dashtak, a man discharged from the army, and his cousin and closest ally Morad. Notably absent were his five brothers, including Abdol Hosain whose herd now grazed Borzu's pasture, and many cousins and other close patrilateral kin.

Over the next two weeks, the number of workers stayed about the same but the composition was always different. Many men came to work once, so that no one, particularly Borzu, could ever say that they had never helped build the road. The issue was sure to arise in arguments and on the chance men unexpectedly needed his truck for an emergency, such as a trip to the doctor. The fourteen men (except the teacher) at Dashtak who originated from other subtribes offered labor at least once to indicate their indebtedness to Borzu, as did Qermezi men who were vulnerable to him. One young man who was eager to marry Borzu's daughter Zolaikha came often, despite the fact that she was engaged to another of her cousins. Visitors to Dashtak, especially Qermezi men from other winter pastures and from villages in summer pastures, often put in half a day's work before continuing their travels through the territory. And some of Borzu's closest kin, while not contributing labor themselves, did occasionally send their sons to work.

The most reluctant worker was Hafez, Borzu's hired driver. Once Borzu figured out a path from the outskirts of Kazerun, he instructed Hafez to meet him there, on the pretext of riding with him into town. But before Borzu went, he put in a day's work, and Hafez could not conscientiously stand by while everyone else worked hard. Being able to exert effort for long periods was one sign of a man's strength. Hafez, however, considered himself a paid professional and not a wage laborer.

In other projects for which Borzu solicited assistance from the group, he would begin work himself, quickly shift into a managerial stance once the project was under way, and then disappear. Now, he worked harder than anyone else on the road. Uncharacteristically, he did not shout unnecessary instructions. He seemed to know that he could not push his luck too far and that men needed to decide for themselves what specific tasks to perform. He simply pointed out the general lay of the road, and others began to clear away large rocks by hand and hand adze and to cut a somewhat flat, axle-wide strip through the roughest terrain. No one owned proper tools for this sort of work; they each brought what they had at home. Borzu eventually bought several long-handled tools which lessened the effort. When he planned to work through midday, he sent several of the children who always accompanied the workers to bring lunch, and they sat at the side of the road and ate bread and rice. Every day the road moved closer to Dashtak and Borzu's campsite, and it was now much easier for him to go to Kazerun that way than via Molla Balut to the south.

Hafez was finally able to move his family, isolated at Molla Balut, by truck to Dashtak. Borzu's pack animals carried the gear from the point the road ended, and Hafez set up his family in a tent (lent by Falak's brother) in Borzu's camp. Hafez's wife immediately assembled a loom and began to weave a pile carpet.

Two weeks after Borzu had begun serious work on the road, Hafez was able to drive the truck to the slope above Borzu's camp. The initial trip from Kazerun took a full day and a truckload of workers, with frequent stops to clear impassable places. For the next several weeks men walking to or from Kazerun learned that if they accepted a ride with Borzu, they would also be obliged to work on the road as they slowly drove along. After a month's labor on the road, the trip to Kazerun took only an hour, and Borzu saw clearly again how useful his new form of transportation would be.

Borzu regarded his truck with pride, affection, and concern, much as he would have regarded a fine horse. He often stood by the truck to survey the terrain, just as he often stood by his herd of sheep. When rain threatened, he covered the cab (but not the engine) with a large blanket and stood anxiously by the vehicle as if to protect it from the elements and other dangers. While Borzu understood how to care for a horse, the workings of the truck were a source of mystery and, often, irritation to him.

Inspired by the cooperation rendered him, for never before had so many people worked for him for such a long period, Borzu decided to improve his campsite. One day after Yadollah dropped off three camel-loads of reeds from Lake Famur, Borzu sent out word that he needed workers to repair a storage hut and construct a new one. Another day, assisted by men who were especially dependent on him, he tried to make a road from the hill overlooking the camp to the animal pen on the far side of the ravine, in the hope of being able to truck out excrement for

23. Borzu building a hut at Dashtak

sale as fertilizer in Kazerun. (Neither the road nor the plan was accomplished that winter.) And on a third day Borzu and his helpers built a shelter in the otherwise uncovered pen for sheep and goats, and they fashioned several troughs out of plastered stones and mud, to conserve the fodder that otherwise sheep trampled into the ground and wasted. On these occasions Borzu fed the workers lunch, and at least the opportunity for general talk seemed to be appreciated.

Once the road was constructed, Borzu drove his married daughter Samarrokh and his only son-in-law Asadollah to Kazerun to see about exempting him from military service. For months the Iranian army had been trying to draft Asadollah, eldest son of Borzu's brother Jehangir, and had sent gendarmes on foot to Dashtak to seize him. Jehangir was usually absent because he had recently begun to work in the Kazerun bazaar as a middleman to pay debts. His only other mature son attended school in Kazerun. Asadollah was therefore desperately needed at home to head the family and herd the animals. Already poor, Jehangir's family would be further impoverished if the large household of twelve (soon to be thirteen) members was deprived of the only adult male present. Borzu hoped the presence of Samarrokh, soon to give birth and still nursing a toddler, would convince the army to pass him by. Army officials were used to this sort of appeal: destitute women and children bearing silent witness to the injustice of the arbitrary draft. First Borzu bribed a key army officer in Kazerun and then brought the young family to his office. The officer was noncommittal, but Borzu hoped Asadollah would be exempted. Often in such circumstances the official would not state his decision. People simply waited for results.

Five days later an army jeep carrying an officer drove up the new road to Dashtak (the first alien vehicle, in fact), and the driver asked directions to Asadollah's tent. Zolaikha began to cry, then had the presence of mind to send Khodabakhsh to warn Asadollah that the army had come for him, to give him a chance to escape. Borzu was in Kazerun and unable to intervene. The road stopped abruptly at Borzu's camp, and so the officer had to walk the rest of the way. When Khodabakhsh returned from his mission, he reported that the officer had come to confirm that Asadollah indeed played the role that Borzu depicted and that his father's household depended on him. Asadollah had no further contact with the army that year, and no one knew if he had been exempted or not. He rarely went to town and, when there, kept a low profile. But every time a government vehicle entered Dashtak (and, thanks to the road, they came more and more frequently), he fled to the mountains above.

24.　Askar in his Qashqa'i hat, cloak, and cummerbund

The army's attempts to draft the sons of Borzu's brother Ali did not have as fortunate an outcome. Askar, a student in Kazerun, had been told repeatedly to report to army headquarters there, but whenever he complied, officers sent him away, apparently because of a bureaucratic snafu. He would always present a letter from his school principal stating that he was a student in good standing, a status that ordinarily allowed a suspension of the draft order until the diploma was conferred. Many years back, as Ali's sons approached school age, he had tried to prevent any of them from being drafted by listing incorrect, misleading information on applications for the identity cards the government required before children could attend school. Three of Ali's sons carried cards with incorrect names and dates of birth, to deceive army officials. In summoning Askar, the army was seeking someone named Dehdar, for that was the name on Askar's card. The real Dehdar was too young for the army. Because the real Askar was still in school, the army went after Haidar, who was also too young for the army but carried Askar's name and age on his card. Several times gendarmes had come by foot to Ali's tent to take Askar away, but he was in school in Kazerun, and they left confused. A third time they had orders to check the cards of as many of Ali's sons as they could find. Haidar, who served as shepherd, had unfortunately returned to the tent for lunch just before the gendarmes arrived, and they took him away, believing he was Askar. Sorrow fell over Ali's tent. Haidar's mother and sisters wept inconsolably, and Ali sobbed into his hands at the injustice of it all. Campmates came to offer condolences and share tears.

Three days later Haidar strolled into camp. He had flunked the physical examination, he said, and everyone rejoiced. A month later the gendarmes were back, this time by jeep, and without words or explanation took him away again. He was inducted into the army, with no apparent consideration for the physical examination or his youth.

Seven young Qermezi nomads were currently serving in the Iranian army, and two of them were reportedly receiving some training in mechanics that might be useful in the future if they chose to leave or were forced to abandon nomadic pastoralism. For Haidar's family and all others whose sons served in the army, the years of their absence were sad and mournful. Often no word at all came from the draftees, and parents especially worried that their sons had been killed. Borzu was not always successful in obtaining information about them, even their whereabouts. When the boys eventually returned, two to three years later, they told of being taken to faraway provinces near the border of the Soviet Union, Afghanistan, or Pakistan (incomprehensible locations to their relatives).

They spoke of physical and psychological abuse, terrible living conditions (bad food, crowded quarters, inadequate clothing), and the alienation of living with non-Qashqa'i people (mostly Persians and nontribal Azeri Turks of the rural and urban poor). As was customary, soldiers returning to their families visited all their relatives and made a special point to see the headman, and then they resumed their lives as nomadic pastoralists. Once they had told their stories, they rarely spoke of service in the army again.

The government required headmen of Qashqa'i subtribes to secure identity cards for all group members. Khalifeh had performed this task in the past and continued to process applications after he transferred the headmanship to Borzu, for he was literate and Borzu only minimally so. During the winter several Qermezi men made a two-day bus trip from their villages near summer pastures to obtain these cards from Khalifeh. Sohrab still held the authority to file for identity cards for his own supporters, and men indicated their political affiliations by soliciting help from Khalifeh or Sohrab in this matter.

The first forty-five days of winter were always the most severe, and this year was no exception. This winter, however, instead of frequent and heavy torrential rains, which would have eventually produced new vegetation, little rain fell at all. As each day passed, people worried increasingly about their animals. Supplies of straw and barley, which sometimes lasted until vegetation began to sprout, were rapidly diminishing, while the price of fodder in Kazerun was increasing. Animals were constantly hungry, and every bout of cold weather exacerbated the problem, for uncomfortable animals would not graze. Ewes and does did not consume sufficient food and water, and their young suffered from inadequate milk. Less than a month into winter, sheep and goats, especially newborns, began to die from illnesses they could have resisted had they been better fed, as well as from diseases, internal parasites, exposure, cold, and injuries caused by predators that attacked the sick and weak. Weak animals died from falls, and others suffocated while huddling together in pens against the cold. Animals also died from snakebites and shepherds' carelessness. Economic disaster loomed for everyone.

Less than two weeks into winter, water basins and pools at the gorges were empty, which again meant the arduous six-hour trips for people and animals to and from the well located below Molla Balut. Goats and especially sheep were in no physical condition to make this trip twice a day without dire results, and the weakest, sickest animals were watered at camp. A month into winter rain fell again, which replenished local supplies and temporarily eliminated these trips. But snow also fell, accompanied by bitterly cold weather.

In the early weeks of winter when government officials had heard about the pressing need for animal fodder in rural areas, they stepped up a long-planned scheme suggested and heavily financed by a United States Aid for International Development project. They began to distribute dried sugar-beet pulp, a by-product of the production of sugar from locally grown beets, from sugar factories located in Fars province. United States AID officials had advised that, after sugar had been extracted, the pulpy residue could be used as fodder. Initially the government allocated the pulp only to people who were settled, to discourage nomadism, but migratory pastoralists were the ones who most needed supplemental feed. The government finally opened the market to people who could afford it. Borzu bought a large quantity in Kazerun for himself, and others at Dashtak bought what they could afford. Any other fodder could be purchased on credit, given the goodwill of creditors, although at ever-escalating and soon to be prohibitive prices. The purchase of sugar-beet pulp required cash, and many nomads were already heavily in debt and unable to secure further loans. Borzu offered to transport the large bulky sacks of pulp for men who had worked frequently on the road.

Nomads feeding dried sugar-beet pulp to their sheep for the first time found it was unpalatable, and they added water to make an edible mush. When Borzu first fed the pulp to his sheep, three were dead by the next morning, and others at Dashtak reported the same result. The animals' stomachs and intestines apparently could not handle the new food. Some nomads mixed in straw or barley to provide substance and nutrition. Although the pulp filled the animals' stomachs, it contained few nutrients, as the nomads soon discovered, and other fodder was still necessary. In the next few months and over the next year, the nomads blamed the high rates of mortality of their sheep on the pulp the government had sold them. Jehangir Khan Darrehshuri reported to Borzu later that excessive consumption caused bone damage because the pulp lacked calcium. Many nomads complained that the animals that had eaten the pulp suffered from broken limbs more frequently than other animals.

Sheep and goats were not the only animals to suffer from the abysmal conditions. Female camels that had contracted smallpox in the autumn had miscarried, and the few that were still pregnant in the winter gave birth to young that soon died of starvation. The mothers did not consume sufficient food or water to produce milk, and the nomads lacked other means for feeding the offspring. Male camels entered a state of rut during midwinter. Ordinarily they were difficult to control during mating season, but when they lacked adequate food they became even more erratic. Hobbled to prevent them from fighting and possibly killing one another, they were further restricted in food gathering. Several competing camels in pursuit of a mate ran off the edge of a cliff and were crushed on the rocks below. Others sustained crippling injuries and had to be killed.

Mules and especially donkeys were more resilient when faced with inadequate vegetation than other animals, but each household bore its own losses of these animals as well. Weakened by the persistent, exhaustive water hauling, horses were particularly vulnerable. Even chickens succumbed to communicable diseases, whose course of travel could actually be plotted from one camp to the next all the way across Dashtak.

A month into winter when it became obvious that the grain seeds planted almost two months earlier were unlikely to sprout because of insufficient rain, many men planted a second crop at Dashtak, Molla Balut, or both places. Not having seed left over for this planting, men had to buy it on credit at high prices in Kazerun.

On the night of the forty-fifth day of winter, each family made a brownish-red dye from acorn skins (a layer surrounding the nut inside the hull) gathered at Wide Mountain, in order to mark a patch on the right side of the bodies or heads of all their mature sheep. Hasel prepared the dye for Borzu and marked his sheep with help from Aqaboa and Yadollah. Some Qashqa'i groups used a color dye for the marking or added color to the acorn-skin dye. On all sheep except white and light-colored ones, the acorn-skin dye was hardly visible. People owning only goats marked their right sides as well. The ritual commemorated the end of the worst period of winter and expressed the hope and expectation that the sheep would now grow fat. The patches of dye served as a talisman and protected animals against evil spirits. Acorn skins were also the main substance used to cure the goatskin and kidskin bags used to process milk and store milk products. Marking the sheep with dye on the forty-fifth day of winter was an auspicious sign of spring and connected this stage of animal husbandry with the crucial productive activities that were soon to follow.

The next day, the first day of the second half of winter, women and children went to a stream gorge to find small puddles of water in order to bathe and wash clothes, also to commemorate the beginning of what they hoped would be better times. They brought along large copper pots for heating water and soaking laundry. If people bathed or washed clothes during a stressful time, such as a period of harsh weather or the serious illness of a family member, they believed that condition would worsen.

Borzu's camel herder Yadollah took a rare trip into Kazerun for supplies and for his annual bath at a public bathhouse. When he returned to his dark tent late that night, his ever-faithful dog leapt at him and bit him. People who heard the story the next day laughed about the man who smelled so clean his own dog did not recognize him.

If sufficient rain had fallen, the forthcoming period was supposed to be the time of "milk and cheese," when sheep and goats avidly ate fresh green grass and produced enough milk that a surplus could be collected for human use. But this course of events was not to occur this year, and the circumstances only worsened. Rain was still expected but none fell. The ground was parched and hard, and even seeds that had managed to germinate were unable to push through the thickening surface crust. The little grass that did emerge was quickly bitten off, and no further growth appeared after it. Lambs and kids, which ought to have been eating fresh grass shoots by now, remained dependent on their mothers' limited supplies of milk. (Calling this the time of "milk and cheese" was just an expression. Whatever the state of grazing, cheese was a product of summer. Yogurt, sour milk, and sometimes fresh and clarified butter were the principal milk products of late winter when fresh grass was abundant.)

In years past, especially during a drought, some Qermezi men had relied on theft to sustain their families. Among the Qashqa'i, a "thief" stole from other Qashqa'i while an "outlaw" or "rebel" stole from non-Qashqa'i society. A code of proper conduct governing intra-Qashqa'i theft did not apply outside a Qashqa'i context. Qermezi men using pastures near the Pass of the Girl southeast of Dashtak enjoyed access to an extra source of income: highway robbery. The less traveled of two branches of the road from Bushehr on the Persian Gulf to Shiraz led through this narrow pass, a mountainous and rocky area perfect for staging holdups. Smugglers who regularly ran this route were the principal targets, both because of goods they carried (arms, ammunition, liquor, cigarettes, opium, watches, radios, imported food stuffs, all of which were easily sold) and because they were unlikely to report thefts to the authorities. They were usually armed and dangerous, however, unlike many other travelers. One notorious Qermezi man confiscated a truckload of eggs and another time hundreds of spoons and forks. Stolen food fed families while luxury and other goods were sold or given or thrown away. Stolen forks, rusted and corroded, could still be seen under bushes and up the mountainside where children had scattered them years before. Although many Qermezi men talked about having been "outlaws" on the road in their youth, only a few continued to engage in this activity in the middle 1960s. By 1971 highway robbery was no longer worth the risk for them because of the increasing likelihood of capture, arrest, and imprisonment by gendarmes.

Taking advantage of the lack of state security in rural areas in 1963, six Qermezi men and a Basseri Khamseh man held up a car at night on the road through the Pass of the Girl. They staged the holdup near the territory of Jarruq Lurs, themselves infamous thieves, with the expectation that the theft would be blamed on them. They might have escaped capture had it not been for a local dispute that put them in jeopardy.

Sharing pastures at Seven Girls for many years with these Qermezi men were Hormoz Basseri of the Khamseh tribal confederacy and three Shesh Boluki Qashqa'i brothers, including Hajj Ali and Zain Ali. Hormoz wanted to marry Hajj Ali's daughter, but his Qermezi neighbors disapproved out of concern that Hajj Ali, bolstered by the alliance, would try to claim the land. When Hajj Ali agreed to the match, several Qermezi men beat him in order to dissuade him. They threatened to expel him from the territory they shared if he gave his daughter to Hormoz. Hormoz withdrew his request and asked for the return of the bridewealth payment. Hajj Ali, lying, said he had never received it.

At this juncture of the dispute, the six Qermezi men and Hormoz committed highway robbery late one night. Hajj Ali's tent was near the road, and his daughter (who had complained she was mistreated by these marriage negotiations) told the gendarmes investigating the robbery exactly who was involved. A gendarme officer, "a bad man with a big moustache," seized Qashqa'i men not involved in the holdup, beat them, and then seized the six Qermezi men. Hajj Ali quickly dismantled his tent and fled to Shesh Boluki territory. His brother Zain Ali joined Masih and Dashti, renowned Qashqa'i outlaws and rebels who were then active in rural protest in Fars, and he was shortly thereafter shot and killed by gendarmes. The third brother was killed while thieving. Hajj Ali's daughter, who had informed on the robbers, was reported to have "played" with a young man, become pregnant, and fled from home. Qermezi people often cited the miserable fates of these four individuals as examples of the bad fortune falling on those who informed on neighbors. The lesson of the affair was to exercise caution in sharing pastures with non-Qermezi people.

The six arrested men were imprisoned for two months and then released when Ziad Khan Darrehshuri interceded and told the authorities that, if they needed contact with the men again, he would be responsible for bringing them in. For years the six men thought the matter was settled, but in 1970 the Tribal Security Force notified them that the Ministry of Justice in Shiraz had reopened the case. The men were supporters of Sohrab and hoped he would mediate. Ziad Khan, elderly by this time and under government restrictions to curtail his tribal involvements, was not expected to assist.

People frequently mentioned another case of theft. In 1951 Bakhtiyari men raided the herds of Qermezi nomads spending the summer near the Bakhtiyari border. Qermezi men put up a defense, during which three Bakhtiyari thieves were killed. Concerned about a blood feud erupting, Darrehshuri khans asked Malek Mansur Khan, brother of the Qashqa'i ilkhani, to settle the dispute. After Malek Mansur Khan and Bakhtiyari khans "excused" the killings, men of the same Bakhtiyari group again came raiding against Qermezi herds and wounded a Qermezi man. Malek Mansur Khan was once more brought in to negotiate. According to the new settlement, the group to which the Bakhtiyari thieves belonged was forced to pay $4,000 to the Qermezi families affected by the raids. The large sum served to punish the Bakhtiyari for pursuing a feud after Qashqa'i and Bakhtiyari khans had settled it.

Shortly thereafter, Sharif Khan and Hamrah of Qermezi went thieving for sheep in Bakhtiyari territory and accidentally killed a man. People in the area reported the men's names to gendarmes. Hamrah fled to Amaleh Qashqa'i territory and was never arrested, and he eventually returned to Qermezi territory after an Amaleh headman forced him to leave. Sharif Khan kept a low profile until a year—to the day—of the killing, when he visited the dead man's family and performed a ritual to certify his innocence. The dead man's mother offered him tea and bread and then led him three times around her son's grave. She said, "If you killed my son, this dust [of the grave] and this blood [the son's] mark you." Several months later Sharif Khan was killed while thieving sheep, proving without a doubt that he was guilty of the earlier killing. His death, people said, was the direct result of his false oath.

Borzu's guests in winter pastures were different from those during the migration or in summer pastures. Inclement weather and the isolation of his campsite on the mountain slope kept all but the most intrepid visitors away. People who called on him in summer were aided by a dirt road running right past his camps. Many potential visitors did not know he had constructed a road to Dashtak, and he did not inform them if he did not want to host them. People who knew of the road found it hard to find and follow and too rough for their vehicles. Because Borzu lived near Semirom and the Tribal Security Force in summer, officials and others could visit him for business and pleasure. The long distance between Dugonbadan and Dashtak, however, kept members of the force from visiting Dashtak, and officials in Kazerun had no reason to travel there in bad weather and on a rough track unless a crisis required it.

Borzu's only high-status visitor to Dashtak was Habib Aqa Zahedi, who accepted Borzu's invitation while on a business trip to Kazerun. Until 1960 he had camped at Famur in winter and hunted in the mountains with Borzu. Men of his family, the Zahedis who held the honorific title of *aqa*, had served as advisors to Darrehshuri khans for generations. Ayaz Kikha Darrehshuri had brought their ancestors, of Turk origin, from Lur territory, and they had become vital members of the Darrehshuri tribe. They had been settled in summer pastures for ten years, had planted apple orchards, and were now moderately wealthy. Desiring to raise his status, Borzu wanted his eldest son Mohammad Karim to marry a daughter of Faraj Aqa, Habib Aqa's brother, and so was always hospitable to the two men. Faraj Aqa, for his part, was unlikely to give his daughter to a man of lower socioeconomic status, a man he considered to be a Qashqa'i commoner, or a nomadic pastoralist. As daughter-in-law of Borzu, the bride would likely become much like a servant in the household. Faraj Aqa held higher expectations.

Still, Faraj Aqa and Habib Aqa continued their contacts with Borzu, particularly because their own elevated position in the Darrehshuri tribe depended on their ability to interrelate with both khans and tribal members. As one of the Darrehshuri tribe's key headmen, Borzu was important to them because of his own position in the tribal hierarchy. The Zahedis relied on men such as Borzu to provide them information about and access to Darrehshuri people at the local level. Although they no longer migrated or resided in winter pastures, they still periodically sought out Borzu. In the past he had helped them find shepherds, and as they contemplated economic changes, they expected that he might be useful if they invested in sheep and sought an overseer of shepherds, a position he had once filled for Jehangir Khan.

On the evening of this visit, Habib Aqa and Borzu talked primarily about the khans. Both aspired to the lifestyle (wealth, leisure, servants, wide networks) these former leaders enjoyed, and they each struggled to cultivate their relationships with them. Habib Aqa was in a superior position to Borzu in this regard, however, and, to set this status right, kept referring to his own close ties to the khans.

Another visitor to Dashtak was the school inspector sent by the Office of Tribal Education in Shiraz. A Naderli Darrehshuri man, the inspector had been Qermezi's teacher in the past, knew everyone at Dashtak, and now lived in Kazerun. His wife and children stayed in Borzu's tent while he went by foot to the school. That night Borzu entertained them over a meal and hoped to influence the report. He fell into a heated argument with the inspector's eight-year-old daughter, who had proclaimed the benefits of living in a house as compared to a tent. Borzu astutely combined this occasion with a formal invitation to the bride of the current teacher, who happened also to be the inspector's sister. The headman customarily hosted a new bride during the first months of her marriage. As part of the event, Borzu made it known via Falak that he was presenting a lamb to the bride. Given that the teacher kept no animals at Dashtak and could not care for any, the gift lamb remained in Borzu's herd.

Other visitors for whom less formality was required included government forest rangers surveying the territory for illegal activities, who would stop by Borzu's tent in hopes of a meal on their way across Dashtak. Their presence inhibited some men at Dashtak who ordinarily produced and sold charcoal, but it did not seem to trouble the Lur and Persian villagers who continued to deforest the nearby mountain slopes. Chiding a forest ranger, Borzu remarked, "You should have come yesterday," for two Persian charcoal makers had just transported filled gunny sacks from Dashtak. A few weeks earlier he had encountered two Lur charcoal makers along the road leading to Kazerun. He told them he would permit them to produce charcoal at Dashtak one more time, but only if they gave him two large sacks of the product. They complied.

Another visitor was Mansur Davodi, a merchant-moneylender with whom Borzu had conducted business since coming to Dashtak, and the two men referred to each other as "friends." Davodi had never been in Borzu's home before, primarily because no road had existed. Despite his longtime business with nomadic pastoralists, he had never even been in a nomad's tent until this occasion. Forty of the sheep Borzu tended were under nimsud contract with him. Ten years previously Davodi had placed two female lambs in Borzu's care, and every year since then Borzu had sold any resulting male lambs, given Davodi half the money, and kept the female lambs in his herd. Although the animals were few, they linked the two men and further involved Davodi in Borzu's economic activities. Neither man depended on the income from these forty animals, but the friendly relationship that their joint ownership created afforded both men, especially Borzu, other favors. Davodi was Borzu's principal source of cash and served as a crucial contact in Kazerun. Borzu killed a kid for the meal and gave Davodi a fat live kid as a gift to take with him when he left.

Two of Borzu's married sisters came from long distances to visit their kin at Dashtak. When Gelboneh arrived by bus in Kazerun, with three of her eight children in tow, she saw her brother Borzu quite by accident. Because he had a day's business yet to conduct in town, he told Hafez to drive her to Dashtak. She spent a few days with Borzu's family and then enjoyed warm reunions with her brothers, sisters, and other kin.

Gelboneh lived in Darrehshuri territory near Dugonbadan. Her husband was a Lur and a member of the Shaikh lineage with which Qermezi subtribe had been linked in the past. Some of his ancestors had received formal religious education, to which the title *shaikh* referred. When some Shaikh Lurs resumed nomadic pastoralism in the mid-1940s, Khalifeh invited them to share pastures with Qermezi. Shaikh Abdishah sought Gelboneh as a bride for his son, and Khalifeh decided that another marriage tie between the two groups would be to Qermezi's benefit. One of Shaikh Abdishah's two wives was Qermezi. Two groups regularly sharing pastures often intermarried. Khalifeh held a meeting of kinsmen to ask, "Does anyone object to giving a girl to the Shaikh Lurs?" No one raised an objection. Khalifeh's real but unstated question had been, "Does anyone want Gelboneh?" No one requested her for his son or brother. Borzu then sought permission from the Darrehshuri khans, as was customary, especially when a marriage involved a Qashqa'i woman and a non-Qashqa'i man. They consented to the match. In 1957 the Shaikh Lurs who had been sharing pastures with Qermezi settled again near Dugonbadan, and Qermezi people saw little of them after that. Qermezi men occasionally talked about using pastures there if grazing at Dashtak was poor, but only several had ever done so. Borzu was one of the few to profit from the marriage alliance.

Expressing anger over the folly of having married Gelboneh to an outsider, people noted that it was unfortunate that no one from among them had spoken out for her. She had been abandoned by her family. The most sorrowful situation for any person was to be without family members, to lose them through death or outmarriage. Poems and songs often equated these two states.

The visit a few weeks later of Borzu's youngest sister Goltamam, with three of her four children, was somewhat different. Her husband Hajji Boa, a patrilateral relative, had disputed with Borzu in the past and had settled in a village far from Borzu's summer pastures. The two men, who rarely met, had not really spoken for years. In the past few months Hajji Boa had emerged as a potential rival to Borzu, for many of the nomads were now talking openly about settling because of their rising debts, loss of full ownership of their herds, and inability to subsist as nomadic pastoralists. Hajji Boa had been one of the first Qermezi, other than Kachili men, to choose to settle permanently. Although his first year as a settler was difficult, he had now quite successfully combined agriculture with pastoralism and was steadily improving his economic position. Viewing the option that Hajji Boa represented as viable, men in dire straits privately sought his advice.

Borzu had no specific plans to settle. He did dream grandly of "a garden at Round Sun, a garden at Polo Field Canyon, and a house in Shiraz" (where he wanted his son to be gainfully employed), but he never planned to live year around at any of these places, and he expected to migrate between winter and summer pastures indefinitely. On occasion he heaped scorn on people who spoke of settling. Some men and women talked about this being their last winter at Dashtak and about the forthcoming spring migration being their last one. Partly in a bid to pull people away from Hajji Boa, Borzu had petitioned government agencies and even the governor-general of Fars province to allow his group to settle at Dashtak and Molla Balut, and he had requested that the government dig wells and construct roads there. On a trip to Shiraz he had paid a visit to Sirus Azarnia, director of the Office of Tribal Development (in function, office for the settlement of nomads). Azarnia spoke about government plans to dig wells in the province and asked him where the Qermezi group needed one. Borzu replied that a location in the mountains at Dashtak would be best. Azarnia snorted and said, "That's impossible. We want you to live in or near the city. You must leave the mountains because you are destroying trees." (Settled Persians and Lurs were the main agents of this destruction in Qashqa'i territory.)

One day when Borzu seemed depressed after hearing indirectly of the plans of close kin to settle, he said he would settle with forty Qermezi families at Molla Balut if the government assisted them in buying the land, currently owned by a Kazerun man. If the government did not help, he said he would settle alone (a most unlikely possibility). Twenty families were ready to settle at the end of winter, he claimed, including Asadollah's and Akbar's and the ten who remained at Dashtak and Molla Balut all year. The next year twenty more families, including those of Borzu and all his brothers, would be ready to settle. The following year yet another twenty would join them. He said he would provide financial and other assistance to help the poorest fifteen families settle.

But no Qermezi people, including Borzu's closest supporters and the families currently living at Dashtak and Molla Balut all year, imagined or spoke of settling permanently in the area. Because of the terrible heat and aridity in winter pastures during other seasons and Hajji Boa's success in settling in summer pastures, men who talked of settling had already chosen summer pastures. Hajji Boa, then, represented to Borzu the loss of his supporters and eventually his headmanship, which contributed to his veiled antagonism.

For Borzu and others at Dashtak, Goltamam was first and foremost a sister, daughter, aunt, niece, and cousin, and she was warmly greeted. Her marriage to Hajji Boa seemed at times a peripheral, even irrelevant, issue. During her visit with Borzu's family she was cautious in describing the circumstances of her life in a village, but with everyone else she proclaimed her satisfaction with having settled, especially given the economic crisis faced by her nomadic kin over the past few years. She regretted not seeing them, but she did enjoy the shelter of a house during winter and especially the income that derived from her ability to weave larger and finer carpets than would have been possible had she still been nomadic. Goltamam was Shir Mohammad and Narges's sixth and youngest daughter. Her name, "No More Flowers" (that is, daughters), conveyed her parents' wish for sons. (Similarly, Borzu and Falak had named their fourth daughter—who was also their fourth child—"Enough." Their fifth child was a son.)

Both sisters were treated well everywhere they went. For one of the few times in their lives, they did no work of any kind, even when assistance with the animals or during a windstorm would have been helpful. They were guests in the full sense of the term. Ordinarily, a woman visiting another woman's home immediately joined in whatever tasks were being performed. But these two sisters on their separate visits sat in places of honor in the tent and watched the activities swirling around them.

One cold evening a week after Goltamam's departure, while Borzu and a few men were sitting around a warm fire talking about the spring migration, Borzu decided to write letters in order to renew ties with his Qermezi kin settled with Hajji Boa. With the passage of time and the physical distance between them, Borzu worried about losing the small degree of influence he still held over them. In sending greetings to each family, he often had to ask Falak the names of the wives and children, and people around the fire were quietly amused. Falak teased him by giving names of children who did not exist. Akbar, one of the few Qermezi men who were literate, turned Borzu's simple message in Turkish into embellished Persian prose, for Qashqa'i Turkish is not a written language. People snickered at the difference between Borzu's straightforward statement and the elaborate formalities in Persian, peppered with Arabic phrases and frequent invocations to God, Mohammad, and the twelve Shi'i imams. Such figures were never part of Borzu's speech unless he was arguing with Persians. Borzu grimaced at the stylized phrases and told Akbar to address the envelopes and post the letters on his next trip to town.

Then Borzu mentioned a troubling legal problem involving a killing. For eleven years Khalifeh, Oroj Qoli, and he had been mired in a court case and were summoned periodically by the Ministry of Justice in Shiraz. In 1960 Jarruq Lur men had stolen sheep from Ja'far Qoli Khan Darrehshuri's entourage, which was near the Pass of the Girl on its way to winter pastures. The khan sent an unarmed force to recover the sheep; a fight ensued but no sheep were seized. He then sent armed men. Another fight ensued, a Jarruq man was killed, and the men confiscated a herd. When gendarmes investigated, Jarruq men implicated Hasan Qermezi, part of the khan's entourage but not part of the fight. They proclaimed that "Qermezi" had killed a Jarruq man to retaliate for the 120 sheep that Jarruq men had stolen from Solaiman Qermezi four year earlier. They named, as responsible for the 1960 killing, Solaiman's son Oroj Qoli as well as Borzu and Khalifeh, the other Qermezi names they knew. All three men had been far from the scene of the fight. Rather than take revenge in blood or attempt to settle the dispute according to tribal custom, relatives of the dead Jarruq man filed a complaint with gendarmes, who seized Oroj Qoli and took him to prison.

Borzu and Khalifeh sought help from Mohammad Bahmanbaigi, director of the Office of Tribal Education. Not wanting to become mired in an intertribal dispute, especially because he viewed his own role as one of creating better ties between the government and the tribes, Bahmanbaigi told the two men that they ought to address their problem to the Darrehshuri khans. Amiramanollah Khan Darrehshuri said he could not help and sent the men to Abdollah Khan Kashkuli. Abdollah Khan, embarrassed that Darrehshuri khans had not helped their own people and had forced them to seek aid from a Kashkuli khan, declined and sent the two men back to Amiramanollah Khan. Amiramanollah Khan located a bail bondsman, Mohammad Hasan Khan Darrehshuri paid the bail, and Oroj Qoli was released from prison. Borzu and Khalifeh paid a Jarruq Lur man, a relative of the dead man, to contact a Jarruq representative in the Ministry of Justice. After they also paid him, he agreed to post another bail and testify in court that the three accused men had not been present at the killing. The case came to court again in the winter of 1971. The Ministry of Justice in Shiraz summoned Borzu, Khalifeh, and Oroj Qoli on three time-consuming occasions, and the case finally appeared to be settled. They were charged court costs of $1,130, which the men split. (Nine months later the ministry reopened the case and once again summoned the three men.)

On his return from Shiraz, Borzu contemplated the forthcoming Feast of Sacrifice (Id-e Qorban), a day marked by Muslims everywhere to commemorate Ebrahim's (Abraham's) willingness to sacrifice his son. This year the feast fell a few days after winter's midpoint. The nomads considered the occasion one of mourning and said that work and play were supposed to be prohibited. Unenthusiastic about observing the customary rituals of the day because of the drought and his resulting foul mood, Borzu asked his brother Khalifeh and his cousin Morad if they wanted to share with him the animal to be sacrificed. Neither did, each unwilling to incur the expense. At the last minute Borzu bought a fat, white male lamb in Kazerun, not having an appropriate animal in his own herds. Once the purchase was made, Morad changed his mind and went to a public bathhouse in Kazerun to perform the required rites of purification. Borzu tethered the lamb near the tent and instructed children to keep other animals away.

The nomads noted that the preparations for and procedures of the sacrifice and feast were strictly prescribed (in contrast with their otherwise often casual attitudes about ritual performances connected in some way with Islam). They did declare that if other (unspecified) circumstances permitted it, they would all year around act in the way they were mandated by Islam to act on this day.

The Feast of Sacrifice required a special animal, people said, and they paid it more attention than any other part of the ceremonial day. The animal needed to be "pure," without sexual experience. A young male sheep or goat of at least a year of age was eligible, except that it might already have entered a state of rut and thereby become unclean and impure. Some considered a young female sheep or goat that had never given birth or been pregnant to be better, although others said a female should never be used. The animal should be a fine specimen, not only fat but lacking anomalous and abnormal traits, and its fleece should be a solid color, either white or black. It should have never fallen down (a trait difficult to prove, people admitted). An animal meeting these specifications was sponsored by three or another odd number of men or older boys, who became partners. The one who had performed the proper ablutions was responsible for the actual sacrifice. Borzu invited Khalifeh to be the third partner, for he was one of the few people at Dashtak able to recite the required Qoranic passages.

In Khalifeh and Morad's presence, with many women and children as onlookers, Borzu instructed his son to dig a knee-deep hole to the side of the tent. Morad unwrapped a knife he had earlier sharpened, which he and a few other families kept for use only on this occasion. He offered the lamb a drink, washed its mouth, nose, and feet, and then tied its four legs with a tasseled multicolored cord, also used only for this event. He carried the lamb to the hole and held its head over it. As Khalifeh recited from the Qoran, Morad faced Mecca and slit the lamb's throat and neck all the way through the spine with one strong even motion, leaving the head attached to the body only by the skin at the back of the neck. Blood pulsed into the hole. Morad held the body tightly for a few minutes, to control the spasms, and then gently laid it by the hole so any remaining blood would drain out. He had tied the lamb's legs so it would not thrash around on the ground spewing blood, as ordinarily occurred, an action that would negate the ritual purity of the occasion and blemish its dignity. The camp's children had earlier restrained all the dogs and chickens, which on other days always pressed in upon a newly slaughtered animal for blood and body parts to eat.

As blood had streamed from the neck, Zali Khan soaked lumps of sugar in it (to be dried and saved for the treatment of illness) and then with his finger dipped in blood marked a line from the forehead to the tip of the nose of each person who came forward. Blood from the sacrificial animal brought God's blessing to the participants, they believed. The men present abstained. More aware of and concerned about Islamic prohibitions than women and children, they worried about ritual pollution resulting from contact with blood and were skeptical about the ritual's efficacy. Zali Khan, a Qasemli man visiting Dashtak, was considered an expert in these and other ritual matters.

Morad inserted a stick used in bread making into a hole in the skin on one leg of the lamb and, by blowing into the hole, separated the skin from the body as an aid in skinning the animal. He discarded in the hole the head and internal parts, almost all of which were ordinarily eaten or used in some way and the rest tossed to the dogs. Mohammad Karim promptly filled the hole with dirt and then placed a large rock on top to prevent dogs and other scavengers from pulling out the remains. Borzu pointed to three other large rocks near the tent, which he said covered previous years' remains. A fourth, he noted, had been inadvertently broken up for use in building the new storage hut. Morad then carefully butchered the animal and divided the meat into three piles, which he placed on clean trays.

Each carrying a tray of meat, Khalifeh and Morad returned to their own camps where they divided their shares with other families. For the herders in Borzu's camp, this occasion was one of the few times in the year when they cooked or ate meat. (They sometimes also received meat when it was plentiful after sick or injured animals were killed.) Each of their families cooked and ate its own meat alone on this day of sacrifice, while in Khalifeh's and Morad's camps the families pooled their shares and enjoyed a collective meal. Everyone including infants was given meat or meat stock, also unusual. If meat were not shared in these ways, people believed that misfortune would occur. Even if only a chicken had been sacrificed, its meat too needed to be distributed equally, with many participants getting only a morsel. People buried the bones of the sacrificial animal and did not crack them open, eat the marrow, and then toss them to the dogs as was customary. They did save the bone from the lower right front leg for a year (or until the family sacrificed another animal for another ritual feast), carefully wrapped in the camel-hair cloth used for rolling out bread dough, in order to bestow good fortune on the family.

The nomads believed that the supernatural benefits this animal and this event granted to the participants would last a year, until the next feast. Some years back Khalifeh had sacrificed a cow, motivated by his sorrow over the recent deaths of two sons and his very real fear that other children would die. People said that the benefits from sacrificing a cow lasted seven years. If the participants omitted or performed improperly any of the preparations or procedures, they believed that the entire Feast of Sacrifice was unacceptable to God and that none of the expected blessings would accrue. This year no one else at Dashtak sacrificed an animal because, everyone said, "The sheep are too thin." Many people did send shares of their own simple noon meals to their campmates.

The day before the Feast of Sacrifice was a customary time to mourn deceased family members. This year the day fell on a Saturday, believed to be inauspicious for a mourning ritual, and so most families at Dashtak (but not Borzu's) remembered their dead in a simple ceremony on Friday. As five men sat talking in Akbar's tent after having eaten lunch, his mother Salatin brought a tray of cooked rice from her tent for them to eat. After they ate, each said an Arabic prayer in memory of loved ones. Kokab, the most recently bereaved camp member, ate the rice remaining on the tray and said her own prayer.

The second forty-five days of winter this year were worse than the first because of the lack of rain and the absence of much new vegetation. Constantly hungry, animals sickened and died or sustained crippling or fatal injuries. Hardly a day passed without some disaster striking the herd and pack animals of each family at Dashtak.

After a bitterly cold night Borzu checked the lambs and kids in the pen at the back of the tent and angrily discovered three dead lambs suffocated in the push to get warm. He blamed Falak for not having gotten up frequently enough during the night to roust the animals. One hundred and fifty (surviving from the two hundred live births) occupied the pen, far too many. Ten nights later another three lambs died in the crowded pen, and Borzu finally acted on his earlier intention by moving the kids to a new pen in the warmest of the huts and expanding the space of the tent's pen to accommodate the growing lambs. Every day older children took lambs and kids for food and exercise. Borzu and some other men let lambs graze the ruined crops of grain to derive at least some small gain from the disastrous planting. Kids fended for themselves on the new shoots of shrubs.

More sheep died than goats, which were more resilient under dry and barren conditions. While Borzu and other herd owners fed their sheep as much sugar-beet pulp, straw, and barley as they could afford, Aqaboa and other shepherds scoured the mountainside for vegetation and came to rely heavily on the branches and leaves of shrubs and small trees. The men carved wooden talismans to hang from the necks of the most valuable animals to protect them from the season's many dangers. Hungry donkeys, mules, and horses dismantled the roofs of their protective shelters as they ate the dried reeds, branches, and leaves.

Several brief rains shortly after the forty-fifth day of winter temporarily filled the basins and pools at the gorges, thus eliminating for a while the arduous trips to the well below Molla Balut. After the last of these rains, a bitter cold descended on Dashtak, and the next morning Aqaboa found three large goats suffocated in the pen. That day ten more animals died, and shepherds threw their bodies into the gully at the bottom of the ravine between the pen and Borzu's tent. Earlier in the season when an animal was on the verge of death, a man cut its throat, and the body provided meat for several days. With many animals sick and dying, however, this effort was not always taken, and whole carcasses littered the refuse area of the camp and surrounding terrain. If an animal appeared to have a disease tainting the meat, the carcass was discarded. Sometimes people said animals were too thin to eat and threw out the bodies, but only when meat was already available. The stench of rotting herd and pack animals hung heavy in the air. Predators abounded, and swarms of insects became a serious problem.

Owners were responsible for slaughtering and butchering their sheep and goats. When decisions about killing a sick animal needed to be made suddenly, other men including itinerant peddlers could perform the act. People said it was a sin to let a suffering animal near death die slowly. They were enjoined by the Qoran, they believed, to end the animal's misery. They killed lambs and kids if they were unable to stand. One day Borzu's daughter Zohreh dragged a dying kid into the gully, and its pitiful bleats could be heard until it quivered, gasped, and died. If a man or older boy had been present, he would never have permitted the kid to die on its own.

Women and girls were prohibited from killing animals, but in an emergency they bent the rules in order to render the meat edible. If no adolescent or adult male was present, a woman could hold the hand of her young son, if he was circumcised, and apply the direction and pressure of the knife cut herself. The meat fell into an ambiguous category and was usually eaten, often surreptitiously, only by women and girls. Butchering was men's work as well, but in men's absence women and older girls cut meat from the carcasses of animals whose throats had been slit before death. One day when six animals with slit throats lay near Borzu's tent, six-year-old Farideh slipped off quietly with one of them. She skinned, cleaned, and butchered the small kid in a secluded gully, roasted the carcass on a stick over a small brush fire, and devoured the meat. Another day when Borzu's daughters were home alone, Samarrokh came for a visit. She had seen a dead kid near the tent, secretly tucked it into the folds of her skirts, and hurried to the cooking hut where she and her three sisters quickly skinned, butchered, broiled, and ate it all. Farideh adamantly refused to eat at first and then gagged on a morsel of the cooked meat, but, worried that the small thin animal was soon to be consumed, she too grabbed a portion. The kid's throat had not been slit, and the sisters said they were prohibited from eating the meat and were committing a sin. But they were hungry and rarely had a chance to eat meat, especially the younger ones who did not yet cook, and so took advantage of men's absence.

Skins (with wool and hair attached) of sick and dying sheep and goats were saved if men were present to slit the animals' throats and had the time and inclination to remove them. The skin, wool, and hair of animals that died in a prohibited state were also considered prohibited and were supposed to be, but were not always, discarded. Women saved whatever wool and hair they could. Zolaikha had yanked the hair from the three dead goats found suffocated in the pen. She might have left one goat untouched, but she said three were too many to ignore. Men expressed disgust in the presence of a prohibited animal and said they would not touch the wool or hair. After pulling out wool and hair from dead, even prohibited, animals, women and girls hid the products for use in trade with peddlers. They kept this wool and hair separate from the wool and hair they would eventually prepare for weaving, and some men knew nothing about these hidden caches.

Persian, Lur, and Arab skin buyers from Kazerun and nearby villages toured Dashtak to take advantage of the nomads' losses. With cash they purchased the skins, sometimes with wool and hair attached, of dead sheep and goats, after trying to ascertain if the animals had been killed in the correct manner. They feared that some skins fell into a prohibited state but eventually overcame their reluctance. Persian and Lur itinerant peddlers also traded for skins, wool, and hair and offered their own goods in exchange. Sometimes skin buyers and peddlers bought and traded meat, although they were generally suspicious about its derivation and ritual state. Some nomads, especially women, did not mind passing off prohibited meat to people they regarded as ignorant and gullible. Skin buyers and peddlers preferred to buy injured and sick animals so that they could properly kill the animals themselves.

Peddlers and skin buyers were sources of information for people at Dashtak, especially women, who lacked the travel and contacts in Kazerun that men enjoyed. They passed along news of other families as they crossed the territory. By these and other means of disseminating information, people knew often precisely the status of others' animals and could tabulate everyone's total losses of the season up to that point. They knew the history of individual animals, especially horses, mules, camels, and rams, and were sad when they heard the news and circumstances of their demise.

Other disasters struck animals. More careless with the flocks than owners tended to be, hired shepherds allowed accidents to occur, particularly when throwing stones at animals that strayed or were on the perimeter of the moving herd. Khodabakhsh accidentally stoned a goat that thereafter seemed disoriented and would wander away from the herd. He tethered the animal near the tent until it appeared to regain its senses, but later it was attacked by a wolf and died of its injuries. Goats, which tended to browse on shrubs and trees rather than to graze on ground vegetation, sometimes endangered themselves. Grazing at ground level, sheep often never bothered to raise their heads (and so their feeding required special attention). Goats, however, went after food more aggressively and could become entangled, especially if they had long or curved horns, in the branches of shrubs and trees. One goat caught in a tree strangled itself before Khodabakhsh saw that it was missing from the herd.

Animals, especially when hungry and weak, fell and broke or twisted their limbs. Two men at Dashtak skilled in treating limb injuries and resetting bones were sought for their services. One of them, Borzu's brother Gholam Hosain, set a broken limb with wood and reed splints that he stabilized with yarn and then tied onto hunks of wool or goat hair above the splint so that it would remain in place. As a final step he wrapped around the set limb a twig or piece of straw until it broke in two, and then he cast away the two pieces in opposite directions. This ritual act was intended to transfer the break from the animal's limb to the twig or straw and cause the limb to heal properly. Men cauterized with a skewer wounds from wolf attacks and other injuries, and they singed the skin around a wound that had not healed. Aqaboa treated a sheep with a severe injury from a wolf, whose bite had split the fat tail and cut into the hind end, by burning the animal with a skewer behind its head and above the tail in order to keep it from smelling the wound and then licking or otherwise disturbing it. Men treated maggot-infested wounds with whatever chemicals (kerosene, insecticide, flea power) they owned. While chemicals did usually rid the wound of worms, at least temporarily, they did not aid healing.

Leeches lived in water basins and attached themselves to the tongues, mouths, and nasal passages of animals who drank there. Men regularly checked their animals and removed leeches, fat with ingested blood, with metal pincers. Leeches entering animals' stomachs were life threatening, especially for unhealthy hosts.

A year-old camel, whose mother had died of smallpox at Wide Mountain, sickened and would not eat. Yadollah carried her on a stretcher to a protected gully near his tent, laid her on a bed of fresh almond branches, covered her with an old tent strip, placed almond-blossom buds by her head, and surrounded her with brambles in order to keep predators at bay. For two days he fed the young camel by hand, and for two nights he slept at her side. On the third day he woke to find vultures standing guard on nearby slopes overlooking the gully, and with sorrow he saw that a wolf had dragged the camel downhill and disemboweled her.

As the days of the second half of winter passed, conditions were in some ways worse for camels than herd animals, for they required larger quantities of food. Many camels had been weakened by smallpox and had not recovered adequately, and all of them were made more vulnerable by scarce vegetation and water. Many camels sickened. Yadollah fed the young ones by hand with buds and flowers picked from wild almond trees, and he chopped up fresh camel thorn specially gathered from an area northwest of Dashtak. Several older camels would not eat and, once collapsed on the ground, would not rise. An old camel refused to eat unless Yadollah and no one else fed him by hand, and he would cry whenever the man left his side. Afsar shrieked and tore her clothes when Borj Ali told her their only camel had fallen, apparently from weakness, and had died. People in camp thought a person had died, possibly her new baby, and ran to comfort her.

Itinerant peddlers carried the news of dying camels to Kazerun, and buyers of camel meat descended on Dashtak to make the rounds of the camps. Selling camel meat in Kazerun was illegal, but these buyers often disguised the meat by mixing it with sheep and goat meat or shipped it elsewhere. Butchers in Kazerun often secretly kept camel meat for loyal customers, who believed that eating it conferred a blessing from the prophet Mohammad and from his grandson Imam Hosain who had relied on camels in his final, fatal battle at Kerbala. Some Persians, Lurs, and Arabs in the region believed that camels were God's special animals. Qermezi people harbored no such notions about camels or their meat. They did eat the meat whenever a camel was properly slaughtered. Because of the animal's size and the absence of any method of preserving the meat, they always tried to sell the surplus.

As time for the spring migration neared, many nomads worried about the health of their camels and about their ability to carry heavy loads. Because of losses earlier in the year, principally from smallpox, many families owned the absolute minimum of pack animals, and the illness or death of even one camel (or donkey) could mean that they would not easily be able to migrate. So, with buyers of camel meat descending upon them, they needed to make difficult decisions. If they sent the buyers away, sick camels might die, and the owners might lose the opportunity to sell the meat and gain a small income. But if they slaughtered sick camels, they might be destroying animals that would have survived and made the migration to summer pastures possible.

Peddlers toured Dashtak frequently because of the trade in skins, meat, and injured animals and profited the most when women and children were alone in camp. One day Zohreh traded a handful of wool for a few dates from a peddler and then, her appetite whetted, gave him three large bowls of barley (a scarce commodity at this time) for turmeric and more dates. He offered her a hen's egg he had received in trade at another camp, and she quietly wrapped it in small pieces of wet cloth, hid it in the ashes of the fire pit to bake, and then secretly, hungrily ate it. Narges asked the peddler to kill a dying ram belonging to Abdol Hosain, and she traded the skin and a large hunk of the meat for sixty cents. She did not bargain with him and simply pocketed the money. Zohreh brought him a dying lamb to kill and then rejected with disgust his offer of only thirteen cents for the skin. Children begged him for sweets and a mirror and scoured thorny bushes in the area for tufts of wool they could trade. As he was leaving, Narges told him to visit the camp of her son Gholam Hosain who had charcoal for sale. With peddlers who came frequently, people at Dashtak were also able to place orders for specific goods.

A few days later another peddler entered Borzu's camp. He said he had traded with nomads at Dashtak for fifty years, long before the Qermezi group arrived, and that his father had done the same work. In autumn he collected and sold nuts and sap from the mountains above. He complained that this year the nomads had denuded so many wild almond trees and bushes in their quest for fodder that he would find few almonds and little tree sap to collect the next autumn. He declared that the crisis people at Dashtak were suffering was the result of Borzu's having bought a truck and sold water to them. He viewed the sale of God-given water as evil; the drought was the consequence. He had apparently heard people griping about Borzu and drew his own conclusions.

Most years at about this time, Borzu and many other men at Dashtak took on short-term animal contracts. They bought male animals in mid-winter if grazing was adequate and fattened them until spring when they sold them. Or they bought male animals at the New Year in March, fattened them during the spring migration, and sold them just before or on arrival at summer pastures. This year, the status of grazing and water being so abysmal, only Mansur planned to assume such contracts, and he would wait until the beginning of the migration.

As the weather worsened and conditions for pastoralism became more dismal, people expressed physical discomfort. Falak, who seemed to complain more than most women about the weather and various aches and pains, increasingly pleaded ill health when chores needed to be done. Her daughters Zolaikha and Zohreh gradually assumed her tasks. One night after a bitterly cold and windy day, Falak lay moaning under a pile of blankets and did not respond when family members asked her what she needed. They, especially Borzu, had learned to ignore her complaints and assumed she was malingering. That night, however, her face was a greenish-gray color, and she repeatedly retched and vomited. As her daughters became agitated, Borzu also became concerned, and soon he rousted Hafez to drive them to Kazerun to find a doctor. The trip took hours, for the road was hard to find in the dark, and the weather grew colder and more windy. Along the way Borzu and Hafez often had to attend to Falak. They had never attempted to travel at night by vehicle on the Dashtak road before.

Personnel at the government hospital in Kazerun refused to admit the semiconscious Falak or have a doctor or nurse examine her. Borzu took her to the home of a merchant. In the morning they returned to the hospital, and she was admitted. She remained there a week, becoming more ill and incoherent and still without a diagnosis, and then Borzu took her to Shiraz on the advice of the merchant. Officials at the Ministry of Health told Borzu that she probably qualified for government assistance but that not a single bed in their clinics or hospitals was available. A doctor at a private hospital diagnosed Falak's illness as brought about by gallstones, admitted her, and operated. He found no stones. Borzu prevailed upon the hospitality of Mohammad Hasan Khan Darrehshuri in Shiraz during her recuperation in the hospital. As soon as she was able to travel, Borzu and Falak returned to Dashtak.

During Falak and Borzu's absence, many people came to offer assistance to their family. Kinsmen such as Morad and Hasel regularly stopped by to check on animals and deliver needed supplies from town. Many families sent adolescent boys to help with animals, keep the family company in the evening, and stay all night as protectors against unexpected events such as a wolf attack. Borzu's mother Narges came for the duration. Still a hard, diligent worker, she spent much of her time spinning goat hair and braiding ropes and bands. Winter rains and the carrying of water had ruined equipment that needed to be replaced before the spring migration, and she put herself to work. Although her poorly healed broken arm was painful, she still found ingenious ways to continue tasks she had been performing all her life.

Narges stayed with Borzu's family until she argued with her grand-daughter Zolaikha. Narges did not approve of the frequent appearance of Khalifeh's son Hosain Ali in camp and complained, "The home of Borzu is for guests, not this boy. Why does he come around?" Zolaikha responded that the home was hers now, with father and mother gone, and that Borzu had placed her in control. She declared that she would do as she wished but added that she had not invited Hosain Ali to visit nor had she spoken improperly with him. Narges left angry, exclaiming that she expected her grandson and not Khalifeh's son to marry Zolaikha. This controversy over who Zolaikha would marry was not to be resolved for a long time.

Before Falak's illness had been diagnosed, and then just before her operation and until the news of her recovery, certain activities in Borzu's camp were prohibited because of the belief that they would cause her affliction to worsen. No one bathed, washed clothes, sang, or operated the battery-powered record player. Anxious to weave, Zolaikha did all the preparations; she washed wool and prepared it for spinning and then spun, twisted, and dyed it. These tasks finished, she contemplated weaving a utilitarian article. An item such as a gelim, jajim, or pile carpet was considered pleasing to the eye and hand of the weaver and could not be woven during a period of crisis. Zolaikha began a sugar bag, but visitors, objecting, proclaimed that it was too attractive and not utilitarian enough. Samarrokh suggested a plain bag for carrying water-filled goatskin bags, and Zolaikha began to weave again. The family discovered that Falak was going to survive through the simple message, arriving via third parties from Borzu, that they could operate the record player again. Women and girls of the camp immediately abandoned their other chores to bathe and wash clothes.

Free to visit others at Dashtak because their parents were gone, Borzu and Falak's children returned to camp one day with the news that Hindi, a year-old goat that had been living independently, had died. Formerly part of the goat herd tended by Khodabakhsh, Hindi had become ill at the beginning of winter and was unwilling to be herded anymore. He lost all his hair and became scrawny; his name derived from his slightness. (Hindi was the name these Qashqa'i had given to the short, lean, dark-skinned Indian soldiers fighting for the British against Qashqa'i forces in south Iran during World War I. Qashqa'i soldiers regarded the Indians with pity, for they were far from home, ill paid, and forced to risk their lives for others' interests. Qashqa'i commanders instructed their troops to avoid shooting Indian soldiers and instead to aim at their taller British officers.) Hindi roamed Dashtak, often stopping at different camps in search of food, and periodically returned to Borzu's camp. People in Borzu's tent would wake to find him resting close to the smoldering embers in the fire pit. When the weather was cold he stayed in the tent. No one paid him much attention, but people were amused by his travels and obvious attachment to people. When several days had gone by and people realized they had not seen him for a while, they asked visitors about his whereabouts.

On the eve of the tenth of Moharram, a month of mourning for Shi'i Muslims, Borzu's children clamored for permission to go to Khalifeh's camp where others were preparing for that evening's *shozenda* ritual. The excitement, building for some days, had reached its peak. The tenth of Moharram is the date in A.D. 680 when Imam Hosain, the prophet Mohammad's grandson and the third imam in Shi'i Islam, was murdered on a battlefield on the plains of Kerbala (now in Iraq). Since then Shi'i Muslims have commemorated the death during the month of Moharram, particularly the first ten days, by performing mourning rituals including the *ta'ziyeh*, a drama reenacting the martyrdom and the events surrounding it. Qermezi people called the eve of the tenth day shozenda (*shab zenda*), "the night people stay awake." They also used the term for ritual observances on the tenth, a day Shi'i Muslims call Ashura.

Returning home from school in Kazerun, Borzu's son Mohammad Karim had brought along a small book of Arabic and Persian chants that he and other children in camp had been practicing and sometimes translating into Turkish. The most enthusiastic, the young goat herder Khodabakhsh had learned other chants from his father Zulfaqar. Children did not treat the occasion solemnly, and a slightly disapproving attitude was apparent in their parents as they heard the high-spirited youngsters practice the chants and motions. Once Borzu gave permission, children ran to the camp to the south. Zolaikha and her two young brothers stayed behind, as he had ordered. She was too near marriage age to be allowed to leave camp at night without a responsible adult along. She told the others she would sneak away once Borzu fell asleep, but through the evening and into the early morning he periodically called her to do some chore, thereby eliminating any chance for her to leave. Using her sister's name, he would yell, "Zohreh, bring me water!" for embarrassment kept him from referring directly to Zolaikha, so near marriage.

Earlier that afternoon, after discussing the wisdom of getting involved at all, Akbar and Asadollah (cousins in their mid-twenties) began to assemble a standard (*alam*) to carry in the ceremony. They made a wooden cross more than two meters tall and more than a meter wide out of tent and loom poles and dressed the figure in a red skirt, black tunic, and black scarf reluctantly loaned by women in their families (none of whom owned a complete change of clothes). They tied the tunic's sleeves to the crossbar with handkerchiefs and then fastened a bell onto the vertical pole. They said the standard represented the banner carried by Imam Hosain's small army. The reason they used women's clothes, they suggested, was that at the time of the prophet Mohammad, clothes worn by his Arab followers were similar to Qashqa'i women's clothes. Aqaboa had earlier told the children that the standard depicted a woman because the prophet had so instructed and that its clothes ought to be black (for mourning) and green (the prophet's color) but never red or white (a bride's colors). The bell, Akbar explained, represented bells on the Arab army's camels and was used to call people to join the ritual.

The standard ready, Akbar and Asadollah along with the youth of their large camp, Borzu's, and a few others convened near one of the cemeteries at Dashtak to perform the shozenda ritual. Mohammad Karim began to chant the Persian verses he had memorized. The others arranged themselves in a circle around him, girls to one side with their arms over each other's shoulders, boys to the other with their hands at their sides, and they slowly stepped sideways around the circle to the rhythm of the chant. The verses were easy to learn and remember, and soon all were repeating them. Mohammad Karim and later Ayaz and Asadollah recited a line in Persian or Turkish, and the others chorused the appropriate response. Some boys rhythmically pounded their chests in unison. When Alibakhsh became carried away with the motion, to the laughter of the others, Akbar temporarily pulled him out of the circle to calm him down. Although Akbar had been standing to the side and never fully participated, he did say that it was wrong to make too much fun of what should be a serious occasion. Other young men the age of Akbar and Asadollah came to watch but did not join in, and no older people were present.

In time the circle disintegrated and the participants, all of whom were now beating their chests, traveled to the ridge separating Khalifeh's land from Borzu's. They carried the standard along and pounded it on the ground, ringing the bell in time with the chants. Children set small brush fires along the way, and the younger ones playfully pushed and shoved one another as they skipped along. Mohammad Karim wanted the group to go to Abdol Rasul's camp beyond Borzu's, but Akbar commented that everyone there would already be asleep. (Waking others, for whatever reason, had never been a problem before.) The group moved toward the ridge between Borzu's and Arghvan's lands where the participants set more fires and then fought for possession of the standard, symbolically representing, they later suggested, the struggle of Imam Hosain's group against the enemy. With this act completed, the group slowly dispersed, no one really wanting to go home. As the youngsters returned to their camps, they talked excitedly about who had chanted the loudest and longest, whose chest and throat were the sorest, and how they were going to stay awake the rest of the night. Adults had told them that people were forbidden to sleep on the eve of the tenth of Moharram. Once back at their camps, everyone went immediately to bed.

The next morning Akbar blamed the small attendance on the cold weather and the drought. In the past, he said, more young adults had joined the ritual, and one household had hosted the group during the ceremony at around midnight and killed a goat, prepared rice, or simply offered bread and yogurt. Akbar mentioned men who had previously been hosts. If an animal was killed, the sacrifice was performed in the name of Imam Hosain, an act believed to benefit the host and his family. This year no one wanted to incur the expense of a meal. In years past the group was offered tea as it traveled from camp to camp enjoining others to participate, which helped everyone to stay awake. No shozenda ritual had been performed the previous winter, also one of drought. Children had gone with expectation to Akbar and Asadollah's camp, but neither man had prepared a standard, and the would-be revelers returned home.

Children identified the shozenda ritual with other children and young adults, and each was able to cite how many times he or she had attended in the past. When Khalifeh, a dignified sixty-year-old, recited a chant he remembered from his youth, children were amazed that he had ever participated. They said they could not imagine him performing the ritual. Farideh flatly denied that her father Borzu had ever been part of a performance and insisted that he was joking when he said he had. Men who had directed the ritual in the past when they were young no longer participated at all. Aqaboa said that a person was permitted to join only seven such rituals in his or her lifetime.

On the morning of Ashura, the tenth of Moharram, most men went visiting at Dashtak. Nine men convened at Borzu's for a brief time to discuss the drought and ponder when and where they should migrate.

Sardar's son Allahyar formally invited Borzu to a ceremonial meal at his father's camp and escorted him and his two eldest sons. Sardar's large camp contained ten tents, two belonging to his economically independent sons, and was one of the most fortified at Dashtak. Stone walls protected the tents. Some huts with stone foundations and roofs made of branches and reeds were suitable for residence during inclement weather. Allahyar ushered Borzu into one whose small single room was decorated with long strips of black and green cloth and several pictures of Shi'i imams. A black banner with verses lettered in white Arabic script was mounted above the narrow doorway inside. It had been purchased years before in Kazerun and was borrowed by men who hosted the meal. Men rose as Borzu entered. Young men and boys who had participated in the ritual the night before stayed outside in the courtyard. Women and girls were not in sight. Sardar's sons served tea and food cooked by women in a nearby tent. The meal, a meat and vegetable stew with rice, was considered a "payment" to Imam Hosain, whom they called "first of the martyrs" on this occasion. By killing an animal for the meal, God's blessing issued to all the household's animals.

Only adult married men were present at the meal, including Khalifeh, Borzu, and men from Sardar's extended family and camp. Men from other families at Dashtak were not invited and did not attend. A ceremonial meal was not held every year, and men who did host one considered their obligation fulfilled for many years to come. Many invited Borzu every year or so, and occasions such as this met that duty. Borzu had never hosted the meal. He frequently served as host to group members for other purposes. More pertinently, perhaps, the event commemorated by the meal held no particular significance for him.

One reason Sardar hosted the meal this year was to establish better ties between his son Allahyar and Borzu. Sardar was Borzu's mother's brother, a kinship relationship that was supposed to be characterized by affection, a quality also to extend to the mother's brother's son. When Borzu had tried to claim Sardar's campsite in 1965, he and Allahyar had fought. The next year he told gendarmes that Allahyar was hiding an illegal gun. Allahyar swore that he no longer possessed one, and the gendarmes dropped the case. But Borzu and Allahyar avoided one another and did not speak for years.

Before the dispute Allahyar had let it be known that he wanted to marry Borzu's eldest daughter, and Borzu had never said he opposed the idea, which was a sign of tentative consent. After their fight Borzu gave his daughter to his brother's son, and Allahyar was angry that she was stolen from him. He then sought Zolaikha, Borzu's second eldest daughter. His mother had spoken to Borzu about the match, and Allahyar had asked a merchant in Kazerun whom Borzu respected to speak for him. Allahyar stressed to all who would listen the amount of work, including cultivating and harvesting, that he and his brothers had performed for Borzu over the years, and he expected a reciprocal gesture. Zolaikha, however, had been betrothed from birth to the son of another of Borzu's brothers, and Borzu would be unlikely to break this promise.

Conversation during the many servings of tea before the meal centered on the disastrous drought, the likelihood of rain in the near future, the plans for the spring migration, and the fate of people at Dashtak who ordinarily stayed through the scorchingly hot summer. After the meal a few men mumbled a prayer in Arabic, one verse for each of the twelve imams, and then conversation resumed. Shortly afterward in the middle of someone's talk, Borzu rose to leave, a standard way of ending a social event. Sardar and Allahyar escorted him and his sons down the path, as was customary of hosts, especially at ceremonial occasions.

People at Dashtak heard about elaborate Moharram activities in Kazerun from men and school boys there, but the month of commemoration was of little significance to them compared with its impact on most other Shi'i Iranians. For the nomads, Moharram meant a night of chanting for some children, a ceremonial meal for some men every few years, and a few restrictions on activities such as prohibitions on washing clothes and weaving on the tenth, eleventh, and twelfth days. A few men wore black shirts on the tenth, in memory of a deceased family member.

Two days later, as people continued to worry about the drought and its devastation, Borzu's son Mohammad Karim suddenly decided that a rain ceremony was in order for that evening. Borzu was in Kazerun and hence could neither forbid nor take control of the activities. Mohammad Karim found Khodabakhsh, Yadollah, and Borj Ali (all shepherds in subordinate positions) and tried to convince one of them to play the part of the thin-bearded bride (*kosah galen*), the central figure and clown in the rain ceremony. Khodabakhsh refused, Yadollah absolutely refused, and Borj Ali was tentatively willing. Yadollah's young son eagerly volunteered but Mohammad Karim pushed him aside. When Khodabakhsh emitted the growling sound characteristic of the clown, people near him responded so enthusiastically that he volunteered after all, although with trepidation.

Mohammad Karim quickly prepared the thin-bearded bride's outfit for Khodabakhsh. He dressed him in a boy's felt cloak and tied a heavy band around his waist, attached a large goat bell to his waist in the back, fastened Borzu's leather slippers with yarn and an old piece of cloth to his head as horns, and made him a beard and moustache of raw wool secured by yarn. He threw white flour into his face and beard, gave him a stick, and told him to memorize the verse: "I am a bride, I ride a pole, I bring the wind, I bring the rain, I don't want anything, I want some sweets." (Later Akbar said that in previous years the thin-bearded bride sometimes rode a tent pole with rein and tail attached and that they had also led him around on a donkey.)

As children of the camp climbed up the slope of the ravine in the light of the full moon, with Mohammad Karim pushing Khodabakhsh in front of him, they all saw how unrecognizable and comical he had become. Someone suggested going north to Barat's camp, but everyone else wanted to go south to Khalifeh's, and off they went at a fast pace. Mohammad Karim held firmly to the thin-bearded bride's rope and occasionally yanked the clown backward. As they ran along the path between the two camps, the children's excitement mounted.

Mohammad Karim propelled Khodabakhsh as the thin-bearded bride first to Akbar's tent where he said they would be welcome. Standing in front of the dark empty tent, the clown recited his verse three times while hopping from one foot to the other and rocking from side to side. Akbar had hid to the side of the tent when he heard the group from a distance and recognized what was coming. Suddenly he threw a dish of water at the thin-bearded bride. As required, the clown held open a large empty sack. When Akbar's wife Dayeh Soltan could not decide what to give, Khodabakhsh thrust his stick through the tent's entrance and growled. Akbar chanted, "Thin-bearded bride, don't ruin my tent, don't ruin my home. I'll give you what you want." The thin-bearded bride responded, "Give me flour, give me sweets, give me clarified butter. I will bring rain." Dayeh Soltan filled a bowl with flour and dumped it into the sack. If people did not give food, the thin-bearded bride was supposed to throw ashes from the fire pit into the tent to scare them.

Ali's tent was dark and quiet. No one appeared to be home, even at this late hour. Mohammad Karim was ready to move on when suddenly a spray of water flew from a corner of the tent and people ran out from where they had been hiding. Nurijan gave flour. Everyone from the two tents enthusiastically accompanied the group to the tent of Khodabakhsh's mother, where people had been asleep. His sister sprinkled the thin-bearded bride with water and gave him dates. Alerted as soon as the exuberant entourage had approached from over the hill, the camp's many dogs were now in a frenzy of barking and attacking, and people tried unsuccessfully to calm them down. At Jehangir's tent, women gave the clown a good dousing. By now a large group had assembled, but everyone except the thin-bearded bride and Mohammad Karim lingered behind as they approached Khalifeh's tent. Khodabakhsh was by now undaunted by even the presence of Qermezi's most respected man, and he threw himself into Khalifeh's tent. Hosain Ali dumped a bowl of water on his head. A still larger group moved on to Bahram's and Safdar's tents and then to several shepherd's tents, where each time the tent appeared vacated until the splash of water. Safdar emptied a goatskin bag of water on the thin-bearded bride.

The procession ended, as Mohammad Karim had decided, at his sister Samarrokh's tent. She and her husband Asadollah had been asleep, but they pushed aside the bedding when they heard the group approaching. Soon thirty people were sitting inside, with none of the usual restrictions on the proximity of women and children to men during social occasions. Samarrokh carefully spilled out the contents of the sack on a large tray and then mixed the flour with water while people drank tea and ate dates coated with flour. Amanollah brought seven pebbles for her to mix into the dough, which she baked on a flat pan over a fire in the tent. While waiting for the thick bread to cook, people performed tricks and told jokes. Several told the story of how their fathers used to lead the thin-bearded bride mounted on a donkey to Kazerun. While townspeople watched his antics, young men slipped away to steal property, and then they all fled back to the mountains. Asadollah joked, "Wouldn't it be easier now, with a pickup truck?"

Akbar distributed the hot bread by breaking off hunks and handing them out. Everyone playfully rejected the piece offered and tried to grab another. Six pebbles were found (the seventh someone must have inadvertently swallowed, to everyone's amusement), and Akbar told each finder to draw a straw to see who would be beaten. Samarrokh pulled the shortest straw, and after Asadollah hit her lightly with a thin branch, she predicted that rain would fall in three days. If rain did not come then, people would find Khodabakhsh, still in the role of the thin-bearded bride, and beat him. (People talking about the rain ceremony described it somewhat differently. They said the participants tried to hit the person who found the one pebble in the bread until three people stood and proclaimed, "Don't hit [the name of the person], because rain will fall in three nights." Then, if rain did not come as predicted, the person who found the pebble would be hit.)

With laughter and noise the group reluctantly dispersed, and the contingent from Borzu's camp slowly made its way back home. Even if the rain ceremony proved to be ineffective, the event provided its participants and onlookers with more merriment than they had enjoyed in a long time. On the way home Mohammad Karim suddenly stopped and then remarked, as if amazed, that this was still a period of intense mourning, being the twelfth of Moharram, and that any kind of entertainment was prohibited. But then he shrugged his shoulders and commented, "What difference does it make?" (Later, Akbar said that he too had known that the fun was inappropriate but that no harm had been done.) Khodabakhsh, who had never before been the center of this much attention and had thoroughly enjoyed it, remained in character even after everyone was bedded down. Setting out to let his goats browse in the moonlight, he could be heard reciting the verse and making the peculiar growl of the thin-bearded bride. In the morning he was simply Khodabakhsh again.

A little less than a month before the beginning of spring, people at Dashtak had begun to make serious plans for leaving winter pastures. Because the Qermezi group there was located far from most other Darrehshuri nomads and would begin the migration alone, its members did not comply with the government's harsh regulations concerning the schedule that other Darrehshuri were forced to follow. They blended with other groups and tribes and, during the early stages, traveled routes not as frequently surveyed by the gendarmes and army as the main routes.

People at Dashtak declared that even if rain fell immediately, they had already lost any chance for new grazing there. Some men grazed their herds near Molla Balut after watering them at the well in the plain below and then returned to Dashtak to feed them on almond trees and bushes, which were lacking at the lower altitude of Molla Balut. The main food for sheep, goats, lambs, kids, and pack animals continued to be fresh almond shoots, and every family spent hours cutting branches to bring back to camp. Sheep and goats were constantly hungry, and people threw piles of branches into the pens for the animals to eat at night. They all owned sick animals that would die if they did not eat proper food soon. People complained that nothing was available for animals to eat except rocks and almond shoots.

Most families had nearly exhausted their supplies of barley, straw, and sugar-beet pulp. Pulp was no longer available in Kazerun and Shiraz, and the price of barley and straw was high. By the first week of March, merchants in Kazerun, anticipating the nomads' imminent departure and having already overextended themselves, refused to give fodder and other goods on credit. A few men bought in Kazerun a broad-leafed plant that grew to the north, and all families sent at least one man or older boy to collect oak leaves a day's journey away. Borzu told Yadollah to pull young stalks of barley from the fields of Davan peasants on the northern border of Dashtak, and other men at Dashtak did the same in the fields of Persians and Lurs closest to them. Everyone worried about the health and well-being of their pack animals, particularly camels, and tried to provide as much fodder as possible. Men who could afford it fed barley flour to their weakest camels. Water basins at Dashtak were emptying, and people talked of soon having to bring all their water from the well below Molla Balut.

During the ceremonial meal at Sardar's, Borzu had announced his plans for moving back to the autumn campsite at Dashtak, then northwest to Polo Field Canyon (Tang-e Chugan) if rain still had not fallen, and finally to Wide Mountain for some days before beginning the spring migration in earnest. The next day, after some thought, he told several men that he would move to Polo Field Canyon in fifteen days if rain did not fall. If rain did fall, he would stay at Dashtak until the twentieth day of spring (when these nomads had often left winter pastures in the past) to fatten and restore the health of his animals before the arduous sixty-day migration. Then he would move directly to summer pastures. In the meantime he wanted to feed sugar-beet pulp, barley, and straw to thin animals, rams, milk producers, and nursing offspring. He hoped that if he could keep them full for ten days, they would not fall sick again and would survive the migration.

Three routes around the mountains just east of Kazerun were possible: one southeast of Kazerun via the Pass of the Girl that the Dashtak group always took, one northwest of Kazerun leading through Polo Field Canyon, and a busy vehicular one just northwest of the second route. In the days to come, Borzu vacillated between the first two routes. All men at Dashtak had already planned to take their customary southeastern route. While never admitting it to others, Borzu obviously would rather lead than follow and hence tried to convince the others to wait until he was ready to migrate and then to accompany him through Polo Field Canyon. He chose this route because it offered both a road for his truck and grazing close by for his herds. Everyone else was uncomfortable at Dashtak and wanted to leave right away by the customary southeastern route. This route, via the Pass of the Girl, first led by Mirror Bridge where Darreh-shuri khans used to set up camp at the end of winter or beginning of spring to collect the subtribes' annual animal tax. In years past Qermezi nomads had usually stopped at nearby Famur pastures for several days or even weeks after leaving Dashtak, but this year the grazing there was poor, and they planned to bypass the area.

People also worried about their cultivation. The first crop of wheat and barley they had planted on arrival in winter pastures was doing poorly, and some men had let ewes and lambs graze the sparse growth. The second crop planted at winter's midpoint might be a total loss. It appeared as if the crop had died in the ground. If either or both crops were to survive to harvest, coming after the nomads' departure from winter pastures, the wheat would provide their staple food, and the barley and straw would be essential animal feed for the following autumn and winter. With poor results now expected and debts already high, they did not know how they and their animals would survive. Men who planted and harvested for others were especially troubled because they usually received a fifth of the harvest. Because the harvest would certainly be meager this year, they would realize little for all their labor.

While deciding how best to proceed and faced with a group ready to bolt, Borzu suffered two setbacks complicating his plans and irritating him. His driver Hafez, who had become increasingly disgruntled with his job, had sat in his tent for two days without emerging and then suddenly announced he was quitting and going to the town of Shahreza to find work. He had found the water hauling during the autumn migration difficult and had decided not to be part of a migration again. During the winter he had disliked waiting in a drafty merchant's shop in Kazerun, sometimes for two or three days at a stretch, while Borzu completed his work in town, and then he had disliked staying in camp, especially during cold weather, until Borzu decided on the spur of the moment to drive into town again. Hafez had wanted to wait out the cold, rainy weather in Kazerun but that was inconvenient to Borzu. He and especially his wife said they were lonely at Dashtak.

Although Borzu talked sadly about selling his truck, he said he would never willingly return to his prior mode of travel. He lacked cash to pay a driver and knew of no one who would drive without payment. His son Mohammad Karim was anxious to learn, and so Hafez reluctantly agreed to delay his departure several days while he taught him. The delay was convenient, in a way, because Hafez's wife said she needed to finish weaving her carpet. Mohammad Karim's school was still in session, but he had already demonstrated little desire to attend regularly. He would often come home either by way of Borzu's truck or on foot (for he feared his father's reaction to his skipping school), and then a day later would return to school. Borzu had expected that his son would learn to drive in summer when school was closed, and he would then be spared the need to find and pay a driver. The spring migration was another matter. Because of losses from smallpox and the ravages of winter he owned insufficient numbers of camels, mules, and donkeys to move his household, and he could not afford to buy replacements. Some people at Dashtak were borrowing pack animals, but he was too proud and too conscientious to borrow from people poorer than himself. Having long ago abandoned the idea of learning to drive himself, he decided to rely on his son, but he was unhappy about his missing school, his inexperience as a driver, and his obstinate character.

Borzu also worried continually about the mounting expenses of running the truck. The pickup was old when he bought it, and it had suffered much abuse since then. He lacked any expertise in mechanics and knew of no one such as a merchant friend who could help him handle problems when they arose. He was forced to rely on semiskilled mechanics in Kazerun and Shiraz. Although always angry and sometimes threatening violence when told of repair charges, he ultimately paid only slightly less than what he was billed. He kept, carefully wrapped in old cloth, broken engine parts and other parts that had been replaced, and he sometimes unwrapped and muttered over them. He said they had been so expensive he could not afford to throw them away.

The second setback came without warning as Borzu was attempting to clear up all outstanding affairs with officials in Kazerun, to avoid having to return during the migration or, worse, while faraway in summer pastures. One day gendarmes came to a merchant's shop to leave the message that Borzu should report to headquarters. A Lur peasant in a village near Wide Mountain had formally charged that Borzu's camel had bitten his son and driven him insane. While the case was a simple one, compared with most of Borzu's others in which many parties and long complicated histories were involved, the new one did receive support from powerful men in Arzhan Plain who were still angry about his extended sojourn at Wide Mountain in the autumn and their inability to extract more money from him. Also unlike other cases, Borzu lacked evidence to support his own position. While resident at Wide Mountain he had heard that a camel had bitten a village boy, but no one had ever asked him for restitution, and no one he knew had witnessed or verified the biting. The allegedly insane boy was an only son upon whom his elderly father depended for a livelihood, which complicated the case. Borzu did not worry as much about the case's outcome as about the inconvenience. The gendarmes were somewhat sympathetic about his imminent departure and told him they would hold the case until he returned in autumn.

Nine days before the beginning of spring Abdol Hosain came to Borzu's camp to help his shepherd Borj Ali move back to Molla Balut in order to prepare for the migration. Narges came along to intervene in case her two sons fought, but Borzu was in Kazerun and did not witness the departure. The next day men from Khalifeh's camp and some others moved their herds into the mountains above Dashtak, the first stage in their own departure from winter pastures. Their tents and families temporarily stayed behind, and the men fended for themselves on the mountaintop, cooked their own food, and slept in the open. Older children brought bread and supplies to them. A pack of five wolves attacked their herds one night, killing five sheep, carrying off a sixth, and injuring others.

Just before leaving Dashtak, the men had driven their herds between two brush fires by beating pans, stomping their feet, and shouting, "Winter, go away!" The ritual marked their escape from cold weather and chased away evil spirits. The heat of the fires symbolized the warm days ahead. When conditions for pastoralism were better, this ritual marked the move from the winter campsite to the spring campsite in winter pastures and was performed sometime after the forty-fifth day of winter.

A few days later Borzu's cousin Abdol Rasul came to tell him that he would soon migrate with his brothers. Borzu appreciated the gesture and the implied respect offered, and he informed him about the location of water and straw at the stages ahead. He had been furious at the men who had left Dashtak without telling him or seeking his "permission." His calm reaction to Abdol Rasul's stated intentions indicated what he expected from others.

Borzu came up with a new plan. According to his calculations, water in his basins at Dashtak would last only four days. Then, for four more days he would bring water by truck from Kazerun, and then he would begin the migration via the southeastern route across the mountain passes. The next day, with the news of the departure from Dashtak of still more families, he became quite agitated again and rethought his plan. His kinsman Abul Hasan came to him about a legal problem at the courthouse in Kazerun, but Borzu told him he would tend to it later and resumed his silent deliberations. He was interrupted by Yadollah who reported that Borzu's prize camel, a fifteen-year-old male, had fallen and would not get up. The two men tried to raise him but were unsuccessful, and Borzu noted with concern that camels in this state never stood again. Later he returned to dig a hole by the camel and, with help from men visiting, tried unsuccessfully to push him into the hole to get him on his feet.

Accompanying his pack animals loaded with possessions, Abdol Rasul passed by Borzu's camp on his way south and shouted at people there that he was leaving, that his water basin was empty. He asked where Borzu was but kept on moving. Borzu, in the tent, did not want to confront him and made himself absent. Abdol Rasul's departure caused him to reconsider his plans, for the man and his brothers had always been the most loyal of his kin. Borzu contemplated sending his herds and camels into the mountains above Dashtak where some others already were, moving his household and infirm animals to Molla Balut, and then migrating southeast after a few days. He said he was not ready to leave Dashtak because his animals were too thin to travel, but he understood that he would soon be alone, an untenable position for a headman. He kept hoping rain would fall, but there was no sign of it in the sky or in the animals' behavior. Borzu sent Mohammad Karim into the mountains to appraise the grazing there.

Part of Borzu's problem in making a decision concerned the ewes and does and their young. His daughters had recently begun to milk the goats and were about to begin to produce yogurt, the first milk product, from which other products derived. Borzu wanted and needed milk and yogurt as food for himself, his family, and guests. If he separated his herds from his household, he wondered who would tend the still-nursing lambs and kids and who would milk the does. Young animals needed special care and protection from predators and could not stay with the main herds day and night. Borzu could not keep them at home, however, because they needed to nurse, and he could not move his whole household to the mountains above Dashtak because no vehicular road existed.

At the same time that Khalifeh and other men had taken their herds into the mountains above Dashtak, Sohrab and his campmates began their own migration by traveling southeast and crossed over the Pass of the Old Woman. At Seven Girls, where Sohrab planned to stay for a few days to restore the strength of his pack animals, seven of his camels died, apparently from the exertion expended while crossing the difficult pass. News of this disaster hit people at Dashtak hard, for they said the health of their own animals was the same as Sohrab's had been.

In the midst of this decision-making process Khodabakhsh announced that he would not migrate with Borzu, that he planned to stay at Dashtak to help his mother and siblings. His shepherding contract ended the last day of winter. This was an impossible time for Borzu to find a new shepherd, and so, by promising Khodabakhsh that his brother Alibakhsh could harvest a plot of grain at Molla Balut (and hence receive a portion of the harvest), Borzu convinced him to stay on as goat herder until they reached Wide Mountain.

The same day Yadollah's wife Golabshar staged a silent protest beside the fire in Borzu's tent. For weeks Yadollah had asked for the flour, tea, and sugar due to him according to his contract, and Borzu kept putting him off. The family of five had completely run out of food, and other families for whom Yadollah tended a few camels had long ago made their payments. Unless she was performing a chore, a hired herder's wife would never sit in the owner's tent in his presence and certainly not in the place reserved for prestigious guests. But there Golabshar sat, nursing her baby and never saying a word. Her strategy worked, for Borzu eventually passed a few bills of small denominations to Falak to give to her. The next day Golabshar, carrying her baby, walked to Kazerun to buy flour and dates. Never before in anyone's memory had a woman from Dashtak gone alone to Kazerun.

In the morning men gathered at Borzu's tent to discuss the migration. Women heard their heated shouting from a long distance away. More dependent on Borzu than the men who had already begun to migrate, these men said among themselves that they needed to coordinate their plans with him if they were to expect his services in the future. The meeting was indecisive, but Borzu later passed the word that he had found a conciliatory plan. First he would send his herds into the mountains where others had already gone. Then, the day after the beginning of spring, his household and ten others would descend to Molla Balut for a few days while he transported their heaviest loads by truck to a merchant's storeroom at Forty Springs village fifteen or so stages from Molla Balut. He offered the transportation as a reward to men who would not abandon him. Then, with lightened loads, Borzu and his traveling companions would migrate over the two difficult passes to Killer of Cows and Wide Mountain. He absolutely refused to leave Dashtak before the first day of spring, an emotionally based decision that created difficulties for him with his group. No one else seemed to care if they migrated before then or not. The well-being of their animals was more important than some random, however symbolically meaningful, date.

A few days before spring, Khalil, one of the men residing at Dashtak who originated from other subtribes, came to pay his respects and offer a chicken to Borzu. Asserting his authority, Borzu kept him busy all day doing chores around camp. A Kezenli Darrehshuri man, Khalil had stayed at Dashtak year around for six years. He planted and harvested Borzu's wheat and barley at Molla Balut in exchange for use of pastures. Borzu supplied the seed, a mule for plowing, and a small sum of money, and Khalil kept a quarter of the harvest. Khalil transported the straw to huts at Borzu's winter campsite and the grain to the safety of a merchant's storeroom in Kazerun. He owned a few donkeys and thirty-five goats, tended by his children while he performed other tasks. He earned a small income by collecting sap from wild almond trees, nuts, and firewood and selling them in Kazerun.

In his youth Khalil had served as a shepherd for Jehangir Khan Darrehshuri. He fell in love with his mother's sister, a prohibited category for marriage, and eloped with her. Eventually they each returned to their respective families, and Khalil's father arranged his son's marriage to his brother's daughter. Poor and without a means of livelihood, Khalil sought help from Borzu. When he came to Dashtak with his wife and small children, they did not even own a tent or any animals. Borzu and other people at Dashtak gave them provisions, Sardar offered him space in his camp, and in time Khalil made a tent of goat hair from animals he now owned, constructed a reed screen for it (a sign of improved economic status), and soon became self-sufficient through various economic activities. He was grateful to Borzu who allowed him to stay at Dashtak and who provided him work in cultivation. Every winter he spent a day helping out at Borzu's camp.

Another man who stayed all year at Dashtak was Naser, who also came to visit before Borzu migrated. He considered himself and was often considered by others to be Qermezi and a member of Aqa Mohammadli lineage. His mother was Aqa Mohammadli; his father, a Chupankara Darrehshuri man, had served as a shepherd for Darrehshuri khans. Naser had grown up and spent his adult years with Qermezi. A few years earlier when his closest maternal relatives settled with Hajji Boa near summer pastures, he stayed behind. Then four or five households remained at Dashtak all year; now ten to thirteen stayed. The main problems in summer, he said, were malaria and the heat, but a cooling wind blew, and his family lived in a hut made of branches, reeds, and grass, which he said was cooler than a goat-hair tent. Twice a day he collected water from the well below Molla Balut. If the heat was too severe, he and other families at Dashtak traveled to the mountains above Arzhan Plain, an area they termed "little summer pastures" (as compared with "summer pastures" at high altitudes far to the north.)

Until 1965 Naser had paid rent to landowners in Davan, but since the nationalization of pastures he had cultivated crops without charge. He owned a donkey for carrying water, a calf he fed straw in the summer, two chickens, and thirty-five goats that he bred three months later than did the nomads who migrated. Kids born just before spring survived better than those born in late autumn and forced to suffer the rigors of winter. He said his goats were healthier than the animals that migrated, and he did not need at present to provide fodder for them. During summer his ten-year-old son, who served as shepherd while he collected sap and nuts for sale, took the goats to browse high in the mountains above Dashtak. Naser sadly noted that he wished he could send his son to school.

The other Aqa Mohammadli man who remained at Dashtak all year was Amir Hosain. He had been an avid nomadic pastoralist until, in a youthful prank, he stole apples from a tree at Zain Ali, a saint's tomb near Hanalishah in summer pastures. The tree and its harvest fell under a religious trust. Early the next spring when his kin were ready to leave winter pastures and migrate back to summer pastures, he could not face returning there. He said he had brought shame on himself and his family. Since then he had never left winter pastures. He was married to Khalifeh's daughter, whose family regretted her predicament and the severe climate she suffered every summer.

On the final day of winter, a blind Persian moneylender named Kalayaz (short for Kerbala'i Ayaz) came from Kazerun to Borzu's tent on the rounds he made of Qermezi territory to remind men of their debts and the terms of repayment. Borzu asked for and received an extension of credit. Kalayaz also hoped to buy weak and injured animals. Like merchants, itinerant peddlers, and skin and meat buyers, he took advantage of the nomads by offering them a pittance for animals they could not take on the migration. With his brother who usually escorted him, Kalayaz went to check on the status of Borzu's large camel, still not on his feet, and tried to negotiate with Borzu about the animal's disposal. Borzu was still hopeful the camel would stand and tried again unsuccessfully to force him to rise. He ordered Golabshar, weaving by her tent, to find fresh camel thorn and chop it up for the animal.

Falak and Zolaikha disassembled in a great disarray the tent's baggage to sort through and then pack items for storage with Kalayaz in Kazerun. Borzu told the herders' children to sweep the animal pen and fill several gunnies with droppings, which he would deliver to a merchant in Kazerun who used this fertilizer in his orange groves. From the pace of activities in and around camp, people saw that he intended to migrate soon, but he still had not announced when. That evening a little rain fell.

Clear skies greeted Borzu and his family in the morning, the first day of spring and the beginning of the Iranian New Year. He abandoned his idea of staying longer at the winter campsite, a decision reinforced by news that few of the families who planned to migrate were still at Dashtak. Basins were muddy and practically empty, so he sent his daughters to the well below Molla Balut and reminded them to gather news about the locations and plans of others. Sulking, Borzu muttered that he had been abandoned. He told Mohammad Karim to go to Khalifeh's camp to ask for meat, but the son returned saying that no one there had killed an animal to commemorate the New Year. The camp's men and herds had already left Dashtak, as Borzu had of course known, and only women and children remained behind. Men, not women, would have decided to slaughter an animal for the New Year.

Seeking practical solutions to the problem he faced, Borzu devised yet another plan for the migration. Because, he said, he thought more rain had fallen near Polo Field Canyon than at Molla Balut (based on a report from Falak's brother who had taken his herd toward the canyon), he would migrate northwest rather than southeast as he had previously announced. He would travel for ten days to Killer of Cows on the other side of the mountains, by way of Polo Field Canyon, a route he said was easier on the pack animals. There the families who would travel over the Pass of the Girl to the east would join him. He had planned to go southeast himself, but having to follow the others irked him. The new plan enabled him to arrive at Killer of Cows first, benefited as he would be by truck transport. By going via Polo Field Canyon, he could travel along with his herds, a contact he always sought. If he had sent his herds into the mountains above and taken his family by way of Molla Balut and the Pass of the Girl, he would have been separated from them for many days. Orchards at Polo Field Canyon would provide fresh grazing for his herd and pack animals. He had never taken this route before, and some were surprised by his decision. Men who needed his help on the migration and in summer pastures complained that his change of plans meant that they too had to migrate by way of Polo Field Canyon, which to their annoyance meant backtracking.

For the New Year's meal, Borzu selected after some hesitation a year-old kid from his herd and killed and butchered it himself, a task he always gave to others. The day being significant to him, he took on the task personally. First he cut up the liver, kidneys, and heart, placed the pieces on a skewer and wrapped cleaned intestines around them, and broiled them over a fire until they were crisp. He gave Falak the head and legs, and she would later singe off the hair and stew these parts in water and herbs for lunch the next day. Zohreh and Farideh collected the stomach, lungs, and other internal parts and roasted them for themselves. Then Borzu broiled four skewers of red meat, and everyone in the family shared the kebab, a rare occurrence. Later they ate rice and a meat stew. He had bought in Kazerun an item of new clothing for each family member and for each herder (as stipulated by contract). New clothes marked the New Year and also served to improve the appearance of his family and hired workers during the migration, when they would be in the public eye and represent him and his position.

Families enjoyed being together on New Year's Day. Ali's family cried together for Haidar "lost" somewhere in the army, and Jehangir's family was disappointed that he had not come from Kazerun to spend the day at home. The day before the New Year, most families (but not Borzu's) commemorated their dead with a simple meal and an Arabic prayer.

Another customary New Year's practice was branding new lambs and kids, but because of the nomads' haste to escape Dashtak they had decided to wait until the spring migration was under way. The New Year was ordinarily a time of happiness, and the nomads wanted to postpone the task until environmental conditions were better. By branding lambs and kids, their owners symbolically declared that they expected them to survive, which at this point was still uncertain. (Similarly, parents did not name their newborn children until the perilous first forty days of life had passed.) But the owners could not wait too long because of the danger of losing these unmarked animals to thieves in alien territory. People packed with their baggage a few pieces of the well-dried wood they had saved since the end of autumn for the branding fires and would burn them later.

In the afternoon Borzu sent word to the nearest families that he needed help with a fallen camel. What he really wanted was some response to his new plans for migrating. Only his cousin Morad came, and Borzu was disappointed. Again he tried to push the camel upright and failed. He struggled with the dilemma. Should he try to load the camel into the truck and carry him to the camp of someone staying at Dashtak? Should he kill him and sell the meat to Kalayaz (who had again stopped by and was quietly listening)? Should he leave the camel where he was and ask others to check on him periodically?

Late that night, sitting alone by a dying fire, Borzu decided he was going to leave the next day, not the day after. He shouted everyone awake to tell them to begin assembling and packing goods. After they all tiredly complied and then relished a few more hours of sleep, he woke up everyone again and ordered the dismantling of the tent and its wrapping for storage. Zohreh reported that one of their two mules was missing, and Borzu complained that it had fled to avoid the work ahead. He muttered that the mule was no better than Khodabakhsh who had threatened to bolt on the first day of the migration. The family's white horse, always inseparable from the mule, ran off in search of her companion.

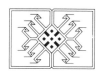

Spring

By dawn Yadollah had corralled Borzu's camels and kept watch on them as he finished dismantling the large winter tent. He unfastened the side panels, removed and rolled up the reed screens and lamb pen, and then knocked loose one by one the stakes holding the tent's guy ropes. The accumulated soot from the winter's indoor fires fell from the roof with each blow. Suddenly the roof and poles crashed to the ground, raising a billow of soot and dust. Goods inside the tent had not yet been packed, and Zolaikha pulled baggage out from underneath the heavy roof as Yadollah detached the ropes and folded it up.

Some days earlier, in preparation for migrating southeast, Borzu had taken the summer tent out of storage in Kazerun and instructed Aliboa, camped near Molla Balut, to pick it up. With plans now to migrate in the opposite direction, Borzu sent Zohreh with a donkey to Molla Balut to retrieve the tent and bring it to camp. With help from Mohammad Karim, Yadollah loaded the heaviest, bulkiest baggage into the pickup truck. Borzu shouted instructions to Zolaikha about items to store in the huts (barrels, reed screens, a camel saddle, poles) and then ran to the truck yelling to Mohammad Karim and Falak to hurry. Anxious to be off, Borzu did not look back as his son awkwardly maneuvered the truck around and headed slowly up the hill away from the winter campsite.

Yadollah rounded up Borzu's camels again and loaded them with baggage. Zolaikha and Hosain Ali, Khalifeh's son who had been sent to render assistance, helped him. While Khodabakhsh packed miscellaneous goods on donkeys, Zolaikha searched once more inside the huts for small items tucked into the roofs' branches and reeds. With a laugh and for no apparent reason, she tossed away the stem of the water pipe her mother enjoyed. With pack animals none too securely loaded, the assembled

174

25. Borzu's winter tent being dismantled

group struggled up the ravine and toward the north. On the way out, Zolaikha remembered forgotten items and ran back to recover them. Katayun and Golabshar were already scavenging in the mess left behind in hopes of finding something useful. No one gave final glances or expressed sadness in leaving the winter campsite. Passing by a basin, Yadollah watered the camels from troughs made of split metal barrels and then threw out the remaining water because he considered it unhealthy for other animals.

Hosain Ali waited by the basin as Borzu's pack animals traveled by. As Zolaikha hurried past him, she was overcome by the desire to linger, and she returned once more to the campsite on the pretext of retrieving some copper pots left behind, which everyone had seen but ignored on their departure. Zohreh, who had just arrived with the summer tent, was old enough to know that her sister ought not to be alone with Hosain Ali, however innocent their meeting would be, and she reminded her that someone from Aqaboa's or Yadollah's family would collect the pots when they left. Not dissuaded, Zolaikha enjoyed an hour with Hosain Ali while they slowly made their way to the new site, out of view of people traveling ahead and behind.

Passing by abandoned campsites at Dashtak, Borzu in the truck and his campmates following on foot saw vividly how delayed he was in leaving winter pastures and how the other nomads had left him behind. While urging the camels forward, Yadollah sadly noted their weakness and expressed concern about their fate during the sixty days of hard traveling ahead.

Ordinarily, several weeks or more before the spring migration and as the weather became warm, Borzu moved from his winter campsite to a spring campsite at Dashtak. The move offered him a clean spot away from accumulated animal dung, rotting animal carcasses, and swarms of insects. During a leisurely period at the spring campsite, he could store goods in Kazerun and at the winter campsite in a more organized way than had been possible this day.

The first day's trip was short, less than an hour for the pack animals, but necessary to test loads and permit returning to the winter campsite if needed. As at the beginning of the autumn migration, the first move was of special significance. The nomads customarily held a small celebration of "changing the stones" when they arrived at the new site. Borzu had chosen a campsite in a small ravine just past the vacated winter campsite of Falak's brothers. It was one the brothers used in autumn, and Borzu said its shelter would protect them in case of rain. As his first gesture, he instructed his son to dig the fire pit deeper and make a fire for tea. After he spread out a carpet under the trees, he prepared kebab on a skewer for himself and sat in the sun to watch his home being reconstructed. He sent Mohammad Karim and Hosain Ali by mule to get water, Golabshar to find browse for the camels, and Zohreh to pull wheat stalks growing in the fields of Davan peasants for the horses. Now that he was leaving the area, he was not much concerned about raising the ire of cultivators. While he repaired an old reed screen he wanted to use for the base of the tent during the migration, to conserve a newer one for summer pastures, he discussed his plans for the migration with three Qermezi visitors. In his usual fashion he soon enlisted their help in the repair.

Borzu instructed Yadollah to turn the summer tent, ordinarily flat-roofed and open along a wide side, into a winter tent. Because of the possibility of rain, he wanted the roof to slope and told Yadollah to use ordinary tent poles, the special boards for this purpose already stored at the winter campsite. One narrow end of the tent became the entrance, and its panel along with the repaired reed screen was used to close the side ordinarily left open. Used to the privacy of the huts at the winter campsite, Falak and her children now had to share the tent with Borzu and his guests and visitors. When he was present, they entered and exited the tent by the lamb pen in the back. A rock wall constructed by a former occupant served to shelter the tent's entrance. Zolaikha dug another fire pit just outside the tent for cooking.

The rest of the day kinsmen and others formally visited Borzu, and they discussed the months to come. Some would migrate with him while others had formed new alliances. Still others planned to remain in or near winter pastures. Ali's son Askar arrived with four donkeys loaded with bulky, heavy baggage that he would take to summer pastures by bus. Short of labor and pack animals, his household was unable to carry all its possessions on the migration. Borzu had offered to transport these goods to Kazerun by truck, as part of an informal agreement he had made to encourage Ali to migrate with him.

Borzu's herds remained with their shepherds near the winter campsite to drink the water still in the muddy basins, and milking was postponed until late afternoon. While Khodabakhsh searched for a lost goat, Borzu told Mohammad Karim to herd in his place. Borzu mixed sugar-beet pulp with the last of the straw from the winter campsite and fed it to the neediest animals.

Early the next morning Borzu woke to find the mule and horse, missing for a day (and no one had even sighted them from a distance), casually eating the remnants of pulp and straw in front of the tent. Packing up and leaving the winter campsite had taken more than six hours, but preparation for the second day's move took less than two. Askar, who had stayed the night and would be driven to Kazerun with his baggage, helped with packing. Yadollah loaded the errant mule with firewood for the stages ahead where fuel was lacking. Unlike the previous day, Borzu remained in camp until all goods were loaded and then drove by truck to the next site, again not far away and less than an hour of traveling time for the pack animals. The new site was located at the very northern edge of Dashtak territory by Hasan's vacated winter campsite. Ears perked and nostrils spread open, the pack animals spotted the green wheat fields of Davan peasants and ran headlong toward them. Borzu's daughters reluctantly chased them away. Borzu later remarked that he would send Khodabakhsh at night to pull up some of the crop for the animals. He shouted abuses at four Persians herding donkeys loaded with wood from the upper reaches of the territory. He complained that Dashtak did not really belong to the Qermezi group at all and that other people invaded the area as soon as he left.

Several families committed to migrating with Borzu camped nearby. Borzu sent Zohreh and Yadollah to fetch water, and Askar helped to pitch the tent, again with a sloped roof but now with one long side left open as an entrance. Zolaikha set up the lamb pen next to the women's side of the tent outside for the first time. Needing to discuss plans with other men, Borzu stood on top of a nearby hill within sight of several tents. This stance serving as a signal, men joined him on the hilltop, a traditional place for discussions that required no host or hospitality and was out of the range of women, children, and especially non-Qermezi visitors.

The blind moneylender Kalayaz stopped by Borzu's tent again. On his rounds of Dashtak, he had purchased three injured goats and sheep that could not travel, and he offered Borzu salt worth a dollar in exchange for the sick camel he had finally decided to leave behind. Borzu reluctantly said he would collect the salt in Kazerun. He packed the truck for the trip to town with goods to store there, Ali's baggage, empty water containers to be filled, and Kalayaz's three animals. Just before leaving with Askar and Kalayaz, Borzu quietly untied a rooster strapped to the back of Kalayaz's mule and substituted a chicken he had bought from him several days earlier. The price he had paid for the chicken had irked him, and he had now acquired a better animal for his trouble. He did not inform Kalayaz, who left the mule for a peddler to lead to Kazerun, of the substitution. (A few days later Borzu had to abandon another sick camel and asked Kalayaz what he would offer. Kalayaz, smiling, said he had already paid for that camel with the rooster Borzu had taken.)

Women milked the does at noon. Two kids had been born in the past several days, and one doe delivered while waiting for the other females to be milked. Some Qashqa'i people planned animal births for early spring, but these Darrehshuri tried to avoid transporting newborn animals on the migration and planned their births instead for late autumn. During Borzu's absence, his sister-in-law Rokhsar brought dried curds as a gift and accepted fresh yogurt in exchange. Many families including hers were not yet milking their animals, for they wanted lambs and kids to benefit by all the milk. Zolaikha promptly made a rice stew with the gift. She had long ago used up her own household's supply of dried curds produced the previous summer. Zohreh collected green branches from bushes to feed the horses and mules. People in nearby tents visited one another, for this site was their last residence in friendly territory. They welcomed the day's relative relaxation, for the next day they would enter lands perceived as alien and hostile. Despite a busy day of breaking and making camp and collecting firewood and water, Katayun still found time to set up her loom and weave for an hour or so in the hope of completing a water-bag carrier for Falak. Women tried to finish weaving projects before leaving winter pastures, because they had little time for weaving during the migration and because the finished product suffered in quality and shape when the loom was dismantled and reassembled.

Borzu returned from Kazerun with only water and a large sack of straw. He had hoped to procure supplies, especially rice, tea, and sugar, but his credit was overextended, and he was able to borrow only a small sum of money for gasoline. While Borzu checked his herds, Mohammad Karim sprayed insect repellent from an aerosol can into the maggot-filled festering wound of a goat whose horn had broken off. By bedtime rain clouds covered part of the sky, and during the night a splatter of rain hit the roof. Borzu woke up everyone to retrieve goods left outside, and Zolaikha draped cloth over the lamb pen. The mule, which had been tethered, was gone again, and her horse companion was nervously chafing at her restraining leg ropes.

The next day Borzu and the six families accompanying him left Dashtak and entered the territory of "strangers." They passed by the still-occupied winter campsites of Qarachai Qashqa'i nomads. Khosrow, son of Borzu's hired shepherd who had spent the winter near the town of Dugonbadan to the northwest, had arrived the previous night to arrange for his father to join Borzu, and he had helped to pack and load. Every day since beginning the migration an extra person had assisted in the day's tasks, a pattern that would be repeated during the next two months. Borzu needed and wanted this extra labor. His status and personality required that he do little or no physical work himself. With Mohammad Karim serving as driver, he lacked the full-time assistance his son would have otherwise (reluctantly) provided. His three hired herders were occupied with their own specific duties. Yadollah was responsible for loading, herding, and unloading the camels and then pitching the tent, but he needed help with the heaviest burdens. Borzu's wife Falak still performed no labor and relied on the sympathy of others during her recuperation. Their two elder daughters could not handle all the remaining work. It was convenient, therefore, when someone arrived, especially to stay the night, for then he was available for work early the next morning. The visitor usually traveled with Borzu's family that day and helped to set up the new camp.

People in Borzu's small group had carefully loaded and adorned their pack animals. They wanted no interruptions in the day's move caused by shifting loads, and they said they also created a pleasing sight for themselves and outside observers. Men tied heavy goods onto animals' backs and then draped on top woven pile carpets and colorful blankets that they secured with braided ropes looped through carved wooden fasteners.

Women hung equipment such as long-spouted water pitchers and wooden mortars from the ropes, and the items swung with the rhythm of the animals' gait. Many possessions had their own special protective covers and bags. Women kept bread-making equipment in a tasseled bag that they hung by a braided cord from an animal's load (and otherwise tied to a tent pole). Tea-making equipment fit into a wooden box called "a thousand things," which was adorned with brass studs and had protective velvet-lined fitted compartments for the porcelain teapot, small glasses, saucers, and spoons. Women slipped the box into a woven bag and tied it on top of an animal's load. They also secured large copper pots filled with miscellaneous items, even an infant camel, there.

The day's trip brought animals in close contact with green fields often on both sides of the path. Herd and especially pack animals were nearly impossible to control, particularly ones heavily weighted with goods and possessing their own momentum as they raced through fields, chased by their tenders, to snatch mouthfuls of greenery. Wads of ripening grain protruded from the sides of their mouths. These animals had not eaten fresh green vegetation like this grain, half a meter tall, for months. Few farmers were nearby, as these plots were cultivated by peasants living a distance away.

The spring migration was more troublesome than the autumn one because of frequent hostile encounters over real and alleged trespass in fields. All along the migratory route cultivators, almost all of whom were Persians and Lurs, stood guard during the day as the nomads passed by. They usually did not defend their fields at night (when most of the destructive activity occurred) because they feared the Qashqa'i then. One cultivator on guard at night announced he was standing vigilance against "wild boars, bears, and Qashqa'i."

Fights and arguments over animal theft and herds of different groups crowding together erupted in both spring and autumn, and the nomads were constantly on alert. People said that when Qashqa'i men had been armed, more fights had broken out and had escalated more rapidly and drawn more men. Men often discussed their skirmishes on previous migrations and pointed out places in the surrounding mountains where they had sought out thieves or taken shelter themselves. They enjoyed telling stories of tracking thieves, of how their horses had spotted or sensed the presence of thieves at night in the dark, and of how they had aimed their guns between the horses' perked, alert ears and fired.

Some women worried about the evil eye during the migration, especially in spring. They believed that evil spirits struck when strangers, prevalent all along the migratory route, were openly envious of others' good fortune. The targets most susceptible to this envy were brides, infants, young boys, camels, and rams, and most families placed talismans on them in order to avert danger. Talismans for children included antique coins, metal disks with imaginary Arabic script, salt crystals, blue beads, cowry shells, beards of wild goats, and wolf claws. People noted that the migration was a time of real peril (theft, loss, accident, attack, illness), and hence any extra protection they could provide themselves was warranted. They perceived the spring migration to be more dangerous than the autumn one because families were dispersed, camps were small, work loads were heavy, young animals were vulnerable to theft, and green fields meant conflicts with cultivators.

Members of the small Qermezi group kept their pack animals in line, usually on the same path, as they left Dashtak. They maintained a steady pace, and no one tried to pass others unless someone was slowed because of a problem with a load or animal. If help was needed, it was always offered. Each household's pack animals stayed together, and people talked with one another when afforded the opportunity. Women and older children usually walked, for they were responsible for keeping donkeys and mules out of fields. Women carried infants and toddlers and strapped small children to loads on the backs of donkeys and mules. Men and adolescent boys were responsible for camels. (Men and boys who herded sheep and goats had left before or at dawn and did not travel with the pack animals). Men who headed households usually preceded the pack animals by horse or mule so they could guide the way and select campsites.

Borzu designated the general camping area for the families traveling with him. Before he had owned motorized transport, he always checked the next day's route on horseback, and then in the morning he would gallop ahead of his own household to be in front of the caravan and to select a campsite for the group. He already reminisced about how he would travel three times the distance of everyone else in the search for a camp and how he would wave his hat on finding a spot and shout "ahoy ahoy ahoy" at the others as they came into view. Now he rode in the truck, and other families had to find him. Roads were scarce and poor, or nonexistent, a problem to be faced throughout the next two months, and already trouble was brewing between men who desired campsites on mountain slopes and Borzu whose truck necessitated access to roads and flat terrain.

The nomads descended some foothills and entered a valley that led into the Kazerun valley. Falak's brother, always somewhat independent, had already set up camp on the slope. Yadollah yelled at other men to ask where Borzu's entourage should go, and then he followed Morad to a track running along the valley floor. Borzu and his truck were at first nowhere to be seen, but then they finally appeared, and Borzu approved the site. The others, disapproving of a site by a road, remained on the slope and set a pattern that would be repeated until their arrival in summer pastures, much to Borzu's increasing irritation. He wanted to occupy a central location in a large camp so he could receive guests and visitors in the midst of the security and support of his group. The others would consistently deny him this privilege of a public display of his power, and he would not forgive them for it. His desire to offer his animals the better vegetation on the mountain slopes (which also avoided conflict with farmers who cultivated below) even, on occasion, cost him the presence of his hired herders' tents. He then camped alone on the valley floor.

Some people pitched tents, others simple shelters. Yadollah and Khosrow set up Borzu's tent with a sloped roof and one wide side as an entrance. A spring was nearby, the first time the nomads had been close to clean, clear water since midautumn. Having been responsible for the supply of water for so long, Zolaikha and Zohreh were delighted by the proximity.

Mohammad Karim had struck a boulder with the truck while trying to locate the others, and his brother Dariush was thrown into the windshield. Falak, Borzu, and Mohammad Karim argued again about his (lack of) driving skills. Neither parent wanted Dariush or especially Bizhan to ride with him, but they also did not want the two boys to suffer the long daily trips on foot or pack animal. Falak insisted that her baby Bizhan, now three years old, should not ride with his brother. Borzu was also concerned about Mohammad Karim driving in Kazerun and other towns. He lacked a license but no one ever mentioned his actually applying for one. Borzu found it ironic that he needed the truck for trips to town but could not drive there with ease for fear of his son's arrest.

Apparently lacking any specific purpose other than a meal, the moneylender Kalayaz arrived once again at Borzu's camp. He was following the small Qermezi group as it left winter pastures and his domain. Mohammad Karim had driven him to Kazerun the previous day, and people were amazed that he had managed to catch up with them so soon—on his mule, no less.

Hasan's young daughter quietly slipped up to Falak to whisper that her father needed help with an injured camel. Always willing to go anywhere to escape Borzu's commands and criticisms, Mohammad Karim accompanied her back home. He found Falak's kinsman Hasan in tears over the catastrophe. The camel, named Two Camels because of his size and the loads he was able to carry, had fallen while trying to browse on a flowering thorny shrub at the edge of a cliff and had shattered a leg. Hasan was sick at the discovery of his favorite animal crying in distress, and he could only pat and talk to him. He knew he would have to kill him but could not, and his wife had sent for help. Hasan was also in despair about the migration, for he had depended on the carrying capacity of his largest camel. He could not easily migrate with his remaining animals.

Sitting sadly on a rock overlooking the site of the accident, Hasan turned his head away as his young kinsman Darab Ali slit the camel's throat and began the long process of skinning and butchering the animal. He had cut the throat in two places, once under the jaw and again where the neck connected with the body, because of ambiguity about where exactly a ritually approved cut should be made on such a long neck to render the act, the animal, and its meat acceptable to God, according to Islamic regulations. Other men helped to butcher and lifted meat out of the crevice where the animal had lodged. Darab Ali carefully preserved the skin in one piece, in hopes that Hasan could sell it for a good price. When the men returned to their camps, they distributed hunks of camel meat to all their neighbors. Hasan gave one of the hind legs to Borzu, and Mohammad Karim and Darab Ali struggled to carry it home in the dark. Although Borzu had been asleep, he was always attentive to activity, especially unusual sounds, and he rousted Khodabakhsh to broil him kebab. The splintered end of the femur jutted through the flesh, and the meat was engorged with blood. Zolaikha had fallen asleep propped up against the baggage; she had said Borzu would order her to work when Mohammad Karim returned, and she was not mistaken.

Later that night, in the only contact Borzu's group had experienced with the Qarachai Qashqa'i nomads still in their winter camps across the valley, a woman called in the dark to ask about a lost goat. Khodabakhsh replied that he had not seen one and that she could check again in daylight. People in the tent were suspicious, but nothing seemed to be missing in the morning.

Kalayaz appeared again at dawn, piqued that Hasan had flatly refused his offer of four dollars for the camel skin and remaining meat. Zohreh placed newborn lambs and kids into folded tent panels laid across a donkey's back. By fastening wooden pins on each side of a young animal's neck, she made a small pouch to hold each animal firmly and keep it from suffocating. Unlike on previous days, Borzu's camels were the first to be loaded and begin the day's trek. Relying now on his truck to deliver him to the new campsite, Borzu was less concerned than he had been during past migrations about being the first household moving in the morning. He and Falak tricked Bizhan into riding a mule with Zolaikha, for they did not want their youngest to ride in the truck with Mohammad Karim anymore.

The youngest son, whom the Qashqa'i called "son of the hearth," was precious, especially because it was his ultimate responsibility to remain in the parental home and care for his parents in their old age, after all his brothers and sisters had left to form their own independent households. The youngest son was better treated than any of his siblings. One of life's first shattering experiences for a boy or young man was to find suddenly that his special status as "son of the hearth" had been preempted by a brand-new baby brother. Some men seemed never to get over this trauma and held grudges against the next younger brother all their lives. Abdol Hosain, and not Borzu, was Shir Mohammad's "son of the hearth."

Wheat and barley fields stretched along both sides of the route, and the pack animals ran frantically from one side to the other to grab mouthfuls of greenery on each pass. A donkey ridden by Morad's young daughter raced through a wheat field while she cried out with frustration and beat him with a stick, unable to halt his course. The morning's move ought to have taken an hour, but everyone was delayed by problems with animals. Camels often ran on downhill stretches, and one of Borzu's fell and rolled over and over on her load. Although the camel was apparently uninjured, Yadollah had to reload the baggage. He said she easily could have snapped her neck. Borzu lost the road and could be seen at a distance driving back and forth along the edge of the foothills. The intended campsite was located at the base of Davan village where the hated former landowners of Dashtak lived. Borzu finally joined his entourage. He told Yadollah not to pitch the tent. The reed screens placed in the usual shape would provide some protection from the night's cold and wind.

As Borzu supervised the setting up of camp, a Lur man from Davan came to watch the operation, guard the nearby water source, and be available for the headman's hospitality. Borzu did not know him, and he appeared to be an ordinary peasant, but Borzu treated him decently in case trouble occurred later. He sent Mohammad Karim and Zohreh to gather weeds growing in nearby grain fields. Little edible vegetation was available in the vicinity, but lush wild growth did stand at the very edges of and within the fields. At least two people from every family, men included, spent most of the day gathering weeds to bring to camp.

Two Lurs were heard yelling from a distance, and they soon came into view. One wore a white shirt with a blue two-piece suit and a turban-shaped felt hat and rode a donkey, while the other wore baggy pants, a tunic, and a felt skullcap and was mounted on a mule. They appeared to be a landowner and his sharecropper. Approaching Borzu's camp, they screamed that people and animals were devastating their fields and that the nomads must leave immediately. Borzu answered curtly that he was legally entitled to camp for twenty-four hours, he was traveling on the next morning anyway, and his people were not in fields but rather collecting weeds nearby. Before the Lurs rode off to check the fields again, the landowner's donkey spun him around six or seven times, and Borzu and the others laughed at the spectacle. A Qarachai Qashqa'i man came to oversee his own fields but was calm and courteous.

The two Lurs returned more agitated than before and yelled that they had found a mule in a field. Borzu replied that it would not happen again, but that he was certain the fault lay with Qarachai pastoralists in the vicinity or with his own group's children who did not fully understand notions of private property. He complained about always being blamed for the misdeeds of the Qarachai. All three men stressed the proper behavior of Muslims, Borzu frequently repeating, "Am I not a Muslim? We don't ruin the fields of fellow Muslims." When the Lurs asked Borzu his name, he retorted, "People call me whatever they want." After he did offer his name, they elevated his status by referring to him as "Mashhadi Borzu" and were slightly more polite. Throughout this interchange, Borzu calmly continued to mix sugar-beet pulp with water and straw. When the herds arrived, he personally supervised their watering at a source guarded by four Lurs. Borzu and the men shouted at one another for a while and then dispersed. He instructed the families camping with him to carry water for herd and pack animals to their tent sites in order to avoid further problems.

In the early evening yet another Lur man from Davan came to sit by Borzu's fire. After offering a pleasant greeting, he said he had been walking along the road when a neighbor reported that Borzu's animals were eating the crops. The visitor remarked that it could not possibly be true. Borzu again blamed the Qarachai. When another man of apparently higher status than previous visitors came to complain, Borzu lost his patience, shouted, "If you find any damage, bill me," and turned away to tend his animals. For the first time in more than eight months, they had eaten to satiation, and he was pleased.

Supper consisted of camel meat. It was tough and chewy, and Borzu said he would like to take what was left to Kazerun to have it ground. He cut meat from the bone to throw to the hungry dogs, which were rarely fed intentionally. Ordinarily they fended for themselves, scrounged for dead animals, and waited for discarded remnants of food. Whenever people ate meat with bones, dogs stayed close and attentive, menacing one another as each bone was tossed away.

Later, out of the darkness and some distance away, a Lur man shouted to Borzu to come to the road. Borzu did not answer, and no one came to the camp. He said people were still scared of the Qashqa'i, especially at night. Later still, a car stopped, and someone called many times for "Borzu Khan." No one answered. Borzu's daughters half asleep under the blankets snickered at the reference.

Borzu spent the next day in Kazerun hoping to complete transactions with merchant-moneylenders and government officials. A Darrehshuri acquaintance of Qermezi men and the father of Qahraman's first wife, Eskandar Bulverdi had sought Borzu's help in a long-running dispute with a merchant over a camel he had used to pay a debt. Borzu appeared at the courthouse on his behalf, and the case was settled in his favor. People in other subtribes occasionally asked Borzu for assistance, especially if a prior link existed between them. He was proud whenever they did so.

Borzu had overseen the breaking up of camp and then instructed his cousin Morad about the day's route. He would join his traveling companions near the entrance of Polo Field Canyon in late afternoon. The area between Davan and Polo Field Canyon was heavily cultivated, and nomads and farmers encountered one another with hostility along the whole stretch. Three families who had been traveling with Borzu took another route to avoid the congestion. Never having gone by way of Polo Field Canyon before, Morad lost the path several times and had to ask directions from cultivators. The shepherd Aqaboa, who had lived with Kash-kuli Qashqa'i nomads when he was young, said he had traveled this way "when Reza Shah was in power and there weren't any khans" (for the shah had held the khans under military control).

After proceeding for more than three hours, Morad found a place to rest and was directing everyone to unload and set up temporary shelters when men brandishing sticks ran from a small camp of tents and huts to attack him. Only Yadollah's wife Golabshar joined the skirmish, and a man struck her. Morad shouted that he only wanted his group to rest for an hour. The men, Kuruni Kurds, yelled that they held a document entitling them to the land and would not tolerate the whole Qashqa'i tribe and "two thousand" nomads descending upon them. Their concern seemed peculiar because the land was dry and barren: no cultivation, no grass, just dry brittle shrubs. Five young Kuruni shepherds waving clubs in the air arrived to help their kin, and they beat the camels to make them rise and move on. Morad tried to placate them but in the end was alone, faced with ten hostile Kurunis. Gholam Hosain and Naser remained by their pack animals and did not support Morad even with their physical presence. Each side in the fight accused the other of being infidels while claiming that they themselves were good Muslims who would not harm another Muslim's property. After the fight and during the argument, Gholam Hosain stood near Morad and then returned to his animals. Yadollah tried to enter the discussion but lacked the capacity of effective Persian speech, and he too rejoined his camels.

Force won out, and Morad moved his small tired group on. Kuruni shepherds kicked the animals that were slow to rise. Seeing that two loaded donkeys still stood behind the Kuruni men, Naser's six-year-old daughter courageously passed through the group to retrieve them. Morad set up temporary camp only a few meters away. Apparently he had crossed over an unmarked boundary that put him in territory the Kurunis did not claim. During the rest, camels and sheep grazed on the other side of the boundary without interference from the vigilant Kurunis. Morad never discovered what the original problem had been, other than the Kurunis' wanting to assert power in the face of what they viewed as oncoming hordes. For security women went in groups to collect water from a nearby channel made of rocks and cement leading from Polo Field Canyon. It was the cleanest water they had enjoyed since summer. Men and boys gathered weeds near distant fields but were careful not to trespass.

After resting and reloading, Morad's group traveled along the gravel road between Kazerun and Polo Field Canyon. From almost every car and truck that passed, someone leaned out to jeer at the nomads. People and animals were frightened of the traffic and remained in a tight group. Borzu was waiting at the entrance to Polo Field Canyon on the road leading to the ancient ruins of Bishapur. He had selected a good spacious site for himself in the narrow gorge, which left only inferior places for others. A few families traveled back the way they had come but soon returned, not having found better sites. Some reluctantly camped close to other Qashqa'i nomads who were also in the gorge, and then they took their animals to graze on nearby slopes. They always went out of their way to avoid close contact with other nomads in order to keep their animals apart. When animals of two or more herds intermingled, herders had difficulty separating them again. When the herds belonged to different groups, animals were lost and stolen.

Borzu unloaded from his truck new tent panels he had picked up in Kazerun that day. The previous summer he had given goat hair and goat-hair yarn to tent weavers in the town of Shahreza, who had just sent the completed panels by truck to the shop of a merchant in Kazerun. Borzu and the weavers would negotiate the cost of the weaving after he arrived in summer pastures. He had debated having Falak and his daughters weave the panels but then decided to contract out the task. After Falak fell ill, he was glad he had decided not to rely on her.

While Borzu was resting by the fire watching others, two Persian merchants from Kazerun drove up near his tent. They had earlier talked with him in the Kazerun bazaar about carpets and had come to see one. Borzu ordered Zolaikha, who had been pitching the tent, to spread out the pile carpet she had labored over during the winter when her mother was ill. The carpet had come to represent her distress and then her relief; she had woven talismans into it to aid her mother's recovery. She had crafted the item with care, for she expected it to be part of her dowry. As Borzu and the two men haggled over the price and method of payment, Zolaikha and her mother and sisters stood dumbfounded. They had never considered that Borzu might sell the carpet. One of the Persians told his young son to fold the carpet and put it in the car. The other Persian gave Borzu a check, and Borzu, acting embarrassed and ashamed, returned a postdated check (written for him by another Kazerun merchant) to be cashed in three months. Having had difficulty securing loans and desperately needing cash for the migration, he had borrowed money from this man earlier in the day on the stipulation that he would throw in a good carpet. On seeing it, the man said he would give him forty dollars. Borzu in essence gave away the carpet in order to get a cash loan. As the men left, they asked who owned a carpet they had seen draped over the load of a camel heading toward Borzu's camp. When Zolaikha and Zohreh went to collect water at a spring at the bottom of the gorge, they spotted the two Persians having a picnic with their families. There, under the feet of romping children, was Zolaikha's carpet laid out with food and a samovar. The sisters put their arms around each other, and tears ran down Zolaikha's face.

For the rest of the day Borzu was noticeably upset and irritated, and he perfunctorily ordered people around. While sitting at the evening fire, little Bizhan slapped his father hard in the face without warning. Borzu roughly pushed him away, and the child fell into a crying fit. Falak also wept, distressed to see her husband punish Bizhan. She was fatigued by the long day and frustrated by the loss of the carpet.

The next day's trip took Borzu and the eleven households now accompanying him through Polo Field Canyon past the ruins of Bishapur and into a valley at the eastern end. As they passed a small gendarme post, gendarmes called to the group to have Morad come forward. Morad responded, argued with them, and then bargained over the fine they said he owed because of the previous day's fight with the Kurunis. Soon the gendarmes opened their billfolds to make change for him. He paid seventy-five cents, a bribe that kept them from formally recording the fight, or so they claimed. Then the nomads traveled by Bishapur where figures carved on rock walls depicted the Sasanian king Shapur's capture of the Roman emperor Valerian in the third century A.D. Qermezi people identified (incorrectly) the figures as characters in the *Shahnameh*, Iran's epic poem of pre-Islamic origins. Ziad Khan Darrehshuri and Abdollah Khan Kashkuli owned land in Polo Field Canyon, and the nomads moving along the road by the houses and orchards remarked at the many cars there and the ornate, sparkling attire worn by women of the khans' families. They saw Ziad Khan's granddaughter Naheed sitting under an orange tree with her daughter Maral while she sewed sequins on a tunic.

Borzu was barely set up in his new camp when a Lur man came to ask for cigarettes and money. After the man left empty-handed, Borzu said he had lost sympathy for non-Qashqa'i people who claimed to have fallen into misfortune and came seeking charity. Burdened by a debt of $8,000 and having no means to pay it, he regarded himself as destitute and resented their appeals. He took Mohammad Karim with him to cut grass along the stream flowing by the ruins, and other families spent the rest of the day cutting grass and bringing it to camp for their animals. Then Borzu paid a visit to Ziad Khan. He brought along a large kid as a gift, which he viewed as his annual New Year's tribute and as payment for permission to collect weeds in the khan's orchards. Springs and streams were plentiful in the area, and women washed children and clothes. A Narrehi Darrehshuri man visited Borzu to ask for a cash loan which he promised to repay from his summer earnings from harvesting gum tragacanth. Borzu told him he had no cash. A black-turbaned young man calling himself a sayyid claimed to Borzu he was a Turk. Borzu was not deceived and ignored his request for money. A Lur man came to sell a radio, a donkey, and tobacco, and two women peddlers waited at the edge of camp until Borzu left to gather grass. A sprinkle of rain fell during the night.

Borzu spent the next day in Ziad Khan's orchards cutting grass to fill the bed of his truck. He had finished his supply of sugar-beet pulp the day before and needed fodder for the days to come. Women and children again took advantage of the respite to bathe and wash clothes. Women peddlers came with figs and herbs. Borzu had planned to travel at noon after collecting grass, but it was raining lightly and so he postponed the trip until the next day. Several Qermezi families who had camped in another location the previous day moved to Borzu's camp.

A Persian man who had wanted Borzu to sell him dung as fertilizer from the animal pen in winter pastures stopped by camp to arrange for the next winter. He argued with Borzu about why nomads did not settle. He kept claiming, "For the price of a camel, a man can build a house." Becoming agitated and defensive, Borzu insisted that the issue was more complicated than that. He said that none of them owned land on which to settle, and he could not convince the government to assist them in any way. He complained about all the bureaucratic problems he had experienced. Other men from camp seeing the jeep approach thought Ziad Khan had sent a representative, and they came to offer Borzu support. Seeing who it was, they left after a glass of tea. Borzu told Zolaikha to bake a second batch of bread to prepare for the hard trip the following day.

It rained from early morning to noon, and Borzu again had to postpone the migration. The previous day, for the first time, he had instructed Yadollah to pitch the summer tent in customary fashion with a flat roof. He noted that making this change never failed to produce rain, and he shouted to Khodabakhsh to dig a channel around the tent. Kalayaz came by mule from Kazerun to arrange contracts, one with Gholam Hosain for a mule and the other with Naser, who was heavily in debt to Kalayaz, for one hundred sheep. Borzu served as mediator, and Mohammad Karim haltingly wrote the contracts.

Many Landrovers and jeeps belonging to Qashqa'i khans, government officials including Bahmanbaigi, and other notables passed by on the road leading to Polo Field Canyon. The day before, Ziad Khan had noted that the commander of Iran's gendarmerie was coming with a large escort to arrange for wheat to be sold on credit to the "hungry tribes" at a price much lower than current bazaar rates. Men of wealth and power descended on his house to hear about the plan and find profit for themselves. For a while Borzu delayed going, intimidated by the company at Ziad Khan's, but then he too went, unable to resist hearing details firsthand and possibly profiting himself. When he returned to camp, he reported that the gendarme captain of the Tribal Security Force for Darrehshuri affairs would distribute wheat at low cost in the town of Arzhan Plain in a few days. He complained that someone in the large gathering had mentioned a fight he had been in many years before, and he was shamed in front of the authorities. Zeki Khan Darrehshuri had come to his defense by saying, "We all had to fight in those days."

Borzu spent the rest of the day gathering grass to load in his truck. Two girls from a nearby village came to trade during his absence. Falak's brother Hemmat, paying a social call, was no help in the transaction, and Falak ended up exchanging a large hunk of camel meat and a sheepskin for only a handful of raisins and two strings of figs. Later the girls returned to give back the meat and demand the (already eaten) fruit. Someone had apparently told them that the meat was probably impure and prohibited to eat. They were still arguing and waving the meat around when Borzu drove into camp, and Falak became agitated, afraid he would see that she had traded away meat, a precious good, and find nothing gained in the exchange. But the girls tucked away the meat just as he entered the tent, and Falak sighed in relief.

In the late afternoon Khodabakhsh reported that a farmer had confiscated some of Borzu's goats because they had reportedly trespassed in a field. Borzu sent Mohammad Karim with a large stick to retrieve them. The farmer was frightened when confronted, and while he shouted for help, Mohammad Karim drove the animals back to camp. Morad said a farmer had seized his mule, and he had fought him to retrieve it. Borzu sent his son to a small camp of gypsy metalworkers and woodworkers on the mountain slope above to get his horse reshod and a harness repaired. He gave Farideh a penny to have two wooden handles made. The gypsies identified themselves as Kashkuli and proudly wore Qashqa'i hats. They said they supervised fields in the valley below for the owners.

The next day's move was almost four hours, to make up time lost in the rain delays. A few kinsmen had complained to Borzu the previous day that their pack animals could not handle such a distance, and he sent his truck to carry their heaviest loads. Animals once again ran though cultivated fields and tried to eat crops. Pack animals chased from the fields bucked under their loads, as if in revenge, and knocked loose their baggage, which caused further delays. The group passed by heavy machinery used for road construction; road crews were in the process of extending the asphalt road west of Arzhan Plain. The nomads were impressed with the technology, and Borzu's first comment was how quickly these machines could have constructed him a road to Dashtak. Two German tourists stopped along the road to photograph the migrators.

Borzu chose a campsite away from the road. Before everyone had a chance to settle in, Lur women heavily decorated with jewelry and marked by tattoos on their faces and limbs descended on the camp from nearby villages to trade walnuts, toasted wheat, raisins, pomegranate seeds, and greens. They did not understand that little or no trading would occur until the men of the camp went elsewhere. Borzu and the other men eventually left to gather grass. He had earlier announced that he would help himself to ripening grain that night because this land used to be their pasture. Men from the nearest village guarded their fields to make sure animals stayed at the periphery. An elderly, congenial farmer presented an armload of grass to Borzu when he heard that the nomads' animals were dying. Borzu was moved by the gesture, the only friendly contact he said he had experienced along the migration so far.

Many women had filled goatskin bags with water when they passed by a spring on the morning's journey, and they all returned to the spring to collect more water. A Qerekhli Darrehshuri man who wanted to harvest gum tragacanth in Borzu's summer pastures stopped by to see him. Falak gave food to a crippled beggar who recited a few lines from the Qoran in response. Borzu and his shepherds took the herds up the mountain slopes to a stand of oak trees. They shook the trees and climbed into the branches to loosen leaves for the animals. Late that night Borzu sent Yadollah and Khodabakhsh with empty sacks to the nearest fields to pull stalks of ripening wheat. He instructed them on exactly how to do it so that little trace of their activity would remain; he cautioned them to be careful to pluck a few stalks here and a few there and not a whole patch. He told them to bypass the field belonging to the farmer who had been charitable to him.

Borzu wanted to leave early in the morning to get a head start on the Khairatli Darrehshuri nomads camped above him. He had seen the Khairatli headman's tent but neither man had visited the other. Darrehshuri headmen competed with one another for status within the tribe, and little social interaction occurred among them. They did meet when they visited the khans, the Tribal Security Force, and markets.

As he departed, Borzu gave the kind farmer a sick sheep and an empty metal container. Later in the day he remarked that this act of charity "excused" his "liberation" of grain the previous night. He said he liked to make friends all along the migratory route so that they would be available for him on the return trip and in the future. "It is good to know everyone, for a man in trouble always has a friend somewhere." Driving later with Morad to collect water, Mohammad Karim passed up a man along the road who needed a ride. Morad told him he should have stopped, for if a fight ever erupted in the vicinity, he might have had an ally.

The day's route took Borzu's group along the path of the road construction to the beginning of the asphalt road and then past Father of Hayat village where farmers were cutting their dry unripe crops of grain to salvage it as fodder. When Borzu arrived at his chosen site partway up a mountain pass and away from the road, he sent the truck back to collect empty goatskin bags from the migrating families. After people made camp, Mohammad Karim and other young men took another water run, and by the end of the day they had filled almost a hundred bags.

Traffic along the narrow asphalt road had been heavy and difficult for the nomads. Drivers of trucks and oil tankers blew their pneumatic horns as they drove abreast of them. Frightened animals ran off the shoulders where they were forced to walk, and three were seriously injured in falls. A car with an urban Persian family on its way to a picnic stopped momentarily by Katayun's pack animals, and a man reached out to untie a puppy strapped to the back of a donkey and drove off with it before Katayun completely understood what was happening. At least one person in almost every passing vehicle jeered, shouted, whistled, or made some lewd or nasty remark. Later, when shepherds arrived with the herds, they reported that people in cars and trucks had stolen eight animals. The nomads had no alternative routes as they approached Arzhan Plain because of the rugged mountainous terrain, the sharp rise in altitude, and the one narrow mountain pass. Along with many tens of thousands of other Qashqa'i nomads, they had little choice but to travel alongside the asphalt road. They often cited this stretch of the migration as reason enough to abandon nomadism. Every year traffic became heavier and drivers more hostile. With the promised extension of the road, the nomads' misery would increase. Once the nomads were past Arzhan Plain, a variety of migratory routes opened up for them, and the crowded, dangerous conditions experienced here would not be repeated.

Borzu liked his campsite for its scenic location, the adequate ground vegetation farther up the mountain slopes for the herds, and the many shrubs and almond and oak trees for the pack animals. He oversaw the arrival of the others from the edge of a cliff. Later he and other men of his group squatted on a hilltop to discuss plans. Earlier Borzu had said that the group would stay at this site for two nights, but then he decided to travel in the morning as usual in order to precede the Khairatli nomads as well as his rival Sohrab and his brother Abdol Hosain who were close by, according to a Lur man he had met at the spring. Later that night he changed his plans again. He decided to wait for a kinsman who had gone to Kazerun to get him supplies and for Abul Hasan who had hitched a ride along the highway early that morning to collect the baggage of Borzu's shepherd from the town of Dugonbadan.

Borzu spent the next day traveling by truck to Arzhan Plain for water and gasoline and to Molla Nari, a few stages ahead of their current campsite, to check on grazing and the presence of other pastoralists. People were glad for the rest and took advantage of the lull in the migration to visit one another. Young children spent the day chewing gum (gathered from wild pistachio trees found at this altitude) while sitting above the highway to watch the traffic go by.

Late that afternoon four Lurs ran into Borzu's camp yelling that his animals had ruined their barley field. One menacingly waved a club with a sharp-edged iron head. They demanded sixty-seven dollars for damage Borzu had allegedly inflicted. If he did not pay, they shouted that they would report him to the Ministry of Justice. Remaining in the cab of his truck to assert his higher status, Borzu calmly informed them that he had more friends at the ministry than they did, that the government would waste three years before it formally registered their report of his alleged misdeed, and that he would bribe the judge in the unlikely event that the issue ever reached court. Smiling, Borzu noted that because of his truck he could report their harassment before they could report his alleged offense. Finally he said, "I'll give you seventy-five cents, and let's call it quits." Daunted by this rapid enumeration of their disadvantages, the Lurs asked him to inspect the crop damage and promised to abide by the mediation of any neutral outsider. To humor them, but only after making them wait several hours, Borzu visited the field in question and then exclaimed that the crop had been ruined by the drought. He told them his economic circumstances were worse than theirs and to leave him alone. He protested that he was not responsible for damage done by other nomads. Again he offered seventy-five cents, and they were outraged. He returned to camp alone. Shortly thereafter, a farmer who had served as mediator came to ask for $1.50, Borzu gave him seventy-five cents after stalling him for hours, and the matter appeared to be closed.

Many Khairatli Darrehshuri nomads traveled past the camp, but Borzu seemed not to pay attention, even after days of worrying that he would have to follow behind them. Early in the evening an oil tanker stopped abruptly on the road, and Abul Hasan jumped out. The driver threw off the shepherd's baggage that Abul Hasan had collected in Dugonbadan and tied on top of the oil tank. Yadollah carried the baggage to Borzu's tent, and Falak inspected it out of curiosity.

It rained hard all night and into the morning, and Borzu postponed the day's migration. He gave Abul Hasan and Hasan, ready to go to Kazerun, errands to run and goods to deliver to the moneylender Kalayaz. Two peddlers, men the nomads had seen at Wide Mountain in autumn, came to trade figs. Borzu exchanged wool from his shepherd's baggage for several strings of the fruit. In a rare gesture he offered the peddlers yogurt and tea and then pressed them for information about grazing and the other pastoralists they had seen between this location and Wide Mountain. It was clear they admired Borzu, whom they saw as a man of power and wealth who could relax, entertain guests, and eat all day long. Borzu and several kinsmen drove to Arzhan Plain to inquire about the government's plan to distribute low-cost wheat. Captain Jamali of the Tribal Security Force for Darrehshuri affairs was there, as were a hundred Darrehshuri men waiting for grain.

Later, one of the Darrehshuri khans' advisors, Faraj Aqa Zahedi, accompanied by his shepherd, arrived as Borzu's guest. Borzu told Morad to kill and butcher a kid and was such an attentive host that it was clear he wanted something from his guest. He had formally introduced his son Mohammad Karim when Faraj Aqa arrived; he hoped that he would eventually be able to arrange his marriage to Faraj Aqa's daughter. To maintain and enhance his status, Borzu needed to marry his eldest son to a girl in a prominent Darrehshuri family. The daughter of a khan was out of the question (for khans married only among themselves), but the daughter of an aqa or even another high-status headman was possible. Barring these alliances to achieve status, the only possibility for Mohammad Karim was marriage to one of his father's brothers' daughters, but no one expected that this would occur.

In an attempt to demonstrate authority in front of Faraj Aqa, Borzu loudly and abruptly commanded his family and others to perform various chores, some of which had been neglected for days. They cleaned and made the lamb pen smaller and placed a reed screen in front of the tent in case of rain. The two men discussed the current race for a seat in the Iranian parliament between Jehangir Khan Darrehshuri and Amiramanollah Khan Darrehshuri (son of Ziad Khan and the ultimate winner). Faraj Aqa's shepherd leapt to his feet every time Faraj Aqa stood up, went outside, or returned to the tent, behavior required of the servants of Darrehshuri khans whose status and lifestyle the Zahedi family admired and emulated. Borzu's herders Yadollah and Khodabakhsh found humor in the

gesture and mimicked the behavior for his every rising, leaving, and returning. Borzu saw exactly what they were doing and smiled to himself.
He did not chide them afterward for their antics.

Another hard rain fell, accompanied by thunder and lightning. Faraj
Aqa did not spend the night. Looking apprehensively at the roof of the
tent, he claimed he had "important work" early the next morning. Other
than a brief visit by Morad and Falak's brother, no one came to join or
assist Borzu as host as had always occurred during the previous migration
when prominent guests arrived. Several times Faraj Aqa asked pointedly,
"Where is Qermezi?" Borzu pleaded bad weather and the necessary dispersal of his group in this rugged terrain on the slopes near the mountain
pass.

The sky was clear at dawn, and Borzu made haste to be on the road.
He was worried again about Khairatli nomads preempting his favorite
campsites, and they were already packing the shoulders of the highway.
When Yadollah brought the camels for loading, Borzu saw that a young
one had a gash on his head full of maggots and was angry that his camel
herder had not told him about the injury. Mohammad Karim sprayed
insect repellent into the wound, causing the camel pain. The route for the
day followed the asphalt highway up the steep grade of the narrow gorge,
an arduous trip for people and animals because of the terrain and the
heavy traffic. Borzu located a campsite on top of a hill by the highway
where he could view people who would camp below and around him. The
truck could not reach the site and was left at the side of the road, and he
waited for others to carry its load to camp. He made a huge fire with all
the wood he could find, this act being the first a man or woman performed
when setting up a new camp. A fire turned a potential campsite into a
home. Tea-making equipment was close by in the truck, but he would not
fetch it himself or brew himself tea.

Well before any of his traveling companions could have possibly
struggled up the gorge, Borzu went to station himself on top of a hill
below his own site to await the coming caravan. He squatted there for
several hours and seemed to enjoy himself. When the first family appeared, he shouted and gestured directions. Competing with one another,
Morad and Barat raced around the area on their horses to find good sites
and then unhappily complained about seeing none. The location itself was
attractive, and people commented how far they could see from this vantage point. They pointed out a valley, now green with wheat, through
which they sometimes migrated, and from this high altitude they could
trace their route from Dashtak. The same two German tourists, who must

have been driving up and down the highway for several days watching the migration, stopped to photograph Borzu's camp. No one spoke to them, and they finally left. Borzu sent Morad and Mohammad Karim to check the availability of water and grazing at Wide Mountain, where he hoped to camp for a few days.

Borzu often allowed his cousin and brother-in-law Morad the privilege of riding in the truck. He sometimes offered him a ride when he searched for the next day's campsite, and he also invited him on errands and other excursions. Of all the men now accompanying Borzu, Morad was his greatest source of competition and a potential threat to his authority. By regarding Morad as an advisor and assistant and by allowing him special access to his vehicle, Borzu kept him under control.

Late in the afternoon several huge herds of perhaps 450 animals apiece, owned by an urban investor and tended by Lur hired herders, passed by the camp on the highway. The tails of the sheep were heavy with fat, and members of Borzu's group marveled at their size and health compared with their own animals. These animals had spent the winter in Qashqa'i and Boir Ahmad territory and were now making a rapid twenty-day trip to Shahreza in the north where they would be quickly sold while still fat. The market was good now; prices were higher than during summer when most Qashqa'i sold animals. Borzu noted with irritation that these hired herders would probably stop at Wide Mountain on their way, and he said he hoped grazing would be left for his group.

Borzu sent Zohreh to pull green stalks from the edges of nearby barley fields, but she returned with little more than weeds. Mohammad Karim trucked in water; no water was close by. Aqaboa's brother arrived in camp to borrow two donkeys so his family could migrate to summer pastures. He had earlier planned to stay in the vicinity of Dashtak and Arzhan Plain all summer, but environmental conditions, expected to be poor, were worsening. (He ended up migrating no farther north than Arzhan Plain.)

Borzu caused another delay in the migration by making a trip to Shiraz. The Ministry of Justice had summoned him, the truck needed repair, and several Qermezi people required identity cards. Truck parts and mechanics would not be available from the point when Borzu traveled past Shiraz until he reached Semirom. He dropped Morad at Arzhan Plain so he could check on the schedule of the government's distribution of wheat; an official said it would be available in three days. The weather was cold at the higher altitudes of Arzhan Plain and all the way to Shiraz, and nomads traveling along the road looked miserable. Dead herd and especially pack animals littered the roadside, and no new vegetation grew.

Borzu saw that he ought to slow down the migration to wait for warmer weather. He was now glad for the day's delay, about which he had worried before. The previous day had been warm and sunny, and fresh green vegetation was appearing at the lower altitude of their present campsite. Past Arzhan Plain Borzu saw the German tourists again, the man driving a Volkswagen bus slowly along the road with five goats strapped to the roof's luggage rack and the woman walking behind a group of nomads.

Rain fell heavily for two days on Borzu's group, and then people moved to Wide Mountain where everyone suffered from the worsening weather. Earthquake tremors struck the region, and the nomads were glad to be living in tents and not houses. Injuries and property damage were reported for some nearby villages. The group found a new campsite at Wide Mountain, under threat from gendarmes, themselves pressured by local landowners who complained that the nomads had overstayed the twenty-four-hour limit. Several days previously Captain Jamali had told Borzu that because of the animals' ill health and the drought's impact on resources along the migratory route, the government was extending the limit to forty-eight hours. The gendarmes forcing the group to move claimed they knew nothing about the extension (and during the weeks to come no other authorities acknowledged it either.) The following day Borzu's group moved near Bear Canyon where it had stayed for twenty-six days in the autumn, for people wanted to be close to town for the distribution of wheat.

A Lur landowner in Arzhan Plain filed a formal complaint against Borzu's brother Abdol Hosain for cutting grass on the mountain slope above the town. The Lur claimed the wild grass growing on government land belonged to him. Using his cousin Abdol Rasul as mediator, Abdol Hosain sought Borzu's assistance. Gendarmes tore up the Lur's complaint and declared that the grass belonged to no one. They did note that Abdol Hosain had exceeded the twenty-four-hour limit on grazing and must move his camp the next day unless it rained. Borzu guaranteed to them that Abdol Hosain would comply.

Borzu was also arbitrating a dispute for Falak's kinsman Hasan who had lost a sheep near the beginning of the asphalt road. Hasan had accused a Lur herd owner and his Khairatli Darrehshuri shepherd of stealing the animal, and the Lur took the case to the Tribal Security Force. The Khairatli shepherd, who kept his own animals in the herd he tended, claimed he owned forty sheep, but the gendarme who investigated, with Borzu as witness, saw that thirty-nine of them were not branded and the fortieth had Hasan's brand. The gendarme seized the animal and returned it to Hasan.

Many Darrehshuri men and women waited in the town of Arzhan Plain. A power struggle among Captain Jamali's Tribal Security Force, the regular gendarmes, the army, provincial officials, and local figures such as headmen and landowners was impeding the distribution of low-cost government wheat. Jamali wanted to provide each subtribe its allotted grain as it passed through the area, but he was experiencing difficulties because members of subtribes did not migrate together in discrete groups. He required subtribal headmen to be present every day to identify group members and verify family size. Responsible for most Qermezi families and others associated with the group, Borzu would be trapped for eleven days by the worsening fiasco. His rival Sohrab, responsible for the other Qermezi families, also waited in Arzhan Plain. No family had yet received any grain. At one point Borzu shook a gendarme and exclaimed, "The government provides this wheat, not you personally, so release it!" Every time he was late returning from town, Falak worried that he had fought with the gendarmes and had been arrested or even shot. At the moment the government was distributing only small quantities of hay and barley, both intended as fodder. Officials said they were enabling the nomads to restore the health of their animals and migrate safely to summer pastures. The amounts supplied were too small to achieve this end, but the nomads were still anxious to acquire what they could. Qermezi's turn had not yet come.

The weather was cold and windy, and it had rained on and off for days. Khodabakhsh lost two goats, and Falak's brother sent a son to tend the goat herd while Khodabakhsh searched. He returned empty-handed two days later. In the meantime the young substitute herder and Yadollah lost three more goats. Theft was suspected, especially given the many nomads congregating near Arzhan Plain for the wheat distribution. Wide Mountain was crowded with nomads and their animals. Local villagers, passersby, and the nomads themselves took advantage of the congestion.

Borzu planned to move his camp closer to Arzhan Plain, but the continuing rain impeded him. Qermezi men traveling with him as well as others ahead and behind spent the days in town. Men who stayed at Dashtak all year arrived to receive a share of the government largess.

Despite the drizzle of rain, a happy Zolaikha surrounded by excited children set up the tripod for churning the first sour milk of the season. She attached a goatskin bag that she half filled with yogurt and water.

Then she built a fire, and when the burning wood had turned to coals, she moved the tripod over the fire pit. She spent a long time readying the apparatus, fixing this and adjusting that. After uttering "in the name of God," she began to propel the suspended goatskin bag back and forth over the coals. Heat helped to sour the yogurt further. When butter was churned by the same process beginning several weeks later, heat would help the butter rise to the surface. A wide grin crossed Zolaikha's face, and children jumped up and down with anticipation. Periodically she added water, and soon, after dipping in a finger and taking a taste, she declared the sour milk ready and offered sips to everyone. The first sour milk of the season was supposed to be too sour, but no one minded.

It was another cold night. In the early morning Amir Hosain, a year-around resident of Dashtak temporarily in camp to wait for wheat, helped Borzu's household pack. The nomads had gathered firewood at Wide Mountain to use during the days ahead when fuel was scarce. With the processing of milk products gearing up, needs for fuel increased, but the extra weight and bulk complicated the task of loading the animals. The mule had abandoned camp to search for the mare Borzu's son-in-law had borrowed, and the other pack animals were overloaded as a result. Borzu drove to Arzhan Plain so he could organize men to chop firewood for the gendarmes at their request.

The day's route took the nomads past Molla Nari, out of the mountains above Arzhan Plain, across the highway, and into the plain in front of the town. People traveled past vacant campsites, some littered with animal carcasses left to rot in the sun. Yadollah's dog scavenged a sheep head and carried it in its mouth the whole trip. Borzu sent Mohammad Karim with the truck back to meet the pack animals and retrieve the tent and poles from Yadollah, for he wanted to pitch the tent before rain began again.

Four army buses full of young soldiers watching "the tribes" pass by were parked on the shoulder of the highway near Arzhan Plain. When Borzu asked what the army was doing, Captain Jamali replied that the government wanted conscripts to see for themselves what tribes looked like, so they would not be afraid when they confronted them. These conscripts were then sent to Kurdistan.

Borzu's daughters arrived at the new camp to face a rare sight: a tent already in place. The plain was filled with the new tender growth of wild prickly artichokes, and Borzu had already eaten some of the leaves, which he had picked himself and tossed into the fire to cook. With Zolaikha's arrival, he called for yogurt and stirred in the steamed plants to make a tasty lunch for himself. He extracted a leech from the horse's mouth and marveled at how much blood the worm had ingested. Khodabakhsh, whom Borzu had sent once more to search for the five lost goats, found them in two herds belonging to Khairatli nomads and retrieved them. Borzu spent the rest of the day in town.

People from Dashtak who had migrated southeast over the Pass of the Girl met up with Borzu's group in Arzhan Plain. While men waited in town, women were free to visit one another. Rarely were all the men gone at once. In the past when fights between groups had been common, women said, men were gone more frequently. Women compared stories about the events of the past twenty-some days. Some wept over the weakness of their pack animals and the difficulties of the migration so far. They wondered how they would transport the wheat the government had promised to sell them. Women and children spent part of the day gathering wild artichokes and gave bowls of the greens, cooked and prepared in different ways, to each other. Women who ordinarily possessed little to give, being too poor, gave wild artichokes. Women giving artichokes returned home with artichokes given by others. Late in the afternoon rain fell again, and a hard chilling wind blew.

Borzu returned from town after dark to report that it had been Qermezi's turn to receive wheat that day, but that no one had received any because Captain Jamali had been in Shiraz. Within a few minutes of Borzu's arrival, his cousin Allahyar came to report that Jamali, just returned, had summoned Borzu to come immediately. While in Shiraz, Jamali had been told by his superiors to prepare for the visit the next day of the commander of the gendarmerie of Fars province who wanted to observe "the tribes" receiving government assistance. According to Allahyar, Jamali was asking Borzu to bring herds and baggage to Arzhan Plain early the next morning so that the brigadier general could see hungry animals being fed government fodder and nomads' possessions being loaded into government trucks for transport to summer pastures. Borzu did not believe what he was hearing, and people sitting around the fire suspected that Allahyar had mixed up the message. Allahyar had come by gendarme jeep, and Borzu went to talk with the driver who readily confirmed the story. He reported that Jamali had hurriedly chosen several Darrehshuri headmen, including Borzu, to provide the people, animals, and baggage for the display. Borzu invited the two gendarmes to his tent for wild artichokes and yogurt and then returned to Arzhan Plain with them.

As the jeep pulled out of camp, people from surrounding tents came to see what the gendarmes had wanted. Some feared Borzu had gotten into a fight in town. Around midnight Borzu returned to camp with two large sacks of hay, one in payment for his bringing herds to Arzhan Plain the following morning and the other taken on his own initiative. The night was bitterly cold and uncomfortable.

At dawn Borzu hurried to go to Arzhan Plain again. The day's planned migration was postponed. He had instructed Aqaboa to remove goats from the sheep herd and drive the sheep to the outskirts of town to await his orders. Government officials had recently proposed regulations that would ban goats from all government land including nationalized pastures; they currently disapproved of the animals because, they said, their eating habits destroyed the environment. (Sheep graze on ground forage while goats browse primarily on shrubs.) Captain Jamali had emphatically declared that no one could bring goats to town. Aqaboa, who kept his own few goats in the herd of sheep he tended for Borzu, put them into Khodabakhsh's herd for the day along with the large male goats that always led the herd. He said it would be difficult to herd the sheep without the lead goats.

Government officials and local notables in Arzhan Plain hastened to prepare the town for the arrival of the dignitaries. Early in the morning Captain Jamali had been told that the governor-general of Fars and other provincial authorities would accompany the gendarme commander of Fars. His growing anxiety added to the rush to prepare for the visitation. For reasons he said he did not totally understand, the government's plan to distribute low-cost wheat to hungry tribespeople, supply fodder for hungry animals, and transport people, sheep, and baggage to summer pastures had apparently attracted wide attention. People in the government-controlled media were said to be coming.

The dignitaries were expected at nine in the morning. At noon the brigadier general arrived with a military escort and a government television crew to record the events. None of the other expected officials appeared. One hundred Darrehshuri men and women, in separate lines as Captain Jamali deemed appropriate and had ordered, received vouchers enabling them to collect wheat. With some unexpected semblance of order, herders and gendarmes fed barley to four herds of sheep and then loaded them into double-deck trucks. Gendarmes piled the baggage of twenty Darrehshuri families into large army trucks for the promised transport to summer pastures. Under Jamali's escort the brigadier general passed down a line of local officials and notables and then was filmed watching the completion of the staged activities. When he walked by the truck loaded with Borzu's herd, Borzu told him falsely, as Jamali had previously instructed, that his sheep had eaten government-issued straw for seven days and were no longer starving and that he was grateful to the government for help in moving to summer pastures.

The brigadier general and his party were in Arzhan Plain for less than ten minutes, and his observations took only five. In a cloud of dust he was gone. Gendarmes drove the trucks loaded with people, baggage, and sheep to the outskirts of town, turned around, and returned to unload them. Borzu and the other animal owners had understood that the sheep would not actually be transported anywhere, that the deception was occurring in order to place memorable images in the general's mind and on film for television. Families with loaded—and now unloaded—baggage had not been told that they would not actually be transported anywhere, and they expressed anger at the duplicity. They had expected to be in summer pastures the next day and had made complicated arrangements for animals and baggage they were forced to leave behind with still-migrating kin. Armed soldiers surrounded the increasingly hostile group and told people to disperse.

Partly because of Borzu's helpful support, Captain Jamali announced that Qermezi subtribe could be registered that afternoon for its allocated wheat. Borzu lined up the men who had gathered, identified them one by one, and declared the size of their families as Jamali and his recording secretary, a tribal teacher, passed down the line. Akbar, whom Borzu had asked to stand by during the past days, was his secretary. Borzu's rival Sohrab had assembled his own list of Qermezi families and served in the same capacity for his supporters. Gendarmes later issued vouchers in exchange for a signed promise to pay for the wheat in summer. In a few days, Jamali said, Qermezi men could collect the stipulated amount of grain from a nearby warehouse. Most men badly needed flour and would have some wheat milled in town, a service for which they would pay in grain. Some men would store part of the remaining wheat there and collect it later during the migration or after they arrived in summer pastures. Because of a desperate need for cash combined with transporting and storing problems, most men would sell some grain to local merchants at a low price reflecting the glut on the market. They said they would have to buy wheat during the migration and certainly on arrival in summer pastures at rates expected to be at least twice what they would receive in Arzhan Plain.

Borzu processed all Qermezi families before families of other origins, including hired herders, who were affiliated to him and his group. These other families almost missed their chance to receive wheat when Captain Jamali turned his attention to other subtribes, but Borzu pressured him to include them, and several days later they also received vouchers. He collected a small sum of money from most of the men he had helped, excluding the poor. He noted the unexpected expenses of having to be in Arzhan Plain so frequently, and no one seemed to mind helping him pay for gasoline.

While Qermezi men were in town, they heard that thieves had struck Arghvan's camp and stolen two ewes and their lambs and a mule and its saddle. Arghvan's campmates and eight men from Borzu's camp hurried home to get clubs and set off on foot to Jarruq Lur territory "where thieves always come from and flee to." They had suffered from Jarruq thievery for years and were always anxious to take revenge. They had wanted to travel in Borzu's truck, but he had been obliged to lend it to a Lur man in Arzhan Plain. The Lur, who had driven Borzu one day while Mohammad Karim took school examinations in Kazerun, was now using the truck to transport firewood from Wide Mountain. The revenge party returned two days later tired and empty-handed.

Mohammad Hosain arrived in camp with his family and Borzu's second herd of sheep. He had spent the winter near the town of Dugonbadan to the northwest. His wife Geljahan, collecting baggage the oil tanker had transported, proudly displayed to Falak the weavings she had completed since they were last together.

Mohammad Hosain was one of the few men of the five Qermezi lineages who served as a hired shepherd within the group and was the only shepherd of mature age. The few other Qermezi hired herders were young unmarried or newly married men. Mohammad Hosain was a grandfather and head of a household containing thirteen people. Eight years previously, as the owner of 180 sheep and goats and many camels, he had been moderately wealthy, according to Qermezi standards, and economically independent. He camped and migrated with his kinsman Ahmad Khan and other Qasemli men. During the drought of 1962 and 1963 almost all his animals died. He cultivated grain for others and then agreed to become Borzu's shepherd. He had remained loyal to Borzu when many other Qasemli men allied with Sohrab during the fight between Aqa Mohammadli and Qairkhbaili men over Dashtak pastures. To help his shepherd and encourage him to remain an employee, Borzu lent Mohammad Hosain twenty goats, their hair and milk his to keep. Until he joined Borzu on the migration, the milk from Borzu's herd was also his. Mohammad Hosain was deeply in debt, and many of his eighty sheep and goats were under nimsud contract with a Kazerun moneylender. His son Khosrow, although formally separated from him and head of his own household, lived with his wife and three children in his father's tent and assisted him. Some people considered Khosrow to be the shepherd, not his father, for he often tended the herd.

From Borzu's perspective, Mohammad Hosain was an excellent shepherd because a large labor force was at his disposal, including two adult men, three adult women, and many helpful children. The shared Qermezi affiliation, with added links of kinship and marriage, helped to produce reliable service.

Women and children went on another spree of gathering, eating, and exchanging wild artichoke thistles. Every family cooked a large pot of the vegetable, and people ate from it all day long. For one of the few times during the year, women and children had as much to eat as they wished.

That night a torrential rainstorm hit the Arzhan Plain area. By morning everyone in Borzu's camp was in a state of shock. Wind had blown apart some tents, and water had streamed into all of them, even cascading over the rocks on which baggage was stacked. Possessions were soaked. No one had prepared for rain, partly because men had been in town the previous day or were tracking thieves, but no effort could have adequately protected them from such a hard, prolonged storm. Animals had scattered, and men could not find and corral them again. Goats had repeatedly pushed into the tents and climbed on top of wet baggage to find shelter, and soon everything was covered with mud. During the night Borzu had instructed his shepherds to lash down the tent by throwing ropes over the roof and fastening them to stakes in the ground. With continuing rain and wind, these and all the other stakes loosened. Everyone feared the imminent collapse of the tent, a physical catastrophe and the worst of omens.

After sitting practically in a stupor for several hours and observing that the rain and wind were not letting up, Borzu suddenly began to talk about an evacuation to the town of Arzhan Plain. The truck made such an action feasible. Refusing to leave his herds behind, he set out on foot in the driving rain to find shelter for them at the only visible house on the plain. Its owner, a settled Talehbazli Darrehshuri man (and coincidentally a distant relative of Hafez, Borzu's former driver), agreed to make room in his outbuildings and courtyard for Borzu's animals. After Borzu sent Khodabakhsh there with the goats, which were more apt to flee and become lost or stolen than sheep, the weather worsened, and he turned his attention to the idea of moving his family and others in camp to town by truck. After several more hours of sitting deep in thought and then eating a hasty lunch in the crush of animals and distraught children, he decided to evacuate. When Mohammad Karim started the engine, a goat screamed, and shepherds ran to help. The animal had sought shelter under the truck, and its horns and hair were caught in the cables. As the goat cried, Aqaboa wrestled the frightened animal loose.

Borzu loaded the truck in a panic, not bothering to pack in the usual careful way, and the baggage became wetter and muddier. Aqaboa tied a canvas tent over the load to protect it from rain. Mohammad Karim drove Borzu, Falak, and the three youngest children toward town. He skidded and slid on the wet muddy track and then became stuck in a formerly dry riverbed. While Falak and the children, waiting in the truck, watched the water rise around them, Borzu and his son ran to the road to flag down a ride to town. There Borzu secured help from Captain Jamali, who lent him two gendarmes and a truck to pull Borzu's vehicle from the water. Borzu then took his family to the home in Arzhan Plain of the Lur man who had borrowed his truck for wood hauling. The Lur had earlier agreed to store excess baggage and surplus wheat for Borzu's group in exchange for a fee and permitted him now to use an empty room and a storeroom for the evacuees. Borzu returned to Jamali to see about aid for others still in camp.

Three hours later, in the worst rain, wind, and cold yet experienced, two trucks drove to Borzu's camp to evacuate women and children. One belonged to a distant relative whom Borzu met in town, and the other was from the gendarme post. Borzu had earlier told Zolaikha and Zohreh to locate and tether the pack animals before leaving but they did not. They did load most of the remaining valuable possessions into the trucks. The tent was left standing, and Khosrow sheltered weak and sick sheep inside. Twelve new lambs and kids huddled in the pen. Some evacuees carried only children, others a blanket or two, and a few brought quantities of baggage. If men wanted to leave, they were expected to go on their own. Only Borzu and two other men went; the others remained to guard their property. Women and children of the hired herders' families were left behind for the next trip. Because of the worsening weather, most doubted that further evacuation would be possible. All day Darrehshuri nomads struggled in the rain back to their camps after having waited futilely in town for grain.

The families of Borzu's herders congregated in his tent, which still held firewood and was larger, warmer, and more secure than theirs. A donkey repeatedly tried to back into the tent, and finally people gave up shooing her out. An hour later, unseen by anyone, she delivered a foal. Other animals also gave birth prematurely, the nomads were to discover. Aqaboa spent the afternoon in the driving rain searching desperately for his brother's young son, whom Borzu had sent to find stray sheep. (The next day he was found in good health; he had sought shelter in a distant tent.) Borzu had left his sheep under Morad's care. Led by goats, the animals walked slowly uphill during lulls in the rain, then ran down again when the rain resumed. Later Morad sought shelter at the Talehbazli man's house for his family and Borzu's sheep. Late in the afternoon the three trucks arrived in Borzu's camp to evacuate anyone else who wanted to leave. Yadollah was the only man who did not send children. Then Borzu sent Mohammad Karim to Khalifeh's camp some distance away, but the route was too muddy for passage. Sohrab, it turned out, had previously evacuated that camp's women and children by a car he had procured in town. Borzu wanted to return to his own camp to "fasten things down" and check on animals, but the worsening weather soon precluded any further trips. Earthquake tremors shook the ground.

Borzu and Falak commandeered the empty room in the Lur's house and allowed in only close family members. The other evacuees sought shelter in the large storeroom where Qermezi men planned to store wheat and had been storing baggage in order to avoid having to carry it for several days. The room soon filled with more than a hundred wet, cold, hungry, and apprehensive women and children. Examining the baggage in her room, Falak removed carpets and blankets belonging to other families to use for the night's beds. In checking her own baggage she discovered that a white jajim was missing, and she talked angrily about that and little else in the following days. The flat-woven textile was never recovered, and she suspected that her Lur hosts had stolen it. Borzu bought bread in town for women and children and then went with his son and son-in-law to a teahouse for a hot meal. As flames in the fireplace slowly dwindled, people settled down to sleep. Talking and intermittent crying of babies and small children filled the night.

People rose before dawn and packed their possessions. The morning was hazy, and the rain appeared to have ceased. Everyone was anxious to return to camp to survey the damage. The previous day Hemmat's daughter had given Falak partridge eggs she had found, and Samarrokh cooked them for breakfast. After eating, everyone left Borzu alone in the room, just as they always left him alone in the tent after breakfast if they were not traveling early that day. He used this time to think, drink tea, and listen to phonograph records of Qashqa'i romantic ballads and wedding music. Sohrab, who rarely saw his rival Borzu, came to offer greetings; Borzu ignored him completely. Mohammad Karim drove some children but no baggage back to camp, for Borzu first wanted to hear about conditions there. The son reported later that the night had been terribly cold and rainy, and many animals had died. Herd and pack animals had scattered and intermingled, and men did not yet know their total losses. Many of Khalifeh's ewes and does had died, and he worried about how he would feed twenty orphaned lambs and kids. Several of his young animals were already nursing from one mother. Nine donkeys belonging to Naser, Nader, and Hasel had died in the hailstorm that had struck their camp. People were sad to hear that a young child of a Bulverdi Qashqa'i family camped near Borzu's site had died during the night.

The evacuees were anxious to return to camp, but Borzu was still unwilling to go. People put wet possessions in the courtyard to dry and moved in and out with baggage. Some wanted to store goods there and collect them when they passed by the town, but the apparent theft of Falak's blanket discouraged them. Borzu sent Mohammad Karim back to camp with Zolaikha and Zohreh, along with equipment for making bread and tea, so they could begin to restore order there. The Lur host, to whom Borzu was once again indebted, asked to borrow his truck and the labor of an adolescent boy for another trip to Wide Mountain for firewood. Borzu could not refuse.

Borzu spent part of the day with Captain Jamali. A distraught Qarachai Qashqa'i nomad had dumped forty dead goats in front of Jamali's temporary office and demanded government assistance. He had lost 170 animals in a mud slide and was destitute. This kind of petition had been successful under the regime of the Qashqa'i khans. The khan to whom the unfortunate man appealed would have given his own animals and collected others from wealthy Qashqa'i. The man's kin would also have offered help. Jamali responded by noting only that the government could not handle such a calamity. The Qarachai man claimed he had slit the throats of the forty goats prior to death, and men in town purchased animals from him to use as meat. Borzu bought one for his family and butchered it. He presented a leg of meat to his Lur host, who suspected that the animal had not been properly killed and hence was forbidden as meat. In refusing the gift he explained that he never ate goat meat because his leg hurt him when he did. Borzu's cousin Allahyar also bought a goat. He poured water over the slit throat so that it ran off the neck tinged with blood. In this way he had caused blood to "flow" from the animal and rendered the meat ritually pure and edible.

Borzu had not wanted to return his entire family to the mud-entrenched campsite. He spent the night with his wife and small children in the same room as before but without the comfort of carpets and blankets. Samarrokh had packed the blanket containers early that morning, and Falak did not want to have to repack them herself the next morning.

The few nomads remaining in town woke early and were anxious to leave. Others of the group had broken camp at dawn and soon arrived with much confusion in the center of town to pick up their stored baggage. Ordinarily they never passed through a town. Pack animals, especially camels, did not like to stand still once they were loaded, and their owners fought to locate possessions and reload. Men and children of the settlement came to watch the spectacle. Borzu packed his truck with people and baggage and drove off to find the next campsite.

Falak and her two youngest children remained in town until Borzu could return for additional baggage. Waiting with them was an elderly Qermezi woman who hoped to find a ride to the home of her daughter in a village near summer pastures. They witnessed a domestic quarrel among women in the family of the Lur host. Hearing a new bride scream obscenities at her mother-in-law, a disturbed Falak sobbed that she was thankful that Qashqa'i people never behaved that way. Between tears she explained the bride's behavior by the fact that she was unrelated to her husband's family. Falak made no effort to straighten or clean the room and courtyard. The evacuees had left a muddy mess and had emptied many goatskin bags of water that the host's wife had carried on her back from a public faucet some distance away. Still suspicious that the family of her host had stolen the blanket, Falak was disinclined to be courteous.

After leaving Arzhan Plain with his remaining family members, Borzu stopped at a shop in Forty Springs village to store goods and pick up supplies. He had visited the same shop during the autumn migration. The nomads usually traveled ahead during the migration to store goods there and later returned to collect them. This year they were glad to have the opportunity because of the difficulties in transport caused by carrying extra loads of firewood on fewer pack animals, some lost in the just-passed storm.

The nomads were delighted to find a profusion of wild artichokes at the new site, and women set out to gather and wash vast quantities of the young and tender thistles as soon as their households were assembled and functioning. Using a stream flowing by camp, people began to clean mud and dirt from their possessions. Borzu returned to Arzhan Plain and spent the rest of the day helping the few families who had not yet been processed to receive wheat and straw. There he heard the news that Lur shepherds from a village near Kazerun had grazed their animals in Khalifeh's fields of wheat and barley at Molla Balut and devastated the crops. Kuruni Kurds had grazed their herds at Dashtak, and Borzu's nephews Hosain Ali and Askar, skipping school in order to harvest, had chased them away.

The next day's migration took only half an hour. Borzu wanted to find a larger site where other families could join him, and he even walked there. Some men who had been traveling separately had said they now planned to join him, in part to acknowledge his efforts to secure wheat for them and his help in the evacuation.

The region of Forty Springs marked the border of winter pastures and the beginning in earnest of the spring migration. The stages of the migration after Arzhan Plain were perceived differently from those before, and people from this point wanted to travel in larger, better protected groups. The region of Arzhan Plain had been a bottleneck with one route running through it, but the migratory path opened up after that, and many different routes were possible. A larger group enabled them to investigate routes more easily. Once past Arzhan Plain, Borzu's route would meet the migratory routes of the many Qashqa'i nomads who were traveling from winter pastures south of Shiraz. The routes of practically all Qashqa'i who migrated would then be in close proximity, and Borzu's group would compete with others for smooth passage, good campsites, and exploitable resources. Until Arzhan Plain, Darrehshuri nomads had migrated primarily with Kashkuli Bozorg and Qarachai nomads. The route Borzu planned to take differed at certain points from the route he had taken the previous autumn. The varying conditions of pastoral resources (grazing, water, fuel) during autumn and spring required different kinds of routes, and migratory strategies were adjusted seasonally and annually.

Arzhan Plain also marked the edge of summer pastures. The areas and altitudes of oak forests were the southern border of Qashqa'i summer pastures. The mountains just north of Arzhan Plain were where Qermezi and other people from Dashtak spent part of the summer if the weather proved to be too hot and dry at Dashtak. Kashkuli Qashqa'i nomads regularly spent summer not far northeast of Arzhan Plain, and other Kashkuli, Amaleh, Shesh Boluki, Farsimadan, and Darrehshuri nomads sought their own summer pastures progressively to the north.

Borzu's kinsman Mansur planned to stay near Arzhan Plain for a while to fatten his animals. He had just acquired four hundred sheep and goats under a short-term contract and planned to sell them in summer. The animals were thin, and traveling with them now to summer pastures would jeopardize any possible profit from their sale.

For the first time since the spring migration had begun, the new camp-site matched the description that people had given during the autumn migration of the spring one: warm sunny weather, fresh green grass (the first seen so far), and plentiful clear spring water. Glad to leave behind the horrors of the storm and the mud and cold, people reveled in the superb conditions. Still traumatized by what they had just experienced and concerned about rain yet to fall, they all set up tents carefully and securely and laid green branches weighted by rocks over the tent's guy ropes and stakes.

Borzu told Yadollah to pitch the white canvas tent for use that day and night and to repair the summer goat-hair tent. He instructed him to re-move the worn panels of the tent's roof and sew on the new ones woven in Shahreza. Then he left camp, having arranged to drive in tandem with Captain Jamali to Shiraz so Jamali could assist him if the police stopped him for not having automobile insurance or a driver's license for Moham-mad Karim. He needed truck repairs.

The next day no one traveled because of Borzu's trip to Shiraz. Samar-rokh and her husband and children returned from making a pilgrimage to the shrine of Shah-e Cheragh in Shiraz and stopped by her mother's tent to leave the small gifts customarily presented after a pilgrimage. Two winters back when her husband Asadollah had been ill, she had vowed that if he recovered she would weave a blanket and offer it to Shah-e Cheragh. She had completed it during the winter. Asadollah and others sadly considered the loss of this property, for the family was poor and could not afford the gift, but no one had wanted her to risk the conse-quences if she failed to fulfill her vow. The previous spring Falak had visited the shrine to donate money she had promised if Mohammad Karim passed the examinations necessary for entering the seventh grade. Borzu had never made a pilgrimage to Shah-e Cheragh and expressed no interest in doing so. Barely tolerant of pilgrims, he considered the trip a waste of time and money.

During the day a harsh wind blew, and rain threatened. Falak in-structed Yadollah to finish sewing and then pitch the goat-hair tent and secure it with two bands over the roof. Earthquake tremors once again shook the ground. Katayun completed weaving a water-bag carrier, to be part of Zolaikha's dowry, and sent it and the surplus yarn via her daughter to Falak. Falak returned the yarn to Katayun, minus several balls, in pay-ment for the weaving. For the first time during this migration, Borzu's brother Abdol Hosain and his cousin Abdol Rasul were close by, and the women visited one another. When Kafayat reported that Lurs in a nearby village had stolen five of their sheep, the women commented that they all should be traveling in larger groups to prevent theft and be better protected. Worried about mud slides, Jehangir and Ali left Borzu's camp to seek a safer site at a higher altitude. They constructed an animal pen to avoid a chaos similar to that experienced in the recent storm. Returning to camp from Arzhan Plain, Gholam Hosain reported that the government was not yet ready to release their wheat. Borzu and Khalifeh came from Shiraz just before midnight. While there they had asked Bahman-baigi, director of the Office of Tribal Education, if Khalifeh's son Hosain Ali could attend the tribal high school in Shiraz.

The next day's campsite could not be reached by road. Borzu planned to ride there by mule in order to situate his family and herders among other group members and to oversee the process of setting up camp. Then he would drive to Arzhan Plain and spend the night there. He told Yadollah to overload the pack animals with goods the truck ordinarily carried. Some rain fell as people began to move. Halfway to the new site, Jehangir set up his own camp and prepared to entertain Borzu and Falak. He was soon to leave his family and the migration in order to go to the city of Isfahan where, to earn cash to pay off debts, he planned to work for four months as a middleman for sellers and buyers of sheep and goats. He relied on Borzu's help during his absence and wanted to demonstrate that he was a good brother and kinsman. On his way to Isfahan, he would first return to winter pastures to pick up his elderly mother Guhar, temporarily living with his kinsman Aliboa at Dashtak, and take her, along with baggage stored in Kazerun, by bus to the home of another kinsman near summer pastures. Guhar was too frail and feeble to migrate. Someone would bring her to summer pastures at Hanalishah once the Qermezi group had arrived there.

Borzu left his truck behind under the guard of a nephew and rode a mule to the new campsite. Settled Kashkuli Qashqa'i men, speaking Persian and not Turkish, argued with him about his animals near their fields. For the first time this migration, many Qermezi families traveled together. Borzu located a spot for his family, the vacant summer campsite of Hosain Khan Kashkuli, and enjoyed filling the khan's place. The summer pastures of some Kashkuli Bozorg Qashqa'i nomads were in the area, while other Kashkuli Bozorg summer pastures were farther north.

Once confident his tent was secured against rain and wind, Borzu returned by mule to Jehangir's camp where Falak and her two young sons had remained. Jehangir had killed a large fat goat, and Borzu readied his knife for making kebab (a task not unusual for a guest) and issued orders to his daughter and son-in-law who served the guests. Falak asked Roqayyeh for yogurt and sour milk, even though she knew her hosts were permitting their lambs and kids to drink all the milk in order to strengthen and fatten them. Ali and Akbar waited on a nearby hilltop for the guests to finish the kebab, and then they joined the gathering for the lunch of rice and meat stew. Afterward, many men from this camp and others returned to the previous campsite where Borzu's truck sat and rode with him to Arzhan Plain to collect the wheat the government was finally ready to release. Falak walked the long distance to her own camp, escorted by Jehangir's daughter (a service customarily offered to women by hosts). Yadollah had made a pen behind the tent's piled baggage and to the side for the newborn lambs and kids. He heard that Hasan's camel had died from eating too many mature, tough wild artichokes, and he cautioned the others to watch the eating habits of their own animals. For supper Borzu's family ate partridge eggs given by Abdol Hosain's daughter.

Yadollah and Zolaikha packed at dawn without the usual urgency, for Borzu was absent. Loading the animals was again difficult because of the extra burdens; Borzu had taken an empty truck to town. The day's trip took the nomads out of the mountains and down to the banks of Black Tree River. Two farmers guarding nearby fields told the nomads where best to cross. They moved at a fast pace, slightly afraid of the water, and told of previous years' drownings of people and animals. Women and young children rode pack animals for the crossing and placed young animals in bags draped over loads. Men and older boys waded across in the swiftly moving current. Naser carefully led his cow loaded with tent panels, for she was not as surefooted as other pack animals. He was the only Qermezi nomad who owned a cow. Borzu had complained that cows slowed down the migration (which was not apparent in the case of this cow) and that, having no useful wool or hair, they were worthless animals. Most of these families had previously owned and migrated with cows. Eight winters earlier they had died of starvation, and men decided not to buy or acquire new ones. The route continued through a floodplain and up into another range of mountains. From the top people could see the mountains around Arzhan Plain and trace the route they had just taken.

Locating the nomads after the river crossing, Borzu commented that he had wanted to join his family the previous night and leave his truck guarded by a nephew on the nearest road but that mechanical problems with the truck had delayed him. He had sought shelter at the home of a Kuruni acquaintance in Forty Springs village. He selected the group's next

26. Qashqa'i nomads crossing the Kor River

site and sent Zolaikha and Zohreh for water and grass. His brother Jehangir came for a final visit before leaving the next day. He had helped Borzu's household to break and make camp the past several days, and Borzu set him to work repairing a reed screen for an animal pen. Jehangir wanted the image of his assistance in Borzu's memory. Borzu and several other men rode to Arzhan Plain to collect wheat, and women were free to visit and exchange gifts. Rokhsar gave her sister-in-law Falak a narrow woven strip for the edging of the reed screen, and Falak told Yadollah to sew it on.

Borzu returned to camp at night, bringing baggage and sacks of flour he had left in Arzhan Plain for a government truck to transport to summer pastures. Since the brigadier general's visit, Captain Jamali had worried about the deception played upon the people for whom he was responsible, and he had finally located a few army and gendarme trucks to carry goods to summer pastures for members of needy Darrehshuri subtribes. He had offered Borzu a truck's transport in appreciation of his aid, and Borzu had told each man in his group to leave several pieces of heavy baggage in Arzhan Plain. The next day when Borzu demanded two trucks, the gendarmes became exasperated with him and withdrew the original offer of one truck. Wanting one truck for Naqneh and another for Narmeh (two villages in summer pastures), he had rejected a truck for Semirom. He was angry at ending up with no transportation at all, but saw no solution but to bring his own stored baggage back to camp. The other men were not so fortunate, for they had to retrieve the goods they had left behind. Sons of Abdol Rasul and Barat had waited in town to carry loads to Naqneh and Narmeh by truck and were now forced to find and pay for private transportation.

The gendarmes had allotted Borzu twice the amount of wheat he was due. He had tampered with the figures by recording more family members for each household than actually existed and then took the surplus himself. Because he needed cash he sold practically all the wheat to two shopkeepers in Arzhan Plain for half the current market value. Men returned to camp with flour milled in town. Bread made from the flour was tough and stale, it turned out, and everyone was irritated to find that their weeks of effort to obtain low-cost government grain were such a waste. Some men had planned to use the wheat for autumn planting but now saw they could not plant old seed.

The night was cold, and new snow covered the nearby mountain peaks. Water in goatskin bags was frozen. Borzu's household was the last to leave camp in the morning. Pack animals were overloaded, especially one camel carrying extra baggage in addition to a sick ewe. Another camel hastening through a deep icy stream tripped and fell, but Yadollah rescued the baggage before it became waterlogged. He asked Zolaikha if she knew the route. Although other families had traveled east around some foothills, she reported that the route lay to the west, and Borzu's small group followed behind her. Khosrow rode ahead to look for Borzu's truck, and Yadollah was perplexed. They traveled alone for several hours, everyone tired and worried. Suddenly, from out of nowhere, Asadollah shouted from a hilltop that the group had lost the way and was going in the wrong direction. Backtracking to the stream they had crossed hours before, they saw all the other nomads camped along its banks near a large Kashkuli Qashqa'i village, including Khalifeh who was near his brother Borzu for the first time this migration.

Borzu was angry at Yadollah for the delay in setting up camp and the needless expenditure of effort, but the camel herder offered no excuse and did not blame Zolaikha who had feared her father would punish her. After Borzu had eaten he calmed down and set to washing a carpet stiff with caked mud. Some men from camp returned to Arzhan Plain on mules to retrieve goods stored there. Jehangir's children and herd had also been lost since morning, and Borzu, responsible for the family with Jehangir gone, was preparing to go by truck to search for them when they arrived. Although happy to be churning yogurt and water to make sour milk, Zolaikha was tired from the day's detour and depressed about her impending marriage. Her mother had yelled at her about her fiancé Hajji Qorban to chastise her for having lost the way.

Falak talked nostalgically about the past when she, her daughters, and shepherds' wives had stayed up practically all night every night during this stage of the migration to churn sometimes as many as fourteen goat-skin bags of yogurt and water to produce fresh butter. Later they clarified the butter and traded the oil for rice in Kurd's Fort village farther along the migratory route. This year the does were not yet producing much milk, the milk's fat content was still too low for the production of butter, and the ewes were not yet being milked. The nomads had just begun to separate the kids (except for newborns) from their mothers during the night so that more milk would be available at the morning's milking. Given the task of herding the kids, older children traveled the same route in the morning as the pack animals but followed slowly behind them to allow the young animals to browse along the way. Khalifeh's son and the sons of his two brothers herded the camels of the three households together, while his younger children and his two brothers' younger children herded the kids together. The three men had cooperated in this friendly manner all their lives. They contrasted with Borzu and his two brothers, who had not assisted one another in this fashion since Borzu married and formed his own independent household.

People rose well before dawn to get an early start because of the long distance to be traveled. The night had been cold, and people packed with difficulty. Clothes and weavings washed late the previous day were frozen stiff, and the carpet Borzu had cleaned was heavy and especially hard to pack. The day's route took the group across an area called Black Pastures where dark-colored grass grew by streams. Qashqa'i villages dotted the landscape, fields were green, and men were plowing new land with tractors. After an hour of traveling, the group stopped to rest the pack animals where Borzu had parked the truck. A settled Bulverdi Qashqa'i man guarding fields complained to him about his animals, and Borzu threatened to hit him and scared him away. Later the man returned, and Borzu accused him of behaving as non-Qashqa'i people did and of not being Qashqa'i anymore. He told him to take a good look at himself before it was too late. Several Qashqa'i men traveling alone, either catching up with their groups or returning to collect baggage, stopped by Borzu's tent for tea and a meal. Taking pleasure in sitting quietly by his sheep as they ate grass growing along a stream, Borzu ruminated about his plans.

After the kids had nursed, the nomads reloaded and traveled for hours. People pointed out the grave of Sohrab's mother (Borzu's father's sister) on a hilltop as they passed by. The route took the group down and away from a range of mountains, across a huge plain and a river, and toward another range of mountains in the distance. Two residents of Shallow Water village stood guard to direct the nomads around the settlement. Zolaikha ran ahead when she saw Borzu's truck, for it was her responsibility to be at the new site when the loaded camels arrived. Borzu had found a site in a valley next to the one his traveling companions chose, and he was well ahead of them with only Morad and Gholam Hosain as campmates. Concerned about the many Imanli Darrehshuri nomads traveling close by, he wanted to camp north of them and precede them the next day. He hoped to be first to reach and cross over the next difficult mountain pass. Affiliated with a man prominent in the Darrehshuri tribe, the Imanli group was wealthy as indicated by its many camels and the fine weavings displayed. Borzu was more aggressive and competitive when confronted with someone of roughly comparable or higher status than when he confronted nomads of more ordinary means. Any two groups the same size posed the same threat of crowding, but he was edgy when he encountered a group that also posed a potential challenge to his social status.

A young boy yelled to Borzu that a Lur man was throwing stones at Morad and Gholam Hosain, and Borzu and his shepherds grabbed sticks and clubs and ran to help. The Lur fled when he saw reinforcements approaching. On the way back to camp, Borzu recovered from a kinsman's herd a lamb that had fallen out of his truck during the day's trip. People were tired from the long distance traveled, and no one bothered to put up tents until it suddenly began to rain. Borzu's fireside was quiet that night. Others were camped too far away to visit, and everyone was exhausted. No further rain fell until just before dawn.

Borzu woke his family and campmates, packed, and was ready to leave earlier than usual, but the Imanli nomads who had crowded the route the previous day were already moving ahead of him. He had worried about this stage of the migration, for he said they had never taken this particular route before. The steep pass was difficult to climb and cross, and the downhill passage was treacherous, especially for pack animals, even without others traveling just ahead and pressing from behind. The route left the mountain range and crossed the Shiraz-Ardekan road, where the Imanli nomads branched off from Borzu. Borzu found a campsite for himself in a valley filled with fields. The rest of his group camped on the mountain slope.

Borzu and several other men had made a side trip to stop at a village to get supplies from a Lur merchant with whom they had traded for eight years. Borzu especially needed shoes for his shepherds. The merchant defined himself as a "village friend," a man with whom nomads traded and visited during the migrations. He sold local products, fruit primarily, and commodities from the Shiraz bazaar, and he sold in Shiraz the pastoral products he received in trade. The nomads bought tea, sugar, grape and fig syrup, and wheat on credit. In autumn, during the return migration, they would pay the going price plus interest (in clarified butter and dried curds). Although they traded commodities, they used the idiom of Iranian currency in their bargaining.

As Morad left the village, he complained that his brother Abdol Rasul had borrowed his mule to collect three blanket containers stored in Arzhan Plain. The skin and muscles on the mule's back had torn from the heavy load, which rendered the animal useless as a pack animal and mount for the rest of the migration. Ordinarily a mule carried only two such bags. Morad's wife Jansanam, who usually rode the mule during the migration, was forced to walk and carry a baby. His eight-year-old son rode alone on a horse. The two brothers had disagreed at the end of winter about how to proceed in the spring migration, and they had not traveled or camped together since then.

After Borzu settled into his new campsite, he commented on the distinguishing marks of the various Qashqa'i tribes. Kashkuli as compared with Darrehshuri people owned many donkeys and chickens and few camels, and he disapproved that their women wore red and orange clothes, inappropriate colors for anyone but new brides. Amaleh people owned gray-fleeced sheep. Gallehzan ("Animal Thieves") men who upheld their warrior image always carried metal-headed clubs prominently. As with all Qermezi women, Falak often noted differences in the dress, jewelry, hair style, and carriage of Qashqa'i women according to their specific tribal membership. They could also distinguish Qashqa'i women from other tribal and rural women, all of whom wore similar clothes.

Borzu sent Morad and Mohammad Karim to Shul village to fill goatskin water bags for the families who brought empty ones to the truck. Two Lurs came to buy animals and old carpets, and Borzu quizzed them about water, grazing, and gasoline. Concerned again about the long way yet to Semirom with no facilities to repair his truck along the route, he abruptly decided to go to Shiraz. Returning to camp about midnight, he was stopped by gendarmes. They did not ask about licenses or insurance but instead about contraband such as arms and other smuggled commodities.

The next day Borzu remarked that a Persian cloth merchant in the Shiraz bazaar had told him that his business with the Qashqa'i this year had been slack. The merchant said that he had offered fabric on credit to nomads until the early 1960s, but that now they were an economic liability for him, unable to pay what they owed. A Persian shoemaker had told Borzu that he could no longer compete against sellers of plastic shoes. Most of his business had come from nomads during autumn and spring when they stopped in Shiraz during the migration. To make extra income, the shoemaker now worked on Fridays as a doorman dressed in ornate Qashqa'i clothes at an expensive tourist hotel.

A severe wind and some rain hit the camp during the afternoon while Borzu was gone. As was often the case when they knew he would be absent for some hours, Falak and Zolaikha cooked a large pot of stewed rice, and everyone ate plenty for a change. They even told the herders' wives to bring empty bowls to be filled.

As people were settling down to sleep and before Borzu's return, Zolaikha spotted small beams of flashlights approaching the camp, and with urgency she alerted the others. Ten Lurs claiming that Qashqa'i nomads had stolen a ram and ewe had come in force, armed with clubs, to search herds. While several of them checked Borzu's herds, three sat in the tent and demanded tea and bread. Falak had been frightened that they would harm her family and steal, but she relaxed when they said they were hungry. Later she noted that they could not possibly have been thieves if they were hungry, for "thieves never went without." The Lurs complained that the government had helped the Qashqa'i this year but had ignored other people who had also suffered from the drought. They did not find the two animals, and as they departed they remarked, "Thank God our property wasn't found among such good people."

The next day's difficult route and schedule meant an early departure. The nomads traveled up through a mountain gorge to a peak and then down a steep slope and into a long narrow unpopulated valley. They then climbed up another steep gorge through rugged terrain toward the top of a pass. A sharp cliff fell to one side of the path. They came out on a peak overlooking Baiza village. The route down the slope was arduous, especially for camels who ran and often risked falling. People dismounted out of concern for accidents. For the first time this migration Abdol Hosain and Abdol Rasul traveled with Borzu's group.

Khalifeh and some others camped by the pass overlooking Baiza, the rest traveled farther down the slope, and Borzu was alone in the plain below. Acknowledging that grazing was better at higher altitudes, he had told his shepherds to find some campmates and not be alone. He stood in the fields and shouted instructions up the slope, but the distance was too great for anyone to hear his words. He set up camp by an orchard and a flowing irrigation channel. Other Qashqa'i nomads also camped nearby. A Qarehqanli Darrehshuri man living in a nearby village, whom Qermezi men had known in the past, had been watching for Borzu's approach and now stopped by his camp with a gift of firewood. Borzu instructed him to make tea and perform chores around the tent before the man went to visit others up the slope. Many fields were nearby, and herders and farmers encountered one another with hostility. Borzu's sister Shahrbanu swore at a Lur man who had told her not to enter his fields, and their exchange rapidly escalated. She was the most combative of all Qermezi women and not only readily entered any skirmish men were in but created her own. When Borzu went to shout at him, the farmer sought reinforcements from the village, including the headman and a gendarme. Asadollah took a club to enter the fight, but no blows were exchanged, and Borzu returned home pleased his group had prevailed. He walked up the slope to check on his herds and on the way argued angrily with farmers. A Persian shoe repairman from Baiza village made the rounds of the tents. He collected shoes to fix in his shop and would return them the following day as the nomads moved on.

When Borzu was returning to camp, he met a Persian man on a donkey who said he was blind and could not find his way home. Borzu invited him into his tent, as he did with many strangers, and the man stumbled and felt his way inside. As the man sat down by the fire, Borzu saw that he had six fingers on one hand, a blind eye, and enough sight in the other eye to tend the fire (a task visitors often performed). His feet were huge and thick, and when he took off his shoes, Borzu could see that one foot had six toes. When Borzu commented, the man responded that a woman had severed the sixth finger from his other hand when he was young, and he had become blind as a result. God's will had been tampered with, he said, and he was punished. His behavior was too smooth for an ordinary passerby, and Borzu soon understood that he was a professional beggar full of tricks. He did not mind offering charity to truly deserving people, but this man was manipulative and taking advantage of him. When Falak served Borzu a meat and potato stew, he told her to give the man yogurt and bread. After the man tasted the food in the bowl and did not find the meat he had smelled, he said he would not eat unless he ate with Borzu. Borzu replied sarcastically, "If only you had come earlier, we would have cooked rice for you," and began to poke fun at him and facetiously call him "Mashhadi," a title the man claimed. After Borzu gave him a bowl of meat stock, the beggar drank and then offered some to Yadollah. Borzu told him not to bother, for Yadollah was content eating yogurt.

Falak and her children did not discover the deformities until well into the evening, and they were horrified and fascinated. The next morning Zolaikha reported that during the night the man had made himself tea (not at all proper behavior for a visitor), and Falak saw that he had emptied the tea jar and sugar bag to steal the surplus. He had relieved himself right in front of the tent, an act that she said insulted her home, and Zohreh had to remove the evidence with a shovel. He might have been scared of the dogs, for they attacked strangers. When Falak asked Borzu why he had not chased the man off, he replied that had he done so, his act of charity would have been nullified. Muslims, he noted, were obligated to offer food and shelter to the unfortunate.

Borzu had been busy before dawn preparing for the day's move, but the sky remained dark and cloudy, and he waited to see if rain would fall. Several hours after dawn Qermezi families in a long caravan made their way down the mountain slope and passed by Borzu's camp. The sight of the others spurred his activity, and he changed his mind about not traveling at all that day. The decision was taken out of his hands, and he was not pleased. His family could not pack up fast enough for him, and he actually performed some of the labor himself. On his way by, Morad stopped to help (the only one to do so) and let his camels wait, then sent them on with the next group of passing camels. Borzu's pack animals were the last to leave. Persian men stood at the edge of Baiza to guard their fields against the passing nomads. Camels collided as they devoured leaves from the branches of oak trees, and herders fought to drive them on. Along the way people pointed out in another migrating group the mother's sister of Qermezi's teacher, and later they saw relatives of the Chardahcharik Darrehshuri man Arghvan's daughter had married.

Borzu camped on a hill overlooking a stream and a small Qashqa'i village. All others, including his shepherds but excluding Yadollah and Khosrow, had traveled in another direction to a site on a mountaintop where grass had been reported, and he was once again alone. Although Borzu had concurred with the others' decision to go another way, where no road existed, and although he had sent his own herds with them, he still considered himself to be diminished in power and authority. Impatient the rest of the day, he stood outside the tent looking beyond the hills at his invisible group. He collected weeds for pack animals and a sick ram he had carried by truck. Sending Yadollah to the mountaintop to check on Aqaboa, Borzu told him to gather information about the others' activities and plans. Yadollah reported later that some men would rejoin Borzu the next day, and so Borzu decided not to move on alone. He worried about the next two stages where his truck could not travel, and he considered placing his family in a village for two days until he could rejoin the migration. A swift river yet to be crossed also troubled him, for it was certain to be too deep for the truck. A gusty wind hit the camp, and he reinforced the tent's ropes.

Borzu's family members rose and were performing chores before dawn, although no travel was planned for the day. The early morning was windy, and the day became colder, windier, and rainy. Many families who had camped in the mountains moved to lower altitudes near Borzu and experienced continued difficulties in the harsh weather. Tents were especially hard to erect in a fierce wind. Ali's pack animals carried a load belonging to Khalifeh because one of Khalifeh's camels had fallen into an empty charcoal pit. It was dead before anyone found it, and the body was abandoned where it was wedged. Khalifeh was depressed about having lost four mature camels in the past three seasons. Morad visited Borzu, and the two men discussed the location of the others as they scanned the horizon.

Qasemli Qermezi nomads were traveling nearby, and people in the two groups visited one another. A delegation of Qasemli men invited Borzu to a mourning ritual in honor of their kinsman Negahdar and added that a kid had been slaughtered for the occasion. Borzu sent Yadollah's son to summon Ali, who rarely received such a request from his brother and did not delay in responding. Borzu then told Ali they were going to a ceremony for Negahdar. He could have sent this specific message when he summoned Ali, but he liked to exert power in this way to keep people guessing about his strategies and motives.

The young daughter of Gholam Shah, also part of the Qasemli group, brought a rooster to Borzu's tent. Falak and her daughters appreciated the gift but did not know who she was until Zohreh finally asked her. Children were difficult to recognize after several years. Zolaikha gave tea leaves and sugar to the girl to take home, and she tied the gifts in the cloth of her skirts. Her family was poor and needy. Her father served as a shepherd for his elder brother. The past year he had owned only one goat, and it had died during the winter. On Borzu's return home he shouted at his wife and daughters for not having prepared the tent for rain, and he noted with irritation that Zolaikha and Zohreh had done no work all day long. He sent them to gather wood and weeds from the fields.

The following morning was bright and sunny. Farideh and Dariush whined to be allowed to walk with the lambs and kids when usually they begged to ride in the truck. The sick ram was loaded once again into the vehicle, and Borzu, noticing its bloody nose, remarked sadly that it would die before nightfall. The day's route for the nomads traversed a difficult mountain pass with slippery gravel on the path, and many animals belonging to other groups jammed the route. People commented on the spectacular view and terrain; oak forests stood at lower altitudes. Khalifeh complained about government forest rangers who were not enforcing laws prohibiting the cutting of trees in the area. Always keeping careful, precise track of the progress of the migration, he announced that summer pastures were twenty-six days away if rain did not delay them and Kurd's Fort, where they always traded, six to seven days away. Traveling nearby with his group was a Farsimadan Qashqa'i man with a gun slung over his shoulder, the only Qashqa'i gun anyone had seen displayed the entire migration. Men were envious, and the sight inspired them to recount incidents involving guns on past migrations.

Borzu chose a site by a stream that ran along the road in a green valley. Seven other tents of his group were close by, a large camp for once, and others were not far away. A few families having problems with pack animals had stopped an hour before the others and made camp. Camped higher up, Abdol Rasul led his animals near fields in the valley. He carried a club with a head containing three iron studs that served "to draw blood." In telling about a recent skirmish with a farmer, he explained how important it was to get blood flowing in a fight, for it marked the weaker party and often stopped the fight. As soon as Borzu left to check his herds near the fields and fill gunnysacks with weeds for the pack animals, Falak chased everyone from the tent, told Zolaikha to boil water, and took a rudimentary shielded bath in the lamb pen. Water being nearby, many women and girls washed clothes. When Borzu returned home he found no fire made and berated Falak. He watched nearby fields and shouted to people to keep their animals away.

Around the fire that night Borzu and a few visitors listened as Falak in the background told the story of the day some years back when her daughter Farideh was lost at this very location. About three years old, she had apparently wandered away from the tent. People searched the mountainous area all day for her and cried, and Falak tore her clothes and pulled at her hair in despair. Calling out the names of her three daughters who had died young, Falak mourned for them too. People thought Farideh had been abducted, for she could not have walked a long distance. Finally Abdol Hosain and Morad found her crouched in a cave. Fulfilling the vows his family had made that day, Borzu killed a lamb and a kid for a ceremonial meal. Hearing the story again now, he joked, "When Farideh dies, no one will cry. We will cry for her only once."

In the morning Borzu was uncertain about the day's route and worried about passage for his truck. No roads covered the next three stages of the migration, which passed through mountainous terrain, and he pondered what to do. He said he could not leave the truck in a village for several days and travel with his herds because he did not have a horse strong or well enough to carry him (and of course a man of his status and personality could not walk). He commented that the group ought to have gone via Sheshbar, where grazing was bound to be better, but that many men had rejected the idea. "Khalifeh and the others were afraid of snow." When a visiting villager asked why the others did not do as the headman proposed, Borzu shrugged his shoulders and replied, "If people suggest we travel this way, we travel this way. If ten men say we ought to go to Sheshbar, and twenty men disagree, we don't go."

Borzu's group passed a large village with houses built close together. Women and children gathered on the rooftops to watch the nomads go by, and some men laughed and jeered. Fields stretched in every direction. Borzu crossed a stream and camped in a valley. Everyone else except Borzu's herders moved past him because the day's trip so far had been short, and they traveled into the mountains near the pass that so worried him. Suddenly he thought of a new plan to travel by truck via Ardekan and be apart from his herds and the group for only two nights. He asked two Qermezi men traveling back to the village for supplies to inquire about road conditions, and he quizzed a tribal teacher who rode his motorcycle by the camp. Katayun went alone to the village to trade. The sick ram finally died, and Borzu said he wanted to cry about the loss.

The next morning Borzu packed what he needed for the two-day absence, including all the tea equipment and a gunnysack of produce, and drove off with Falak and his two youngest sons by way of Ardekan. A peddler of handmade shoes had offered to trade Borzu a pair for a sick ewe being carried by donkey, but Borzu had rejected the offer, and the animal died an hour into the day's move. Zolaikha stopped to pull out and save its wool. On Borzu's detour around the mountains, he spotted and stopped at the tent of Faizollah, a Talehbazli Darrehshuri man, who killed a kid in his honor. Faizollah's wife was the daughter of the uncle of Falak's father, and the two families felt comfortable with one another because of the link. A Persian man guarding his wheat fields against Faizollah's sheep provided information about pasture in the area, Qashqa'i people settled nearby, and nomads who had already migrated past.

The day's trip took the migrating group, without Borzu, up and down a series of ridges. Green fields filled the landscape, and farmers were plowing with cows. Lone houses of recently settled Kashkuli Qashqa'i families dotted the terrain. The nomads commented upon a large camp of Lur hired herders who used canvas tents and had made pens of thorny bushes for their animals. The terrain at higher altitudes was typical of the scene Qermezi people had described of summer pastures: flowering meadows, steep mountain slopes, snow-covered mountain peaks, springs, streams, and quiet punctuated only by bird songs. Borzu had said the group would break the long day's trek with a rest in the middle, but after traveling for over four hours, Morad took charge, called a halt, and set up a tent, which was an obvious sign of an overnight stay. Borzu had allocated authority to Morad who located tent sites for Borzu's family and herders. For the first time this migration the camp was surrounded by grass, and the setting was pleasing with a gurgling stream nearby. In charge of the household, Zolaikha did not pitch the tent but piled baggage as shelter and then worked on a goatskin she was preparing and curing for eventual use as a bag for storing water. She scraped out the flour and salt she had placed in the skin a month earlier, yanked out the hair, turned the skin inside out in order to sew shut the four leg openings, and then put heated acorn skins into the bag to remove odor and strengthen the skin.

Jehangir's young son came to request Borzu's mule, for Asadollah had accidentally stoned and broken the leg of a ram and needed transport for Samarrokh, who ordinarily rode the mule, now burdened with the injured animal. Borzu's absence made this bold request possible. Zolaikha delayed before turning over the mule to the boy. To discourage borrowing, people sometimes stalled, claimed the item was elsewhere or broken, or gave it grudgingly. Katayun tended the herd while Aqaboa walked back to the previous campsite to search for a lost lamb. At dusk Morad stopped by to see if Borzu's pack animals were fed and tethered, and he yelled at Zohreh to get to work. He told a Lur woman who was searching for eight lost goats to try another group.

The night was too cold for anyone to sleep well, especially without the protection of a tent. Zolaikha rose several hours before dawn to churn the season's first butter, and she woke up Zohreh to bake bread. She told Khodabakhsh to slaughter a lamb and then made kebab for herself and others for breakfast, actions she never could have taken if Borzu or Falak had been present. Morad was packed before Borzu's household was, and he sat and drank tea while waiting to lead the group on the day's move.

The caravan crossed a small meandering river several times and then climbed a steep trail in a long winding pass. The body of a donkey that had died under its load lay at the summit. From the top people could scan the route of the next several days. A tree nomads had filled with stones over the years grew at the pinnacle, and several young girls added stones of their own as they passed by and made a wish. Once over the pass and descending to rocky rounded hills, men in the small group lost the way and disagreed about the correct direction. Morad, who had acted as leader earlier in the morning, abandoned this role and looked after only his own animals. The group retraced its steps.

Khosrow, a young man of low status who had not previously played any kind of leadership role, announced he had found a campsite and chose the best spot for himself. Other families settled close by in the surrounding valleys. No one set up tents, only sun shelters. The landscape was pitted with small holes and piled with mounds of dirt, evidence left by wild boars rooting in the ground for truffles with their tusks. Hasan, who had lagged behind Borzu's group because several of his camels had died, finally caught up and joined the camp. Naser's household had temporarily joined Nader's, also present in camp, while Naser took their elderly mother to summer pastures by bus. She had begun the spring migration, but the rainstorm at Arzhan Plain had weakened her.

Katayun, Golabshar, and women in nearby camps continued to prepare goatskin bags for storing water. This stage of the process required quantities of firewood, and everyone took advantage of places along the migratory route where fuel was plentiful. Their own summer pastures lacked firewood. Katayun hung in a tree a nearly completed bag inflated to stretch the skin, and then she set up a small dark shelter around it to smoke and cure the skin. Hunched under two felt cloaks and over a fire inside the shelter, she rubbed sticks in the dirt to extinguish the flames, inserted the smoking ends into the bag's opening, and held them there until she replaced them with freshly smoking sticks.

Asadollah and a few other men branded their lambs and kids on the snout, ears, or side of the head; the victims uttered distressed cries, and the odor of burning flesh and hair hung in the air. Two Lur hired herders from Shul visited camp to search for two sheep, lost, they claimed, when the Qermezi group had passed through their area. Asadollah told them they were free to check any herds but that they would probably find the animals back at their own camp. His wife Samarrokh visited her sisters, and they gave her lamb meat, sugar, and wool. She returned home seeming embarrassed and ashamed about needing help, with bundles of food tucked and hidden in her clothes and in her baby's wraps. Borzu had no idea how much Falak and her daughters contributed to Samarrokh's household.

Taqi finally located the camp after some searching. He was a settled Amaleh Qashqa'i man married to a Qermezi woman near whose village Borzu had stayed the previous night. He had come by foot bearing the message that Borzu wanted the group to travel again in the afternoon and that he would meet them at a certain location the next day. Taqi went first to Khalifeh and then to Morad who passed the news to Zolaikha. The men disregarded Borzu's instructions and said they would stay right where they were for the rest of the day and then move in the morning. The morning's trek had been long and difficult, and the pack animals were not yet sufficiently rested. They did acquiesce to Borzu's route, however. Asadollah remarked, "If it weren't for Borzu, we would travel another direction tomorrow." Khodabakhsh brought a skinned and partially butchered kid to camp and made himself kebab. He said he had found the animal choking to death and had slit its throat. No one questioned him about the facts, but everyone suspected that he had simply wanted meat to eat and had slaughtered the kid.

Zolaikha stayed up late to churn a second batch of butter. She had hardly slept the previous night and had worked hard all day with no rest. After she retired, Khodabakhsh and Yadollah's son sat by the fire, drank tea, and cavorted. Goats climbed up the reed screen and onto the piled baggage and then ripped open a sack of flour and ate and scattered the contents, leaving white powder ground into carpets and bags. The night was cold, and no one slept comfortably.

People woke early and packed hurriedly. The route was almost entirely a descent, hard on their legs and on their animals. The track left the tree-filled gorge and approached some hills planted with grain, then traveled down into a valley and over a steep hill to a stream. Zolaikha and other women stopped briefly to collect wild watercress and other edible water plants. A loaded donkey lost control of its hind legs on a precipitous incline, and Nader had to lift it by its tail and then remove its load and tie the donkey onto the back of a mule. People who saw the donkey collapse exclaimed, "Flee, evil," meaning, "Don't let this misfortune happen to us!"

The route led next across rolling wheat fields to Shekaft, Taqi's village. A Kohba Amaleh Qashqa'i man, Taqi had come to live with his kinsman Khalifeh, Qermezi headman, when his parents died. Khalifeh, whose mother was Kohba Amaleh, had relied on Taqi as a shepherd and treated him as a son, and after two years he arranged his marriage to Manizhah, an Aqa Mohammadli Qermezi woman. For two years the young couple lived in Khalifeh's tent, and then Khalifeh and Khanom gave them enough equipment for their own independent household. For a year they shared Khalifeh's camp until suddenly one night the headman of Taqi's subtribe arrived on horseback with twenty armed kinsmen to take Taqi back to Kohba Amaleh territory. Hamzah, the headman, had viewed Taqi's presence in Qermezi as a threat to his own authority. Crying with anger and sorrow, Manizhah was placed on a donkey and taken away with them. Taqi and Manizhah never lived with the Qermezi group again.

Manizhah and her children were waiting by the road to greet everyone in the Qermezi group as it passed by. She saw her family of origin only once or twice a year when it took this particular migratory route. When part of the caravan approached her, she greeted each person in order of sex, age, and status. Some men dismounted as did all the women, and as she kissed each and every child, she marveled over the young ones she had not seen before. Having said their greetings, people one by one hurried to catch up with their pack animals. No one said good-bye, and Manizhah turned toward the next oncoming group. Everyone was moved by the poignancy of the meeting, such a brief encounter with a beloved kinswoman. People stated again the importance of marrying within the group to avoid creating these distances among them.

Borzu sat by his truck along the road near Shekaft village. As people came near, they saw that Falak, apparently sick again, was lying under blankets by the truck. Each passing person stopped to greet Borzu and inquire after Falak, some dismounting, and then returned to their animals. As Samarrokh approached, she was frightened by the scene and ran to her mother's side while crying and hitting the sides of her head. Taqi and Manizhah, who had waited to greet the last of the caravan, joined Borzu and Falak and accepted further greetings. From Falak's groans and demeanor, everyone thought she was dying, and Borzu gradually became agitated although earlier he had been unperturbed. Wearied by her complaints and appeals for sympathy, he often simply ignored her. The others' reactions made him fear she was indeed ill. He rejected Taqi's suggestion that he take her to Shiraz. He had no money for a trip and doubted that a journey there would effect any change in her condition. He explained her illness and operation to anyone who would listen and noted that the past two nights of cold weather had caused a relapse.

Borzu directed that the tent be pitched some distance away, well back from the dusty road, and Zolaikha and Zohreh readied the home. A lone Amaleh Qashqa'i woman seeking charity approached the tent but was not acknowledged, and she moved on to Borzu and the gathering by the road where she asked what was happening. She complained that she had sought help at his tent but had received none. Apologizing, Borzu replied that only shepherd women were there and did not know any better. He gave her a few coins.

Borzu's kinsman Mohammad, whom Borzu had hit during their disagreement in late autumn about campsites at Dashtak, walked up to him. Borzu kissed him three times on the cheeks, and Mohammad kissed the palm of his hand in a ritual of reconciliation. Borzu saw that twenty-one Qermezi households had camped in the vicinity, the largest group he had enjoyed so far this migration, and he relished the moment, a public display of his importance and the resumption of the actual exercise of his position.

A Persian man from Shekaft village who had arranged an animal contract with Borzu on a previous passage through the area came to see him. Borzu took him to the tent, made tea, and then instructed others to bring Falak. He spent the rest of the day negotiating with him about the contracted animals. Taqi offered assistance as did men in Borzu's group who were unexpectedly present; some had wanted to greet Taqi and Manizhah. Having anticipated trouble, the Persian had brought along a friend, and a third Persian, cultivator of a nearby bean field, became mediator.

A year and a half previously during the autumn migration, Borzu had taken 34 lambs and goats to winter pastures for the Persian man on the agreement that he be compensated in rice. On Borzu's passage through the area the previous spring, the Persian had given him a portion of the rice. Borzu enumerated the autumn's and winter's heavy expenses (water, rents, bribes, truck, driver, sugar-beet pulp, other fodder) and demanded compensation. Five of the 34 animals had died and were considered no one's responsibility. The Persian agreed to pay but not an amount close to Borzu's demanded sum. Borzu's shepherds stayed close to the tent, let their herds graze nearby, and waited to see the fate of the remaining 29 animals. At a point when a resolution seemed close, the Persian claimed that half the animals belonged to his brother for whom he was unable to negotiate. Exasperated by the delaying tactic, Borzu yelled to the shepherds to remove the 29 from the herds. The two men stood divided by the animals and shouted at one another. Finally, after demanding 2 goats and 2 lambs for his expenses in caring for the 29, Borzu accepted 3 goats and 1 lamb. Dissatisfied with the transaction, he proclaimed that he would never conduct business like this again and would always demand money and goods in advance.

With this matter settled, the assembled men turned to the issue of the goat Borzu's brother Abdol Hosain had left with the same Persian man during the last autumn migration. The goat had broken its leg, and Abdol Hosain could not have easily carried the animal to winter pastures. The Persian had agreed to take the goat on a half-and-half partnership basis. He now claimed the animal had died, but Abdol Hosain and his kin were dubious, and the Persian finally agreed to give Abdol Hosain a goat of the same age and to receive half the local price of such an animal, his fee for having cared for the goat, as stipulated in their verbal contract. After the Persian left, Borzu declared, "I should have beaten up the man."

The negotiations had served to draw attention away from a "dying" Falak who lay under a heavy cover of blankets. Men who visited either left her alone or woke her up to shout a question about how she was feeling, for they expected the ill to be hard of hearing and difficult to communicate with. Samarrokh served as host. Manizhah and her children returned home with two animal skins and a scarf as gifts. Farideh found two mushrooms, the first of the season for these nomads. Borzu steamed them in the fire and then broke them into bites for people. Two local "khans" of a nearby village came for a short visit. Borzu told Aqaboa to pack his tent and travel ahead with the herd to find better pastures. Taqi performed tasks for Borzu and stayed the night.

In the morning Taqi helped Borzu to pack. The day's route took Borzu's large group of twenty-one families up and down a series of steep hills, across a valley, and up another steep hill to a place overlooking the huge Saran Plain bordered by the snowy mountains to the west that people had seen for four days. The entire plain was plowed into what appeared to be a single field. The area had once been luxuriant Qashqa'i pastureland. It

27. Milking the sheep. Borzu is in the background.

was famous for its wild mushrooms, but people saw few this year and blamed not only the plowing but also the nomads who had already passed through and plucked them. Many other Qashqa'i groups were migrating through the area. Borzu camped near Serenjeli village, located in a small valley at the northern edge of the plain, and most others moved a distance away. Seventeen tents of his group were visible. Lunch for Borzu's family consisted of one huge mushroom offered by Falak's kinsman Hasan. Borzu salted it and laid it upside down on the coals to bake, and much of its moisture remained inside. Inspired by its taste, children ran to find more. Farideh carried matches to make a fire, and they cooked mushrooms as they found them.

By midmorning Falak had returned to normal health and was soon laughing and retelling the details of her illness. Golabshar quietly commented that Borzu would certainly not permit Falak to feign dying again. Hungry for attention, she had basked in people's kindness when she had returned from the hospital some months before. According to Golabshar, Falak had now exploited a momentary recurrence of ill health at a place along the migratory route where the nomads would pass by in single file.

Falak's brother Barat rode by to tell Borzu he had experienced trouble with a farmer over flocks in a field. Khodabakhsh brought him tea, and he drank from the saddle with the shepherd standing at attention with the tray. Borzu snorted that the image reminded him of "the era of the khans," when servants had hastened to bring tea on the khans' return to camp after war or hunting. Khalifeh's shepherd Kordikhan sought refuge with Borzu and complained that Khalifeh's son Bahram had threatened to strike him. Borzu directed him to return to work when the man admitted that he had not actually been hit. Borzu told him to tell Khalifeh to break camp and move because the rain that was imminent would be snow at that higher altitude. Khalifeh had been unable to travel with the others that morning because of the shepherd's flight.

A small village of twenty Qashqa'i, Lur, and Persian families, Serenjeli was the home of Mashhadi Hamzah, headman of the Kohba subtribe of the Amaleh Qashqa'i tribe and the mother's sister's son of Borzu's father. He was also the man who had forced Taqi to return to Kohba Amaleh territory many years before. Hamzah had built a house and planted an orchard at Serenjeli in 1936 during Reza Shah's forced settlements. Since then he had stayed there part of the summer, and Qermezi people had occasionally visited him when they migrated through the Saran Plain. Ten years had passed since the last visit, and Borzu was anxious to reestablish contact. Hamzah had always migrated seasonally between the Saran Plain and winter pastures near Firuzabad south of Shiraz, but he had just made his last migration and now planned to stay permanently in Serenjeli. He said, "I have had enough. No more mules, no more camels, no more baggage." For the time being his son would migrate seasonally with his flocks, which he had reduced from 600 to 150 head. Land reform officials were currently distributing much of the cultivable land Hamzah had formerly controlled in the Saran Plain to the Persian farmers who had served as his sharecroppers.

Borzu summoned his nephew Akbar, who dressed in his best clothes, to go to the village to invite Hamzah to be his guest that evening. He butchered a kid, ordered the finest carpets laid out, and unwrapped a new porcelain teapot (the old broken one repaired with metal bands being unseemly for an honored guest). Soon Hamzah arrived on foot from the village accompanied by four kinsmen, his wife, a kinsman's wife, and three children. The women wore new clothes of vividly contrasting colors and fabrics ornamented with sparkly trim. Falak looked shabbily dressed by comparison. Morad, Abdol Hosain, and Barat came to offer Borzu support, Akbar and Asadollah provided physical help, and Samarrokh prepared meat stew and rice. Borzu had a superb time all evening playing host and entertaining the guests with stories of the past and plans for the future. Inspired by Hamzah's own success in combining pastoralism with agriculture, Borzu spoke expansively about how he would buy a tractor, cultivate grain, and plant orchards with labor provided by his brothers and their many sons. Because the guests lived so close they did not stay the night as guests usually did. After they left, Borzu and his kinsmen talked around the fire. Barat told the long story of his fight with the farmer, and Morad complained about his brother Abdol Rasul who continued to travel apart from him.

Borzu had magnanimously told his family they could sleep until noon, for no one was traveling that day because Hamzah had invited him and other Qermezi men as guests. Before dawn Borzu shouted everyone awake. By sunrise he was dressed and eager to ride by truck into Serenjeli (only several minutes' walk away), but then he stalled, saying it was much too early, and went to see Morad's newborn mule. Morad was excited about this increase in his wealth and talked grandly about buying land at Serenjeli and planting an orchard. Borzu sent Farideh and other children to deliver to Hamzah a live goat and her kid as gifts.

By midmorning Borzu was again ready to proceed to Serenjeli, and off he and his family went by foot. They saw that the villagers, benefiting from plenty of water, had planted shade trees and pleasant gardens. On the way he was met by Hamzah's kinsman sent to escort him to Hamzah's house, and other Qermezi men arrived soon thereafter. Men and women were ushered into separate reception rooms, a practice common in Iranian villages. Half the day men of the two groups unobtrusively watched Gholam Hosain's mule browsing in the wheat field in front of Hamzah's house, the animal absolutely refusing to be chased away. Falak found her female hosts to be boring, especially Hamzah's second wife who attempted to joke away her own apparent infertility. "He wanted a lamb but bought an old ewe," she laughed, but then she tearfully noted that a woman was nothing without children and might as well be dead. Borzu's company was lively and pleasurable, and Hamzah provided elaborate hospitality greatly exceeding Borzu's efforts the night before.

That evening Borzu's brother Abdol Hosain hosted Hamzah and seven kinsmen, the first guests of this stature he had ever entertained. He also invited Borzu, as was required, and other Qermezi men. In contrast to his relaxed mood during the previous two meals, Borzu was agitated and offensive. He stressed the effort and expense he had lavished on everyone since the water hauling at Wide Mountain in the autumn and as recently as the wheat distribution in Arzhan Plain, and he blamed Qermezi people for being ungrateful and not reciprocating. A few kinsmen responded that he could carry the burden of being headman because of his wealth. He began to shout at individuals and criticize them, particularly Abdol Hosain, for not helping him. He hurled abusive names at them and worked himself into a hostile frenzy. Abdol Rasul came to Abdol Hosain's defense, and then, when Abdol Hosain tried to defend himself and return the occasion to its proper tone, Borzu leapt at him and struck him. Men jumped to their feet to stop the attack, and Hamzah and Akbar pulled apart the two brothers and took them to separate sections of the tent. Naser quietly left the scene for he feared a fight between his own two brothers Morad and Abdol Rasul, who were incited by the attack. He did not want to have to take sides. Abdol Rasul criticized Borzu for his behavior. Borzu was so angry at Abdol Hosain that he stormed out of the tent and returned home to bed. Hamzah and Abdol Rasul were too upset to eat, the others quickly and silently choked down their food, and then everyone left. Women had tried to intervene in the fight but were pushed aside and ostensibly ignored, and they continued to discuss the event loudly after the men had left.

Men and women who had witnessed the enmity and then others as they heard the story declared that Borzu had behaved abysmally. They said he had beaten up and belittled his host in the presence of an honored guest and then fled before the meal was served. He had caused a loss of honor for himself and, by extension, the people he represented. He had dwelt on problems internal to the group (family, lineage, subtribe) when the event honored an outsider. He had ruined Abdol Hosain's attempt to host his first distinguished guest. He had fought with and struck his younger brother on an occasion that was also intended to forge better ties between them. And he had ruined a potentially productive relationship with Hamzah. Being simultaneously a Turk, a Qashqa'i, a distant relative, and a moderately wealthy settler, Hamzah might have offered contacts and services for Borzu and his group. He was useful for people who migrated, for they always needed friends along the migratory route, and might have helped men who wanted to settle. With these ends in mind, Borzu had courted Hamzah by hosting him lavishly, giving him gifts, and then being his guest.

In the morning Hamzah's young kinsman helped Borzu with packing. Embarrassed about the fight, the two men did not speak. By the time Borzu's family and the shepherds were ready to leave, all the other Qermezi families who had camped nearby were already gone and were no longer in sight. The short route that Borzu's entourage took to the next camp traversed hills and rolling fields and ended in a small protected valley. No villages were nearby.

Borzu was depressed and alone in thought all day. He did not make a fire, as he always did on arrival at a new site, not even when Yadollah unloaded and began to pitch the tent. Dejected, he sat by himself and then idly walked around. He shooed away two women peddlers, but Falak later traded tea leaves for popcorn, cooking greens, and herbs. During milking, women and shepherds talked about the tragedy of "brothers striking one another." Yadollah reported that he had heard that Abdol Hosain and Abdol Rasul would no longer talk to Borzu. Borzu took several walks alone, to no particular place, and then napped in an empty tent. No one visited or spoke with him.

As soon as all the other nomads had camped and settled in, out of sight of Borzu's camp, most of the men gathered at Abdol Hosain's tent to discuss the fight. They wanted to know what Borzu was doing and who had come to see him. In talking about whose fault the fiasco the previous night had been, they saw they did not disagree. Commenting at length about Borzu's wide-ranging complaints that no one ever helped him, they offered many examples of how they had often laid aside their own work in order to perform his. Morad was the only man who did not speak strongly against him, but he did not particularly ally himself with either side. By sitting in Abdol Hosain's tent and not Borzu's, he offered some indication of his sentiments.

A few men declared that they had known since the days at Arzhan Plain that Borzu would hit Abdol Hosain sometime soon. The two men's first face-to-face encounter during the spring migration had been only three days previously, and the men said that Borzu had struck out at the first opportunity. They discussed the recent history of the conflict. After leaving winter pastures, Abdol Hosain had joined Borzu's rival Sohrab and migrated with him, and Borzu was angry at that alliance. One man said the trouble had begun earlier, at the end of winter, when some of Borzu's kinsmen took their herds to the mountains above Dashtak and began the migration from there without talking strategy with him. Abdol Hosain had not supported Borzu's plans for migrating as he should have done. No one mentioned in this meeting that Borzu had shared his own sparse pastures all winter with Abdol Hosain's herd and that Abdol Hosain had never acknowledged this generosity. The final straw for Borzu, the men concluded, was that Hamzah reportedly had invited Abdol Hosain to live with him in Serenjeli and promised to provide him land there for cultivation. Borzu heard about the invitation and asked Abdol Hosain in front of Hamzah about his plans. He took offense at Abdol Hosain's equivocation and hit him.

(Months later as Qermezi men continued to discuss the conflict, they noted that Hamzah had shown interest in their group in order to stir up trouble among them, to split up Qermezi as he had split up his own Kohba subtribe when some Kohba men had fled from him and joined another Amaleh subtribe. Hamzah, like Borzu, was threatened by the loss of political support as members of his group settled. If he could entice several Qermezi men to join him, he could regain some influence.)

For the first time on this migration, no extra person helped Borzu and his family pack and load the animals in the morning, and the process went slowly. During the day's travel, women and children in his entourage discussed the fight briefly with the few other families they met along the way. Roqayyeh talked sadly about Jehangir being gone, his large debt, and his request that she weave a jajim to sell. She carried her youngest child in her arms as she walked, and her son Asadollah rode the family's mule carrying the injured ram while her daughter-in-law Samarrokh rode Borzu's mule. The route took the group once again across rolling hills and fields and then down to a river. Once lush pastureland, the large plain above the river was being plowed with tractors into one huge field. Another group of Qashqa'i nomads was crossing the river when the Qermezi group approached, and people held their animals back until the others were gone. They loaded lambs and kids into bags on the pack animals, and boys making many trips across the river carried the rest. Borzu's elder brother Khalifeh stood on the riverbank to direct movement. Although he said he was helping the animals, it was clear he was also informing each family where to go once across the river. The nomads headed up the hill and past Jamalbaigi village.

Restricted by the road, Borzu had no choice about his route and direction, and he set up camp along a stream leading to the river. He told Yadollah to pitch the tent, and his herders put up theirs too. He expected others to join him. Farsimadan Qashqa'i nomads traveled by, and some camped near him. Anxious to process the first curds of the season, Falak and her daughters rolled the moist curds they had prepared during the past two days into small balls and set them on reed mats to dry in the sun. Children came to beg for chunks of curd to eat. Calm when camp was being set up, Borzu became increasingly agitated. He seemed to be too embarrassed to ask where the rest of the group was, but no one with him had seen where any of the other families had camped. He slowly realized that he would not be joined by anyone, that the other nomads had ignored him and found their own site.

Suddenly in an excited state, Borzu shouted that they were traveling

28.   Falak and Yadollah's daughter Zahreh rolling curds to dry in the sun

again right away and to pack up in a hurry. Falak was astonished, then angry, for the household was completely set up, and she was in the middle of processing curds with half the mixture already set out to dry. Tents were never pitched or major productions begun if the day's travel was only partly completed. She argued with Borzu, but he retorted that grazing was poor at the site, which was untrue, and that his shepherds had told him to move. On previous days when grazing was inadequate nearby, he had simply sent his herds and shepherds elsewhere. His shepherds would not be so brazen as to tell him to move. Borzu also claimed that he needed to be closer to Jamalbaigi for trading, but he did not need to move the whole camp in order to go by truck to the village. He complained that thieves might be among the Farsimadan nomads camped so close by. He faced such a concern about other Qashqa'i practically every day, but he had never before packed up and moved away from a site because of a potential threat. And, as if he had not already concocted sufficient justi-fication, he pointed out that the present site was unfavorable in case of rain. He did not mention that it was imprudent to camp alone in alien territory (although thieves would think twice about robbing a headman's camp). Everyone was irritated to have the day's labor needlessly doubled and understood that his reasons for moving again were bogus.

Borzu wanted at least to catch up with the others or, better yet, to move past them so he could be in a position of leadership the following morning. He did not know where the others had traveled or camped, however, and he knew they could have bypassed him completely or might still be able to do so. With the exception of Morad who also chose to move a second time and who again camped alone, Borzu did not see any other Qermezi people. Borzu found a new campsite beyond Jamalbaigi at the edge of its fields and returned alone to the village to trade. Later, several women on their way to a well called to Zolaikha and Zohreh, who were out collecting grass, and joked with them about the urgent need to move again.

Except for two families, all the other nomads had traveled to a site some distance beyond Jamalbaigi. There they had spread out under Khalifeh's leadership, with his tent in the center. They had acted as a group independently of Borzu. On most other days when men had needed or wanted to move or camp separately, they notified Borzu directly or via third parties. This day he had received no communications of any kind. Many men had often acquiesced to his need to be near a road, but on this day they had all climbed to higher altitudes where grazing was almost always better and where they said they should have been all along. Borzu's attack on his younger brother was the catalyst to their acting in their own interests.

The two men not camping with either Khalifeh or Borzu were Morad and Barat. They maintained a special relationship with Borzu and did not want to break it, but they were also disturbed enough about his behavior not to be at his side either. Assuming a politically ambiguous position, they each camped alone.

Arriving in Jamalbaigi village, Borzu saw that many Qermezi men had gathered at Hajj Ivaz's shop to trade, and he entered the guest room where he expected others to join him. Other than his son-in-law Asadollah who needed to ask him about his father's debt from the previous autumn, Borzu sat alone and then conducted trade after the others had left. He and his family were Ivaz's guests that evening, but other Qermezi men who might also have been included in the gathering had told the merchant that they had work back at camp and an early departure the next morning.

Ivaz had settled in Jamalbaigi in 1962. His Lur ancestors had joined the

Qashqa'i confederacy in the nineteenth century, and his brother was now the headman of the Bolgar subtribe of Amaleh. Ivaz was one of only two merchants along the migratory route who provided goods on credit to these nomads, most of whom relied on him to replenish their depleted supplies of flour, sugar, salt, and rice. He was the only Qashqa'i merchant with whom they traded during the year. Largely because of the tribal tie they shared, he trusted them to pay their debts, and they were more likely to comply. Other merchants with whom they traded during the migration were not as trusting. Ivaz owned a mill that ground their wheat free of charge. In previous years and when conditions for pastoralism had been better, many men had traded fresh and clarified butter for supplies. This year only Borzu, Abdol Hosain, and Abdol Rasul had produced sufficient quantities; they each brought a kidskin bag of fresh butter. The others bought on credit and promised to pay either cash or clarified butter on the return autumn migration.

Ivaz was well off. He owned land that he cultivated, herds, orchards, and a house in Shiraz for his family. Borzu and his group had traded with him for only a few years, but they and their fathers had earlier traded with a similar partner in a nearby village. Although Ivaz was a Qashqa'i and fluent in Turkish, he chose to speak only Persian, and all conversation directed to him in Turkish he answered in Persian. His Qashqa'i wife spoke Turkish but their children did not know it at all. Borzu and Ivaz discussed the drought, the money spent on fodder, and the merits of sugar-beet pulp. Ivaz reported that several Qashqa'i nomads had recently stored their surplus pulp with him, and the two men laughed at the foolishness of having bought so much. By now most Qashqa'i were disillusioned with the feed and planned never to use it again.

When Borzu had first arrived at Ivaz's shop, he had issued instructions via the merchant about the next day's route for the nomads. They all planned to take another route, however, and they claimed "no grazing" was available the way Borzu had specified. They flaunted their own independence and ignored his authority. They also noted that because of his two-stage migration the previous day, he had moved one day ahead of them, and they were unable to catch up. They complained about the restrictions created by his use of the truck and expressed their displeasure about his expecting them to camp near roads.

Borzu wanted to travel early in the morning as usual, despite there being no one nearby with whom to compete. Falak walked around the campsite searching for a donkey's missing woven cover, and Borzu was delayed in leaving. He told others to look and drove off with Falak. Although she suspected thieves from the village, it was possible the animal had rolled somewhere and the cover had come unfastened. The previous spring when Borzu had picked up supplies in Jamalbaigi, a village woman had untied the decorative woven strip around the lead camel's neck and walked away with it. Falak said she would never trust these thieving villagers again.

Borzu's family and shepherds traveled through a rolling plain, entered a mountain gorge, and crossed over yet another range of mountains that had separated them from their own summer pastures. They approached a small grassy valley where Borzu's flocks were lazily grazing and then traversed some hills to a place overlooking the valley containing Kurd's Fort village. During the trip no other Qermezi families except Morad's were in evidence, unlike on previous days when caravans of people and pack animals had stretched out as far as the eye could see in front and behind and herd animals had dotted the terrain on all sides. The only herds they saw were Borzu's. In sight at a distance behind them, Morad soon caught up with the tail end of Borzu's entourage and maintained a slight separation. People kept looking back futilely for the others.

Borzu waited beside the truck at the bottom of a hill and shouted up to the small group. When people came closer they heard him yell, "Is this not a good place?" It was the first time anyone could remember him seeking advice about a site he had already apparently chosen. And he certainly never sought such advice from shepherds, women, and children. He seemed to want someone to tell him about the location of the other nomads but could not ask directly. Because he had come by another route, he did not yet know that no others were following behind. When people heard the question they all stopped, presumably to wait to continue down the slope as soon as Morad did. But Morad was in no mood to follow Borzu's lead, and he busied himself with "adjusting" his stirrups. Borzu looked helpless and small from the higher vantage point. Assuming that no one approved the site (when no one had said anything either way), Borzu drove on, and his entourage was forced to travel a long way farther, into the valley of Kurd's Fort and skirting the village buildings and most cultivated fields.

A Persian farmer guarding his fields became agitated on seeing the small group of nomads approach, and he shouted, with pauses in between, when no one changed direction: "You must be Muslims, so of course you won't allow your animals to enter my fields. You must not be Muslims, because your animals are in my fields. You must be unbelievers, because

you are ruining my fields. Unbelievers! You destroy fields everywhere
you travel!"

Women and girls picked a green plant along the way; they noted it
grew nowhere else and was tasty in cooking. The group traveled up a
rocky gorge and down into another valley, past a village cool with trees
and flowing water. There they located the road again and at the same time
saw the truck approach. Borzu chose a site up a hill along the road. When
Morad arrived he selected a site across the road some distance away. Many
other nomads were migrating through and camping in the area. Borzu
was angry about the congestion and began to talk about moving on, but
Falak persevered about staying put, the first time people had seen her
make the final decision, especially against his wishes. He seemed inca-
pable of making even small decisions in the face of the major problem he
had created for himself, and he collapsed on a carpet. Falak built a fire and
served him tea. Yadollah said he could not remember the last time she
had done either.

Later Borzu went to watch for the arrival of his flocks, and he found
Morad at a distance doing the same thing. He asked him if he had seen
any Qermezi people traveling, and Morad said he had not. The two men
separated, each climbing to a different hilltop to scan the horizon. For
several hours Borzu sat immobile. Many nomads followed the route his
family had just taken. As each group and then family came into view, he
thought he identified Qermezi individuals and animals, but as each came
closer he saw that they were strangers. The rest of the day Borzu and
Falak frequently asked the shepherds and children, "Is the group coming?" and they would peer in the expected direction. Since his attack on
Abdol Hosain, Borzu had seen no members of his group except Asadollah
and Morad, each of whom was maintaining his own distance and not
confiding in him. Borzu had no idea what was happening to the others in
his absence.

On one of Borzu's walks as he surveyed the landscape for his group,
he saw Iraj Khan Darrehshuri driving on the road and invited him to his
tent. Although Iraj Khan was a minor khan with virtually no tribal followers, Borzu fell into a frenzy of hospitality. He urgently summoned
Morad to kill a kid and then hastily spread out carpets, made a fire,
brewed tea, and ordered his family and shepherds to serve his guest.

As Iraj Khan settled down comfortably to receive this hospitality, Yadollah herded Borzu's camels in front of the tent and attempted to treat
and administer antidotes to them. The camels had attacked a large patch

of broad-leafed wild artichokes and eaten voraciously despite Yadollah's frantic efforts to drive them away. The first growth of wild artichokes in early spring was tender, but as the plant matured the leaves and stalks became tough and thorny. The camels were still starved for adequate vegetation and had stuffed their mouths. The plant caused the animals to bloat, and in extreme cases the gas could suddenly rupture their stomachs and intestines, killing them instantly. Two camels were sicker than the others, and Yadollah directed his attention to them. Alternating between the two, he rhythmically pumped with his feet on their folded forelegs to rock them gently, to make them belch the gas. He yelled at his wife Golabshar to come and do the same. Aqaboa and Khodabakhsh were out of sight with their herds and could not help, and Borzu was obligated to attend to his guest. Iraj Khan made no effort to assist and expressed no interest in the crisis.

All the camels were emitting bad smells, had severe diarrhea, and were moaning and trying to roll on their sides. The ones less stricken stood stiffly with their back legs stretched apart. The stench in the air was terrible, and Yadollah kept looking incredulously at Borzu and Iraj Khan who were sitting relatively calmly in the tent sipping tea and attempting to ignore the disaster. Yadollah tried to force the camels to eat a plant with anti-gas properties, and he shoved their own dung and handfuls of loose dirt into their mouths to make them vomit. The animals did not even retch.

As soon as Morad had finished butchering the kid for Iraj Khan, he ran to help, hands and arms still covered with blood. The sickest of the camels collapsed on its side and stretched out its legs. It was moaning and obviously in pain, and Golabshar kept repeating, "Oh my God." Seeing that Borzu was not going to act, Morad felt the bloated stomach and abdomen, yanked out wool and hair in two places, and scratched an X on the skin with a knife. With a muttered "in the name of God," he plunged in his long knife to the hilt and worked it around inside. The camel gave no indication of pain. Suddenly a loud hiss and then the noise of a muffled explosion came from the animal, followed by massive quantities of green mushy liquid oozing from the knife hole. The camel twitched once and was still. Morad pumped at the neck to ensure that blood flowed there and then quickly slit the throat in two places. Blood spurted out and foamed on the ground. At this point Borzu called Morad to make more tea for the khan. When Morad finished that task he began the arduous process of skinning and butchering the camel. Haste was essential because the stench of the contents of the stomach and intestines would soon penetrate the meat.

The other camels were still sick but none as desperately as the now dead one had been. Yadollah's pumping on the folded forelegs seemed to help the others, and soon he saw they were recovering. He was then able to assist Morad with the butchering. When Iraj Khan finally departed, Borzu came to watch the proceedings. Morad hastened to check the condition of his own camels, for his son had come to tell him that they were sick too. He pumped on the forelegs of one, saw that the others were stricken but not severely, and then returned to the butchering. The shepherd Khosrow arrived in camp and joined the two men in the arduous task. While they were removing the skin from the trunk of the body, the belly suddenly became more swollen. When Morad accidentally slit the membrane under the skin, intestines popped out and rapidly inflated from the pressure of the gas. It was obvious to all that the animal would soon explode. Just previously the men had kidded one another about being afraid, and now no one wanted to act cowardly by moving away. Sitting on a rock at a distance, Borzu did back off on some pretext, at exactly the right time. The sound of the explosion was shattering; its force blew open the camel. The three men and the children who had been watching jumped in fright and ran scared, but not before being sprayed with a foul-smelling liquid.

Borzu noted later that if a camel afflicted with this malady was not skinned and cut open but simply left where it died, it swelled to an enormous size, and the subsequent explosion could be heard a long distance away. The customary treatment for stricken camels was a combination of three plants with anti-gas properties, then kerosene (which Borzu did not own) forced down their throats if no change in their condition occurred, and finally a puncture.

After attempting to wipe themselves off, Morad and the other two men checked what was left of the internal organs and other internal parts but saved nothing because of contamination from the gas. Investigating the mangled body cavern, Morad observed that if he had jabbed the knife in a slightly different place, the camel might have recovered. Borzu placed no blame on Morad and instead told Yadollah that the death was his fault, for he had obviously not watched what the camels had eaten. But he also said that the camels' stomachs were still in such a poor state from the hunger of winter that the animals were not strong or well enough to tolerate illness or distress of any kind. Seven of his mature camels had died since autumn, and he noted that he had never seen a year as miserable as this one. The three men severed the camel's legs at the knees, to throw to the waiting dogs, and then cut off the remaining portions of the legs. As they butchered the animal they piled the meat on large trays. Morad went to check on his own camels again before riding into Kurd's Fort on errands. He had rolled up the camel skin and took it with him to sell.

Borzu stayed in camp the rest of the day. The air hung heavy with the camels' stench. He asked news of the whereabouts of Qermezi of all passersby, whether Qashqa'i nomads traveling through the area or Persians and Lurs with plows and draft animals or loads of firewood. No one could provide any information.

Morad returned after dark accompanied by a Lur "village friend" whom Qermezi men had known from previous migrations. The man had bought the camel skin for less than a dollar and had come to buy the meat. In the days when shoemakers had used camel skins, a whole skin sold for much more, but a market no longer existed for the product. Nomads and villagers were more apt to buy factory-made shoes. Borzu asked the villager about the price of flour in Kurd's Fort and commented that earlier on the migration he had purchased it for half the cited amount. After drinking tea and eating a meal, the man agreed to take the meat off Borzu's hands and said he would accept as payment a fifth of the money he received from selling the meat to others. He would pay Borzu in flour, part the next day and the rest in autumn when Borzu migrated through the area again. They did not put their agreement in writing. The transaction seemed fair to all parties, and Borzu gained another friend for the future.

Borzu rose at the usual early time and ordered people to pack, but he was disorganized and did not rush. The route for the pack animals was short, north through several valleys, one green with grass and marked by ridges from plowing. Borzu's desired campsite was occupied by another Qashqa'i group, and he found an alternative site farther on. Zolaikha pointed out campsites of previous years and the spot where they had eaten meat after Qorban Ali's camel died from too heavy a load. Morad camped in the same valley but at a distance again. Several Lur men reported that Borzu's rival Sohrab had been in the area but was now gone. Borzu slept the rest of the morning, heated water for tea but lacked energy to complete the task, and scanned the valley for Qermezi. No one appeared. His kinsmen Arghvan and Safdar passed by at a distance but did not stop. They had never been part of his migrating unit. Qahraman, another son of Arghvan, was one stage behind. He had been delayed by problems with pack animals and had not yet been able to catch up. Lonely, Falak also watched the valley while she rolled another batch of curds to dry in the sun. Rain fell with intermittent hail, delighting the children.

Later in the day Safdar's wife Fatemeh came to pay her respects to Falak in the customary visit made after someone had been seriously ill. She reported that some members of Borzu's group were following behind him along a different route, the first real news the family had heard in days. Borzu sent Khosrow back to Kurd's Fort for gasoline and the flour from the sale of the camel meat. Twice the previous day he had been unsuccessful in buying gasoline; the village had exhausted its supply. A few other Qermezi men, also not part of Borzu's group this migration, passed by on horseback on their way to Kurd's Fort but did not stop to see him. The lone tent of Falak's kinsman Hasan was at a distance; he often traveled alone. Borzu spent the afternoon with the herds, not herding but just watching them graze and drink. He talked with a Persian man driving by who wanted to buy fat sheep and told him he had none. Khosrow returned from Kurd's Fort with flour and wheat but no gasoline, and Borzu worried that he would not be able to drive on much farther.

In the morning Borzu found much at fault in his family's behavior. Aqaboa reported that a ewe had disappeared from an area where Lur hired herders were camped, and Borzu grabbed a club and ran off to confront them. His family could hear him shouting from a long distance away. The animal was later found in his other herd of sheep. Again the route he chose was short, across the valley, up a gorge, over a mountain pass, and then down into the rolling plain of Khosrow Shirin, the former summer headquarters of the ilkhani, paramount leader of the Qashqa'i confederacy. The expansive plain was dotted with springs surrounded by lush grassy patches. Borzu planned to exploit the rich resources of Khosrow Shirin for several days. He noted later, as did others, that when the Qashqa'i ilkhani had been in office (and not under arrest or in exile abroad), Qashqa'i nomads who needed to migrate through Khosrow Shirin on their way to their own summer pastures to the north were forced to travel quickly. Some years they were not allowed to stop or even to collect water at the many springs. Armed men from the ilkhani's entourage made certain the nomads kept moving. The pastoral resources of Khosrow Shirin had been used exclusively by the ilkhani, his family, and their immediate supporters who were members of the Amaleh tribe.

Khalifeh later told the story of how, when he was a young boy, his father Shir Mohammad and six other Qermezi men had sought sanctuary at Khosrow Shirin. Ayaz Kikha Darrehshuri, whom Qermezi men supported, had fought with Nasrollah Khan Darrehshuri and then requested aid from the Qashqa'i ilkhani at Khosrow Shirin. When Nasrollah Khan tried to force the Qermezi group to join his entourage, the seven Qermezi men fled from Darrehshuri summer pastures, traveling at night and hiding by day. They stole twenty donkeys from wood collectors to transport their goods. On the run for seven days, they finally reached the sanctuary of the ilkhani's camp at Khosrow Shirin where Ayaz Kikha was temporarily residing. On another occasion, to escape being drawn into the dispute between Ayaz Kikha and Nasrollah Khan, the Qermezi group sought sanctuary in summer pastures in Bakhtiyari tribal territory.

Darrehshuri khans were often part of the oral history recounted by Qermezi people, as in these cases. And Qermezi people were sometimes a small part of the stories Darrehshuri khans told about their own history. The two groups had interacted for as long as they could remember.

In the early twentieth century Ayaz Kikha, kalantar or preeminent khan of Darrehshuri, had expanded his tribe's winter pastures. He had moved against Boir Ahmad Lurs to the north and Kashkuli Qashqa'i to the south. One day in the winter of 1917 a Qermezi woman at Paku, his winter campsite, shouted that Boir Ahmad Lurs were attacking in an effort to regain land. Ayaz Kikha's youngest son Shahbaz, a good rifleman and fighter, did not respond to the alarm. His father chided him, "Why do you sit when Lurs attack? Lurs are taking the skirts of Darrehshuri women" (that is, raping them). Shahbaz leapt on a white horse and rode to the scene of the attack. As he crested a hill, a Lur rifleman shot and killed him. Grieving, Ayaz Kikha sent a message to Shir Mohammad Qermezi to ask for gunmen to seek revenge against the Lurs. Shir Mohammad's brother Khan Mirza responded, contracted cholera during the mission, and died.

Shir Mohammad had occasionally visited the camp of Esma'il Khan Soulat ed-Douleh, the Qashqa'i ilkhani, at Khosrow Shirin. As headman, Khalifeh had also gone there once to see Naser Khan, the new ilkhani. The ilkhani's camp was surrounded by tents belonging to his retainers and other Amaleh supporters. Each Qashqa'i tribe had its own reception tent; Khalifeh and other Darrehshuri men ate separately from other guests. Men in a long cooking tent prepared meals over a row of fire pits, and sometimes as many as one thousand guests were fed in a single day. Women of the ilkhani's family, called *bibis*, greeted some guests and moved freely about the camp. Khalifeh, who had brought several sheep as gifts for Naser Khan, received in return a voucher stamped with the ilkhani's seal for 250 kilograms each of rice and wheat. Borzu, a young man at the time, collected the commodities in Semirom. Khalifeh said he had not gone to see the ilkhani at Khosrow Shirin other than on this one occasion, for visiting meant he offered loyalty, and he had lacked any other reason to go there. Khalifeh, Borzu, and a few other Qermezi men had attended Naser Khan's military camps (*ordus*) during times of war.

On the way down the steep path into Khosrow Shirin plain, young girls tied cloth strips they had prepared earlier to a bush already filled with many others. They did not linger at the bush or utter any words out loud. Grinning, they spotted and pointed out the exact strips they had left the previous migration. Farther down, Zolaikha saw the grave of Khalifeh's son Bahlul who some years back had sickened during the migration and then died suddenly three days later from a swollen throat that cut off his breathing. The next migration Khalifeh had set up an inscribed gravestone. Every spring and autumn Bahlul's mother went to the grave and cried.

Borzu camped by a lovely spring, its waters lush with different kinds of edible plants that women and children gathered avidly. Grass by the spring was good for the pack animals, and shepherds took their herds up the nearby mountain slopes to graze. Across the valley Morad pitched a tent with a sloped roof in anticipation of rain, and Borzu was once again alone. Falak and the shepherds' wives rolled curds and set out the balls to dry. Morad sheared a few sheep and talked of what he would buy with the wool, but his wife Jansanam informed him that she planned to use all the wool for weaving. Morad noted that shearing the sheep at this time made the animals so cold that they ate more and became fat. Borzu met him on a hilltop, and they exchanged a few words. They spotted camels belonging to Abdol Hosain, Abdol Rasul, and Gholam Hosain at a distance, but the three men did not come near Borzu's camp. Several peddlers on their return trip to Semirom passed by with donkeys laden with goods they had acquired. They did not stop to trade. Borzu sent Khosrow on Morad's mule to Khosrow Shirin village to try to purchase gasoline, and he was finally successful. Borzu could leave that source of anxiety behind for a while. Borzu gave him camel meat for his efforts.

Morad, who hated to have people borrow his pack animals, took Borzu's horse to return to the previous campsite to find, he said, a missing horse cover. Women noted that the cover was not lost, that he only wanted to visit the others from whom he had been isolated because of his loyalty to Borzu. After greeting the men who were now traveling separately from Borzu, Morad supported his own actions. He declared that, even though he believed Borzu had misbehaved, the families who began the migration together ought to stay together. Their primary purpose, he reminded the others, was to reach summer pastures safely, and they each held a commitment to one another. He pointed out that now everyone traveled more or less alone, and he complained about his two brothers with whom he had always migrated in the past. Abdol Rasul was allied with Abdol Hosain, and Naser would not ally with either brother for fear of antagonizing one or the other.

That evening Amaleh Qashqa'i shepherds driving from Firuzabad to Semirom by car to join their herds stopped by the road and began to set up camp. Borzu was absent, attending his herds, and Falak exclaimed that the cars contained khans who were coming to visit him. Panicking, she set her family and herders' families frantically to work straightening up the tent and camp to prepare for guests. Borzu saw who they were and sent Golabshar to offer the use of a tent, which they declined. Later he sent butter and yogurt, and when they returned the dish filled with cabbage and beans, they discovered a distant kinship tie with Borzu.

Borzu had said he would move late the next morning in order to let the sun warm the tent first, for it had been cold in the mornings, but he was up and active at the usual early time. He announced that threatening rain clouds required as early a departure as possible. The route north through Khosrow Shirin plain was short, and Borzu camped in an area of springs, edible water plants, and grass similar to the previous day. Rain began, and Yadollah quickly pitched the tent. During the trip Borzu had seen a few Qermezi families traveling at a distance, but no one camped within view, and he was as alone as ever. Borzu's herders and their families had by now sorted out who was traveling and camping with whom, and they were surprised by some of the alliances. They often talked of little else. Women again gathered water plants; they said some grew here that did not grow elsewhere. Yadollah collected hardwood from the mountains for making tent stakes. Camping somewhere in the expansive valley, Naser sent word to Yadollah and Morad's shepherd to ask for help in finding a lost camel. Borzu was furious at the affront. How dare Naser ask help from his herder when no one bothered to give him any!

Although Borzu had announced where he would travel the next morning, he changed his mind sometime during the night, and his tent stayed up when the herders expected to hear it fall to the ground. People in their tents kept peeking out to see if any preparations to move were evident. Given Borzu's mood, no one would ask him directly. Over breakfast he explained that he needed to give his tired animals a rest and that plenty

of water was available at this location but not the next. The real reason
for not moving, however, was obvious in his behavior through the morning. He wanted to let the other nomads behind him catch up, for he kept
scanning the southern horizon for their appearance. By traveling short
distances on each of the past few days, he had tried to allow the others,
some of whom took meandering routes in order to find good grazing, to
join him. Some of the families for whom he waited delayed moving while
Naser searched for his camel.

Two gypsy tinners arrived at the camp of Morad, who had respected
Borzu's wish not to travel that day, and they set to work applying tin to
worn copper vessels. The younger gypsy scoured the vessels with sand
and water by standing in or on a vessel, holding onto a tripod, and scrub-
bing with his bare feet by twisting his body back and forth. Then he
worked the goatskin bellows. After heating pure tin and sal ammoniac,
the elder gypsy applied the liquid mixture with a cotton pad to each clean
vessel as he heated it over a fire, and then he solidified the fresh coating
with cold water. The tinners accepted wool or cash in exchange. Next they
moved on to Borzu's tent. In Borzu's absence, Falak "borrowed" wool
from Morad to pay the tinners, to Morad's irritation (the price of his
loyalty, he mumbled), and she also gave them tea leaves. The gypsies said
they spent every winter in southeast Fars tinning among Arab tribes
there. They spoke Turkish, Luri, Persian, and Arabic in their travels
among various groups in the province.

Ali and Barat entered the valley and located campsites, and a few others
followed. Barat sent a son to invite Borzu and Falak as guests. Barat and
Hemmat were soon to diverge from Borzu's migratory route, for their
summer pastures were not at Hanalishah. They always hosted Borzu as
headman and brother-in-law before their departure. As Falak's only close
kin in the group, they were also the most appropriate people to celebrate
her recovery. Some people viewed the event as an attempted reconciliation
between Borzu and the others. Young Farideh donned her best skirt, for
she hoped to accompany her parents to the camp of her mother's brothers
(usually a person's favorite relative because of the affection and informality possible in the relationship), but they ignored her as they left, and she
stood tearfully in their wake.

Men in Barat's tent stood, in an act Borzu initiated, as Khalifeh entered
and was given the place of honor. The gypsy tinners were also present
and sat as guests for a long while before tinning the vessels there. An
elderly Talehbazli Darrehshuri woman who was traveling alone to summer pastures sat in the background. Barat and Hemmet viewed them-

selves as good Muslims and hence did not turn her away when she sought someone with whom to migrate for a while. Strained in their relationship, Khalifeh and Borzu did not talk to one another. Borzu dominated the conversation as usual and tried to impress the others with his plans, but the men sat stiffly and silently with heads bowed and talked quietly about the migration to their immediate neighbors when they had a chance. No one mentioned Borzu's attack on Abdol Hosain, and everyone kept a level head except Borzu who became excited as he announced his own plans.

After the meal and Borzu's departure, the men became animated. They discussed with Barat how best to slit the skin of the swollen neck of a donkey to relieve the pressure. Asadollah had brought a pony with a stomach ailment, and they considered various treatments. Akbar sadly reported that the best of his two camels had died from eating wild artichokes four days previously. Bahram told how he had suspected that Farsimadan Qashqa'i nomads near Jamalbaigi had stolen a lamb, and he had ridden to their camp to confront them. He found his lamb covered by a blanket behind a tent and took it with him when he left. Barat and Hemmat argued with the tinners about payment, in particular how to weigh the wool they intended to trade for the work. Other men entered the argument and offered help as they usually did in such negotiations. Khalifeh told the gypsies to come to his tent if they would accept dried curds. If they insisted on cash, he told them they could go elsewhere.

Back at Borzu's camp some distance away, two Persian men complained bitterly to Borzu about his donkeys in their fields. He invited them into the tent to pacify them. While women and girls milked the ewes and does, assisted by shepherds and their children, Falak boasted about the meal her brothers had held in her honor and about Khalifeh's attention and kind words to her. He had actually offered only a routine greeting. Jansanam and Katayun were eager to know if fighting among the men had broken out at lunch. Returning to his shearing, Morad explained to an itinerant peddler that if he did not hobble his camels at night they would flee. They dreamed of green grass in winter or summer pastures, woke, and set off in one of the two directions. His job then was to decide which was the pasture of their dreams and search in that direction.

Borzu continued to be angry and irritated at everything and everyone, but he had calmed down somewhat because his group was with him again. Although the other families were widely dispersed, at least he now knew they were in the same valley and could keep track of them. At lunch he had said a few curt words to his son-in-law Asadollah about the mule he had borrowed and never returned. He complained that Asadollah had not even asked him if he needed the animal back. Late that afternoon Asadollah's young brother brought the mule to Borzu, but Falak prevailed upon him to let Asadollah have it again. She said his family needed it and hers did not.

The next morning Borzu wanted to be packed and on the road earlier than usual because most of the Qermezi families near him had camped farther ahead. The route, north toward the end of the spring-filled Khosrow Shirin plain, was short and easy, and for once the truck and pack animals traveled the same road. Passing by Khalifeh's and Bahram's camp, Borzu heard that three of their camels had disappeared, and he took their heaviest baggage in his truck and told Zolaikha to load additional items on his mule. He left Zohreh and Farideh to help out while men searched for the camels, and he told Yadollah to load the remaining pack animals. Anxious to be near the parents of Hosain Ali whom she desired to marry, Zolaikha pushed herself in Zohreh's place and sent her sister with the caravan of pack animals. Driving by Asadollah on the road, Borzu was irritated to see that he was riding his mule on the search. People often used a borrowed pack animal for arduous traveling and transporting in order to protect their own animals, and for this reason owners disliked loaning animals.

Borzu found a pleasant camp with plenty of grass but no water nearby, and he complained that Yadollah was not present to pitch the tent. The snowy peaks of Dena (approximately 4,400 meters), highest mountains in summer pastures and dominating the area, stood to the west. This region was Farsimadan Qashqa'i territory. Seeing Mount Dena, everyone in Borzu's group was reminded that they were close to their own summer pastures. They remembered being in this locale seven years previously when hungry camels had eaten excessive amounts of mature wild artichoke plants; twenty-two of them had died in one day. Morad camped farther away from Borzu than he had been camping recently, freed now by the proximity of others to be more independent. Bahram and Akbar finally located the three errant camels and came to Borzu's camp to collect the goods he had transported for them. Borzu had earlier inspected the baggage and commented that he was practically out of salt. After pausing to finger Khalifeh's salt bag, he poured out a panful for himself and later spread it out on rocks for the animals to lick.

Khalifeh came to pick up his own baggage, and Falak had to prompt Borzu into inviting him in for tea. Zolaikha took special pains over lunch in order to impress Hosain Ali's father. She served him and her father rice, cabbage, and the one mushroom children had found that morning. Khalifeh had purposely avoided contact with his younger brother Borzu the whole migration, but he was now obliged by the assistance Borzu had rendered to pay his respects. Borzu had probably offered help with this end in mind and took advantage of the opportunity to tell Khalifeh how clever his own plans for migrating were and where Khalifeh should travel in the morning.

Most men stayed clear of Borzu whenever possible so that they could avoid instructions like these. Men preferred making up their own minds or at least hearing of Borzu's plans secondhand, even though they might desire the very same schedule and route and might still "follow" his lead in the morning. To maintain control, Borzu tried to be first to travel in the morning and then to find a campsite first and halt that day's trek. If he were not first to leave, others ahead of him could easily choose their own routes and campsites without expressly ignoring or flouting his desired itinerary. People needed to travel together for protection, but they still chafed under Borzu's instructions. They compromised by acting as if they decided independently while also remaining part of a group.

Sometimes when men and women talked about Borzu and the problems of the migration, they told a humorous old story about a Shesh Boluki Qashqa'i group. During the migration the group's headman died suddenly, and men assembled to select a new one. When they could not reach a decision, the most intelligent man suggested that the first one to be packed and moving the next morning should become the new headman. As dawn was breaking, people peeked out of their tents to see who had been first to awake. They saw a black dog running up the path. So they hastily broke camp and followed the dog. Every time the dog stopped to scratch or rest, people selected tent sites and unloaded their pack animals. Before they could pitch their tents, however, the dog was on the move again, and they had to reload and hasten to follow him. They tried to keep up with him the rest of the day.

On returning to his own campsite, Khalifeh commented that no one had been present to pitch his tent. Bahram's tent stood close by, but the son maintained his independence by not setting up his father's tent. Khalifeh complained about the choice of campsite, usually his responsibility but this day left to Ali, and he said he envied Borzu's site. He pointed out a campsite he had occupied twenty years previously when Ziad Khan Darrehshuri had sent him meat from four wild rams he had shot on Mount Dena. Still angry at his shepherd, Khalifeh yelled at him about another lost kid.

Later Khalifeh performed purifying ablutions and said his prayers. He and Jehangir were the only Qermezi people who prayed regularly. Their brother Ali occasionally did, especially when Khalifeh was nearby. People sometimes joked that Borzu did not even know the correct Arabic phrases. Men his age noted that they had seen him go through the motions only three times in his life, and each of these had occurred at village weddings when he apparently was embarrassed to be the only man not engaged in noon prayers. Wedding guests had asked him, "Aren't you going to say your prayers?" Explaining to a Persian peasant one day why he did not make a pilgrimage to Mashhad, even though he could obviously afford it, Borzu pointed out that pilgrims were obliged to pray at least three times a day for the rest of their lives. He said he was too busy and could not afford the luxury of that much free time.

Abul Hasan and Hajji Qorban stopped to see their kinsman Khalifeh before returning to winter pastures to harvest their families' grain. Akbar came to visit and talked about wanting to find work in Shiraz, any job that would pay at least seventy-five cents a day (which he said was more than he earned as a nomadic pastoralist). His herd of eighty animals had been reduced to thirty by the famine and cold of winter. He was ashamed to mention how small his herd was. In no position to help him, his father Ali had lost more than half of his own herd of 170 animals in the past two seasons. Akbar wanted to attend the tribal teacher training program in Shiraz but did not quite meet the qualifications. Morad asked Akbar to write letters to merchants in Kazerun and to his son in school there, which the two men going to winter pastures could personally deliver. Men rarely wrote or sent letters, but when they did, they did not trust the government mail service and avoided it whenever possible. Even when letters did actually arrive at town shops, they often became lost there.

A Farsimadan Qashqa'i khan traveling by car from winter to summer pastures sent a servant to Borzu's tent to ask for yogurt. To avoid complying, Falak told him they were not yet producing dairy products. When Zolaikha filled a glass with yogurt and handed it to him, Borzu told her to fill a large bowl instead and to include butter and then lectured her about not giving enough, primarily in reaction to Falak's objecting to any dairy products being given at all. Falak angrily muttered, "Khans, khans, khans." She complained that Mohammad Karim went hungry living alone in Kazerun while Borzu wasted valued food. Later Borzu wondered aloud why he had given so much.

Borzu went to watch his sheep grazing, and as usual he whistled to them while they ate. He said they ate more, and more contentedly, when he whistled. Pointing north, he commented that his summer pastures at Hanalishah were ten days away and that the nomads could be there in three days if it was necessary. The remark was unintentionally portentous.

All night horses and donkeys browsed in nearby wheat fields. They were becoming difficult to control, for they had been gradually replenishing their stores of fat and were now entering the mating season when they became unruly. Early in the morning Borzu was impatient to load the pack animals and truck, and his entourage managed to leave ahead of other Qermezi families. The route left the Khosrow Shirin plain and crossed a hill into another valley. Borzu chose the best and greenest campsite, and everyone else spread around the valley at the base of hills at some distance from him. Nearby were unoccupied rudimentary settlements of hired herders who stayed at this location during late autumn despite the cold and snow. They had built stone-fortified animal shelters and stone foundations a meter high for their huts. Deep fire pits lined with stone indicated that they made charcoal in their spare time. A Lur man on horseback came to complain to Borzu that two sheep had been stolen the previous night, and Borzu replied that the thief was certainly among the nomads ahead of him.

Assisting with milking, Khodabakhsh announced from behind the tent, "By God, I'm leaving today." Overhearing the remark, Borzu flew into a rage and leapt from the tent to scream at him and beat him with a stick. He had just been contemplating his many problems and shouted that he could not possibly replace a shepherd on a day's notice. Earlier that morning Khodabakhsh had told Borzu's children that he was quitting that day, and Borzu, informed of the intention, had waited to see what would happen. He had said he would strike the shepherd if he threatened to leave.

When Khodabakhsh's contract had finished the last day of winter, he had wanted to stay with his mother and siblings in winter pastures. Borzu had told him to continue as herder during the first stage of the spring migration, as far as Wide Mountain. At Wide Mountain Borzu informed him he could leave when they reached Kurd's Fort, and at Kurd's Fort he instructed him to stay until Semirom. Motivated by Abul Hasan and Hajji Qorban's imminent departure for winter pastures, Khodabakhsh wanted to accompany the two because he was frightened to travel alone from Semirom. Borzu had already paid his salary for the previous year but had not given him money since and had promised none. He had explained that the wheat he had taken on credit from the government for his family was sufficient payment for the extra time he worked. He had also reminded him that he had given his brother the right to harvest a plot of grain at Molla Balut as an additional payment for his services.

Khosrow and his mother Geljahan tried to restrain Borzu in his physical attack on Khodabakhsh. After many swift blows, Borzu continued to shout at him. Terrified, Khodabakhsh crouched on the ground and cried. Borzu accused Aqaboa, who had also announced his intention to quit once they reached summer pastures, of inciting the young shepherd to leave. Falak informed Borzu that he had behaved badly, and the other women sat stunned at the sudden attack. (Borzu had found over the years that the element of surprise was effective in the assertion of power and application of force.) Falak unsuccessfully tried to get Khodabakhsh to his feet and then sent Zohreh to tend the goat herd. Khodabakhsh followed later and sat huddled and crying on the mountainside. Aqaboa went to soothe him, and soon Zohreh was able to return to her own chores. Later she tried to find him, for he had not yet eaten anything that day. That evening Khodabakhsh, submissive and with eyes downcast, appeared in camp and assumed his regular tea-making position.

Borzu sent Zohreh to retrieve the mule from Asadollah and then rode the animal to check the next day's route, as he said he always used to do. He had become so reliant on the truck that this was only the second time this migration he had ridden an animal. He hoped to find plentiful grazing at the next site in the mountains and planned for the group to stay there several days. Asadollah visited later hoping to borrow the mule again, but Borzu said nothing to him about it, and he returned home on foot. Camels had eaten wild artichoke plants, and their stomachs were distended. To keep them quiet as they sat, Yadollah talked with them while he carved wild pistachio branches into pins for fastening tent panels together. Then he tightly wrapped goat-hair yarn around the bundle of pins and soaked them in water in order to straighten and harden them. Zolaikha spread out the past several days' collection of wild garlic on a mat so the bulbs could dry in the sun.

A man in tattered clothes rode into camp on a mule to retrieve his son Borj Ali, Abdol Hosain's hired shepherd. He was Borzu's mother's sister's son. His wife had broken her hand and was unable to milk, and he needed another woman at home. He wanted to substitute a younger unmarried son for Borj Ali, whose wife could then perform a woman's chores, but he had been unable to find Abdol Hosain's camp.

Borzu rose earlier than usual, impatient to load the truck and leave. The route for the vehicle was circuitous, and he was nervous that he

29. Morad and his shepherd Behruz shearing sheep. Borzu's tent and truck stand in the background.

would not arrive first at the intended campsite. Zohreh, who had been herding lambs and kids, reported that a cultivator had confiscated Asadollah's mule he had found browsing in his fields. Falak tried to convince Borzu to lend their own mule again, but he flatly refused, fed up with arguments about the animal and the trafficking between the two households. Because the area of the day's planned campsites lacked water, one woman from every household took an unloaded pack animal in a direction opposite that of the day's route in order to fill water bags. Falak worried that her daughter Samarrokh would be unable to go along; she would have no pack animal to take.

Although Borzu had said that the people who had camped near him would travel the way he instructed Yadollah and Zolaikha to go, no one did. The short route for Borzu's entourage ran up a gorge and out onto a plateau. Morad, the group's only companion, located campsites for Borzu and himself, and people quickly unloaded the pack animals. Too late, Borzu appeared on the crest of a hill and shouted some now superseded instructions. Yadollah set up the tent, and Falak forgot her weakness in order to guard the family's food supply from him and came trudging down the hill with Bizhan on her back. Zolaikha had gone for water, Zohreh was herding young animals, and Falak (needlessly) feared Yadollah being alone with her household supplies. He was more concerned about his uncomfortable pants than with stealing a handful of tea leaves, and he said he had not worn worse trousers since he was in the army. The ones Borzu had procured for him from Kurd's Fort, straight-legged "Western" trousers with no give in the waist, did not allow him to move or squat in the accustomed manner.

Women returned from their water run happy to have found many partridge eggs along the way. Complaining that nomads previously passing through the area had plucked all the mushrooms, they said the region had always been bountiful enough for them all in the past. Borzu settled into the new site and made kebab for himself. Anxious to exploit the fuel this location provided, Katayun spent part of the day smoking a kidskin bag to be used for storing dairy products. Morad invited Borzu to an informal lunch; he was the only person ever to feel this comfortable with Borzu. He fried small strips of goat meat with local mushrooms and wild garlic leaves in fresh butter in the concave side of the bread-baking pan placed over the fire. Later Borzu's kinsman Hasel came to pay his respects. He and a few others were soon to branch off from Borzu's migratory route and travel in the direction of Naqneh village where he intended to settle. His brother was already there making arrangements. Borzu planned not to move the next day, for he said he wanted time to fatten the flocks and gather firewood to take to Hanalishah. More pertinently, he wanted the other nomads, somewhat behind again, to catch up and join him.

The next morning Borzu branded lambs in the herd tended by Mohammad Hosain. He said that the day (a Thursday) was auspicious for this work. Hasel had stayed the night in order to help, as men often did when they were about to depart from Borzu, and Mohammad Hosain and Khosrow stood ready to assist. Borzu marked each animal on its right ear or snout with one of three brands—his own, Mohammad Karim's, or Bizhan's. He placed Bizhan's brand on animals under nimsud contract with a Semirom merchant-moneylender. After providing the customary lunch of rice to his helpers, he divided the wood Yadollah had gathered into loads for the truck and a camel. Zohreh returned with water after several hours, and shepherds watered their herds from this supply. Samarrokh came seeking a remedy for the sick pony. Ordinarily she stayed a while and was given food for her family, but because Borzu was present she took the medicine and left quickly. Rules of social distance between men and their newly married daughters still held for Borzu and Samarrokh. Later her husband Asadollah brought the pony to Barat for treatment, but it was too late, and it died in the afternoon.

Buzzards circled in the air above the nearby mountains, and Khosrow

30.   Borzu branding a lamb with help from Yadollah

unsuccessfully searched for the dead or dying animal that had attracted them. Barat visited Borzu, for he too was preparing to branch off from Borzu's migratory route. He had stopped to collect Morad before coming so as not to have to visit Borzu alone. A rumor circulated in the small group that a Lur man had shot a Qermezi man on the Saran Plain because animals had trespassed in his fields. Gendarmes had reportedly sent the injured or dead man's companions to their headquarters in Ardekan village. Borzu, Barat, and Morad discussed the probability of the rumor's accuracy and the possible identity of the Qermezi man involved. (Later they heard that Mir Gharati, a renowned Qashqa'i warrior of Lur background, had shot at Ahmad Khan.) Because ewes and does were now producing more milk, women were increasingly busy, especially in the evening and in the early morning before dawn, processing milk into yogurt, sour milk, butter, clarified butter, curds, and whey.

Borzu had said he wanted to leave earlier than usual in the morning, but he was delayed by having to rearrange the baggage to accommodate the firewood. A third of the truck's load was now wood, and a camel and a donkey also carried heavy burdens of wood. Some stages ahead lacked fuel, and Borzu also wanted to take as much firewood as possible to his summer pastures, for good fuel was lacking there. With new space needed for the many milk products being generated, packing and loading had become complicated.

The day's route led across a valley and a series of hills to a steep decline and then through a narrow valley leading into a plain south of the town of Semirom. When passing through the narrow valley, Morad turned around to shout happily to the long caravan behind him that the region of Semirom was now within view. He and the other nomads remarked that they immediately felt more at ease, for they now fell under the authority of the Darrehshuri khans and the government officials in Semirom with whom they were familiar. Any disputes that occurred from this spot on would involve familiar personnel, unlike on earlier stages of the migration.

Borzu took a different route that passed through cultivated valleys. He was irritated to discover that Khalifeh had already occupied his chosen site. His pride would not permit him to be the second man to arrive at a new site, but he and the other nomads also considered it inappropriate to infringe on another's spot. Because of his large entourage, he needed space where he and his herders could spread out and where the three herds would not merge or mix with other herds. Muttering that he could have beaten Khalifeh to the spot, Borzu cursed to himself for not having left as early as he had desired. Searching for another site, he approached an area with no vegetation and spotted his weary pack animals cresting a hill. Once again a decision was forced upon him, a circumstance he disliked. The site was the worst he had occupied this migration. No one else, not even Morad, camped near him. Borzu remained in an irritable state the rest of the day.

An unusual peddler entered Borzu's camp, and Falak welcomed him to the tent. Despite a minor comic accident as he came close, in which the heavy load on his donkey slipped and swung upside down from the animal's belly, he was more professional than any other peddler with whom these nomads traded. A Persian based in Borujen to the north who spoke fluent Turkish, he carried a vast array of goods and two sets of seemingly accurate weights and scales. His son preceded him into the tent with a small carpet that he smoothed out for himself, and then he waited as his son brought him bags of trade goods. Falak needed a grape syrup for treating the inside of new goatskin bags, to eradicate the smell and taste of the acorn skins and smoke that had cured them. The syrup was also tasty mixed with yogurt and sour milk. With Borzu's approval she traded raw wool for several kilograms. Borzu also traded wool for nuts and dried fruit which he ate and tossed to his sons. Yadollah's daughter needed matches and traded wool she had yanked from a dead sheep abandoned by a well. The peddler opened a container of sewing notions, but Borzu waved his hand in disinterest. If alone, Falak would have traded wool or tea leaves for what she wanted. Borzu asked the peddler about other nomads traveling through the area and wanted him to identify the Qermezi families ahead.

A Qashqa'i man on mule-back, carrying a stick as he would a gun, came to inquire about a lost animal. Several Lur hired herders checking animals in the area found one of their own sheep in the flock tended by Borzu's shepherd Mohammad Hosain. The nomads were glad to be able to water their herds at a nearby well. Borzu wanted to keep his young animals in the mountains for the night because of good grazing there but was unable to find anyone to tend them. During the day small children cared for them.

Packing up the next morning again took more time because of excess firewood and milk products. Early on the route, one of Borzu's donkeys fell under her heavy burden and would not rise, even when beaten, until she was unloaded. Other families also experienced difficulties with their pack animals, for they all carried wood to summer pastures. The animals were in wretched shape; everyone hoped they would last the few remaining days. The route took Borzu's group toward the mountainside across a flat valley floor strewn with flowering wild irises. Several families including Morad's were ahead of Borzu while others were behind, and he was again alone. Khalifeh had remained where he was because he said he wanted to exploit the excellent site he had found the previous day—a subtle jab at Borzu who had wanted the same site. Anticipating that Borzu was not going to travel that day, Asadollah also planned to take advantage of the grazing, but when he watered his animals he saw Borzu's deserted campsite and so returned home to break camp and move. Ali and Akbar stayed at their site until noon to graze and water their animals and then traveled in the direction Borzu had taken.

Borzu found, again with difficulty, a campsite in a valley where the terrain was a little greener than elsewhere. It was another poor site with minimal grazing, and he was so irritated that his family and herders kept their distance. Water was a long distance away, and his daughters took four trips to bring supplies to camp. Because of the shortage and cost of gasoline, he no longer used the truck for any travel other than the daily move to a new camp. Several Qermezi families traveled well past his camp and settled down out of sight. The daughter of Khalifeh's shepherd came to Falak in tears, having been sent by her father to ask for tea leaves. As she shamefacedly left with tea tied in her tunic cloth, Falak asked if she had any wooden pins (for fastening tent panels) at home, a fairly explicit request for repayment. Later Falak and Zolaikha realized they ought to have given sugar too, but their own supplies were low. A well-dressed Bulverdi Qashqa'i man on horseback came to pay his respects to Borzu. A Lur shepherd who knew Borzu asked for tea glasses and saucers. Giving him a single glass, Borzu commented that the others had broken en route.

The families of Ali, Akbar, and Jehangir, who usually camped together, located a site farther north. Their members performed chores such as milking and water hauling together, yet each person ordinarily did only her or his own work. They always politely asked permission to borrow an item and then promptly returned it. They stayed in contact and frequently engaged in conversation. When Ali or Salatin went to their son Akbar's tent, they always waited to be invited in before entering and were treated with the same respect as would be given outsiders. Ali's and Akbar's families also helped Bahram and his wife, who was Ali's daughter; they usually camped nearby with Khalifeh. Ali and Akbar, although formally two independent households, had recombined herds for convenience during the migration. Akbar's herd was too small to tend alone, and two of Ali's sons, his best sources of labor, were absent—Haidar serving in the army for Askar while Askar attended school in Kazerun.

Together a man and his married son decided when to form two independent households. The son received part of his parents' herd, a portion determined by the number of sons and sometimes daughters still at home and by the bridewealth payments the family expected it would receive and need to pay. Nimsud animals were included. Under ordinary circumstances, a man with five sons at home gave forty of his two hundred sheep and goats to the first of his sons to form an independent household. When the second son became independent, he received a fourth of the parents' herd, and so forth. The last son, remaining with his parents, shared the final portion with them. Animals (and their offspring) given to the bride as wedding gifts also went into the newly formed herd. When a young husband and wife set up their own independent tent for the first time, they sacrificed an animal for a ceremonial meal and invited the husband's parents, elders in camp, and the headman. After the meal, the elders helped to divide the parents' herd and select animals for the couple. Even though he had been independent for several years, Akbar had not yet invited Borzu to be his guest. Borzu occasionally complained about this slight and for the duration refused to recognize Akbar's household as a separate unit.

That evening found Borzu morose. He enumerated his immediate problems: no water, no food, no gasoline, his children asleep hungry, his

31. Akbar preparing to shear a sheep

daughters and wife and hired workers worthless, his flocks thirsty, and Zolaikha and Zohreh exhausted from water hauling.

The next morning's route followed the valley bottom north, and for the second time the roads for the truck and pack animals converged. The route was crowded with Darrehshuri and Amaleh nomads, and the Qermezi group was pushed on all sides. Pack animals loaded with protruding firewood jammed together and became tangled. Borzu had retrieved a donkey he had lent to Mohammad Hosain the year before, for he wanted the animal to carry wood, and Geljahan who had always ridden the donkey was now forced to walk. The route passed by some Qashqa'i living in canvas and goat-hair tents who herded sheep owned by Persians in nearby Hanna village. Borzu pointed out the exact spot where a camel had died several years previously from eating too many wild artichoke plants. When his shepherds had taken the camel meat to Semirom to sell, the police arrested them for selling tainted meat. He went to Semirom to get them released, and in the fracas his brother Gholam Hosain was also arrested.

Borzu stopped to camp in the foothills and then watched angrily as everyone else in his group traveled farther into the mountains. He felt pinched by the dilemma. If he permitted the group to travel ahead of him in the morning, he had to accept the campsite others chose if he wanted to be near them. But if he traveled at the head of the group, the others enjoyed the option of bypassing the campsite he chose and leaving him behind and alone.

Arghvan and Qahraman, Aqa Mohammadli men who had formed their own nomadic group during the past two months, came to pay their respects to Borzu before diverging from their common route to travel on to their own summer pastures. People considered it courteous and customary to bid farewell to the headman. The weather was becoming warm, and it was no longer comfortable at noon even in the shade of the tent. An irrigation channel to the fields below was close by, but the flow was unexpectedly shut off in midafternoon, and Zolaikha had to seek a new source of water. Katayun gathered wild watercress along the channel to mix with yogurt for the evening's meal.

Borzu sent Khosrow to Hanna, the nearest village, for gasoline and other supplies. Returning to camp without gasoline, he encountered along the road a small party composed of Ziad, his veiled Persian wife, and other family members who were coming by donkey to visit Ziad's Qermezi relatives. Ziad was a Kachili Qermezi man whose father had settled in Hanna in the 1920s. The father had taken a Qermezi wife, an Amaleh Qashqa'i

wife, and a Persian wife from Hanna. His summer pastures had been close
to the village. During the spring migration he would travel ahead to be
with the Hanna wife (who continued to live with her family because "she
did not know how to migrate and be a nomad"), and at the beginning of
the autumn migration he would stay behind with her for a while. One
year he remained in Hanna and never migrated again.

Ziad was distressed that no one had come to invite him for a visit.
Visibly irritated that he had to perform as host, Borzu had been sleeping
in the shade and planned to take it easy all day. He quickly became bored
with Ziad and for once lacked interest in regaling guests with stories and
plans for the future. Ziad seemed not to listen anyway, and no one else
was present with whom Borzu could talk. He sent Zohreh by horse to
collect a kid from the herd to be killed for the meal, and he told her to
find Ali's camp to invite Salatin (Ziad's closest relative among the nomads)
and the men there. He sent a message to Morad to bring his lantern.
Morad no longer chose to camp nearby now that some semblance of a
group had formed around Borzu again. He returned the message that the
lantern was broken (possible but unlikely), and he never came nor did any
other men, to Borzu's dismay. Borzu cared little about impressing what
he considered a nonentity from Hanna, but he did worry about his obvious loss of support.

While Zolaikha spread the finest carpets, Borzu prepared tea. Khosrow
served the guests, a role Morad usually played. Salatin arrived and exchanged the customary greetings with Ziad. The number of phrases spoken and the length of time spent saying them depended on how long it
had been since the two people had seen one another and how closely they
were related. They uttered these formulaic questions and answers simultaneously and without pause.

"Welcome!" "May you be happy too."

"How are you?" "We are well."

"I hope you're not too tired." "Long life."

"Are your children well?" "Blessings to you."

"I wanted so much to see you." "And I wanted to see you."

"Are your brothers well?" "They are healthy."

"How is your father?" "Thanks be to God."

"How are your animals?" "They aren't bad."

"Did your sons have wedding celebrations? Did your daughters find
husbands?" (meaning, "I haven't seen you in such a long time that I don't
know if your children are married or not"). "Thanks be to God."

"Did your youngest son grow up?" "Thanks be to God."

While they drank tea Salatin and Ziad discussed the merits of settlement. Ziad declared that village life was deleterious to the production of offspring, especially sons. He frequently asked about other Qermezi people by name and wondered why none had yet come. Embarrassed, Borzu could say only that everyone was busy with the daily chores of the migration. The absence of supporters was a direct insult to him. During the autumn migration guests had always drawn many men to his tent to demonstrate his position and power, appreciate the fireside discussions, and eat meat.

When dinner was served, Salatin experienced a dilemma. She was an invited guest and the only representative of Qermezi subtribe outside Borzu's entourage, but she was unaccustomed to eating alongside male guests. At first she hesitated to eat, then turned her head and body away from the communal food tray while she shyly ate a few bites. The veiled young bride of Ziad's son did not eat at all, but such modest behavior was expected of someone of her status. When Ziad asked Salatin about Haidar, she broke into tears. Borzu uncharacteristically reassured her by gently (but untruthfully) saying that army conscripts were not beaten or otherwise mistreated anymore and that Haidar would undoubtedly learn some skill during his service. Her son Dehdar came with a lantern to escort her home, and she said farewell. Zolaikha, upon whom the home's work load rested, cleaned up after the meal, set out bedding for the guests, and turned to hours yet of milk processing and bread baking. Pleading ill health, Falak had not served the guests and had enjoyed relaxing by the fire all evening.

In the morning the guests sat unobtrusively while Borzu silently contemplated the day and then packed the truck. They asked again where other Qermezi families were, and Zohreh pointed out several tents on the distant mountain slope. "But what about the others?" Ziad's wife asked pointedly, complaining that she had not seen any Qermezi people for years. She presented Falak a large bag of foodstuffs and hinted for milk products and meat in return. Falak gave her dried curds and the wool from three sheep Yadollah had sheared the day before. Ziad readied their donkeys, and the guests sadly and quietly left. Falak slipped behind a pile of baggage to sort through the contents of the bag of gifts. She distributed the beans, popcorn, nuts, dried fruit, and "village" bread throughout the baggage, and only she knew what and how much had actually been given.

The truck and camels were loaded and ready to leave, but Zohreh was still trying to round up the horses and mules. The route for the pack animals, once again following the road because Borzu had camped by it and was alone, passed through a plain and over a hill where people received their first sight of the town of Semirom on the mountain slopes to the north. The small group stopped by a spring to fill goatskin bags and then traveled down a hill and along the edge of a mountain. The landscape of green fields contrasted with the dry uncultivated land of the past few days. Surprisingly, Borzu selected a campsite near the tents of other Darrehshuri nomads but still in his own niche in the mountainside. Pasture on the slopes above took the form of long thin-bladed grass, the first seen this migration. The grazing here, although not lush, was better than that encountered anywhere else during the previous two months.

In an irritable mood, Borzu slept under the truck while Yadollah pitched the tent. He sent Khodabakhsh to retrieve three goats that had joined someone else's herd when nomads of different groups were crowded together at Wide Mountain in April. He thought he knew the identity of the culprits and had heard they had arrived in summer pastures in the area. Later a Lur hired herder passed by and promised to give Borzu a kid in exchange for use of winter pastures at Famur. Borzu had allocated him grazing land in the past, and every year he gave Borzu a kid for the favors he had done. Falak was angry and suspicious about their own hired herders and families because all four men had announced plans to quit once they reached summer pastures. She complained that Yadollah's wife Golabshar had stolen salt for her own use while feeding Borzu's camels. She noted that a person could give anything except salt to another, and now as a result of the theft a person or sheep would die. Salt was the essence of all edible, God-given provisions, she said, and if a household gave away salt, God's blessing would leave too.

A pickup truck pulled up along the road some distance away. Hearing the sound, Borzu was momentarily angry that his second nap of the day was to be interrupted. Then he saw that the pickup truck was the virtual twin of his own truck and that the driver was Hajj Kalhaidar, his principal merchant-moneylender in Semirom and the man who had sold him his own truck. He had come to welcome Borzu upon his arrival in summer pastures. The two men greeted one another affectionately. Kalhaidar owned a general store and a car-parts shop in Semirom and a house in Shahreza where he spent the winter. He held a nimsud contract with Borzu for eighty sheep. Borzu was obligated to trade his clarified butter, dried curds, and wool with him.

The two men discussed the dismal year. Borzu reported that his sheep had gone so long without green grass that, not having much of an appetite, they did not eat it when they encountered it. Their stomachs had been damaged by hunger. Less harmed by the winter, the lambs were eating well and getting fat. Listening to Borzu's enumeration of animal losses, Kalhaidar commented that Borzu had survived the year well in comparison with other nomadic pastoralists. Borzu was frequently told this and staunchly refused to accept it each time. Kalhaidar reported that grazing in summer pastures was apparently adequate and that the Dar-rehshuri khans had already arrived for the season at Round Sun, north of Semirom. Borzu questioned him about prices in Semirom and about his current stock of goods. When he inquired about mail, Kalhaidar replied that nothing of consequence had come. Kalhaidar needed to visit else-where, and before he left Borzu asked him for gasoline. Kalhaidar hesi-tated and then said he would give a little when he passed by later that night.

Gholam Hosain was camped alone as usual but closer to his brother Borzu than any other person. They were the only Qermezi men to use Kalhaidar's services. Gholam Hosain had seen Kalhaidar arrive but was unwilling to go to Borzu's tent to greet him. He said the reason he gen-erally avoided Borzu was that he did not want to answer questions about his activities and plans. He noted that their brother Abdol Hosain had provoked trouble by not avoiding Borzu. Gholam Hosain and Rokhsar remarked on what they considered to be the unbreakable bond between their son Hajji Qorban (now in winter pastures harvesting grain) and Zolaikha. They said their wedding might occur in the summer.

Anxious to inspect their summer pastures at Hanalishah and to prevent other pastoralists from exploiting the land, Abdol Hosain and Abdol Ra-sul had traveled ahead of the other Qermezi families and would have just now arrived at their campsites. Anticipating their own arrival in a few days, the people still migrating wondered what these two men had en-countered. Khalifeh, who had been traveling a day ahead of Borzu, moved farther ahead.

When the merchant Kalhaidar returned to Borzu's camp, the two men discussed the plight of nomadic pastoralists and the means by which their circumstances could be improved. Dealing intimately on a daily basis with the economic affairs of many pastoralists from different groups and loca-tions, Kalhaidar was excellently situated to view the broad context. Just when Borzu was warming to the discussion and his own argument (for he loved these interchanges), Kalhaidar abruptly inquired why his two broth-ers Abdol Hosain and Gholam Hosain were no longer speaking to him. When Borzu offered an innocent reply, Kalhaidar asked him why he had hit Abdol Hosain, and then he began to laugh uproariously and to hold his sides in mirth. Borzu looked ashen, sputtered that someone must have lied, and then quizzed him about the dastardly source of the rumor.

One of Borzu's worst fears had just been realized. Since striking Abdol Hosain he had worried that news of the attack would spread, and he especially feared the story reaching Semirom and Round Sun before he arrived and was able to present his own side of the event and the context in which it occurred. He still argued to himself that he had been justified in hitting his brother because of Abdol Hosain's unwillingness to help him with water hauling at Wide Mountain in the autumn, his refusal to acknowledge his sacrifice of winter pastures, and his disinclination to accompany and assist him during the spring migration. Because Borzu had been so isolated since the attack, he had no way of knowing how far and wide the story had spread or how others viewed his behavior. He was sickened by Kalhaidar's revelation.

The lights of Semirom twinkled in the distant mountains. Kalhaidar stayed the night, and packing and loading the next morning went smoothly and calmly because of his presence. Mashhadi Hasan, an itinerant peddler Qermezi people knew well and one of the few with whom affectionate ties existed, welcomed each family on its entrance to summer pastures. The trip for the pack animals was short, north across a series of hills toward Semirom. Borzu camped in a grassy place by springs.

Just as Borzu's tent was going up, people saw his cousin and brother-in-law Abdol Rasul racing toward camp on horseback. Because of the total lack of contact between Abdol Rasul and Borzu and the ongoing state of avoidance, everyone stood transfixed by the sight. Moaning that a close relative must have died, Falak collapsed on the ground muttering incoherent lamentations. Abdol Rasul shouted as he raced by and then circled the tent, "Ayaz Khan's shepherds and three thousand sheep and goats are pillaging the grazing at Hanalishah!"

Abdol Rasul and Abdol Hosain had traveled ahead to Qermezi summer pastures to protect them from nomadic pastoralists passing through the area, but they had not expected such an organized and apparently sanctioned invasion or one that would be so difficult to repel. They were shocked to discover Ayaz Khan Darrehshuri's shepherds, Lak Darrehshuri men, occupying their very own and other Qermezi people's campsites. Because his own interests were also at stake, Borzu galvanized into action to plan strategy with Abdol Rasul. Suddenly assuming his headmanship again, he seemed not to give a second thought to the residual problems with Abdol Rasul and Abdol Hosain. He told Abdol Rasul to notify Morad and other Qermezi men in the vicinity. One of Ayaz Khan's shepherds had told Abdol Rasul that he would slit open Borzu's stomach if he brought even a single sheep to Hanalishah. Although Borzu viewed the threat as verbal warfare and was more than ready to respond with physical force, he was also sensitive about his girth and took that part of the threat as a personal attack to which he was vulnerable. After hearing Abdol Rasul's message, Akbar, Bahram, and Asadollah raced on horseback to Hanalishah.

Kalhaidar sympathetically agreed to postpone a trip south in order to accompany Borzu to Semirom. Borzu was torn between driving immediately to Hanalishah to stake his claim or driving first to Semirom to report the incursion to government officials and then to Round Sun to seek the intercession of his patron Jehangir Khan Darrehshuri. He packed enough goods and food in the truck to set up a rudimentary household at Hanalishah and then drove with Kalhaidar and Falak to Semirom to evaluate the situation from there.

The peddler Hasan had accompanied Borzu's family to the new site and had assisted in household affairs while news of the crisis unfolded. He offered dried fruits and nuts to people and brought news of other Qermezi families who were traveling ahead of Borzu. As soon as Borzu and Falak departed, Borzu's daughters dug through the baggage to see what they could possibly trade for the nylon undershirts, plastic key chains, snaps, and thread they wanted. They and the herders' wives cooked food, and it seemed as if everyone in the vicinity swooped down to eat. Morad stopped by periodically, as he often did when Borzu and Falak planned to be gone overnight, to check on the household and yell at people to retrieve animals from the fields. A Persian boy ostensibly herding two cows kept watch on the nearby cultivation and shouted continually at the nomads. Mohammad Hosain's daughter, an expert in bread baking and milk processing, stayed in Borzu's tent all day helping with chores.

Khosrow assisted Borzu's family in packing and moving the next day. Borzu had attempted the previous morning to lighten the load by carrying heavy goods by truck, but the pack animals were still overburdened. Darrehshuri nomads crowded the day's route, which passed over hills and alongside extensive bean fields. Persians astride donkeys rode to their fields for the day's work, and some took cows to graze. Khosrow and others commented that the Persians and Lurs in summer quarters were of "bad quality" and more unpleasant in temperament than Kazerunis. Morad traveled ahead to find a campsite and then directed Borzu's entourage across plowed fields to a hillside.

Jansanam stopped by after the milking was done, and Katayun narrated the story of Zolaikha's innocent rendezvous with Hosain Ali at Dashtak during the winter and the resulting anger of her grandmother Narges. Jansanam, Narges's daughter, had not heard the account before, to her amazement. Because Morad often chose to camp alone and his two brothers had formed other alliances during this migration, Jansanam did not benefit from the presence of other women with whom to share information.

Some incidents such as the rumored shooting at Saran Plain spread to every family quickly, while others traveled slowly. People were so widely separated in space and time and so many events occurred that some stories took a long time to be disseminated. Women especially were isolated, and even when they did meet, they were often restricted by limited time or restrained in what they could say by men or outsiders present. Stories were often told in detail, and sometimes people did not even begin the telling if they knew time was short. Once a story was told, it was endlessly retold and elaborated with details from the teller's own perspective and background. Men transmitted certain news immediately; women did not ordinarily have this ease of communication. Men had discussed without hesitation the rumor of the shooting. They would not have discussed, and would have claimed disinterest in, the casual encounters of Zolaikha and Hosain Ali.

A sayyid came begging, and Katayun, who had less to give than anyone else, offered him butter. Later she said that misfortune befell the home of someone who ignored a man of Islam, especially a sayyid. He questioned Katayun about Morad's empty tent because he wanted an offering from there too, and Katayun replied that everyone had gone to collect water. But he had recognized Jansanam sitting beside her, and Katayun was caught in a lie. She worried about having negated her act of charity.

A well-dressed Persian hired herder, visiting Borzu's camp to inquire about two lost donkeys, entered Borzu's tent even though only the daughters were there, behavior that would not have been tolerated in his own village or if any Qermezi men had been within view. Zolaikha spent hours collecting dried animal dung from the surrounding terrain to use as fuel. Borzu had conspicuously inspected the supply of wood just before he left for Semirom, and she feared using more than a few pieces. The current demand for fuel was great; at least one fire burned continuously for various stages of milk processing.

Nasrollah, a Bulverdi Qashqa'i man who was a khan's retainer, drove Borzu's truck back to camp with Falak, accompanied by her sister-in-law Rokhsar who had gone to Semirom to have badly decayed teeth pulled.

Borzu stayed in town. He had not gone to Hanalishah, despite his previously stated intentions, and had only run errands including shopping for nonessentials. Seeing the truck, Qermezi men hurried to Borzu's tent to hear news of Hanalishah and Borzu's actions and were surprised to discover that he had apparently done nothing to resolve the problem of Ayaz Khan's sheep expropriating their legal pastures.

Borzu had tried, however, to see Captain Jamali of the Tribal Security Force in charge of Darrehshuri affairs, but the force's season of residence in Semirom had not yet begun, and none of its gendarmes had arrived from Dugonbadan. He had visited the secret police with no results. He had heard that Ayaz Khan was in the city of Isfahan and hence could not contact him directly. The several Darrehshuri khans he had seen in Semirom were not the ones who could help him.

Nasrollah then took Borzu's truck to drop off a Qashqa'i man who had accompanied him. Saying he had "become tajik" (non-Qashqa'i) when he settled in the Semirom plain and planted an orchard, the man was a tracker of thieves and a mediator for their victims. He remarked that it was fairly easy to discover who exactly had thieved, especially if both thief and victim were Qashqa'i, and he told of a case he was currently pursuing. For every case he settled, he received a percentage of the returned property. The shepherd Mohammad Hosain noted that such a mediator was called "a friend of thieves and a partner of the caravan," that is, someone who conspired with both thief and victim. As part of the settlement, thieves customarily received a percentage of the stolen property to compensate them for the effort they had expended in the act of theft, for "the wear and tear to their shoes." Nasrollah drove back to Semirom to pick up Borzu.

Akbar and Asadollah returned from Hanalishah where they had toured the area identifying themselves as "Bulverdi" to whoever asked. They came with Morad and Gholam Hosain to see Borzu. For the first time in many weeks a gathering of Qermezi men was present at the evening fire. A common cause had brought them back to the headman. Borzu quizzed them about Ayaz Khan's ten herds and asked how many men they would need to expel them. Akbar reported that they saw "no grass" at Hanalishah, a condition resulting more from lack of rain and snow, apparently, than from other pastoralists having already grazed it. Nevertheless, they feared the destruction of the sparse grass that did grow and the resulting loss of secondary growth. They discussed the probability of violence and the extent to which other khans and the Tribal Security Force would back their legal claims. If herders of another subtribe comparable to theirs were

occupying Qermezi pasture, Qermezi men would have immediately expelled them, with force if necessary. Hired shepherds of a Darrehshuri
khan, however, posed different problems, especially when this particular
khan claimed rights to Hanalishah. Morad complained that if a fight was
to break out, his brother Naser was still several stages behind them and
would be unable to help. "It's like having no brother at all," he grumbled.
Before the men left, Borzu could not resist airing his grievances about
Abdol Hosain's past behavior and Khalifeh's refusal to attend the meal
hosting their kinsman living in Hanna.

After the men left, Borzu worried about the reports that grazing at
Hanalishah was poor and that the khan's herds had already depleted the
sparse growth. He said his animals would be hungry and would not fatten. As a result he would be unable to sell them, and they would die in
winter pastures. Other men could graze their small herds between cultivated fields, but he lacked sufficient labor to rely on this plan for his own
three herds.

Akbar packed before dawn and left for Hanalishah, stopping first to
check with Borzu about strategy against Ayaz Khan's shepherds. Morad
and a few others would also arrive there later in the day. Borzu planned
one more stop for his own entourage before entering Hanalishah. Nasrollah, who had stayed the night, helped with packing, and Borzu was the
last of the small group to leave. The route ran north through a valley,
then up a hill to an easterly view in the early light of a surprisingly close
Semirom. The group traveled along a mountain slope and into another
valley. Nader Bahmanbaigi, brother of the director of the Office of Tribal
Education, stopped his Landrover to talk briefly with Borzu, who had run
out of gasoline, and he gave him enough to drive to his next camp and
then to Semirom. The two brothers owned land in a valley just northwest
of Hanalishah, and Borzu met them informally during the summer.

Borzu camped in a niche on the mountain slope above the road, and
his herders had to level places for their own tents farther up the slope.
The site was poor, but he wanted to be close to the road in case of trouble.
Once camp was set up, he asked Nasrollah to drive him to Semirom. Falak
and the children visited her brothers Barat and Hemmat who had camped
nearby. The two men had planned to branch off from Borzu's route several
days previously, to travel on to their own summer pastures, but instead
had stayed close to offer him physical and political support.

Rain began to fall, and then a hard gusty wind suddenly arose, blowing
down several tents. A collapsed tent was a most inauspicious sign and a
harbinger of death, and people thought in terror about the fight over

Hanalishah expected to be occurring at that very moment. Tripods holding reed mats arrayed with curds set out to dry in the sun tipped over, and donkeys ate what they could before being chased off. Once the wind died down and order had been restored in camp, Zolaikha and other women went to collect dry shrubs for fuel. They burned too quickly to be of much use, and so dried animal dung would be the main source of fuel available locally for the next three months. Two gendarmes sent by the newly arrived Tribal Security Force in Semirom came by jeep seeking Borzu in order to investigate the dispute over land. Borzu returned to camp late at night with no solution to the presence of Ayaz Khan's herds at Hanalishah.

The various government authorities with whom Borzu had talked claimed that the case belonged in some other office. They all suggested that he settle the conflict with Ayaz Khan personally. The khan, however, was still in Isfahan. The Tribal Security Force had told Borzu that the issued rested with the Ministry of Agriculture's forest rangers. When he went to their local office, the man in charge obstinately refused to listen to him and open a new case, for he was ending his term of appointment in Semirom and waiting impatiently for his replacement. In routinely checking Borzu's file, the official spotted corrections and additions on documents that had not been registered with his headquarters in the distant city of Isfahan. He declared that before anyone in his office could even think about assisting Borzu, Borzu had to take the file personally to Isfahan to have the changes formally registered. Some of them were years old, and Borzu was irritated that no one had ever said anything to him about this procedure.

Whenever Borzu stepped into a government office and had to confront men of an unknown degree of power, the self-assurance and physical strength he exuded while in tribal territory withered away. He was uneasy, subdued, and humble on unfamiliar ground where neither the rules nor the consequences of breaking them were completely known. The other men of his group were even more at a loss and often stood tongue-tied when faced with officials' rapid-fire questions and accusations. One reason Borzu and the other men still sought out the Darrehshuri khans, despite their diminishing power and authority, was that they handled such encounters more effectively. Officials were more apt to listen and respond to the khans, primarily because they still bestowed coveted material rewards.

Borzu planned to enter Hanalishah the next morning and see what would unfold. Partly because he would have to handle the consequences personally, he was not looking forward to a violent solution, unlike other Qermezi men. He doubted that he would prevail over a Darrehshuri khan, and he expected that government officials would back a khan over a headman, that is, a person too poor to bribe them much. He also understood only too well how furious he could become if provoked, and he said he knew beforehand what would result if he personally entered the fight with Ayaz Khan's shepherds. No one came to Borzu's fire that night.

Borzu woke the family and herders at the usual early time, but the pace of activity in and around his tent was slow. The herders watched quietly to see what he would do. After several hours of torpor he told Yadollah to remove the side walls of the tent, an indication of the intention to migrate, and only then did the families of the three herders begin to dismantle their own tents. Practically every morning during the past two months Borzu had stomped around the camp ordering people to do this or that chore and had engaged in his own frantic efforts to load the truck, but this morning he sat silently by the fire and hardly observed the action around him. The process of packing moved slowly. People understood that he did not want to be the first to arrive at Hanalishah, and it seemed he hoped the fight would be over before he arrived. Other men nearby, puzzled by the slow pace, sent Asadollah to seek instructions before the confrontation, but Borzu was lost in thought and did not answer him or acknowledge his presence. Asadollah got up from the fire and left. An unrelated Qashqa'i man on his way through the area stopped by Borzu's tent for tea and talk, as he had done in the past, but he also roused no response from Borzu, and he left perplexed. Barat paused on his way to find a campsite at Hanalishah near Borzu's intended site and talked briefly with his sister Falak. In order to support Borzu, Falak's brothers had decided to wait a few days more before moving on to their own summer pastures. Neither was a fighting man, but they told her their departure would later be seen as desertion and cowardice if Borzu was caught up in physical violence.

Finally, seeing that no other Qermezi families were coming up the road, Borzu sent his family along with the loaded, restless pack animals. He stayed behind to tinker with the truck. The route for the pack animals was short, only an hour of travel through the valley to a summit. As they reached the top, people were struck by the wind characteristic of summer pastures at these high altitudes. They crossed several other hills and then branched off to the east from the dirt road heading northwest to Vanak village. Ahead of them Hanalishah nestled in a valley surrounded by high mountains. Abundant springs, streams, and green cultivated fields filled the valley floor. The families traveling ahead of Borzu moved into the valley and dispersed as they made for their own campsites. To everyone's surprise, Borzu called a halt just at the valley's mouth and instructed his entourage to set up camp on a hillside away from the dirt track.

The location Borzu chose was some distance from one of his customary spring campsites, which he ordinarily occupied on entering Hanalishah. No grazing or water was near the new site on the barren slope, but from this vantage point he could easily watch the entrance to Hanalishah and the dirt track leading into the territory. As with his winter pastures at Dashtak, access to Hanalishah was restricted by the topography, and he wanted to surveil the crucial southern entrance. Once Borzu saw that his pack animals were unloaded in the proper spot and the tent positioned well, he set off for a hilltop farther into Hanalishah to watch for signs of a possible fight. He descended briefly to tell Mali's wife Dokhi, who had unloaded close to the dirt track, to find another site higher up in order to stay clear of the pastoralists who would be traveling through Hanalishah.

Before returning to the hilltop, Borzu offered further instructions about the setting up of his household. He planned to stay at this site for ten days and wanted the tent and camp arranged properly. Given the strong probability of violence, he expected government officials from Semirom and khans from Round Sun to come in the aftermath. A pragmatist, he was preparing for guests.

The air was crisp and the sky a bright blue. Glad to be in a familiar place, Borzu and his family gazed with satisfaction at the surrounding, protective mountains.

Shouts suddenly erupted from the base of the valley to the north. Borzu yelled at Khosrow, Yadollah, and Khodabakhsh to abandon the herds, grab clubs, and run toward the noise. Falak, groaning, collapsed against a pile of baggage. A young man unknown to Borzu came running along the track from the direction of the shouting. He lamented rhythmically again and again: "My father is burning [in hell], Abdol Hosain killed my brother, my brother is dead." Borzu sent Aqaboa, who had hurried down the mountain slope, to find out from the man what had happened, but the man, dazed, did not respond and ran on toward Semirom continuing his chant. Further wailing was heard from the valley, and soon an elderly woman, also unknown to Borzu, hastened along the road after the young man. She chanted and wailed, "My son is dead, killed by Qermezi, killed by Borzu Beg. Qermezi women raped us with sticks."

Summer

Borzu ran down to the road to ask the elderly woman what had happened. Within seconds they were shouting and swearing at one another. Unable to get a coherent account, Borzu was livid with rage. The woman yelled, "I offered bread to Qermezi, but Qermezi ate the bread and stole the rolling pin," which meant, someone later suggested, that Qermezi had stolen Lak land and plundered the pasture. Borzu yelled back, "Stick the rolling pin up your vagina!" Another woman and then a man walked swiftly by without answering Borzu's shouts, and the elderly woman followed after them.

Back in the tent, Falak was certain that someone had indeed been killed. Agitated by the suspense, Borzu sent Zohreh on horseback to Abdol Hosain's camp for news. Both mules bolted after the horse, and Borzu sent a shepherd's daughter to try to retrieve them in case he needed to go to the town of Semirom quickly.

But Zohreh soon returned home, followed by the mules, for she had seen both Abdol Hosain and Abdol Rasul galloping toward Borzu's camp. Arriving first, Abdol Hosain offered no greeting nor was given any, and Falak and Katayun fired questions at him. Breathless, he reported that a fight had broken out between Qermezi men and women and the Lak men herding Ayaz Khan's sheep at Hanalishah. No one had been killed or seriously injured. He rubbed his own bloody head where he said a Lak man had struck him with a tent pole. Borzu sat in silence and looked in all directions but at his brother, then asked Falak about the fate of Morad and Khalifeh. Hearing the query, Abdol Hosain remarked that many Qermezi men and women had gathered near his camp. Unable to continue to ignore him, Borzu finally asked him if further fighting would erupt. He complained that he had warned everyone not to fight.

276

Falak informed Abdol Hosain that Lak people were already well on their way to Semirom, and he cut short his comments to race after them to stop them before they reached the authorities. He also wanted to report on their violation of his pasture space.

Abdol Rasul arrived at a gallop, delivered his own message to Borzu, and also hastened to intercept the Laks. Men quickly congregated at Borzu's, the herders he had sent returning among them. Only Ali could offer a detailed account of the fight and its outcome. By now, everyone except Borzu was laughing about the discrepancies between the facts of the fight and the Laks' incoherent shouts. Borzu wanted to tell the story himself to each person who arrived, and soon he was laughing as well and repeating with gusto the curses of the elderly Lak woman.

The actual fight had pitted Abdol Hosain, Abdol Rasul, Borzu's sister Shahrbanu, and several shepherds against the men and women of three Lak households. Shouting escalated to swearing (the usual prelude to physical violence) and then to hitting with tent poles. Abdol Hosain scored some hits with stones he shot from a sling. Everyone was cut, bleeding, and bruised. Qermezi people who heard the noise came running and stopped the violence, and by the time people from farther away arrived, the fight was over and a deputy of Laks was on its way by foot to Semirom.

In what everyone in Borzu's tent regarded as a remarkably short time, a large truck from the Tribal Security Force in Semirom pulled up along the road. Three gendarmes holding their rifles prominently rode in front; the four Laks and Abdol Hosain squatted in the back in the bed of the truck. Borzu walked down to the road, yelled at the Laks who now acted submissive, and took control. He invited the gendarmes to his tent and jovially apologized for the disturbance these Laks had caused to their day. The Laks followed and, being poor and of low status, crouched outside the tent, men in the gravel near the entrance and women "unseen" behind the reed screen. They were soon joined by their relatives who were also camped at Hanalishah.

Clearly relishing his commanding role as host, Borzu ordered a goat slaughtered and rice cooked. He loudly proclaimed that he would have killed anyone he had found ravaging his pastures. Addressing the gendarmes, he reported that in the morning's dispute, "Someone hit, someone fell and died, someone was buried, someone was put in prison. These are everyday occurrences. Why all the fuss?" The Lak men unsuccessfully tried to state their case. They asserted that they had been forced to defend themselves against 350 hostile attackers. They complained that because they were impoverished and Borzu had twenty-five dollars in his pocket (that is, money to bribe), gendarmes were subservient to him and always carried out his wishes. Borzu dismissed their pleas to point out indignantly that a khan protected them while he benefited from no outside support and that gendarmes were subservient to khans. He declared that many Qermezi boys served the government as soldiers but that no one served Qermezi. He searched through his briefcase for government documents entitling his group to use Hanalishah pastures and waved them in the air. Lak women sitting behind the reed screen became louder in their denials and retorts, and the gendarmes told them to shut up. Figuring it already a lost cause, they sullenly returned to their own camps.

While the gendarmes and others consumed bread, yogurt, and tea, Borzu ordered three young kinsmen to ride horses up the road as near as possible to the camp of Abdol Hosain and Abdol Rasul. The gendarmes, Borzu, and a few Qermezi men in the gendarme truck followed the horses, and then Borzu and the other men walked beside the mounted gendarmes to the two men's tents on a hilltop overlooking a ravine where three Lak tents stood. The gendarmes needed to investigate the site of the fight and write a report.

Enjoying the attention, Abdol Hosain stayed behind in the headman's tent for a while. He kept exhibiting proudly his split head and torn jacket, and then he too left for the scene of the dispute. Abdol Rasul returned from Semirom on horseback, heard that gendarmes were already at the site, and hurried off. Qermezi women remaining behind were more interested in discussing the Lak women than anything else and were sympathetic toward the one who had complained that riding in the gendarme truck had ruined her clothes.

In front of a Lak tent, four Lak women were wailing beside a body covered with a blanket, only the feet exposed. Three men and some children moved about agitatedly. They shouted to the gendarmes to avenge the death of their kinsman. A stretcher made of tent poles lashed together was lying near the body to transport the dead man for washing and burial. Borzu, turning pale, muttered about the trouble he would have all summer because of the death.

The gendarmes asked for someone to uncover the body for inspection. Underneath was a young Lak man who unexpectedly moaned, grimaced, and then whispered that he was dying. When a gendarme asked him what had happened, he let loose with a tirade against Qermezi. When questioned about the precise territory he claimed for his herds, he raised himself up with no hesitation or difficulty to point out the area. The gendarmes burst into laughter and whispered to Borzu that they frequently employed this trick to determine the extent of injuries. Borzu began to yell at the Laks, but the gendarmes successfully contained everyone's tempers and kept all parties from fighting again. They said it was their duty to write a report of the dispute and told everyone to desist from creating a new one. They took statements of complaint from each injured person. People who had gone to Semirom had already given statements, all conflicting. The Lak men swore that Jehangir, Borzu, and other named Qermezi men, none of whom had even been at the scene of the fight, were among their attackers. While a gendarme inspected the wounds inflicted on Shahrbanu, Abdol Hosain wondered aloud whether he should kill an animal or cook a pot of rice. Others told him that the gendarmes would soon return to Borzu's for a meal already in preparation. Offering "bread and butter," the Laks defiantly declared, "*We* have butter too."

Calm by now and accurately judging the direction of the gendarmes' sympathies, Borzu told them that blame for the dispute lay not with these poor unfortunate shepherds but with Ayaz Khan Darrehshuri who had told them to graze these lands. The gendarmes agreed that the Laks would never continue to use these pastures unless they were so instructed by someone in authority (a khan). They asked all parties to sign a general statement. Only Borzu and a Lak youth who had been to tribal school could write their names; the rest offered fingerprints. The gendarmes told the Laks that their lies were easy to disprove and noted that they would be in trouble if the dispute reached the Ministry of Justice. They were especially harsh with the young Lak man who had hit Shahrbanu. Reinforcements from Semirom arrived at the site by jeep and gave the other gendarmes and Borzu a ride back to the headman's camp.

As the jeep pulled up along the road by Borzu's tent, people spotted a Landrover approaching from the direction of Semirom. Borzu recognized the car as belonging to Mohammad Hasan Khan Darrehshuri. A Lak involved in the fight had run to Round Sun to report to the khans that a man had been killed at Hanalishah, and Ziad Khan had promptly sent Habib Aqa Zahedi in hopes of settling the dispute before it escalated and the government was alerted. Habib Aqa was a member of the Zahedi family which had served Darrehshuri khans as advisors for generations. Well acquainted with Borzu, he had been his guest at Dashtak in the winter, and Borzu still nursed hopes that Mohammad Karim could marry into the Zahedi family.

From the Darrehshuri perspective, the ideal situation was to settle the dispute without involving any government authorities. Once the dispute reached the Tribal Security Force, as it had done in this case, control over its resolution was placed in part in non-Darrehshuri hands. The gendarmes' principal role was to establish a written record, and the case need not go beyond them if Darrehshuri people themselves or mediation by the gendarmes settled it. All parties including the gendarmes wanted to avoid the next level, the Ministry of Justice, for a case there was certain to last years and cost money, time, and effort with no likely positive outcome.

Borzu's household was ready for guests, and everyone in the large group was served a meal except five Lak men who once again crouched outside the tent in the gravel. Still in a state of ritual avoidance with Borzu and not yet formally reconciled with him, Abdol Hosain did not eat nor did Borzu invite him. The gendarme officer joked that he was astonished to see Borzu eat with a fork, by which he implied Borzu always ate with his fingers (which, in fact, Borzu often did). Borzu was not amused.

The meal was quickly concluded, and discussion of the dispute began again. Borzu, yelling, tried to dominate, and Habib Aqa led him from the tent for a private discussion. Reza, Ziad Khan's driver who had brought Habib Aqa to Hanalishah, served the khans as these shepherds did, and he urged the Lak men to drop their complaints. When Borzu and Habib Aqa returned, the gendarme officer attempted to summarize the case, but Borzu disagreed with many points of the statement. The officer asked Habib Aqa to write the statement and demanded total silence. Habib Aqa wrote a succinct, straightforward account. The officer then asked Habib Aqa, Reza, and a young Dunduli Darrehshuri man who was passing through Hanalishah to serve as witnesses. The Dunduli man objected to his name being included, because if the dispute escalated and fell under the Ministry of Justice's authority, he would have to appear in court. The officer began to include the phrase "Borzu Qermezi and Qermezi sub-tribe" at the end of the statement, but Borzu protested, and so he wrote only "Qermezi people." He wanted Borzu to sign the document, but Borzu objected again (for he was already involved in many such cases), and so the officer slipped the paper into his briefcase. In order to have the last word, Borzu continued to yell in protest against the inclusion of his name.

The gendarme officer ordered the Laks to vacate Abdol Hosain and Abdol Rasul's campsite and to cease physical violence. He warned the young Lak man that he would report him to the Ministry of Justice if he ever hit a woman again. Caught in many lies, the Laks appeared frightened, and the man who had feigned death and then become the butt of joking after the discovery of his remarkable resurrection was uneasy. The officer told Abdol Hosain and Abdol Rasul to stay away from the disputed area until the conflict was resolved. He stated that any resolution was postponed until Ayaz Khan returned from Isfahan, and he implied that he hoped the problem could be solved internally among the disputants. The various parties again dispersed to talk in small groups, and the Laks left without further comment. Falak tried unsuccessfully to interest the gendarmes in her illness and operation as they walked toward their vehicles. Before Reza left with Habib Aqa, he asked Falak for dried curds. To avoid complying, she said she would give some later.

Although Borzu was pleased that the day's dispute had apparently ended well for him, he did not look forward to the next stage, which would entail direct negotiations with Ayaz Khan and possibly other Darrehshuri khans. He suspected that several other khans would support Ayaz Khan's claims to Hanalishah. He hoped that government authorities would intervene to uphold their own policies concerning the use of these pastures, and he disliked having to be in a position of dealing directly with the khans on the matter. He said he would have to make concessions to them, even though new government laws were on his side, and he complained that the negotiations would cost him several sheep at the very minimum.

The next day Borzu was moody and sat silently in the tent. He had pressing business to conduct in Semirom, Shahreza, and Isfahan, but he lacked cash to make these trips and was still bothered by the prospect of negotiating with Ayaz Khan. He had earlier announced that he would wash and shear his sheep as soon as he settled into summer pastures. He enjoyed marking each stage of the yearly pastoral round and always looked forward to hosting "volunteer" workers and overseeing activities. But this morning he sent Aqaboa alone to begin washing the sheep, and his previous enthusiasm was gone.

Borzu spotted Lur hired herders with their large commercial herds entering Hanalishah along the dirt track, and he sped off to chase them back the way they had come. "Let them find another route," he snapped. When Qashqa'i nomads also entered Hanalishah, he told them to turn around and camp back up the road and not migrate through Hanalishah until the next morning. Borzu's power prevailed, and both groups complied without argument. Unlike the more isolated Dashtak, Hanalishah was a passageway to other summer pastures to the north. Qashqa'i pastoralists, Lur and Persian hired herders, and others often traveled through the area, and Qermezi people were constantly alert for animal thieves.

Next Borzu went to offer polite greetings to the Persian and Lur cultivators nearest his camp. After exchanging stylized phrases with him about each other's families and fortunes during the past year, the cultivators reported on the number of herders and herds that had grazed his land since they had arrived to prepare the soil. In an attempt to gain an upper hand and out of spite (for they had fought bitterly with him the previous summer), they appeared to exaggerate the extent to which outsiders had devastated his grazing.

Anxious to return to his family in winter pastures and determined once again to leave Borzu's employment, Khodabakhsh began to shear the goats. He did not want an incomplete task to be used by Borzu as one more excuse for keeping him on the job longer. He tied each goat's left rear leg and right front horn with ropes to pegs pounded firmly into the ground. Straddling the standing animal, he cut the hair with two metal blades held together by a wooden handle.

Aqaboa drove the herd of sheep to a small pool in a mountain stream in order to wash them for the shearing. One by one he grabbed a sheep, pulled it protesting into the frigid water, twisted its neck to flip the animal over on its back, and then sloshed the terrified animal back and forth by using its front legs as a lever. After water rushing through the sheep's dirty wool turned clear, he forced the animal to its feet, squeezed handfuls of wool to release more dirt, submerged the head to clean the face and nose, and then ran his hands over the wool to pull out accumulated dirt and dung. Aqaboa's children helped to keep the wet sheep on their feet so that they would stay clean while the sun dried the wool. After Aqaboa had spent several hours of hard work in the chilling, fast-moving water, Khodabakhsh, Yadollah, and Khosrow came to help. They moved upstream to a pool that had been constructed for this purpose years before and finished washing most of the sheep. The men spent a long time over a brush fire trying to get warm. They all complained of illness and discomfort the next few days.

Women and girls spent all day collecting wild plants of various kinds growing on the mountain slopes for use as food, medicine, and dye. This activity was always their first when they reached summer pastures. They were anxious to harvest plants before the herd and pack animals ate them. They especially sought out a tasty wild onion; the plant had a large round purple flower and was easy to find. Snow still rested in rocky crevices, especially at higher altitudes, and the gatherers searched for plants growing nearby. One variety grew just at the edge of the snow cover. Herders kept their animals away from land below snowy patches, for the ground was muddy and hooves would pack the mud and jeopardize that year's and the next year's growth.

Late that night Yadollah's son brought to Borzu's tent a sheep that had died after, and probably as a result of, its frigid bath. Once again meat was available. In a rare gesture, apparently to recognize the difficult job of washing the sheep, Borzu gave the herders meat.

Many Qashqa'i nomads passed through Hanalishah early the next morning, and Borzu, ever vigilant, shouted at people who strayed from the dirt track. He commented that he could not go to town because he needed to stand guard. Hemmat came to say good-bye. Falak's two brothers were finally able to travel to their own summer pastures without the appearance of abandoning Borzu. Three of their sons would live with Borzu all summer while they attended school at Hanalishah. Mohammad Qoli, Qermezi's teacher, came on motorcycle to find out why Borzu had not picked up his bride, tents, and baggage from Semirom as he had promised. Borzu procrastinated, not wanting to face the various problems the town held for him, then suddenly decided to leave and instructed Falak to pack fresh butter for him to take to his main merchant creditor. He could not easily procure supplies without providing pastoral products in return. As soon as he was gone, women and girls hurried off to gather wild plants, and they spent the afternoon cleaning, chopping, and drying the two days' collection.

Borzu, the teacher, and the teacher's bride entered camp late that night. Shahbaz, son of Borzu's kinsman Khanboa who stayed all year in winter pastures, was asleep on top of the baggage in the truck. Khanboa wanted Shahbaz to continue his education and had agreed to have him help the teacher in exchange for food while school was in session. Twenty boys would attend school at Hanalishah. Parents of nine of them lived in other summer pastures, and the boys would stay with their closest kin at Hanalishah.

The next day Borzu's herders washed the sheep in the second herd, and the following day men gathered at his camp to begin shearing the two herds. Borzu had let it be known that he was ready to shear, and the men most obligated to him sent help or came themselves. In addition to his herders, this group included Morad, Akbar, Abdol Rasul's son, boys on

32.   Men shearing Borzu's sheep at Hanalishah

vacation from school in Kazerun, and two non-Qermezi men (Mali and Haidar) who depended on Borzu for pasture at Hanalishah. As men had approached the camp to join others already at work, they exchanged greetings spoken on the occasion of communal shearing, "May God increase the wealth."

Each shearer laid a sheep on its left side and tied its four legs together with a decorative, braided, tasseled cord he had brought from home. He sheared the right side first, then flipped the sheep over to shear the left side. After flipping the animal once more so that the right side was up, he untied the legs and released the animal. As the sheep escaped, he grabbed a rear leg and yanked it in order to "straighten the digestive organs in case they had twisted during the shearing." Men considered it dangerous for the animal to begin to shear on the left side and to release the animal with its left side up. Borzu ordered a kid to be killed for lunch; it was customary to provide volunteer workers a good meal. For the next three days the shearing continued. After the men completed the two herds of sheep, they sheared the remaining goats.

Borzu complained that because of the drought the quality of wool was inferior and the quantity low. Twenty sheep had lost all their wool, and the rest had lost some. Wool was one of the main marketable products in late spring, and Borzu was obliged to sell most of it to a Semirom merchant in order to pay part of his debt to a Kazerun moneylender. He saved half the wool sheared from sheep under nimsud contract for his partners. Falak and her daughters kept some wool, sorted by color and quality, for weaving. Borzu intended to use the remainder to rent an alfalfa and clover field at Hanalishah. He would sell some goat hair and give most of the rest to women in Shahreza who had woven new panels for his summer tent. Falak kept some hair for weaving and rope making.

Borzu and other men used to shear during the spring migration and then travel from Mount Dena to Isfahan to sell the wool. During the past several years, however, their Semirom merchant-moneylenders had demanded that they trade the wool with them if the nomads expected to receive further credit and loans. Creditors gained a 50 percent profit by selling the wool immediately thereafter in Isfahan.

Three days after arriving at Hanalishah, Borzu had met Ayaz Khan Darrehshuri and some of his Lak shepherds in Semirom. The khan told the Laks to leave Hanalishah, and he agreed to come in a few days to inspect the land. He said his sheep were being sheared the following day and asked Borzu to send Qermezi men to help. Borzu privately noted that the request was ridiculous, especially because these very sheep had been fattened on Qermezi grass. He would volunteer shearers only if all the khan's herds left Hanalishah. The next day the Lak herders did vacate the disputed section and took the ten herds to graze in the mountains just east of Hanalishah, but Borzu chose not to send help. A few days later Ayaz Khan accompanied by Habib Aqa Zahedi came to Hanalishah. Borzu killed a goat for lunch, and many Qermezi men came to show their support. The issue of Hanalishah pastures appeared to be settled for the season.

That evening, pleased with the outcome, Borzu instructed Aqaboa and Mohammad Hosain about the patterns of grazing he wanted them to follow in the weeks ahead. Because his section of pasture at Hanalishah would be inadequate for three months of grazing for all his sheep and goats, he told Aqaboa to use land near that of Gholam Hosain during the daytime, close enough to Borzu's camp that ewes could be milked at noon, and to use land at night just across the border of Hanalishah to the west. Bahmanbaigli Amaleh and Lak Darrehshuri pastoralists occupied these western territories. Borzu had agreed to pay the Bahmanbaigli headman one hundred dollars so that he could graze on a portion of Bahmanbaigli land for a month.

During the last stages of the spring migration when Borzu had heard that pasture at Hanalishah would be sparse, he had said he would rent an irrigated wheat field at Hanalishah from a Persian cultivator. When the wheat ripened, he would cut the crop and let his animals eat the grain where it lay, but grazing at Hanalishah had proved to be better than expected, and he had also located another grazing area.

Soon after Qermezi people arrived at Hanalishah, Sayyid Ramazan, a Persian man in the retinue of Ayaz Khan, chose a day to visit when many of the nomads were in Semirom. He told women alone in their camps that he had guarded their pastures during the spring, and some, including Falak, gave him a sheep's fleece in payment. He had guarded only Hanalishah Pass to the east, however, land Ayaz Khan claimed. When Ramazan came to Khalifeh's tent to collect, Hosain Ali chased him away.

During the first two weeks at Hanalishah, Borzu sent men to shear the sheep of other Darrehshuri khans, as he, Khalifeh, and their father had done for many years. When Borzu had served as the supervisor of shepherds for Jehangir Khan, he organized and attended the annual shearings and received a lamb for every herd sheared. This year Borzu said he could not attend because the event was distant from a road. He sent four Aqa Mohammadli men and his sister's son. The men brought the wool in gunnysacks by mule-back to Borzu's camp, and Morad and Mohammad Karim, whose classes in Kazerun had just ended, delivered it to Jehangir Khan at Round Sun. The khan gave Morad a lamb for his efforts and sent another one for Borzu. When Ziad Khan's supervisor of shepherds scheduled the khan's sheep shearing, Borzu brought five Aqa Mohammadli men to assist. He attended as a guest and did no work as his status required. Noting that he had offered labor to the khans on five occasions so far this summer, Morad also helped shear Mohammad Hasan Khan's sheep. Until the mid-1960s Qermezi men organized by their headman had periodically volunteered labor and military support to the Darrehshuri khans, and in 1971 they were still contributing labor for constructing orchard walls and shearing.

Three days after Ayaz Khan's visit, Borzu moved his tent and camp farther into Hanalishah. He did not need to be as close to the territory's entrance as he had been, for the dispute had been settled, and most of the Qashqa'i and other herders expected to travel through Hanalishah had already made their passage. Ordinarily he remained in his first spring campsite as long as other nomads were passing through. It was now time for a clean camp closer to water.

History of Qermezi in Summer Pastures

Before coming to Hanalishah in 1958, members of Qermezi subtribe had used summer pastures in many other locations. Their movement from place to place reflected competition among Darrehshuri khans, wider Qashqa'i politics, and expanding needs for pastureland.

Qermezi men were part of the entourage of Gudarz Kikha Darrehshuri in the latter part of the nineteenth century and used summer pastures near Narmeh where the khan was located. At the end of the nineteenth and the beginning of the twentieth century, including the time when Shir Mohammad was young, members of Qermezi subtribe spent summers near the town of Dehaqan in northern Darrehshuri territory. They cultivated land controlled by Ayaz Kikha Darrehshuri and his son Hosain Khan and paid them a fifth of the harvest. Few Qashqa'i planted grain at that time. Hosain Khan then gave the Qermezi group summer pastures at Nosratabad and Molla Qoli near Round Sun. There, also, they cultivated. Hosain Khan moved the group to pastures at Black Mud, but later Yar Mohammad Qermezi fought with Hemmat Ali Kikha, a minor Darrehshuri khan who eventually forced Qermezi to leave. The location was too small for two groups. Qermezi people noted that the major Darrehshuri khans had favored the minor khans, with whom they were intermarried, over members of a subtribe.

In 1933 Reza Shah forced all Qashqa'i nomads to settle, and Qermezi people remained year around at Girl's Grave in winter pastures or Narmeh village in summer pastures. When Reza Shah abdicated in 1941, most Qermezi people resumed their seasonal migrations. Ziad Khan and Zeki Khan gave new summer pastures to the Qermezi group at Narmeh where people remained until 1951, when Faraj Khan and Amir'ata Khan, based there, forced the group to leave. The two khans, grandson and great-grandson of Gudarz Kikha, lacked political standing and did not need the support or want the burden of the Qermezi group. They also viewed the group as the client of the major Darrehshuri khans and did not desire it in their midst.

In the 1940s, as part of the struggle for power between the Qashqa'i ilkhani and the Darrehshuri khans in the aftermath of Reza Shah's abdication and the resumption of Qashqa'i nomadism, the Darrehshuri khans pushed the ilkhani's Amaleh subtribes from the northernmost section of Qashqa'i territory. They claimed that their ancestors in the late eighteenth century had forced a similar expulsion of an earlier ilkhani's supporters. The Darrehshuri khans bought land at Wolf Hill (Qurdtapaseh) in northern Darrehshuri territory from the Igdir Qashqa'i tribe. Until the late 1920s the ilkhani had controlled the land, and the Darrehshuri khans were anxious to assume control. Aqakikha khans, men of one of the two major branches of the Darrehshuri khan family, controlled the wider region at Wolf Hill and placed their own Bulverdi supporters there. Ziad Khan, Zeki Khan, and Jehangir Khan, who were Ayazkikha khans of the other major branch of the khan family, wanted to challenge the Aqakikha khans and place in their midst their own supporters.

The two sets of Darrehshuri khans were united in wanting to assert their collective Darrehshuri power in the area not only against the Qashqa'i ilkhani and his Amaleh supporters but also against the Bakhtiyari tribal confederacy just to the north. These khans placed reliable supporters along the northern border of Darrehshuri territory to repel and inhibit incursions from Bakhtiyari tribes. Wolf Hill was the northernmost section of Darrehshuri tribal lands and of the wider Qashqa'i territory. The Qashqa'i ilkhani also needed a strong force along the Bakhtiyari border, but the Darrehshuri tribe, strengthened by its reinforcements in the area, posed a threat to the ilkhani's control of the Qashqa'i confederacy.

In 1951 Ziad Khan, Zeki Khan, and Jehangir Khan gave summer pastures to Qermezi subtribe at Canyon of the Cow Herd (Tang-e Galleh Go) and Row of Willows (Bid-e Qetar) just west of Wolf Hill. They claimed they had seized Canyon of the Cow Herd by force from Malek Mansur Khan, brother of the Qashqa'i ilkhani, who had placed Mussulli Amaleh nomads there. Row of Willows had been occupied by Igdir Qashqa'i pastoralists who were loyal to Khosrow Khan, another brother of the ilkhani. Ja'far Qoli Khan Darrehshuri, resident at nearby Wolf Hill, tried to force the Igdir to leave, and the Igdir turned over control of the land to Khosrow Khan. Favoring Ayazkikha Darrehshuri khans over Aqakikha Darrehshuri khans, Khosrow Khan in turn gave Jehangir Khan the right to assign pastures at Row of Willows. Jehangir Khan allocated the area to Qermezi and Bulverdi Darrehshuri nomads and expelled the Bulverdi Darrehshuri nomads whom Ziad Khan and Ja'far Qoli Khan had placed there.

When Mohammad Reza Shah exiled the Qashqa'i ilkhani and his brothers from Iran in the mid-1950s, Ja'far Qoli Khan and Ziad Khan purchased or seized the rest of Row of Willows from the Igdir. Then they offered to rent a section to Qermezi subtribe. Only Sohrab, whom the khans charged less rent than other Qermezi men because of his loyalty, stayed at Row of Willows, while other Qermezi, including most Aqa Mohammadli men, went to nearby Canyon of the Cow Herd. They rented pastureland from Ayazkikha khans and paid Jehangir Khan a share of the harvest netted from land he controlled.

As the Qermezi group expanded in numbers, it needed further pasture space. Ziad Khan and Jehangir Khan located new land to the southeast at Hanalishah for Khalifeh and his closest supporters, most of whom were Aqa Mohammadli men. In 1958 and during the next few years, Qermezi people at Canyon of the Cow Herd moved to Hanalishah, while Sohrab and other Imamverdili men remained at or moved to Row of Willows. Qermezi men stated that the Ayazkikha and Aqakikha khans divided the Qermezi group into two parts through these land allocations. Without much support from any Darrehshuri khans, Qairkhbaili and Qasemli men found pastures south of Semirom.

Hanalishah had been at the center of disputes over pasture and power between the Qashqa'i ilkhani's family and the Darrehshuri khans. The territory also figured in internal Darrehshuri conflict. Khalifeh and Borzu became a small part of these larger struggles.

Since at least the nineteenth century, Hanalishah and pastures to the north and west had been controlled by the Janikhani family, leaders of the Qashqa'i confederacy, who had used the area for their own herds and Amaleh supporters. Sarqaz Mountain just east of Hanalishah was the border between Janikhani land and Darrehshuri khan land. In 1941 Naser Khan, Qashqa'i ilkhani, assigned Hanalishah and territories to the west to the Bahmanbaigli subtribe of Amaleh, as a reward to Mahmud Khan (Mohammad Bahmanbaigi's father) for his loyalty during Reza Shah's persecution of the Janikhani family. In 1950 Naser Khan gave permission to Hasan Khan Kikha, a minor Darrehshuri khan, to use part of Hanalishah.

In the mid-1950s when Mohammad Reza Shah exiled the ilkhani and his brothers from Iran, Darrehshuri khans forced Amaleh pastoralists to leave Hanalishah and nearby areas and placed their own herds and supporters in the territory. They sent their flocks to Hanalishah under the care of Rakkeh Darrehshuri shepherds. Jehangir Khan's supervisor of shepherds, a Rakkeh man, established a campsite there. Darrehshuri khans had proclaimed, as they took control of the area, "Naser Khan and Khosrow Khan are Qashqa'i khans, but they left Iran. We are Qashqa'i khans, and therefore the land is ours." Hanalishah was close to Round Sun, the Darrehshuri khans' summer residence, and convenient for their use. Their main pastures were close by in the mountains to the east and north of Hanalishah. Several Darrehshuri khans competed for control over Hanalishah, each trying to exploit the territory for his own flocks and assign grazing to his own supporters.

Just before he left Iran, Mohammad Hosain Khan Qashqa'i, brother of Naser Khan, gave a letter to Ayaz Khan Darrehshuri in which he assigned him responsibility for Hanalishah and two nearby areas for the Janikhani family. Ayaz Khan thus came to hold an ambiguous position rife with potential conflict. Darrehshuri people noted, "Ayaz Khan served the il-khani but he was still Darrehshuri." Jehangir Khan wanted Hanalishah to fall under Darrehshuri control and competed against his brother Ayaz Khan who was also serving the interests of the exiled Janikhani family. Jehangir Khan was attempting to build his own power in the Darrehshuri tribe, to counter the power of his uncles Ziad Khan and Zeki Khan. Hanalishah became a site where these conflicting interests were expressed.

In 1958 Ziad Khan and Jehangir Khan gave Khalifeh, then Qermezi headman, rights to use Hanalishah pastures in exchange for an annual payment of eighty to one hundred dollars. The first year Khalifeh came to Hanalishah alone and grazed his herd and cultivated there. The second year several close kin joined him, and the third year Borzu and a few others followed. Some Qermezi men objected to Hanalishah because it was on a migratory route. They wanted more isolated pastures. Summer grazing land was scarce, however, and they eventually came to appreciate Hanalishah's advantages.

Despite the Darrehshuri khans' occupation of Hanalishah in the mid-1950s, the Iranian government continued to regard the land as property of the Janikhani Qashqa'i family. When the shah exiled the ilkhani and his brothers, he also confiscated the family's extensive landholdings, including Hanalishah. In the 1960s national land reform opened up Hanalishah for cultivation. Settled Persians and Lurs in Semirom and Vanak (a nearby village) quickly acquired rights from the government to cultivate at Hanalishah below the water channels issuing from springs. No Qashqa'i people were entitled to use, lease, or purchase any of this cultivable land. The government decreed that land above the water channels was nationalized pastureland, and competition among the Darrehshuri khans continued.

Ziad Khan and Jehangir Khan assigned Hanalishah to Qermezi pastoralists, while Ayaz Khan, bolstered by the mandate he held from the Janikhani Qashqa'i family, announced that the territory was his to assign and claimed the area for his own shepherds and supporters. "War" between Ayaz Khan and Qermezi men waged for two years. Borzu, who had become headman, negotiated the dispute. Ziad Khan, preeminent Darreh-shuri khan, and Ayaz Khan toured Hanalishah on horseback. At the conclusion of the survey Ziad Khan proclaimed that the majority of the land was Borzu's (Qermezi's), that Ayaz Khan ought to stop claiming that portion, and that Ayaz Khan could continue to use grazing land in Hanalishah Pass in Sarqaz Mountain to the east. Borzu was pleased that Ziad Khan had ruled in his favor, when he could have allocated all of Hanalishah to Ayaz Khan. He accepted Ziad Khan's judgment and did not dispute publicly with him over the smaller section given to Ayaz Khan. Borzu killed two animals for a meal, which marked the resolution of the dispute, and hosted the two khans.

Every year thereafter, as Ayaz Khan attempted to seize control of the entire expanse of Hanalishah, Borzu busily accumulated government documents supporting his own rights to the land. The government was becoming his main source of power on this issue.

Although Qermezi people, especially Borzu, were anxious to stake their own claim to Hanalishah, they did often note that the land still rightfully belonged by tribal mandate and a long history of occupation to the Janikhani Qashqa'i family, in particular Guhar Bibi and Rudabeh Bibi. Each of these two daughters of the former Qashqa'i ilkhani Abdollah Khan owned half of Hanalishah, and Qermezi men could point out the boundary between their halves. Borzu and other men noted that if Naser Khan and Khosrow Khan were ever to return to Iran from exile abroad, they would seek the khans' permission to continue to use Hanalishah pastures.

In 1971 Borzu had not yet acquired the definitive government document ruling that he and his group were entitled to exclusive use of Hanalishah as summer pasture, for the government had not yet completed land reform in this area. But he did possess preliminary papers from the Tribal Security Force and the gendarmerie concerning the land and its use that officials had said would be necessary for the acquisition of the formal deed. The most important documents were records of disputes over land at Hanalishah, which proved that certain Qermezi men had occupied the territory at specific periods and that members of Qermezi subtribe had experienced an uninterrupted (seasonal) residence there. In the meantime forest rangers and gendarmes in Semirom stated that no other group of pastoralists could exploit these pastures during the summer.

Borzu determined which families could use pastures and campsites at Hanalishah. Most men who had come there shortly after Khalifeh's arrival in 1958 continued to use the territory. Government documents in

Borzu's possession listed the men who were legally entitled to pastures: Borzu and his five brothers, Morad and his two brothers, Abul Hasan and a brother, Aqaboa and his brother, and Lachin and two of his brothers. Aqaboa (Borzu's hired shepherd) and Aliboa (Aqaboa's brother who stayed at Dashtak all year) did not claim their rights. Lachin and his brothers had recently settled in Naqneh village and had abandoned their places. The other men listed continued to come to Hanalishah, and Borzu assigned a few others space there on a year-to-year basis.

Hanalishah was also under dispute by twenty-three Persian and Lur men who cultivated land below the water channels issuing from springs. Some of them claimed they would soon receive legal, permanent ownership of the land through the implementation of land reform. The rest claimed they leased the land from the government according to the amount of seed they expected to plant. Qermezi men did not know which cultivators were legally entitled to cultivate and which were squatters, for they all alleged the land was already registered in their names. They planted areas in excess of what they said were their legally designated plots. Every year the cultivated land expanded at the expense of pastureland.

In 1971 Hanalishah pastures contained 30 households organized in ten camps. Camps contained from 1 to 7 households. Qermezi men headed nine of these camps, and the tenth belonged to a man from another Darrehshuri subtribe. The core of Aqa Mohammadli lineage occupied Hanalishah in the summer; Aqa Mohammadli men dominated the territory. Of the 30 households, 15 belonged to Aqa Mohammadli men, and 7 more belonged to their hired herders. Four of the 7 hired herders came from other Darrehshuri subtribes, 1 was a Mussulli Amaleh Qashqa'i man, and 2 were Qasemli Qermezi men. (During the summer of 1971, 2 shepherds from other Darrehshuri subtribes replaced 3 of the 7 shepherds.) Five households at Hanalishah belonged to men of other Qermezi lineages (2 Imamverdili, 1 Qairkhbaili, 2 Qasemli who were also hired herders).

Four men (excluding four hired herders) at Hanalishah originated from other Darrehshuri subtribes. These included two members of Ipaigli subtribe, which had closely associated with Qermezi for many years. Once powerful, the subtribe had disintegrated, and its few remaining members who were still nomadic found sanctuary in other Darrehshuri groups. Khalifeh allowed Ilmas, one of the Ipaigli men, to share his pasture. Two of Ilmas's sons served as shepherds for Aqa Mohammadli men. The third non-Qermezi man, Haidar of Zargar subtribe, had camped alone at Hanalishah for sixteen years, beginning two years before any Qermezi families had entered the area. Mohammad Hasan Khan Darrehshuri had issued him a document attesting to his long-term residence. Khalifeh and then Borzu permitted him to stay. Haidar's mother's mother was Qermezi as was his wife's mother. Other men of the Zargar group were similarly dispersed and lived alone or in small groups in Qashqa'i and surrounding tribal territories. They often married people with whom they shared pastures. Members of the Zargar subtribe traced their ancestry to the Qizilbash. (Qizilbash was the name given to warriors, usually Turkish and of tribal background, who followed and fought for the Safavi religious brotherhood in the fifteenth century. The term came to be generally used for the Safavid dynasty's tribal followers. Under Shah Esma'il Safavi, Qizilbash forces conquered Fars province in 1503, and some settled there.) The fourth non-Qermezi man, of Naderli subtribe, was Qermezi's teacher.

The one non-Qashqa'i pastoralist at Hanalishah was Mali, a Lur and a member of the Shaikh lineage from the area where Qermezi used to have winter pastures. Part of a nomadic group that had settled near Dugonbadan fourteen years previously, Mali was migrating for the first time in many years. Borzu had offered him pastures at Hanalishah. In the 1940s and 1950s a few members of Mali's lineage had shared winter pastures at Dashtak and summer pastures at Row of Willows with the Qermezi group. Despite Mali's non-Qermezi, even non-Qashqa'i identity, he enjoyed close ties of kinship and marriage with Borzu and others at Hanalishah. He was a kinsman of Borzu's sister's husband, his wife was Qermezi (Qairkhbaili), his sister was the wife of Naser (an Aqa Mohammadli man resident at Hanalishah), his mother was the sister of Mohammad Hosain (a Qasemli Qermezi man currently Borzu's shepherd), and his brother was soon to marry Borzu's sister's daughter.

Qermezi people who migrated between winter and summer pastures were found in seven different locations in summer pastures: Hanalishah, Row of Willows (11 Imamverdili men, 3 Qairkhbaili, 3 Aqa Mohammadli, 1 Kachili), Canyon of the Cow Herd (2 Imamverdili), Black Mud (2 Qasemli), Narmeh (2 Kachili), south of Semirom (11 Qasemli, 5 Qairkhbaili), and Red Canyon (10 Qairkhbaili). These places were dispersed throughout Darrehshuri and other Qashqa'i summer pastures. People in one place did not have much contact with people in the other places unless they met in Semirom or at Qermezi weddings. The primary affiliations and loyalties of all these individuals, however, were with fellow Qermezi. Qermezi men in summer pastures other than Hanalishah paid rent to use pastures and cultivate, even though these lands were nation-

33.   One of Borzu's summer campsites at Hanalishah. The government forbade the planting of trees on nationalized pastureland, and forest rangers later cut these few trees down.

alized and renting was illegal. Men at Hanalishah with Borzu paid no rent.

Hanalishah and Vicinity

Hanalishah consists of a long narrow valley surrounded by tall mountains. Pastures extend up the mountain slopes. The valley curves toward the northwest at its northern reaches. Several streams originating from nearby springs converge at the base of the valley where the Persians and Lurs cultivated. The name Hanalishah, some said, was an abbreviated form of Hasan Ali Shah who was possibly a dervish who lived in the vicinity at some now-unknown time. The area of Semirom was once the haunt of many dervishes.

Borzu's campsites were located in open, fairly flat terrain, for he wanted to keep an eye on activities in the area and on all people traveling through it. He also wanted constant surveillance over the entrance to Hanalishah Pass leading east through Sarqaz Mountain to Round Sun. His main summer campsite was located at the mouth of the pass. All other camps at Hanalishah were tucked into ravines and shallow depressions leading up the mountain slopes. People traveling through Hanali-shah along the valley bottom did not see most of the tents and camps. Borzu's territory dominated the southern part of Hanalishah, and the nearest neighboring camp to the north was more than a kilometer away. A kilometer or less separated each of the other camps from its neighbors.

Each of the fifteen Aqa Mohammadli men at Hanalishah who headed independent households held rights to use a section of the territory for campsites and pastures. The other fifteen households were allowed to use resources on the basis of contractual ties with Aqa Mohammadli men there or special arrangements with Borzu. Aqa Mohammadli men could invite others to share their pastures if Borzu permitted it. Only he could entitle additional households to reside at Hanalishah.

Most campsites, particularly the favored summer one by a spring, were used exclusively by specific households. Boundaries of the surrounding pastures were not precisely drawn at Hanalishah as they were at Dashtak. Pastoralists at Hanalishah used the slopes of hills and mountains near their camps for their animals. As at Dashtak, grazing at the highest altitudes was open to all who held rights (via Borzu) to Hanalishah. Unlike Dashtak, outsiders did not exploit these higher altitudes for resources. The only exceptions were the collectors of gum tragacanth who paid Borzu for the privilege of exploiting shrubs growing on the slopes. Pastoralists at Hanalishah relied on naturally growing vegetation on the slopes for two months after their arrival and then, this vegetation depleted, used the stubble of their own and others' cultivation and the fodder they cultivated and purchased.

The pastoralists occupied three to four campsites during their stay at Hanalishah, and they moved from one to another for clean locations and better access to grazing and water. They built no permanent structures, and the only improvements they made were to the sources of water. Men lined the mouths of springs with stones to create small pools and sometimes constructed stone-lined channels directing water a short distance from the source. These efforts kept the springs clean and provided easy access for people and animals. To avoid contamination, animals were not allowed to drink from the heads of springs but rather were led to the channels below. Women and girls collecting water from the pools were careful not to pollute or muddy the water. They washed clothes, cooking equipment, and yarn in the channels downstream. Every time the pastoralists planted shade trees by their springs, government forest rangers or cultivators cut them down. Government law forbade any planting on national pastures, and the cultivators wanted to erase any trace, however minor or symbolic (such as a few trees), of the pastoralists' hold on the land.

The pastoralists constructed no enclosures for their animals, unlike in winter pastures. Weather was usually warm and mild, rain was rare, and few predators were present. The herds slept at night by the owners' and shepherds' tents, and people responsible for herding kept surveillance along with the ever-vigilant guard dogs. At night horses, mules, and donkeys were ordinarily tethered, while camels either roamed freely to be rounded up in the morning or were hobbled by a short rope.

One of the few environmental problems in summer pastures was the sudden gusty wind that rose up and could blow down tents and scatter possessions. Whirlwinds were especially troublesome. People could do little but pick up loose objects and hold onto tent poles and ropes when a whirling tower of wind and dust approached.

Men with independent pasture rights at Hanalishah cultivated small plots of wheat and barley by dry farming, although they would have preferred to cultivate with irrigation because of the higher and more predictable yields. Some of them had irrigated when they first came to Hanalishah, but shortly thereafter the government forbade them to use land below the water channels. Fields, usually located near camps, were not enclosed or protected in any way, unlike the stone-walled fields at Dashtak. The totality of the harvest belonged to them. The government's nationalization of pastures meant they were no longer obligated to pay rent or a share of the harvest to people who had once controlled the land. Cultivation was, however, forbidden by law on nationalized land, a law everyone including government officials disregarded. Lacking independent pasture rights, hired shepherds and camel herders could not cultivate at Hanalishah nor did they have time to help others cultivate for a share of the harvest.

By the mid-1960s all irrigable land at Hanalishah was controlled by twenty-three Persian and Lur men from Semirom and Vanak. These men refused to cooperate in cultivation on an equal basis with the pastoralists for fear they would later claim the land. Persians and Lurs plowed and planted grain in autumn to harvest in summer, and they planted beans, peas, alfalfa, and clover in spring. They harvested the crops themselves, occasionally with help from some of the pastoralists, usually adolescents and young men. They paid these workers in kind by the day or job. They sometimes paid workers who held no pasture rights at Hanalishah, such as Mali or a shepherd's son, a fraction of the crop, for these men and boys were in no position to claim the land. The cultivators kept the products for their own consumption and sold the surplus in Semirom. Some pastoralists bought ripe alfalfa and clover from them, to harvest and dry the crop themselves for use as fodder in autumn. The cultivators constructed protective stone walls around their fields, which helped to keep out the pastoralists' animals but also restricted their movement and access to water.

Every summer the cultivators and the pastoralists engaged in violent disputes. Each group encroached on what the other considered its own land. The cultivators grazed their own animals on pastureland before the nomads arrived and tried to block access to springs and streams. The pastoralists tried to claim all vegetation in the area that was not planted (and to take some that was), and they wanted to pull up weeds in and between cultivated fields and to graze their herd and pack animals nearby. The cultivators confiscated animals they claimed were in fields. They severed the ears of donkeys if they repeatedly found them trespassing.

Vegetation growing wild between fields, along irrigation channels, and by streams was a source of constant conflict between the pastoralists and the cultivators. The pastoralists declared that they had freely used all vegetation in the vicinity until the mid-1960s and were still entitled to it. The cultivators claimed that wild vegetation grew on their legally entitled land and was necessary for the draft and pack animals they used in cultivation. They also insisted that their own labor in constructing irrigation channels and irrigating fields produced this wild vegetation, which they therefore viewed as a crop in the same sense as their grains and legumes. Some cultivators owned or cared for small herds of cows that grazed this wild vegetation. Many of them also brought other animals to graze the pastures before the nomads arrived in spring. While the cultivators waited for fields to ripen, they cut wild grass growing along water channels for sale in Semirom. The pastoralists indignantly maintained that while it might be appropriate for the cultivators to feed this vegetation to animals they employed in cultivation, it was not acceptable for them to exploit it as grazing for other animals or to sell it. They proclaimed that a valuable base of their own livelihood was being expropriated and sold out from underneath them.

One day Borzu yelled at a cultivator who passed by his tent on his way to Semirom herding donkeys laden with cut wild grass. "Farmer [in this context, a pejorative label]! Your work is in the fields. I am a herder! That grass is mine! I owned that grass long before your father was born, long before you ever came here to cultivate!"

The Persian and Lur cultivators owned or rented houses in Semirom (eight of them) and in Vanak (fifteen) where their families stayed all year. From the time of preparing the soil in spring and planting, the men lived alone in small stone huts, some partly subterranean, which they constructed by their fields in order to guard them. They remained there until they transported harvested crops to town or village. Many stayed even longer so that their draft, pack, and herd animals could eat the fresh, rich stubble. The pastoralists were angry about this constant vigilance, for it impeded their own attempts to cut wild vegetation, graze animals in fields, and pull up crops for fodder. They strongly resented this intrusion into their territory.

Each year the cultivators steadily improved the land by increasing the area cultivated and constructing better irrigation channels, walls, and shelters. These efforts fortified their attachment to the land and made it less likely that they would succumb to the pastoralists' pressure.

Lack of fuel was the major ecological limitation of summer pastures for the nomads. Whatever trees had once grown at Hanalishah had long ago been cut down. Like almost all other Qashqa'i summer pastures, the terrain was devoid of vegetation that could be used as fuel. Only ubiquitous hardy shrubs proliferated. These shrubs, which burned rapidly and without concentrated heat, were not an effective fuel for most purposes. During late spring and most of summer, women processed milk products, almost all of which required quantities of fuel. For these and other needs they relied almost exclusively on camel and donkey dung, which was produced in pellets and dried where it dropped. Young girls spent part of each day collecting dried dung. The firewood men had transported to summer pastures from the last stages of the migratory route did not last long into the season. A few men traveled to wooded areas near summer pastures, particularly at Canyon of the Cow Herd, to collect firewood for use at Hanalishah.

The lack of vegetative cover was one reason why few predators were found in summer pastures as compared to winter pastures. Occasionally a lone wolf attacked a stray sheep or lamb. Vultures, although present, did not usually attack live animals. Snakes, some of which were poisonous, were said to be more prevalent in summer than in winter pastures. Bears, wild boars, and striped hyenas inhabited some Qashqa'i summer pastures but not Hanalishah.

Darrehshuri summer pastures were the most northern of the summer pastures of the Qashqa'i tribes. Hanalishah is located in the central western section of Darrehshuri territory near the border of Lur tribes to the west. High mountains separate Qashqa'i and Lur territory and impeded contact between the two groups. During the summer Qermezi people at Hanalishah associated primarily with fellow Qashqa'i, especially other Darrehshuri. Semirom was the principal market town of Amaleh, Farsimadan, some Shesh Boluki, and most Darrehshuri. Qermezi people living in northern Darrehshuri territory bordering Bakhtiyari territory interacted with Bakhtiyari, Yalameh, and Basseri (a different group from the Basseri of the Khamseh confederacy) tribespeople.

For business, Qermezi men frequently traveled by horseback, muleback, and foot to the town of Semirom, located two hours southeast by foot from Hanalishah. Merchants and moneylenders from whom they acquired loans and commodities (mostly on credit) were located in Semirom, and the nomads owed their animal products to them. Semirom also housed the Tribal Security Force for Darrehshuri affairs, and headmen such as Borzu needed to go there several times a week. Officials of the gendarmerie (the regular force, separate from the Tribal Security Force's gendarmes), Ministry of Agriculture (forest rangers, Land Reform Organization), secret police, and army were also found in Semirom. Semirom is located in Isfahan province, and Borzu and other men were required to travel to the provincial capital, Isfahan, a day's journey by bus, in order to complete governmental administrative tasks.

In the midst of Qashqa'i territory, Semirom was a town inhabited predominantly by Persians. Many of the Persian merchants, moneylenders, and craftsmen (blacksmiths, leather workers, makers of felt rugs and cloaks) tended principally to Qashqa'i customers. Some of them also owned or rented homes and shops in Shahreza, Borujen, and Isfahan, where they went once the nomads were well on their way to winter pastures and once Semirom and the wider area became snowbound. None of the shopkeepers or craftsmen in Semirom were Qashqa'i. Several wealthy Qashqa'i men owned shops there, which Persian shopkeepers ran. Some Qashqa'i people whose summer pastures were in the vicinity had settled in the town.

Historical patterns of Qashqa'i settlement favored summer over winter pastures, and most Qashqa'i people who were settling in the 1960s and early 1970s were choosing summer pastures. Although much of the area was isolated and snowbound in the cold months, protection against the elements was possible, whereas protection against the severe heat and aridity of winter pastures in the hot months was not as feasible. Small villages and even single houses of recently settled Qashqa'i dotted summer pastures, including the area around Semirom.

Thirty or so Qermezi men and their families were permanently settled in summer pastures. Most Kachili men had been settled in three villages for many years. Some lived in Round Sun and Narmeh villages near the summer camps of Darrehshuri khans and worked land for them or performed other services. Eight Aqa Mohammadli men had settled during the past nine years in two villages near the town of Borujen.

The village closest to Hanalishah is Vanak, some fifteen kilometers through mountainous terrain to the northwest and inhabited by Persians and Lurs. Vanak's headman was a Lur as were the dominant families. Their principal crop was opium. When opium production became government controlled in 1955, landowners in Vanak received permission to continue to cultivate the crop, and they had become wealthy. Men in Vanak grazed their ten thousand sheep and goats in the vicinity. These animals did not enter Qermezi land while Borzu's group resided at Hanalishah, but they did exploit the area before and after. Their proximity made it difficult for Qermezi herders to find pasture beyond Hanalishah. Qermezi men experienced indirect contact with Vanak through the Persian and Lur cultivators at Hanalishah, and some created "village friend" relationships with Vanak men in order to store goods and find guards for their fields when they were absent and to sell, buy, and board pack and herd animals.

A narrow dirt track north of Hanalishah valley led to Zain Ali shrine, a small saint's tomb nestled in the mountain folds several hours away by foot. Persians and Lurs from Semirom and vicinity traveled on donkeys to Zain Ali for pilgrimages, especially on religious holidays, and some used the track leading through Hanalishah. A better road bypassed Hanalishah and led through Vanak. Qermezi people did not frequent Zain Ali or consider it important. No vehicular road passed through Hanalishah; the farthest north vehicles could easily travel was on the valley bottom where several streams converged.

Round Sun (Mehr-e Gerd), summer residence of many Darrehshuri khans, is located just less than an hour's drive northwest of Semirom. The high rugged Sarqaz Mountain separates Hanalishah and Round Sun, and a footpath leading through a pass connected the two areas. Borzu and Sohrab met frequently with the khans in Round Sun and in Semirom where they all conducted business. Once every summer or so, one or two khans, sometimes with their families, came to visit Borzu at Hanalishah.

A small village, Round Sun was inhabited in summer by about six hundred people, almost all of whom were Darrehshuri Qashqa'i. Ziad Khan and Zeki Khan Darrehshuri had built the first houses there in 1941. By 1971 the village contained the homes and orchards of all Ayazkikha

Darrehshuri khans. Members of the Zahedi family and many of the khans' retainers and servants also lived in houses there. Some Darrehshuri men, as well as several Persian men from Semirom, operated a few small shops stocked with essentials. Most residents of Round Sun moved to towns and cities before winter when the village was snowbound. On the hills and mountain slopes above Round Sun, many Darrehshuri khans set up large elaborate tent encampments for their main period of residence in the area. They lived in their houses in the village in the cold weather of midspring and early autumn and stored goods there year around. Some of the khans' servants also pitched tents near their employers' tents. As many girls as boys of the families of Round Sun attended three tent schools established by the Office of Tribal Education. Their teachers, Darrehshuri men and one woman, came from families who served the khans.

Soon after Borzu settled into his spring campsite at Hanalishah, he took his family to Round Sun to visit Faraj Aqa Zahedi and Habib Aqa Zahedi and then Falak's brother Shir Ali at Narmeh, a village northwest of Round Sun. He still desired Faraj Aqa's daughter for Mohammad Karim and wanted to keep their ties active. Also, he had entertained each of the men at least once in the past three seasons and wanted reciprocal hospitality.

Summer was a time of consuming and diverse economic activities for the Qermezi people at Hanalishah. They viewed the season as the culmination of a year's efforts to practice profitable animal husbandry. They sold surplus animals once a year, in late spring or early summer, and reduced their herds to a manageable size able to survive the autumn migration, the harsh winter, and the return spring migration. The cash the nomads derived from this sale was their only major source of income all year. In summer they paid some debts incurred during the previous three seasons. They renewed and took on new animal contracts for the following year or more. Some assumed short-term contracts for the three months of summer. Men usually hired shepherds or renewed their contracts on the first day of summer. They sheared sheep and goats in late spring and sold the wool and hair they did not keep for weaving. Spring and summer were the seasons of milk production. The most profitable of the products, clarified butter, was sold along the migratory route and in summer. People also sold fresh butter and dried curds and preserved other milk products for their own consumption in late summer, autumn, and winter. Most men cultivated wheat and barley in summer. Wheat provided their staple food, and barley, straw, alfalfa, clover, and hay were fodder for the sheep and pack animals in late summer and autumn when grazing was sparse. Women wove a gelim, jajim, or pile carpet and several smaller, more utilitarian items in summer. Women and children scoured the terrain for wild plants to use as food, medicine, and dye.

Twenty days after their arrival in summer pastures, most men at Hanalishah, but not Borzu, prepared to sell sheep and goats. They had wanted to fatten them on new vegetation before their sale. The spring migration had been hard on the animals, especially following the hunger and stress of winter, and a sedentary period at summer pastures helped to restore their health and increase their weight. The nomads were desperate for cash. Creditors in Semirom were pressuring them to discharge their debts, and creditors in Kazerun would soon descend on summer pastures to demand repayment of the loans and credit they had given since the autumn migration. In years past men had sold year-old male lambs and kids toward the end of the spring migration as they neared summer pastures, but this year the animals had been too thin. Also in years past men had sold most of the animals they intended to sell by the beginning of summer when they added new nimsud animals to their herds.

Qermezi men at Hanalishah sold their sheep and goats in different ways. Most transported animals to Isfahan for sale at caravansaries and government slaughterhouses. They included nimsud animals in these sales or turned them over to their partners for sale or reassignment. Men appreciated the animal buyers (Persians, Lurs, Shahsevan, and Qashqa'i) who came to Hanalishah, for the prices offered were sometimes competitive with what they expected the government to pay in Isfahan, and the nomads avoided the effort, expense, and risk of taking their animals to the city. Sometimes they sold a few animals to merchants and moneylenders in Semirom if they liked the price or felt obligated. Finally, some men sold a few animals to their kinsmen and neighbors. A man needing a ram, for example, might buy one from someone close. A hired shepherd needing cash to pay a debt might sell a few animals to someone wanting to augment his herd.

Men preparing to sell animals in Isfahan checked their herds and marked with dye or ashes the animals they wanted or needed to sell. Under ideal conditions they sold only year-old male lambs and kids and animals deemed unfit to reproduce or migrate. Under current conditions, however, with animal losses and debts so high, men dipped into their capital stock and sold animals that did not fall into these categories. Men who had agreed to cooperate in the venture assembled their animals, and several men herded them near Semirom and slept in the open that night.

At dawn they drove the animals to the other side of Semirom near the road leading to Shahreza and Isfahan. Another man rented a truck in Semirom and directed the driver to a prearranged location. The truck, sometimes double-deck, transported the animals to a caravansary in Isfahan where they slept the night, while men found cheap lodging there or nearby. Early the next morning men arranged to sell some or all of their animals to buyers who congregated at the caravansary. If they considered the offered price low, they drove the animals to a government slaughterhouse where they took their chances.

Workers there sorted animals into groups of ten, then "randomly" selected one group for slaughter. They removed the heads, internal organs, and skins and hung the carcasses by the legs. The total weight of the ten carcasses determined the price of each of the other groups of ten animals. If the ten "randomly" selected animals were low in weight compared to other groups of ten, the seller sustained a loss. If the ten animals were heavy in comparison, he sustained a gain. No seller ever reported his heaviest animals being selected. Qermezi men viewed the transaction as a matter of chance but were also skeptical about the procedure's fairness. Someone, not the seller, profited from the sale. The government-controlled price per kilogram decreased as the number of animals brought to the city increased. Because so many nomadic pastoralists (Qashqa'i and others) were settling and needing to rid themselves of animals, the market was glutted and the price low. It was illegal to sell animals directly to butchers or meat wholesalers. Workers at the slaughterhouse sold for their own profit the heads, internal organs, and skins. Animal owners lost their rights to these parts. Animals sold at the slaughterhouse were taxed, an income said to be intended for the Ministry of Agriculture's forest rangers who supervised nationalized pastureland.

While many Qermezi men were selling animals in Isfahan, people back at Hanalishah talked incessantly about Borzu's herders. Khodabakhsh was finally able to return to his family at Dashtak, and Borzu was left without a goat herder. When Yadollah refused to tend the goat herd as Borzu ordered, Borzu struck him. Remaining firm in his resolve, Yadollah staunchly proclaimed that he was a herder of camels, not goats, and that goat herding was demeaning. Camel herding was a specialized occupation requiring more knowledge and skill, people said, than goat herding. Borzu had been asking young men at Hanalishah to fill in until he hired a new herder, but he was running out of people who owed him favors. He tried to send Mohammad Karim with the goats, but his son always balked and then performed irresponsibly as a herder. As soon as Borzu left camp, especially for trips to Semirom, Mohammad Karim abandoned the herd, let the goats stray, and returned to sit in the tent.

Aqaboa, Mohammad Hosain, and Yadollah all claimed they were serious about leaving Borzu's employment the first day of summer. Mohammad Hosain, his son Khosrow, and Yadollah wanted to earn cash harvesting grain south of Semirom. The pool of prospective shepherds that had been available until this year had dried up, and no one knew of possible replacements for the four herders Borzu was losing. Hired shepherds were finding that part-time agricultural labor was more profitable than full-time herding, and they had been severely tried during the difficult last year. Borzu and other men needing herders were not raising wages adequately to compete against other kinds of employers in the wider labor market in south Iran. A few herders hired by Qermezi men were tied by kinship and marriage to the Qermezi group or were Qermezi themselves, and they were urged to remain as herders to help their kinsmen. Such emotionally based appeals were not effective for herders who lacked kin ties with Qermezi.

Borzu contracted to rent a ripe alfalfa and clover field from a nearby Persian cultivator, who accepted wool in trade after insisting on cash, and he asked Hajji Qorban to help cut it. Along with a reluctant Mohammad Karim, Borzu occasionally contributed labor. He fed fresh alfalfa and clover to the rams that would mate in midsummer, and Zohreh took lambs to graze in the ripe crop and then to eat the fresh stubble. The previous summer Ali had agreed to take six sheep to winter pastures for a Persian cultivator in exchange for clover this summer. Harvested three times a summer, alfalfa and clover were essential animal fodder for the pastoralists, who cut, dried, and packed the crops for use later in the summer and autumn. Persian and Lur cultivators at Hanalishah said that if their alfalfa and clover fields were closer to town and the price were higher, they would harvest, transport, and sell the crops themselves.

Government forest rangers and Qashqa'i collectors of gum tragacanth came by truck to Borzu's camp to negotiate with him. Gum tragacanth was the marketable sap of a shrub growing on the mountain slopes of summer pastures. To extract the gum, collectors dug a small hole to expose part of the main root of the shrub, made incisions in the root, covered the hole with a rock to protect the root, and returned later to scrape off the exuded dried sap for eventual transport to Shahreza. Exporters sold the sap, used as a thickener, to foreign industry. In 1966 forest rangers had begun to control the extraction of gum tragacanth by limiting the number of collectors and setting the sale price. Collection of the gum was illegal without government permission, and forest rangers controlled access to the resources of summer pastures. The harvested crop was supposed to be sold only to the government at a controlled price. The system was corrupt at all levels. Forest rangers extorted cash bribes in addition to the required government fee before they permitted collectors to work. Men in control of territory, such as Borzu at Hanalishah, solicited payment before allowing collectors on their land, and they arranged other private deals with them for their mutual benefit. Collectors tried to produce more gum than they had estimated to forest rangers when the season began, so that they could sell the surplus privately. In Darrehshuri territory, the collectors were the poorest members of several economically disadvantaged subtribes. No Qermezi men were among them.

In exchange for permission to tap Hanalishah's resources, Borzu made use of the collectors' labor. When the firewood he had transported from the last stages of the migratory route was gone, he sent Yadollah, two collectors, and camels to Canyon of the Cow Herd to gather more. In a headman's tent, firewood and not animal dung was required for use during the entertainment of guests and visitors. It was not seemly for guests to sit around a dung fire, Borzu said. He told the collectors to harvest the ripe alfalfa and clover he had purchased, and one of them wove a reed screen for the tent. When a collector came to see him, he invariably gave him a chore or an errand. The previous year when a different group of collectors had worked at Hanalishah, they had tried to bring their small herds, but Borzu banished the animals and refused to permit the group to return. He accepted a new group consisting of seven Qerekhli Darrehshuri men who were anxious to be in his favor so they could return the next year. They each agreed to give him six kilograms of gum, which he would sell privately.

Men who had left the spring migration to harvest crops in winter pastures rejoined their families at Hanalishah. They brought with them goods they had stored in Kazerun at the end of winter. The harvest had been meager. Some fields had been total losses. Men who remained in winter pastures all year had grazed their goats in other fields, to salvage the crop, according to prior agreement. Non-Qashqa'i herders had ravaged still other fields. Damage inflicted by birds was greater than usual. Crop yields this year generally averaged a sevenfold increase over the amount of seed planted, but Khalifeh, Ali, and Akbar had achieved only a threefold increase. Men noted that such low yields made the whole effort pointless.

Abul Hasan, one of the returning cultivators, reported to Borzu that the former landowners of Dashtak had plowed Dashtak pastures with tractors to prepare for planting. They took advantage of the road Borzu had built, a recent rain that had softened the soil, and the temporary absence of most families in Borzu's group who stayed in winter pastures all year. These families had moved to higher altitudes to escape the heat and were not present to prevent the encroachment. Borzu wrote letters of protest to government agencies in Kazerun and to the Tribal Security Force, and he hoped Hajj Khodaparast, member of the Kazerun town council, would help him by wielding influence.

Milk production was at its peak toward the latter part of spring. Women milked each animal twice a day and were busy processing products. They made the first dried whey paste of the year, a sharp-tasting extract of sour milk that took a full day of cooking and stirring over a fire to produce. Several large slabs of the dark hardened paste, used primarily as flavoring in food, would last into winter. Prices for fresh and clarified butter and dried curds were unusually high because of the scarcity of these commodities in markets, but men at Hanalishah were forced to trade them at below-market prices to pay off debts to their merchant-moneylenders in Semirom.

Falak, her daughters, and the wives and daughters of the shepherds organized six separate milkings a day. Each time a herder brought animals to camp to be milked, women and girls put aside their other work to gather up large pots, and children and others who were present hurried to help corral the herd. The herder had just previously grazed the animals some distance away so they would be tired and more apt to stand close together and still. Never employing any kind of physical structure to contain the animals to be milked, the herder held two animals at his sides with their heads facing him and used them as a barrier. Other people stood at the herd's periphery to control the waiting animals. Women and older girls stationed themselves with pots near the herder who directed animals toward them. The milkers slapped the sides of the animals when they finished, and they leapt and sped away to graze or stand at a distance until the herder rounded them up to rejoin the rest of the herd. After the shepherds' wives and daughters milked Borzu's animals, they retrieved their own few animals from the herds.

Once again Jambazli Darrehshuri nomads tried to travel through Hanalishah. The first time their herds had strayed from the dirt track, eaten vegetation that Qermezi men were conserving for later, and grazed in the fields of the Persian and Lur cultivators who tried to hold Qermezi men responsible for all crop damage. Borzu, Mohammad Karim, and Borzu's nephew Fathollah forced the Jambazli group to reverse direction and chased them from Hanalishah. The next day other Qashqa'i nomads camped for the night at the bottom of the valley, but Borzu said he knew they would leave early the next morning.

Armed gendarmes from Semirom, along with the Lur headman of Vanak village and several Vanak farmers, dropped by at Borzu's. They left one gendarme there to write a report on a dispute a Persian cultivator had brought to the attention of the secret police, and then they continued on to oversee the collection of Vanak's opium crop. Borzu and the gendarme drove in Borzu's truck to the scene of the trouble, where Fathollah had allegedly hit a cultivator who had blocked his path as he led animals to drink from a stream. Borzu and the gendarme later returned to his tent with three cultivators who were needed as witnesses, and with animation they discussed the conflict for hours.

When the gendarme finally left, Borzu put Yadollah, Fathollah, and two other boys to work rubbing linseed oil on goats whose skin had become itchy after they had been sheared, and then he went to cut clover. Heating the oil in goat milk, Yadollah and the boys applied the warm liquid with an old piece of tent fabric to the goats' hind ends and legs and then along their backs against the direction of the growth of hair. They rubbed oil on the goats' horns and noses, so that when they scratched and sniffed their bodies they would spread more oil. The sun's warmth would also disperse the oil and soften the skin. The treatment helped the goats to be less distracted, and they were supposed to become fat more quickly.

Falak and her daughters, including Samarrokh who had come for a visit, prepared a place behind the tent where they could process goat hair for spinning. They pulled apart chunks of hair fresh from shearing, piled it on a cloth, and beat and lifted it for hours with thin wooden sticks to separate the strands. Then they gently twisted and wound clumps of loose hair around a thick stick to prepare bundles for spinning. People approaching the work group said, "May God increase the wealth," so as not to cause misfortune. The task lasted two days, Samarrokh staying until it was done. For one lunch Katayun cooked a rice stew and offered some to each tent in the camp, in one last act of community sharing. In five days she and her family planned to leave Hanalishah. Falak gave processed goat hair for spinning to the shepherd Khosrow's wife and to the wife of a Qerekhli collector of gum tragacanth. After these women had spun the yarn, she would pay them in goat hair.

Qermezi men returned from Isfahan disappointed and depressed about the low price they had received for their animals. The government's price was lower than expected, and ten of the smallest animals of each man had been chosen as the supposedly representative sample of all the animals he had brought for sale. The thousands of acts each man had performed to ensure the health, security, and proper feeding and watering of his animals were all reduced to a random, government-controlled operation netting them no economic profit for the past year's work and, for many, a substantial loss. They remembered Borzu's assertions that they would recover the cost of transporting water to Wide Mountain in the heavier weights of animals at the time of sale. This expectation had not been realized. The drought had kept the animals thin, and the price was substantially lower than in previous years. No one blamed Borzu.

While in Isfahan one man had lost a sheep, probably through theft. People commented, "It was as if he had killed and eaten the animal himself." Men were careful not to use herd animals for meat, even when they and their families were hungry. When an animal was lost or stolen, they often remarked that they might as well have enjoyed eating it—the end was the same. A Persian craftsman toured Hanalishah hoping to take orders for felt rugs and cloaks from nomads who had earned money from selling animals. He found no takers.

On their way back to Hanalishah, men had encountered Kazerun merchants and moneylenders who had arrived in anticipation of the beginning of summer, the customary time for nomads to pay debts incurred in winter pastures. Expecting hospitality and food, these creditors would travel from tent to tent time and again during the next six weeks. Several of the most parasitic ones, including the blind Kalayaz, stayed more than two months living off the hospitality of Qermezi and other Qashqa'i nomads to whom they had lent money and credited goods. Because of the nomads' continued indebtedness and their certain need for loans and credit in the autumn and winter to come, they were unable to dislodge their creditors. Kalayaz and a few others announced that they had increased interest rates for loans and credit already given, beyond the amount their debtors had earlier agreed upon. These new demands caused arguments everywhere they went. Qermezi men often gathered at a kinsman's tent when they heard that Kalayaz or another moneylender was on his way so that they could offer moral support and argue against him.

Most creditors held nimsud animals with one or more Qermezi men at Hanalishah, and they came also to renegotiate or discharge the contracts. All the nomads were unable to repay their total debts, and almost all of them were forced to engage in new or extended nimsud contracts with their creditors. As partial owners of animals tended by these pastoralists, merchants and moneylenders proclaimed that their stay at Hanalishah was necessary because they needed to make decisions concerning their property. The nomads' recent increased expenditures on fodder, water, and grazing, combined with the high rate of animal deaths, had complicated the process of concluding or extending nimsud contracts. These costs and losses had previously been considered the pastoralists' responsibility, but they were no longer willing to carry the entire burden. Merchants and moneylenders claimed that the pastoralists must have practiced improper animal husbandry if their reports of expenditures and mortality rates were correct. These discussions and arguments lasted for weeks.

Responsible for Hanalishah pastures, Borzu was angry about the increased number of animals partially owned by merchants and moneylenders but tended by Qermezi families. He did not want pastoral resources, already limited, to be exploited for the profit of outsiders. He was especially disturbed by men whose herds consisted increasingly of nimsud animals. For example, Kalayaz held half-ownership of two hundred of Naser's animals. "Hanalishah is Qermezi land, not Kalayaz's," Borzu often shouted. Because of scarce resources at Hanalishah and Dashtak, he had turned away Qermezi men who had sought use of grazing land. When he allotted pastures to Qermezi and other nomads, he gained economically and politically. But he gained nothing by "giving" pastures to Kalayaz. Kalayaz, who did not pay for the land and seemed not to appreciate the favor, was interfering more and more in the economic, even social, affairs of people at Hanalishah and Dashtak.

Aqaboa invited Kalayaz for dinner one night and, in his honor, killed one of the few goats he owned. He was indebted to him for more than twice his annual shepherd's salary, and he also owed money to a Semirom merchant. One of the poorest men at Hanalishah, he could not afford rice to serve with the meat. Katayun bought tea and sugar, which ordinarily they could not afford, from Rokhsar. Mindful of their own reliance on help from others, Katayun and Aqaboa were unusually generous with their sparse wealth. Some years back, Katayun said, they had owned two goatskin water bags (when at least four were necessary). When they saw a family with none, they compassionately gave it one of their own. "What is a man without a goatskin bag?" Aqaboa queried.

One sunny afternoon at the end of spring Qermezi men gathered in Borzu's tent to discuss pressing issues. His elder brother Khalifeh had heard from Sohrab that the government might give pastureland to Qermezi at Wolf Hill in northern Darrehshuri territory. Borzu debated the rumor with the men and then decided to go there sometime soon with Khalifeh to investigate.

Qermezi nomads who had exploited summer pastures at Row of Willows near Wolf Hill for nineteen years held no legal documents to prove their presence. Ja'far Qoli Khan Darrehshuri, who had formerly controlled much of the area and still exercised considerable power, had often told them that he would secure government deeds for them when the time came. He had instead helped wealthy Lur investors in Borujen, in exchange for a monetary reward. For many years the khan had collected a fifth of the harvest netted by Qermezi men at Row of Willows as if he owned the land. The government, however, had nationalized the land in the early 1960s, and he had been illegally expropriating a fifth of the harvest since then. When confronted by Qermezi men who had threatened to report him to the government, he replied that if they did he would refuse to help them obtain legal rights to the land and would allocate the land to others. He had just carried out this threat, and Sohrab sought the help of his rival Borzu. Aware of improprieties on the khan's part, government officials had apparently decided that Qermezi people residing at Row of Willows and others in their group who had lived near there in the past should be allotted part of the area. One problem facing Borzu was that Row of Willows fell under the jurisdiction of Shahr-e Kord, capital of the province of Chahar Mahal Bakhtiyari, and not under that of Isfahan or Shiraz where he was more accustomed to handling land problems.

The men sitting with Borzu also talked at length of settlement. Borzu always claimed personal disinterest in settling and argued with the men who stressed its benefits. Because he had heard that some close kinsmen had already announced definite plans to settle at the conclusion of their stay at Hanalishah, he worried about others joining them and did not know exactly how to hold onto them.

Borzu raised the issue of the pasture rights of other Qermezi people who were currently south of Semirom. The government had just decreed that Qashqa'i nomads who had used pastures in that region twenty years ago could now claim the land as theirs. If implemented, the decree would displace people of three Darrehshuri subtribes (including Qermezi) and move Amaleh people into the area. The land had been controlled by the Qashqa'i ilkhani Naser Khan and his family. When he was exiled, Darrehshuri khans moved their own pastoralists into the area and displaced some Amaleh. Currently Amaleh and Darrehshuri shared the region. Amaleh pastoralists were now claiming the entire region for themselves, and the two groups had fought. Borzu declared that the Darrehshuri khans were currently assisting these Amaleh in order to pauperize their own Darrehshuri supporters. The khans depended on Darrehshuri people as agricultural laborers (in their fields, orchards, and gardens), shepherds, and domestic servants and wanted, so Borzu argued, to keep members of the tribe poor so that they would remain a pool of cheap labor.

Early in the morning on the last day of spring, Borj Ali, his family, and their seven sheep and goats left Hanalishah. When Afsar stopped by Katayun's tent to say good-bye, Katayun quickly searched through her possessions to find a gift but could locate only a few strands of yarn. Afsar then paused briefly at Borzu's tent. Borj Ali and Afsar were Bulverdi Qashqa'i, and he wanted to return to his family and then find other work rather than continuing as a shepherd. Abdol Hosain, who was selling or lending most of his herd animals and actively preparing to settle, no longer needed or could afford a shepherd.

Khalifeh led his newly contracted nimsud lambs to a clover field, careful to see that they ate from the edges first and then slowly entered the plot. The previous year he had planted poplar trees beside a spring at his summer campsite at Hanalishah, but in his absence in the autumn someone had cut them down. He suspected that the nearest Persian cultivators were the culprits, for they abhorred any physical sign that Qermezi claimed the land. He said he so wished to have a place to drink tea in the shade. More than any other man at Hanalishah, Khalifeh loved his part of the territory and tried constantly to improve it. He constructed channels leading from the spring, cut steps in one channel for animals to gain better access to the water, and created pools where animals could drink. His, Borzu's, and a few other men's wheat and barley fields were near his tent. He had planted clover and then paid a Vanak peasant to water the field before he arrived at summer pastures, but apparently the man did nothing, and Khalifeh lost most of his investment. He had paid another Vanak peasant to oversee his pastures and keep alien herds away. The Vanak man reported that whenever he had spotted commercial herds grazing on Khalifeh's land, he threatened to cry and tear his clothes until the hired herders drove away the animals. Khalifeh talked about his heavy debts and destitute state. He needed a shepherd, for his sons still at home were at school much of the year, but he had no income to pay for one. His independent son Bahram, who had left that morning to find his own shepherd, returned unsuccessful several days later.

The first day of summer found Borzu yelling about Aqaboa, to no one in particular, but loud enough for the shepherd and his family to hear. He

threatened to obliterate Aqaboa's pasture rights at Hanalishah and Dashtak if he quit his job. (An Amaleh Qashqa'i man, Aqaboa was the only
hired shepherd to hold independent pasture rights at the two places, rights
he held because of long-term kinship, marriage, and residential ties with
Aqa Mohammadli men. His father's sister Guhar was Khalifeh's mother.
When Guhar married Shir Mohammad, she brought her brother's sons
with her to the Qermezi group, and they became members.) At Borzu's
request Khalifeh had asked Aqaboa to continue as shepherd but he had
refused. Morad told him he ought to stay at Hanalishah with his "brothers" (his father's sister's sons) and warned that he would be among strangers if he took another job.

Borzu sorted through his herds and told Mohammad Karim to mark
with a mixture of ashes and water the animals he was ready to sell. He
examined carefully the year-old male goats he had earlier told Khodabakhsh not to shear, for he wanted to choose two to groom as lead animals
for his herds. The other two he would sell, and he instructed Yadollah to
shear them. Each of Borzu's herds contained two or three lead goats, superb specimens of the breed, tall-standing animals with long curved
horns. Their hair was never cut, and the long hanks moved rhythmically
with the animals' majestic gait. They wore leather neck straps and large
brass bells of different shapes, each making a distinctive sound so animals,
shepherds, and others could recognize them in the dark and at a distance.
When they were adults, they were castrated.

Borzu's nephews Hosain Ali and Hajji Qorban prepared the animals he
had selected for sale, along with animals belonging to Khalifeh and Gholam Hosain, for the long trip to Isfahan. The combined animals slept by
Borzu's tent, and Hajji Qorban and Khosrow would drive them to Semirom before dawn the next morning. By waiting until now to sell his animals, Borzu had once again marked symbolically the first day of a new
season. But he had also temporarily escaped having to deal with the problems of his herders, all three of whom had expected to quit the first day
of summer, the end of their contract year. They could not leave if Borzu
was absent.

Yadollah had long been planning to quit but was currently unable to
do so because of a debt he held with Khalifeh. In the winter Khalifeh had
given him wheat on credit from Kalayaz in Kazerun and expected to take
goats in exchange, but the price of goats was too low to repay Khalifeh
adequately. Yadollah said he would sell a sheep and a goat in Semirom,
pay the debt, and then harvest wheat in the area on a sharecropping basis.

Merchants and moneylenders refused to give him loans or goods on credit because of his poverty.

A series of separate hostile incidents erupted during the day. Sayyid Mohammad, a Persian cultivator, ran to Borzu's tent in a crazed state to shout that Mohammad Karim had hit him. He said he had sent his own son to report the attack to the gendarmes. At Sayyid Mohammad's fields another son claimed that Khalifeh's animals had ruined the crop. Hosain Ali threw a stone at Golzar, wife of Khalifeh's shepherd, because she had not prevented a donkey from grazing in Khalifeh's fields. An itinerant peddler cut clover from Ali's field for his animals. Morad's shepherd hit him, and he had fled by the time Ali arrived at the scene. A Persian cultivator demanded money from Ali for grain his animals had allegedly eaten.

Saying he was glad to escape these problems, Borzu left early the next morning by truck to oversee the animal sale in Isfahan. Falak rode along in order to see a doctor in the city. As they drove slowly through the steep and narrow dusty lanes of Semirom, the brother of Borzu's main creditor spotted several large gunnysacks in Borzu's truck and asked him what he was carrying. It was obvious that the lumpy sacks contained dried curds. Borzu had intended to sell them in Isfahan for needed cash at the current high market rate, but the brother reminded him of his obligation to give Kalhaidar all his milk products. Borzu was irritated that he had not taken precautions to hide the curds; he had no recourse but to hand over the sacks to him. Kalhaidar would calculate a lower price for the curds, deduct that sum from Borzu's debt, and then take the curds to Isfahan himself to sell for a profit of over 60 percent.

Yadollah's wife Golabshar, free now with Borzu and Falak gone, made the rounds of the tents at Hanalishah in farewell. Women offered her flour, tea leaves, and sugar. She and her family were regarded as "unfortunate," and people felt obliged to act charitably to her, especially now that she was leaving. Golzar also traveled through Hanalishah telling stories of her family's economic difficulties and exhibiting the wound caused by Hosain Ali. People openly condemned him for stoning a woman and a member of an impoverished shepherd family. Morad's shepherd Behruz herded animals until exactly noon, the time his annual shepherding contract ended, and he left Hanalishah a few minutes later after bundling his few possessions in a cloth and throwing it over his shoulder. Morad sent his eldest son to care for the flock. Katayun herded for Aqaboa while he sold a few animals in Semirom to repay part of his debt to Kalayaz.

Borzu, Falak, and Khalifeh returned after three days in Isfahan. Borzu was sullen, depressed because of low animal prices, and said he had become ill from Isfahan water. He had sold ninety-seven animals and complained, "I didn't even receive thirteen dollars apiece for them." The previous year a sheep had sold for twenty-six dollars. Personnel at a government clinic told him that Falak needed X rays for a postoperative examination. Because he had lacked time for that procedure, she was not examined at all. Time and again Borzu and Falak had avoided getting what passed for "modern" medical treatment. He understood its importance; faced with reality, he often backed away from the encounter. Medical care was shoddy, inappropriately applied, and often dangerous, especially for people like Falak who were formally uneducated, considered to be poor, not fluent in Persian, and members of an often despised minority.

The moneylender Kalayaz sat in Borzu's tent all day expecting to be repaid loans and enjoying the quality and quantity of food there as compared with that offered at other tents. He often appeared "by chance" at mealtime, and rules of hospitality (plus Borzu's outstanding debt) required that he be invited to share the food. Borzu hailed from a distance a shepherd of Mohammad Hasan Khan Darrehshuri who was passing through Hanalishah after shopping in Semirom. He invited him to eat, an act of good public relations with the khan and useful for the purpose of finding shepherds. Yadollah formally asked Borzu to settle their accounts, and Borzu told him to come that evening. Katayun reported that Aqaboa would also be leaving in a few days. The family was waiting for an auspicious day.

Women produced the year's first cheese, and families gathered in celebration around the tripod where fresh cheese wrapped in cloth was draining. Before cheese was preserved for storage, it was soft and mild and considered a great treat. Women made cheese only when milk production was at its peak and a particular quality of milk had been reached. They processed cheese for ten days when grazing was abundant and for only three to five days when milk was scarce.

The adolescent daughters of Khalifeh, Jehangir, and Naser were responsible for their families' camels and cared for them collectively. In the early morning they packed bread for lunch and raw wool they would spin into yarn that day and left camp with the animals. They sang songs, made up poetry, and told jokes as they walked along. They stopped when they found good browse and secured their bundles on rocky ledges to keep camels from eating them. The close ties established among these girls, brought about in part by such cooperative work, would be a basis for their lifelong affections. When they became slightly older and nearer marriage age, they would no longer enjoy this spatial freedom and would usually stay near the tent. Their younger siblings would assume many tasks that needed to be done away from camp. Elderly women still talked about the individuals with whom they had tended camels as young girls.

Mali invited Borzu to be his guest that evening, a hosting that was customary and expected of someone who received pasture rights solely on the basis of a private arrangement with the headman. A Lur who had not migrated or come to summer pastures in fourteen years, Mali was connected by kinship and marriage to Borzu and others at Hanalishah. Borzu had placed Mali's tent near the southern entrance to Hanalishah and relied on him to surveil the territory. Currently he wanted reports on the collectors of gum tragacanth, who were often presumed also to be animal thieves. Mali had killed and butchered a kid, and his Qermezi wife had straightened up and cleaned the tent. Tea was ready when Borzu arrived, and then Mali served a meal of meat and rice. As was proper for a host who occupied a lower socioeconomic position in relation to his guest, he did not eat or drink anything except for the first glass of tea. In the past, Borzu noted, a tea maker always drank the first glass to prove that he had not poisoned the pot and planned to murder a khan. Now it was simply a custom. Borzu spent the evening in relaxed conversation and joked about his day's problems with Persians.

Borzu went to Semirom early the next morning to conduct business but soon had to return, accompanied by a gendarme and Sayyid Mohammad, the Persian cultivator at Hanalishah who was pursuing his conflicts with Qermezi. The sayyid had become disgusted with the gendarmes in Semirom because they appeared to support Borzu, and he had reported the dispute to SAVAK, the secret police. Most people in the area, Qashqa'i and non-Qashqa'i alike, no matter how severe the discord, did not solicit assistance from SAVAK. Its agents often pried into other issues with deleterious effect on people they investigated. In this dispute even the gendarmes were disturbed about the case going to SAVAK because their own personnel, actions, and written reports were being scrutinized. The previous day a Persian man wearing gendarme pants but a civilian shirt had walked through Hanalishah asking questions about Sayyid Mohammad and Borzu. When queried if he was a gendarme, he lied that he was. Frightened, people quickly understood he was a SAVAK agent. He asked for butter at every tent, and they were afraid to refuse.

Borzu, the gendarme, and Sayyid Mohammad drove to the scene of the dispute where the sayyid had blocked Borzu's access to a stream. The gendarme lectured the sayyid about his behavior, told him to remove the stone obstruction, and then swore at and hit him when he proved obstinate and argumentative. He then hit another Persian cultivator who had come to argue alongside the sayyid. He ordered the sayyid never to involve SAVAK again and threatened that he would remove his rights to cultivate at Hanalishah if he did. The sayyid appeared to relent. He and Borzu agreed to stop fighting, and all parties kissed. Borzu drove the gendarme back to Semirom after offering him a bountiful lunch. Earlier in the day he had slipped him a cash bribe. Engaged in their own conflicts with cultivators, Ali and Morad later gave Borzu money to offset the amount he had paid. Ever since Borzu had first begun to use pastures at Hanalishah, he had found it useful to bribe the gendarmes periodically so that they would serve his interests when disputes occurred. The other nomads occasionally contributed to these payments.

In past summers Borzu's brother-in-law Esfandeyar had camped with fellow Qairkhbaili men in the mountains south of Semirom. This year, lacking sufficient browse for his camels, he needed to find pastures elsewhere. He lacked rights of his own in summer pastures. A few years back he had paid a Persian landowner who promised to help him acquire pasture rights, but the man had assisted another nomad instead, and Esfandeyar had to leave the area. He had not sought help from Borzu then because of conflict between Qairkhbaili and Aqa Mohammadli men. Currently he relied on close relatives for aid. In autumn he planned to settle with other Qermezi families. While he went ahead to make plans and arrange to harvest grain, he sent his wife, household, and animals to Hanalishah.

A shepherd told Borzu that Esfandeyar's wife Samanbar was camped just south of Hanalishah. Borzu watched for someone going in that direction. When Gholam Hosain stopped by on his way to Semirom, Borzu told him to tell Samanbar to enter Hanalishah. An hour later she and her family arrived, and Borzu told her to join Gholam Hosain's camp. Although Esfandeyar and Borzu had discussed his problem in general terms, Esfandeyar had not wanted to confront Borzu directly about pasture space at Hanalishah and did not want to presume on his generosity. Rather, he placed his wife, who not incidentally was also Borzu and Gholam Hosain's sister, in a situation where Borzu became obliged to help. Within a few days Borzu was relying on Esfandeyar's son as an unpaid herder.

An itinerant peddler passed through Hanalishah, the first in weeks, and stopped at Katayun's tent. A Persian man who knew Turkish through his contact with Qashqa'i people, he carried mostly fabric which women and girls hastened to examine. This was one of their only opportunities to see diverse fabric, and it enabled them to tell men what to buy in town. Katayun brewed tea for the peddler, and he generously added tea leaves from his own supplies to the second pot. He complied with Falak's demand for a "gift" of mixed nuts and raisins. He accepted from Yadollah's son a large pile of wool in exchange for a small box of matches and a ballpoint pen, which the boy needed for schoolwork. The peddler stayed the night at Aqaboa's, and in the morning he visited other tents at Hanalishah. He had with him Bahram's radio which he had taken to Isfahan for repair after his previous trip to Hanalishah.

After examining the peddler's large supply of fabric, Akbar and Salatin chose material for a skirt and tunic for Akbar's wife. Dayeh Soltan had wanted yellow and pink cloth, but her husband and mother-in-law chose purple for the skirt and dark blue for the tunic. This simple act seemed to be a turning point for her, and she went to her own small tent and wept silently. She and Akbar had been married for three years, and she had not yet produced a child. She was still dressed as a new bride in white, red, and other bright colors, but Akbar and his mother worried that this scheme was no longer appropriate. By choosing subdued colors they indicated that she could not continue to be dressed as a bride forever and that she had entered a new category. Dayeh Soltan wondered later whether she could still cut short her bangs and forelocks, another symbol of a bride, or whether her new darker clothes would contradict this hair style. Akbar and Dayeh Soltan were not getting along well, and his family and some others blamed her for their apparent infertility. His family was talking about getting him another wife.

Paying for the fabric with cash and dried curds, Akbar complained about the cost of women's clothes and the number of meters needed. Prices charged by this peddler were cheaper than those in Semirom shops, however, and the nomads were glad to take advantage of his tour. He tried to tempt Salatin and her daughters with sparkling rickrack that they could sew on their jackets, but she said Akbar had already spent too much.

The long-awaited inspector of tribal schools from the Office of Tribal Education in Shiraz arrived in Hanalishah to evaluate Mohammad Qoli and his students. Children rose to their feet and clapped as he entered the round canvas school tent. Borzu, Khalifeh, and Mansur wanted to witness the evaluation and sat in the back of the tent. A Qashqa'i man who had formerly been a tribal teacher, the inspector gave a short speech in Persian about the importance of education, delivered in a stylized manner similar to that often used by Mohammad Bahmanbaigi, director of the program.

Continuing in Persian as the government required, rather than in his and the children's native Turkish, he asked each of the five classes to recite in turn from their lesson books. He wrote his report during the evaluation.

The first three classes did poorly, with some children unable to respond at all. The inspector criticized their awkward reading and the formal stance they took while reciting. When he questioned the students about the content of what they had just stated, they did not answer, and he told them they were parrots. He was noticeably irritated that many children appeared not to know subjects Mohammad Qoli said he had covered and that a few required books had not been studied at all. None of the younger children could do any arithmetic. Each wrote a long problem on the blackboard, dictated by the inspector, and then stood puzzled. Observing that their arithmetic books were clean and unwrinkled, the inspector drew the conclusion that they had never been used. He proclaimed that the teacher had not taught these students, that their performance was unacceptable.

Chagrined by the reprimand in front of his students and the three Qermezi elders, Mohammad Qoli offered a string of excuses: previous teachers had not taught well, classes at Hanalishah had started late, the year of drought had been catastrophic for everyone, and certain children whom he identified were deficient. Khalifeh tried in Turkish to help the children. Agitated by what he saw as an attack on Qermezi subtribe, Borzu was visibly angry. He told a student to bring him a glass of water but did not offer any to the inspector, and then he tried to impress the inspector's driver as if that would strengthen the evaluation.

The inspector asked whether Mohammad Qoli or the previous teacher had struck students more, and the children chorused that the previous one had. When he questioned them if they brushed their teeth and frequently washed their hands, they demonstrated how they performed each act of hygiene. It was obvious that he knew they were lying. He noticed one student's wheezing and asked if he had received any medical attention. Khalifeh's son Filamarz recited "Iran," the standard poem used for such occasions, and everyone applauded. Khalifeh was proud, and Borzu said, "Hurray!" The inspector handed a copy of his finished report to Mohammad Qoli as he prepared to leave. When he exited the tent, the children rose and clapped; in a standard formula he told them to study, not clap.

The inspector gave Borzu and Khalifeh a ride back to Borzu's tent in his car. Mansur had gone ahead to prepare tea. Borzu called for "bread" (meaning any food), and Falak, unseen behind the tent's reed screen, responded that they had none, which angered him. Complaining to the inspector about Mohammad Qoli, Borzu and Khalifeh reported (correctly) that he frequently left Hanalishah on his motorcycle and did not teach and that students often studied on their own. Borzu quickly added in Mohammad Qoli's defense that his new bride and household needed attention. Both men stated that he hit the students. They pleaded for a teacher who was Qermezi, one who could teach an hour a day during the migrations. Borzu noted that a Qermezi teacher would be helpful to him, implying that he would serve the headman, which he said Mohammad Qoli did not and would not do. The inspector replied that a Qermezi teacher would be a possibility in a year or so, especially because the group had not yet produced one of its own. As Borzu returned from escorting the inspector to his car, he saw that a lush, ripe melon had been in full view to his guest the whole time, and he groaned that he had not offered even it to him.

Later in the day four government forest rangers from Shahreza came seeking Borzu's hospitality while they searched the area for illegal collectors of gum tragacanth and arranged to purchase the harvest of the legal collectors. Leaving their truck by his tent, they borrowed mules from Borzu, who borrowed from others at Hanalishah, and went off to conduct their business in the mountains.

Borzu and Khalifeh left early the next morning for Semirom, for Borzu had heard that the Tribal Security Force had summoned him. He was increasingly reluctant to visit this office or the gendarmerie, because gendarmes insistently asked for fresh meat and dairy products. He complained that they lacked any understanding of the economics of pastoralism and the difficult times he was experiencing. Later in the morning the two men drove to the camp of Mohammad Bahmanbaigi, director of the Office of Tribal Education and an Amaleh Qashqa'i man. His summer residence, fields, orchards, and herds were in the valley to the northwest of Hanalishah. Borzu brought a lamb as a gift. Both men wanted to talk with Bahmanbaigi about the possibility of Akbar and Hosain Ali being accepted as teacher trainees.

Although Bahmanbaigi was of non-elite origins, his encampment was as elegant as that of any of the Qashqa'i khans. He actively played a role similar to the one many khans had played in the past. He had in fact taken their place. Situated in the middle of a green flowering meadow under tall shade trees was a compact unit of dwellings: four small stone houses, a mud-brick kitchen, a school tent, three large goat-hair tents, and an immense canvas pavilion with open sides for receiving distinguished guests. All the tents contained large Qashqa'i carpets of the finest quality. Bahmanbaigi used his own personal tent to entertain close relatives, and there his wife and a servant cared for his infant son. Bahmanbaigi's Lur wife was not as elegantly dressed as many women of the Qashqa'i khans' families. As guests and visitors arrived in camp, servants and assistants ushered them to one of the tents and then brought them to Bahmanbaigi according to their status and mission. Forty or so visitors were present when the two Qermezi men arrived.

Borzu and Khalifeh, ushered to a guest tent, were then directed to the edge of the pavilion where Bahmanbaigi was presiding over business. The two men knelt close together, sitting on their heels on the fringe of a huge Kashkuli Qashqa'i carpet, and silently waited to be acknowledged. Their hands placed in identical fashion on their knees, they were the very image of submission and supplication. Bahmanbaigi's relatives and many other Qashqa'i came and went. His brother Nader mediated, often identifying people and stating the purpose of their visit. A Qashqa'i foreman reported on the grain crop. Bahmanbaigi asked a young man who had brought a lamb whose son he was, and they engaged in polite talk. A third man came to beseech Bahmanbaigi to reaccept his son in the tribal high school; the boy had been expelled for stabbing a fellow student. Hearing an argument at a distance, Bahmanbaigi motioned over one of the men involved. The argument concerned a marriage, and after Bahmanbaigi learned that both families agreed to the match, he gave permission for the wedding to occur.

Bahmanbaigi acknowledged Borzu and Khalifeh and thanked them for the lamb. Both men pressed the case for Akbar and Hosain Ali to be accepted as teacher trainees. He replied that he would allow Akbar (who did not quite meet the prerequisites) to take the examination along with Hosain Ali and that if they both did well he would accept both.

Later Bahmanbaigi said he did not know why the Qermezi school was deficient, for he always assigned the best teachers. He noted that Mohammad Qoli had performed well during training but that the results of his teaching were dismal. He concluded that the social environment and citizenry of Kazerun, close to Qermezi winter pastures, were a negative influence on Qermezi people, especially students, and pointed out that in summer, too, the nomads were near a Persian town and under its influence. "Qashqa'i culture" was corrupted by the close association. He noted that Qermezi people needed to live within a wider Qashqa'i territory and not be as isolated as they were.

Servants served lunch to the forty guests, each receiving a particular quality and quantity of food depending on his or her status. Bahmanbaigi invited Borzu and Khalifeh to eat with him. Their lunch consisted of many different meat dishes, rice, and melon. Bahmanbaigi used a fork and spoon while Borzu and Khalifeh, not provided any utensils, ate with their fingers. After the meal a renowned Qashqa'i singer whom Bahmanbaigi said he had rescued from impoverishment and ill health sang poignant Qashqa'i songs. She remained unseen behind a reed screen. Bahmanbaigi and others gently rocked with the music, visibly moved by what they heard. A Persian carpet buyer visiting from Shiraz smoked opium with ritual pomp. Surrounding himself with the many accoutrements of opium smoking and summoning servants to produce pillows, charcoal, tea, and sweets, he and not Bahmanbaigi appeared to be head of the household. He played backgammon with Nader until the opium took full effect and he became too giddy to continue.

On the drive back home Borzu recognized a man herding a donkey, and he stopped to ask him if he wanted to work as a shepherd. The man replied that he had no household of his own but might come with another one. Borzu preferred hiring a shepherd who had a wife and children so that extra labor would be available.

Many newly shaven and cleanly dressed Qermezi men were waiting in Borzu's tent in expectation that he might bring Bahmanbaigi back with him. As they attempted to shout over the music from the recently repaired record player, Borzu and Khalifeh eagerly competed to tell the story of the day's successful visit. They proclaimed that Akbar would definitely be accepted as a teacher trainee and then be assigned to Qermezi subtribe.

In the midst of this cheerful discussion, Borzu suddenly lashed out at Mohammad Karim to say how ashamed he had been that Bahmanbaigi had criticized him for being a poor student. Once Borzu became agitated he did not calm down easily, and soon he was raising all sorts of other grievances against his son. He told him he had no right to wear the Qashqa'i hat, a symbol of bravery and power, and he blamed his defective character on Falak. During this tirade Mohammad Karim sulked in a corner of the tent without comment. Accustomed to being criticized in front of others, Falak seemed to be more sorry for her son than for herself. Men added comments here and there that did not seem to affect Borzu's agitation. Mansur raised the record player's volume, and simultaneously men began to talk among themselves, both signs that they had heard enough. Katayun and Golabshar had come to sit quietly behind the reed screen to listen, and the camp's women later discussed the father's grievances against the son.

Borzu left to check on his herds. When he returned to the tent, composed, he sorted through and cleaned out his briefcase, an act he performed with ceremony every few months. He took advantage of Akbar's presence to have various documents read for him. Khalifeh used the occasion to write a letter to three government agencies in response to a new law stipulating that nomadic pastoralists must sell all their goats and half their sheep. The law, aimed more to force nomads to settle than to lessen the impact of herd animals on the natural environment, did not restrict the number of animals that commercial investors in cities, towns, and villages could send onto national land. Khalifeh's letter stated simply that he and the other men were poor, were deeply in debt, and could not possibly survive on a fourth of the few animals they presently owned. All Qermezi men at Hanalishah signed the letter except Borzu. He said that because it came from the grassroots level, it would have more impact if he did not sign it. Borzu planned to write his own letter stating that he could not afford to sell his animals now but that he would donate them to the government if it would find him other employment. He joked to the men sitting at the fire that it would take the government two years even to process his letter, and by then he would have fattened the animals in question and sold them himself.

The previous summer officials from the Ministry of Agriculture had toured Hanalishah to count and record the sheep and goats each man owned. Not understanding the purpose or implications of the registration, the nomads had not known if they should produce flocks larger or smaller than their actual ones or if they should state that some animals were partially owned by others. Only when the officials completed the registration did they divulge their aims. They said they had estimated the amount of pastureland available at Hanalishah in order to comply with a new government decree stating that herd size must be regulated by the land available. Every four hectares of pasture could support either four sheep or one goat, they had ruled, which would force the pastoralists to rid their flocks of goats. The officials had declared that goats were destroying Iran's natural vegetation. The new law stipulating that pastoralists must sell all their goats and half their sheep was a further step in greater government control.

Khalifeh and the others expressed concern about their future livelihoods. They despised these new and proposed regulations concerning pastures and animals. They never met any government agents who were knowledgeable about pastoralism or the environment, and they remarked that the distinction the officials tried to make between the eating habits of sheep and goats was ludicrous. Of course the two species did graze and browse differently, but not with the effect the officials claimed. Goats often ate vegetation that sheep did not, and the nomads systematically rotated grazing areas and allowed vegetation to replenish itself before returning there. They pointed out new green shoots on the bushes that goats had previously browsed and took credit for the growth. These bushes, in turn, protected more fragile surrounding ground vegetation upon which sheep relied. The nomads proclaimed that their own pastoral practices did not destroy the natural environment; rather, other processes were at fault, particularly urban-based commercial herding and the destruction of vegetation for fuel by settled people.

Government officials had said they would soon be ready to issue individual grazing permits to each Qermezi man at Hanalishah on the basis of their surveys the previous summer. They would force all non-Qermezi men and their families to leave. Grazing permits, which could be obtained only by each man applying personally (and not through the headman), were intended to control the number of animals each man could keep at Hanalishah. No man could herd more than two hundred or fewer than one hundred animals. Officials said they would confiscate the animals of men who lacked permits. The number of animals they had recorded in 1970 was to remain fixed. If herd size changed in the future, especially if the number exceeded two hundred, the owners would have to sell any surplus. If these animals were not eliminated, officials would confiscate them. They would also force nomads owning less than one hundred animals to vacate their pastures and settle, on the (incorrect) principle that men with few animals were not viable pastoralists, produced nothing of value for the market, and engaged in other, now illegal, exploitative activities on nationalized land. Officials said they would find jobs for these men on road crews and pay them a dollar's worth of wheat a day. Government agents had not yet registered men, pastures, and animals in most winter areas; Qermezi men expected them to reach Dashtak in the coming winter.

The government planned to require the nomads to sell their too few or their excess animals at government slaughterhouses at a controlled price. For each $13 of animals sold, the government would pay the nomads $3 cash, $3 worth of sugar-beet pulp, and $7 worth of barley. By providing this fodder they hoped to encourage settlement.

In the 1960s government policy aimed at settling nomads on uninhabited land outside their tribal territory. The government provided few if any services to the new settlers. New government policy in 1971 was to incorporate the nomads in existing villages. As part of a larger plan to exert political control over the Qashqa'i, the government would not create all-Qashqa'i villages. Services (roads, wells, schools, bathhouses, and loans for building houses) would be provided only to existing villages, at least half of whose inhabitants were Persians or nontribal Lurs.

A few days previously, lacking knowledge about new policies, Akbar had written letters to government agencies requesting help in settlement, and all men at Hanalishah except for Borzu had signed them. Akbar had asked the government to allow them to settle at Hanalishah and to offer them low-interest, delayed-payment loans.

Officials had recently told Borzu that the government would soon pass a law forbidding nomads to own or use camels. They proclaimed that goats and camels destroyed the natural environment. Borzu decided not to relay this news to members of his group and would wait for official notification to reach them independently. He worried that knowledge of this new policy would drive additional men to settle.

As Borzu and the men sat talking about their predicament, Mohammad Qoli rode by on his motorcycle from the direction of Semirom. He had given instructions to his students early that morning, left them alone to do their lessons, and had been gone all day. It seemed he could not face them or the task of teaching after the previous day's public chastisement and humiliation.

People's anger at Mohammad Qoli surfaced after the inspector's visit, when before no one expressed much concern about him. The inspector's criticisms were fresh in everyone's minds, and they complained about the teacher's absence. They now said he was ineffectual; even when he hit the students, they did not learn. They said they would tolerate such punishment only if the children learned their lessons after being hit. They did not approve when he told the students to perform his household chores; they said he regarded them as his personal servants. Students could collect brush for fuel but other tasks were unsuitable. They blamed Amanollah's wheezing, noticed by the inspector, on the teacher who had told the boy to bring water. Some had spilled, gone to his chest, and made him ill, they said.

Summoned by Borzu, Ilmas had come to see him during the day. A resident of Hanalishah and an Ipaigli Darrehshuri man who had long associated with Qermezi, he first asked Falak what Borzu wanted. When he heard the word "shepherd" he promptly left. He proclaimed to Falak and then to everyone he met on his way home that he would slit his own throat before becoming Borzu's shepherd. When Borzu discovered that

Ilmas had come and gone, he yelled at Falak for not keeping him there and for divulging the purpose of the summons. After many appeals from Qermezi men sent by Borzu, Yadollah finally agreed to stay another year as camel herder in exchange for permission to collect gum tragacanth at Hanalishah.

Early the next morning Borzu's brother Abdol Hosain and his cousin Abdol Rasul rode by horseback to Jehangir Khan Darreshuri's camp at Round Sun to borrow a gun so they could shoot a wild ram. With soup made from the ram, they hoped to cure Abdol Rasul's goats of an illness that had dried up their milk, made them thin, and caused swollen joints. They brought along a kid as a gift. Jehangir Khan reported that his son Manucher had taken the gun to Tehran. Mohammad Hasan Khan, visiting his brother Jehangir Khan, offered the men a gun but said they would have to wait until later in the day. Not certain the gun would actually be forthcoming, the men did not want to wait, and they returned to Hanalishah. To substitute for the wild ram, they found a live turtle and kept it weighted down with stones until they were ready to boil it to make soup. Some years back when Ali's and Jehangir's animals had contracted the same illness, they bought a calf from Khalifeh to make soup for the goats and cooked a dead goat for the sheep. Sheep were cured with a goat soup, and goats were cured with a sheep soup, people believed.

Borzu persuaded the Tribal Security Force to telegraph Kazerun for the results of Mohammad Karim's school examinations. He had failed four out of twenty subjects. Parents of other students in Kazerun noted that if Borzu had not paid cash bribes to each of four teachers, his son would have failed at least eight subjects. Several other fathers had also bribed their sons' teachers by going to their houses at night to give them money. A week later a letter containing the marks of all six students arrived in Semirom from a Kazerun shopkeeper. Although no student had done as poorly as Mohammad Karim, several had failed one or two subjects. Students with failing marks would have to return to Kazerun to repeat these examinations in order to continue in school.

In the second week of summer Borzu drove to Wolf Hill in northern Darreshuri territory to investigate the possibility of pastureland there for Qermezi people. At nearby Row of Willows he made a rare visit to his rival Sohrab who asked his help in arranging a marriage. Sohrab accompanied Borzu back to Hanalishah, and Borzu appeared pleased that Sohrab had sought him out for a favor. Coming to greet Sohrab, Qermezi men and women each in turn kissed the palm of his hand, and he cupped each face as he kissed people's cheeks, sometimes many times. Borzu pre-

sided over the greetings and was friendly and jovial with the visitors. In
a tent filled with people, the shepherd Mohammad Hosain told a detailed
story about engaging in highway robbery ten years previously. People
sat hushed and fascinated, and no one, not even Borzu or Sohrab, interrupted him.

Borzu had invited the chief officer of the gendarmerie in Semirom and
his family for the next day but was not sure they would come. Early in
the morning he sent Mohammad Karim alone to Semirom on an errand
so he could be available at home. Just before noon his son returned with
a truck full of Persian women and children. The major was unable to
attend because he was investigating an intratribal dispute, but he had sent
his family for an outing. Borzu was disgusted with having to waste food,
a goat, and a lamb on women. Many Qermezi men had come to demonstrate their support while he entertained the officer, and they too were
irritated at the exclusively female company. At first the women, dressed
in trousers and shirts, clutched their transparent veil wraps around them,
but soon they relaxed, inspired by the open environment and the unveiled
Qashqa'i women moving freely about, and eventually left the veils in a
heap in a corner of the tent. They offered Falak cookies, candy, and nuts
which she tried to hide in the baggage, but Borzu saw and demanded them
for himself.

Borzu, Sohrab, and the assembled men soon ignored the women and
turned to their own discussions of pasture rights and heightened government control. The Persian guests ate kebab, the men ate the scraps, and
later the thirty visitors enjoyed a lunch of meat and rice. A Persian
woman and two girls wandered off to Yadollah's small tattered tent for a
nap, and the men joked about the camel herder's "guests."

In front of his Persian visitors, Sohrab, and Ahmad Khan (leading man
in Qasemli lineage who was also visiting Hanalishah), Borzu began to
become argumentative. Soon he was shouting over the piled baggage toward Katayun's tent where the teacher's wife Ma'asumeh was sitting. He
accused her of inciting his shepherds to quit and of turning Qermezi boys
into her personal servants. A few days previously she had complained
about Borzu and Falak to Zolaikha, Zolaikha had relayed her comments
to Falak, and Falak had been whispering the stories to Borzu whenever
the opportunity arose. Having finally heard enough, he erupted. He also
yelled at Golabshar, blaming her for Yadollah's wanting to quit and collect
gum tragacanth. This tirade appeared to be his attempt to demonstrate
assertiveness in front of Sohrab and Ahmad Khan.

To deflect Borzu's anger, Sohrab astutely began to discuss the details of the marriage negotiations. During the winter the son of Sohrab's uncle had gone on Sohrab's behalf to Mortaza Talehbazli Darrehshuri, a prominent man, to ask for his daughter's hand in marriage for Sohrab's son Ebrahim. Mortaza had tentatively agreed to the match, and it was now time for someone of higher status to formalize the arrangements. Sohrab needed Borzu's assistance as Qermezi's headman and a near-equal and acquaintance of Mortaza. Borzu and Sohrab chose to present a unified face for the sake of ties between Qermezi and Talehbazli subtribes and their most powerful men. Borzu was apparently willing to set aside his problems with Sohrab for a wider political aim. Sohrab had not asked Borzu to suggest the marriage to Mortaza initially because a refusal would have damaged Borzu's honor and the reputation of the subtribe he represented. After Mohammad Karim drove the Persian women and children back to Semirom, he took Borzu and Sohrab to Mortaza's home north of Round Sun to negotiate the bridewealth payment.

As the men drove away, Falak hurried to Katayun's tent to dispel any thoughts that Katayun and Ma'asumeh would have about her being the provoker of Borzu's anger. The two women were not convinced. Falak addressed her remarks on the conflict to Golzar, visiting Katayun for treatment of a festering wound, and used her as a means of relaying sentiments to Katayun and Ma'asumeh. Ma'asumeh did not try to defend herself and explained only that she was a stranger at Hanalishah, without kin, and had no reason to cause trouble. Falak and Ma'asumeh were near tears on occasion, each moved by the confrontation. Several times they reconciled and were ready to kiss when some new topic erupted and the anger resurfaced. Katayun said nothing to indicate her opinions. She commented later that Falak had no right to disturb and provoke Borzu with women's squabbles. A good wife, she noted, was one who did not tell her husband every petty irritation, who kept women's conversations to herself.

Borzu returned from his trip several days later. A crisis was coming to a head for him, for unresolved problems were becoming increasingly troublesome, and his anxiety and tension were heightening. He had not yet been able to locate replacements for the four shepherds he had lost or was losing. The goat herd was often left to roam the surrounding hills unless a man or boy had the bad luck of stopping by Borzu's on other business, in which case Borzu sent him to herd until he found a legitimate excuse to leave. Borzu's heavy debts were steadily rising due to high interest rates, new expenses (partly because of the truck), and loss of expected income from animal sales. Some of his closest supporters were talking openly about settling permanently. Other supporters were struggling to secure pasture rights and relied on the assistance he was finding increasingly hard to provide. As an example, Darrehshuri khans at Narmeh had promised but now refused to give permanent pasture rights to Falak's brothers, who solicited Borzu's aid in filing a complaint with the Ministry of Agriculture. The Ministry of Justice in Shiraz had summoned Borzu about an incident of highway robbery years ago, and Arghvan and Qahraman, the accused, wanted his help. Borzu worried that he could not afford to take the necessary trips to Isfahan and Shiraz to handle these problems, and other business required his presence in summer pastures.

Borzu also continued to fret about Falak's health and the consequences if she were to fall ill again or die. She needed a medical examination in Shiraz from her surgeon, but Mohammad Karim absolutely refused to take her by bus. Borzu, who did not trust him with the truck, was unwilling to go there himself.

Borzu spent the evening arguing with a Zailabli Darrehshuri man who had come as a prospective shepherd. The man wanted half again as much salary as Borzu was offering. Borzu said he needed help from someone who would not be concerned only with himself, but the man replied that he also deserved succor. During lulls in the negotiation Falak came to sit by Borzu and repeat and embellish statements the teacher's wife Ma'asumeh had made during their argument. He was angry already and now became furious, goaded by her words. She continued to feed him stories until he was nearly hysterical with anger, and then she told him to calm down and let the issue drop. He shouted at Shir Ali to order the teacher to remove his tent from camp, but Falak's brother sat unresponsively and quietly. In the midst of the tirade Borzu suddenly asked the Zailabli man about his decision. When before the man had been self-assured, even bold, now he was hesitant and apprehensive, having witnessed the anger for which Borzu was famous.

Borzu's shepherd Aqaboa sat by the fire in a silent vigil as he had done on many previous nights. Whenever he asked Borzu to settle his accounts so that he and his family could leave, Borzu either ignored him or told him to return later. Falak had informed Katayun that Borzu expected Aqaboa to pay him eighty dollars for water he had transported for Aqaboa's family and animals at Wide Mountain the previous autumn and for fodder for these animals. Eighty dollars was slightly less than the cash portion of Aqaboa's yearly salary, which meant that if he paid it he would have worked for a year as a virtually unpaid shepherd. Every second day (in addition to some Muslim and Shi'i Muslim holidays) was considered inauspicious for beginning a migration or ending or starting a job, and Aqaboa and Katayun kept postponing and moving ahead by two days their departure. He sometimes muttered, "The home of Mehdi Khan can burn." Many years ago, he said, Qermezi's headman went to Mehdi Khan to find shepherds to work for Qermezi men. Since then shepherds had regretted coming to Qermezi and had cursed Mehdi Khan for their fate. After Borzu fell asleep for the night, Falak began to whisper again about Ma'asumeh's remarks, and soon he was on his feet shouting abuses over the piled baggage toward the teacher's tent.

At the breakfast fire Aqaboa was again waiting for an accounting. Falak was dressed for the trip to Shiraz despite Mohammad Karim's continuing refusals. Although openly critical of his son, Borzu was frequently unable to force him to perform a task. Soon Mohammad Karim lay down and began to moan. His mother placed a heavy load of blankets on him and then concocted an elaborate brew as medicine, which he refused to drink. Even Borzu seemed taken in by the charade for a while and sat worried at his son's side.

Without warning Borzu began to shout at Aqaboa and refused to allow him to respond. The other people present sensed a physical attack coming and stood at a distance to watch. Borzu suddenly leapt at Aqaboa, hit him and knocked him down, and then attempted to strangle him. At this point Aliboa ran to pull Borzu away from Aqaboa. (Late the previous night Borzu's kinsman Aliboa, returning to Hanalishah from Semirom, had hoped to pass by Borzu's tent without notice. Borzu saw him, told him to come to the tent, and kept him there for the night. It was now clear that Borzu had anticipated the attack and needed at least one additional man to intercede. "Hold me back! I'm going to kill him!" embodied his apparent strategy. Falak's brother Shir Ali, still present, was considered to be passive and could not be expected to intervene. Aliboa thus filled the interventionist role Borzu had specifically intended for him.)

Katayun screamed from her tent, and everyone else in camp found a spot to watch (except the teacher and his wife who remained out of sight). Borzu released Aqaboa who stomped off to his tent. Incited further by Aqaboa's words as he retreated, Borzu chased after him wielding a club. Aliboa, now with Shir Ali's assistance, grabbed the club and stopped him. As soon as the men let him go, Borzu once again chased after Aqaboa until the men impeded him one more time. The Zailabli man was on his feet but did not interpose. Borzu's two young sons cringed on the ground and wailed in fear. Aqaboa continued to yell back at Borzu's tent as he and Katayun dismantled their own. They sent a daughter to retrieve their donkeys so they could pack and leave. Borzu shouted at Mohammad Karim, who forgot his illness in the excitement, to find Hajji Qorban so he could herd in Aqaboa's place. Mohammad Karim walked a short distance away, then returned, and Borzu sent him instead to bring Morad to mediate.

Quite coincidentally, two armed mounted gendarmes passed by Borzu's tent. Borzu went immediately to the road to greet them, to prevent them coming to his tent where they might hear about the attack or sense the tension in the air. They asked if he needed their services. He thanked them for offering, and they continued on their way. Later Katayun said she had wanted to seek their help, but Aqaboa had not permitted it; he knew he stood no chance with the authorities against Borzu. Khalifeh, on his way to see Borzu about other business, heard the clamor of the fight and turned around to avoid becoming involved.

After hearing the details, Morad told Borzu that the problem was of his own making, that he ought to have collected money from Aqaboa when he had incurred those expenses. He noted that if Borzu was angry because he had to pay the gendarmes when animals under Aqaboa's care had trespassed in someone's fields during the migration, then that issue was long past and should be forgotten. Borzu kept insisting on Aqaboa paying him eighty dollars for water and fodder. Morad then sought out Aqaboa, who had hurriedly left camp with his family and all their possessions, and brought him back to Borzu's fireside. The threat of another physical attack did not seem imminent. Despite his fear, Aqaboa was able to state his case clearly. Because Borzu acted as if he were not listening, Aqaboa directed his remarks to Shir Ali with frequent use of the honorific title of Mashhadi. He held reverence for pilgrims and thought that a beneficial judgment might result from Shir Ali's intervention. Claiming that he would leave the financial settlement to Morad and noting that he had no money, he declared that Borzu could seize as many of his thirty animals as he wished. When he saw that the dispute was winding down, Mohammad Karim resumed the pretense of illness to avoid accompanying his mother to Shiraz, and Borzu was again distracted by him. Seeming to have lost all interest in Aqaboa, he appeared suddenly to be very tired.

Morad, Aliboa, and Aqaboa went to Borzu's herd to remove Aqaboa's animals and count the remaining ones, a standard procedure at the conclusion of a shepherd's employment. Morad arranged the settlement; Aqaboa was to pay, in sheep, the equivalent of eighty dollars to offset expenses Borzu claimed he had incurred by transporting water and providing fodder for Aqaboa. Aqaboa turned over to Morad three sheep, and another that Borzu had seized earlier completed the sum said to be due. During the year Borzu had also killed for food or given as gifts four of Aqaboa's kids, but Borzu would not consider these animals in the accounting. He gave Aqaboa a sheep from his other herd, a standard part of a shepherd's salary. Shepherds were paid cash and a sheep or goat at the end of a year's service.

Aqaboa returned to sit by the fire, for he wanted a decent parting, but Borzu refused to acknowledge his presence and then fell asleep. Morad told Aqaboa to leave. Aqaboa delayed and then slowly walked away with tears in his eyes. Months earlier Katayun had remarked that Borzu's shepherds always left his employment this way, after a fight and without a farewell. Katayun had already moved the family to another part of Hanalishah to prepare to travel north to Atakola and Naqneh villages where their relatives were settled. Borzu spent the late afternoon and evening herding the sheep Aqaboa had tended.

Mohammad Karim finally relented. If Borzu had allowed him to drive Falak to Shiraz in the truck, he might have complied more quickly, but Borzu was afraid of his son's driving and did not trust the dilapidated vehicle to survive the long round-trip journey. He also wanted to have the truck available for his own business. Several weddings were in the offing, and he anticipated attending in style. He instructed his son to drive Falak to Semirom, leave the truck at a merchant's shop, and from there take buses first to Shahreza and then Shiraz. Disturbed about the implications of her mother's trip, Farideh emotionally kissed the hem of her skirt as she departed. The two young sons out playing did not see her leave and cried inconsolably when they saw she had gone. The two older daughters silently watched her depart. Because internal stitches that ought to have been self-dissolving protruded from the red infected scar of the incision, Borzu worried that Falak might need more surgery to repair the area.

Three days later Falak and Mohammad Karim returned to Hanalishah driven by Kalhaidar, Borzu's closest Persian associate. The merchant had not yet visited Borzu at Hanalishah this season, and he brought gifts of food and some supplies Borzu had requested. Also loaded down with gifts from her trip, Falak began to display and distribute the jewelry, scarves, shoes, plastic-handled knives and forks, fruit, cucumbers, candy, and toothpaste. Borzu was appalled at the obvious expense. When she saw Borzu's face, she tried to hide some items from him to disburse later, but her children wrested all the goods from her hands. Borzu saw the totality of her shopping.

Borzu asked what the doctor had said. Falak casually replied that he had not been at the hospital when she visited and that she would return to Shiraz in two weeks to see him. She had made no effort to see another doctor or to wait for her own. Borzu was shocked by the disclosure and her stupidity and was now even more dismayed about the expense and trouble involved. She had made the whole trip for baubles, he complained. For months he had fretted about the follow-up on her operation, and he had assumed that this trip would end his worries. He was also angry at Mohammad Karim who, as the man along, should have taken responsibility.

Falak and Mohammad Karim had spent two full days and nights on buses traveling to and from Shiraz. They had found a cheap hotel near Shah-e Cheragh, Shiraz's most venerated shrine, and Falak had made three pilgrimages there during her one day in the city, each of which counted as a separate act of piety. Many of her gifts were ones appropriate from a returning pilgrim. For the first time she had gone to a bathhouse.

Borzu killed a kid in appreciation of Kalhaidar's assistance. When the meal ended and Kalhaidar left, taking presents of fresh meat and cheese, Falak and Mohammad Karim competed to tell stories of their journey. Falak was so exhilarated and her children so caught up in her expansive mood that when Borzu suddenly erupted at her, she was stunned into silence. Women were no better than gypsies and donkeys, he yelled. Men kept women at home because of this kind of stupid behavior, he shouted. After he stormed off, she resumed her stories and broke open yet another melon. Mohammad Karim modeled a new shirt and played a new flute. By the time Borzu returned, he had found another reason to be angry. His son had bought a shirt for himself but not one for Borzu, who needed to visit the Darrehshuri khans in Round Sun the following day and lacked presentable clothes to wear.

The day after Aqaboa's abrupt departure, Borzu's kinsman Hasel had come to pay his respects and receive a blessing for his forthcoming marriage. Borzu greeted him perfunctorily and sent him to tend Aqaboa's herd standing idle on a hillside. Men and boys often avoided coming to see Borzu because of this type of reception. By contrast, they frequently dropped by Khalifeh's, the previous headman, and the mood there was one of relaxed informality. Khalifeh never put anyone to work.

Hasel had experienced a difficult winter and was impoverished; twenty of his thirty-two goats were under nimsud contract. He had received a lucrative herding contract for the summer, however, and was currently making more money than any other Qermezi man. His job was to fatten rams for sale for a wealthy Persian investor who owned eighteen herds. His salary and benefits for three months were more than triple what a shepherd for a Qashqa'i nomad would have earned in a year. Hasel grazed the herd in the mountains near Borujen, just north of Darrehshuri territory. Borzu would not have permitted Hasel to bring these animals to Hanalishah because their grazing would have profited an outsider.

The money Hasel had received as a hired herder enabled him to marry. He had come to Hanalishah to ask Khalifeh and Bahram to seek Mansur's permission for him to wed his daughter. Once at Dashtak and then again at the New Year, close kinsmen had gone on his behalf to seek Mansur's consent, and Sohrab had also formally brought up the issue with Mansur during his visit to Hanalishah. Mansur had tentatively agreed to the last request. Khalifeh and Bahram would formalize the match, settle the bridewealth payment, and enable Hasel and his close kin to plan the ceremony.

Borzu spent the day muttering about two sheep that were unaccounted for in the herd that Aqaboa had tended. Finally he was so certain that something was amiss that he sent Hajji Qorban to summon Aqaboa so that he could confront him. The two men discussed in chronological order each loss to the herd during the preceding year. Although they had done a complete accounting when they arrived at Hanalishah at the end of the spring migration (when animals were most apt to be lost and stolen), Borzu wanted a recount. The two "missing" animals turned out to be the lambs he had given Bahmanbaigi and the gendarme major. He looked disgusted with himself for having forgotten these animals and sent Aqaboa away. Able to describe each animal, Aqaboa had known precisely when and why animals had been removed from the herd.

At dawn on the nineteenth day of summer Borzu moved his tent and camp over a small hill and farther into Hanalishah to the first of two summer campsites. Mohammad Qoli was temporarily absent, and Ma'asumeh, not informed of the change, did not know if she should move too. When Morad asked Falak why the teacher had not accompanied Borzu and was now camped alone, Falak lied that Ma'asumeh had been busy baking bread at the time. The next day Mohammad Qoli decided on his own to move the school and his own tent near Borzu's camp, and he borrowed a camel and used students to help. Mali, whose tent had been within sight of Borzu's, dismantled it and traveled toward Vanak to seek other pastures for a while. He planned to return to Hanalishah for the agricultural harvest. Zolaikha and Zohreh washed clothes in a nearby stream, a job women did when they occupied a new campsite.

An agency of the Ministry of Agriculture in Isfahan summoned Borzu, who journeyed by bus from Semirom armed with documents covering land use at Hanalishah. After four days of futilely sitting in and traveling between offices, he finally received a signature that an official in Semirom had demanded. Other matters remained unresolved, including the possibility of some Qermezi people using pastureland at Wolf Hill.

Unable to find adequate pastures for even his immediate group, Borzu increasingly worried about the negative consequences if many more Qermezi nomads settled. Settlement was no longer a vague possibility for some time in the future. His kinsman Hajji Boa and some other Qermezi men and their families had settled over the past nine years at Atakola, a small village just north of Darrehshuri summer pastures near the town of Borujen and the Bakhtiyari border. Many Qermezi nomads now said they planned to settle in Atakola and the neighboring larger village of Naqneh, where other Qermezi families had recently settled. Atakola housed 124 people, most of whom were Qermezi and the rest Persians. Naqneh contained three thousand people, Persians, Lurs, and a small number of Qashqa'i. The landowners of the cultivable land of Atakola and Naqneh were Persians.

More than any other problem, Borzu feared the disintegration of the group upon which he relied, and much of his tension over the past year was explained by this concern. Men such as Abdol Hosain and Abdol Rasul, formerly staunch supporters, had fought with him and now definitely planned to settle when people at Hanalishah began the autumn migration. Aqaboa had gone to Atakola after Borzu struck him. Others such as Hasel, still friendly with Borzu, had found it economically impossible to continue as nomadic pastoralists, and they too had decided to settle. Some men had already moved to Atakola and Naqneh, planted crops, and taken on short-term shepherding or nimsud contracts with wealthy Persians and Lurs in Borujen and Naqneh. A few men still resident at Hanalishah had planted crops at both Hanalishah and Atakola or Naqneh and planned on soon moving to one of the two settlements. Other men at Hanalishah had not yet decided what to do when it came time to leave toward the end of summer and were discussing different options. The most viable proposition for some families, they said, was to combine households, sending some members with herd and pack animals on the migration to Dashtak and settling others at Atakola or Naqneh where they could cultivate as sharecroppers for the Persian landowners, try to find wage work, and rent or begin to build houses.

Despite Borzu's competence in overcoming other problems, he seemed unable to find adequate solutions to these changing circumstances. Broad economic conditions were the principal motive for settlement, not general or specific grievances against him. He did not possess the means to change these wider circumstances and was unable to slow the downward spiral that had drawn in all Qermezi nomads. He was losing control.

Settled for nine years at Atakola, Hajji Boa was de facto leader of the Qermezi people in the two villages. (Hajji was part of his personal name; he had not made a pilgrimage to Mecca.) He had understood sooner than most Qermezi men the need to place greater reliance on settled agriculture than on nomadic pastoralism because of the transformations brought about in Iran by land reform, the nationalization of pastures, the changing balance of power between the Qashqa'i and the state, and economic change. As a powerful personality with an independent spirit, he had resented being controlled by Borzu; problems between them had also been important in his decision to settle.

When Qermezi people talked about the conflict between the two men, they often referred to a past dispute. When Hajji Boa was a young boy, Borzu's father Shir Mohammad had forced Hajji Boa's sister to marry Shir Mohammad's eldest son Abdollah. Her brothers appealed to Darrehshuri khans to prevent the marriage, but they upheld Shir Mohammad's decision. Salatin fled from Abdollah soon after the marriage and returned home to her brothers. Then Abdollah died. Many years later Shir Mohammad forced her to marry Ali, another of his sons, and once again she went unwilling into marriage. In 1971 Hajji Boa often remarked with frustration that he had been too young and helpless to confront Shir Mohammad and protect his sister. Rather than acquiescing to Borzu now, he had resolutely decided to act on his own behalf.

In 1961–1962, which was known as "the year that Hajji Boa left Qermezi," he had shared Borzu's campsite at Dashtak for the winter and had become convinced that he could not easily coexist with him. He was married to Borzu's sister Goltamam, a tie that Borzu used to command his labor and cooperation. Borzu's father's father's brother's son, Hajji Boa was also a member of Aqa Mohammadli lineage.

A fight between Falak and Goltamam in the summer of 1962 further soured the relationship between the two men. Serving as supervisor of Jehangir Khan Darrehshuri's shepherds, Borzu told Hajji Boa to take some of the khan's sheep to Isfahan to sell. Hajji Boa wanted to attend the wedding of his sister's daughter, about to commence, but followed Borzu's instructions. He sold a few of his own sheep on the trip and with some of the money bought fabric for new clothes for his family. When Falak saw

Goltamam's fabric, she jealously remarked, "The wife of the khan's supervisor should be better dressed than the wife of Hajji Boa." Goltamam replied, "My father [Shir Mohammad] was more prominent than yours. Why am I not entitled to good clothes?" Hajji Boa became weary of the situation and decided to leave Hanalishah. He gave all the money from the sale of the khan's sheep to Falak, packed his possessions, and traveled with his family to Narmeh. When Borzu returned home, Falak complained that Hajji Boa had spent Borzu's money from the sheep sale on fabric for Goltamam. Borzu became angry about the money and Hajji Boa's leaving. The four individuals avoided one another for years.

Hajji Boa decided to settle in Round Sun village near the Darrehshuri khans and expected to receive help from Kachili Qermezi men who had moved there many years before. He had often served Jehangir Khan, usually on Borzu's behalf, and assumed that the tie between them would facilitate his settlement. After laying in a store of firewood and straw in a rented house in Round Sun, he discovered that Falak had told people that Borzu had promised Jehangir Khan that Hajji Boa's wife would be a servant to the khan's wife Sara Bibi. (Borzu would not have made this offer unless as a threat he never intended to carry out, because Goltamam was his own sister.) Fearing the rumor might be true, Hajji Boa decided not to settle in Round Sun that autumn. Anger prevented him from migrating with Borzu to winter pastures. He borrowed pack animals, for he had already sold most of his own while preparing to settle, and traveled to Wolf Hill where he spent autumn and winter in a rented house. All his sheep and goats died. In the spring he looked for a place to settle.

At Atakola, then an empty landscape, Hajji Boa met Mohammad Sadeq, a Persian landowner who was beginning to build houses and establish a village there. The two men discussed a potential economic tie, and Sadeq agreed to let him live in an unfinished house if he helped to build two more. Because of Hajji Boa's services, Sadeq gave him rights over pastoral and potentially cultivable land in the mountains nearby and rights for water for a garden and orchard the two men would create together at Atakola.

For two years Hajji Boa spent late spring and summer at Atakola, and in autumn he and a shepherd migrated with a nimsud herd to Mirror Bridge near Kazerun and stayed there through the winter. His wife and children remained at Atakola. He established his orchard and cultivation at Atakola and from then on lived there all year in a house he built himself. The second year he encouraged two of his brothers, who were nomadic pastoralists with Borzu, to cultivate at Naqneh. The previous season Hajji Boa had harvested an abundant grain crop, which provided bread for his family and brothers, seed for the next planting, and enough left over for sale. After the next harvest the two brothers migrated to Dashtak, and the following spring they joined Hajji Boa permanently at Atakola. Every year thereafter one or several Qermezi men and their families joined them. Qermezi people at Atakola and Naqneh soon became closely intermarried; they found spouses for their marriageable sons and daughters among themselves. Hoping to create "a little peace" with Hajji Boa, Borzu told him he could still use pastures at Dashtak, but Hajji Boa never resumed residence there.

Personal interactions figured in how people chose to settle and the way in which they did so. Settlement in Hajji Boa's case and in many others was not simply an economic issue. It was a politicized process, and for Hajji Boa it related to issues of personal leadership. General economic factors together with the personal ties developed from Borzu's style of leadership were relevant in Hajji Boa's and other people's decisions to settle or continue to migrate.

The land of Atakola was owned by Sadeq, principal holder, and five other Persian men who lived in Naqneh. Because of the impending implementation of land reform, these men were anxious to diversify their holdings and bring existing and new land under mechanized or irrigated cultivation, which would thereby exempt the land from government confiscation. Hajji Boa and then the Qermezi men who joined him served these men's and their own interests. Sadeq and the other owners provided seed and tractors for plowing, while the Qermezi men performed all the work of cultivation and split equally the grain and straw with them. Later Hajji Boa and the others provided their own seed, rented their own tractors, and provided all the labor, at which point they owed one-sixth of the proceeds to the landowners. The landowners built houses to rent to the Qermezi newcomers, and some, including Hajji Boa's brothers, were eventually able to build their own houses on land given or sold to them by the owners.

Hajji Boa continued much of the life of a nomadic pastoralist by moving his family into the mountains near Atakola for the second half of spring and most of summer. Snow at his campsite prevented him from going there earlier. Outsiders who observed his camp, tent, and possessions would not have known he was not a full-time nomadic pastoralist. He maintained all the trappings. The only items that possibly set him

34.   Hajji Boa, Goltamam, and children in front of their tent in the mountains above Atakola village. Hajji Boa staged this scene to represent "the American family," after a discussion about Qashqa'i versus American families.

apart were bags made of the skins of cows rather than goats and a large tripod made of tent poles, both used to handle the large quantities of milk his cows produced.

Hajji Boa found a ewe during his first year at Atakola and bought four more with money from the sale of grain. Hajj Abdollah, a landowner in Naqneh and brother of Sadeq, bought five goats, and the two men combined these animals and formed a partnership from which they profited. The next year Hajji Boa obtained eighty animals on a nimsud contract with a Naqneh man. He hired a shepherd to care for his growing herd and took on other short- and long-term contracts with Borujen men in order to gain additional animals and milk products. He acquired cows so he could produce quantities of milk. The market for meat animals and milk products in nearby Borujen and in Isfahan was favorable. Qermezi nomads lacked such a dependable, accessible, year-around market. Hajji Boa sold yogurt, which his migratory kin did not and said they could not do. He cultivated his own grain on his mountain pastures, and he cultivated grain at Atakola as a sharecropper with Sadeq. Flat and close to good roads, land at Atakola was easily worked by tractors, unlike land at Dashtak and Hanalishah, and products were easily transported to market. Hajji Boa planted fruit trees and after some years was producing a marketable crop. His garden brought in other food, mostly for his family's consumption. His initial effort to plant poplar trees met with failure when Naqneh men stole them for firewood, but his second attempt resulted in fifty tall sturdy trees which he planned to sell and to use in building. His donkeys were prolific, and he profited on the sale of the offspring.

Of course some years were better for Hajji Boa than others. But by 1971 when Qermezi nomads were in such desperate economic straits, Hajji Boa's relative success and his secure and diversified economic base presented an attractive option. Because he had close ties to Sadeq and other men in the area who owned land available for sharecropping and house building, he was able to make it possible for Qermezi people to join him. The supportive community he had already formed around him was proof of his economic and social skills. Borzu could not offer any of these benefits. It would take him years to reach the same landed security and economic position that Hajji Boa had already achieved.

The first houses at Atakola, constructed from sun-dried bricks made of mud and straw, were two-storied with one or two rooms at ground level for animals and one or two rooms at the second level for people. Supported by wooden beams, roofs were flat, layered with reed mats, and packed with mud and straw. A fire pit and a small kitchen were located under the stairs leading to the second story. Most newer houses and those being built in 1971 were one-storied with two rooms, one providing living quarters and the other for storage, cooking in inclement weather, and weaving. The settlers constructed separate buildings for herd and pack animals. They kept herd animals indoors for weeks, sometimes months, at a time, depending on the depth of the snow, and brought food and water to them twice daily. Some old and new houses were partly or totally enclosed by walls, creating a courtyard for work and play.

The family room in the house was set up as a tent would be, with baggage piled in a row at the back. Large woven cotton rugs over which were sometimes placed felt or woven wool rugs lay on the dirt floor. Some walls had shallow built-in alcoves where possessions were stacked. People hung clothes and other items from nails in the walls. No windows were made because of the winter's cold and summer's heat; the room's only opening was a single door. People in two-storied houses congregated on the balcony in good weather, and those in one-storied houses on the porch. No one spent any time inside unless the weather was uncomfortable. Rooms were dark, and dust hung in the air. The floor, walls, and ceiling were made of mud and straw, and any movement in the room raised dust. Particles fell from the dried mud packed between the ceiling beams. The frequent eye infections and respiratory illnesses, from which the nomads did not ordinarily suffer, seemed to derive from this habitat. Most people at Atakola and Naqneh who did not move to tents at higher altitudes in warm weather set up tents in their courtyards and lived there as if no house at all existed.

One room in some houses was devoted to weaving, and a horizontal loom, much larger than that found among the nomads, filled the space. The pile carpets that settled women wove were larger and of finer quality than those of nomad women. Unhappy about dismantling and resetting their looms because of the resulting irregularities in the shape and quality of the finished product, nomad women ordinarily wove only items they could complete in one sedentary dry-weather period. Village women lacked this restriction and could also use heavy metal devices that helped to create a tightly woven final product with even edges. Some women at Atakola said they could complete three large carpets a year. By setting up a loom indoors they could weave in poor weather and in the evening by the light of kerosene or pressure lanterns, and their potential productivity was much greater than that of nomad women. These settled women wove primarily for commercial purposes. Usually a moneylender advanced their husbands money, minus the interest of the loan, and later claimed the completed carpets. If the weavers had taken their carpets to sell to carpet dealers in Isfahan, which they did not do, they would have received up to ten times the money they currently were given.

Women who settled often complained about the new social environment. Nomad women, usually quite isolated in their camps, ordinarily experienced few regular social contacts with other people. Rules of behavior limited both women's and men's interactions within and beyond camps, and notions of privacy in the open tents and spacious habitat were held to be important. Once settled in houses, however, people were concentrated and their numbers increased. Women said they lost their privacy in a village. Settled men often stressed the new economic advantages; within courtyard walls and closed-door houses they were no longer responsible for providing food and drink to every passerby. Settled women by contrast regretted the loss of their autonomy; they resented the fact that so many people interfered in daily and personal activities. The social contacts of men who settled continued as in the past. As nomads they usually met other men away from their tents, and as settlers they met other men away from their houses. Settled women fell vulnerable to the constant scrutiny of the many other women present. Recently settled women said they liked to move to tents at higher altitudes in summer to recreate conditions of privacy; they could better control their social setting. They especially appreciated being away from the Persian and Lur women and children who lived in Atakola and Naqneh. (They also liked the cooler weather, the clean air, the spring water, and the absence of bothersome insects.) Nomad women enjoyed frequent and seasonal changes in the composition of local social groups. Settled women found themselves stuck permanently within one social group.

Akbar and Dayeh Soltan, nomads from Hanalishah, temporarily stayed in Hajji Boa's house at Atakola while Akbar harvested wheat. Women and children of the village gathered there in large groups and stayed for long periods. At first Dayeh Soltan treated them each as she would any visitor, but then she saw she could not extend such protracted hospitality to so many. When the same women returned again and again to the house, she did not know what to do. The Persian woman living in the room next door spoke of the social unit of coresidents as if the term meant the same thing for two households separated by a mud-brick wall as it did for two tents in a camp. Dayeh Soltan found the women to be meddlesome gossips and discovered with dismay that her minor comments were soon common knowledge to everyone in the small community. She did not like women prying into the details of her and Akbar's life or into her possessions. She remarked that small girls, who among the nomads were socialized to be inconspicuous and quiet when accompanying their mothers on visits, were even more accomplished meddlers than their mothers.

The interaction these settlers, especially women, experienced with Persians and Lurs had also increased substantially. The Qashqa'i were still a small minority in the region. Although Hajji Boa had created an economically viable niche for himself and successfully interacted in the wider social environment, even he said that Persians and Lurs resented Turks (that is, the Qashqa'i) coming to the area and that they had "fought" him every step of the way. He and other early settlers told the Qermezi newcomers to behave appropriately and to understand that any improper acts by individuals affected them all. When Bahador broke a limb of a Persian landowner's mature apple tree while playing, the settlers told Akbar to warn him and others against any further such disruptive behavior.

Because of the wider Persian-controlled, staunchly Shi'i-Muslim environment in which women and girls were subject to strict behavioral and dress restrictions, Qermezi women and girls fell under special scrutiny and were quickly forced to change their practices. They could not travel alone beyond the edge of the small village, and much greater attention was paid to male escorts than ever before. Collecting water and fuel and tending animals, tasks that nomad women and girls performed daily, often far from camp, were done by boys and men to comply with the dominant society's notions concerning women's mobility and extra-community contacts. The natural resources that nomad women and girls gathered throughout the year in their various habitats were not present in this relatively heavily settled, overexploited area. Settled women were no longer able to scour the countryside for food, medicine, and dye. Under strong pressure from their Persian neighbors, Qermezi girls were obliged to dress in the fashion of Persian girls, in loose pants, knee-length and full-skirted dresses, and head scarves tied under the chin. They became instantly indistinguishable from them.

Borzu's brother Ali was one of the Qermezi men who had tentatively planned to settle at Atakola in the autumn, and he was relying on his wife's brother Hajji Boa to help him. In preparation his son Akbar had asked a kinsman to plant wheat and barley there for him the previous autumn, and when the crops ripened Akbar, his brother, and two cousins went to harvest. They lived with relatives in Atakola until Akbar, missing his own household, sent his brother to help his wife Dayeh Soltan move their possessions from Hanalishah to Atakola. His few herd animals remained with Ali's animals under the care of another brother. The wheat Akbar was harvesting would be used for bread in autumn and winter, and the barley and straw would provide feed for the few necessary pack animals. Ali's wife Salatin and several daughters would soon move to a rented house in Atakola. Ali, two sons, and possibly a daughter would migrate as usual with their herd to Dashtak and stay there the winter. Hoping to attend a teacher trainee program in Shiraz beginning in autumn, Akbar would leave his wife at Atakola. With Askar in school in Kazerun much of the year and Haidar still in the army, Ali's household was seriously short of labor.

One day at the end of the first month of summer, Hajji Boa's shepherd yelled from a hill that two people were coming up the mountain slope on horseback to his campsite. Hajji Boa had been preparing to go to town but decided to wait. Parviz and Monavvar, son of Sohrab's wife's brother and wife of Sohrab's brother, soon came into view. Their obviously new clothes and ceremonial demeanor meant they had a message to deliver. Hajji Boa understood that they had come to invite him to the much anticipated marriage of Sohrab's son Ebrahim. Once Mortaza Talehbazli had agreed to the amount of a bridewealth (four hundred dollars, to be paid in wheat, tea, and cash), negotiated by Borzu, the wedding was quickly arranged as was customary.

35. Fathollah harvesting a sparse crop of wheat near Atakola village

By allying with a prominent man in another Darrehshuri subtribe, Sohrab hoped to raise his status, buttress his position in the Qermezi subtribe, and demonstrate his independence. Because he had lost his battle for winter pastures at Dashtak and lacked other pastures, and because it was unlikely that his rival Borzu would help him in the near future, he was glad to have the implicit support of a powerful man in another major subtribe. Mortaza's uncle was the supervisor of Ziad Khan Darrehshuri's shepherds and was thus in a position to help Sohrab find new winter pastures. The marriage alliance between Sohrab's son and Mortaza's daughter demonstrated the two men's desires for new strategies, wider networks, and an orientation beyond subtribal borders. It signified Sohrab's move away from Borzu and the dominant sector of Qermezi subtribe, and it proved that Sohrab could create some political capital of his own.

Sohrab's family and supporters traveled in pairs by horseback to every summer pasture to invite Qermezi people to the wedding, scheduled to begin the next day. The pair at Hajji Boa's quickly described the circumstances of the celebration and listed the men and women who were issuing invitations. They were proud of Sohrab's (and Qermezi's) alliance with a prominent Talehbazli man and noted that "all Qermezi people" would attend and offer assistance to make the ceremony memorable. If the wedding was elaborate and many guests came, people would speak favorably about Qermezi subtribe. Many guests symbolized the extent of Qermezi honor. Because the inviters still needed to visit other people before returning to the wedding camp that night, they ate only a quick meal of bread and butter and then resumed their journey. On parting, Hajji Boa gave Monavvar the customary gift of money, half to defray wedding expenses, the other half for the inviters. The pair had come to Hajji Boa first, as a mark of respect, and then rode to Atakola and Naqneh. They sought out Akbar, still harvesting wheat near Atakola.

The next morning Qermezi people at Atakola and Naqneh excitedly prepared for the wedding celebration. Akbar and Dayeh Soltan dismantled their tent and stored their possessions at Hajji Boa's house, for they did not want to leave an empty tent during the expected three days of the wedding.

Sohrab's camp at Row of Willows, several hours' ride by horse southwest of Atakola, had been prepared specially for the celebration. He and his brother Mokhtar had formed a long reception tent by joining their tents and adding extra panels. Three kinsmen pitched tents nearby for guests and fixed a kitchen and a shelter for tea making. On hillsides

36. Sohrab (with the club) at the wedding celebration of his son Ebrahim

37.   Qermezi women and children at the wedding

behind the long tent stood six more tents of relatives, all of whom had moved there to provide Sohrab support.

As guests arrived, members of Sohrab's camp greeted them and escorted them to one of the tents. Children led their mounts away to be fed and secured. Hosts and guests watched excitedly for each new arrival, and everyone talked with anticipation about who was expected to attend. They wondered about Mokhtar who should have already returned to camp. As Sohrab's brother, it had been his responsibility to notify Mortaza Talehbazli of the day the wedding was to begin. He was also supposed to invite Qermezi families at Hanalishah. When new arrivals appeared at a distance, people guessed who they were and from where they were coming. Women trilled loudly for each new group. Some guests brought gifts of sheep and goats, and children led them away for feeding. Sohrab personally greeted the most distinguished guests and invited them into his large tent. Other guests were brought to him, and he rose, kissed, and welcomed them. Most female guests were greeted by other women and escorted to a tent where women gathered.

People watching the road saw Mokhtar and Ebrahim appear at a distance. They were traveling slowly, and it took them a while to reach the camp. They stopped at a distant tent, and then Mokhtar came alone to the kitchen. Everyone was quiet as he delivered his message. When he had gone to Mortaza Talehbazli's home to inform him that a party would come for his daughter in three days, he discovered that Mortaza had gone to winter pastures on business. In his absence, the bride's mother would not permit her daughter to be taken. Mortaza had left the message that Sohrab should postpone the wedding for ten days until he returned from his trip. People hearing this were angered and spoke of Qermezi's honor being stolen. Sohrab had paid the bridewealth and incurred other expenses, the wedding camp was already set up, and guests were present or on their way. His personal honor and prestige were at stake. Mortaza appeared to want to assert his own superiority over Sohrab.

People now openly criticized Sohrab for seeking an outsider for his son Ebrahim (for almost all Qermezi people married their children to fellow Qermezi), and they ran through the list of available Qermezi girls. Some individuals, including his wife Khadijeh, pressed him to forget about Mortaza Talehbazli and marry within Qermezi, while others said he ought to arrange for a Qermezi bride in case the alliance with Mortaza fell through completely. For years people had expected that Ebrahim would eventually marry the daughter of Sohrab's brother Cheragh, but one time Ebrahim had said he did not want her. Cheragh was incensed, and people remarked that he would never permit the marriage after that initial rebuke. Sohrab's sister's daughter had been a second choice, but she had just been promised to another man. A third girl, daughter of Sohrab's wife's brother, was discussed, and most people seemed to agree that she would be a good choice. They did note that she was younger than most girls when they married. People stood in a circle around Sohrab and listened to him consult with those he respected.

Sohrab decided to confront Mortaza Talehbazli directly. He entertained some doubts as to whether the man had actually taken a trip. If Mortaza was gone, Sohrab wanted to ask influential Talehbazli men if they accepted Mortaza's decision. Assuming a deferential pose, Sohrab politely sought aid from a wedding guest, a Persian merchant who promptly sent his assistant to Borujen to locate a car and driver. In the meantime Sohrab chose two close kinsmen, his sister Shamayol, and Marjan (the most influential and articulate woman present) to accompany him. The two women were to try to convince Mortaza's wife to release her daughter. The driver arrived and stated his fee, which Sohrab accepted without argument, and the small party left immediately for Talehbazli territory.

People had lost their earlier excitement about the wedding and sat in small groups deciding what to do. Those who lived nearby went home, to return if news came of the celebration's resumption. Some men from

Atakola and Naqneh who had been harvesting also left. Others decided to stay. At Sohrab's request, Akbar went to the closest village to find musicians who could entertain the guests until his return. There either was or was not to be a wedding, and the presence of musicians would indicate that a wedding would occur regardless of Mortaza's actions. Akbar returned later, not able to locate musicians anywhere, even Lur or Persian ones. People continued to talk about Qermezi honor. A few Persian men, including landowners from Atakola and Naqneh, were present as invited guests, and Qermezi men were embarrassed to face them. Except for a few men and boys harvesting at Atakola, no one from Hanalishah was present. Mokhtar reported that when he had gone to Hanalishah, he told Borzu and the others not to bother to come to the wedding because there was no bride.

Ebrahim, the clean-shaven, well-dressed potential groom, circulated among the guests as his father's representative. When Sohrab had been present, Ebrahim had stayed in the background. He was the oldest son at home; his elder brother was serving in the Iranian army. Guests sitting around plastic cloths laid on the carpets in the guest tents were served meat and rice. As soon as one group finished, people rose quickly, and others removed the platters and cloths to lay new ones for the next group. Young men played records of Qashqa'i wedding music on a phonograph, and women rose in a group to dance in front of the large reception tent. When Mokhtar replaced the dancing music with music for the stick-fighting game, some men hurried to don their ceremonial cloaks. The dancing, stick fighting, and socializing continued until the early hours.

The aged Arghvan arrived late that night. He had just returned from Arzhan Plain, having traveled from summer pastures all the way back to winter pastures and Jarruq Lur territory to find a mule stolen from him while nomads had gathered at Arzhan Plain in April to buy government wheat. The mule's theft had irked him for months, and he had decided to act. He had not located the animal. After he hungrily consumed tea and food in the crowded tent, his son Qahraman asked him a pointed question about his trip. The question inspired Arghvan, as Qahraman had anticipated, and he began the long narrative of his adventure. People sat silently and listened, and a few mothers woke their children to hear.

At first light everyone in the large camp was up and about. From somewhere the sound of someone churning butter could be heard. Men went to check their horses tethered on a grassy area just beyond the camp. Guests ate kebab and yogurt.

The previous night several men had gone on horseback to find musi-

38. Women and girls dancing at the wedding

cians, and a young boy shouted that he heard them approaching. It was said to be bad luck to watch for the arrival of musicians, that if they saw people looking for them, they would turn around and not come to the wedding at all. One musician on horseback drummed their arrival. An oboe player rode a bicycle, and a second drummer rode a mule. An open-sided tent was readied for them, and they were offered a hearty breakfast. The musicians were part of a small caste within the Darrehshuri tribe of ritual specialists called *ussa*. Many of them also performed circumcisions and served as dentists and barbers.

Young men hurriedly dressed again for the stick-fighting game. Most wore Qashqa'i cloaks (*arkhaloq*), now men's ceremonial attire. Until the 1930s these lined, brightly patterned cloth cloaks held closed by a wide cloth cummerbund had been men's standard daily dress, and men had worn the *choqqa*, another kind of cloak, during war, for hunting, at weddings, and when attending meetings at the Qashqa'i ilkhani's camp. As a few men still did, Safdar chose the choqqa, a loose cloak of diaphanous beige fabric, because the stick his opponents would use against him would become tangled in its cloth and he would not be hit as hard. He secured the cloak with cords around his arms and shoulders and tied the multicolored tasseled ends in back. Three young Aqa Mohammadli men from Hanalishah took elaborate measures to bind their legs in hopes of not becoming badly bruised. Because their lineage was represented at the wedding by only a few men, each of them expected to play and be hit frequently. They wrapped strips of cloth around their legs and ankles, put on long socks, and then wrapped another strip around their legs. Fathollah packed his socks with rags, cotton batting, and raw wool.

The oboe player began a solo, the customary beginning of the music and an invitation for people to gather. As one of the wedding's principal hosts, Mokhtar was the first to dance, and he proudly performed alone in the large open space. He held a stick used in the stick-fighting game, to announce he was ready to begin the competition. Then the drummer joined in, and stick fighting began. Men and boys, especially those well practiced in the sport, were anxious to compete. Steps and movements were patterned, with the element of aggressive surprise added. Dancing in time to the music, an attacker with a short thin willow stick circled a defender holding a long thick poplar pole upright. In the midst of nonchalantly strutting to the music, the attacker tried to catch the defender off guard or break through the barrier of the pole by suddenly aiming a sharp blow at his shins. Swinging the pole to parry the hit, the defender tried to block the blow. If he was hit, someone in the circle of watchers

39.   Musician playing the drums at the wedding

ran to take his place. If the attacker missed, he was forced to quit, and defender became attacker, ready to confront the first man who was able to come from the circle and grab the thick pole abandoned on the ground.

The musicians changed to music for women's dancing, and most women and girls gathered up scarves to participate. Fathollah, Mokhtar, and a musician joined them. Small girls who did not yet quite know all the motions kept the rhythm and were encouraged to continue. A musician invited the groom's mother Khadijeh to dance and pulled her off protesting. She danced awhile and then resumed her hosting. People saw a Persian cultivator sitting alone at a distance to watch the festivities. Mokhtar sent a young boy to invite him to join, and he came and danced with the women. A Bakhtiyari cultivator came by himself and joined the stick fighting. He was hit often and hard, and the other men laughingly noted that he should not have come alone if he had no one to retaliate for him.

With the expectation of more guests, men pitched a small tent for tea making in place of the shelter used the day before. Men of low status gathered there to help. They completed the kitchen tent, and newly married women and adolescent girls had more space for their work. Other women gathered there while men were stick fighting. Khadijeh was in charge, and her daughter-in-law Mahtalab, the busiest of all, performed much of the physical work. At one point Mahtalab carried her young son limp and hot with fever to the kitchen. Crying, women gathered around him. In their collective experience, children this ill often died. One woman concocted a purple medicine and put drops of it on his forehead, his cheeks, and the palms of his hands and then dipping her finger in the medicine circled his left wrist and left ankle.

Lunch of meat and rice was served to the men, the most distinguished guests receiving special portions. Women ate a stew without rice. Two of the three musicians played continuously, while the third would rest and then take the place of the one who had played the longest. Sohrab's campmate Hasan arrived from Bakhtiyari territory where he had gone to invite Bakhtiyari sayyids and shaikhs to the wedding. He had brought back with him three kids, clarified butter, and rice as gifts and a letter explaining that a fight over land prevented the invited Bakhtiyari from attending. A moving line of dust indicated that a vehicle was approaching, and everyone was alerted for Sohrab's return. Sohrab's kinsmen quickly herded all the Persians and Lurs into a guest tent to eat by themselves, so that serious discussion with Sohrab about choosing another bride for Ebrahim could occur without outsiders present. The jeep turned out to hold government forest rangers overseeing the collection of gum tragacanth.

Sohrab finally returned with his four companions. The music stopped, and everyone went to discover what had happened. He had earlier said that if by noon of that day the Talehbazli group had not permitted him to take Mortaza's daughter, he would let her go. Parviz had been first to race to the car; his jumping and clapping with happiness made it clear that Sohrab had succeeded. Everyone accompanied Sohrab to the large tent, and on the way he greeted guests who had arrived during his absence. He sat down and told his story in Persian, directed at one of the Persians but intended for all. On hearing his report and realizing that the supposedly unscrupulous Talehbazli had not caused the trouble, Sohrab's brother Darab proclaimed angrily that the blame was Qermezi's. People dispersed to talk in small groups about the situation.

Apparently, Sohrab's brother Mokhtar had not properly informed Mortaza Talehbazli, father of the intended bride, of the schedule of the wedding. He had visited Mortaza's kinsman Gholam Hosain Talehbazli, who was mourning an uncle, and presented a woman's scarf, a customary gift to a mourner from someone preparing a wedding. (If a close family member died, a wedding had to be postponed. Mourning for immediate family members lasted a year.) The bride's father Mortaza was at Gholam Hosain's home when Mokhtar visited, but Mokhtar said nothing to him about the upcoming wedding. An irritated Mortaza returned home, and Mokhtar spent the night at Gholam Hosain's. When Mokhtar went to see Mortaza the next day to announce formally the date, he found him "gone to winter pastures." Mortaza had purposely been at a distant tent, and not in winter pastures, to slight Mokhtar whom he said had slighted him. When Mokhtar told Mortaza's wife that a party would collect her daughter in three days, she denied permission and reminded him that she needed at least several days to assemble dowry goods, buy fabric, and sew the bride's wedding clothes.

People listening to Sohrab agreed that it was an established Qashqa'i custom to notify a girl's parents ahead of time so they could prepare for her marriage and departure. Taking the collective blame, the listeners readily admitted the mistake and kept repeating that Mortaza was exonerated. The day before, when news had come that Mortaza had made himself absent, everyone had immediately faulted him. Mokhtar, not present at this gathering, was not asked to account for his error.

Sohrab had gone first to see Gholam Hosain Talehbazli, who was absent, and then another kinsman, Amir Hosain Talehbazli. Together they went to Mortaza's. He was not at home, and it was not disclosed where he was, but they assumed he was probably avoiding Sohrab. The two men talked with Mortaza's wife and son and received their permission to collect the daughter and proceed with the ceremony. They agreed on the day they would return for her. Mortaza's wife and son and Amir Hosain went immediately to Shahreza to buy fabric for the bride's clothes, and Sohrab returned to Row of Willows.

As host of the celebration Sohrab greeted the musicians and briefly performed at stick fighting in order to restore normal appearances. A few of his age-mates playfully sparred with him. Younger men took over the playing field and competed for a chance to show off for him. The few Aqa Mohammadli men and boys had been told by their elders not to play much, to prevent a conflict from erupting during the game, and not to play at all unless Safdar and Mohammad were present. These two Aqa Mohammadli men currently residing with Sohrab mediated between the two Qermezi groups and added their physical presence to the small Aqa Mohammadli contingent. Aqa Mohammadli and Imamverdili men had disputed in the past, and stick fighting was sometimes an occasion for their animosities to flare publicly. The sparring served as entertainment, but it was also a form of competition among the five Qermezi lineages and between the Qermezi subtribe and outsiders.

In the afternoon Mokhtar performed one of the sports of skill that characterized Qashqa'i weddings. Circling the playing field, he rode a horse at a fast canter, leapt off to run alongside the horse for a few steps, and then leapt back on. A musician rode Sohrab's elegant horse at a fast gallop around and around the playing field and then pantomimed shooting a rifle backward while galloping, another customary performance.

Dancing and stick fighting alternated all evening, the most festive period of the long celebration. Before Sohrab's return, everyone had been worried and anxious. With his good news, people relaxed, danced, and sported, then collapsed in exhaustion. Music continued until midnight, and then somehow everyone found a place to sleep and blankets for warmth. The eleven residential tents were overflowing, and many people slept in the open in front and to the sides of the tents. Safdar hosted people from Hanalishah, along with the aged Saif Ali who had fallen ill that afternoon. Hearing about his condition, people went to sit briefly at his side. His wife held his hand. Noting that he was an old man, people talked about his dying. When Saif Ali heard that Sohrab had returned, he asked to see him.

Because Mortaza's wife had said that the next day was too soon to come for her daughter, Sohrab had agreed to wait three days. Every second day was considered inauspicious for collecting a bride, and so Thursday was the first possibility. Sohrab had asked the driver of the rented car to return Wednesday afternoon with another driver and two small trucks so that a group from his camp could collect the bride. Because of the two-day postponement, many guests went home, some with plans to return the day the bride would arrive.

The musicians began playing again at dawn, and a few women and men performed. Sohrab and other elders gathered in Safdar's tent, and others came to sit and listen. Still in poor health, Saif Ali lay inside, and people asked about him. Men and women consulted with Sohrab about various topics including other marriage alliances. In listing several prospective couples, he remarked that he favored one particular pair. Soltan Ali came to ask permission for Lashkar to marry Dastan's daughter, and Sohrab enthusiastically approved. He displayed scars from wounds he had suffered in the Semirom war of 1943, and he told a boy to feel shrapnel still in his arm. Darab began to blame his brother Mokhtar for the fiasco concerning the bride, but Sohrab silenced him by saying that the issue was resolved.

Sohrab's personal style of leadership differed from Borzu's, as indicated by the tone of this small gathering. He welcomed visitors and was patient with their questions. People came to him about ordinary issues, whereas they usually came to Borzu only in case of trouble or crisis. Sohrab relied on elders, "white beards," in ways that Borzu did not; Sohrab did not seem threatened by them, as Borzu was. Borzu refused to let Khalifeh play an active role as elder, except when literacy was required. Borzu sometimes complained that several Aqa Mohammadli elders (Arghvan, No Ruz Ali, Saif Ali) were close to and helped Sohrab, but he also jokingly noted that Sohrab was forced to rely on these men because his own Imamverdili elders were of no account.

An intelligent, wise, and even-headed twenty-five-year-old, Ali's son Akbar approached the celebration as an occasion to talk with one or two men at a time, his strategy for building up power and gaining the confidence of men individually. He participated in stick fighting but never joined the circle of watchers as most other young men his age did. In his recent move to Atakola village, he had become both a useful ally for Hajji Boa and a potential rival for group leadership, and the political dynamics there had already altered.

Akbar and his brother decided to leave the celebration to resume harvesting at Atakola and then return to Row of Willows the day the bride was to arrive. He said the event was actually over and everyone satiated. He wanted his cousins to accompany him but they decided to stay, happier playing than laboring in the fields. During Akbar's ride to Atakola, a shepherd yelled, "Did the girl appear?" Apparently word of the problem had spread, and Akbar wondered about the damage caused to Sohrab's and Qermezi's reputation.

When Akbar returned to Row of Willows the next afternoon, he saw that many guests had left, and only a few participated in stick fighting. New guests had arrived, including Qermezi men and women, Darrehshuri ritual specialists, Persian and Lur merchants and moneylenders, and Bakhtiyari and other Lur cultivators and hired herders. Borzu still had not come. Mirza, who had gone to Hanalishah to reinvite Qermezi people there, reported that the merchant Kalhaidar had taken Borzu's malfunctioning truck to Isfahan for repair. Borzu had said he would not attend the wedding unless his truck was fixed in time.

Children yelled that a jeep was approaching, and Sohrab stood to see who it was. Three gendarmes from Gandoman village pulled up as close to Sohrab's large tent as possible. People abandoned the musicians and gathered nervously. The gendarmes had come about a dispute over cultivation that involved Sohrab, Qahraman, Dastan, and Bulverdi Qashqa'i men. Issuing the three Qermezi men a letter, and ignoring the fact that a wedding celebration was in progress, the officer told them to report to gendarme headquarters in three days. Sohrab noted ingratiatingly that he had sent him an invitation to attend. The officer was aggressive, and whenever Sohrab denied an allegation of misdeeds, the officer mentioned yet another dispute. This technique placed Sohrab and the others on the defensive, and they were unable to address calmly the details of the current dispute. Smirking, the officer declared that the group ought to be called "The Black Ones" and not "The Red Ones" (Qermezi) for the trouble it always caused. He reminded Sohrab of his dispute over pasture rights with the Bakhtiyari hired herders in the neighboring valleys. Mentioning another conflict in which Ebrahim had allegedly hit a Lur hired herder, he told Ebrahim to come in on Saturday as well. Sohrab protested that his son Esma'il was serving Iran as a soldier, so why should Iran harass him? The officer was unmoved.

During the encounter Qahraman served as Sohrab's spokesman by sitting in front of the other men and answering questions first. He spoke Persian well and was enough at ease to joke and laugh with the gendarmes. His father Arghvan sat right behind him, a little to the side, and occasionally added a comment that Qahraman either incorporated or ignored. The son was gradually taking over a position of leadership and influence from his elderly father. After a while Sohrab retreated from the discussion, concentrated on smoking a water pipe, and left the business to Qahraman. The debate covered ravaged wheat crops, rustled animals, and physical violence. When the officer mentioned one conflict, Sohrab reentered the discussion to protest that they had still been migrating from winter pastures when that incident occurred and could not possibly have been involved. People drifted away as the argument lessened in intensity, and the officer sent his two subordinates to the jeep so that he could be bribed in privacy. While he wrote a report he motioned to Ebrahim to sit close by (so that Ebrahim could slip him money), and Qahraman provided some detail. A Persian moneylender helped to phrase the report. After the gendarmes left, people noted with disgust that they came only for money and created occasions to extort it.

Two small hired trucks pulled to a sudden halt in a flurry of dust downhill from the reception tent. People hurriedly ate bread and yogurt as they decided who would collect the bride. Sohrab asked Goltamam and Dayeh Soltan to accompany him, for he wanted Aqa Mohammadli women, especially Borzu's sister, in the entourage. He expected Borzu and other Aqa Mohammadli people to meet the group at Mortaza Talehbazli's the next day. People needed Sohrab's permission to go along and asked one another if they had spoken to him yet. Men loaded food into the trucks for the meal at Mortaza's the next noon. Sohrab's sister and Mokhtar's wife had already taken positions in one of the front seats. Other women and girls of Sohrab's camp and group pushed to find space in the open beds of the trucks. The musicians climbed into one and played short tunes. Sohrab asked Akbar's permission for the young men of Hanalishah to go along. Small children being left behind cried for their mothers in the trucks. Qahraman ousted a woman from the front seat in order to sit there himself. Assuming control in this seeming chaos, Akbar climbed into each truck to eject people he thought should not go, rearrange the seating, and instruct those who were subject to motion sickness to forget about going. People seemed to decide to go spontaneously. Many coming to the trucks to say farewell climbed in themselves. As the trucks pulled away, others suddenly hopped in.

Most members of Sohrab's camp and most Qermezi guests ended up going along. Many women especially wanted the chance to see relatives. Such an occasion was regarded as a legitimate excursion for women and was one of the few they were permitted. Most young men went. A few people wanted a ride back home. The itinerary included a drive to the home of a settled Kachili Qermezi man in Sakkiz for a night's sleep and then an early morning drive to Mortaza's home. Women of Sohrab's party were to prepare lunch there, and then the entourage would bring the bride to Sohrab's camp that afternoon.

A small group stayed behind, with Mahtalab, wife of Sohrab's eldest son, serving as the head of the camp. People enjoyed a relaxed, calm evening and soon went to sleep.

No one rose early, and the morning was quiet. Men sat in a small circle around the fire where tea was brewed, and women and girls gathered in the kitchen. Ali Mirza, member of the Darrehshuri musician caste and considered Qermezi's own ritual specialist, organized the camp's children to move an orange canvas tent close to the cairn of stones that marked the wedding site and to set it up as the bridal tent. An older child carried the central pole and others held the ropes taut. After Ali Mirza pounded in the stakes and secured the tent, he threw candy on the sloped roof, and children scrambled for pieces. Small girls carried large stones into the tent and arranged them in a row to create the symbol of home and family where the bride would pile her dowry. Then they cleaned a felt rug to lay on the ground. Children played in the tent the rest of the day and periodically teased the adults by pretending to see the wedding party return. Ali Mirza readied the horse to carry the bride to the bridal tent.

In the late morning Ali Mirza walked over to the tent of Sohrab's brother and prepared to circumcise Cheragh's two-year-old son Azizollah. He carefully removed instruments and materials from his bag, while family members cuddled and soothed the boy. A few children came to watch the circumcision; they stood quietly at a distance. Ali Mirza sent for Borzu's sister Senobar, the boy's mother, who had sought refuge in another tent. He reassuringly reminded her that he had cut her hair the day she married. She removed her son's pants, pinned back his cloak, and wrapped him in a large cloth. Ali Mirza cut and shaped a reed, sharpened a razor on a stone, and washed both tools in alcohol. When he called for a dish of clean water, Senobar carefully rinsed a bowl with boiling water and sent a child for fresh spring water. She assumed he needed it for the operation and was surprised to see he simply wanted a drink. He sifted ashes from the fire pit into a fine powder, set it aside in a dish, and then made a wash of Mercurochrome from powder.

As Ali Mirza moved close to the small boy, everyone apprehensively intoned "in the name of God." He said he needed a man to help, and Cheragh called for Oroj Qoli along with another, younger man "for luck."

Ali Mirza poured alcohol on the boy's penis and rubbed the area. He instructed Oroj Qoli to hold the child facing him and told the younger man and Cheragh's twelve-year-old son each to spread one leg and hold it down. Ali Mirza pushed back the foreskin to expose the head of the penis, applied more alcohol, and then replaced and extended the foreskin. As he inserted a blunt wooden tent pin cleaned with alcohol into the foreskin's opening, Azizollah squirmed and protested against the assault. Unable to face the actual operation, Senobar left the tent and squatted outside, her back to the tent and head down. Cheragh repeated "my precious child" and "in the name of God" each time he thought Ali Mirza was about to cut.

Holding the foreskin with the wooden pin inside, Ali Mirza drew both through a slit in the reed. With a razor he quickly cut off half an inch of foreskin at the point of the slit. Simultaneously he said with feeling, "In the name of God, the most merciful, the most compassionate." Azizollah shrieked with pain and struggled to get free. Blood flowed from the wound. Ali Mirza then pushed back the remaining foreskin to expose the penis head and worked the skin into place. He applied turmeric and ashes from rabbit flesh to the wound and then the wash of Mercurochrome. Finally he threw the sifted ashes from the fire pit onto the whole area. Azizollah gulped water from a bowl Oroj Qoli offered him.

Ali Mirza removed the severed foreskin from the wooden pin, threaded red yarn through it, and then tied it to the boy's left ankle. Just as the severed skin would quickly dry, so too, he said, would the actual wound dry and heal. He arranged under the boy the large cloth in which he had been wrapped and then dumped the remaining ashes on the wound. He replaced the cloth around the child and wrapped a braided goat-hair cord again and again around him from under his arms to his knees as a newborn was swaddled and tied. In a way, the boy had become a vulnerable infant again. Senobar returned, tears running down her face, and took the boy to nurse and calm him. A circle of blood marked the felt rug where the child had sat. Ali Mirza told Senobar to keep her son wrapped and quiet for two days. On the seventh day she was supposed to untie the yarn on his ankle and throw out the dried severed foreskin. Ali Mirza washed his hands in a stream and put away his equipment.

Cheragh called for his son, to hold and comfort him, and then asked Senobar to sit at his side. Together, in a family scene emotionally moving to the few others present, they cuddled their son. The operation had been traumatic for the parents. Everyone always feared for their sons.

As Oroj Qoli prepared tea, Ali Mirza remarked that over the years he had circumcised practically all the men and boys now in Sohrab's camp. He pointed out the precise tent sites where some of the operations had occurred. He also mentioned Qermezi men and boys elsewhere whom he had circumcised. He operated on either one or three boys on the same day but never two, which he considered unlucky. If a family had two boys ready, he would do one operation and then another seven days later. If three boys were circumcised, they had to come from different families. (These customs insured that only one son at a time was threatened by infection, illness, and possibly death.) The family or families with sons being circumcised customarily killed an animal and hosted a feast for the community. Sometimes they brought musicians to play. Because of the wedding Cheragh and Senobar decided not to host a ceremonial meal.

Ali Mirza's father had performed these and other ritual functions for Qermezi subtribe, and now Ali Mirza's three sons were doing so as well. Also a dentist and barber, Ali Mirza had shaven and given haircuts to many men in the wedding camp during lulls in the activity. Until this year Borzu and his father Shir Mohammad before him had each employed a Salmanli Darrehshuri ritual specialist as a groom and tea maker, and this man had also tended to Qermezi's weddings and circumcisions. This year Ali Mirza and his son had visited Borzu's group several times. He had lived at Dashtak in earlier years, but one winter no rain fell, and he went to live with Shaikh Lurs near Dugonbadan. He had remained there for the past several winters. During summer he lived with Sohrab's group at Row of Willows. He owned six sheep and goats and subsisted on the food and small fees that people offered him. Some years back he had owned a large herd but the animals had died in a snowstorm.

Late in the afternoon children shouted that they spotted the two trucks returning, and Ebrahim quickly fled up the hillside to find shelter in a distant tent. The groom was not supposed to be present when the bride arrived. The trucks noisily approached the camp; musicians played their instruments, and young boys and men riding on top of the dowry clapped with the rhythm. The truck carrying the bride was allowed to enter first. Ali Mirza helped her from the cab and raised her completely covered onto a horse for the short trip to the bridal tent. People pelted apples, symbols of fertility, at one another. Women and girls crowded into the tent after the bride. A troop of Bakhtiyari Lur women and girls from the camp of hired herders over the hill pushed into the tent to inspect her. They said nothing, stared, and then in a silent group trudged back up the hill. In an act believed to promote fertility, someone put a small boy into the tent with the bride, who kissed him. Monavvar gave her a mirror in a bowl of water into which to look, a symbol of light and happiness. Dayeh Soltan, a recent bride herself, took charge of the bride's comfort, removed two of her head coverings, and adjusted her hair and clothes. She untied a bundle of bread and money wrapped in cloth around her waist, and Monavvar instructed her to put the money in the bride's saddlebag and relock it. Dayeh Soltan and other women, empathizing with her, said later they had remembered the day they had been brought to their own bridal tents.

The negative feelings toward Mortaza Talehbazli and his subtribe as a group of outsiders, which had been manifest in the early stages of the celebration, were nowhere in evidence in people's behavior toward or words about the Talehbazli bride. Everyone seemed to accept her, even without having seen her, and people were happy simply for the reason that a kinsman had taken a bride.

Men who had gone on the trip gathered with men who had remained behind, and they eagerly talked about the games of stick fighting that had occurred at Mortaza Talehbazli's. Sohrab had lost his voice from the fatigue and discussion of the past days and sat helplessly, anxious to contribute his thoughts but physically unable to do so. Men around him discussed who had participated and who was hit by whom. Some reported scornfully that Borzu had played only the part of the attacker and never the defender, the one to be struck, and that he hit unfairly at all parts of the body, not just at the lower legs as the game required. Several men, standing up for Borzu, said that other Aqa Mohammadli men there, his son-in-law especially, had grabbed the pole when it was time for Borzu to take his turn as defender. Asadollah "ate many hits for Borzu." Particularly because another subtribe was involved, it was not acceptable for the Qermezi headman to be struck. His lesser-status kin took his place.

During the stick fighting Borzu and others had distinguished between "Semirom Qermezi" and "Bakhtiyari Qermezi," a distinction especially heightened by the plans of some "Semirom Qermezi" to settle with Hajji Boa and other "Bakhtiyari Qermezi." Tension between representatives of the two groups was high. Witnessing the loss of some key supporters, Borzu had been especially agitated. Through their competitive stick fighting, men expressed antagonisms and hostilities that did not usually find other expression. The game allowed them an exchange that did not otherwise take place.

The noon meal at Mortaza Talehbazli's was customarily the responsibility of the groom's family. Although Sohrab had brought food and supplies with him, Mortaza's kin had insisted that they would host the meal. Mortaza himself was not present at the event, still angry, it was said, about the slight he had suffered when Sohrab's brother had neglected to inform him directly about the wedding date. He spent the day in Semirom. Of the women of Hanalishah, only Falak had attended, and members of Sohrab's party were disappointed not to have seen their female kin. The day before, Borzu had sent a donkey loaded with firewood (a scarce commodity in summer pastures) to Mortaza's home, as his contribution to the festivities. The donkey then disappeared. Borzu was irritated but he joked that the donkey had gone on its own to Ja'far Qoli Khan Darrehshuri. In the past, he said, people always gave a large animal to a khan when they sought permission to marry a son or daughter. Mortaza had not given any gift to Ja'far Qoli Khan, and Borzu's donkey had sacrificed itself for the purpose.

Back at Sohrab's camp, the musicians had not been planning to play again but were urged to do so. Women and men danced and sparred. Hasan escorted the bride from the bridal tent, without her enveloping veil but with her mouth and nose covered, and put her into the dance line. She refused to dance, and Monavvar took her back to sit with the women outside the bridal tent. A bride customarily remained out of public view for three days, and the bridal tent was supposed to remain closed, with the bride inside, until after the first night. Some people were surprised at this breach, and one young man was angry about her visibility. The groom, also supposed to be absent, had returned to camp and sat grinning in the musicians' tent.

The mood of the large gathering was one of a delighted, contented family relaxed at last. Most of the Persians, Lurs, and other outsiders had departed, which contributed to the informality. Qermezi people were pleased that one of their sons had taken a bride, an event that signified more sons to come. Alluding to the consummation to occur that night, Sohrab whispered, "Look how far and wide Ali, Vali, and Yuli [ancestors of the three main Qermezi lineages] have spread their seeds, from Dugonbadan to Bakhtiyari territory to Shiraz." He added, "I have brought milk to my camp today." (I have added a woman to my family; I have found a woman to nurse my descendants.)

After midnight when practically everyone in camp was asleep, Ebrahim went to the bridal tent to consummate the marriage. To lessen the tension, the bride and groom washed each other's right hand and right foot, and the bride fed the groom bread she had brought from her mother's hearth. When Ebrahim left the tent, his mother and his father's sister went to check the bridal cloth for blood, a sign of the bride's virginity.

Happy with what they found, they told a musician who beat a rhythm on the drum, and people in camp stirred with contentment.

No music was played at dawn. Several men noted that playing the drum after the consummation was something new and not a Qermezi or Qashqa'i custom. To commemorate the formation of a new home and family and their symbol, the hearth, the musicians played and a few women and men danced while the ritual specialist Khurshid dug a fire pit in front of the bridal tent and placed three stones around it. Introducing Ebrahim to his home, Khurshid led the groom three times counterclockwise around the fire pit, then helped him to kneel and press his forehead to the stones. His bride stayed inside with other women and girls. The ritual paralleled the one the bride had enacted as she departed from her parents' home; the groom greeted his new home, while she had said farewell to hers.

Because the bride was an outsider, not Qermezi, and because Qermezi's honor had earlier been threatened by what had been perceived as Mortaza Talehbazli's insult, people talked more about the demonstration of her virginity than they usually did at Qermezi weddings. They needed to be certain about her physical condition in order to be reassured that her first child would be Ebrahim's. Although not publicly displayed, the bridal cloth was available for any woman who wanted to see it. The last event of the long wedding celebration now complete, guests quickly took their leave. A member of Sohrab's family gave each guest sweets, socks, or handkerchiefs.

After the wedding several young men said that it would have been better if Sohrab had found a Qermezi bride for his son because she would have been a hard worker. Sohrab's status was increased because the Talehbazli bride was the daughter of a prominent man, but everyone else in his household was now said to be working for her. "Sohrab's bride" would not perform certain tasks, including work, such as bringing water and fuel, that involved donkeys. The young men were certain that she had not done much hard work back in her father's home. Her father had employed a camel herder who also collected water and fuel. As a bride she did perform tasks in and near the tent such as bread baking and weaving. The young men commented that when the couple formed its own independent household, she would be burdened by work.

Once the wedding was over, people at Row of Willows, Atakola, and Hanalishah again turned their attention to the summer's productive activities. At Hanalishah most Qermezi men who had cultivated grain had finished cutting the crop, had transported it to a threshing ground, and were just beginning to thresh. Some Persian and Lur cultivators had already finished their threshing, and a few were pressing Borzu to transport their grain and straw to Semirom. Mali, the Lur nomad who had camped with Borzu in late spring and early summer, had returned to Hanalishah to help harvest the Persians' and Lurs' grain. They paid him a portion of the harvest instead of a daily wage because he was not Qermezi or Qashqa'i and did not pose a threat to their attempted control of the land.

At the beginning of August Borzu moved to his fourth and final campsite at Hanalishah, right next to the long-talked-of spring. Twice in the past several weeks he had sold a few sheep and goats to Shahsevan men, formerly nomadic but now settled in the religious town of Qom near Tehran. They toured summer pastures to buy animals and then sold them individually in Qom for a good price, they said. Women milked the goats once a day at noon, but they were milking the sheep only every other day now, and the quantity of milk had greatly decreased. In a few days ewes would be dry. Hajj Khodaparast, visiting Borzu, said he was depressed because he was unable to collect money owed him. Two other Kazerun moneylenders also dropped by Borzu's, but he hardly spoke to them. For six weeks they had haunted summer pastures and forced themselves upon the nomads who were their debtors. The gendarme major in Semirom sent his adolescent son for a vacation with Borzu, who did not quite know what to do with him or how well to treat him.

Some men at Hanalishah decided to try to avoid the previous winter's high losses of lambs and kids by postponing this year's mating. They herded rams and bucks separately, which had entered a state of rut at the end of the first month of summer, or they placed them in herds lacking adult females. Mansur, who had acquired many year-old rams on an animal contract, volunteered to herd the rams and bucks of three other men. When mating occurred in midsummer, young were born at the end of autumn and suffered the rigors of winter. If the year was one of drought, their mothers received insufficient food and water and did not produce enough milk. By postponing mating until the beginning of autumn this year, men planned births for the sixtieth day of winter when new grass was expected, and they hoped the mothers would then produce adequate milk. Young would stay with their mothers until they reached summer pastures. The main disadvantage of the new strategy was that no milk or milk products would be available for human consumption and trade until after the nomads' arrival in summer pastures. Borzu did not change the schedule of mating and allowed rams and bucks to mate in midsummer.

40. Abdol Hosain and his son and daughter at Atakola village

He had fed barley and other fodder to the rams before they rejoined the herd, and he kept them well fed for the duration.

After intense bargaining, Borzu had finally hired the Zailabli Darrehshuri shepherd who had witnessed his attack on Aqaboa, but the shepherd soon quit in disgust. Hired to herd in Aqaboa's place, he had spent the cash portion of his salary received in advance to pay debts and purchase supplies. Falak had fought with him, and he had sworn at Qermezi. He left his family at Borzu's camp while he borrowed money to repay Borzu, and then they left without a farewell. Borzu made no comment, but Falak looked content that she had driven away yet another family that had displeased her and not done her bidding. After weeks of searching, Borzu hired a new shepherd, a Chardahcharik Darrehshuri man named Haibat who was an opium addict. Already there was beginning to be trouble with him.

News spread quickly that Borzu's younger brother Abdol Hosain was migrating for the last time the next day, and people went to say good-bye. Although he had made it clear for months that he was abandoning nomadic pastoralism, and people knew the concrete steps he was taking in that direction, they were still surprised by the news and shocked that he was leaving so soon. Others at Hanalishah were not planning to begin the autumn migration for another three weeks. Jansanam hurried with all her children to say farewell to her brother and her mother Narges, who would settle with him. The two women cried together, sad and uncertain when they would see one another again. That morning Abdol Hosain had asked Gholam Hosain to take his sheep and goats to winter pastures, but his brother had refused because he could not incur the expense of caring for them. He also feared that Borzu would prohibit him from grazing these animals on Dashtak pastures. Weeks later Abdol Hosain commented dispiritedly, "Qermezi said they wouldn't take my animals."

Sitting with men in his tent and hearing women's laments outside, Abdol Hosain talked sadly about his decision. He readily recognized that he was leaving most of his kin and abandoning a way of life he cherished. He felt driven out by Borzu, he said, and forced to escape. The men discussed his decision and wondered whether it was a prudent one or not, and he kept asking for their opinion. He and some other men who also expected to settle reassured themselves that other families would shortly or at least eventually join them. Abdol Hosain planned to settle in Atakola village, although he said he would first stop at Narmeh village, where his wife's father Darab had been settled for years, and might remain there.

Abdol Rasul brought a horse for Abdol Hosain to shoe, and other men came to benefit from his specialized skills for possibly the last time. Jansanam kissed her mother and all of Abdol Hosain's children, and Narges kissed all her daughter's children. No one was without tears, including the men who were trying to act oblivious of the women's farewells. Jansanam walked slowly away. Gholam Hosain's daughter came to collect the dog that Abdol Hosain did not want to take along, and the men joked that it also wanted to flee from Borzu. Narges hit the dog and yelled at it to leave, and then, wiping the tears streaming down her face, she went off to be by herself for a while.

Before dawn the next day Gholam Hosain came to Abdol Hosain's camp to offer to take some of his sheep and goats to winter pastures. Abdol Hosain had hoped he would take them as a courtesy, without explicit remuneration, but Gholam Hosain asked for a nimsud arrangement. Abdol Hosain reluctantly agreed to turn over thirty animals to him. Still burdened with pack animals, he lent his brother four camels to thank him for taking the herd animals. He had earlier lent three donkeys to Mali. The day before when Morad had heard that Gholam Hosain had refused his brother's request, he had volunteered to take thirty of Abdol Hosain's animals without recompense. When Abdol Hosain left Hanalishah for the last time, forty sheep and goats accompanied him. Several days later he left four with Darab at Narmeh. He then lent thirty sheep and goats, a horse, and three camels to Abdollah, a Qurd Darrehshuri man who was a longtime acquaintance of Qermezi men and Gholam Hosain's wife's brother. Qurd winter pastures near Dugonbadan were said to be better than Dashtak, and the animals would be more likely to survive there. He lent his sister's husband Cheragh a camel as he passed by Row of Willows. After he settled in Atakola village, he took his last camel to Isfahan to sell and then turned his attention to the difficult task of suddenly having to find a new livelihood.

The celebration marking the marriage between a Rakkeh Darrehshuri man and the daughter of Borzu's new shepherd Haibat began at a Rakkeh camp in a valley in Sarqaz Mountain to the east of Hanalishah. Urged to attend, Borzu stalled all day, for no Qermezi supporters had yet arrived to accompany him.

Borzu was also concerned that, once his truck was at the wedding, he would be pressed to put it into service and would be unable to refuse. "What excuse could I give?" he wondered. Because of the low socioeconomic status of the families of the groom and bride, he (rightly) assumed that no other vehicles would be present. He had incurred expensive repairs in the past month and was unwilling to permit others to use his truck for their own purposes if he was restricting his own use of it. He kept running out of gasoline far from any town, for he hated to spend even the small sum for fuel and often thought he could take "one more trip" before buying any. Now, he worried, people at the Rakkeh wedding were planning to run his truck all over summer pastures at his expense and for their pleasure. Falak had become quite irritated about all the carrying of goods and running of errands that Borzu had been doing recently, and she rarely let a chance go by without letting him hear her opinions. To her anger, he had even promised a Persian cultivator the use of his truck to collect a bride, which to her was the ultimate folly. The argument she often used with him was, "Why should Mohammad Karim go hungry in Kazerun while you are wasting money on strangers?"

A Rakkeh man delivered the bridewealth payment of $320 and twenty-five ewes to Haibat and asked Borzu to permit his shepherd to have the day off. Borzu replied that Haibat could ride with him in the truck to the wedding the next morning. The Rakkeh man had also brought a goat as a gift for Borzu. When the man was out of earshot, Borzu exuberantly exclaimed, "I am a kikha [khan]!" He always appreciated receiving recognition of his status and position. Until the mid-1960s and only rarely thereafter, people wanting to arrange the marriage of a son or daughter asked permission from the khan with whom they were most closely connected. They always accompanied their request with the gift of an animal.

In the morning Borzu stalled again, for he was still without any Qermezi supporters. As the headman of Qermezi he could not arrive alone with only his non-Qermezi hired shepherd at his side. When Haibat walked by with studied casualness to see what he was doing, Borzu asked him why he had not gone to the wedding. Suddenly, solving the problem of the truck, he called for a horse and a mule to be saddled, and off he rode with Haibat. Angry to be left behind, Mohammad Karim complained bitterly that a shepherd and not he was given a mount. Other family members had also planned to attend, and Zolaikha and Zohreh had been sewing new clothes in preparation. Mohammad Karim, Asadollah, and Hosain Ali dressed in their ceremonial cloaks and set off on foot to the wedding. That evening the camp's children and young girls gathered at Haibat's tent to sew the bride's clothes. Ordinarily a bride's female relatives assisted in the preparations but none lived nearby.

Mohammad Karim returned from the wedding by foot late that night and left again at dawn with the truck. Falak assumed that Borzu, who had not returned the previous night, had instructed his son to drive the vehicle to the wedding. She said it was absurd to take it now, after two days of maneuvering to avoid it. Mohammad Karim had told her that Borzu claimed he had business to conduct in Semirom, and she asked everyone what that could possibly be. No one knew. She complained that he wanted to attend the wedding in style and be respected as the owner of a vehicle.

Soon word came via various sources that Borzu had caused a fight at the wedding the previous night. Rumor had it that he had competed unfairly during the stick-fighting game by hitting his opponents' heads and shoulders. Before anyone could discover the details or learn of his current whereabouts, Falak and the others heard drums. They ran to see who would be first to spot the entourage from the Rakkeh wedding camp coming to collect Haibat's daughter, and then they hurried back to their tents to dress in their best clothes. Borzu was temporarily forgotten.

Thirty people on horseback, including musicians playing instruments, charged into Hanalishah via the stream gorge leading from the pass. They had assembled out of sight and then mounted their mock attack on the home of the bride-to-be. As they approached Borzu's camp, many men and boys galloped their horses back and forth, and some leapt off and on in the customary Qashqa'i sport. Men pantomimed firing guns into the air as they raced into camp, as they had actually done before the Qashqa'i were disarmed. They circled the bride's tent and shouted warnings. Women trilled. By the time Falak and her daughters reached Haibat's tent, the entourage had already dismounted. The bride huddled beside the tent under a large cloth and wailed loudly. Women and girls gathered around her to clap and dance and then moved her behind the tent where she collapsed against the back of the piled baggage. Stumbling around with her head down, her mother lamented, "Don't cry, my baby." Her father Haibat sat inconspicuously in the tent.

A young Rakkeh man who was a servant to Jehangir Khan Darrehshuri prepared and served tea with equipment the entourage had brought along. Two musicians set up instruments in the small tent and began to play. Mohammad Qoli arrived, earlier instructed by Borzu to write the marriage contract, but the Rakkeh group had brought their own teacher for the purpose. The many dogs that had accompanied the entourage fought noisily with the dogs in Borzu's camp.

Symbolic of the bride's transfer to a new family and group, Rakkeh women took charge of dressing her. She had bathed the previous night, and her hands and feet had been dyed with henna. Her clothes were not of high-quality material, and people later commented how unfortunate she was to have a father who "ate" the bridewealth for his own debts and opium habit and did not spend it on the dowry as was customary and expected. Consoling herself, the girl's mother said to Falak later, "God gave my daughter to strangers," but then admitted that her husband had actually sold her. After Samarrokh cut the bride's bangs and forelocks, a Rakkeh woman braided her hair and helped her put on a cap decorated with coins. She covered the bride completely with a whitish veil and then a small red scarf. The groom's family offered money to the bride's mother as payment for "milk" she had given her daughter, but she refused it as was proper, and Samarrokh tied it in a cloth around the bride's waist. The groom's party distributed candy and served tea, and in a rush people found their mounts and prepared to leave. Women lifted the bride onto a decorated horse and placed a young boy behind her as a charm for fertility. Her mother stood at her side, but she was led away too quickly for any possible farewell between them. Her father was nowhere in sight. Zolaikha later joked that it was customary for the bride to cry when she left her parents' home, but that when she sat alone in the bridal tent at the groom's camp she laughed, thinking about all the work her younger sister now had to perform.

41. Bridal tent at the Rakkeh wedding celebration. People watching the ritualized chase and capture of the bride.

The few Qermezi men who had come to Haibat's tent had left their mounts at Borzu's, and they raced to see who would accompany the party on which animals. Zohreh leapt on a horse with her cousin Fathollah, and they joined the group that was already riding quickly through the mountainous gorge to the Rakkeh camp in the first valley to the east. At the beginning and end of the trip, Rakkeh men and boys raced back and forth and whooped. A Rakkeh man led the bride's horse on the journey, and the boy seated behind her held down her veils. One of the two musicians riding together on a mule fell off during a difficult downhill stretch; he remounted and resumed playing the drums. Near the Rakkeh camp a shepherd tried to make a large curved-horn ram pass in front of the bride's path, another ritual intended to promote fertility, but the animal ran in the opposite direction. (A man visiting Borzu the next day erroneously reported that the bride had fallen off the horse three times on the trip to the wedding camp. He conveyed the displeasure people felt about the marriage and especially about Haibat selling a daughter for his own financial gain. Such accidents, if they had actually occurred, were believed to signify the inauspiciousness of the match and even indicate that the bride was impure).

The wedding party excitedly entered the Rakkeh camp, and many

42. Morad and a Rakkeh man competing in the stick-fighting game at the Rakkeh wedding

people chased after the bride to capture her. A man snatched the apple from the pole marking the tent of the groom's father and pelted the unprepared bride with it, hard enough to make her cry out in surprise. Other men raced after him to pelt him. A musician lifted the bride off the horse and led her to the bridal tent made of colorful flat-woven textiles otherwise used to cover a tent's baggage. The groom's family had piled salt and flour bags and camel saddles in the small tent to compensate for the paltry amount of dowry goods they knew the bride was bringing with her. Qermezi men from Hanalishah, especially Morad and Abdol Rasul, acted as distinguished guests and sat importantly in the guest tent. Borzu was not present. No Chardahcharik people, members of Haibat's group, had come to the wedding or to Haibat's tent when his daughter was collected, another indication that he had fallen into disfavor with them. Angry that he had not sought their permission, they refused to attend the ceremonies.

Women danced, and then the music for stick fighting began. Qermezi men and boys leapt up to participate. When a Rakkeh man hit a Qermezi man in the game, another Qermezi man grabbed the pole to challenge the attacker, and the sport rapidly became a serious Rakkeh-Qermezi competition. When someone was hit hard, men had to restrain the victim from seeking revenge. Each side was eager to respond to the loss of honor that had occurred the previous night when Borzu had played unfairly. Abdol Rasul used tactics to confuse his opponent, while Morad disconcertingly shouted at his as a diversion. Asadollah kept a thin stick tucked in his cummerbund to deflect the stick aimed at his thighs. Young men had once again elaborately wrapped their legs for protection.

Abdol Rasul pretended to strike his opponent's head but instead struck only the pole the Rakkeh man held, as a scare tactic and to put the man off guard, and then he was able to whack his leg hard. This move angered the Rakkeh men who, recalling Borzu's actions the night before, attacked Abdol Rasul in a group. Simultaneously they saw that Abdol Rasul's powerful blow had split the thick pole, and one of them grabbed a pole from the musicians' tent as a replacement. Removing the pole, however, put too great a strain on the front tent stake, which pulled loose, and the whole tent fell on top of the musicians. The music and stick fighting stopped immediately, and everyone was stunned, faced with such an inauspicious occurrence. Qermezi men laughed at the spectacle, and a few Rakkeh men joined in. Irritated, the musicians acted for a while as if they would refuse to play another note. Only a few young men returned to the game. When Abdol Rasul had made the threatening hit, Morad angrily told the other Qermezi men and boys to cease playing and sit down. Rakkeh men sitting in the guest tent vacated it in anger as the Qermezi group approached, and they moved to the groom's father's tent where they argued with one another. Qermezi men sat tensely in the guest tent.

Morad tried to talk calmly to the Rakkeh group's teacher, the one guest who was neither Qermezi nor Rakkeh. When he uttered the word "hit," however, Rakkeh men who were listening from the next tent became even more angry and refused to speak with the Qermezi men. Then Morad tried to justify Abdol Rasul's hit, but coming as it did after Borzu's unfair playing, Rakkeh men were not convinced. One complained loudly, "Why bother to have a nice event when it only becomes ruined?" Everyone sat silently and waited for lunch.

Purposely ignoring the Qermezi guests, a young Rakkeh man offered water to the teacher for washing before he ate. Piqued by this breach of hospitality, the Qermezi guests refused to wash when the pitcher was belatedly brought to them, and they ate lunch without washing. The teacher proclaimed impolitely that the rice was burnt. Morad announced, "It's finished," and said it was time to go home. Before the stick fighting, members of the groom's family had placed braided cords with tassels on all the horses and mules from Hanalishah. Now, only one man from the Rakkeh camp came to say farewell to the Qermezi group. No one spoke during the slow-paced return trip. Abdol Rasul and Morad avoided one another and rode apart. Amidst the Rakkeh, Morad had defended his brother; once away from Rakkeh territory he was free to be angry at him. Back at Borzu's tent, Falak reported that the bride's mother had cried profusely after her daughter was taken away.

The next day the story of Borzu's behavior on the second night of the wedding was told more completely. He had hit a Rakkeh man's head, and everyone had become angry. The gendarmes present told him to stop playing, and he left the celebration in a huff. In front of visitors two days later, he rolled up his pant leg to display bruises where he had been hit, as if to justify his illegal playing. Morad's and Abdol Rasul's attitude at the wedding was clear to others, for the two men had gone to restore Qermezi honor. They said they would not have bothered even to attend such a minor wedding had it not been for Borzu's actions.

Qermezi men were aware that their group honor was in jeopardy. When they traveled outside Qermezi territory, they were frequently confronted about their "hitting." Stories that they struck their brothers in front of high-status guests, beat their defenseless shepherds, and forgot to notify the fathers of brides about the wedding date circulated widely and were subjects of joking. News had spread that Borzu's close kinsmen were abandoning him to settle in villages. People even discussed the implications of the negative evaluation of the tribal school inspector. A wedding was a place to demonstrate that the group was powerful and yet capable of sporting behavior. Qermezi men had hastened to the Rakkeh wedding to prove themselves and had again fallen out of favor. People at Hanalishah complained that Borzu's and Abdol Rasul's actions undermined the efforts of other Qermezi men to present a better image. In the past when they had exhibited their physical prowess during wars, raids, territorial disputes, and intertribal competitions, they were widely praised. Now they saw they were mocked for their inappropriate use of force.

At breakfast the next day two schoolboys came to tell Falak that the teacher's wife Ma'asumeh had "fallen." Falak set off immediately. The previous day she had been full of curses about this "shitty woman." Ma'asumeh, whose husband had taken students to Round Sun for fifth-grade examinations, was lying under blankets, moaning, and complaining of back pain. Falak set right to work making a stew. Hearing that a Persian itinerant peddler who carried medicines was at Hanalishah, Ma'asumeh's brother went to get a pill from him. A schoolboy brought two home remedies from an elderly Chardahcharik woman living in the next valley and reported that her saddlebag was full of medicines. Falak said she did not recognize the two he had brought but knew they were efficacious from their smell.

Sayyid Javad, the peddler who was from the town of Dehaqan, came to see what Ma'asumeh's ailment was. He sat a short distance from her and then moved closer to look at her tongue. Feeling her pulse for a few seconds, he asked if she had a hot water bottle or Vicks VapoRub and then dispensed a fancy aspirin. He inquired if she had eaten any pickled vegetables and asked about other food, then wondered if she had been sick in this fashion before. She explained that she had recently walked a distance; ordinarily she never left the confines of her tent and its immediate surroundings. He did not know she was two to three months pregnant, and she did not mention it.

During these inquiries Sayyid Javad watched Ma'asumeh carefully. He announced that she had caught a cold caused, definitely, by the evil eye. Most sickness was the result of the evil eye, he proclaimed, and he offered several examples. Ma'asumeh and Falak accepted and agreed with his diagnosis. When he had first arrived, Falak asked him to look in his book to see what cure Ma'asumeh needed. He asked for a large piece of paper from which he tore a long strip and prepared to write a prayer. He wrote "in the name of God" at the top, then took a small book from his pocket and flipped through the handwritten pages to find the appropriate passage. After putting on glasses he filled in the long strip with the passage. At the end he asked for her and her mother's names which he added with a flourish. He folded the long sides of the paper toward the center and then slowly and precisely folded up the paper from the bottom, ending up with a neat square packet. He wrote "oh God" on the outside. He recited for a few minutes, partly in Arabic from the Qoran and partly in Persian about the evil eye. He concluded, "As I am from the family of the prophet Mohammad, I speak from him and God."

Earlier, when Sayyid Javad had diagnosed Ma'asumeh's illness as caused by the evil eye, he declared that any silk or blue-colored clothes were injurious to wear. Looking up at the cord where she hung clothes, Ma'asumeh pulled down a silky blue tunic and blamed her sickness on it. He had obviously spotted the tunic before his pronouncement, but he made it seem as if he held mysterious powers. He called for scissors and cut a narrow strip from the tunic's right front side from the hem to where the front and back panels joined. He reassured her that he was cutting a straight line and only removing a narrow piece so as not to ruin the garment. While he continued reciting he fondled the strip, then folded it and cut it in two, saying he was cutting the power of the evil eye over her. He folded the two cut pieces and cut and folded again and again, ending with a pile of small squares of blue cloth. Holding the pile in front of his mouth, he recited, "By the power of the first imam, by the power of the second imam," continuing up to the sixth imam, and then blew on the pile. He recited, "By the power of the seventh imam," and blew again several times. He inserted the squares into the folded paper packet. Everyone said, "In the name of God."

Placing the packet into Ma'asumeh's hands, Sayyid Javad instructed her about her duties. She should make a cloth pouch and insert the packet along with a white crystal (alum, used in dyeing to set colors), five chickpeas, and a new needle that had never been used. She should then sew the pouch shut, melt beeswax on the outside to seal the seams, and pin it on the upper right arm of the tunic she wore. He listed the foods she should avoid for a week. He told her to burn wild rue and other dried herbs in the fire. He wrote "in the name of God" and a short prayer on a small square of paper, dropped it into a glass of clean water, and told her to drink it. He suggested that she wrap camel's wool (which is very soft) on the side of her body where it hurt, and Falak offered to bring her some. He declared that she would be well by the next afternoon.

Falak complained of a headache and asked for a cure. Sayyid Javad wrote a short prayer and gave her instructions about burning dried herbs and drinking a potion (neither of which she followed). He explained the qualities of the medicines dispensed by the Chardahcharik woman. After he left, Ma'asumeh and her brother wondered if they should pay him. Falak said she had given him two dollars after he had saved Dariush's life. Katayun had donated a donkey the previous summer after he had cured her infant son.

Sayyid Javad, whose principal income derived from peddling, bought commodities in Isfahan where prices were low and then returned to the city after a month to sell the goods (mostly wool and dried curds) he had accumulated in trade. Some items he acquired during his rounds, such as chickens and eggs, he traded along the way. A young helper who loaded and unloaded the commodities accompanied him. During winter he bought and sold carpets in Shahreza, which had been his father's occupation. His brother Sayyid Abul Qasem, who also wrote prayers and treated illness but was not a peddler of wares, traveled through summer pastures in the same general territory. He had recently passed by Khalifeh's tent with a donkey and a pony in tow, offered by people discharging vows uttered in his name in the past. Looking resigned, Khalifeh had given him money, and his son had donated a kid. Katayun had often stated that one could tell from a sayyid's face whether he was genuine or not. She noted that sayyids were placed on earth to encourage righteous behavior.

Falak and Ma'asumeh talked about the evil eye. They declared that when someone said a woman or child was beautiful, the woman or child would fall sick. Of one hundred people, one or two were so powerful that if they praised, "What a splendid mountain!" it would split and collapse. They were certain that speaking badly of a person did not cause sickness. Ma'asumeh's brother, however, implied that "the talk of women" and Falak's harmful words had resulted in his sister's illness, because Falak and Ma'asumeh had been so hostile and vituperative for weeks. Ma'asumeh blamed the illness on Haibat's daughter who had exclaimed, seeing her at the spring, "What a lovely bride!" just before she herself was to become a bride. That evening Ma'asumeh had fallen ill. A few days before that, a stranger had asked who she was while she was washing clothes in a stream, and she thought it might also have been his notice of her that had made her ill. She remarked that prayers to cast off the effects of the evil eye had been written for her on two previous occasions.

Early the next morning after Falak pressured Borzu to offer aid, Mohammad Karim drove Ma'asumeh with her brother to Semirom to see a doctor. At a government clinic a paraprofessional with minimal training gave her an unidentified injection drawn from an unlabeled bottle and four types of pills (all thought to be attractive, in different colors and packaging) and proclaimed that she probably had a stone in her kidney. He offered no instructions or suggestions for further treatment. Ready to return to Hanalishah, Ma'asumeh remembered an elderly Kezenli Darrehshuri woman who provided medical treatments, and they made a detour to visit her camp. The woman manipulated a vein in her right shoulder in order to dislodge a piece of meat that she was certain had stuck in her stomach. Pleased with this treatment, Ma'asumeh and her brother offered her twenty cents for which she seemed grateful. They stopped at their sister's tent for lunch and then returned to Semirom for shopping. After driving her home, Mohammad Karim killed the chicken her sister had given her because of her illness. The day had provided a stimulating outing for Ma'asumeh, who ordinarily went only a few steps from her tent; the excursion and attention seemed to clear up her symptoms. When Mohammad Qoli returned from Round Sun and spotted the charm that Sayyid Javad had prepared, he snapped at his wife and declared that the sayyid had put "dog shit" inside.

Borzu returned to camp with one Persian and three Qashqa'i men. He had carried loads for two of them, and he told the Persian he would send someone to his house the next day to see if he had found "ten large chicks" for him (that is, payment for the transportation). One Qashqa'i man laughingly asked him about the Rakkeh wedding, and Borzu went to pains to explain his version of the conflict. He swore that he had hit his opponents' legs and not heads and that when a Rakkeh man hit him, gendarmes had come to his aid. Critical of the Rakkeh groom, the visitors described him as so sickly he looked as if he "drank water from a water pipe and ate dirt." They reported that the ritual specialist who had helped the groom to bathe and had marked him with henna had declared that it was against his better judgment to prepare the man for marriage. They said no Rakkeh family wanted to give him a bride, and they were critical of Chardahcharik men for allowing Haibat to sell a daughter. One visitor laughed about Borzu's luck with hired shepherds, and Borzu had to explain that problem too, case by case. He lent the man a mule to ride the rest of the way home.

After waiting a month for Borzu to offer him a better shepherding salary, Mohammad Hosain had finally quit work and taken his large family to the plains south of Semirom where he planned to find agricultural labor. He had left Hanalishah while Borzu was attending the Rakkeh wedding in order to avoid a confrontation with him. Two of Borzu's herds were now tended by children and visitors or otherwise left to fend for themselves. Goats browsed on their own, while sheep usually stood motionless, heads drooping. Appreciating the fact that Hanalishah was enclosed and protected, Borzu daydreamed about how in the future he would hire guards for the south and north entrances to the territory and let his herds roam freely. He said he would take on additional nimsud animals and still not need more than one shepherd.

When Borzu returned from a stint of herding, he spoke about settling at Hanalishah. He sadly remarked, "I have spent forty years in these mountains. What difference has it made? Where is proof that I have been here? What have I left behind?" He indicated that if he had partners, he would buy the rights to the irrigable land from the Persian and Lur cultivators and pay the government for rights to the pastureland (which was nationalized and not for sale). He talked of planting poplar trees along the stream at the base of the valley, to be harvested for building. He would construct his own house, plant an orchard, and continue to travel to winter pastures. He would seasonally move his family and possessions by truck, via the asphalt road running from Shahreza to Shiraz and then to Arzhan Plain, and send his herds on the migrations with a kinsman and several hired shepherds. "All of Qermezi would be together here," he noted plaintively, as if he knew it would never occur.

A few days earlier Borzu had outlined his own three-part plan for "a better life." First he would sell all his pack animals except for two mules and use a vehicle to transport goods, water, and fuel. Then he would buy land for a house and for grazing and secure government documents attesting to his exclusive and permanent ownership. His herds would graze on natural pastures, crops he would plant specially for them, and stubble. He would cultivate his own wheat and barley. Finally, he would require all government officials to hold a high school diploma. "Men lacking intelligence and literacy are running my life," he complained. Educated men would listen to his problems, he thought, treat him and his group fairly, and not demand bribes.

Visiting from Row of Willows, Borzu's brother-in-law Cheragh came to see him the next day. He cursed the ritual specialist Ali Mirza because his recently circumcised son had been running a fever. He said he had been afraid all along and had known his son was too young to be circumcised. Falak and Mohammad Karim questioned him about who was settling. He reluctantly told them some news in sparse detail and avoided other questions. When Borzu returned, he too grilled him and received the same response. People were afraid to tell Borzu their plans. Cheragh hesitated and then suggested that his brother Sohrab would travel to winter pastures by rented truck, when in truth Sohrab was planning to rent a house somewhere in summer pastures for the winter. As if to change to a subject less charged with emotion, the two men discussed the moon having been "taken away" a few nights earlier when an Apollo spacecraft had been launched from Cape Canaveral in Florida. They had heard about the event via Bahram's radio and had remembered that the moon that night had become black and then red.

Hajj Khodaparast also visited, and Borzu killed a kid for him. The merchant was returning from Tehran where he had just taken a loss in selling the sheep and goats he had transported from Hanalishah as the partner of the many nomads with whom he held nimsud contracts. Unexpectedly, the Tehran price had been the same as in Isfahan, and he had needlessly incurred expenses in transporting, feeding, and housing the animals. He asked Borzu for a special rice and herb stew, and Borzu instructed Falak to prepare some. Borzu had never engaged in animal contracts, borrowed money, or taken goods on credit from him and never intended to. He wanted to keep him as a useful ally in Kazerun without having the relationship tainted by economic transactions, especially ones placing him at a disadvantage. Khodaparast was a member of the Kazerun town council and was influential locally. Several years previously he had supported Sohrab when he claimed rights to Dashtak pastures, and Borzu had struck him in an argument about it. Since then they had reconciled.

Monavvar, who like Cheragh was also visiting Hanalishah from Row of Willows, wanted to see her relatives before they left for winter pastures. Mokhtar and Monavvar were settling, possibly in Naqneh. Borzu asked her the same questions he had asked of Cheragh, to check the information he was receiving. She was guarded and more so when alone with Falak, but soon Borzu was shouting about the man (Sohrab), whose father was a dog, who was not going to migrate.

Men and boys gathered where the wheat and barley of Borzu, Ali, Khalifeh, and Bahram were being threshed. Asadollah and Abul Hasan had harvested Borzu's grain in exchange for a portion of the crop. Khalifeh washed barley that had mixed with dirt from the threshing floor. On top of a pile of threshed wheat Bahram wrote with a stick the words Allah, Mohammad, and Ali in Arabic script and then, not losing contact with the grain, drew a circle around the pile and muttered a short prayer to bless the harvest and give thanks for God's bounty. Then he and Khalifeh carefully pushed the grain into shallow copper pans and leveled them off. In a singsong rhythm they counted each panful as they poured it into a large sack. At planting they had also carefully measured the seed, and by this technique they determined what yields they had received. For every wheat seed planted, Khalifeh harvested nine seeds. Other men who had cultivated nearby achieved ratios between one to six and one to ten. Barley yields were slightly higher than wheat yields. In the three previous years Khalifeh's wheat yields from the same plot were one to twelve, one to twenty-five, and one to eight.

The totality of the harvest at Hanalishah belonged to these cultivators. Like their agricultural efforts at Dashtak (but unlike at Molla Balut), they owed no rent or share of the harvest to anyone. Qermezi men in other summer pastures paid a fifth to a quarter of their harvest to men who still illegally controlled what was now nationalized land.

High-spirited because the harvest was almost complete, the men joked about many topics, including the news Monavvar had brought concerning the intentions of the aged widowed Arghvan to take a new wife. He had found a divorcée who would be ready to marry him once she completed the carpet she was weaving, and her kinsmen had agreed to a small bridewealth. She had been married to Hormoz Basseri who had shared pastures with Qermezi many years back. Divorce was rare among Qermezi and other Qashqa'i people, and older divorced women were even rarer. When it occurred, divorce usually resulted from apparent infertility or intrafamily disputes.

The next day adolescent boys and girls in a festive playful mood gathered at the threshing ground to pack and transport the grain and straw. They heard a Persian cultivator yell that Borzu was in a "stone fight" and saw that many Persians had clustered around one of their own threshing grounds. Sayyid Mohammad had apparently not permitted Mohammad Karim to herd animals close by, and the boy had hit him twice with a stick. Waiting until a restraining force of fellow Persian cultivators could arrive, the sayyid struck matches and attempted to burn his own unthreshed piled grain. He wanted the authorities to see that Borzu had destroyed the harvest. A long heated discussion followed. Tempers were high as the season's productive activities were concluding, and the cultivators and pastoralists had not resolved their problems.

In years past the Persian and Lur cultivators had left Hanalishah as soon as they completed the harvest, and Qermezi pastoralists had grazed their herd and pack animals on the stubble in the cultivators' fields. This fresh stubble was rich in quantity and nutrients and was especially appreciated for the grain heads and seeds that had fallen to the ground. "Dry stubble" was less prized. This year the cultivators proclaimed that they would remain at Hanalishah until the Qermezi group migrated south. If any men wanted the fresh stubble for their animals, they would have to pay for it. Depending on this vegetation, the pastoralists were outraged, for they needed to conserve the fodder they had been accumulating for the autumn migration. They complained that the cultivators were so spiteful that they would willingly sacrifice animal fertilizer in order to deprive the pastoralists of the use of the harvested fields.

Borzu especially, but most other men at Hanalishah as well, had offered few pastoral products to the cultivators this year, unlike in previous years. Living alone and isolated by their fields, the cultivators had a limited diet and thus appreciated invitations to meals and gifts of fresh dairy products and meat. Qermezi women commented that the reason their men were currently having such difficulty with the cultivators was that they had not warmed the relationship with gifts. Katayun had often noted that she customarily gave small gifts of pastoral produce to the cultivators nearest her tent and water supply and that when they discovered her donkey in their fields, for example, they did not raise a commotion but simply called for a child to chase the animal away. A month after Borzu's arrival at

Hanalishah, he was heard shouting at cultivators who had blocked his access to a stream. Then a shepherd's child came to Falak with the message that she should send a bowl of fresh butter to Borzu. Such gifts from him had become rare.

Kalayaz, the blind moneylender from Kazerun, had come again to Hanalishah because the nomads had produced another commodity, this time grain, and he wanted to collect. He sought out Khalifeh first. Khalifeh was unwilling to give him grain and claimed he lacked money. Finding no other options, he finally agreed to a four-year nimsud contract for eleven animals. The two men argued for hours about the price as they inspected and reinspected the animals. They finally compromised, using Mansur and Bahram as mediators, and Kalayaz subtracted half the agreed-upon value from Khalifeh's outstanding debt.

Khalifeh had been talking with his new shepherd when Kalayaz arrived. Now bolstered by being part owner of Khalifeh's herd, Kalayaz meddled in the discussion and tried to assume control. Asking the shepherd about his contract, Kalayaz discovered that Khalifeh had not yet stated the quantities of sugar and tea that were often part of such contracts, and he urged him to do so immediately. Unhappy about being pressured by an outsider, Khalifeh retorted that he would help his shepherd when necessary and that he was unable to state specific quantities at this time. Kalayaz pressed him to promise tobacco; Khalifeh replied that it was not part of a shepherd's contract. Submissive and humble when first talking with Khalifeh, the shepherd was now strengthened in his resolve and insisted on certain items. Khalifeh reluctantly agreed to give him money for tobacco.

Kalayaz had proclaimed that he was not going to stay long but, obliged by his presence, Khanom had cooked rice. Having completed his business, which included asking about the affairs of other Qermezi families at Hanalishah, he insisted on leaving and acted irritated that he was invited to stay for lunch. When he was finally gone, Khalifeh noted with disgust that Kalayaz had sat as if he were the homeowner, ordering this and that for his comfort. He had turned imperious within minutes of becoming part owner of Khalifeh's herd.

When Khalifeh discussed his debt he juxtaposed the economic facts with comments about honor. He remarked that as a man of honor he was obligated to be hospitable, well dressed, and a giver of gifts, but he could not afford these actions. "I greet a stranger or visitor and then make rice, as honor requires, but I can't afford the expense." He needed to visit the khans but could not go empty-handed, without a lamb or kid. He sadly commented that he was burdened daily by his heavy debt, currently $2,000 and soon to increase to $2,400 if he did not pay it by winter.

Morad's son ran to Khalifeh's camp yelling that Borzu and the Persian cultivators were fighting again, and people grabbed their clubs and hastened to the scene. The cultivator Sayyid Mohammad had struck Borzu in the nose with a stone, and Mohammad Karim and a shepherd had driven to Semirom to report the incident. Borzu then decided he ought to be in Semirom as well and told the teacher to take him on his motorcycle. The teacher returned alone after dark to say that three Persian men wielding stones and sticks had attacked them as they rode to town. When the teacher had pulled a knife and threatened to use it, the Persians scattered. Alone in the tent with her children, Falak was afraid that Persians would come to assault her sons, and Zolaikha cried in fear as the tension mounted. Mali came to report that he had seen a bloodied Persian man on the road who yelled that Borzu was making war. Long after midnight Borzu returned to Hanalishah with three gendarmes and a Persian cultivator. With flashlights the gendarmes investigated the scene of the dispute. Keyed up, Borzu shouted all night, and the camp and its animals were restless with the noise.

At dawn Borzu was still shouting. Qermezi men had gathered in his tent along with many gendarmes and cultivators. He was angry that no Qermezi men had joined the fight or come to his aid in Semirom, but because of the presence of outsiders all he could do then was complain about having been alone. Morad, Abdol Rasul, and others had hastened on their own accord to his tent when they heard that a dispute had brought the gendarmes to Hanalishah. Despite the internal disagreements they still presented a unified front when officials investigated a conflict. They all quarreled with the cultivators and needed to be present in case points about other confrontations were raised.

Borzu still had dried blood on his face from the cut on his nose. For dramatic effect he had not wanted to wash it off. (Ordinarily, traces of human blood caused great concern because of notions of ritual impurity and were immediately removed.) He pleaded to the gendarmes and others that he was a poor innocent victim of a ruthless attack by Persians, and he told and retold how they had mercilessly beaten him. A cultivator to whom he directed his story and who seemed sympathetic soon left, not wanting to become more involved. Borzu kept displaying his bruises, and his kinsmen were quietly amused to see him also exhibit the contusions he had received some days earlier during stick fighting at the Rakkeh wedding. He tried to raise his pant legs and sleeves farther to exhibit the worst contusions higher up, but he noted that his clothes were too tight. The gendarmes seemed uninterested in the display. The officer was busy filling out a report, and then Morad accompanied them to the scene of the dispute. Whenever any authorities came on this kind of business, Qermezi men always fully saddled their horses and mules when otherwise they would have walked or ridden bareback, because the officials often needed mounts to ride for their investigations. The gendarmes returned, wrote another report, and left for Semirom after eating the lunch Borzu had provided.

Borzu's and the herders' families were now busy processing agricultural produce. For several days Falak and Zolaikha had been washing wheat, dirty from the threshing floor, and drying it on cloths laid in the sun. Domestic animals and wild birds kept eating the grain. Busy at some other chore, Zolaikha would casually glance up to see donkeys feasting on the grain, and she would run shouting at them and brandishing a stick. Zolaikha, Zohreh, and others carried many loads of hay on their heads to camp. Borzu had commandeered Khalifeh's son Hosain Ali for herding but then told him to abandon the sheep so that he could process the crop. With help from young children, Hosain Ali led three donkeys around a pile of hay as he pulled stalks for them to tread upon and cut. Then he filled large sacks with the fodder, some to be kept by the tent and the rest to be stored in Semirom for Borzu to draw upon during the early stages of the autumn migration. Young Filamarz cautiously approached Borzu to say, in a carefully rehearsed statement, that if he did not require Hosain Ali any longer, Khalifeh wanted him home. Borzu was disgusted, having had further plans for him, and reluctantly told him he could leave when the day's work was finished.

Many people dropped by to see Borzu in order to tell him their intentions for the migration, autumn, and winter. Qermezi and other men who shared Dashtak, but not Hanalishah, with him came to reaffirm their plans as an act of courtesy and also to make certain their places were still available. One was never sure with Borzu, they said privately. Some wanted to add to or subtract households from their campsites. Because many families planned to settle toward the end of summer, others were eager to gain access to the grazing land these settlers were abandoning. Nader came to invite his kinsman Borzu to his brother Hasel's wedding, to begin at Atakola in three days, with a party coming to Hanalishah to collect the bride in five days.

Borzu sent a donkey and her offspring to Narmeh village to be cared for by Shir Ali, Falak's brother, until Borzu returned to summer pastures the following spring. The animals had spent the summer with Jehangir Khan Darrehshuri's shepherd who had access to better pastures, but they were still too thin to migrate. Shir Ali was to send Borzu a mule in exchange. Borzu noted that they would have made a nimsud contract if they had not been relatives. As it stood, each would care for the other's animals without payment. One of Borzu's mules had recently been lost, probably stolen, and he needed a replacement for the migration.

Borzu and Falak were angry at the shepherd Haibat, who was unaccountably delayed in returning from Vanak village where Borzu had sent him to sell a thin mule. Haibat had placed a kinsman in charge of the herd during his absence. He was not demonstrating the subservient attitude and behavior that Borzu expected of his hired workers. Borzu yelled at Falak, blaming her for his former shepherd's leaving. He declared that she had done nothing but complain about Mohammad Hosain and his family and suspect them of stealing milk products, and so the family had just packed up and left. He noted that the man had been a dutiful shepherd with many sons and daughters to help. His anxiety about Haibat was increasing, for he was the shepherd who would be out of his sight and unsupervised for months. Haibat, he said, was worthless and pompous. Borzu had not yet found a second or a third shepherd and was worried because the time to migrate was quickly approaching. Just then, a young man who appeared to be a prospective shepherd arrived to see Borzu, who erupted angrily about Haibat as he discussed the job with him. Haibat's kinsman, also present, would certainly relay his dissatisfactions.

In the third week of August (the beginning of the third month of summer), Amaleh Qashqa'i nomads traveled through Hanalishah on their way south. People at Hanalishah commented that the autumn migration had begun. If they were allowed to migrate in accordance with ecological conditions and economic cycles rather than government whim, they would be ready to leave Hanalishah now. Grazing was depleted, and their crops were in. Before Iran's military controlled their movements, they usually left Hanalishah twenty to thirty days before the beginning of autumn. A few years they left around the thirtieth day of summer and then exploited other summer pastures in the mountains south of Semirom before migrating slowly to winter pastures. One year they left Hanalishah on the forty-fifth day of summer and traveled directly to Dashtak to prevent other pastoralists from grazing the reportedly superb pastures there. The recent loss of this flexibility seriously impeded their efforts to succeed as pastoralists. Borzu reported that the Semirom plain was already full of tents belonging to Bahmanbaigli Amaleh nomads, always the first in the Semirom area to receive government permission to migrate. This privilege derived from the group's connections with Mohammad Bahmanbaigi.

Later in the day Morad talked about the predicament experienced by many Qermezi men, especially those at Hanalishah and close to Borzu. He commented that someone like himself should try to organize the others to petition the government for permanent land rights, to buy land themselves, and to form economic cooperatives. These actions were the headman's responsibility, however, and others were afraid to exercise leadership independently of him. Morad especially felt alone, now that his brother Abdol Rasul was settling. Men needed the cooperation of their brothers, he insisted. Still content to migrate, Borzu was making no plans to settle and was unsupportive of people who were. Nevertheless, some men were waiting for Borzu to take the initiative. Just as he had suddenly bought a truck to solve the problem of scarcity of water at Wide Mountain, and just as he had built a road to Dashtak, so too, they said, they expected him to buy land, begin to build houses, and buy a tractor, changes from which they all expected to benefit. Many men counted on his incentive, his guidance, and, importantly, his financial acumen. Faced with his inaction, others were deciding to rely on their own initiative.

Morad indicated that the most feasible plan, in lieu of Borzu's leadership, would be for a group of them to buy land. Then every household would contribute money and labor to the building of a house for one family, which would live there and guard the area. The following year every household would contribute to the building of a second house, and this cooperation would continue until every family had a house and was settled. The problem, he said, was that Borzu would want to take control once they had acted on their own, and they would all become workers in his fields, orchards, and building projects. Morad concluded that no Qermezi man would ever engage in any cooperative venture and that, if the coming year were like the dismal one just experienced, they would all be "nothing" at this time next year.

Abdol Hosain's and Abdol Rasul's plans for settling had threatened the community. Both men were vital members of the group and socially well integrated in it. Other men were now forced to make decisions they had been putting off, whether or not they too should settle. All were experiencing conflicting feelings. Men who were taking action to settle regretted it. Men who were not settling said that they should, that settlement was the most prudent economic move. People who were settling were angry about having to settle "alone." People who were not settling were angry about being abandoned.

People's decisions to settle affected Borzu not just personally but also in his role as headman. In order to be leader of a thriving polity, he needed to assume a semblance of control over group members, particularly close kin. By making an independent decision to settle, Abdol Hosain and Abdol Rasul had threatened Borzu's hold over others in the group.

No wider political aspirations than to be headman of the subtribe were possible for Borzu. He could have expanded his followers, as he had done successfully in the past, if he had gained access to and could control more pastoral and agricultural land. Changes in land policies in Iran made such expansion impossible, however, and Borzu was forced to make do with diminishing land. Currently his main motivations were to retain his followers and enhance his own economic fortune. He was having difficulty in both areas. He needed a body of supporters, readily available men and their families, to maintain and strengthen his political and economic position. But he was apparently unwilling to settle, a direction in which practically all his kinsmen were driven. They were deadlocked.

Borzu loaded into the truck five large sacks of wheat to carry to Semirom to be taken to Kazerun by bus by the next Qermezi man unfortunate enough to have planned that moment to go there. Riding with him were Akbar and Hosain Ali, on their way to Shiraz to take the qualifying examination for entrance to the tribal teacher training program. They had known he was driving to Semirom that morning and had come to sit by his fire. Only when he suddenly prepared to leave did they ask him if he was going and could they ride along. As a signal, they whistled to Filamarz, waiting at a distance out of view of Borzu's tent, who then brought a mule loaded with grain sacks belonging to Ali and Khalifeh to be stored in Semirom. They had not wanted to arrive at Borzu's tent with baggage as if they had presumed he would transport their goods. Mansur's wife Khadijeh and brother Abul Hasan had gone to Semirom to buy fabric for the bride-to-be and gifts for the wedding guests, and they rode with Borzu when he returned to Hanalishah later in the day.

Falak, her daughters, and the children of Yadollah and Haibat spent the day washing and drying wheat and twisting yarn. Zolaikha and Samarrokh finished a horse blanket they had begun weaving two days before. Falak cooked a stew for the many helpers, and all ate heartily, never possible with Borzu or Mohammad Karim around. Khanom finished a pile carpet, the design of which she had adapted from a small bag she had borrowed years earlier from a Qashqa'i woman of another tribe. She had used its designs for blanket containers and had created a variation for the pattern of her new carpet. Other women at Hanalishah were also spending as much time as possible at their looms in order to finish projects before the migration. In action and mood, people were gearing up for beginning the long autumn migration.

A collector of gum tragacanth, exhausted from his work, came to visit Borzu. Entitled to part of the harvest, Borzu agreed to transport the gum to Semirom. Another prospective shepherd, this one a Nimardli Darrehshuri man, argued with him about a salary. Borzu's first question was, "How many able-bodied workers are available?" When the man responded that an elderly father and a lame wife lived with him, Borzu became less enthusiastic. A problem he experienced with hired herders, in fact with anyone in his camp, was that he wanted to commandeer the labor of everyone present, while the person hired resented having the labor of his own household expropriated for Borzu's and Falak's profit and convenience.

Men at Hanalishah were cutting the size of their flocks so that losses in autumn and winter would be lessened. At the beginning of summer most men had rid themselves of many animals held under nimsud contract, an arrangement they anticipated being unprofitable during the coming year. With smaller herds, more grazing for each animal would be available, and they would have to exert less effort in hauling water. They expected that the conditions for pastoralism during autumn and winter would be poor. Mansur, who relied on income from nimsud animals more than others at Hanalishah, had unburdened himself of all of them. If the grazing during winter proved to be better than expected, he would take on nimsud animals then and bring them to summer pastures to sell.

Borzu spent part of the day with his herds, deciding once again which sheep and goats to sell in Isfahan, his second trip of the summer for the purpose. He told Abul Hasan, who planned to take a few animals of his own and Mansur's to sell, to mark the eighty candidates with a mixture of ashes and water and to herd the combined animals near Semirom where he would rent a truck and driver to transport them to Isfahan. Morad, Ali, and Gholam Hosain coordinated their activities with Borzu in order to share the transport and to profit from the clout they expected him to exercise at the government slaughterhouse.

Borzu rode a mule to Semirom, unwilling to leave his truck there where it might be used in his absence by the merchant to whom he would have to entrust it. He had ordered the mule saddled before dawn, then sat by the fire and looked at the animal. Several hours later when he finally decided he had to leave, he looked around carefully to see if anyone would see him mount, and then with reluctance he got on. As a truck owner he was ashamed to appear in Semirom on mule-back. When he met someone he knew on the outskirts of town, he told him to lead the mule to the merchant's, and he walked the rest of the way.

Borzu had fought with Falak and others before he left. Zolaikha commented that he always became tense and agitated before the migration. She added that he was disturbed because Mohammad Karim had gone to Kazerun in a state of anger, and the harsh words they had shouted at one another were still hanging in the air (and she motioned around the tent). Also going to Kazerun to repeat an examination, Bahador had agreed to take the Persian language examination in Mohammad Karim's place. Mohammad Karim had not studied since the last examination but still hoped to pass the other three examinations by paying cash bribes to the teachers. Askar and Fathollah had to retake the physics examination and planned to bribe the teacher with the clarified butter they were bringing with them. (They gave him the butter but he failed them again anyway.)

Borzu's cousin Abdol Rasul, his brother-in-law Esfandeyar, and their families temporarily joined Jehangir and Naser's camp to prepare for their move to Atakola and Naqneh villages. The most organized of the men planning to settle, Abdol Rasul had accumulated quantities of firewood, straw, barley, and wheat. He sold all but twenty-three of his herd animals, sold three camels, and lent three camels each to his brothers Morad and Naser. He sold his horse to a Vanak man, Bahram writing the contract of sale. He hired a truck to come from Semirom to transport his supplies and possessions, and then with heavily laden pack animals his family and Esfandeyar's made their way to Atakola and Naqneh.

The wedding party from Atakola was due to arrive in the morning to collect Mansur's daughter Aftab, who was to marry Hasel. Zolaikha readied the home and grounds, and Falak took a rudimentary bath. Practically all the men and older boys of Hanalishah were gone, and a few women wondered if some of the absences were intentional in order to demonstrate displeasure at Hasel's having abandoned his kin to settle at Atakola. Other absences were regarded as legitimate. Akbar and Hosain Ali accompanied by Khalifeh were in Shiraz taking scheduled examinations. Older boys who attended school in Kazerun were repeating examinations. Jehangir worked full-time in Isfahan. Borzu, however, could have scheduled his animal sales in Isfahan earlier or perhaps later. By not being present at Hanalishah or attending the wedding at Atakola, he indicated his disapproval of Hasel's decision to abandon nomadic pastoralism. Hasel and his brother Nader had been dependable workers for him, and he already wondered who he would find to take their place. The four men accompanying Borzu to Isfahan to sell animals could also have scheduled another time, except that they depended on his influence there. Abdol Rasul and Esfandeyar were moving to Atakola and Naqneh that morning. They too could have delayed their departure a day, but they appeared to want to avoid a confrontation at Hanalishah with people opposed to their plans. Weddings, which provided these dispersed nomads with their only large gatherings, were often the settings where people met who did not otherwise interact and where disputes were aired publicly. The bride's father Mansur, Bahram, and Naser were the only Qermezi men remaining at Hanalishah.

By noon people saw that the wedding party was probably not coming. A bride should be collected and delivered in a single day; no time was left this day for the celebration and return trip. Napping, Falak dreamed that Saif Ali, resident of Naqneh village, had died and told everyone her premonition. Sometimes such presentiments proved correct but no corroboration for hers appeared. The death of a patrilateral kinsman of both groom and bride and a group elder would have forced a postponement of the wedding.

The elderly father of the new Nimardli Darrehshuri shepherd Borzu had finally hired came to return the advance money. He reported that his son's wife refused to serve as a shepherd's wife, and the son was therefore forced to withdraw his services. How truthful the excuse was remained unknown. Most likely, the shepherd-to-be, a man currently collecting gum tragacanth, had reconsidered after talking with people who knew or knew of Borzu, and his elderly father may have refused to be part of his job.

That night Mohammad Qoli and another teacher from Talehbazli subtribe came to invite Borzu's family to a Talehbazli wedding. Borzu had apparently promised the use of his truck to collect the bride, but when the Talehbazli man saw its poor condition, he decided to wait until morning so as not to be stranded somewhere in the dark with an inoperative vehicle.

Returning from Shiraz, Khalifeh reported that Akbar and Hosain Ali were still in the midst of examinations. He had heard that of the fifth-grade students who had taken examinations at Round Sun, his son and Khanboa's had passed at high levels and were allowed to take qualifying examinations for the tribal boarding school in Shiraz. Khalifeh had also been in Isfahan where he had seen his nimsud partner and then his brother Jehangir. Jehangir's son Amanollah had qualified for entrance to the seventh grade in town schools, and Jehangir had said he wanted to stay in Isfahan for the autumn and winter and have the boy study and live with him there. Khalifeh stopped by Jehangir's tent to report the news to the family. The previous autumn Jehangir had migrated with them and then worked in Kazerun during the late autumn and winter. His plan to remain in Isfahan distressed everyone, for his family would not see him. Greater burden was placed on Asadollah as the only man at home. The next younger son, Fathollah, would be in school in Kazerun most of the year. Samarrokh was especially disturbed to hear that Amanollah would not migrate or be with them during winter. Caring for two small children, she depended on his labor and would now have more work herself. Listening to the discussion, aged Guhar asked Khalifeh about her "young child" (Jehangir, who was a grandfather).

On his return home Khalifeh was irritated to find that his newly hired shepherd had left during his absence to cut wheat for cash and had placed a young son in charge of the herd. Unable yet to hire his own shepherd, Bahram still herded his own animals. This father and son, as with many such pairs, were each independent. They could have easily combined their herds to create a single manageable one but chose not to do so. Bahram complained that when his father was gone so long, the camp was unprotected.

Long after midnight the noise of people greeting one another and talking filled Borzu's tent. Others in camp understood that the wedding party from Atakola village had finally arrived. The people had left the previous afternoon in a rented truck which had broken down near Wolf Hill. Able to rent only a tractor and an open-bed wagon as a substitute conveyance, they had moved along slowly and bumpily. They had not been able to come two days earlier as planned because the mother of a Persian landowner in Naqneh village had suddenly died. Out of respect for her mourning relatives, they canceled plans for bringing musicians to Hanalishah.

The core of the wedding party was twelve men and women, all Aqa Mohammadli and close patrilateral kin of the groom and bride. Hajji Boa came as the leader of the Qermezi families settled in Atakola and Naqneh. He wanted to impress people at Hanalishah, to demonstrate that the nomads who settled had already formed a strong solidarity group composed of individuals who supported one another. Hajji Boa's wife Goltamam, Borzu's sister and closely related to people at Hanalishah, was also along. Several Persian men from Atakola and Naqneh who were Hasel's friends came too. Two Persian tractor drivers completed the group. The groom-to-be had remained at Atakola, as was customary.

The entourage from Atakola, joined by people from Borzu's camp, climbed onto the tractor and into the wagon and were on their way to Mansur's camp before the sun appeared over the mountains. Lachin from Naqneh raced by on a mule he had borrowed from Falak. He had been inviting people at Hanalishah to come to Mansur's and then to Atakola for the culmination of the celebration. On the way he had collected one of the goats that Bahram tended for him and put it in the wagon; the goat was to be killed for lunch. Lachin and a few others had assumed that the noon meal would be at Borzu's (and Zolaikha had prepared for the event several days earlier). They especially wanted to impress the Persians by having the Qermezi headman host the meal. It did not matter that Borzu was absent; the prestige accrued would be the same. The rest of the entourage preferred to hold the meal at Mansur's. Goltamam, who had fought with Falak in the past, reported that Falak was ill and would be unable to host the gathering. Besides, she noted, the young women and girls who would help Falak were already in the wagon on the way to Mansur's. Hajji Boa also did not want the meal at Borzu's, and people argued together as the tractor moved forward.

Women individually and together sang sad songs about wedding days, many women crying. The pain of seeing relatives from whom they were separated and the pain of further separations to come were intense. The day's event—taking away a daughter who would never live at home again—evoked and symbolized other separations people experienced, and everyone was deeply moved by the songs and emotions. People from Atakola and Naqneh were sentimental about seeing Hanalishah and their Qermezi relatives again, and everyone talked then and later about the time when "all Qermezi" had been together. For people such as Hajji Boa who had purposely cut themselves off from their Qermezi kin, the return to Hanalishah was stressful. The Persian tractor driver asked the Atakola faction, "How many parts is Qermezi divided into now?" Fariborz defensively replied, "Only one." Mortaza quickly added that their territories were widely separated and the space at each one restricted. Goltamam shed new tears whenever someone pointed out the camp or tent of her relatives. No one came from these tents, but people there peeked at the passing vehicles. They would arrive ceremoniously at Mansur's in due course.

Women in the wagon trilled as they approached Mansur's camp where his two brothers Abul Hasan and Qorban Ali, as well as Ilmas, resided.

People there were busy straightening up tents and the grounds, and all looked sad. First Ilmas and then everyone else came to greet the entourage. Zainab and the bride-to-be Aftab were crying behind Mansur's tent. Zainab then led Aftab to her tent to be dressed.

Having brought all the supplies with them as was customary, the Atakola entourage immediately began to prepare tea and the noon meal. Several large bags contained food, gifts for the guests (candy, socks, handkerchiefs), and new clothes for the bride. Mortaza took charge by killing the goat and starting another fire. An objection one man had raised to having the meal at Mansur's rather than at Borzu's was that Mansur's camp would not have firewood, and cooking would be difficult with only animal dung and quick-burning shrubs to use. A headman, he implied, would have firewood. Marjan, the most powerful Qermezi woman at Atakola and Naqneh, directed the cooking. Aftab's mother Khadijeh and father Mansur periodically performed small tasks but otherwise sat sadly and talked with no one. The groom's party was in charge of the hosting.

Groups of mostly women and children came from all over Hanalishah to Mansur's, and women trilled to announce each arrival. Members of the wedding party greeted and escorted each one. Female kin seeing one another after a long separation cried together. Men filled half of Mansur's tent and women and children the other half. When the bride's mother's sister Khanom arrived she made a short speech about "daughters going away." She cried about Fatemeh, her own daughter married to Safdar who migrated and spent summer at faraway Row of Willows with Sohrab's group. Hajji Boa and Fariborz assured her that Fatemeh was well. By the time many women had gathered in the tent, they found they could not easily talk together or exchange news because men were close. They were more comfortable talking one-on-one and in small groups than in large groups where interlinking ties of kinship, marriage, and coresidence meant that topics of interest to them could not be discussed for fear of causing insult to people present. A woman asking with concern about her married daughter, for example, might be heard as implying that her daughter's in-laws—whose siblings might be present to hear the query—were not treating her well. Women sat quietly and talked with one another's small children.

Girls and young married women went to sit with Aftab in Zainab's tent. One made a henna paste that they spread on each other's hands and then on the bald head of a baby boy. Aftab's hands were already marked with henna from the previous night's preparations. A few women and girls sang, danced, and clapped. Aftab sobbed. Her father's sister Jeran with two small children went immediately to her side, and the four sat in a tight circle and cried together. Zainab handed Aftab her baby brother, and the two cuddled under the cloth that covered her.

Dressed in a clean white shirt for the occasion, Bahram had been asked to write the marriage contract required by Islamic law. He was the only person present who possessed the necessary degree of literacy. Using Mansur's own marriage contract as a model, Bahram copied out with care and neatness a new one for Hasel and Aftab. Mansur had earlier requested a guaranteed sum if Hasel divorced his daughter, and Bahram prepared to write the amount when Hajji Boa suggested a lower amount. Mansur agreed. Five Qermezi men (Mansur and Hajji Boa among them) and the two Persian tractor drivers (one of whom claimed to be a sayyid) signed the document or made a thumbprint in lieu of their names. No Ruz Ali brought the contract to Aftab to sign. He put ink on her finger and then Zohreh pressed it to the paper where he indicated. So thoroughly covered up that she was unable to see well, she smudged it, and he told her to be neat. (The next day or several days later a kinsman of the groom would take the contract to the town of Borujen where a *molla* would certify and register it. The marriage was then official according to Islam. No other religious figure played a part in the wedding. According to Iranian civil law, the marriage must be registered in a government office.)

Taking charge again, Marjan invited Khanom to attend the dressing of the bride. Refusing, Khanom said sadly that she would weep. Women and children went to the tent where Aftab sat sobbing and gathered around her. She was uncovered for the first time. When it was quiet almost everyone except very young girls wept. Khanom, appearing after all, sobbed loudly for her sister's daughter and sang a sad song about the separation of loved ones. Girls soon to marry wept into their hands. Younger ones sprinkled water, in which dried aromatic flowers and necklaces of dyed wild pistachios were soaking, on the bride's head and then playfully splashed everyone else. Marjan, Jeran, and the groom's brother's wife combed and braided the bride's hair. They separated off the front sections and put a cap on her, and then Marjan cut the bangs and sidelocks short. She gave the severed locks to the bride's sister to give to her mother (who would, in remembrance of her daughter, hang them on a myrtle shrub when she reached winter pastures).

Girls held a large cloth over the bride while she was dressed in new clothes. When Aftab's first skirt was ready, Marjan helped her to her feet, placed the skirt over her head, and then allowed it to fall around her ankles. Aftab stepped out of the skirt, and the ritual was repeated two more times, for what reason, other than "custom," no one could say. The fourth time Marjan fastened the skirt at her waist and placed two fancier, prettier skirts on top. She helped Aftab's brother cut open the neck of her new tunic (an act symbolically releasing her from girlhood). The neck opening was supposed to remain unhemmed until after the marriage. For sentimental reasons Marjan gave the bead necklace the bride had worn to her mother and then adorned her with the new pistachio necklaces.

Women and girls sang solos, and everyone wept again. Recently married women said they remembered how sad they had been when they left their own parents' homes. Older women were distraught because of the separation of families, and this particular year was especially distressing because so many people were changing residences and lifestyles. Simply being together again was a cause for emotional expression and release. Most of these women had not been in the company of many other female kin at one time for at least several years. So many life-transforming events had occurred for each of them in the interval, and they had not had a chance to share in or recount them.

Khadijeh sat quietly in the tent with her infant son during her daughter's dressing. No Ruz Ali presented the money customarily given to a bride's mother, and Khadijeh took it after a slight hesitation. Newly married women neatly folded sheets of fresh bread from her hearth and placed the money with the bread and wrapped them in a head scarf. Ordinarily they then tied the bundled scarf around the bride's waist, but Marjan suggested they wait until they had arrived at Atakola because it would be hot to wear. The bundle was temporarily packed with the dowry goods. The last garments the bride donned were a white head scarf, a pinkish-white flowered veil, and finally a purple scarf covering her head and face completely. The three coverings were pinned to the cap the bride wore underneath. She would remain concealed until after she arrived at the bridal tent many hours from now. A bride's face was hidden so no one would unintentionally comment on her beauty and thereby attract evil spirits who would cause harm. Marjan made a game of hiding candy, symbol of sweetness and good fortune, so that children would scramble for pieces. After most women left the tent, Khanom went to sit beside her sister's daughter. She put a hand on Aftab's head and told her not to cry anymore.

Lunch was served to the women, the men having eaten while the bride was being dressed. The tractor started up, and everyone was alerted to the imminent departure. Mortaza and Jeran brought Aftab to her parents' tent. The fire pit where tea was made had been covered with a bread-baking pan and a carpet. Mortaza led Aftab three times counterclockwise around the hearth, and each time she knelt, facing the tent, to press her forehead on the hearth. Her father leaned against the piled baggage inside and wept into his hands. The ritual symbolized Aftab's permanent departure and expressed her gratitude to her parents and their home. Mortaza then led Aftab to the wagon where she and her mother kissed farewell. Others helped her climb in and seated her on the small pile of baggage containing her dowry. A few people said good-bye. Her family stayed by the tent, and Mansur kept wiping his eyes. The groom's entourage boarded the tractor and wagon, along with many people from Hanalishah who wanted to accompany the party for a short distance.

With the invocation, "In the name of God," the tractor and wagon pulled away from the camp. A sad scene was left behind. Women knelt on the ground and cried. Khalifeh's shepherd led five goats in front of the vehicle, and as a reward No Ruz Ali gave him a handkerchief after searching through the baggage. The tractor stopped near Morad's camp, and Hajji Boa collected a large sack belonging to Ali to take to Atakola. Then he, Goltamam, and Hajji Qorban galloped by on horses to add drama to the departure. Lachin hopped off the wagon by a field to say hello to the Persian Sayyid Mohammad whom he had known when he used to reside at Hanalishah. The tractor could not reach Borzu's tent, and so everyone aboard who wished to or felt obligated (including Hajji Boa, Goltamam, and Marjan) went by foot to greet Falak, who had not gone to Mansur's. A few minutes later the tractor started up again, and people ran to catch up with it.

As soon as the wedding party was gone, Samarrokh told Falak what Borzu's sister Shahrbanu had said about Falak the previous day as Shahrbanu's family was leaving Hanalishah to settle at Atakola. Flying into a rage, Falak shouted and swore about Shahrbanu and added criticisms of Goltamam. She snorted, "If Borzu hit Abdol Hosain, and now Abdol Hosain and Abdol Rasul want to flee, so what?" She complained about Akbar, Khalifeh, and Bahram and then threw a knife into the ground in fury. This tirade took place in front of the adolescent girls of Hanalishah who had ridden in the wagon as far as Borzu's; they would undoubtedly repeat her statements to their mothers (and hence fathers). Falak asked Khalifeh's daughter if Borzu had ever fought with Qermezi, and the girl dutifully replied that he had not. Zolaikha made tea but the girls fled without drinking it, and Samarrokh had to leave with them so that someone could carry one of her two small children. Falak called and called for the girls to return in order to rectify her mistake but they continued as if they had not heard her. She worried aloud about what tales the girls would tell at home. So rarely did she have a female audience that she had gotten carried away. She was aware she had behaved improperly in front of this one.

Men who had accompanied Borzu to Isfahan to sell animals returned to Hanalishah by foot the next morning, and Falak and her daughters hastened to ready the tent and grounds to forestall Borzu's certain complaints that they had done no work the whole time he had been gone. At noon as Falak was serving herself meat stew, she heard a vehicle approach. Assuming that Borzu had returned, she uttered a curse and dumped the bowl of stew back into the pot. (She could not be found eating when Borzu arrived. She rarely ate in his or other men's presence.) The vehicle was, however, only a tractor driven by a Talehbazli man who wanted to invite Borzu's family to a wedding. He said he had heard that Borzu was in Semirom and might go from there directly to the wedding. Falak offered a cash gift and apologized that it was so small a sum. When the man had gone, she said she was ashamed not to have given a kidskin bag of butter. "An important family ought to have given more."

Aged frail Guhar, mother of Khalifeh, Ali, and Jehangir (and stepmother of Borzu), visited all her close kin at Hanalishah. She told each family that she expected to die during the winter and wanted to see everyone one last time. She was disturbed that her "children" were dispersing and afraid that they would not be present to bury her. After each visit an adolescent girl helped her onto a donkey and escorted her to the next tent. With poignancy women of each tent brought all their children to her to kiss as she departed. Guhar held the babies tightly and then pushed them back into the arms of their crying mothers.

Returning from gathering shrubs for fuel, Zolaikha and Zohreh joked that Borzu must be home if Haibat was actually shepherding again. He had done no herding during the four days Borzu had been gone. He had either left the sheep to wander on nearby slopes or found a kinsman to do short stints of herding. At her first opportunity Falak came to sit by Borzu to whisper what she had heard while he was gone. He was angry at her for agreeing to loan his truck to Talehbazli men unrelated to him when unsuitable conveyances, a tractor and wagon, had carried a Qermezi bride and a member of his own lineage. He also complained about Lachin having ridden his mule at a gallop all over Hanalishah inviting people to the wedding. He still lacked a decent mount for the migration and worried about his own transportation if something were to happen to the truck. Once again he was sensitive about others using his pack animals. Haibat, who in Borzu's absence had acted as if he were head of the household, assumed a humble demeanor and came to Falak's defense.

The last few nights had been cold, and people commented on the harshness of the colder, windy nights yet to come before they could begin the migration and enter lower altitudes. Borzu spent the morning with his herds, as he often did after an absence. He wanted to go to the Talehbazli wedding to restore his honor and prove he was a fair player in sports, but Kalhaidar had taken the truck to the town of Shahreza for repair. He could not arrive at the wedding on foot or mule-back, nor could he appear alone, without a Qermezi entourage. No one at Hanalishah except the teacher, who was Talehbazli himself and a kinsman of the groom, had shown any interest in attending. A gift would be required if anyone went, and no one wanted that needless expense. Borzu, Falak, and their children spent all afternoon washing wheat and filling sacks with barley. Zolaikha had just woven a new bag to carry goatskin water bags, but Borzu sewed it in such a way that it could be used to transport grain to winter pastures, at which time he would restore its intended use.

At the fire that night Borzu detailed his plans for autumn, winter, and early spring. He said he would migrate from Hanalishah to the plains south of Semirom shortly before he expected the military to permit the Darrehshuri to leave. He planned to travel at a comfortable pace and take advantage of good grazing and water when he found them. When he reached Wide Mountain near Arzhan Plain he would stay ten days, every day stalling the landowners and headmen by claiming his legally entitled twenty-four hours, by promising to move the next day and then not doing so, and then by moving a short distance until the ten days were over. He had hoped to remain there twenty to thirty days by paying local notables as he had done the previous year, but he had recently heard via a kinsman at Dashtak that an investor in Shahreza had already purchased this privilege for his own hired herders.

From Wide Mountain Borzu would travel to the mountains above Dashtak until the rains began. Then he would seek the shelter of his winter campsite at Dashtak until grass began to grow, when he would return to the mountains above to allow this vegetation to mature. Descending again to Dashtak, he would remain there until the beginning of spring. As an alternative plan, if rain failed to fall at Dashtak or fell insufficiently, he would travel toward Dugonbadan and either stay near there until spring and chance a migration through the Bakhtiyari mountains or return before spring to Dashtak and migrate by the customary route. He wanted a man to guard the grazing at Hanalishah from March on, but when he considered who that might be, he concluded that no one was available.

During this long discussion Falak, sitting to the side but not in the circle around the fire, dismissed most of Borzu's comments with snide remarks and scoffing noises. She muttered several times that he would do as he always did and would never alter his patterns. Borzu ignored her.

The next day Ali and Salatin deliberated their own plans. Concerned about their five sons, they worried that they were financially unable to send them all to school and unable to send all who finished five years of tribal school to school in town. Their accumulated debts of the past two years totaled $3,470 and were rapidly rising, and they saw no way of extricating themselves from the debilitating payments. Ali said he could not sell any more of his eighty-five herd animals, for he needed the few he had left to produce young. He had rid himself of most nimsud animals to avoid incurring more losses. When he tried to sell his horse and mule in Vanak and other villages, he was offered insulting prices. So many Qashqa'i and other nomads were settling this year that the market was flooded with pack animals. The only other form of capital in their possession was their woven goods, and all items were in use and necessary.

Ali and Salatin's plans for autumn and winter were complicated and as yet not decided, and they were disturbed by the uncertainties. They especially worried about the dispersion of their family members and the economic difficulties they would face. Their eldest son Akbar would not know for some weeks if he was accepted as a teacher trainee. If he was admitted, the program would pay his room and board, and he would receive a salaried job on his successful completion of the course. If he was not admitted his future was unclear. He would probably try to find work in Isfahan. In either case his wife Dayeh Soltan would live in Atakola village near her parents who had just settled there. Askar, the second son, was trying to switch schools from Kazerun to Borujen in order to be near Atakola and assist with cultivation there. Haidar remained in the Iranian army somewhere.

In a few weeks Ali, along with his youngest sons Dehdar and Sarvar, would migrate with the herd, a small tent, and minimal possessions to Dashtak. There they would set up the winter tent currently in storage in Kazerun. Dehdar would serve as shepherd as before, and Sarvar would attend tribal school. Ali talked about having one daughter old enough to bake bread, gather fuel, and collect water accompany them, but Salatin opposed the idea. The family decided that Ali, Dehdar, and Sarvar would migrate and camp alongside Bahram whose wife was Ali's eldest daughter, and she could bake their bread and help with domestic chores. After serious deliberation, Ali and his nephew Bahram finally decided to combine herds. Dehdar would serve as shepherd, which would save Bahram the expense of hiring one. During the previous months Ali and his brother Jehangir had talked about combining herds, and they had said that eventually only one responsible man (probably Asadollah) and a hired shepherd would migrate seasonally with the herd, while the other men cultivated and found work in cities.

Before the autumn migration and as soon as Akbar returned from Shiraz, Ali planned to take Salatin and their three daughters to Atakola where they would live in a rented room. Salatin's brother Hajji Boa would help to care for them. Askar would do agricultural work when he could, along with Akbar if he was not accepted as a teacher trainee. Ali remarked that he would settle at Hanalishah if ten other Qermezi families decided also to do so. He saw no point in settling alone and noted that it would be too difficult. His alternative strategy was to rent a house in Naqneh village and wait to see where the other nomads would eventually settle.

Other families planning to settle were also unsure about the arrangements. As time for the autumn migration approached, men frequently changed their minds about the details. Safdar decided to settle at Naqneh, sell his animals, buy a motorcycle (the first Qermezi nomad to intend to do so), and find wage work somewhere. Then he had second thoughts. In particular, he disliked the notion of doing manual, low-paid wage labor, and others often commented, "Safdar can't work as a laborer; his heart isn't in it." (Several weeks after others at Row of Willows migrated south, Safdar hurried to join them. He claimed he was forced to migrate for the sake of his camels. Other men planning to settle had long before sold or lent their camels; Safdar had kept his.) Several other men, including Nader, who had definitely decided to settle and had taken concrete steps in that direction also migrated at the last possible minute. They claimed they had not put aside sufficient fodder for their animals for winter. Aqaboa had chosen to settle despite others' protests that he still owned too many animals and lacked fodder to feed them. Qahraman, one of only several Qermezi men to have two wives simultaneously, planned to send the older, less-favored wife, minimal possessions, and his herd and pack animals on the migration with his brother and father and then rent a house in Borujen for himself and his second wife.

Many Qermezi men, especially from other summer pastures, came to see Borzu in his few remaining days at Hanalishah. Some wanted to coordinate their plans for migrating with his or at least discuss them with him. These and other men who shared Dashtak confirmed their presence for the forthcoming winter. Borzu wanted to be informed about others' activities, and men who made the gesture enjoyed better relationships with him than men who did not. Because some families were not migrating at all, the remaining nomadic families needed to form new cooperative associations for the migration itself, camps at Dashtak, and cultivation.

Falak's brothers Barat and Hemmat who ordinarily migrated with Borzu sent word that they would not leave until the first of autumn. They wanted to exploit the grazing still available at Narmeh and assumed that conditions in winter pastures would be poor. They were in no rush to migrate. Qasemli Qermezi men in the mountains south of Semirom and at Red Canyon ordinarily mingled with Amaleh and Kashkuli Qashqa'i nomads during the autumn migration and ignored government regulations about the Darrehshuri schedule. A few Qasemli families remaining in these two locations were planning possibly to migrate when the Qermezi group from Hanalishah passed by on its way south.

A few men including Morad discussed migrating through Bakhtiyari territory to the north and west and then finding winter pastures there or near Dugonbadan. Traumatized by the previous harsh and dry winter at Dashtak, they wanted to avoid a recurrence. Morad was convinced that, as a solitary household, he could find grazing in Bakhtiyari territory if he paid local gendarmes and landowners. He said he thought he could avoid securing government permission. When Bahram asked him if he would carry out this new strategy, he responded with a simple negative. The supportive ties of kinship and coresidence were too strong and too necessary to be abandoned. Falak's kinsman Hasan, who had migrated with Borzu since he had received pastures at Dashtak, planned to migrate through Bakhtiyari territory with his wife's brother who knew the route. Then he would find new winter pastures. He owed Borzu money that he was currently unable to repay, and he could avoid seeing him by migrating and sharing pastures with someone else. Borzu viewed Hasan's new plans as attempts to "flee."

Although the news did not reach Borzu until later, his brother-in-law Cheragh also planned to migrate by way of Bakhtiyari territory in the company of Mortaza Talehbazli. People noted that Cheragh was weak without the presence of his brother Sohrab (who was settling) and was unwilling to seek support from Borzu. "How quickly Sohrab and Cheragh acted upon the brand-new marriage alliance with Mortaza," people commented. After changing his mind many times about where to stay during autumn and winter, Sohrab finally settled at Narmeh with his brother

Darab. He entrusted his herd and pack animals to Mortaza. His son Ebrahim and his new bride (Mortaza's daughter) would remain at Narmeh until Mortaza had arrived in winter pastures, and then they would travel by bus to meet him. Ebrahim would supervise the care of Sohrab's animals.

Rakkeh Darrehshuri nomads were now poised at the edge of Hanalishah, and several elders sought Borzu's permission to camp by the stream at the base of the valley for a few days before they moved farther south. Borzu responded positively to the polite request.

Every family at Hanalishah was busy washing grain and packing grain and straw. Men stored in Vanak village the grain they would plant at Hanalishah in several weeks, after they had begun the migration, and they stored grain and straw in the storerooms of merchants and moneylenders in Semirom for use during the migration and for transport to Kazerun and eventually Dashtak. Women hurriedly finished their weaving projects. With ewes dry since midsummer and goats no longer producing much milk, few milk products were prepared anymore.

Because of his deepening debt and his problems in finding shepherds, Borzu finally decided to take an action he had postponed since arriving at Hanalishah. He reduced the number of his herds from three to two. The third herd had consisted of goats, which were less profitable than sheep under average environmental conditions, and he decided to get rid of most of them. New government regulations about goats, as yet not implemented, were also on his mind. Earlier in the summer he had sold goats in Isfahan and turned over others to his nimsud partners. Now he divided the rest among his close kinsmen Gholam Hosain, Asadollah, and Abul Hasan under an arrangement in which they tended the animals in exchange for their milk and hair. They were not held responsible for deaths and injuries. The three men had remained loyal to Borzu and continued to offer him services, and he rewarded them. Gholam Hosain had told him he wanted to add animals to his herd and was looking for a nimsud partner. Borzu saved him the effort.

Borzu still wrestled with another problem concerning his herds. For years he had physically separated his two herds of sheep during winter and had sent one of them near Dugonbadan with a shepherd he trusted, usually a kinsman. He was uneasy about Haibat's handling this herd for months without supervision; he was an opium addict and unreliable, and Borzu already had reason to doubt his honesty. After much deliberation Borzu thought of a solution, and he jumped up from where he had been sitting by the fire. The Lur pastoralist Mali, who owed him a favor for receiving pasture at Hanalishah, could accompany Haibat and the herd to winter pastures near Dugonbadan, Mali's intended destination. There Borzu could entrust the management of Haibat and his herd to his sister's husband Esfandeyar Shaikh. Mali could camp nearby as additional oversight.

Borzu faced one more crucial decision. After much thought he abruptly told Yadollah he did not need his services as camel herder anymore. As Yadollah sadly left Hanalishah with his small family, he commented that he did not know what he was going to do. He owned only nineteen goats and lacked pasture rights anywhere. He desperately needed paid employment. If he had left Borzu when he had wished, at the beginning of summer, he could have spent several months harvesting grain for cash or a share of the crop. Leaving now, near the beginning of autumn, no similar wage work was available.

Just before Borzu left Hanalishah he contracted with a Zailabli Darrehshuri man named Khalifeh to live and migrate with him. Khalifeh would plant and harvest Borzu's grain at Dashtak and Molla Balut for a fourth of the crop and for grazing rights there, and his son would tend Borzu's camels. Borzu would pay him no money. Hasel and Nader had cultivated for Borzu in the past, but they had just settled, and he needed new labor. No other Qermezi men were available.

Ali's son Akbar returned from Shiraz and helped his mother and sisters move to Atakola where they took up residence in the room of a house loaned by Hajji Boa. Later they moved in with Alinaz, another of Salatin's brothers there. Bahram invited Ali and his two sons to migrate with his family and share his tent.

Some Qermezi settlers, including Borzu's brother Abdol Hosain and his nephew Ayaz, found temporary manual labor in the sugar-beet fields near Borujen. Adult men and older adolescent boys shoveled beets, cut off leaves, and loaded beets into trucks for a daily wage of $1.30. Children who cleaned and piled beets all day received fifty cents.

Borzu's former shepherd Aqaboa accepted a lucrative herding contract from a Borujen investor after having rejected another offer. He had declared that he thought he could find a higher-paying job. Men were amazed and amused that his fortunes had so dramatically improved after he left Borzu's employment that he was suddenly free to weigh available offers and choose the best. He had been one of the most impoverished of the group. The investor provided his family the free use of a house in a village. The goats for which he was responsible remained in the village, which did not get much snow in winter, and slept in stables at night. He let them browse every morning and fed them fodder at other times. A skillful weaver who had always lacked adequate quantities of high-quality materials, Katayun was able to begin weaving a large carpet with yarn purchased against the carpet's eventual sale.

Borzu's kinsman Qahraman spent the last weeks of summer digging two hundred holes for planting apple saplings. He was one of the few Qermezi men to possess some legal claim from the Ministry of Agriculture to his summer pastures at Row of Willows, and he was attempting to further his hold on the land by establishing an orchard. Bakhtiyari Lur hired herders who shared part of these pastures and their Borujen employers filed a complaint against him with the ministry. Qahraman's brothers and Sohrab eagerly awaited the outcome, for they also wanted to establish orchards at Row of Willows. The government banned the use of these nationalized pastures for any activity other than grazing and collecting gum tragacanth, but many people, particularly the Qashqa'i elite and Persians, were rapidly planting orchards in summer pastures on land to which they held some prior claim.

Sohrab loaned Akbar his fine horse to ride from Atakola to Hanalishah to invite people there to the wedding of Abdol Rasul's son Ayaz to Cheragh's daughter Monavvar. Still angry at his cousin and brother-in-law Abdol Rasul, Borzu refused to go and denied permission to his son who wanted to take the truck with others at Hanalishah as riders. He did not send a gift to commemorate the marriage of his nephew and niece. Only Morad, Bahram, Asadollah, and Hosain Ali from Hanalishah attended the wedding. Morad and Bahram wept profusely there, moved and disturbed by the split-up of Qermezi.

During the previous month Abdol Rasul had sent emissaries to Cheragh and Sohrab concerning Cheragh's daughter. Cheragh had first said "later" and then "next year." Abdol Rasul asked Sohrab to ask Mortaza Talehbazli, who was at Row of Willows to collect Sohrab's animals, to visit Cheragh with him. Cheragh finally agreed, saying, "Because Mortaza came, I'll give my daughter now." The next day Cheragh and Senobar bought fabric for their daughter's new clothes, and four days later the wedding celebration began.

Men at Hanalishah carefully evaluated their herds one more time to check the fitness of each animal for the long migration and difficult winter. Many sold a few animals in Semirom. Most men traveled at least once more to Vanak and nearby villages to try to sell, exchange, and bor-

43. Nomads on the migration

row pack animals and to arrange to leave animals there for the winter. Unhappy with the current price of pack animals, Ali traded a young donkey for a small felt rug.

In the first week of September Borzu, his herders, and twelve Qermezi families left Hanalishah. People had expected a confrontation between Borzu and the men who had decided not to continue as nomadic pastoralists. But the principal irritants (Abdol Hosain, Abdol Rasul, Sohrab, Akbar, Qahraman, Hasel) were absent, and Borzu proceeded in his plans as he had done in the past. He did seem glad that as many families as these twelve accompanied him, at least at this stage of the migration, and men observed that he was strangely subdued. They had expected a hostile eruption from him.

The tensions that had built up during the spring migration had been partly dissipated in the summer because of the season's many distractions (conflict over pastures, culmination of pastoral and agricultural production, deepening debts, low animal prices, and weddings). As summer came to a close, however, the underlying tensions reemerged as people were forced to decide if they would continue with or abandon nomadism. These tensions were partly resolved when Borzu left Hanalishah, for he was finally faced with visual evidence of who was and who was not to proceed as in the past.

The first day's migration, to the next valley to the south, was customarily short so that people and animals could become accustomed to migrating again. The Tribal Security Force had not yet permitted the Darrehshuri tribe to leave summer pastures. As in the previous autumn, Darrehshuri nomads congregated in the plains of Semirom to wait.

Large herds belonging to urban investors descended on Hanalishah as soon as Borzu's group left. They ranged over the whole area to eat whatever vegetation had remained and then moved on to the just-vacated summer pastures of other Darrehshuri nomads. Borzu heard that thousands of goats from villages near Kazerun were browsing at Dashtak on vegetation his group would need upon its arrival there. Askar and other students in Kazerun expelled the herders but lacked the means to prevent them from returning. Borzu and the other men angrily complained that they were invaded from two directions.

Ten days after Borzu left Hanalishah, as he was idling on the dry barren plains south of Semirom, the newly appointed head of the Tribal Security Force announced a stunning decree. The military was prohibiting all Qashqa'i nomads from migrating until Mohammad Reza Shah had concluded his celebration of twenty-five hundred years of the Iranian monarchy. The event was to be held northeast of Shiraz at Persepolis, an ancient capital of the Persian empire and an area near the customary migratory routes of many Qashqa'i. The government planned other ceremonies at Pasargadai and the tomb of Cyrus the Great (559–530 B.C.), also by Qashqa'i migratory routes. Officials considered the migration of the Qashqa'i, whom they viewed as a military and political threat, to be hazardous to the shah and his many illustrious guests (including kings, queens, emperors, presidents, and prime ministers from around the world). Security would be extraordinarily tight even without consideration of the Qashqa'i. The government's solution was therefore to ban all Qashqa'i from the vicinity of the celebration.

Qashqa'i nomads were already spread out all along the migratory route. People close to Persepolis and Shiraz were subjected to searches by the army and then were ordered to move through the area quickly. The military forced all other nomads to remain where they were. Because Darrehshuri was the last of the Qashqa'i tribes to be given government permission to migrate, its members were still in summer pastures when the order came forbidding the migration. Almost all Darrehshuri people,

Qermezi included, ordinarily migrated south and then westward as they descended from summer pastures and did not enter the area near Persepolis. They passed by Shiraz at some distance to the northwest, unlike most other Qashqa'i who passed close by to the west of Shiraz after nearing Persepolis. Still, these different itineraries did not matter to government officials, who wanted nothing to do with any Qashqa'i until the celebration concluded.

For six weeks Borzu and his small group were forced to remain stationary at a site south of Semirom where they had been traveling when the military suspended the migration. Several hundred thousand Qashqa'i nomads were frozen in similar circumstances. Borzu's site was one of the worst of the whole migratory route, an area he and his group had always hurried through before. Little grazing and water were available. The weather grew increasingly severe as the days and then weeks passed. Harsh, chilling winds blew almost continuously, a condition inhibiting the sheep and goats from eating and drinking. Nights especially were difficult as the temperature dropped well below freezing and decreased steadily night by night. Water in goatskin bags was frozen solid in the mornings.

Seeking protection and security in this hostile physical and political environment, Borzu's companions clustered closely around him, uncertain what the future would hold. He had helped them to face similar crises in the past, and they turned to him once again.

Snow fell on Borzu's small group as the nomads waited for the shah to complete his celebration.

Appendix A

People Mentioned in the Text

Under Reza Shah in the 1930s and again under the bureaucratizing reforms of Mohammad Reza Shah in the 1960s, Qashqa'i people were required to take family names. These last names were placed on their identity cards required by law for school, conscription, and marriage. Borzu and some of his close patrilineal kin used Qermezi as their legal family name, and other people in the Qermezi group took or were assigned other names. Within a Qermezi and a wider Qashqa'i context, these last names were not used, and people often laughed about them. In the following list, the few family names mentioned belong to Persians, Lurs, and urbanized and state-assimilated Qashqa'i. If a last name is pertinent, a person is listed by that name. Members of the Darrehshuri khan family carried different legal last names; because these are not germane to this account, I exclude them here. I identify members of the khan family by the Darrehshuri name, which was how Qermezi and other Qashqa'i people identified them.

When government officials registered names, they altered personal and family names if they disliked them or thought them to be inappropriate or politically charged. For example, an official said Salatin ("Sultans") was too important a name for an unimportant Qashqa'i woman, and he gave her a new name. In the 1960s as part of a policy to subjugate and control the Qashqa'i, the government forbade Qashqa'i khans to use the title "khan." Any Qashqa'i person holding "khan" as part of his personal name (Ahmad Khan, for example) could not have this name officially recorded.

Qermezi and other Qashqa'i people chose Turkish, Persian, and Arabic personal names. Some parents named all their children after individuals in the *Shahnameh,* Iran's epic poem of pre-Islamic origins. Some used only Turkish names, while others used names of people notable in Islam, particularly Shi'i Islam. Many parents gave their sons Arabic/Islamic names and their daughters Qashqa'i Turkish ones. Some Turkish names were Persianized; some Persian names were Turkicized.

Some titles used to convey pilgrimage (hajj) or positions of power within the tribal system (khan, beg or baig, aqa) were also used as personal names. In this list, a title used as a title follows the personal name (Ivaz, Hajj), and a title that is part of a personal name is shown as such (Hajji Qorban).

All people in the list were members of the Qermezi group unless otherwise indicated. Their lineage or group of origin is indicated. I include the affiliations and identities of Qashqa'i people who were not members of the Qermezi group or who were associated with the Qermezi group but still retained their group of origin as an identity.

Four names on the list (Afsar, Dokhi, Golzar, Zainab) are fictitious.

Abdishah, Shaikh: Shaikh Lur, father-in-law of Gelboneh
Abdol Hosain: Aqa Mohammadli, full brother of Borzu
Abdollah: Qurd Darrehshuri, brother of Rokhsar
Abdollah, Hajj: Persian landowner of Atakola village, brother of Mohammad Sadeq
Abdollah Khan Kashkuli: Kashkuli Bozorg khan
Abdollah Khan Zargham ed-Douleh: Janikhani Qashqa'i, ilkhani of the Qashqa'i confederacy (1898–1902, 1902–1904), executed (1904)
Abdol Rasul: Aqa Mohammadli
Abul Hasan: Aqa Mohammadli, brother of Mansur
Abul Qasem, Sayyid: Persian itinerant healer
Afsar: Bulverdi Darrehshuri, wife of Borj Ali
Aftab: Aqa Mohammadli, daughter of Mansur, bride of Hasel
Ahmad Khan: Qasemli
Akbar: Aqa Mohammadli, son of Ali
Ali: Aqa Mohammadli, half brother of Borzu
Ali: reputed ancestor of Imamverdili lineage, deceased
Alibakhsh: Ipaigli Darrehshuri, son of Zulfaqar
Aliboa: Aqa Mohammadli, son of Kiamars
Aliboa: Mussulli Amaleh Qashqa'i
Aliborz: Aqa Mohammadli, resident of Atakola village
Ali Mirza: Salmanli Darrehshuri, Qermezi's ritual specialist
Alinaz: Aqa Mohammadli, resident of Atakola village
Allahyar: Qairkhbaili, son of Sardar
Amanollah: Aqa Mohammadli, son of Jehangir, fifth-grade student
Amiramanollah Khan: Darrehshuri khan, Ayazkikha branch, son of Ziad Khan
Amir'ata Khan: Darrehshuri khan, Gudarzkikha branch
Amir Hosain: Aqa Mohammadli
Amir Hosain: Talehbazli Darrehshuri
Aqaboa: Mussulli Amaleh Qashqa'i, Borzu's hired shepherd
Aqa Kikha: Darrehshuri khan, founder of the Aqakikha branch, deceased
Arghvan: Aqa Mohammadli
Asadollah: Aqa Mohammadli, son of Jehangir, husband of Samarrokh
Askar: Aqa Mohammadli, son of Ali, student in Kazerun
Ayaz: Aqa Mohammadli, son of Abdol Rasul
Ayaz Khan: Darrehshuri khan, Ayazkikha branch, brother of Jehangir Khan
Ayaz Kikha: Darrehshuri khan, founder of the Ayazkikha branch, deceased
Azarnia, Sirus: Persian man, director of the government's Office of Tribal Development in Shiraz
Azizollah: Imamverdili, son of Cheragh

Bahador: Aqa Mohammadli, son of Naser, student in Kazerun

Bahlul: Aqa Mohammadli, son of Khalifeh, deceased

Bahmanbaigi, Mohammad: Amaleh Qashqa'i, director of the Office of Tribal Education in Shiraz

Bahmanbaigi, Nader: Amaleh Qashqa'i, brother of Mohammad Bahmanbaigi

Bahram: Aqa Mohammadli, son of Khalifeh

Barat: Kachili, brother of Falak

Behruz: Ipaigli Darrehshuri, son of Ilmas, Morad's hired shepherd

Bizhan: Aqa Mohammadli, son of Borzu

Borj Ali: Bulverdi Darrehshuri, Abdol Hosain's hired shepherd

Borzu: Aqa Mohammadli, headman of Qermezi subtribe

Cheragh: Imamverdili, brother of Sohrab

Darab: Imamverdili, brother of Sohrab

Darab Ali: Kachili, son of Barat

Dariush: Aqa Mohammadli, son of Borzu

Dashti (Dastan): Gallehzan Qashqa'i, outlaw and rebel, deceased (1966)

Dastan: Imamverdili

Davodi, Mansur: Kazerun merchant-moneylender

Dayeh Soltan: Aqa Mohammadli, daughter of Abdol Rasul, wife of Akbar

Dehdar: Aqa Mohammadli, son of Ali

Dokhi: Qairkhbaili, daughter of Solaiman, wife of Mali

Ebrahim: Imamverdili, son of Sohrab

Esfandeyar: Qairkhbaili, son of Sepahdar

Esfandeyar: Shaikh Lur, husband of Gelboneh

Eskandar: Bulverdi Darrehshuri

Esma'il: Imamverdili, son of Sohrab, conscript in Iranian army

Esma'il Khan Soulat ed-Douleh: Janikhani Qashqa'i, ilkhani of the Qashqa'i confederacy (1904–1933), executed (1933)

Faizollah: Talehbazli Darrehshuri

Falak: Kachili, daughter of Rostam, wife of Borzu

Faraj Khan: Darrehshuri khan, Gudarzkikha branch

Fariborz: Aqa Mohammadli, resident of Atakola village

Farideh: Aqa Mohammadli, daughter of Borzu

Fatemeh: Aqa Mohammadli, daughter of Khalifeh, wife of Safdar

Fathollah: Aqa Mohammadli, son of Jehangir, student in Kazerun

Filamarz: Aqa Mohammadli, son of Khalifeh, fifth-grade student

Gelboneh: Aqa Mohammadli, sister of Borzu, wife of Esfandeyar Shaikh Lur

Geljahan: Qasemli (by association and through her mother), wife of Mohammad Hosain

Gharati, Mir: Amaleh Qashqa'i

Gholam Hosain: Aqa Mohammadli, full brother of Borzu

Gholam Hosain: Talehbazli Darrehshuri, supervisor of Ziad Khan Darrehshuri's shepherds

Gholam Shah: Qasemli (by association and through his mother)

Golabshar: Khairatli Darrehshuri, wife of Yadollah

Goltamam: Aqa Mohammadli, sister of Borzu, wife of Hajji Boa

Golzar: Darzi Darrehshuri, wife of Kordikhan

Gudarz Kikha: Darrehshuri khan, founder of Gudarzkikha branch, deceased

Guhar: Mussulli Amaleh Qashqa'i, wife of Shir Mohammad

Guhar Bibi: Janikhani Qashqa'i, daughter of Abdollah Khan

Hafez: Talehbazli Darrehshuri, Borzu's hired driver

Haibat: Chardahcharik Darrehshuri, Borzu's hired shepherd

Haidar: Aqa Mohammadli, son of Ali, conscript in Iranian army

Haidar: Zargar Darrehshuri

Hajj Ali: Shesh Boluki Qashqa'i

Hajji Boa: Aqa Mohammadli, resident of Atakola village

Hajji Boa Khan: Darrehshuri khan, father of Ayaz Kikha, deceased (1873)

Hajji Qorban: Aqa Mohammadli, son of Gholam Hosain, fiancé of Zolaikha

Hamrah: Qairkhbaili

Hamzah, Mashhadi: Kohba Amaleh Qashqa'i, headman of Kohba subtribe

Hasan: Kachili

Hasan: Persian itinerant peddler

Hasan Khan Kikha: minor Darrehshuri khan, Taherkikha branch

Hasel: Aqa Mohammadli, brother of Nader and Naser

Hemmat: Kachili, brother of Falak

Hemmat Ali Kikha: minor Darrehshuri khan, Bahramkikha branch, deceased

Hormoz: Basseri Khamseh

Hosain Ali: Aqa Mohammadli, son of Khalifeh, student in Kazerun

Hosain Khan: Darrehshuri khan, son of Ayaz Kikha, father of Jehangir Khan, executed (1937)

Hosain Khan Kashkuli: Kashkuli Bozorg khan

Ilmas: Ipaigli Darrehshuri

Iraj Khan: Darrehshuri khan, Gudarzkikha branch

Ivaz, Hajj: Bolgar Amaleh Qashqa'i, merchant in Jamalbaigi village

Ja'far Qoli Khan: Darrehshuri khan, Aqakikha branch

Jamali: captain in the gendarmerie, head of the Tribal Security Force for Darrehshuri affairs

Jani Khan: ilkhani of the Qashqa'i confederacy (1779?–1823), deceased (1823)

Jansanam: Aqa Mohammadli, sister of Borzu, wife of Morad

Javad, Sayyid: Persian itinerant peddler and healer

Jehangir: Aqa Mohammadli, half brother of Borzu

Jehangir Khan: Darrehshuri khan, Ayazkikha branch, Borzu's patron

Jeran: Aqa Mohammadli, daughter of Shaikh Ahmad, wife of Mahmad

Kafayat: Imamverdili, daughter of Darab, wife of Abdol Hosain

Kalayaz (Kerbala'i Ayaz): Kazerun moneylender

Kalhaidar (Kerbala'i Haidar): Semirom merchant-moneylender

Kashefi, Mohhi ed-Din: Persian industrialist in Isfahan

Katayun: Aqa Mohammadli, daughter of Saif Ali and Marjan, wife of Aqaboa

Khadijeh: Qairkhbaili, daughter of Taher, wife of Mansur

Khadijeh: Qasemli, daughter of Rostam Khan, wife of Sohrab

Khalifeh: Aqa Mohammadli, half brother of Borzu, former headman of Qermezi subtribe

Khalifeh: Zailabli Darrehshuri, sharecropper for Borzu

Khalil: Kezenli Darrehshuri

Khanboa: Aqa Mohammadli

Khan Mirza: Aqa Mohammadli, brother of Shir Mohammad, deceased (1917)

Khanom: Qairkhbaili, daughter of Taher, wife of Khalifeh

Khodabakhsh: Ipaigli Darrehshuri, son of Zulfaqar, Borzu's hired shepherd

Khodaparast, Hajj Nur Mohammad: Kazerun merchant-moneylender, member of Kazerun town council

Khosrow: Qasemli, son of Mohammad Hosain, Borzu's hired shepherd

Khosrow Khan: Janikhani Qashqa'i, leader of the Qashqa'i confederacy, brother of Naser Khan (ilkhani), executed (1982)

Khurshid: Salmanli Darrehshuri, ritual specialist

Kokab: Ipaigli Darrehshuri, wife of Zulfaqar

Kordikhan: Darzi Darrehshuri, Khalifeh's hired shepherd

Lachin: Aqa Mohammadli, son of Saif Ali, resident of Naqneh village

Lashkar: Imamverdili, son of Ziad Khan

Ma'asumeh: Naderli Darrehshuri, wife of Mohammad Qoli

Mahmud Khan: Bahmanbaigli Amaleh Qashqa'i, overseer for the Qashqa'i ilkhani, deceased

Mahtalab: Imamverdili, daughter of Darab, wife of Esma'il

Malek Mansur Khan: Janikhani Qashqa'i, leader of the Qashqa'i confederacy, brother of Naser Khan (ilkhani)

Mali: Shaikh Lur

Manizhah: Aqa Mohammadli, daughter of Kiamars, wife of Taqi

Mansur: Aqa Mohammadli, brother of Amir Hosain, Abul Hasan, and Qorban Ali

Manucher Khan: Darrehshuri khan, Ayazkikha branch, son of Jehangir Khan

Maral: Darrehshuri khan family, Ayazkikha branch, daughter of Manucher Khan and Naheed Bibi

Marjan: Ipaigli Darrehshuri, wife of Saif Ali, mother of Katayun

Masih: Bulverdi Amaleh Qashqa'i, outlaw and rebel, deceased (1965)

Mirza: Qairkhbaili

Mohammad: Aqa Mohammadli, son of Arghvan

Mohammad, Sayyid: Persian cultivator

Mohammad Hasan Khan: Darrehshuri khan, Ayazkikha branch, brother of Jehangir Khan

Mohammad Hosain: Qasemli, Borzu's hired shepherd

Mohammad Hosain Khan: Janikhani Qashqa'i, leader of the Qashqa'i confederacy, brother of Naser Khan (ilkhani)

Mohammad Karim: Aqa Mohammadli, son of Borzu, student in Kazerun

Mohammad Qoli: Naderli Darrehshuri, Qermezi's teacher

Mohammad Reza Shah Pahlavi: ruler of Iran (1941–1979), deceased (1980)

Mohammad Sadeq: Persian landowner of Atakola village

Mokhtar: Imamverdili, brother of Sohrab

Molla Qoli: Imamverdili, former Qermezi headman, deceased

Monavvar: Aqa Mohammadli, daughter of Beg Mirza, wife of Mokhtar

Monavvar: Imamverdili, daughter of Cheragh, bride of Ayaz

Morad: Aqa Mohammadli

Mortaza: Aqa Mohammadli, son of Saif Ali, resident of Naqneh village

Mortaza: Talehbazli Darrehshuri, father of Ebrahim's bride

Mosaddeq, Mohammad: prime minister of Iran (1951–1953), deceased

Na'amatollah: Aqa Mohammadli, deceased (1945)

Nader: Aqa Mohammadli, brother of Naser and Hasel

Naheed Bibi: Darrehshuri bibi, Ayazkikha branch, daughter of Amiramanollah Khan, wife of Manucher Khan

Narges: Qairkhbaili, wife of Shir Mohammad, mother of Borzu

Naser: Aqa Mohammadli, brother of Abdol Rasul and Morad

Naser: Aqa Mohammadli, brother of Nader and Hasel

Naser: Aqa Mohammadli (by association and through his mother)

Naser Khan: Janikhani Qashqa'i, ilkhani of the Qashqa'i confederacy (1920s–1984), deceased (1984)

Nasrollah: Bulverdi Darrehshuri

Nasrollah Khan: Darrehshuri khan, Aqakikha branch, deceased

Negahdar: Qasemli, deceased (1971)

No Ruz Ali: Aqa Mohammadli, resident of Naqneh village

Nurijan: Aqa Mohammadli, daughter of Ali

Oroj Qoli: Qairkhbaili

Parviz: Qasemli

Qahraman: Aqa Mohammadli

Qorban Ali: Aqa Mohammadli, brother of Mansur, Amir Hosain, and Abul Hasan

Qorban Ali: Qairkhbaili

Ramazan, Sayyid: Persian man in Ayaz Khan Darrehshuri's entourage

Reza Fuladi: Mokhtar Khani Amaleh Qashqa'i, Ziad Khan Darrehshuri's driver

Reza Shah Pahlavi: ruler of Iran (1925–1941), deceased (1944)

Rokhsar: Qurd Darrehshuri, wife of Gholam Hosain

Roqayyeh: Aqa Mohammadli, daughter of Beg Mirza, wife of Jehangir

Rostam Khan: Qasemli, short-term Qermezi headman, deceased

Rudabeh Bibi: Janikhani Qashqa'i, daughter of Abdollah Khan, wife of Naser Khan

Safdar: Aqa Mohammadli

Saif Ali: Aqa Mohammadli, resident of Naqneh village

Salatin: Aqa Mohammadli, daughter of Yar Mohammad, wife of Ali

Samanbar: Aqa Mohammadli, sister of Borzu, wife of Esfandeyar

Samarrokh: Aqa Mohammadli, daughter of Borzu, wife of Asadollah

Sara Bibi: Darrehshuri bibi, Gudarzkikha branch, wife of Jehangir Khan

Sardar: Qairkhbaili

Sarvar: Aqa Mohammadli, son of Ali

Senobar: Aqa Mohammadli, sister of Borzu, wife of Cheragh

Sepahdar: Qairkhbaili

Shahbaz: Aqa Mohammadli, son of Khanboa, fifth-grade student

Shahbaz Khan: Darrehshuri khan, Ayazkikha branch, deceased (1917)

Shahrbanu: Aqa Mohammadli, sister of Borzu, wife of Abdol Rasul

Shamayol: Imamverdili, daughter of Khan Ali, wife of Musa Khan

Sharif Khan: Imamverdili, deceased

Shir Ali: Kachili, brother of Falak, resident of Narmeh village

Shir Mohammad: Aqa Mohammadli, former headman of Qermezi sub-tribe, father of Borzu, deceased (1943)

Sohrab: Imamverdili, challenger to Borzu

Solaiman: Qairkhbaili, deceased

Soltan Ali: Kachili, resident of Atakola village

Taqi: Kohba Amaleh Qashqa'i

Vali: reputed ancestor of Qairkhbaili lineage, deceased

Yadollah: Khairatli Darrehshuri, Borzu's camel herder

Yar Mohammad: Aqa Mohammadli, father of Hajji Boa, deceased

Yuli: reputed ancestor of Aqa Mohammadli lineage, deceased

Yunes Ali: Kachili, the first known Qermezi headman, deceased

Zahedi, Faraj Aqa: advisor to Darrehshuri khans, resident of Round Sun (Mehr-e Gerd)

Zahedi, Habib Aqa: advisor to Darrehshuri khans, resident of Round Sun (Mehr-e Gerd)

Zainab: Aqa Mohammadli, daughter of Boa Ahmad, wife of Abul Hasan

Zain Ali: Shesh Boluki Qashqa'i

Zali Khan: Qasemli

Zeki Khan: Darrehshuri khan, Ayazkikha branch

Ziad: Kachili, resident of Hanna village

Ziad Khan: paramount Darrehshuri khan, Ayazkikha branch

Zohreh: Aqa Mohammadli, daughter of Borzu

Zolaikha: Aqa Mohammadli, daughter of Borzu, fiancée of Hajji Qorban

Zulfaqar: Ipaigli Darrehshuri, deceased (1970)

Appendix B

Figures

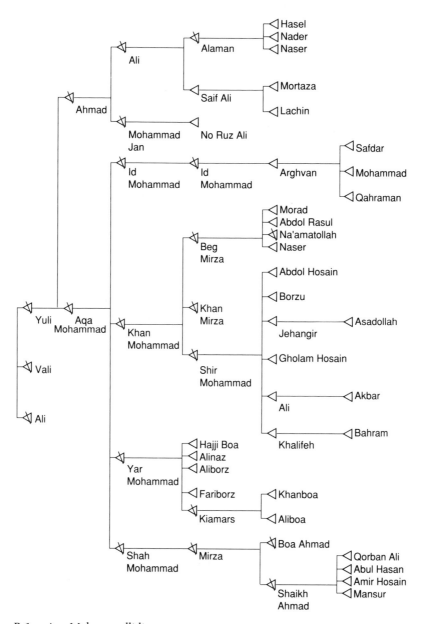

B-1. Aqa Mohammadli lineage

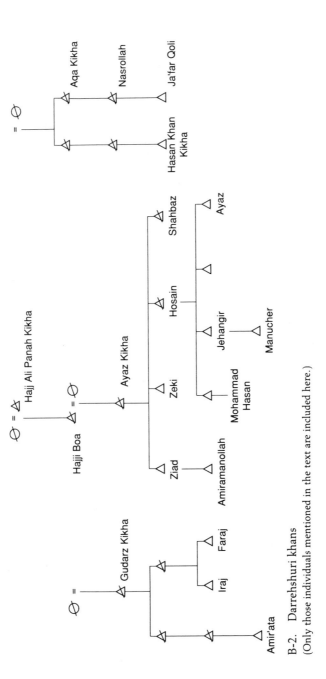

B-2. Darrehshuri khans
(Only those individuals mentioned in the text are included here.)

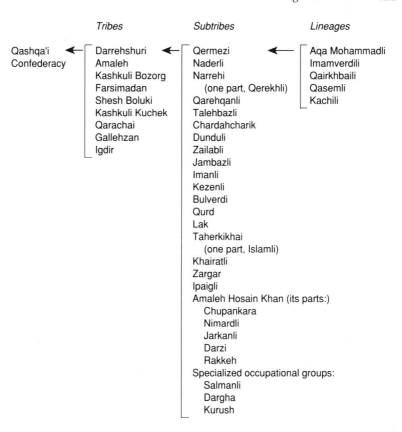

B-3. Qashqaʹi confederacy and its component parts
(Only those groups mentioned in the text are included here.)

B-4. Schedule of activities: August 1970 to September 1971

August	25	Leave summer pastures at Hanalishah; begin the autumn migration
	30	Goats no longer produce milk; end of milking and milk processing
September	1	
	5	
		Iranian military permits the Darrehshuri tribe to migrate to winter pastures
	10	
	15	
		Some men return to Hanalishah to plow land and plant wheat and barley
	20	
		Beginning of Autumn (23rd)
	25	
	30	
October	1	
	5	
	10	
	15	
		Some men travel ahead to winter pastures at Dashtak and Molla Balut to thresh grain
	20	A few men produce charcoal at Wide Mountain
	25	
	30	Finish threshing grain at Dashtak and Molla Balut
		Beginning of Ramadan (month of fast in the Muslim calendar)
November	1	
	5	
	10	
	15	
	20	
	25	Arrive at autumn pastures at Molla Balut; finish the autumn migration
		First lambs born
	30	Move to the autumn campsite in winter pastures at Dashtak
		Begin planting wheat and barley at Dashtak and Molla Balut
December	1	
	5	
		Winter rains begin
	10	First kids born
		Some families move to the winter campsite at Dashtak
		Finish planting wheat and barley at Dashtak and Molla Balut

	15	
	20	
		Beginning of Winter (22nd)
	25	
	30	
January	1	
		Begin to herd lambs
	5	
		Begin to herd kids
		Camels arrive from Famur
		Begin to feed sugar-beet pulp to sheep
	10	
	15	
	20	Feed fodder to lambs
		Plant second crop of wheat and barley at Dashtak and Molla Balut
	25	Finish planting wheat and barley
	30	
February	1	
		Forty-fifth day of winter; dye sheep with a ceremonial patch
	5	
		Camels born
		Feast of Sacrifice (Id-e Qorban)
	10	
	15	Lambs and kids nurse only once a day
		Plant third crop of wheat and barley at Molla Balut
	20	Herd lambs and kids with adult animals, after morning nursing
	25	
		Beginning of Moharram (month of mourning for Shi'i Muslims)
March	1	
	5	
		Ashura (tenth of Moharram) ceremonies
	10	Rain ceremony
		Milk goats for the first time; first milk for human consumption
		Some families leave winter pastures at Dashtak
	15	
		Lambs stay with ewes at night
		Produce the first yogurt
		Some men brand lambs
		Kids nurse only after does are milked

20

Beginning of Spring (21st); beginning of the Iranian New Year
Leave the winter campsite in winter pastures at Dashtak; begin
the spring migration
Lambs and kids born

25

30

April 1

5

Begin to harvest wheat and barley at Molla Balut

10 Churn yogurt to produce sour milk for the first time
Find the first wild artichokes

15

Separate kids from does at night
Herd does and kids separately until after the morning's
milking

20 Begin to harvest wheat and barley at Dashtak

25

Some men brand lambs and kids
Produce the first fresh butter
Begin to cure and process goatskin bags

30 Find the first mushrooms

May 1 Milk ewes for the first time
Separate lambs from ewes until after milking
Milk does twice a day; kids not allowed to nurse anymore
Produce the first dried curds

5 Some men shear sheep

10 Some men return to winter pastures to harvest grain
Horses mate; donkeys mate
Clarify butter for the first time
Some men brand lambs and kids

15

Milk ewes twice a day

20 Arrive at summer pastures at Hanalishah; finish the spring
migration; set up camp at the first spring campsite
Wash sheep
Shear goats
Gather and process wild plants as food, medicine, and dye

25 Shear sheep
Move to another spring campsite at Hanalishah

30

June 1

5

10 Peak of milk production; milk ewes and does twice a day
Some men take sheep and goats to Isfahan to sell

15 Harvest alfalfa and clover (first of three harvests)
Finish harvesting grain in winter pastures
Produce the first dried whey paste
Process goat hair for spinning
Merchants and moneylenders arrive in summer pastures to collect debts

20

Beginning of Summer (22nd)
Pay some debts incurred during the previous seasons
Shepherd contracts begin and end
Animal contracts begin and end
Some men take sheep and goats to Isfahan to sell

25

Produce the first cheese

30

July 1 Collectors of gum tragacanth begin work
Begin to harvest wheat and barley at Atakola and Naqneh

5 Milk ewes only once a day
Move to the first of two summer campsites at Hanalishah

10

Begin to harvest wheat and barley at Hanalishah

15

Begin the wedding celebration of Sohrab's son Ebrahim

20
25
30

August 1 Move to the second summer campsite at Hanalishah
Milk ewes once every two days; milk does once a day

5 Bring grain to the threshing grounds at Hanalishah
Ewes no longer produce milk
Rams and ewes mate; some men postpone this mating until the beginning of autumn

10
15

Wash grain; process alfalfa, clover, and hay as fodder
Begin to sell, trade, buy and board pack animals as preparation for the migration

20 Some Qashqa'i nomads begin the autumn migration
Collectors of gum tragacanth finish their work

Some men take sheep and goats to Isfahan to sell
Begin to feed dried alfalfa, clover, and hay to sheep
Milk does once every two days

25

30

September   1 Does no longer produce milk; end of milking and milk
processing

5

Leave summer pastures at Hanalishah; begin the autumn
migration

10

15

Iranian military prohibits Qashqa'i nomads from migrating
Some men return to Hanalishah to plow land and plant grain

20

Beginning of Autumn (23rd)
Rams and ewes mate

25

30

B-5. Autumn 1970 migration

August   27 leave summer pastures at Hanalishah [Hasan Ali Shah
{personal name}]

28 Gallehvar [Owner of Flocks]

29 Cheshmeh Ali [Ali's Spring]

30 Chah Arzhan [Well of Wild Almond Trees]

31 Chah Arzhan (no migration)

September   1 Chah Arzhan (no migration)

2 Mazar-e Shaikh Ali [Tomb of Shaikh Ali]

3 near Zarghamabad [Zargham village]

4 near Zarghamabad (no migration)

5 Arzhenak [Place of Wild Almond Trees]

6 Arzhenak (no migration)

7 Arzhenak (no migration)

8 near Kumeh [Settlement] village and Mehrak [Grapes] village

9 near Kumeh and Mehrak villages (no migration)

10 Tang-e Jelu [First Pass]

11 Cheshmeh Naz [Beautiful Spring]

12 Shah Neshin [Shah's Place; that is, the best place]

13 Aq Cheshmeh [White Spring]

14 Bairambaigi [Honorable Spring] and Qurri Dutti [Dry Hilltop] (two-stage migration)

15 near Dez-e Kord [Kurd's Fort] village

16 near Dez-e Kord village (no migration)

17 near Deh Bujar [Village of Farmers]

18 near Jamalbaigi [Honorable Jamal] village

19 Shur [Salty] River

20 Serenjeli [Place of Serenj {a plant}] village, Darreh Haman [Valley of the Witch]

21 Garmeh [Warm Place]

22 Rah Khersah [Road of the Bear]

23 *Autumn Equinox*; Chighah [Low Land]

24 Mashhad-e Bili [The Place Where Bili Appeared], Palangari [Place of the Leopard]

25 Palangari, Khorrakan

26 Tang-e Tir [Arrow Pass]

27 Javaherak [Little Treasure]

28 Tang-e Bezangan [Pass of the Victor]

29 Qurridan [Dry Place], near Baiza village

30 near Jian village

October 1 Tang-e Khollar [Pass of Green Peas] (afternoon migration)

2 Chehel Cheshmeh Ghalat [Forty Springs, near Ghalat Canyon] (night migration)

3 Aji Qanat [Bitter Qanat {underground water channel}]

4 Tang-e Sorkh [Red Pass]

5 Tang-e Sorkh (no migration)

6 Kherak [Pass], Jamal-e Pir Imamzadeh [Shrine of Saint Jamal]

7 Kuh Nar [Pomegranate Mountain], Kotel Dan [Dan Pass]

8 Qara Aqaj [Black Tree] River

9 behind Chehel Chesmeh [Forty Springs] village

10 Dasht-e Arzhan [Plain of Wild Almond Trees]

11 Dasht-e Arzhan (no migration)

12 Molla-ye Nari [Molla of the Pomegranates]

13 Molla-ye Nari (no migration)

14 Molla-ye Nari (no migration)

15 Kuh Pahn [Wide Mountain], Tang-e Khers [Bear Canyon] (remain there 26 days)

	16	
	17	
	18	
	19	
	20	
	21	
	22	
	23	
	24	
	25	
	26	
	27	
	28	
	29	
	30	
	31	
November	1	
	2	
	3	
	4	
	5	
	6	
	7	
	8	
	9	
	10	lower slopes of Kuh Pahn [Wide Mountain]
	11	lower slopes of Kuh Pahn
	12	lower slopes of Kuh Pahn
	13	Molla-ye Nari [Molla of the Pomegranates]
	14	Pol-e Hava'i [Aerial Bridge], near the end of the asphalt road
	15	near Gukoshak [Killer of Cows] village
	16	near Gukoshak village (no migration)
	17	near Gukoshak village (no migration)
	18	Haft Qez [Seven Girls]
	19	Haft Qez
	20	Sorkhi {name of tribal group} territory
	21	Pol Ab Gina [Mirror Bridge]
	22	Kuh Mahmud Begi [Mahmud Begi Mountain]
	23	Dasht-e Barm [Plain of the Pond]
	24	Dasht-e Barm
	25	arrive at Molla-ye Balut [Molla of the Oak Tree], in the foothills below winter pastures at Dashtak

B-6. Spring 1971 migration

March	21	*Spring Equinox*
	22	leave winter campsite at Dashtak, travel north
	23	Tikuh [edge of the mountain] (edge of Dashtak)
	24	Obidi [Water Willows], north of Kazerun
	25	below Davan village
	26	entrance to Tang-e Chugan [Polo Field Canyon], Sar-e Dokhtar [Spring of the Girl]
	27	upper reaches of Tang-e Chugan
	28	upper reaches of Tang-e Chugan (no migration)
	29	upper reaches of Tang-e Chugan (no migration)
	30	below Bul Hayat (Bu al-Hayat) [Father of Hayat] village
	31	Bul Hayat Aq Ara [White Valley of Bul Hayat]
April	1	Bul Hayat Aq Ara (no migration)
	2	Bul Hayat Aq Ara (no migration)
	3	near Kuh Pahn [Wide Mountain], by the asphalt road
	4	near Kuh Pahn, by the asphalt road (no migration)
	5	Kuh Pahn foothills
	6	Kuh Pahn foothills
	7	Kuh Pahn
	8	Kuh Pahn
	9	Kuh Pahn, Tang-e Khers [Bear Canyon]
	10	Kuh Pahn, Tang-e Khers (no migration)
	11	plain in front of Dasht-e Arzhan [Plain of Wild Almond Trees] town
	12	plain in front of Dasht-e Arzhan town (no migration)
	13	plain in front of Dasht-e Arzhan town (no migration, rainstorm)
	14	plain in front of Dasht-e Arzhan town (no migration)
	15	behind Chehel Chesmeh [Forty Springs] village
	16	Barm-e Sepid [White Pond]
	17	Barm-e Sepid (no migration)
	18	Bon Rud [River's Origin], across from Zanganeh village
	19	Kuh Nar [Pomegranate Mountain], across Qara Aqaj [Black Tree] River
	20	{place not named}
	21	Qara Chaman [Black Pastures], Kotel Dan [Dan Pass], Opardeh [Shallow Water] village (two-stage migration)
	22	above Giyum village, across the Shiraz-Ardekan road, Sar-e Sangar [top of the Trench], near Jian village, near Shul [Mud] village

	23	Dutti-ye Sangar [Hilltop of the Trench], Tang-e Bono [Pass of the Water's Source], near Baiza village
	24	near Baiza village, below Javaherak [Little Treasure], Bezangan [Victor]
	25	below Javaherak, Bezangan (no migration)
	26	Javaherak
	27	{place not named}
	28	Sulli [Muddy; Watery], Duli Khan {personal name}
	29	Bugod, Kakarum
	30	near Shekaft [Cave] village
May	1	Dasht-e Saran [Plain of the Flocks], Serenjeli [Place of Serenj {a plant}] village
	2	Dasht-e Saran, Serenjeli village (no migration)
	3	Tul-e Zarneh [Zarneh Hill]
	4	below Jamalbaigi village, above Jamalbaigi village (two-stage migration)
	5	Bar Aftu [Toward the Sun], near Dez-e Kord [Kurd's Fort] village
	6	Dutti-ye Bairambaigi [Bairambaigi Hilltop]
	7	Khosrow Shirin {shah and his beloved}, Cheshmeh Bairambaigi [Bairambaigi Spring]
	8	Khosrow Shirin, another spring {not named}
	9	Khosrow Shirin (no migration)
	10	Khosrow Shirin, Darreh Kuh Pahnak [Valley of Wide Mountain], in the plain below Mount Dena, Dutti-ye Majak [Hilltop of Wild Almond Trees]
	11	Qeli Yal [Hairy Hill], Zama Karosi {personal name}
	12	Saqezli [Place of the Gum Trees]
	13	Saqezli (no migration)
	14	plain south of Semirom town, Chehel Chah [Forty Wells]
	15	Chah Zahra [Zahra Well]
	16	Tul-e Farajollah [Farajollah {personal name} Hill], near Hanna village
	17	near Zarghamabad [Zargham village], hills of Banah
	18	Darreh Baqer Khan [Valley of Baqer Khan {personal name}]
	19	Chah Arzhan [Well of Wild Almond Trees]
	20	behind Gallehvar [Owner of Flocks]
	21	arrive at summer pastures at Hanalishah [Hasan Ali Shah]

Appendix C
Tables

Table C-1. Heads of households of Aqa Mohammadli lineage

Name	Nomadic		Settled
	Winter Pastures	Summer Pastures	
Khalifeh	Dashtak	Hanalishah	
Bahram	Dashtak	Hanalishah	
Ali	Dashtak	Hanalishah	
Akbar	Dashtak	Hanalishah	
Jehangir	Dashtak	Hanalishah	
Gholam Hosain	Dashtak	Hanalishah	
Borzu	Dashtak	Hanalishah	
Abdol Hosain	Dashtak	Hanalishah	
Naser	Dashtak	Hanalishah	
Abdol Rasul	Dashtak	Hanalishah	
Morad	Dashtak	Hanalishah	
Mansur	Dashtak	Hanalishah	
Amir Hosain	Dashtak	———	
Abul Hasan	Dashtak	Hanalishah	
Qorban Ali	Dashtak	Hanalishah	
Aliboa	Dashtak	Hanalishah	
Khanboa	Dashtak	———	
Arghvan, Mohammad	Dashtak	Row of Willows	
Qahraman	Dashtak	Row of Willows	
Safdar	Dashtak	Row of Willows	
Naser	Dashtak	near Atakola	
Nader	Dashtak	near Atakola	
Hasel	Dashtak	near Atakola	
Saif Ali			Naqneh
Lachin			Naqneh
Haidar			Naqneh
Fariborz			Atakola
Aliborz			Atakola
Alinaz			Atakola
Hajji Boa			Atakola
No Ruz Ali			Naqneh

433

Table C-2. Heads of households of Imamverdili lineage

Name	Nomadic		Settled
	Winter Pastures	*Summer Pastures*	
Sohrab	Dashtak	Row of Willows	
Darab			Narmeh
Cheragh	Dashtak	Row of Willows	
Mokhtar	Dashtak	Row of Willows	
Kaka Khan	Bakhtiyari	Pasmakan, Canyon of the Cow Herd	
Bahram	Bakhtiyari	Pasmakan, Canyon of the Cow Herd	
Gholam Shah	Famur, Sweet Well	———	
Gholam Ali	Famur, Sweet Well	Row of Willows	
Tarkhan	Seven Girls	Pasmakan	
Ziad	Seven Girls	Row of Willows	
Hosain	Seven Girls	Canyon of the Cow Herd	
Javad	Dashtak	Canyon of the Cow Herd	
Abdol Shah	Seven Girls, Dashtak	Row of Willows	
Vali	Seven Girls, Dashtak	Row of Willows	
Mahmad, Ahmad, Ali	Seven Girls, Dashtak	Row of Willows	
Masih	Famur	Row of Willows	
Khaibar	Famur, Sweet Well	Row of Willows	
Karim	Famur	Row of Willows	
Aqa Khan	Famur, Sweet Well	———	
Dastan	Famur, Sweet Well	Row of Willows	
Galandar	Famur, Sweet Well	Row of Willows	
Gholam Hosain	Famur, Sorkhi	border of Hanalishah	
Kazem	Famur, Sorkhi	Chardahcharik territory	
Bahar	Famur, Sorkhi	Chardahcharik territory	
Nader	Seven Girls	Canyon of the Cow Herd	

Table C-3. Heads of households of Qairkhbaili lineage

Name	Nomadic		Settled
	Winter Pastures	Summer Pastures	
Mirza	Sweet Well	Row of Willows	
Oroj Qoli	Dashtak	Row of Willows	
Qorban Ali	Dashtak	south of Semirom	
Hormoz	Sweet Well, Seven Girls	Red Canyon	
Parviz	Sweet Well, Seven Girls, Dashtak	Row of Willows	
Hamrah	Seven Girls	Wide Mountain	
Mortaza	Seven Girls	Wide Mountain	
Alhaidar			Red Canyon, Seven Peaks
Sharif	Sweet Well	Red Canyon	
Masih	Dashtak	Red Canyon	
Sepahdar	Dashtak	south of Semirom	
Ebrahim	Dashtak	———	
Esfandeyar	Dashtak	south of Semirom, Hanalishah, Hamqin	
Delavar	Sorkhi, Dashtak	south of Semirom	
Sardar	Dashtak	Red Canyon	
Mehdi	Dashtak	Red Canyon	
Shahriyar	Dashtak	Red Canyon	
Kordi	Dashtak	Red Canyon	
Ahmad	Dashtak	south of Semirom	
Mahmad	Dashtak	south of Semirom	
Mokhtar	Dashtak	Red Canyon	
Ziad Khan	Famur	Red Canyon	
Mohammad Ali	Famur	Red Canyon	

Table C-4. Heads of households of Qasemli lineage

Name	Nomadic		Settled
	Winter Pastures	Summer Pastures	
Musa Khan	Famur	Black Mud	
Ahmad Khan	Famur	south of Semirom	
Zeki	Famur	south of Semirom	
Ardeshir	Famur	south of Semirom	
Ziad Khan			Basht, Khan Ahmadi
Malek Hosain	Basht	south of Semirom	
Gholam Hosain			Basht, Khan Ahmadi
Kaka Khan	Famur, Sorkhi	Darrehshuri territory	
Mohammad Hosain	Basht	Hanalishah, south of Semirom	
Khosrow	Basht	Hanalishah, south of Semirom	
Ferdus			Dugonbadan
Kaikavus	Famur	south of Semirom	
No Ruz	Famur, Molla Balut	south of Semirom	
Qorban Ali	Famur, Molla Balut	south of Semirom	
Khaibar	Famur	south of Semirom	
Zali Khan	Sorkhi	south of Semirom	
Sorkhab	Famur	Black Mud	
Mohammad Shah	Famur	south of Semirom	
Gholam Shah	Famur	south of Semirom	

Table C-5. Heads of households of Kachili lineage

Name	Nomadic		Settled
	Winter Pastures	*Summer Pastures*	
Shir Ali			Narmeh
Hemmat	Dashtak	Narmeh	
Barat	Dashtak	Narmeh	
Hasan	Dashtak	Row of Willows	
Naser	Dashtak	Darrehshuri territory	
Hamdollah			Bear Canyon, Wolf Hill
Valiollah			Atakola
Manuchehr			Naqneh
Soltan Ali			Atakola
Sayyid-e Khan			Mehr-e Gerd (Round Sun)
Ivaz Khan			Mehr-e Gerd (Round Sun)
Amir			Mehr-e Gerd (Round Sun)
Panj Ali			Mehr-e Gerd (Round Sun)
Abdishah			Mehr-e Gerd (Round Sun)
Qorban Ali			Narmeh
Morad Ali			Narmeh
Mohammad Ali			Narmeh
Yusuf Khan			Narmeh
Va'ez Ali			Narmeh
Amirollah			Narmeh
Masih			Narmeh
Matahar			Sakkiz
Ganj Ali			Arzhan Plain

Table C-6. Camps at Dashtak (from north to south)

Camp	Household Head	Lineage in Qermezi	Other Affiliation	Tie to Camp
1	Hasan	Kachili		
	Naser	Kachili		
2	Amir Hosain	Aqa Mohammadli		
3	Ahmad	Qairkhbaili		
	Bahman	Qairkhbaili		
	Mokhtar	Qairkhbaili		
	Mokhtar	Imamverdili		
	Cheragh	Imamverdili		
	Mansur	Aqa Mohammadli		
	Abul Hasan	Aqa Mohammadli		
	Qorban Ali	Aqa Mohammadli		
4	Gholam Hosain	Aqa Mohammadli		
	Nader	Aqa Mohammadli		
	Hasel	Aqa Mohammadli		
	Aliboa		Mussulli Amaleh	
5	Barat	Kachili		
	Hemmat	Kachili		
6	Abdol Rasul	Aqa Mohammadli		
	Morad	Aqa Mohammadli		
	Naser	Aqa Mohammadli		
	Khodakhast		Islamli Darrehshuri	Shepherd for Abdol Rasul
7	Qahraman	Aqa Mohammadli		
	Arghvan, Mohammad	Aqa Mohammadli		
8	Borzu	Aqa Mohammadli		
	Aqaboa		Mussulli Amaleh	Shepherd for Borzu
	Yadollah		Khairatli Darrehshuri	Camel herder for Borzu
	Borj Ali		Bulverdi Darrehshuri	Shepherd for Abdol Hosain
	Hafez		Talehbazli Darrehshuri	Driver for Borzu
9	Ali	Aqa Mohammadli		
	Akbar	Aqa Mohammadli		
	Jehangir	Aqa Mohammadli		
	Alibakhsh		Ipaigli Darrehshuri	
10	Khalifeh	Aqa Mohammadli		
	Bahram	Aqa Mohammadli		
	Safdar	Aqa Mohammadli		
	Kordikhan		Darzi Darrehshuri	Shepherd for Khalifeh
	Mohammad Qoli		Naderli Darrehshuri	Teacher

Table C-6. *(continued)*

Camp	Household Head	Lineage in Qermezi	Other Affiliation	Tie to Camp
11	Khalil		Kezenli Darrehshuri	
12	Sepahdar	Qairkhbaili		
	Ebrahim	Qairkhbaili		
	Esfandeyar	Qairkhbaili		
	Delavar	Qairkhbaili		
	Sardar	Qairkhbaili		
	Mehdi	Qairkhbaili		
	Shahriyar	Qairkhbaili		
	Hamrah	Qairkhbaili		
	Khanboa	Aqa Mohammadli		
	Mohammad Hosain		Bulverdi Darrehshuri	
13	Masih	Qairkhbaili		
	Oroj Qoli	Qairkhbaili		
	Qorban Ali	Qairkhbaili		
	Parviz	Qairkhbaili		
14	Kordi	Qairkhbaili		
	Mahmad	Qairkhbaili		
	Abdollah		Bulverdi Darrehshuri	
15	Abdol Hosain	Aqa Mohammadli		
	Aliboa	Aqa Mohammadli		
	Naser		Chupankara Darrehshuri	
16	Abdol Shah	Imamverdili		
	Vali	Imamverdili		
	Mahmad, Ahmad, Ali	Imamverdili		Shepherds for Sohrab and Javad
17	Sohrab	Imamverdili		
	Javad	Imamverdili		
	Mizra Hosain		Kurush Darrehshuri	Camel herder for Sohrab
18	No Ruz	Qasemli		

Table C-7. Camps at Hanalishah (from south to north)

Camp	Household Head	Lineage in Qermezi	Other Affiliation	Tie to Camp
1	Borzu	Aqa Mohammadli		
	Aqaboa		Mussulli Amaleh	Shepherd for Borzu
	[Replaced by Khalifeh]		Zailabli Darrehshuri	Shepherd for Borzu
	Mohammad Hosain	Qasemli		Shepherd for Borzu
	Khosrow	Qasemli		Shepherd for Borzu
	[Replaced by Haibat]		Chardahcharik Darrehshuri	Shepherd for Borzu
	Yadollah		Khairatli Darrehshuri	Camel herder for Borzu
	Mali		Shaikh Lur	
	Mohammad Qoli		Naderli Darrehshuri	Teacher
2	Gholam Hosain	Aqa Mohammadli		
	Esfandeyar	Qairkhbaili		
3	Abdol Hosain	Aqa Mohammadli		
	Abdol Rasul	Aqa Mohammadli		
	Borj Ali		Bulverdi Darrehshuri	Shepherd for Abdol Hosain
	Khodakhast		Islamli Darrehshuri	Shepherd for Abdol Rasul
4	Haidar		Zargar Darrehshuri	
5	Ali	Aqa Mohammadli		
	Akbar	Aqa Mohammadli		
	Morad	Aqa Mohammadli		
6	Naser	Aqa Mohammadli		
7	Jehangir	Aqa Mohammadli		
8	Khalifeh	Aqa Mohammadli		
	Bahram	Aqa Mohammadli		
	Kordikhan		Darzi Darrehshuri	Shepherd for Khalifeh
	Aliboa	Aqa Mohammadli		
9	Mansur	Aqa Mohammadli		
	Abul Hasan	Aqa Mohammadli		
	Qorban Ali	Aqa Mohammadli		
	Ilmas		Ipaigli Darrehshuri	
10	Gholam Hosain	Imamverdili		
	Kazem	Imamverdili		
	Khodakaram		Ipaigli Darrehshuri	

Table C-8. Hired shepherds and camel herders at Dashtak and Hanalishah

Name	Affiliation		Employer	Independent Household?
	Qermezi Lineage	Other		
Qobad		Khairatli Darrehshuri	Cheragh	no
Son of Shir Khan		Dargha Darrehshuri	Gholam Hosain	no
Son of Abdollah		Bulverdi Darrehshuri	Mansur	no
Cheragh Ali	Qairkhbaili		Hemmat	no
Khodakhast		Islamli Darrehshuri	Abdol Rasul	yes
Behruz		Ipaigli Darrehshuri	Morad	no
Haibollah		Qerekhli Darrehshuri	Qahraman	no
Aqaboa		Mussulli Amaleh	Borzu	yes
Yadollah		Khairatli Darrehshuri	Borzu	yes
Khodabakhsh		Ipaigli Darrehshuri	Borzu	no
Borj Ali		Bulverdi Darrehshuri	Abdol Hosain	yes
Ilyas		Ipaigli Darrehshuri	Bahram	no
Kordikhan		Darzi Darrehshuri	Khalifeh	yes
Ali		?	Safdar	no
Mahmad	Imamverdili		Sohrab	yes (with brothers)
Ali	Imamverdili		Sohrab, Javad	yes (with brothers)
Vali	Imamverdili		Hosain	yes
Mirza Hosain		Kurush Darrehshuri	Sohrab	yes
Khalifeh		Zailabli Darrehshuri	Borzu	yes
Mohammad Hosain	Qasemli		Borzu	yes
Khosrow	Qasemli		Borzu	yes
Haibat		Chardahcharik Darrehshuri	Borzu	yes
Payedar		Zailabli Darrehshuri	Khalifeh	no
Koroqoli		Islamli Darrehshuri	Bahram	no
unknown		Lur Chupankara Darrehshuri	Khalifeh	?

Table C-9. Recently settled Qermezi

Village	Head of Household	Lineage or Other Affiliation
Atakola	Hajji Boa	Aqa Mohammadli
	Fariborz	Aqa Mohammadli
	Aliborz	Aqa Mohammadli
	Alinaz	Aqa Mohammadli
	Valiollah	Kachili
	Saifollah	Mussulli Amaleh
	Soltan Ali	Kachili
	Abdol Hosain*	Aqa Mohammadli
	Abdol Rasul*	Aqa Mohammadli
	Nader*	Aqa Mohammadli
	Hasel*	Aqa Mohammadli
	Aliboa*	Aqa Mohammadli
Naqneh	Saif Ali	Aqa Mohammadli
	Lachin	Aqa Mohammadli
	Haidar	Aqa Mohammadli
	Manuchehr	Kachili
	No Ruz Ali†	Aqa Mohammadli
	Qahraman*	Aqa Mohammadli
	Mortaza*	Aqa Mohammadli
	Naser*	Aqa Mohammadli
	Esfandeyar*	Qairkhbaili
	Jelodar*	Qairkhbaili
Abro	Aqaboa*	Mussulli Amaleh
Narmeh	Darab	Imamverdili
	Shir Ali	Kachili
	Sohrab*	Imamverdili
Borujen (town)	Mokhtar*	Imamverdili

Note: Other Qermezi families have been settled for many years in Round Sun (Mehr-e Gerd), Narmeh, and Hanna.
*Settling in 1971.
†Settling in 1970.

Bibliographical Essay

The political organization of tribes and tribal confederacies in Iran is discussed at some length by a number of authors, including: Garthwaite (1972, 1981, 1983a, 1983b) and Digard (1987) on the Bakhtiyari, R. Tapper (1971, 1979b, n.d.) on the Shahsevan, Irons (1971, 1974, 1975) on the Turkmen, Barth (1961) on the Basseri of the Khamseh confederacy, van Bruinessen (1978) on the Kurds, Fazel (1971, 1979) on the Boir Ahmad, Salzman (1971a, 1978) on the Baluch, and Salzer (1974) and Beck (1986) on the Qashqa'i. Barth (1962), Salzman (1967), and Towfiq (1987) offer brief general comparisons of the political systems of Iranian tribes. R. Tapper (1979b) examines local-level political processes in detail.

Anthropologists and historians (for example, Garthwaite 1977, 1983b; van Bruinessen 1983) discuss tribal leaders in Iranian history. Detail about specific tribal leaders in contemporary times, particularly local-level leaders, does not exist. R. Tapper (1979b, in press, n.d.), Brooks (1983), and Salzman (1973) examine the issue of authority and power in tribal society in Iran. Caton (1987) discusses the exercise of power and persuasion by Middle Eastern tribal leaders. The role of tribal leaders as mediators and brokers between tribal and nontribal society is the focus of Salzman's (1973) essay on the Baluch and of Beck's (1986) sociohistorical study of the Qashqa'i. Loeffler (1971) examines the role of a mediator in a tribal village in south Iran. Salzman (1974) provides a general discussion of leadership as mediation in the Middle East. Bestor (1979, n.d.) studies the role of a Kurdish tribal elite in Baluchistan.

The relationship between tribes and states in Iran and other parts of the Middle East has recently been the focus of scholarly attention. For Iran, R. Tapper (1971, 1983b, in press, n.d.), Garthwaite (1972, 1983a, 1983b), Digard (1979b), van Bruinessen (1978, 1983), Irons (1974), Black-Michaud (1974), Salzman (1973), Spooner (1988), and Beck (1983, 1986) examine the historical development of tribe-state relationships in the case

of specific tribal groups. Bradburd (1987) and Caton (1990) critique some
of these new studies. R. Tapper (1983a) provides a general discussion of
the issue relating to Iran and Afghanistan, as does Beck (1990) for Iran.
Helfgott (1977) raises historical issues with regard to socioeconomic patterns and tribal associations in Iran. Useful studies of tribe-state relationships for other parts of the Middle East include Dresch (1990b), Davis
(1987), Anderson (1986), Khazanov (1984), Lindner (1983), and Gellner
and Micaud (1972). A general discussion of the nature of tribes in the
Middle East is found in Eickelman (1989: 126–50) and Tapper (1990).
Tribes and state formation in the Middle East are discussed in Khoury and
Kostiner (1990). The issue of the continuing relevance of tribal identities
and affiliations in contemporary Iran is examined by R. Tapper (1988a)
and Beck (1986). Dresch (1984, 1990a, 1990b) and Lewis (1979) examine
this topic for the Yemen Arab Republic and Somalia, respectively, and
Gellner (1983) presents a general discussion.

Nomadic pastoralism in the Middle East has drawn the attention of
many scholars. For works on Iran with a focus on cultural ecology, Barth
(1961, 1962), Martin (1982b, n.d.), and Sunderland (1968) provide discussion. A general examination of nomadic pastoralism and cultural ecology, with examples from Iran, is found in Spooner (1973). Despite the
importance of nomadism in Iran, only a few scholars offer detail on the
migratory patterns and processes of specific groups. R. Tapper (1979b)
discusses the spring migration of Shahsevan nomads, Barth (1959,
1961:147–53) comments briefly on the Basseri spring migration, and
Swee (1981) outlines Kordshuli migratory patterns. Digard (1977) offers
an overview of the Bakhtiyari migration, and Cooper (1925; see also the
classic film *Grass*) presents a popular account. The current study is the
only existing detailed account of an entire migratory cycle. Despite
the title, *The Last Migration* (Cronin 1957) does not offer much information about Qashqa'i migrations. Irons (1974) examines historical and
political factors in the nomadism of Yomut Turkmen. Singer (1973) discusses historical patterns of tribal migration along the Iran-Afghanistan
border. Salzman (1971b, 1972) connects patterns of subsistence and nomadism in the case of the Baluch.

Most studies of nomadic pastoralism in Iran focus on local-level social
and economic patterns. Digard (1979a, 1987) discusses the social organization of nomadic pastoral tribes. Salzman (1975) examines local social
organization among nomadic Baluch. Tapper (1979a) discusses grazing
rights as they relate to social organization. Bradburd (1980, 1981, 1990)
describes and analyzes the economic patterns of a small nomadic group in
central Iran. Irons (1972, 1975) examines Yomut Turkmen social and economic organization. Lur economic systems are discussed in Black (1972)
and Black-Michaud (1986). Barth (1964) examines Basseri economics.

Afshar-Naderi (1968, 1971) and Fazel and Afshar-Naderi (1976) comment on economic patterns among Kuhgiluyeh Lur tribes (particularly the Bahmeh'i and Boir Ahmad). Safi-Nezhad (1966, 1975; Safi-Nezhad et al. 1969) has also studied economic systems found in Boir Ahmad and other Kuhgiluyeh tribal areas. Salzman (1979) notes the wider political implications of different kinds of economic relationships at the local level of Middle Eastern pastoral and nomadic societies. Pourzal (1980, 1981b) demonstrates political and social patterns among Koohaki nomads in southwest Iran. Digard (1981) and Roux (1970:239–44) discuss seasonal patterns among Bakhtiyari and Taurus mountain nomadic pastoralists, respectively; Digard (1981:240) provides a schematic drawing. Irons (1979) considers political structures among nomadic pastoralists.

Nomadic pastoralists and settled agriculturalists, as well as nomadic pastoralism and agriculture, have been vitally connected throughout Iranian history. These relationships are not well covered in the literature. The link between nomadic pastoral economies and urban, market, commercial economies is a related significant topic worthy of further attention. Irons (1975) is one of the few scholars to examine the relationships between pastoral and agricultural components of the same tribal group. Comments on this topic for Luristan are found in Black (1972) and Black-Michaud (1986). Martin (1982a, 1982b, 1987a, 1987b, 1988, n.d.) looks at pastoral and agricultural processes and decision-making strategies in small pastoral and agricultural communities on the desert fringe in northeast Iran. Lambton (1953, 1969) provides detailed information on historical patterns of land use in rural Iran.

Few scholars have examined in detail the process of the settlement of nomads in Iran. Swee (1981), one exception, discusses patterns among the Kordshuli, a tribe neighboring the Qashqa'i to the east. Qerekhlu (1989) summarizes patterns found among Darrehshuri Qashqa'i settlers. Salzman (1980) comments on Baluch settlement. Fazel and Afshar-Naderi (1976) critique Barth's (1961) model of settlement for the Basseri with information drawn from the Lur tribes of the Kuhgiluyeh region. Bradburd (1989) compares Basseri settlement with patterns found among Turkmen and Komachi pastoralists. The extent to which recently settled people maintain contact with their still-nomadic kin and cotribalists is not well examined in the literature on Iran. One exception is Irons (1975). Bates (1973, 1974) studies these issues for the Yoruk of southeast Turkey.

The detailed descriptions of livelihoods and economic processes in this book also provide information about ecology, technology, and material culture. Keddie (1984) points to the need for such detail. Digard (1981) describes the material culture of the Bakhtiyari. Wulff (1966), Gluck and Gluck (1977), and Bier (1987) offer detailed discussions of traditional technologies and techniques in Iran. Safi-Nezhad (1977) presents a comprehensive study of peasant agricultural cooperative work groups.

The current study, in the attention given to relationships among the environment, technology, and socioeconomic patterns, has importance for the study of history, archaeology, and ethnoarchaeology. In pioneering ethnoarchaeological studies in Iran, Hole (1978, 1979), Watson (1979), and Kramer (1982) examine the interrelationship of pastoralism and agriculture in southwest Iran and the relationships between settled and nomadic peoples. Horne (1988) discusses this topic for desert settlements in northeast Iran. Nyerges (1977, 1980, 1982) provides detailed information on the behavior of domesticated sheep and goats and their herders in the same area. Cribb's (1991) general study of nomad archaeology includes examples from Iran.

It is useful to place this study of a small Qashqa'i group within the wider context of nontribal rural society in southwest Iran. Studies on nontribal rural communities include the work of Hooglund (1982) and Hegland (1980, 1982, 1983a, 1983b, 1987), who conducted research in a nontribal Persian village just north of Shiraz on the migratory route of many Qashqa'i. Beeman (1986) explores social interactional patterns in another Persian village north of Shiraz. Kielstra (1971) comments on a Persian village south of Shiraz. Kortum (1976) examines historical and contemporary settlement patterns in Marv Dasht, northeast of Shiraz.

Political, economic, and social changes in Iran in the 1960s and 1970s are discussed by Katouzian (1978, 1981), Abrahamian (1982), Keddie (1981), and many others. Studies on the impact of these changes on tribal society in Iran include: Amanolahi (1985) and Black-Michaud (1974, 1986) on nomadic and settled Lurs in Luristan, Fazel (1971, 1973, 1985) on nomadic Boir Ahmad, Loeffler (1973, 1976, 1978) and Friedl (1989) on settled Boir Ahmad, Safizadeh (1984) and R. Tapper (1979b) on nomadic and settled Shahsevan, Bradburd (1981, 1983, 1990) on Komachi nomads of Kerman, Stober (1979, 1988) on Afshar nomads of Kerman, and Beck (1981a, 1981b, 1986:249–347) on nomadic and settled Qashqa'i. Land reform, a major agent of change in rural Iran, is examined by Lambton (1969) and Hooglund (1982). Goodell (1975, 1986) discusses the impact of the modernizing state on two types of nontribal villages in Khuzistan province. Bill (1988) provides a comprehensive account of the intensifying relationship between Iran and the United States during the 1960s and 1970s.

The few existing accounts of the impact on tribal society of the 1978–1979 Iranian revolution and the subsequent establishment of the Islamic Republic of Iran (both events following the historical period covered in this book) include: Harrison (1981), Loeffler (1982, 1988), van Bruinessen (1986), Fazel (1985), Friedl (1989), anonymous authors (1982, 1983a), and Beck (1980b, 1980c, 1986:296–347). Since the revolution, Iranian scholars have published on specific tribal groups in Iran and on general topics concerning tribal and nomadic pastoral society. Scholars publishing in Iran have received government support in these efforts, a collaboration or at least nominal approval that invites further investigation. Why officials of the Islamic Republic were interested in the 1980s in tribes and nomads in Iran deserves study. Works recently published in Persian in Iran include Qashqa'i (1986), Bayat (1986), Bahmanbaigi (1989), and Parham (1983) on the Qashqa'i; Goli (1987) on the Turkmen; Shahshahani (1987) on Mamassani Lurs; and Karimi (1987) on the Bakhtiyari. General works include Amanolahi (1981); Afshar Sistani (1987); Iran, Tehran University (1987); Safi-Nezhad (1989); and an anonymous editor (1983b). Chapters in Afshar Sistani (1987, vol. 2, 615–52) and Safi-Nezhad (1989:59–101) concern the Qashqa'i. Kasraian (1988) offers photographs taken in the 1980s of nomads, including the Qashqa'i.

The role of women in tribal and nomadic pastoral societies in Iran has been the topic of some studies. For tribally organized nomadic pastoralists, they include N. Tapper (1978, 1980, n.d.) on the Shahsevan, Fazel (1977) on the Boir Ahmad, and Beck (1978) on the Qashqa'i. For settled tribal people, studies include Friedl (1978, 1980, 1981, 1983, 1989) on the Boir Ahmad and Shahshahani (1986a, 1986b, 1987) and Wright (1978, 1981) on the Mamassani. Oehler (in press) offers a fictional account of a woman of the Bakhtiyari tribal elite; the historical and sociocultural context is factual.

In this account I include some information about the religious beliefs and practices of members of a small Qashqa'i group. Other studies on Iran offer a more systematic treatment of Islam and its universal and local expressions than I have provided. Loeffler (1988) studies local expressions of Islam in a tribal village in south Iran in both the prerevolutionary and postrevolutionary periods. Other discussions of Islam in tribal societies in Iran are found in R. Tapper (1984), van Bruinessen (1978), Friedl (1980), Bradburd (1984), and Pourzal (1981a). Hegland (1980, 1983a, 1983b, 1987) details the resurgence of Islam in the late 1970s in a nontribal village north of Shiraz. Betteridge (1980, 1983, 1985) studies the importance of pilgrimage for Shi'i Iranians and describes Shah-e Cheragh, the major shrine in Shiraz frequented by some Qashqa'i. Various facets of the commemoration of the martyrdom of Imam Hosain during the month of Moharram are presented in Chelkowski (1979).

Although Iran contains many different tribal, ethnic, national-minority, religious, and linguistic groups, few anthropological accounts of intergroup relationships exist. Rosman and Rubel (1976) present a general essay on interethnic exchange. Beck (1982) describes patterns of asymmetrical social exchange between Qashqa'i nomadic pastoralists and urban Persians. No study of intertribal relationships (such as between the Bakhtiyari and the Qashqa'i, for example) in Iran exists. Studies on ethnic identities and processes among tribally organized nomadic pastoralists in Iran include R. Tapper (1988a, 1988b), Singer (1982), Spooner (1983, 1988), and Beck (1986). Helfgott (1980), Keddie (1983, 1986), and Higgins (1984, 1986) discuss national minorities in Iran.

Sources on Qashqa'i history include Oberling (1974), Qashqa'i (1986), Bayat (1986), and Beck (1986). Cronin (1957) offers a fictionalized, partly accurate account of the paramount Qashqa'i khans' stand against the Iranian government in 1953. Works discussing Qashqa'i society in the 1960s and 1970s include Barker (1981), Bahmanbaigi (1971, 1989), and Beck (1980a, 1980b, 1981a, 1981b, 1986:249–95, in press). Beck (1986:296–347) examines the impact on the Qashqa'i of the Iranian revolution and the establishment of the Islamic Republic of Iran. Amir-Moez Qashqai (1985) describes Qashqa'i material culture and technology in general terms, and Paiman (1968) discusses economic and sociocultural systems. Works on the introduction of formal education to the Qashqa'i include Hendershot (1964), Shafii et al. (1977), and Beck (1986:271–85). Salzer (1974) discusses the social organization of the Kashkuli Kuchek, a small Qashqa'i tribe.

The weaving of the Qashqa'i has drawn the attention of scholars and others. Accounts of Qashqa'i weaving are found in Amir-Moez Qashqai (1985), Parham (1985), Allgrove (1978), Gluck and Gluck (1977:289–344), Bier (1987:317–24), and a publication of the University of Manchester's Whitworth Art Gallery (1976). Many publications catering to the interests of dealers and collectors of woven goods contain fanciful and incorrect information about the origin, production, and symbolism of Qashqa'i woven goods. Hillmann (1984) presents a survey of carpets and weaving in Iran, and Spooner (1986) and Helfgott (1987) offer general comments on the development of the carpet industry and trade in Iran.

Attention in anthropology and other social sciences has recently been given to critiques and new styles of ethnographic writing. Clifford and Marcus (1986) and many other authors provide a critical appraisal of different styles. Fernea's *Guests of the Sheik* (1965) was one of the first works on Middle Eastern society that took a nontraditional yet scholarly and objective approach to explaining social and cultural patterns. A sensitively written portrayal of people in a tribal village in south Iraq, the book remains, many years after its publication, well appreciated by teachers and others. Biography is another approach that has gained in importance. Crapanzano (1980) presents an account of a spirit-possessed subproletarian tilemaker in Morocco, while Munson (1984) recounts the lives of members of an urban Moroccan family. Mottahedeh (1985), a historian, adroitly mingles the biography of a fictionalized molla in Iran with an insightful analysis of Iranian culture and society. Abu-Lughod (1986) accounts for the power of oral poetry in the lives of settled bedouin women in Egypt. Authors of the best of these and other new works effectively move the discussion among the levels of the individual and family, a historically specified political economic context, and patterns and processes found in culture and society as a whole. They also often offer the opportunity for Middle Eastern people to speak for themselves.

Bibliography

Abrahamian, Ervand
  1982   Iran Between Two Revolutions. Princeton: Princeton University Press.

Abu-Lughod, Lila
  1986   Veiled Sentiments: Honor and Poetry in a Bedouin Society. Berkeley: University of California Press.

Afshar-Naderi, Nader
  1986   Il-e Bahmeh'i (Bahmeh'i tribe). Report no. 7. Tehran: Institute for Social Studies and Research, Tehran University.
  1971   The Settlement of Nomads and Its Social and Economic Implications. Tehran: Institute for Social Studies and Research, Tehran University.

Afshar Sistani, Iraj
  1987   Ilha, chador neshinan va tavayef-e ashayeri-ye Iran (Confederacies, nomads, and nomadic tribes of Iran). 2 vols. Tehran: Homa.

Allgrove, Joan
  1978   The Qashqa'i. In Yoruk: The Nomadic Weaving Tradition of the Middle East. Anthony Landreau, ed. Pittsburgh: Museum of Art, Carnegie Institute.

Amanolahi, Sekandar
  1981   Kuch neshini dar Iran (Pastoral nomadism in Iran). Tehran: BTNK.
  1985   The Lurs of Iran. Cultural Survival Quarterly 9(1):65–69.

Amir-Moez Qashqai, Yassaman
  1985   Quelques aspects d'une culture matérielle: techniques des pasteurs nomades Qasqayi. Ph.D. dissertation, Ethnologie, Ecole des hautes études en sciences sociales, Sorbonne, Paris. 2 vols.

Anderson, Lisa
  1986   The State and Social Transformation in Tunisia and Libya, 1830–1980. Princeton: Princeton University Press.

Anonymous
1982   Report from an Iranian Village. MERIP Reports 12(3):26–29.
Anonymous
1983a   Current Political Attitudes in an Iranian Village. Iranian Studies
            16(1–2):3–29.
Anonymous, ed.
1983b   Ilat va ashayer (Tribes and nomads). Tehran: Agah.
Bahmanbaigi, Mohammad
1971   Qashqa'i: Hardy Shepherds of Iran's Zagros Mountains Build a
            Future Through Tent-School Education. In Nomads of the World.
            Washington, D.C.: National Geographic Society.
1989   Bokhara-ye man, il-e man (My Bukhara, my tribe). Tehran:
            Agah.
Barker, Paul
1981   Tent Schools of the Qashqa'i: A Paradox of Local Initiative and
            State Control. In Modern Iran: The Dialectics of Continuity and
            Change. Michael Bonine and Nikki Keddie, eds. Albany: State
            University of New York Press.
Barth, Fredrik
1959   The Land Use Pattern of Migratory Tribes of South Persia. Norsk
            Geografisk Tidsskrift 17:1–11.
1961   Nomads of South Persia: The Basseri Tribe of the Khamseh Con-
            federacy. London: Allen and Unwin.
1962   Nomadism in the Mountain and Plateau Areas of South West
            Asia. In Problems of the Arid Zone. Paris: UNESCO.
1964   Capital, Investment and the Social Structure of a Pastoral Nomad
            Group in South Persia. In Capital, Saving and Credit in Peasant
            Societies. Raymond Firth and B. S. Yamey, eds. Chicago: Aldine.
Bates, Daniel
1973   Nomads and Farmers: A Study of the Yoruk of Southeastern
            Turkey. Anthropological Paper no. 52. University of Michigan
            Museum of Anthropology. Ann Arbor: University of Michigan.
1974   Shepherd Becomes Farmer: A Study of Sedentarization and Social
            Change in Southeastern Turkey. In Turkey: Geographical and So-
            cial Perspectives. Peter Benedict, Erol Tumertekin, and Fatma
            Mansur, eds. Leiden, Netherlands: E. J. Brill.
Bayat, Kaveh
1986   Shurash ashayer-e Fars, 1307–1309 (The uprising of the tribes of
            Fars, 1928–1930). Tehran: Zarin.
Beck, Lois
1978   Women Among Qashqa'i Nomadic Pastoralists in Iran. In
            Women in the Muslim World. Lois Beck and Nikki Keddie, eds.
            Cambridge: Harvard University Press.
1980a   Herd Owners and Hired Shepherds: The Qashqa'i of Iran. Eth-
            nology 19(3):327–51.
1980b   Revolutionary Iran and Its Tribal Peoples. MERIP Reports
            10(4):14–20.

1980c	Tribe and State in Revolutionary Iran: The Return of the Qashqa'i Khans. Iranian Studies 13(1–4):215–55.
1981a	Economic Transformations Among Qashqa'i Nomads, 1962–1978. *In* Modern Iran: The Dialectics of Continuity and Change. Michael Bonine and Nikki Keddie, eds. Albany: State University of New York Press.
1981b	Government Policy and Pastoral Land Use in Southwest Iran. Journal of Arid Environments 4(3):253–67.
1982	Nomads and Urbanites: Involuntary Hosts and Uninvited Guests. Middle Eastern Studies 18(4):426–44.
1983	Iran and the Qashqai Tribal Confederacy. *In* The Conflict of Tribe and State in Iran and Afghanistan. Richard Tapper, ed. London: Croom Helm.
1986	The Qashqa'i of Iran. New Haven and London: Yale University Press.
1990	Tribes and the State in Nineteenth- and Twentieth-Century Iran. *In* Tribes and State Formation in the Middle East. Philip Khoury and Joseph Kostiner, eds. Berkeley: University of California Press.
in press	Rostam: Qashqa'i Rebel. *In* Struggle and Survival in the Modern Middle East. Edmund Burke III, ed. Berkeley: University of California Press.

Beeman, William O.

1986	Language, Status, and Power in Iran. Bloomington: Indiana University Press.

Bestor, Jane

1979	The Kurds of Iranian Baluchistan: A Regional Elite. Master's thesis, Department of Anthropology, McGill University.
n.d.	The Kurds of Iranian Baluchistan. Naples: Committee on Baluchistan Studies, University of Naples. In preparation.

Betteridge, Anne

1980	The Controversial Vows of Urban Muslim Women in Iran. *In* Unspoken Worlds: Women's Religious Lives in Non-Western Cultures. Nancy Falk and Rita Gross, eds. San Francisco: Harper and Row.
1983	Muslim Women and Shrines in Shiraz. *In* Mormons and Muslims: Spiritual Foundations and Modern Manifestations. Spencer Palmer, ed. Provo, Utah: Religious Studies Center, Brigham Young University.
1985	Ziarat: Pilgrimage to the Shrines of Shiraz. Ph.D. dissertation, Department of Anthropology, University of Chicago.

Bier, Carol, ed.

1987	Woven from the Soul, Spun from the Heart: Textile Arts of Safavid and Qajar Iran, Sixteenth-Nineteenth Centuries. Washington, D.C.: The Textile Museum.

Bill, James
1988   The Eagle and the Lion: The Tragedy of American-Iranian Relations. New Haven: Yale University Press.

Black, Jacob
1972   Tyranny as a Strategy for Survival in an "Egalitarian" Society: Luri Facts Versus an Anthropological Mystique. Man 7(4):614–34.

Black-Michaud, Jacob
1974   An Ethnographic and Ecological Survey of Luristan, Western Persia: Modernization in a Nomadic Pastoral Society. Middle Eastern Studies 10(2):210–28.
1986   Sheep and Land: The Economics of Power in a Tribal Society. Cambridge: Cambridge University Press.

Bradburd, Daniel
1980   Never Give a Shepherd an Even Break: Class and Labor Among the Komachi. American Ethnologist 7(4):603–20.
1981   Size and Success: Komachi Adaptation to a Changing Iran. In Modern Iran: The Dialectics of Continuity and Change. Michael Bonine and Nikki Keddie, eds. Albany: State University of New York Press.
1983   National Conditions and Local-Level Political Structures: Patronage in Prerevolutionary Iran. American Ethnologist 10(1):23–40.
1984   Ritual and Southwest Asian Pastoralists: The Implications of the Komachi Case. Journal of Anthropological Research 40(3):380–93.
1987   Tribe, State, and History in Southwest Asia: A Review. Nomadic Peoples 23:57–71.
1989   Producing Their Fates: Why Poor Basseri Settled but Poor Komachi and Yomut Did Not. American Ethnologist 16(3):502–17.
1990   Ambiguous Relations: Kin, Class, and Conflict Among Komachi Pastoralists. Washington, D.C.: Smithsonian Institution Press.

Brooks, David
1983   The Enemy Within: Limitations on Leadership in the Bakhtiari. In The Conflict of Tribe and State in Iran and Afghanistan. Richard Tapper, ed. London: Croom Helm.

Caton, Steven
1987   Power, Persuasion, and Language: A Critique of the Segmentary Model in the Middle East. International Journal of Middle East Studies 19(1):77–102.
1990   Anthropological Theories of Tribe and State Formation in the Middle East: Ideology and the Semiotics of Power. In Tribes and State Formation in the Middle East. Philip Khoury and Joseph Kostiner, eds. Berkeley: University of California Press.

Chelkowski, Peter, ed.
1979   Ta'ziyeh: Ritual and Drama in Iran. New York: New York University Press and Soroush Press.

Clifford, James, and George Marcus, eds.
1986   Writing Culture: The Poetics and Politics of Ethnography.
            Berkeley: University of California Press.
Cooper, M. C.
1925   Grass. New York: G. P. Putman.
Crapanzano, Vincent
1980   Tuhami: Portrait of a Moroccan. Chicago: University of Chicago
            Press.
Cribb, Roger
1991   Nomads in Archaeology. Cambridge: Cambridge University
            Press.
Cronin, Vincent
1957   The Last Migration. London: Rupert Hart-Davis.
Davis, John
1987   Libyan Politics: Tribe and Revolution, An Account of the Zuwaya
            and Their Government. Berkeley: University of California Press.
Digard, Jean-Pierre
1977   Caractères et problèmes spécifiques du nomadisme en Iran:
            L'exemple Baxtyari. In Séminaire sur le nomadisme en Asie
            centrale. Berne: National Commission of Switzerland for
            UNESCO.
1979a   De la nécessité et des inconvénients, pour un Baxtyari, d'être bax-
            tyari. Communauté, territoire et inégalité chez des pasteurs no-
            mades d'Iran. In Pastoral Production and Society. Equipe écologie
            et anthropologie des sociétés pastorales, ed. Cambridge: Cam-
            bridge University Press.
1979b   Les nomades et l'état central en Iran: Quelques enseignements
            d'un long passé d' "hostilité réglementée." Peuples Méditerra-
            néens 7:37–53.
1981   Techniques des nomades baxtyari d'Iran. Cambridge: Cambridge
            University Press.
1987   Jeux de structures: Segmentarité et pouvoir chez les nomades
            Baxtyari d'Iran. L'Homme 27(2):12–53.
Dresch, Paul
1984   Tribal Relations and Political History in Upper Yemen. In
            Contemporary Yemen: Politics and Historical Background. B. R.
            Pridham, ed. London: Croom Helm.
1990a   Imams and Tribes: The Writing and Acting of History in Upper
            Yemen. In Tribes and State Formation in the Middle East. Philip
            Khoury and Joseph Kostiner, eds. Berkeley: University of Cali-
            fornia Press.
1990b   Tribes, Government and History in Yemen. New York: Oxford
            University Press.
Eickelman, Dale F.
1989   The Middle East: An Anthropological Approach. 2d ed.
            Englewood Cliffs, N.J.: Prentice-Hall.

Fazel, Golamreza

1971   Economic Organization and Change Among the Boir Ahmad: A Nomadic Pastoral Tribe of Southwest Iran. Ph.D. dissertation, Anthropology Department, University of California, Berkeley.

1973   The Encapsulation of Nomadic Societies in Iran. *In* The Desert and the Sown: Nomads in the Wider Society. Cynthia Nelson, ed. Berkeley: Institute of International Studies, University of California.

1977   Social and Political Status of Women Among Pastoral Nomads: The Boyr Ahmad of Southwest Iran. Anthropological Quarterly 50(2):77–89.

1979   Economic Bases of Political Leadership Among Pastoral Nomads: The Boyr Ahmad Tribe of Southwest Iran. *In* New Directions in Political Economy: An Approach from Anthropology. Madeline Barbara Leons and Frances Rothstein, eds. Westport, Conn.: Greenwood Press.

1985   Tribes and State in Iran: From Pahlavi to Islamic Republic. *In* Iran: A Revolution in Turmoil. Haleh Afshar, ed. Albany: State University of New York Press.

Fazel, Golamreza, and Nader Afshar-Naderi

1976   Rich Nomad, Poor Nomad, Settled Nomad: A Critique of Barth's Sedentarization Model. Unpublished manuscript.

Fernea, Elizabeth

1965   Guests of the Sheik: An Ethnography of an Iraqi Village. Garden City, N.Y.: Doubleday.

Friedl, Erika

1978   Women in Contemporary Persian Folktales. *In* Women in the Muslim World. Lois Beck and Nikki Keddie, eds. Cambridge: Harvard University Press.

1980   Islam and Tribal Women in a Village in Iran. *In* Unspoken Worlds: Women's Religious Lives in Non-Western Cultures. Nancy Falk and Rita Gross, eds. San Francisco: Harper and Row.

1981   Women and the Division of Labor in an Iranian Village. MERIP Reports 11(3):12–18, 31.

1983   State Ideology and Village Women. *In* Women and Revolution in Iran. Guity Nashat, ed. Boulder, Colo.: Westview Press.

1989   Women of Deh Koh: Lives in an Iranian Village. Washington, D.C.: Smithsonian Institution Press.

Garthwaite, Gene

1972   The Bakhtiyari Khans, the Government of Iran, and the British, 1846–1915. International Journal of Middle East Studies 3(1):24–44.

1977   The Bakhtiyari Ilkhani: An Illusion of Unity. International Journal of Middle East Studies 8(2):145–60.

1981   Khans and Kings: The Dialectics of Power in Bakhtiyari History. *In* Modern Iran: The Dialectics of Continuity and Change. Michael Bonine and Nikki Keddie, eds. Albany: State University of New York Press.

1983a   Tribes, Confederation and the State: An Historical Overview of the Bakhtiari and Iran. *In* The Conflict of Tribe and State in Iran and Afghanistan. Richard Tapper, ed. London: Croom Helm.

1983b   Khans and Shahs: A Documentary Analysis of the Bakhtiyari in Iran. Cambridge: Cambridge University Press.

Gellner, Ernest

1983   The Tribal Society and Its Enemies. *In* The Conflict of Tribe and State in Iran and Afghanistan. Richard Tapper, ed. London: Croom Helm.

Gellner, Ernest, and Charles Micaud, eds.

1972   Arabs and Berbers: From Tribe to Nation in North Africa. Lexington, Mass.: D. C. Heath.

Gluck, Jay, and Sumi Hiramoto Gluck, eds.

1977   A Survey of Persian Handicraft: A Pictorial Introduction to the Contemporary Folk Arts and Art Crafts of Modern Iran. Tehran and New York: Survey of Persian Art.

Goli, Aminollah

1987   Sairi dar tarikh-e siasi ejtema'i-ye Torkamanha (Survey of the sociopolitical history of the Turkmen). Tehran.

Goodell, Grace

1975   Agricultural Production in a Traditional Village of Northern Khuzestan. Marburger Geographische Schriften 64:245–89.

1986   The Elementary Structures of Political Life: Rural Development in Pahlavi Iran. New York: Oxford University Press.

Harrison, Selig

1981   In Afghanistan's Shadow: Baluch Nationalism and Soviet Temptations. New York: Carnegie Endowment for International Peace.

Hegland, Mary

1980   One Village in the Revolution. MERIP Reports 10(4):7–12.

1982   "Traditional" Iranian Women: How They Cope. The Middle East Journal 36(4):483–501.

1983a   Aliabad Women: Revolution as Religious Activity. *In* Women and Revolution in Iran. Guity Nashat, ed. Boulder, Colo.: Westview Press.

1983b   Two Images of Husain: Accommodation and Revolution in an Iranian Village. *In* Shiism from Quietism to Revolution. Nikki Keddie, ed. New Haven: Yale University Press.

1987   Islamic Revival or Political and Cultural Revolution? An Iranian Case Study. *In* Religious Resurgence: Contemporary Cases in Islam, Christianity, and Judaism. Richard Antoun and Mary Hegland, eds. Syracuse: Syracuse University Press.

Helfgott, Leonard

1977   Tribalism as a Socioeconomic Formation in Iranian History. Iranian Studies 10(1–2):36–61.

1980   The Structural Foundations of the National Minority Problem in Revolutionary Iran. Iranian Studies 13(1–4):195–214.

1987   Production and Trade: The Persian Carpet Industry. *In* Woven from the Soul, Spun from the Heart: Textile Arts of Safavid and Qajar Iran. Carol Bier, ed. Washington, D.C.: The Textile Museum.

Hendershot, Clarence

1964   White Tents in the Mountains: A Report on the Tribal Schools of Fars Province. Tehran: Communications Resources Branch.

Higgins, Patricia

1984   Minority-State Relations in Contemporary Iran. Iranian Studies 17(1):37–71.

1986   Minority-State Relations in Contemporary Iran. *In* The State, Religion, and Ethnic Politics: Afghanistan, Iran, and Pakistan. Ali Banuazizi and Myron Weiner, eds. Syracuse: Syracuse University Press.

Hillmann, Michael

1984   Persian Carpets. Austin: University of Texas Press.

Hole, Frank

1978   Pastoral Nomadism in Western Iran. *In* Explorations in Ethnoarchaeology. Richard Gould, ed. Albuquerque: University of New Mexico Press.

1979   Rediscovering the Past in the Present: Ethnoarchaeology in Luristan, Iran. *In* Ethnoarchaeology: Implications of Ethnography for Archaeology. Carol Kramer, ed. New York: Columbia University Press.

Hooglund, Eric

1982   Land and Revolution in Iran, 1960–1980. Austin: University of Texas Press.

Horne, Lee

1988   The Spatial Organization of Rural Settlement in Khar O Tauran, Iran: An Ethnoarchaeological Case Study. Ph.D. dissertation, Department of Anthropology, University of Pennsylvania.

Iran, Tehran University, Institute for Social Studies and Research

1987   Manabe' va ma'khez-e ashayer-e Iran (Resources and origins of the tribes of Iran). Tehran: Office of the Prime Minister, Bureau of the High Council of the Nomads of Iran.

Irons, William

1971   Variation in Political Stratification Among the Yomut Turkmen. Anthropological Quarterly 44(3):143–56.

1972   Variation in Economic Organization: A Comparison of the Pastoral Yomut and the Basseri. *In* Perspectives on Nomadism. William Irons and Neville Dyson-Hudson, eds. Leiden, Netherlands: E. J. Brill.

1974   Nomadism as a Political Adaptation: The Case of the Yomut Turkmen. American Ethnologist 1(4):635–58.

1975   The Yomut Turkmen: A Study of Social Organization Among a
              Central Asian Turkic-Speaking Population. Anthropological Pa-
              per no. 58. University of Michigan Museum of Anthropology.
              Ann Arbor: University of Michigan.
1979   Political Stratification Among Pastoral Nomads. *In* Pastoral Pro-
              duction and Society. L'Equipe écologie et anthropologie des so-
              ciétés pastorales, ed. Cambridge: Cambridge University Press.
Karimi, Asghar, trans.
1987   Fonun-e kuch neshinan-e Bakhtiyari (Techniques of Bakhtiyari
              nomads). Tehran: Astan-e Qods Rezavi. (Translation of Jean-
              Pierre Digard's Techniques des nomades baxtyari d'Iran.)
Kasraian, Nasrollah
1988   Endless Jouney. Tehran: AX Press.
Katouzian, Homayoun
1978   Oil Versus Agriculture: A Case of Dual Resource Depletion in
              Iran. The Journal of Peasant Studies 5(3):347–69.
1981   The Political Economy of Modern Iran: Despotism and Pseudo-
              Modernism, 1926–1979. New York: New York University Press.
Keddie, Nikki
1981   Roots of Revolution: An Interpretive History of Modern Iran.
              New Haven: Yale University Press.
1983   The Minorities Question in Iran. *In* The Iran-Iraq War: New
              Weapons, Old Conflicts. Shirin Tahir-Kheli and Shaheen Ayubi,
              eds. New York: Praeger.
1984   Material Culture and Geography: Toward a Holistic Comparative
              History of the Middle East. Comparative Studies in Society and
              History 26(4):709–35.
1986   Religion, Ethnic Minorities, and the State in Iran: An Overview.
              In The State, Religion, and Ethnic Politics: Afghanistan, Iran, and
              Pakistan. Ali Banuazizi and Myron Weiner, eds. Syracuse: Syra-
              cuse University Press.
Khazanov, A. M.
1984   Nomads and the Outside World. Cambridge: Cambridge Univer-
              sity Press.
Khoury, Philip, and Joseph Kostiner, eds.
1990   Tribes and State Formation in the Middle East. Berkeley:
              University of California Press.
Kielstra, Nico
1971   A Dialectical Model of Attitudes Towards Authority in a Persian
              Village. Unpublished manuscript.
Kortum, Gerhard
1976   Die Marvdasht-Ebene in Fars: Grundlagen und Entwicklung einer
              alten iranischen Bewässerungslandschaft. Kiel: Department of
              Geography, University of Kiel.
1980   Zagros (Iran): Bergnomadismus und Anbsiedlung der Qašqai.
              Tübinger Atlas des Vorderen Orients Map A, 12.2 Wiesbaden:
              Tübinger Atlas des Vorderen Orients, Universität Tübingen.

Kramer, Carol
1982   Village Ethnoarchaeology: Rural Iran in Archaeological Per-
            spective. New York: Academic Press.
Lambton, Ann K. S.
1953   Landlord and Peasant in Persia: A Study of Land Tenure and Land
            Revenue Administration. London: Oxford University Press.
1969   The Persian Land Reform, 1962–1966. Oxford: Clarendon.
Lewis, I. M.
1979   Kim Il-Sung in Somalia: The End of Tribalism? In Politics in
            Leadership: A Comparative Perspective. William Shack and Percy
            Cohen, eds. Oxford: Clarendon.
Lindner, Rudi Paul
1983   Nomads and Ottomans in Medieval Anatolia. Bloomington:
            Research Institute for Inner Asian Studies, University of Indiana.
Loeffler, Reinhold
1971   The Representative Mediator and the New Peasant. American
            Anthropologist 73(5):1077–91.
1973   The National Integration of Boir Ahmad. Iranian Studies 6(2–
            3):127–35.
1976   Recent Economic Changes in Boir Ahmad: Regional Growth
            Without Development. Iranian Studies 9(4):266–87.
1978   Tribal Order and the State: The Political Organization of Boir
            Ahmad. Iranian Studies 11(1–4):145–71.
1982   Economic Changes in a Rural Area Since 1979, Supplementary
            Remarks, and Discussion. In The Iranian Revolution and the Is-
            lamic Republic. Nikki Keddie and Eric Hooglund, eds. Washing-
            ton, D.C.: Middle East Institute.
1988   Islam in Practice: Religious Beliefs in a Persian Village. Albany:
            State University of New York Press.
Martin, Mary
1982a   Case Studies of Traditional Marketing Systems: Goats and Goat
            Products in Northeast Iran. Dairy Goat Journal: 45–49.
1982b   Conservation at the Local Level: Individual Perceptions and
            Group Mechanisms. In Desertification and Development: Dry-
            land Ecology in Social Perspective. Brian Spooner and H. S.
            Mann, eds. London: Academic Press.
1987a   City and Country: Rural Textile Production in Northeastern Iran.
            In Woven from the Soul, Spun from the Heart: Textile Arts of
            Safavid and Qajar Iran. Carol Bier, ed. Washington, D.C.: The
            Textile Museum.
1987b   Production Strategies, Herd Composition, and Offtake Rates:
            Reassessment of Archaeological Models. MASCA (Museum Ap-
            plied Science Center for Archaeology) Journal 4(4):154–65.
1988   The National and Regional Context of Local Level Agricultural
            Strategies: The Case of Small Holders in Northeastern Iran. In
            Human Systems Ecology: Studies in the Integration of Political

Economy, Adaptation, and Socionatural Regions. Sheldon Smith and Ed Reeves, eds. Boulder, Colo.: Westview Press.

n.d.   The Changing Socio-Economic Context and Impact of Resource Use Among Mixed Agriculturalists in a Steppic Region of Northeast Iran. Ph.D. dissertation, Department of Anthropology, Washington University, St. Louis. In preparation.

Mottahedeh, Roy

1985   The Mantle of the Prophet: Religion and Politics in Iran. New York: Simon and Schuster.

Munson, Henry

1984   The House of Si Abd Allah: The Oral History of a Moroccan Family. New Haven: Yale University Press.

Nyerges, A. Endre

1977   Traditional Pastoralism in the Middle East: The Ecology of Domesticated Sheep and Goats in the Turan Biosphere Reserve, Iran. Master's thesis, Department of Anthropology, University of Pennsylvania.

1980   Traditional Pastoralism and Patterns of Range Degradation. *In* Browse in Africa: The Current State of Knowledge. H. N. Le Houerou, ed. Addis Ababa, Ethiopia: International Livestock Centre for Africa.

1982   Pastoralists, Flocks and Vegetation: Processes of Co-adaptation. *In* Desertification and Development: Dryland Ecology in Social Perspective. Brian Spooner and H. S. Mann, eds. London: Academic Press.

Oberling, Pierre

1974   The Qashqa'i Nomads of Fars. The Hague: Mouton.

Oehler, Julie

in press   Bibi Mariam: A Social History. *In* Struggle and Survival in the Modern Middle East. Edmund Burke III, ed. Berkeley: University of California Press.

Paiman, Habibollah

1968   Tausif va tahlili az sakhteman-e eqtesadi ejtema'i va farhang-e il-e Qashqa'i (A description and analysis of the economic, social, and cultural aspects of the Qashqa'i confederacy). Publication no. 34. Tehran: Institute of Health, Tehran University.

Parham, Sirus

1983   Il-e Qashqa'i ki va az koja beh Fars amadeh ast? (When and from where did the Qashqa'i tribe come to Fars?). *In* Ilat va ashayer (Tribes and nomads). Tehran: Agah.

1985   Dast-baftha-ye ashayer-e va rustai-yeh Fars (Hand-weavings of nomads and villagers of Fars province). Vol. 1. Tehran: Amir Kabir.

Pourzal, Rostam

1980   Nomads Without a Chief: The Baraftowi Koohaki of Southern Iran. Master's thesis, Department of Anthropology, University of Pennsylvania.

1981a Ethnic Politics and Religious Change Among Arab Iranians: A Case Study. Unpublished manuscript.

1981b The Other Nomads of South Persia: The Baraftowi Koohaki of Jahrom. Nomadic Peoples 8:24–26.

Qashqa'i, Mohammad Naser Soulat

1986 Salha-ye bohran: khaterat-e ruzaneh-ye Mohammad Naser-e Soulat-e Qashqa'i, 1329–1332 (Years of crisis: the daily memoirs of Mohammad Naser Soulat Qashqa'i, 1950–1953). Tehran.

Qerekhlu, Mehdi

1989 Rovand mohajerat va ofaq-e kuch neshini il-e Qashqa'i (tayefeh Darrehshuri) (The immigration process and the migrational horizons of the Qashqa'i confederacy [the Darrehshuri tribe]). Faslnameh-e Ashayeri 8–9:53–65.

Rosman, Abraham, and Paula Rubel

1976 Nomad-Sedentary Interethnic Relations in Iran and Afghanistan. International Journal of Middle East Studies 7(4):545–70.

Roux, Jean-Paul

1970 Les Traditions des nomades de la Turquie méridionale. Paris: Librairie Adrien-maisonneuve.

Safi-Nezhad, Javad

1966 Sisakht-e Boir Ahmad (The Boir Ahmad village of Sisakht). Tehran: Institute for Social Studies and Research.

1975 Khan nameh tahqiqi dar ashayer-e Kuhgiluyeh va Boir Ahmad doran-e khankhani (A study of the Kuhgilu and Boir Ahmad tribes during the time of khan rule). Daneshkadeh: A Journal of Culture and Human Sciences 1(2):182–204.

1977 Buneh (A study of bunehs). 3d ed. Tehran: University of Tehran Press.

1989 Ashayer-e markazi Iran (Nomads of central Iran). Tehran: Amir Kabir.

Safi-Nezhad, Javad, et al.

1969 Jam'eyyat va shenas nameh-ye ilat-e Kuhgiluyeh (Demographic and social characteristics of the Kuhgilu tribes). Tehran: Institute for Social Studies and Research.

Safizadeh, Fereydoun

1984 Shahsavan in the Grip of Development. Cultural Survival Quarterly 8(1):14–18.

Salzer, Richard

1974 Social Organization of a Nomadic Pastoral Nobility in Southern Iran: The Kashkuli Kuchek of the Qashqa'i. Ph.D. dissertation, Anthropology Department, University of California, Berkeley.

Salzman, Philip Carl

1967 Political Organization Among Nomadic Peoples. Proceedings of the American Philosophical Society 3(2):115–31.

1971a Adaptation and Political Organization in Iranian Baluchistan. Ethnology 10(4):433–44.

1971b   Movement and Resource Extraction Among Pastoral Nomads: The Case of the Shah Nawazi Baluch. Anthropological Quarterly 44(3):185–97.

1972   Multi-Resource Nomadism in Iranian Baluchistan. *In* Perspectives on Nomadism. William Irons and Neville Dyson-Hudson, eds. Leiden, Netherlands: E. J. Brill.

1973   Continuity and Change in Baluchi Tribal Leadership. International Journal of Middle East Studies 4(4):428–39.

1974   Tribal Chiefs as Middlemen: The Politics of Encapsulation in the Middle East. Anthropological Quarterly 47(2):203–10.

1975   Kin and Contract in Baluchi Herding Camps. Unpublished manuscript.

1978   The Proto-State in Iranian Baluchistan. *In* Origins of the State: The Anthropology of Political Evolution. Ronald Cohen and Elman Service, eds. Philadelphia: Institute for the Study of Human Issues.

1979   Inequality and Oppression in Nomadic Society. *In* Pastoral Production and Society. L'Equipe écologie et anthropologie des sociétés pastorales, ed. Cambridge: Cambridge University Press.

1980   Processes of Sedentarization Among the Nomads of Baluchistan. *In* When Nomads Settle: Processes of Sedentarization as Adaptation and Response. Philip Salzman, ed. New York: Praeger.

Shafii, Forough; Manouchehr Mohseni; and Mansour Motabar
1977   Formal Education in a Tribal Society, Iran. Sociologia Ruralis 17(1–2):151–57.

Shahshahani, Soheila
1986a   Mamasani Women: Changes in the Division of Labor Among a Sedentarized Pastoral People of Iran. *In* Women's Work: Development and the Division of Labor by Gender. Eleanor Leacock and Helen Safa, eds. Granby, Mass.: Bergin and Garvey.

1986b   Women Whisper, Men Kill: A Case Study of the Mamasani Pastor [sic] Nomads of Iran. *In* Visibility and Power: Essays on Women in Society and Development. Leela Dube, Eleanor Leacock, and Shirley Ardener, eds. New York: Oxford University Press.

1987   Chahar fasl aftab: zendegi-ye ruzmarreh zanan eskan yafteh ashayer-e Mamassani (The four seasons of the sun: the daily life of settled tribal Mamassani women). Tehran: Tus.

Singer, Andre
1973   Tribal Migrations on the Irano-Afghan Border. Asian Affairs 60:160–65.

1982   Ethnic Origins and Tribal History of the Timuri of Khurasan. Afghan Studies 3–4:65–76.

Spooner, Brian
1973   The Cultural Ecology of Pastoral Nomads. Addison-Wesley Module in Anthropology, no. 45. Reading, Mass.: Addison-Wesley.

1983   Who Are the Baluch? A Preliminary Investigation into the Dynamics of an Ethnic Identity from Qajar Iran. *In* Qajar Iran: Political, Social and Cultural Change, 1800–1925. Edmund Bosworth and Carole Hillenbrand, eds. Edinburgh: Edinburgh University Press.

1986   Weavers and Dealers: The Authenticity of an Oriental Carpet. *In* The Social Life of Things: Commodities in Cultural Perspective. Arjun Appadurai, ed. Cambridge: Cambridge University Press.

1988   Baluchistan. Encyclopaedia Iranica, vol. 3, fascicle 6, 598–632.

Stober, Georg von

1979   Zur sozio-ökonomischen Differenzierung der Afšar Kermans. *In* Interdisziplinäre Iran-Forschung. Günther Schweizer, ed. Wiesbaden: Tübinger Atlas des Vorderen Orients, Universität Tübingen.

1984   Die Gawdaran: Sozio-ökonomischer Wandel bei Rinderhaltern in Sistan (Iran) im 20. Jh. Sociologus 34(1):47–73.

1988   The Influence of Politics on the Formation and Reduction of "Ethnic Boundaries" of Tribal Groups: The Cases of Ṣayad and Afšar in Eastern Iran. *In* Le Fait ethnique en Iran et en Afghanistan. Jean-Pierre Digard, ed. Paris: Centre National de la Recherche Scientifique.

Sunderland, E.

1968   Pastoralism, Nomadism and the Social Anthropology of Iran. *In* The Cambridge History of Iran. Vol. 1, The Land of Iran. W. B. Fisher, ed. Cambridge: Cambridge University Press.

Swee, Gary

1981   Sedentarization: Change and Adaptation Among the Kordshuli Pastoral Nomads of Southwestern Iran. Ph.D. dissertation, Anthropology Department, Michigan State University.

Tapper, Nancy

1978   The Women's Subsociety Among the Shahsevan Nomads of Iran. *In* Women in the Muslim World. Lois Beck and Nikki Keddie, eds. Cambridge: Harvard University Press.

1980   Matrons and Mistresses: Women and Boundaries in Two Middle Eastern Tribal Societies. European Journal of Sociology 21(1):59–79.

n.d.   Ziyaret: Gender and Shrines in Three Communities of the Muslim Middle East. Unpublished manuscript.

Tapper, Richard

1971   The Shahsavan of Azarbaijan: A Study of Political and Economic Change in a Middle Eastern Tribal Society. Ph.D. dissertation, University of London.

1979a   Individuated Grazing Rights and Social Organization Among the Shahsevan Nomads of Azerbaijan. *In* Pastoral Production and Society. L'Equipe écologie et anthropologie des sociétés pastorales, ed. Cambridge: Cambridge University Press.

1979b	Pasture and Politics: Economics, Conflict and Ritual Among Shahsevan Nomads of Northwestern Iran. London: Academic Press.
1983a	Introduction. *In* The Conflict of Tribe and State in Iran and Afghanistan. Richard Tapper, ed. London: Croom Helm.
1983b	Nomads and Commissars in the Mughan Steppe: The Shahsevan Tribes in the Great Game. *In* The Conflict of Tribe and State in Iran and Afghanistan. Richard Tapper, ed. London: Croom Helm.
1984	Holier Than Thou: Islam in Three Tribal Societies. *In* Islam in Tribal Societies: From the Atlas to the Indus. Akbar Ahmed and David Hart, eds. London: Routledge and Kegan Paul.
1988a	Ethnicity, Order and Meaning in the Anthropology of Iran and Afghanistan. *In* Le Fait ethnique en Iran et en Afghanistan. Jean-Pierre Digard, ed. Paris: Centre National de la Recherche Scientifique.
1988b	History and Identity Among the Shahsevan. Iranian Studies 21(3–4):84–108.
1990	Anthropologists, Historians, and Tribespeople on Tribe and State Formation in the Middle East. *In* Tribes and State Formation in the Middle East. Philip Khoury and Joseph Kostiner, eds. Berkeley: University of California Press.
in press	The Tribes in Eighteenth- and Nineteenth-Century Iran. *In* The Cambridge History of Iran. Vol. 7, The Afshars, Zands and Qajars. Peter Avery and G. Hambly, eds. Cambridge: Cambridge University Press.
n.d.	The King's Friends: A Social and Political History of the Shahsevan Tribes of Iran. Unpublished manuscript.

Towfiq, F.

1987	Ashayer (Tribes and nomads). Encyclopaedia Iranica, vol. 2, fascicle 7, 707–24.

University of Manchester, Whitworth Art Gallery

1976	The Qashqa'i of Iran.

van Bruinessen, Martin M.

1978	Agha, Shaikh and State: On the Social and Political Organization of Kurdistan. Ph.D. dissertation, Utrecht University, Netherlands.
1983	Kurdish Tribes and the State of Iran: The Case of Simko's Revolt. *In* The Conflict of Tribe and State in Iran and Afghanistan. Richard Tapper, ed. London: Croom Helm.
1986	The Kurds Between Iran and Iraq. Middle East Report 16(4):14–27.

Watson, Patty Jo

1979	Archaeological Ethnography in Western Iran. Viking Fund Publications in Anthropology, no. 57. Tucson: University of Arizona Press.

Wright, Susan
  1978   Prattle and Politics: The Position of Women in Doshman-ziari.
                Journal of the Anthropology Society of Oxford 9(2):98–112.
  1981   Place and Face: Of Women in Doshman Ziari, Iran. *In* Women
                and Space: Ground Rules and Social Maps. Shirley Ardener, ed.
                New York: St. Martin's Press.
Wulff, Hans E.
  1966   The Traditional Crafts of Persia: Their Development, Technology,
                and Influence on Eastern and Western Civilizations. Cambridge:
                MIT Press.

Index

References to illustrations are set in italic type.

Abdol Hosain, 61, 75, 119, 127, 153, 166, 184, 194, 211, 213, 220, 224, 230, 232, 235, 239, 247–48, 255, 325, 404; Borzu attacks, 233–35, 238, 250, 267–68, 395; and crisis in summer pastures, 275, 276–78, 280–81; dispute with Borzu, 63–64, 110–11, 235, 267–68, 280; entertains Hamzah, 233–34; feels driven out by Borzu, 366; inspects summer pastures, 267–68; Lurs file complaint against, 198; makes preparations to settle, 311; Morad takes his animals for the winter, 366–67; settles in Atakola, 335, *365*, 365–67, 385, 395; works in sugar-beet fields, 402

Abdollah: dies, 335

Abdollah Khan: as ilkhani, 291

Abdollah Khan Kashkuli, 144; land at Polo Field Canyon, 189

Abdol Rasul, *31*, 111, 157, 211, 215, 220, 223, 233–35, 239, 247–48, 283, 325, 366, 404; Borzu's anger at, 403; and crisis in summer pastures, 276–78, 280–81; inspects summer pastures, 267–68; leaves winter camp, 167–68; Morad's disputes with, 218, 373; negotiates his son's marriage, 403; settles in Atakola, 334, 385, 388–89, 395; in stick-fighting game, 372–73; supports Borzu in dispute, 382; as wedding guest, 371–73

Abul Hasan, 167, 194–95, 253, 254, 305, 379, 386, 391; Borzu gives goats to, 401; pasture rights at Hanalishah, 292; sells surplus animals, 387

Acorns, 52, 135, 225, 259

Afsar, 123, 152, 311

Aftab: marries Hasel, 388, 390–95

Agriculturalists: Borzu disputes with, 35, 110, 114, 220, 250, 282, 297–98, 380, 381, 382–83; encroach on pastures at Dashtak, 306; encroach on pastures at Hanalishah, 292, 296–98; fear Qashqa'i, 180, 186; guard fields during spring migration, 180, 213, 216, 220–21, 223, 225, 240–41, 256, 269; guard fields in summer pastures, 298; hostility toward Qashqa'i, 186–87, 220, 223, 241; and migration, 28, 46–47, 53–54; mutilate trespassing animals, 297. *See also* Peasants

Agricultural labor, 65–66, 115–16, 304, 311–12, 344, 364, 377, 399, 402. *See also* Sharecropping

Agriculture: pastoralism gives way to, 333–42; vs. pastoralism, 4, 79–80, 142, 380–82

Ahmad Khan, 97, 98, 204, 326; Mir Gharati shoots at, 258, 270

Aid for International Development (U.S.), 134

Akbar, 142, 147, 156–58, 203, 213, 232,

DATE DUE

4-9-2015	

GAYLORD   PRINTED IN U.S.A.

Compositor:	Graphic Composition, Inc.
Printer:	Malloy Lithographing, Inc.
Binder:	John H. Dekker & Sons
Text:	10/13 Aldus
Display:	Aldus